SELLING OUR SECURITY

SELLING OUR SECURITY

The Erosion of America's Assets

MARTIN AND SUSAN J. TOLCHIN

ALFRED A. KNOPF   NEW YORK

1992

THIS IS A BORZOI BOOK
PUBLISHED BY ALFRED A. KNOPF, INC.

Library of Congress Cataloging-in-Publication Data

Tolchin, Martin.
    Selling our security: the erosion of America's assets / by Martin and Susan Tolchin.—1st ed.
        p.   cm.
    "A Borzoi book"—T.p. verso
    Includes bibliographical references and index.
    ISBN 0-394-58309-4
    1. Technology transfer—Economic aspects—United States. 2. Investments, Foreign—United States. 3. United States—National security.   I. Tolchin, Susan J. II. Title.
    HC110.T4T65   1992
    332.6'73'0973—dc20   92-4499
                                                                              CIP

Manufactured in the United States of America

First Edition

To
Astrid E. Merget
and
Steve & Nancy Schlossberg

CONTENTS

Contents

x   *Contents*

ACKNOWLEDGMENTS

We are indebted to the Rockefeller Foundation for providing sanctuary and sustenance at the Villa Serbelloni, in Bellagio, Italy. The grant afforded us a month's solitude and the resources that encourage reflection and creation, as well as the benefit of the perspectives of our fellow scholars in residence.

We thank George Washington University's research program for providing a travel grant that helped fund fieldwork in the United States. Research assistance was expedited by the School of Business and Public Management. For their support and encouragement, we give special thanks to Dean Ben Burdetsky; Public Administration Department Chair Kathryn E. Newcomer; and Vice-President Rod French, who provided the support for a special seminar in "National Security and International Economic Policy," which tracks many of the themes in this book. To Professor William Adams, who first introduced us to the 386 chip and remained good-naturedly at the ready end of the "help" key, we extend our heartfelt gratitude.

Five graduate research assistants from the Public Administration Department contributed their time and enthusiasm to this book. For the skill with which they checked facts, tracked down leads, surmounted obstacles, and still kept their good humor, we thank Dion Anderson, Amy Birgensmith, Linda Feinstein, Andrew Sachs, and Cynthia Stachelberg. We are also grateful to the department's executive assistants, Jerry Paxton and Bushra Finsish, for their help.

The book benefited greatly from the extensive comments of many of our friends, family, and colleagues, who read chapters of the book in manuscript form. For their insights and criticisms, we thank the following members of the Washington Bureau of *The New York*

Times: Janet Battaile, Adam Clymer, Jack Cushman, Clyde Farnsworth, Caroline Herron, Robert Hershey, Stephen Labaton, and Robert Pear. We also are indebted to Frederick Amling, William Becker, John Boswell, Pat Choate, Wendy Frieman, Dorothy Goldsmith, Michael Green, Kent Hughes, Brian Krier, Henry Nau, Robert Pitofsky, Charles Tolchin, Karen Tolchin, Frank Turek, and Richard Van Atta.

A substantial part of the book is based on original interviews in the United States, Great Britain, and Japan. Interviews were conducted between 1988 and 1991 with members of Congress, business leaders from U.S. and foreign corporations, officials from the executive branch, congressional staffers, trade-association representatives, scholars, and journalists. All direct quotes in the text that are not cited in notes are drawn from these interviews. We thank the following U.S. and British respondents for sharing their knowledge, experience and insights with us:

Jose Alvarez, Alf Andreassan, Bernard Ascher, Norman Augustine, Susan Bales, Ronald Barks, Juan Benitez, Representative Helen Bentley, Senator Jeff Bingaman, Jim Blackwell, Larry Blair, John Booth, Mike Boss, Jamie Boucher, Fred Branfman, Representative John Bryant, Steven Burbridge, George Burns (of Dataquest, not the actor), Andrew Button, Joseph Campbell, Representative Tom Campbell, Stephen Canner, Pat Choate, Jack Clifford (of the Department of Commerce), Christopher Coburn, Victor Cohen, Debi Coleman, Robert Costello, Kenneth Courtis, Richard E. Donnelly, Jim Douglas, Joseph Duncan, Loretta Dunn, Al Eisele, Stephanie Epstein, Keith Erickson, Senator J. James Exon, James Fallows, Charles Ferguson, Craig Fields, Frank T. Finch, Steven Forbes, Gail Fosler, Ellen Frost, Frank Gaffney, Jacques Gansler, William Graham, Paul Gray, Peggy Haggerty, John Hall, Peter Hansen, Turner Hasty, Representative Jimmy Hayes, Erland Heginbotham, Donna Heivlin, Charles Herzfeld, Senator Ernest F. Hollings, William Holstein, Richard Iverson, Al Joseph, Representative Marcy Kaptur, Kevin Kearns, Michael Kelly, Victor Kiam, Charles Kimzey, Milton Kirkpatrick, John Kline, Joseph Krenski, Burgess Laird, Bradley Larschan, Judy Larsen, Robert Z. Lawrence, Representative Jim Leach, Carl Ledbetter, Reuven Leopold, Martin Libicki, Steven Linke, Jeff Lins, Gary Madden, Ira Magaziner, Michael Maibach, Representative John Markey, Horace G. McDonnell, Joan McEntee, Ed McGaffigan, Chris McLean, John McPhee, Allan I. Mendelowitz, Robert Mercer, Tim Miles, Henson Moore, Theodore Moran, John Morley, Norman Morse, Ronald Morse, Thomas J. Murrin, Mark Nelson, David Noble, William C. Norris, Robert Noyce, Representative Mary Rose Oakar, Avtar Oberai, James O'Connell, Robert A. Perkins, William G. Phillips, Robert Pitofsky,

Allan Platt, Clyde Prestowitz, J. C. S. Priston, John Richards, Elliot Richardson, Maurice Roesch III, Glenn Rudd, Peri Sabety, Howard D. Samuel, Senator Jim Sasser, Bernard Schwartz, Tom Seidel, Michael Sekora, Jean Jacques Servan-Schreiber, Rhod Shaw, Greg Shephard, Michael Skarzynski, Charles Smith, Michael Smith, William Snyder, Linda Spencer, Roger Steciak, Paula Stern, Joseph Stroop, William Triplett, John Tyler, Richard Van Atta, Raymond Vernon, Pat Wait, Representative Theodore Weiss, Michael R. Wessel, Deborah Wince-Smith, Malcolm Winter, and Jerome M. Zeifman.

In addition to those named above, there were many individuals whose help we cannot acknowledge publicly, but who have our gratitude nonetheless. They know who they are.

Chapter IV, the FSX chapter, benefited greatly from fieldwork conducted in Tokyo through the auspices of the Policy Studies Group. Mr. Motoo Shiina, the leader of the group, in conjunction with three staff members—Michael J. Green, Toshio Sumi, and Masako Masuda—set up interviews and provided valuable translation services. Our knowledge of the complexities of the FSX was greatly enhanced by the insights of Messrs. Shiina, Sumi, and Green and Ms. Masuda, and we extend our thanks to them as well as to: Tadashi Abe, Misao Asakura, Joseph Bresher, Bruce Edward Carter, Kiyofuku Chuma, W. Kent Combs, Richard E. Coyle, Rust M. Deming, Y. Ichihashi, Yoh Kurosawa, Hiroshi Morikawa, Atshushi Nakajima, Seiki Nishihiro, Hajime Ohta, Shinichiro Ohta, Hirohiko Okumura, David Sanger, Seizaburo Sato, Toshinori Shigeie, Kazuhiro Suzuki, Yoshihiro Tamura, Tomoyoshi Uranishi, Stephen R. Weisman, Kazutami Yamazaki, and Toshimichi Yanashima.

Our editor, Jonathan Segal, contributed his considerable skills as well as his perceptive insights to the book. We especially thank him for the great care he took with the manuscript from start to finish, and his unflagging encouragement and enthusiasm. For providing us with valuable editorial suggestions, we thank the copy editors, Terry Zaroff and Melvin Rosenthal, and Mr. Segal's editorial assistant, Ida Giragossian.

We are also grateful to our literary agent, Gloria Loomis, for her thoughtful critiques of our work and her sound judgment.

Our children, Charles and Karen, have now lived through five books co-authored by their parents. We cherish their steadfast love and support, and take great pride in the fact that they have both turned into very talented writers.

Bethesda, Maryland, 1992

SELLING OUR SECURITY

CHAPTER I

From Slingshots to Computer Chips

WHY TECHNOLOGY IS DESTINY AND WHAT AMERICA CAN DO ABOUT IT

We became a truly great nation and a world power in the twentieth century because we were always on the cutting edge of technology. The question is, where will we be as a nation in the twenty-first century?

—Senator J. James Exon

There is no difference between computer chips and potato chips.

—A White House official

Senator J. James Exon was incredulous. The Nebraska Democrat implored President Reagan to block a British corporate raider's November 1986 bid for the Goodyear Tire and Rubber Company, the largest American tire manufacturer and a major defense contractor, with a plant in Lincoln, Nebraska. But the president refused, saying there was nothing he could do to stop Sir James Goldsmith, short of declaring a national emergency, a draconian step that Reagan feared would have worldwide repercussions.

Never mind that Sir James was eyeing an industry in which two of the three top manufacturers were already foreign-owned. His takeover attempt occurred after Bridgestone, a Japanese company and the third-largest tire producer in the United States, had acquired the tire-production facilities of Firestone, America's second-largest tire manufacturer. If Sir James was allowed to purchase Goodyear, the combined effect

of these acquisitions would be to leave the United States with less than
20 percent of its previous tire-manufacturing capacity. Goodyear also
was a major defense contractor that supplied the military with sophisticated computers, F-15 flight simulators, radar, and missile-guidance
systems.

Was it good public policy, the senator asked, to have the world's
leading industrial power dependent upon foreign-owned companies
for something so basic to national security as tire production? Was the
government really powerless to stop the foreign acquisition of a major
military contractor? Although Goodyear bought off Sir James and was
eventually spared despite the absence of government help, the company
was almost destroyed in the process.

Was the United States really incapable of preserving industries
vital to both military security and economic competitiveness? The
Department of Commerce reported in 1990 that the United States was
losing ground to Japan in all but three of twelve key technologies.[1]
The report was among dozens of government studies warning of the
erosion of the nation's technological dominance, an erosion that
spelled disaster for U.S. industries that relied upon those technologies
and therefore lost their competitive edge. It meant lost jobs, lost national income, lost market share, a lower standard of living, and an
increased trade deficit. It meant greater dependence upon foreign
sources that could raise prices or even withhold products to assist
their own industries. The stakes were higher yet: America's political,
economic, moral, and military leadership in a world in which it was
losing prestige along with market share.

America's trade and investment policies have blunted its technological edge. Gone is the last major U.S. producer of robots, sold to
overseas investors. Foreign investors have also purchased the last major U.S. producer of silicon wafers, vital to the production of semiconductors, along with the crown jewel of American biotechnology
companies. Lost is the nation's lead in semiconductors, supercomputers, optoelectronics, and digital imaging, among dozens of other critical technologies. Want a link trainer to simulate the F-16 fighter plane?
The American company that makes them was sold to a Canadian firm.
Need an optical encoder? Try a British company. And how about some
rarefied gases critical to the manufacture of almost all semiconductor
equipment? The firm that produces them was sold in 1991 to a Japanese manufacturer, despite protests from U.S. manufacturers and an
antitrust action by the Department of Justice.

McDonnell Douglas, the aerospace giant and the nation's largest
military contractor, meanwhile negotiated the sale of 40 percent of its
commercial-jetliner business to a government-backed firm in Taiwan

in November 1991, raising fears that the United States might lose its technological edge in one of the few manufacturing industries still dominated by U.S. companies.[2] In a letter to President Bush, twenty-nine senators protested the sale as against the national interest. "It strikes us that this sale raises the prospect of the transfer of a tremendous amount of aerospace technology to Taiwan (and possibly other Far East equity partners) for a small fraction of the cost it has taken to develop that technology, much of which was paid for by the taxpayers of this country," said the letter, organized by Senator Jeff Bingaman, Democrat of New Mexico.[3]

Accompanying these technological losses was the incredible shrinking American industrial base. Our automobile industry, which once provided most of the world's cars, saw a foreign competitor, Honda, produce the most popular car in the United States in 1991. In the 1970s, U.S. companies made 95 percent of the telephones and 80 percent of the television sets for U.S. homes; by 1991, they made 25 percent of the telephones and 10 percent of the television sets sold here. Ten years ago, the United States had 100 percent of the world's lithography market; by 1991, this had shrunk to 20 percent. In 1970, the Japanese had none of the world market share in dynamic random-access memories (D-RAMs), a semiconductor device; by 1988, the Japanese share of the marketplace had reached 80 percent. Japanese firms also made great inroads in autos and machine tools, while German firms successfully targeted industrial machinery. Once the world leader in semiconductor production, the U.S. saw its worldwide market share decline steadily from 57 to 35 percent from 1980 to 1989, while Japan's share increased from 27 to 52 percent.[4]

Congress paid scant attention until the Goodyear debacle. The president's impotence in the face of the threatened erosion of the American tire industry and the loss of Goodyear's military production galvanized Senator Exon. "I thought it was a terribly bad precedent to be setting," the senator recalled.

To prevent such acquisitions in the future, Exon sponsored a bill giving the president authority to block foreign acquisitions that imperiled "national security" without having to declare a national emergency. But how define "national security"? Exon's bill touched off a lively congressional debate. Should the president have the authority to block only those foreign acquisitions that imperiled military security, involving companies with defense contracts? Or did "national security" encompass companies that produced technologies critical to the nation's economic development, technologies needed to assure that the United States remained economically competitive in the twenty-first century? Was there a distinction between these two concepts of "national security"? Did domestic ownership still make a difference in a world where national borders were receding in importance, so long as key technologies were available from our allies and trading partners?

Major defense contractors, such as manufacturers of flight simulators and missile-guidance systems, would surely be covered by the bill, but what about technologies vital to economic competitiveness, such as robotics, biotechnology, computers and supercomputers, and advanced television systems? And more mundane industries, such as the electronics and machine-tool industries, which are central to the development of new technologies? What about the role of banks and other financial institutions in funding the development of new technologies? And what about the old basic smokestack industries? Is the steel industry vital to national security? What about automobiles, or tires? Can the world's leading industrialized nation survive without such basic industries, and depend instead upon foreign governments and companies to supply these products?

Most important, would a definition of national security that encompassed economic competitiveness serve to protect obsolete and inefficient industries, the proverbial buggy-whip manufacturers? Was "national security" the last refuge of inept corporate executives whose blunders had led their companies toward well-deserved extinction? Could "national security" be a pretext for protectionism, with virtually every industry found to be defense-related? Could a "national-security" case be made for the food industry, textiles, transportation, and a host of other enterprises without which our nation would be sorely handicapped in the event of war? After all, George Washington's troops suffered mightily at Valley Forge because they lacked an adequate supply of boots, and had to wrap their feet in bandages. "National security" has, moreover, been invoked by all manner of scoundrels to justify everything from the Reagan administration's secret deals to divert funds to the Contra rebels, to FBI surveillance of rock stars, to John Sununu's use of a White House car to drive to New York City to attend a stamp auction.

Although "national security" is a much-abused concept, a nation's first imperative is indeed to protect itself. Even without an immediate Soviet threat, the world remains a perilous place: a Saddam Hussein with nuclear weapons, an ossified and aging Chinese oligarchy that holds power by firing on its own students, an Azerbaijani physicist lured out of his chaotic region by a terrorist dictator eager for tactical nuclear weapons, and the ever-present threat that an American will be swept off the streets and taken hostage—all could threaten us.

With the ending of the Cold War, however, military security

began to assume less national importance, while the need for economic security, prodded by a worsening recession and fears that America had lost its competitive edge, brought productivity and economic issues to the forefront. With no immediate challenge to its military pre-eminence, America began to focus on its economic morass, and the extent to which this had been created by shortsighted trade and investment policies that had undermined the country's technological strength. Militarily secure, the United States faced the prospect of becoming a second-rate economic power.

Exon's bill initially defined "national security" as not only military preparedness but also "essential commerce and economic welfare." In the final version, however, Exon and Representative James Florio, New Jersey Democrat, the House sponsor (who subsequently went on to become governor of his state), yielded to the objections of the White House and the lobbyists for foreign investors. The definition was left intentionally vague, with the proviso that economic security was to be considered, and that "national security is intended to be interpreted broadly without limitation to particular industries."

The congressional debate was punctuated by expressions of concern over how America's future as a world power would be affected by the erosion of the strength and health of industries critical to national security, called the "defense-industrial base," as well as by the loss of cutting-edge technologies. Could the United States continue to be the leader of the free world, and assert political, moral, economic, and military leadership, if it kept losing industries that were vital to both national and economic security?

Critics of the Reagan and Bush administrations feared the nation's increasing dependence upon foreign manufacturers for technologies crucial to national and economic security. They viewed both presidents as victims of their own laissez-faire, free-market rhetoric.

The issue crosses ideological lines. Though many conservatives agree on the importance of America's continued ability to determine its own national-security interests, they are uncomfortable with the degree of government intervention needed to assure such self-reliance. On the other hand, many liberals who generally support government intervention in domestic programs oppose increases in spending for national security, fearful that the additional funds would come at the cost of housing, education, and health programs. It is, therefore, not surprising that political moderates took the lead in bringing the issue to public attention. To them, a nation was not secure unless its economic base was healthy and expanding, and able to enhance the lives of all Americans.

Enactment of the Exon-Florio amendment in 1988 was one of

the earliest signs that America was becoming concerned about the loss of its technological edge, and the erosion of its defense industrial base. Why should anyone care? After all, ever since President Eisenhower warned the nation in his farewell address against the growing power of the "military-industrial complex" there has been concern over the *expansion* of the defense industrial base. It took a military hero elected president to warn against the excessive power of the alliance between the government and defense contractors, which in the eyes of critics skewed national policy in favor of the expenditure of hundreds of billions of dollars that could be better used for domestic purposes.

However, one need not agree with Mao Zedong that power grows out of the barrel of a gun to appreciate the relationship between technological superiority and political, economic, and military power. This has been demonstrated throughout history, from the slingshot with which David slew Goliath, to the Spanish Armada, to Britannia ruling the waves, to America's harnessing of nuclear energy. David's slingshot ultimately catapulted him onto the throne of Israel; the Spanish and British navies were key to their nations' explorations and colonizations, enabling small garrisons in remote outposts to control large civilian populations, and bringing the riches of the Orient and the Indies to London and Madrid. More recently, technology played a key role in the peaceful Soviet revolution of August 1991, when opponents of a right-wing coup used cellular telephones, fax machines, and a communications satellite to mobilize resistance both within the Soviet Union and around the world. As shown by the Soviet upheaval, civilian technological prowess was more important than the Kremlin's military power. In fact, technology is gradually proving itself more useful for keeping the peace than for wartime uses, by providing leverage and influence in a range of disputes that includes everything from human rights to border disputes.

Similarly, America's ascent as a world power began with its development of the assembly line and basic industries, and was secured when the United States unleashed the power of the atom. The nation's development of the atomic bomb not only assured victory in World War II, but established the United States as the political and economic leader of the free world.

A key issue today is whether the United States can remain the leader of the free world if it loses its technological edge and depends increasingly on other nations for technologies vital to its military security and economic competitiveness. One may disagree with specific aspects of America's values—most notably its nuclear stance—and take issue with various laws, regulations, programs, or initiatives. But what other society is as democratic—as open, diverse, innovative, progressive, and responsive to change? The Gulf War was but the latest initiative in which the United States mobilized the world's leading powers to thwart a major threat.

Now, there is evidence that America's economic leadership has already eroded, and that its officials no longer command the respect they previously enjoyed in the community of nations. To be sure, Washington speaks with many voices. The State Department, which often prevails in trade and national-security cases, is primarily concerned with building and maintaining alliances and is reluctant to offend U.S. allies. The Treasury, responsible for financing the federal budget deficit, is also fearful of offending our allies and anxious to encourage foreign investors to purchase Treasury notes. The Department of Commerce, representing the often conflicting interests of U.S. business, wants to promote trade without burdensome restrictions, and also is heavily involved in protecting critical industries. And the Pentagon has many factions, including those concerned with maintaining foreign bases, those worried about the loss of critical technologies, those eager to share technology with allies like Japan and South Korea, and those alarmed about the security risks represented by lax export and investment controls.

On Capitol Hill, some lawmakers complain that they no longer feel free to express concerns about trade issues because of the foreign money that has poured into their states, districts, and re-election campaigns. Congressional voices have nonetheless offered the strongest warnings against the foreign acquisition of critical industries. Senator Ernest F. Hollings, South Carolina Democrat and chairman of the Commerce Committee, warned his colleagues in a floor speech in June 1991 that "This decline in the U.S. leadership position has tremendous consequences for all Americans. The erosion of critical U.S. industries means fewer jobs for American workers. Increasing investment in the United States by foreign companies means that profits from American activities flow overseas. The lack of an industrial and high technology base within the United States threatens our military capabilities and our national defense.

"The economic, social and political ramifications of the continued deterioration of U.S. strength in these crucial industries could be devastating."[5]

Representative Richard Gephardt, the majority leader, a Missouri Democrat, noted that, "While the free market has great value, it places no special emphasis on our national security, it does not take into account our standard of living, and it does not adequately value the national interest." He said that in today's world of "adversarial trade, foreign investment is a means toward strategic political and industrial

ends. Thus, our continued benign analysis of foreign investment practices is rapidly leading to our economic isolation, as we refuse to
confront the realities of foreign economic systems which are not consistent with our view of capitalism."[6]

The alliance between government and industry in the interest of
technological progress is as old as the nation. Alexander Hamilton's
influential "Report on Manufactures," in 1791, recommended the
development of a domestic industrial base, to avoid excessive reliance
on foreign suppliers. Hamilton recognized that the difference between
a colony and a first-rate power rested on technological capability and
industrial strength. A government contract awarded to Eli Whitney to
produce rifles with interchangeable parts led to the development of the
first machine tools and the basis for "industrial growth in the new
century."[7] Military funding also subsidized the research of Thomas
Blanchard, whose invention of the industrial lathe proved as critical
to the nineteenth century as supercomputers will be in the twenty-first.
The first digital computer, intended to plot artillery strikes, was funded
by the army as well. Throughout the nineteenth century, the federal
government supported tariffs to encourage and protect U.S. industry
and its workers.

More recently, the government has invested billions in space exploration, the modern equivalent of Queen Isabella's funding of the
Niña, the *Pinta*, and the *Santa Maria* in pursuit of new worlds and
their riches. Ironically, there is no longer commercial shipbuilding in
the United States, which had thirty-seven shipyards capable of building
large ships in 1982, but only twenty by 1990.

It was also the military that provided seed money for many new
technologies with civilian "spin-offs," including the computer, avionics (electronics used in aviation, missilery, and astronautics), and robotics industries. Furthermore, in the era after World War II, the
country's more encompassing theory of national security, blending
national and economic security, sent defense dollars into highways,
education, basic science, raw materials, and technological innovation.
Not until the 1980s did a narrower concept of national security take
hold, one confined to "things that go bang," in the words of United
Technologies executive Dr. Ellen Frost.

It is a paradox that in the 1980s, when the defense budget doubled
and the government poured hundreds of billions of dollars into research and development, when space exploration captured the nation's
imagination and "Star Wars" became a household phrase, America
suffered the loss of dozens of cutting-edge technologies, many developed at taxpayers' expense.

The United States government has long encouraged the development of science and technology, and spent billions—$66.3 billion in 1991 alone—on basic and applied research. Yet, unaccountably, the government remained idle as many technologies developed here were commercialized overseas, or acquired by foreign governments and companies. By 1991, signs of concern were beginning to emerge from business groups, the White House, and other constituencies that had been ambivalent about protecting critical industries.

"Throughout America's history, technology has been a major driver of economic growth," noted a March 1991 report by the Council on Competitiveness, an influential blue-ribbon panel of academics, corporate executives, and labor leaders known for its commitment to maintaining the nation's competitive advantage. "It has carried the nation to victory in two world wars, created millions of jobs, spawned entire new industries and opened the prospect of a brighter future. In many respects, technology has been America's ultimate comparative advantage. Because of our great technological strength, U.S. manufacturing and service industries stood head and shoulders above those of other nations in world markets.

"That comforting view is under assault," said the council, warning that the U.S. was no longer a player in such fields as robotics, silicon manufacture, liquid-crystal displays, memory chips, and structural ceramics. "As a result of intense international competition, America's (once commanding) technology edge has eroded in one industry after another. The U.S.-owned consumer electronics and factory automation industries have been practically eliminated by foreign competition; the U.S. share of the world machine tool market has slipped from about 50 percent to 10 percent; and the U.S. merchant semiconductor industry has shifted from dominance to a distant second in world markets. Even such American success stories as chemicals, computers and aerospace have foreign competitors close on their heels."[8]

The council's findings echoed other influential voices, both within the government (including the Pentagon) and outside it. Many of these groups, committees, and agencies issued warnings about the erosion of the defense industrial base, along with lists of the imperiled technologies that constitute the nation's key industries. The warnings were either quashed or ignored.

How should America respond? Should the government try to save a broad range of industries, only those with "critical" technologies, or none at all? And if the government intervenes, what should be its role? Should it provide subsidies, tax breaks, low-cost loans, money for research and development, and government contracts, and encourage private customers? Or should the government recognize that it is no longer possible to retain technological superiority in all critical industries, but assure that the United States develop and retain some technologies that are needed by other nations, as a bargaining chip? Should the government at least guarantee an American presence in all industries vital to national security, so that the nation could gear up in wartime and not have to depend either on the kindness of allies or the uncertainties of transportation?

Or are such efforts doomed to failure because of the "intractable" laws of international economics, which supposedly deem that the marketplace knows best and that government intervention can only make matters worse? Would government help go mainly to industries with political clout, rather than to those crucial to the nation's economic survival? To what extent was the erosion of America's defense-industrial base and its technological edge caused by the shortsighted practices of American companies, and their assumption that they would remain superior despite weak quality control and an emphasis on quick profits? To what extent was it attributable to fickle and greedy institutional investors trapped by a fixation with the quarterly report? Finally, are government efforts to nurture these industries and technologies unnecessary, since it no longer matters who owns what in the global economy?

THE LONELY PLAYING FIELD

None of America's major trading partners subscribe to the U.S. vision of free trade. None regard technology with the cavalier notion that ownership doesn't matter—unless *they* are the owners. Instead, each nurtures technologies it deems vital to its economic competitiveness in the twenty-first century. The U.S. semiconductor industry's steep loss of market share in the 1980s, for example, a loss that will be felt for years to come, resulted in large measure from the gains made by Japanese competitors supported by government subsidies.

The declining U.S. market share of such critical technologies as semiconductors (often known as "enabling technologies" for their role in the development of other products and technologies) puts the nation into an unaccustomed condition of dependence. The effects of the increasing reliance by U.S. manufacturers on foreign suppliers of semiconductors emerged in 1990, in an informal poll of American manufacturers of semiconductor equipment, taken by SEMATECH, the government-industry consortium of these manufacturers. The poll revealed that many manufacturers had to wait up to two years to obtain needed computer chips from Japan, and that those chips were often not among the most advanced being produced. The delay affected thousands of products that relied on microchips, from automobiles to personal computers, motion-picture equipment, machine tools, and robotics. A year later, SEMATECH's findings were corroborated by a General Accounting Office (GAO) study which found that 42 percent of the fifty-nine semiconductor companies surveyed reported "specific examples of instances in which Japanese suppliers had rejected their offers to buy advanced equipment, parts, or technologies or had delayed their delivery by more than 6 months."[9]

"The basic design of shoes has not changed in two hundred years," noted Norman Augustine, chairman of Martin Marietta, a major military contractor, "but semiconductors change on the average of every two and one-half years." It follows, then, that Japan's policy of saving the newest and best computer chips for itself means that American products which depend on computer chips will become less versatile—and hence less competitive—than their overseas counterparts.

In this context, it should not surprise observers if American cars are outperformed by foreign cars, as they soon will be if they lack sensors that warn of traffic jams ahead, or are unable to advise on the best route to a particular destination—to name two capabilities of advanced Japanese automaking. As a consequence, American cars will suffer in the marketplace, production will decline, workers will be laid off, the GNP reduced, and the trade deficit heightened.

One need not be a visionary to see the domino effect of the loss of a cutting-edge technology. Nor is the semiconductor the only advanced technology that can have such an effect. Recent studies warn that the United States has lost primacy in robotics, another technology central to hundreds of industries, and this loss will affect the manufacture of a broad range of American products and weaken their global competitiveness. Other twenty-first-century technologies that are threatened include fiber optics; high-temperature/high-strength, lightweight composite materials; sensitive radars; "advanced" ceramics needed for high-temperature applications, such as advanced engines; aeronautics; energy technologies; and biotechnology, including gene therapy.

"We became a truly great nation and a world power in the twentieth century because we were always on the cutting edge of technology," Senator Exon said. "The question is, where will we be as a nation in the twenty-first century?"[10]

Overseas investors even seek to gain control of motion-picture technology, an industry totally identified with the United States. With Sony's purchase of Columbia Pictures and Matsushita's purchase of MCA, four of the seven Hollywood studios are now controlled by foreign interests. The Japanese acquisitions were intended to give the two companies control over the industry's hardware as well as software—the films that are part of the nation's cultural heritage. The industry itself is America's largest net exporter, after the aerospace industry, accounting for $8 billion in trade surplus. The morning after the announcement of the MCA deal, an official from Matsushita told the Nikkei Telecom wire service that "The decision means there will be two Japanese companies controlling both hardware and programs in the audiovisual field."[11] The acquisitions are viewed as an inroad into American culture. Indeed, despite Japanese promises to leave creative control in Hollywood, after Matsushita acquired Universal Pictures as part of the MCA deal, the studio changed the plot of a pending movie, *Mr. Baseball*, to make its hero—a former American baseball star who joins a Japanese team and clashes with his teammates over their characteristically Japanese devotion to martial spirit and group harmony—eventually "accept" their approach to the sport.[12] Soon after, another Hollywood studio (this one owned by Sony) was forced to drop a film that had already been in production for fifteen months because it was opposed by the Sumo Association of Japan, which found its "portrayal of sumo wrestlers to be unflattering." The film, *Hell Camp*, was being produced by Tristar Pictures and directed by Oscar-winner Milos Forman.

The impact of trade and investment policies on national security presented a philosophical problem to both the Reagan and Bush administrations. Both presidents were strongly committed to free trade and national security, but both found it difficult to reconcile these concepts. Nor could they relate the loss of technology to a loss of national security. When free trade and control of critical technologies were in conflict, they invariably gave the edge to free trade.

"We are in deep trouble because of our ideology, the ideology of the free marketplace," cautioned Bernard Schwartz, chairman of the Loral Corporation, one of America's largest defense-electronics and aerospace firms. "We are not a free marketplace. I cannot sell my stock without abiding by the rules of the SEC. I accept that for the public good. Why should I not accept the fact that I cannot sell something for the good of the country, and for the welfare of the country? If current trends continue, we may be approaching a time when decisions about the defense of the United States will be made by foreigners."

Signs of U.S. dependence were already in evidence during the Vietnam War—for example, when two Japanese producers refused to supply American troops with needed high-technology equipment. Kyocera refused to supply ceramic parts for cruise missiles and nuclear warheads, and Sony declined to sell TV cameras for missile mounts, prompting long debates in the Japanese Diet and denunciations of America's prosecution of the war. The supplies were eventually obtained, after lengthy delays.[13]

The paradox of the exploding military budget and the erosion of the defense industrial base was one of the conundrums of the 1980s. In the interests of national security, President Reagan doubled the defense budget between 1980 and 1986, with Pentagon spending soaring from $140.7 billion annually to $281.4 billion. But the Reagan and Bush administrations watched silently as many American manufacturers of critical technologies were acquired by foreign investors, while others struggled to survive in an environment far less hospitable than that enjoyed by their foreign competitors. A great number of the purchases were hostile takeovers like the Goodyear attempt, leading Representative Byron Dorgan, North Dakota Democrat, to call the U.S. a "giant feedlot for international speculators."

During this period, many subcontractors went out of the defense business, victims of tough economic times and lax U.S. policies. An estimate by the Center for Strategic and International Studies put the loss at eighty thousand companies.[14] Defense officials testified in hearings on the Defense Production Act that this could spell disaster for our fighting forces; in real terms, it meant that the U.S. Army strike force could be sent anywhere in the world, but after only three months of intense fighting would run out of crucial supplies.[15]

Finally, in the waning months of the Reagan presidency, the Defense Department issued two reports warning that national security was being compromised by the administration's laissez-faire policies. Initiated by Dr. Robert Costello, the undersecretary of defense for acquisition, a former General Motors executive, the reports were unusual for their candor. They became a rallying point. "While the strengths of the United States economic system have not changed," said the more famous of the two reports, *Bolstering Defense Industrial Competitiveness* (known also as the Costello Report), "the market environment for American industries has." Along with the growth of the global economy, "foreign governments have adopted aggressive strategies of economic development, through direct and indirect subsidies to develop and maintain indigenous industries, the promotion of exports, and the creation of import barriers." The Costello Report was the first official statement from the executive branch that linked national defense to economic strength, although it diverged sharply from White House policy in its criticism of escalating foreign acquisitions of U.S. assets. It was also the first official document that questioned the administration's unabashed enthusiasm for foreign investment, along with its underlying theory that ownership of critical assets didn't matter: "This view overlooks economic issues, such as the long-term impact on the current account of a continuing flow from the U.S. of repatriated profits and other fees. More importantly, it overlooks the fact that ownership tends to dictate the geographic location of the underlying technologies. Security concerns are not resolved by domestic manufacturing facilities that are dependent on technologies controlled by other nations."[16]

The Defense Science Board, a separate advisory board of leading academics and CEOs which advises the secretary of defense, confirmed the findings of the Costello Report, adding its own concerns that the loss of technological leadership undermined the national strategy of deterrence. "Deterrence relies on convincing a potential aggressor that the U.S. is fully capable of countering any form of aggression," wrote the authors, Robert A. Fuhrman and Robert M. Gardiner. To maintain a credible strategy of deterrence, they said, the U.S. had to "eliminate the apparent loss of leadership in key defense technologies," and "maintain our technological leadership for the foreseeable future."[17]

The White House steadfastly ignored such warnings. "Industrial policy" remained anathema to Reagan and Bush appointees, who refused to intervene even in the most extreme cases of foreign acquisitions of critical technologies. To counter this attitude, concerned scientists, businessmen, and bureaucrats began to speak of "technology policy," prompting Representative Lee Hamilton, Indiana Democrat and chairman of Congress's Joint Economic Committee, to note that " 'Technology policy' is a way of getting away from 'industrial policy,' isn't it?"

The United States stood alone among industrialized nations in its strict interpretation of free trade, and its determination to play on a "level playing field" on which only America's end was "level." Both Japan and the European Community have long supported their critical technologies, incredulous that any nation would even question the utility of supporting industries that promise to keep their nations on the cutting edge of future technologies.

There are those who suggest that, in the increasingly global economy, ownership and national economic interests no longer matter. In a utopian world, perhaps. The adversarial trading practices of some of the United States' major trading partners confirm that we are indeed a long way from an economic Utopia, with Japan rejecting American beef as unfit for Japanese stomachs and American-made skis as unsuitable for Japanese snow. Nor is the U.S. a stranger to protectionist barriers, such as recent government action on liquid-crystal displays for lap-top computers to protect domestic manufacturers.

Concerns over America's difficulty competing in the international marketplace, and the accelerated erosion of America's lead in cutting-edge technologies, finally caught the attention of the White House. In a ground-breaking speech on November 13, 1990, President Bush linked technology and economic competitiveness, saying: "If America is to maintain and strengthen our competitive position, we must continue not only to create new technologies but to learn to more effectively translate those technologies into commercial products."

But the president was silent on government's role in achieving these ends, and his administration generally followed the policy direction of his predecessor. Bush threatened to veto a strong bipartisan effort to improve U.S. competitiveness, the American Technology Pre-eminence Act of 1991, largely because it would provide government loans to selected companies, a program that smacked of "industrial policy"—and "picking winners and losers."

Congress disagreed. "There is now widespread agreement that American prosperity cannot be separated from technological preeminence, and that government policies play a crucial role—either positive or negative—in delineating the economic environment in which new technologies are developed and marketed," said the report accompanying House passage of the legislation.[18]

At least the Bush administration—unlike Reagan's—included some eloquent spokesmen for government involvement, such as Commerce Secretary Robert Mosbacher, science adviser Allan Bromley, occasionally the U.S. Trade Representative Carla Hills, and various sub-Cabinet officials, mostly from the Commerce Department and the intelligence agencies. Although these officials were able at times to emerge victorious—a better deal on the FSX-fighter-plane coproduction agreement with the Japanese, for example—they were generally outmaneuvered by their counterparts at the Office of Management and Budget (OMB), Treasury, and the Council for Economic Advisers, which resisted government assistance to American industry.

Others expressed concerns that reflected their special needs and constituencies. Some members of Congress, like Senator Exon, feared the loss of constituent jobs. The Pentagon expressed national-security concerns, and warned against overreliance on foreign suppliers of needed military hardware. Labor leaders feared the loss of jobs, business leaders the loss of America's economic competitiveness. All these expressions, however, though strikingly similar, were isolated from one another, and therefore less effective than if they had been orchestrated in concert. Even the business community spoke with several voices, reflecting the immediate needs of corporate executives rather than the long-term health of American industry.

Despite occasional lip service in defense of critical technologies,

White House officials were actually proud of their cavalier attitude toward the rescue of Perkin-Elmer, a key semiconductor-equipment manufacturer, which came close to being sold to the Japanese company Nikon. "If IBM is so unhappy, let them buy it," said one White House official. "There is no difference between computer chips and potato chips in this White House," said another official—reputed to be Council of Economic Advisers Chairman Michael Boskin, although he denied it—at a widely quoted private meeting at the White House. Right after the potato-chips/computer-chips episode, Andrew Grove, president and CEO of Intel, an American manufacturer of semiconductors, sent a violin to OMB Director Richard Darman, an allusion to Nero and the burning of Rome.

It took the Gulf War to reveal the costs of complacency: American embassies beseeched foreign governments for needed military equipment. In the spring of 1991, the Bush administration temporarily departed from its long-standing ideological opposition to industrial policy in a report by the Office of Science and Technology Policy urging that critical technologies be identified and nurtured. The report noted that "the spectacular performance of U.S. and coalition forces in the Persian Gulf" was a reminder of "the crucial role that technology plays in military competitiveness." The report then asserted that "It is equally clear that technology plays a similar role in the economic competitiveness among nations." The report identified twenty-two critical technologies that should be nurtured by government policies. Under orders from the Congress, the Pentagon and the Energy Department had for the past three years issued annual reports on critical technologies and where the nation stood in terms of gains and losses. This was the first time those in the White House inner circle lent their official support to the concept.[19] Opponents within the administration struck quickly, however, and Bush swiftly disavowed the report, saying that it reflected only the views of its authors, who happened to be the White House technology experts.

In identifying critical technologies, the United States was somewhat belatedly following the lead of its trading partners, who routinely identified and subsidized certain technologies according to their perceived national needs. Japan's Science and Technology Agency publishes a biennial *Technology Forecast Survey*, and in 1990 the European Community released a list of key technologies that its leaders felt merited strong Community support.

Another sign that the winds were shifting in the U.S. was the surprising and uncharacteristic May 1991 protest from the Bush White House against the Japanese government's effort to enlist American scientists in a ten-year project aimed at achieving breakthroughs in computer design. Failing initially to get U.S. government cooperation, the Japanese approached U.S. scientists and engineers through their professional groups. Eugene Wong, associate director of the White House Science Office, charged that the project seemed to "pose a serious competitive threat" to the United States. American universities, generally considered to be world leaders in computer-science research, should, he said, be concerned about the consequences of accepting foreign support for their research.[20]

In fact, some type of industrial policy has been in effect throughout most of the nation's history. The tax system, for example, always an instrument of social and economic policy, boasted a long tradition of picking winners and losers through preferential treatment for selected industries—usually the ones with the most political clout. When the Tax Reform Act of 1986 streamlined the system and revoked tax breaks to smokestack industries, all industries were affected, especially companies with cutting-edge technologies, who missed the years of tax benefits that gave older industries their head start. But although the critical technologies were offered little help, the tax code continued to provide benefits to other investors, including homeowners and builders. The Reagan and Bush administrations did support a reduction in the capital-gains tax that would help U.S. industry—especially emerging technologies, starved for capital—but, given the political briar patch surrounding this issue, reform will probably come too late to make much of a difference to many high-tech companies.

In praising the "spectacular performance" of American and allied troops in the Gulf War, the Bush White House report neglected to mention that the victory owed much of its success to outdated technologies. The Patriot missile, for example, which proved so effective against Saddam Hussein's Scud missiles, used a microchip that was ten years old and no longer produced by its original manufacturer, Intel. If the Iraqi leader had gained access to more modern chips, the Gulf War might have been prolonged, at a much higher cost in American lives.

Assessments of the Gulf War by numerous government agencies noted as well America's technological dependencies on foreign suppliers. In fact, the military was "dangerously dependent," according to the Defense Science Board.[21] "Almost all U.S. weapon systems contain component parts from foreign sources," noted a 1991 report from the Office of Technology Assessment, the scientific-research arm of Congress.[22] Even with the full cooperation of foreign governments, reliance on foreign suppliers complicated the smooth flow of U.S. supplies to the Gulf, and left policymakers seriously concerned about how to ensure future U.S. military readiness in the event of a shortage of foreign components from countries that might not be so cooperative in the future.[23]

Vital parts of the military equipment that helped win the Gulf War were made in Germany, Japan, and other foreign countries.[24] The mad scramble for needed parts sent allied officers to Paris and Tokyo for special battery packs for their computers; Teledyne executives enlisted the cooperation of French diplomats to fill a rush order for "one of the most critical items of Desert Storm," a transponder that beamed electronic signals necessary for differentiating between enemies and allies; U.S. officials sought help from the Japanese embassy to compensate for shortages of critical parts for display terminals used to analyze intelligence data. Tactical cockpit displays came from Britain, and video panels as well as critical components for search-and-rescue radios and navigation systems came from Japan. To their credit, U.S. allies came through, but the need to beg foreign embassies for essential parts was chilling to many who favored a greater degree of technological independence.[25]

Desert Storm led many to recall that it was the strength and health of the nation's basic industries that made the difference between victory and defeat for the Allies in World War II. More than half the munitions produced by the Allies were stamped "Made in America," and experts say that without U.S. help the Soviets would never have survived the Nazi assault. American aid included 1,981 locomotives, 3,786,000 tires, 52,000 jeeps, 35,000 motorcycles, 415,000 telephone sets, 15 million pairs of soldiers' boots, and 4 million tons of food. "No other nation in the world could have done it," wrote Bernard Baruch, the investment banker who helped President Roosevelt raise the money to finance this effort. "That we could undertake two . . . operations, at opposite ends of the world, at the same time, has never ceased being a source of marvel to me." No longer "Fortress America," or even an "arsenal of democracy," the nation still recognizes the need to mobilize in the event of a global threat, such as the Iraqi invasion of Kuwait. To achieve that capability, the United States needs a new concept of national strength that includes a greater degree of technological independence.[26]

THE OVERSEAS INVESTMENT CHALLENGE
Interdependence or Vulnerability

How did it happen? How did the greatest military build-up in peacetime, in the 1980s, coincide with the nation's loss of its technological edge? How can a nation claim its economic system is strong and still lose over 35 percent of the worldwide semiconductor market? How can a nation that invented the computer chip, VCRs, and a host of other innovations lose control of those lucrative industries to countries smart and aggressive enough to commercialize them? How do these losses relate to the slow but steady decline of America's standard of living in the early 1990s? The United States was the only industrialized nation in the world to face such a decline, a strange state of affairs for the nation with the world's largest Gross National Product, largest consumer market, and richest store of natural resources.[27]

One reason for this is that America is not investing in itself, at least in amounts sufficient to retain control over the most valuable sectors of its economy. Other nations scurry to acquire U.S. assets and technologies while U.S. investors and governments neglect them. Many explanations spring from what columnist Robert J. Samuelson calls the "excuse industry"; a brief glance at some of them helps explain why the nation no longer can pride itself on its innovation and initiation.

Presidents Bush and Reagan feared that restricting the sale of America's technological base would send a negative message to foreign investors, on whom the United States had become increasingly dependent for money to underwrite the deficit and buoy the stock market. As a result, foreign money flowed freely into the country, surging from $196 billion in 1974 to a cumulative total of more than $2.5 trillion by 1991. Foreign investment accelerated swiftly in the second half of the 1980s, thanks to the drop in the value of the dollar, which made American assets cheap for overseas investors, and the nation's transition in 1983 from net creditor to net debtor, which required increased borrowing from abroad to finance the burgeoning debt.[28]

Foreign investors were delighted with this turn of events. The steep drop in the dollar was brought about by the Plaza Accords of 1985, at which Treasury Secretary James A. Baker joined his European counterparts in agreeing to devaluation. Although this helped U.S. exports by making them more affordable, it also had the unanticipated effect of making U.S. assets cheap to foreign buyers. Add to that the attractions of the lucrative U.S. market, and a political system that provided one of the most stable business environments in the world, and you had the ingredients for the biggest fire sale held by any advanced industrialized country in history. Americans became addicted to foreign capital, willing to sell any asset to the highest bidder, unconcerned they were selling their assets faster than their goods.

Americans didn't care where the money came from, or where it went. The U.S. took money from Filipino President Ferdinand Marcos, Haitian President Jean-Claude Duvalier, and other third-world despots, including money that American taxpayers had sent to these poverty-ridden countries as foreign aid. The Soviets made a down payment on several small banks in Silicon Valley, the better to obtain information on U.S. executives and projects. In June 1988, nothing prevented CitiSteel USA Inc., an agency of the People's Republic of China, from purchasing the Phoenix Steel Corporation of Wilmington, Delaware, which manufactured heavy armor plate for submarines.[29]

A few mavericks warned that this trend was eroding the nation's independence, and that major decisions affecting the lives of Americans were increasingly being made in Tokyo, Bonn, London, or Riyadh. Others cautioned that the nation should discriminate a bit to preserve its critical industries; or perhaps put a ceiling on foreign ownership of banks, machine tools, or land to preserve an American component, or a degree of domestic ownership, for national-security reasons. But policymakers felt that the influx of capital outweighed any disadvantages. After all, foreign investors brought new technology, jobs, and fresh managerial approaches to American firms facing obsolescence, not to mention desperately needed long-term, or "patient," capital. And, thanks to currency shifts, foreign money could mean fatter profits to those with golf courses, skyscrapers, wheat fields, semiconductor equipment, and other assets to sell.

National-security questions were brushed aside with the rationalization that, since the major foreign owners of U.S. assets were allies, the United States didn't have to worry; after all, our interests would always coincide, and therefore our allies and trading partners would act in our interests. This argument became especially embarrassing during Desert Storm, when the Customs Service seized a number of high-tech companies owned by Iraqi officials, one of whom was Saddam Hussein's brother-in-law. The Iraqi investments dramatized the vulnerability of U.S. technologies to the nation's rivals and enemies, given the indiscriminate U.S. policy of welcoming virtually anyone with the francs, marks, rubles, or yen to pay for them.

An array of public officials and private entrepreneurs played the role of midwife. Hungry for jobs and encouraged by the policy vacuum at the top, governors and mayors circled the globe seeking to lure foreign money to their states and cities, shaping American international economic policy. American investment bankers made millions by targeting companies that would appeal to foreign investors, and almost all of them followed one Wall Street house in forming "Bargain Basement Committees" to identify vulnerable U.S. companies. For their part, offshore investors hired a small army of lobbyists, many of them former high U.S. government officials, to protect their American subsidiaries from periodic congressional attempts to provide oversight. Among these lobbyists were Elliot Richardson, former attorney general, secretary of defense, and ambassador to Great Britain; Lloyd Cutler, counsel to President Jimmy Carter; and William E. Brock, former U.S. trade representative, secretary of labor, and U.S. senator. Together with their allies, they succeeded in blocking congressional efforts to improve data collection on foreign ownership, protect technologies thought to be essential to national security, and close the revolving door to influence peddlers like themselves. They pointed out that this nation's greatest strengths were its openness and diversity. How that rationale translated to open season on its assets mystified even offshore investors, many of whom privately scorned the policy but marveled at their good fortune.

The United States had, indeed, benefited from being the most open country in the world, inviting foreign money as well as immigrants. Foreign money built the nation's railroads, canals, factories, mines, and overall industrial capacity, particularly in the last century. Freedom of opportunity is the bedrock upon which America was built. Supporters of unrestricted foreign investment in the United States argued that, although such investment had grown rapidly, it amounted to only a small fraction of the nation's wealth. They noted that foreign investment furthered the country's historic goal of reducing the restrictions on the free flow of goods, services, and capital throughout the world. Since World War II, the United States has been the leading advocate of free trade and the reduction of tariffs worldwide, as well as the prime mover behind the engines that power those goals: the GATT (General Agreement on Tariff and Trade) negotiations, the International Monetary Fund (IMF), and the World Bank. The continued free flow of investment plays a vital role in the success of the global economy, they argued, and President Reagan expressed the prevailing view in 1983 when he said, "We believe that there are only winners, no losers, and all participants gain from it."[30]

But the foreign money that helped build this country when the United States was a developing nation served a very different purpose from the one it serves today, when overseas funds pour into the world's greatest industrial nation to acquire technology and economic power. The ease of acquiring assets in a nation that refuses to differentiate between potato chips and computer chips virtually invites the rest of the world to snap up its choice industries.

The U.S. has the dubious distinction of remaining the only industrialized country in the world without a policy governing foreign investment. In the vast majority of cases, the decision to sell defense technologies to foreign owners rests solely in the hands of the owners of those technologies. A glance at the rest of the world reveals how isolated the U.S. is in its approach to protecting its critical technologies.

When the Kuwaitis increased their holdings in British Petroleum from 9 percent to 22 percent over a four-month period, the British bounced them back below 10 percent. Using the vehicle of antitrust law, the free-market British argued that they regarded BP—a government-owned company—as a critical asset, worthy of protection against a takeover by an offshore investor (particularly the Kuwaitis, who, the British pointedly recalled, had not exactly acted in British national interests when they led the OPEC cartel).

Contrast the British reaction to the very different approach of the U.S. toward its energy assets. CFIUS, the Committee on Foreign Investment in the United States (the interagency group led by Treasury with the responsibility for overseeing the sale of security-related companies), allowed a company owned by the Saudi Arabian government to purchase 50 percent of Texaco's refining and marketing assets, concluding that the sale represented no threat to U.S. national security. The Saudi purchase included three refineries, fifty product distribution terminals, fourteen hundred owned and leased service stations, and ten thousand franchise gasoline stations in Eastern and Gulf Coast states. The effect of the Saudi purchase was compounded by the earlier British purchase of Standard Oil of Ohio, which gave BP access to vast U.S. oil reserves in Prudhoe Bay, Alaska. How much of our oil reserves can the U.S. afford to lose before national security is imperiled? Fifty percent? Seventy-five percent? One hundred percent?[31]

Even the Canadians held up the acquisition of one of their aircraft companies, De Havilland, by a consortium of French and Italian investors, on the grounds that the purchase seemed not to be in the national interest. Investment Canada, the federal agency that screens foreign investment, reflected concerns on the part of government leaders that the sale would be a blow to the Canadian aerospace industry and risked the loss of jobs and technology.[32] What a contrast to U.S. policymakers, who seek to overturn regulations limiting foreign-equity ownership of airlines to help the nation's ailing airlines. In view of the critical role of U.S. airlines during the Gulf War, when a number of commercial planes were drafted for wartime use, one would think this policy deserves careful review.

An American Component

In fact, the surge of acquisitions of critical technologies led the late William J. Casey, when director of Central Intelligence, to call foreign investment "a Trojan horse," superficially attractive, but inimical to long-term U.S. interests.[33] During this period, America sold off some of its prime assets, including cutting-edge technologies needed to keep the nation competitive. In the absence of government constraints, foreign acquisitions made deep inroads into industries ranging from semiconductors to machine tools to biotechnology. In 1990, a Japanese manufacturer, Nippon Sanso, purchased Semi-Gas, the only American manufacturer of the rarefied gases needed to produce semiconductors. Another foreign investor purchased the American manufacturer of precise machine tools that affect the explosive force of nuclear weapons and control the risk of accidental detonation. These sales went through easily.[34]

In a comprehensive and chilling study, Linda Spencer of the Economic Strategy Institute identified the hundreds of high-tech companies sold to foreign firms during the last decade, including: one hundred U.S. computer companies, forty-five U.S. semiconductor companies, thirty-five U.S. advanced materials companies, and twenty U.S. aerospace companies.[35] Of course it is all a matter of degree. There is no need, nor is it possible, to retain 100 percent of the production of every vital technology. But surely the United States should retain some production capability in technologies that were developed in this country, and not allow foreign investors to cart off 70, 80, or 90 percent of an American industry.

Sadly, no industry seems immune to foreign efforts to acquire control of its leading corporations. Foreign acquisition of banking assets, for example, went from 16-percent ownership in 1988 to 25-percent ownership by 1990. Problems in regulating these international institutions were highlighted in 1991, with the revelation that the Bank of Credit and Commerce International (BCCI), a Pakistan-based institution involved in widespread drug traffic and money laundering, had secretly purchased control of the First American Bank, a Washington-based institution, along with the National Bank of Georgia and the Independent Bank of Encino, California.

Much foreign investment was intended to tap into the world's greatest consumer market—the United States. Foreign companies set up automobile plants in the United States, the better to sell and service American customers. Some foreign investors were motivated by a "search-and-destroy" strategy—acquire an American company to destroy a leading competitor—and others sought to acquire American technology. Regardless of the motive, little attention was paid to which investments were beneficial to the national interest, which had no effect, and which were downright harmful. Although there were sporadic protests related to some dramatic foreign purchases—Mitsubishi's Rockefeller Center acquisition, or Sony's purchase of Columbia Pictures, hardly critical technologies—there was scant national debate about the surge of foreign investment, and whether there were any industries that warranted government protection because they were vital to American security. Nowhere is this clearer than in the ongoing implementation of the Exon-Florio amendment, which the White House has rendered as unnecessary as an appendix. Dispositions in case after case indicate that the administration is unconcerned about sales of a number of companies representing the "last" manufacturer of a security-related technology.

America's technology has been raided by the West as well as the East. The last American manufacturer of silicon wafers, described by Representative Florio as "building blocks for all the sophisticated equipment required for national defense," was purchased from Monsanto Electronic Materials Company by the West German firm of Huels AG, a subsidiary of the Veba AG chemical group.[36] Similarly, Hoffman–La Roche, the Swiss pharmaceutical giant, purchased Genentech, the crown jewel of America's companies in the biotechnology field, considered a critical industry for America's economic well-being in the twenty-first century. France's Compagnie de Saint-Gobain acquired the Norton Company, a leading manufacturer of abrasives, advanced ceramics, and chemical-process products. Again, the absence of policy makes it easy for overseas investors to purchase choice U.S. assets, especially when domestic investment is scarce.

These acquisitions were rubber-stamped by CFIUS, which critics have called a "paper tiger." CFIUS has reviewed more than seven hundred cases since the passage of Exon-Florio in 1988, and rejected only one: a Chinese government agency, suspected of being a front for spies, which sought to acquire a Boeing supplier. Absent any strengthening of the language in the amendment from Congress, or any interest from the White House, U.S. security interests will continue to be compromised, and U.S. tax dollars wasted. In fact, why continue to finance SEMATECH and other research consortia if the government refuses to curb business deals that give overseas competitors the fruits of its efforts?

Political Intervention and U.S. Sovereignty

To protect their investments, foreign investors have become increasingly involved in the American political process. Their lobbyists, who patrol the corridors of Congress and state capitals, have created more than a hundred political-action committees (PACs), which pumped more than $2 million into the 1990 congressional campaigns.[37] Indeed, the foreign investors' American lobbyists defeated congressional efforts to obtain reliable data on foreign investments, including the extent of the investments and the ultimate recipients of foreign money.[38] In May 1991, these lobbyists persuaded the Senate to reverse itself and defeat a bill—sponsored by Senator Lloyd Bentsen, Texas Democrat, and overwhelmingly passed in 1990—that would have barred PACs created by American subsidiaries of foreign companies. It does remain illegal for foreign citizens, companies, or governments to contribute directly or indirectly to the election campaign of a candidate for federal office.

On the state level, lobbyists for foreign multinationals, led by Sony, convinced state legislatures across the nation to repeal the unitary tax, a state tax on multinational corporations. State finance experts estimate that repeal cost the state of California alone between $300 and 600 million annually. On the national level, foreign lobbyists have been heavily involved in persuading the White House not to implement the Exon-Florio amendment, and to turn a blind eye to foreign acquisitions that might threaten national security. The system perpetuates itself: the more investments, the greater the necessity for political involvement. If a nation loses control over significant measures of its tax, trade, and national-security policy, its sovereignty will inevitably also erode, bit by bit.

Of all our trading partners, the Japanese are the unquestioned masters of "adversarial trade," according to Peter Drucker, one of the nation's leading scholars of modern management. And although Japanese businessmen, diplomats, and their American lobbyists protest criticism of Japanese trade and investment practices as "Japan-bashing," the fact remains that Japan not only refuses to extend to American companies comparable reciprocity in trade and investment, but also aggressively uses trade and investment to acquire technology and eliminate global competition. Nor are Japan's critics assuaged by that nation's tradition of giant *keiretsu*—interlocking organizations of companies, including banks, manufacturers, suppliers, and distributors—which are a throwback to the giant prewar conglomerates that created Japan's military machine. Great Britain, the Netherlands, Canada, France, and Germany allow a greater degree of reciprocity, and their approach is generally more collegial and benign.

"Japan is on a wartime economy," warned the late Robert Noyce, co-inventor of the integrated circuit (forerunner of the computer chip) and CEO of SEMATECH. "They are exporting their industry. They are out acquiring assets. This is the most massive transfer of assets that has occurred in any war."

America has not yet figured out how to deal with an economic adversary that is also an ally and a major trading partner, and whose trade practices follow a very different course from our own. All too often America's response becomes hostile and impotent, the worst combination of all. Years after the Japanese cartels and *keiretsu* expanded their reach across the United States, isolated pockets of activity finally emerged in the offices of the United States Trade Representative and the Justice Department to deal with some of the imbalances caused by domestic firms trying to compete against the deep-pocketed cartels. In the FSX coproduction agreement, the inadequacies of U.S.-government trade policies showed that uncoordinated and untimely responses do not serve the national interest, especially when competing against a coordinated Japanese government acting on behalf of its own industries and labor force.

HOLDING ON TO THE TECHNOLOGICAL EDGE

One of the earliest and most vocal advocates of linking economic and national security was Senator Bingaman. As chairman of the Defense Industry and Technology Subcommittee of the Armed Services Committee, the studious and softspoken Bingaman sponsored the legislation requiring the Department of Defense to identify critical industries, which set the stage for the national debate.[39]

"We need to retain within our borders the ability to innovate on those technologies most critical to future generations of weapon systems," the senator said, even if that meant identifying and nurturing them. "If semiconductors are one of them, should we be disturbed when Monsanto sells the only silicon-wafer production plant in the U.S. to a German firm? Should we be concerned about the Hitachi–Texas Instruments joint venture on sixteen-megabit D-RAMS?"

Bingaman's views were supported by Congress's Office of Technology Assessment in a study entitled *Holding the Edge*, appropriately suggesting someone holding on by his fingertips: "Technological superiority has been a cornerstone of United States security and industry since World War II. That cornerstone is not crumbling, but over the past decade it has weathered significantly. Foreign companies have made deep inroads into high technology markets that had been more or less the exclusive domain of U.S. industry. In addition to causing economic problems, this has fostered dependence on foreign sources for defense equipment at a time when the technology in defense systems comes increasingly from the civilian sector."[40]

Foreign companies and their governments should not be blamed for acting in what they consider to be their best interests. Unfortunately, the United States has not followed suit.

What should be the government's role? Pentagon studies have noted that the Defense Department now depends upon our trading partners for virtually every sector of the manufacturing base. Ninety-five percent of the manufactured goods purchased by the Pentagon came from a broad spectrum of 215 industries. "Clearly, the Department of Defense cannot provide massive financial assistance for every American industry characterized by a lack of international competitiveness, nor can we effectively provide incentives for every manufacturing industry critical to our defense."[41]

Some experts point the finger at American industry, accusing American manufacturers of becoming overly dependent on defense contracts and failing to develop the aggressiveness needed to compete in the global marketplace. Some defense contractors actually jettisoned their civilian products, believing the defense contracts would provide greater profits at less risk.[42]

Many defense specialists point out that it is no longer possible for the United States to be technologically self-sufficient. The objective, they say, is to have the United States retain enough key technologies to use as leverage to assure access to other technologies that are needed. That's the difference between interdependence and dependence, a distinction that is critical to U.S. future technological leadership. To be a player, you have to bring something to the table, so that other nations are as dependent on us as we are on them.

Losing a technology, however, also means losing control over its development. "If we decide we're not in the sixteen-megabit business, then it means we're not in on the follow-on, the sixty-four-megabit business," said Mike Kelly, former director of manufacturing of DARPA (Defense Advanced Research Projects Agency), the agency that funds much of the advanced research for the military. Kelly emphasized that flexibility in the manufacturing process was critical in times of crisis. "You don't have to make 100 percent of the product," he said. "It's even okay to buy 90 percent of the product as long as you have the technology and the ability to make this in times of crisis, that is, as long as you have flexible factories." Richard E. Donnelly, assistant deputy undersecretary of defense (manufacturing and industrial programs) agreed, adding that "We must discriminate between foreign sourcing and foreign dependency."

America's policymakers are belatedly recognizing that the nation's defense industrial base and cutting-edge technologies are up against a stacked deck. With eroding government support, U.S. producers have been left to compete against foreign companies that receive a broad range of assistance, including subsidies, tax breaks, low-cost loans, government grants, money for research and development, and protection against overseas competitors.

In mid-1992, Congress took action to safeguard the industrial base when faced with the impending sale of LTV's missile and aircraft divisions to corporations owned and controlled by the French government. LTV is heavily involved in highly classified weapons and defense systems, including the Stealth bomber, missile launch systems, and a short-range tactical ballistic missile system. This was the first time a U.S. prime defense contractor had come up for sale to a foreign corporation: Thomson-CSF bid for the missile division, and Crédit Lyonnais, through the Carlyle Group, was financing the acquisition of the aircraft division. Two U.S. multinationals, Martin Marietta and Lockheed, were outbid by the French, with both companies competing against the unlimited resources of a foreign government. This seemed highly unfair to many members of Congress, who noted that U.S. citizens had financed this aerospace technology with billions of their tax dollars.

It is hard to see how America's interests are served by the selling off of its energy resources, manufacturing base, and financial independence. Goodyear hardly became "leaner and meaner" and more efficient by experiencing the Goldsmith assault, which left it saddled with debt and forced to close down plants, fire workers, and reduce research and development. Would any of our trading partners have permitted such a raid on a major company?

The failure of American firms has been blamed on the shortsightedness of American management, but there has been complicity on the part of government officials who are wedded to outmoded and unrealistic laissez-faire ideologies. Such ideologies focus on short-term political needs rather than on the collective long-term need to end the erosion of American technological superiority.

Fortunately, there seems to be an awakening. Enactment of the Exon-Florio amendment, the Defense Department studies, the 1991 Bush White House report, and a host of warnings from congressional leaders and experts in the academic, business, and labor communities suggest that the United States is becoming aware of the perils of technology erosion. America, the sleeping giant, is slowly awakening. The question is, by the time the nation finally decides to act, will it be shorn of sufficient strength to reverse the complacency of the past decade? Bold steps are needed, and promptly, to retain the industry and technology that have made America the envy of the world.

CHAPTER II

Shooting Down the Goodyear Blimp

HOW WE DEFEND THE DEFENSE INDUSTRIAL BASE FROM FOREIGN RAIDERS

If I were Qaddafi, I'd put a dozen Libyans in three-piece suits, send them to Wall Street, assign them to different American industries, bankroll them with junk bonds or petro-dollars, and watch them destroy America's industrial base without firing a shot.

—Robert Mercer,
former chairman of Goodyear[1]

Bud Fox: "But why do you need to wreck this company?"
Gordon Gekko: "Because it's wreckable."

—from *Wall Street*, 1987

THE RAIDER

"Goldsmith leaps out of the Cayman Islands, with two wives and a mistress, children from France and England, and *he* accuses *us* of diversification," mused Robert Mercer, the feisty former chairman of the board of Goodyear. Now in retirement in Akron, Ohio, Mercer remembered his company's unhappy tangle with international financier Sir James Goldsmith as clearly as if it had occurred the day before—although the event took place in October and November of 1986.

A champion of the global economy, Goldsmith is a swashbuckling corporate raider of British nationality, whose companies encircle the

globe from their tax havens in the Cayman Islands, Bermuda, Liechtenstein, the Bahamas, and Panama. His U.S. corporate trophies include
Grand Union grocery stores and Crown Zellerbach, a paper company
with extensive timber holdings. Like American corporate raiders,
Goldsmith targets vulnerable companies, quietly buys up their stock,
and then pounces, convinced that bloated businesses like Goodyear
benefit from takeover experiences by becoming leaner, meaner, and
more "efficient."

As a strategy it is foolproof, with the raider assuming few risks
if he plays the game right. Sir James was a master at such win-win
tactics, and Goodyear proved him successful. When he finally departed
for home, he had lost the company but won its cash box: he received
$93 million for six months' work, while the investment-banking firm
that raised his junk bonds pocketed $250 million. Only Goodyear lost
out. The company was forced to fire four thousand people, farm out
its research-and-development activities to universities, "hollow out"
many of its key operations, and sell its aerospace division.

THE "HOW-TO" GUIDE TO BIG-TIME TAKEOVERS:
THE GOODYEAR VIEW

Mercer casts Goodyear in the role of victim, not target of opportunity.
"You're talking about a raid on a company that had a major defense
role," said Mercer, referring to the loss of Goodyear's aerospace division. Despite that role, the company became an easy target thanks in
part to the U.S. government's conspicuous absence from the fray.
Mercer detailed the steps of the attempted buy-out; his story makes a
perfect primer for anyone interested in launching a corporate takeover.

From a purely economic perspective, Goodyear was no beanbag
operation. It was an $11-billion corporation, the largest tire company
in the world, with 133,000 employees, of whom 60,000 were in the
United States, and 46,000 shareholders. It was the last major American
tire manufacturer, whose product was vital to the automobile industry.

Like Carl Sandburg's fog, Goldsmith's troops came on little cat
feet. Sir James slowly and quietly began buying up Goodyear stock
until he reached the 12-percent mark. His purchases were made
through a confusing concoction of limited partnerships and parent
companies that enjoyed virtual anonymity. "Limited partnerships
don't adhere to Hart-Scott-Rodino antitrust protection," explained
Mercer. "All raiders use it. If we as a corporation want to go after
someone, we have to go through Hart-Scott-Rodino, while partner-

ships don't. It drives a truck through the free-enterprise system." (The Hart-Scott-Rodino law requires companies planning to acquire assets of $15 million or more, or a 15 percent stake in another company's securities, to get the approval of the Federal Trade Commission.)[2]

To buy the amount of Goodyear stock needed for a serious take-over attempt, "Goldsmith attracted a bunch of junk bonds" raised by his investment banker, Merrill Lynch. "Merrill Lynch did the spade-work. They said Goodyear was undervalued, a euphemism for break-ing up a company into pieces where you can get more for each of them individually, and then selling them off separately.

"The group then started buying up the stock, carefully keeping the amount under 5 percent—the limit for filing with the Securities and Exchange Commission. They bought timidly under Merrill Lynch. We asked, 'What's the interest [in buying up the company]?' Merrill Lynch was not telling. You smell something, but can't do anything about it. . . . They line up stock, then they buy the rest quickly in a ten-day period before the SEC notification."

Finally, Sir James filed with the SEC and registered his intent to buy the company. At that point, continued Mercer, "their PR firm came in with the standard jargon: 'Get rid of entrenched management'; 'fight corpocracy,' with corpocracy defined as an unholy alliance of big business, big labor, and big government; and finally the holy grail comes out—'We're enhancing shareholder value by unlocking the value of the shares.' "

Goldsmith was able to escape government intervention up to this point by an ingenious organizational structure, a portent of the creative possibilities of the new freewheeling, global economy, where owner-ship escapes scrutiny and defies the imagination. Thus, two newly formed partnerships were able to purchase half a billion dollars' worth of Goodyear stock without filing any documents. Once the details were ferreted out, it appeared that one limited partnership was based in Bermuda, the other in Delaware. The labyrinth continued: The general partner of each of those partnerships was a corporation—one in Dela-ware, the other in the Cayman Islands. Both of these were owned by a second Cayman Islands corporation, which was owned by a third Cayman Islands corporation, which, in turn, was controlled by two interlocking Panama corporations. At the center of the maze rested a Liechtenstein-based trust named Brunneria, which controlled the Panama corporations.

Thanks to Liechtenstein's secrecy laws, the identities of the princi-pal owners at all layers of the corporate structure were kept anony-mous. "They could be owned by Qaddafi or the Russians," remarked

Mercer. Conceivably, even another tire company, a competitor of Goodyear, could be protected under these laws—a clear violation of U.S. antitrust laws, but who would know and who could find out?

ENTER THE GOVERNMENT

Immediately after Goldsmith filed his intention to buy out Goodyear, Mercer and his top managers decided it was time to seek government help. "I talked to John Shad [chairman of the SEC] right after the ten days, in October 1986," said Mercer. "I said, 'John, here's what's happening. Goldsmith is a knight in shining junk bonds. I have an uneasy feeling that what he's doing is somewhere illegal. Because of the maze of partnerships, it would take us quite a bit of time to find out what's illegal. *Put a halt on the proceedings until we can find out . . . to see if it's illegal.* Once you knock Humpty-Dumpty down, you can't put him back together. There are going to be thousands unemployed.'

"Shad said there was nothing he could do. It was beyond his power. His best advice was to have Congress handle this. They weren't in session. I got hold of Representative John Seiberling, our congressman [Ohio Democrat]. He is a former Goodyear lawyer and the grandson of the founder of Goodyear. Seiberling got hold of Rodino [Peter Rodino, Democrat of New Jersey and chairman of the House Judiciary Committee], who held a postadjournment hearing on November 18, 1986.[3]

"Jimmy was the star of the hearing. He told me, 'I called you names, but I didn't mean them.' I told him, 'The profession you're in is obscene.'

"He's a great actor. He should have gotten an Oscar. He called me an 'idiot.' Seiberling asked Goldsmith, 'Who the hell are you?' Jimmy answered: 'I happen to be an investor, and I don't want to see what happened to England happen here.' If Jimmy was that good, why didn't he save the U.K.?

"It was a great public-relations setup. I was the bad guy. Goldsmith was going to unlock the value of the company. Merrill Lynch came up with $1.9 billion, plus an analysis of what's wrong with Goodyear. Kerry Packard, another investor, had half a billion, and Hanson Trust of England was in the background.

"They borrow all that money short-term, take over the company, put it up for sale, then they can sell the pieces for less than market value to competitors . . . then get rid of the competition."

At the hearings, Mercer tried to negotiate privately with Goldsmith. Given his strong feelings, perhaps he wasn't as tactful as he should have been. When Goldsmith, peering out over the hearing at a room full of Goodyear workers wearing union caps, asked Mercer, "Who are all those people?," Mercer responded: "They came in on the bus this morning. They sat up all night to get here. They don't want you here. You can't find anybody who thinks you belong."

According to Bruce Thompson, an aide from Merrill Lynch who helped orchestrate Goldsmith's appearance at the hearings, Goldsmith became fearful of a riot in the halls of Congress, spurred by the angry Goodyear workers. After the hearing, he stopped and spoke to the group and to his surprise found them interested in what he had to say, and courteous to a fault. Sensitive to the mounting public-relations disaster, Goldsmith then left the Rayburn Building, where the hearings were being held, and found TV cameras surrounding his stretch limousine. Ignore them, he told his aides, and they walked past the limousine and hailed a cab.

Clearly nervous by this time, Goldsmith asked Mercer out to lunch. Mercer responded with a counteroffer: "Can you be bought out? Let's get our groups together tonight." Goldsmith couldn't make it, because he was spending the evening with President and Mrs. Reagan, who were hosting an event in his honor at the Kennedy Center, according to Mercer.

While Goldsmith, a foreign corporate raider, was being fêted by the president, Mercer was still trying to get government help. He was not without contacts. "I was trying to beat my way through the administration and find someone sympathetic. I played baseball at Yale and knew Bush. Bush called me back and in refusing to help said: 'I think you know this administration is strongly in favor of the free-enterprise system, but you've given me something to think about.'

"I then called Baker," said Mercer, referring to then Secretary of the Treasury James A. Baker III. "I was handling his national campaign for savings bonds. He gave the same answer Bush gave about the free-enterprise system. I called but I couldn't get through to Reagan. I got Regan [White House Chief of Staff Donald Regan] instead."

No help there either. Regan was a former head of Merrill Lynch, Goldsmith's investment banker, and his answer was a foregone conclusion. Mercer felt outgunned—not by a foreign investor, but by his own government, whose leaders were, by dint of ideology and their own ties to a foreign investor, unwilling to help an American multinational fend off a hostile offshore takeover attempt.

COUNTEROFFENSIVE

Mercer finally gave up on the government and launched a counter-attack that will be recorded as one of the most convoluted defenses in the history of corporate raids. Besides using the company's own internal SWAT team of financial and legal experts, Mercer hired outside help straight from the enemy camp at a cost of $35 million in fees: He engaged a New York lawyer named Joseph Flom, who at that time was being retained as the personal attorney of Sir James Goldsmith. According to Mercer, Flom was also representing Corn Products Corporation, which makes Hellmann's mayonnaise and Skippy peanut butter, against a well-known American takeover artist, Ronald Perelman. Flom was also Perelman's attorney.

This arrangement may boggle the minds of laymen, but Flom, Mercer noted, "didn't see it as a conflict of interest. This is the ethics of the business. It's hiring wolves to keep the fox out of the chicken coop. There is a fraternity of lawyers, public-relations companies, and investment bankers. They work both sides of the street. It is a matter of who calls first. On the same principle, we also hired Drexel Burnham. Flom told us, 'I'm going to the ball game tonight with Perelman. I'll see what he says.'"

THE HOLLOW CORPORATION

Despite, or because of, this highly inbred and high-priced talent pool, Mercer saved the company. His efforts to enlist Washington and the takeover establishment lined the pockets of everyone except the company. "I personally would have been way ahead financially if I had let Goldsmith buy," Mercer pointed out in retrospect. The financial side of the deal left Goodyear saddled with debt for years to come.

Goldsmith ran the stock up to $76 a share, claiming that his efforts enriched shareholders. The company then spent $2.6 billion to get the stock back, including $600 million for the investment bankers and Sir James; the latter eventually walked away with a clear profit of $93 million. To avoid charges of greenmail, a form of bribing to get raiders to desist, the company made a tender offer to its other shareholders for $50 a share for 40 percent of the shares they owned at a time when the stock sold for $41 a share. (Goodyear was later sued for engaging in greenmail, but the suit was thrown out.) Goldsmith signed a "standstill agreement," which guaranteed that he would not launch another raid on the company for five years, after which all bets were off and he could repeat the attempt. Goodyear then restructured the company to pay off its debt and raise the value of its stock.

Goodyear's restructuring program reduced the company by 12 percent and included such measures as:

- the firing of four thousand employees;
- the assumption of $4 billion in debt that leveraged the company to an unprecedented 82 percent of total debt to capitalization, up from a pre-raid figure of 42 percent;
- the sale of three major subsidiaries;
- the closing of three plants—in Menominee, Michigan; Cumberland, Maryland; and New Toronto, Ontario;
- the reduction of R-&-D activities;
- a cutback in advertising;
- the reduction in force of forty-three hundred hourly employees through early retirement and special programs;
- a new approach to capital spending and R & D "weighted toward projects with short term payout";
- the reduction of training activities;
- cutbacks in plant and equipment; plans for plants in Korea and in the United States were abandoned.[4]

LEAN AND MEAN: GOLDSMITH'S VIEW OF "CORPOCRACY"

Sir James, an eloquent spokesman for an unpopular cause, made his case before Congress in defense of his assault on Goodyear. His view: Goodyear should "stick to its knitting" instead of entering businesses about which it was totally ignorant. The company was seriously weakened, he charged, by management's ill-considered decision in 1983 to acquire Celeron, an owner of oil and gas assets and a manufacturer of natural-gas transmission systems; they forgot the admonition of the company's most successful CEO, Paul Litchfield, to "build better tires, cheaper, and sell them harder."

Goodyear's foray into the oil-and-gas business ultimately cost the company nearly $1 billion, an investment that turned sour as the price of crude oil dropped. Coupled with the Celeron purchase came the announcement of plans to build a three-hundred-thousand-barrel-per-day transcontinental pipeline from California to Texas—the "most expensive capital project in Goodyear's history . . . and "as ill-considered as it would be for an oil company to build a major tire factory."[5]

An article three years later in *The New York Times* by Michael

Lev buttressed Goldsmith's judgment, concluding that the pipeline was simply a gamble that failed to pay off. Since the company was "faced with mounting competition and sluggish growth in its core tire business," wrote Lev, the decision in 1983 "to smooth out the bumps and potholes in its earnings performance by diversifying . . . seemed to be a sound strategic move." Events, in the form of declining oil prices, proved them wrong, and the "$1 billion (1,225 mile) pipeline Goodyear built to be a cash cow [became] its white elephant."[6] It was an honest mistake—even oil companies like ARCO and Shell were burned—but it was a costly one. With the wisdom of hindsight, the SEC later identified Goodyear's entry into the oil business as the major reason the company became a takeover target.

Goldsmith accused Goodyear of failing to follow the common business practice of taking precautions to ensure that the pipeline would operate profitably. Of course, acquisitions are rarely risk-free, but Goldsmith felt that the size and complexity of the operation, along with the history of previous failures (by Standard Oil of Ohio and Getty Oil) to build similar pipelines, should have led Goodyear to proceed with caution. It was an idea that was "wholly lunatic," testified Goldsmith, "building a transcontinental pipeline which no major oil company could build; without syndication, without finding out whether there was going to be enough oil, . . . left with this white elephant crossing the country."[7]

White elephants breed "white knights," the name accorded to corporate raiders in the Sir James mold. White knights dub themselves entrepreneurs, representing the shareholders against the vested interests of entrenched and incompetent managers. Management, claimed Goldsmith, simply "lost its way. The approximately $2 billion spent in the oil and gas business should have been invested to build the most modern, state of the art, frontier breaking industrial infrastructure to produce better tires . . . and to ensure that Goodyear's operations could compete with anything, including imports, no matter their origin."

Goodyear's attempt to seek government help was especially abhorrent. The entrenched corporocrat, charged Goldsmith, "calls on government for help . . . when the free market exerts pressure on his corporation. . . . The appropriate response to competition is to compete, not to seek artificial protection. That means reorganizing, cutting out fat, and concentrating on building better tires."

As far as trying to discredit him as a foreign investor, said Sir James, "Goodyear's views [welcoming foreign investment] are the same as mine. . . . Goodyear is justifiably proud of operating 101 manufacturing facilities in 28 countries. That means that Goodyear has believed foreign investment to be right for at least 27 countries."[8]

In response to Mercer's accusations about spinning off the company's divisions, dissipating its assets, and causing the loss of jobs, Goldsmith declared that such actions would not square with the realities of his investment. "We are putting up $1 billion of our own equity," he told the committee chairman, "and the total management investment in the company is $8 million. So why we would dissipate with $1 billion invested, as opposed to the present management with $8 million, is somewhat unclear to me."

But the line between dissipating and divesting is fuzzy. "Yes, indeed," added Goldsmith. ". . . we have made it quite clear that we would return Goodyear to its core business and concentrate on it. That means selling noncore diversifications. Goodyear management has now announced that it will do the same thing. Selling diversifications does not mean dissipating assets or jobs."

Goldsmith offered his own record to show how divestment could lead to enhanced corporate health and increased profits. The sale of unprofitable divisions of the Diamond International Corporation, a company that failed to fend off Sir James and his allies, proved the ultimate success of the "diversification strategy" to any remaining doubters. Five of the company's unprofitable divisions were now making dramatically higher profits, freed at last of their "tired conglomerate." One such example: "The Packaging Division of Diamond . . . was in deep financial trouble. . . . Since the sale, production at the mill is up 50 percent, wages and benefits are up 33 percent, and capital investment has increased fourfold."

Sir James leveled his final volley at Mercer, challenging the view that the stock market does not recognize long-term value and forces management to concentrate on the short term—the core dispute between "corporocrats" and "raiders." "If [that] were true," testified Goldsmith, "then the market would disregard quality of earnings and would value all companies at the same price-earnings multiple. In reality, the market does the opposite. . . . When the market believes that management is good and that it will make earnings grow, then it places a premium on the market price of the shares so as to take into account future growth. When, on the other hand, the market believes that management is poor and will dissipate assets and earnings, it places a discount on the market value of the shares so as to take into account future stagnation or decline.

"If Goodyear management has failed to convince the marketplace that it deserves a good rating and instead receives a poor one, then it has only itself to blame, along with its failed strategy," he added.

Questioned harshly by Representatives Seiberling and Glickman, Goldsmith stoutly defended his position. The obvious question—What did *he* know about tires?—went straight to the heart of his argument: that Goodyear's management should make tires, instead of diversifying into areas outside of its expertise. What irony: Raiders actually know very little about specific areas of manufacturing; they attack any vulnerable target; and they have no expertise beyond high finance, and the increasingly discredited methods of raising money through junk bonds and other instruments. In retrospect, it is difficult to see how the government accorded their views so much legitimacy for such a long and critical period of time.

Seiberling also pointed out that Goodyear had been in the aerospace business since World War I, with no visible harmful effects from such diversification. Indeed, it is almost antientrepreneurial to suggest that companies should not branch out, particularly if the branches relate to the trunk of the tree. One thing that quite naturally links up with the tire business is precisely oil, which is consumed in enormous quantities in tire manufacture—for instance, it takes over 740 gallons of petroleum to produce a single 7,670-pound tire for a giant earth-moving vehicle.

Seiberling declared Goldsmith's attacks on Goodyear's excessive borrowing for the purchase of Celeron to be a case of the pot calling the kettle black: Goldsmith, he said, didn't exactly raise the money for his acquisitions from his own bank account; Sir James admitted, for example, to borrowing two-thirds of the money for the purchase of Crown Zellerbach.

Although under attack for what several congressmen regarded as ill-gotten gains from his successful corporate raids, Goldsmith defended his profits—which he claimed were overstated—as pillars of the capitalist system: $1.9 million for Crown Zellerbach, plus a special dividend of $213 million, and $503 million for Diamond International, according to information released at the congressional hearing.[9]

In fact, however, Goodyear was no stranger to lean and mean methods of corporate fat-trimming. "Sometimes it is necessary to tear down in order to create wealth," claimed Dennis Rich, director of business planning. "We closed twenty-six plants in the preceding ten years. That's an average of 2.6 every year. We're not proud of that, but the point is that business has been restructuring all along. We didn't need the takeover artists to show us how to do that."[10] During that same period, Goodyear had also opened eleven new facilities and made eight acquisitions, investing nearly $1.5 billion in state-of-the-art production facilities and the development of new products.[11]

THE TWO FACES OF NATIONAL SECURITY

Whatever the quality of its business practices, Goodyear was not just another knitting factory. Even the raiders admitted its critical role in the defense business. What is curious is why government failed to recognize Goodyear as an industry vital to the nation's economy and national security. A decade ago, there were five world-class American-owned tire producers: Firestone, Goodyear, Uniroyal Goodrich, Armstrong, and General Tire. Today, Goodyear is the last U.S.-owned major tire producer: Firestone was acquired by the Bridgestone Corporation of Japan; Uniroyal Goodrich by Groupe Michelin, of France; General Tire by Continental A.G., a German company; and Armstrong by Pirelli S.P.A., of Italy.

While Mercer fought and government slept, there was virtually no public debate at the national level—with the exception of Congress—on such vital questions as:

- whether tire production was important to the national defense;
- whether aerospace was important to the national defense;
- whether either aerospace or tire production was critical to the nation's economic security or industrial base; and
- whether the U.S. world position in tire production mattered.

The dilemma for the U.S. government is how to address these issues without compromising the nation's steadfast dedication to the twin doctrines of free trade and comparative advantage: If the French, the Italians, the Germans, and the Japanese make better tires, what difference does it make, as long as we can buy tires from them? If we can buy them cheaper, all the better.

But should the U.S. be totally dependent on overseas suppliers for something as basic as this? After all, tanks, trucks, jeeps, and other military vehicles do not roll into battle on blueberry muffins. Nor should the American automobile industry be dependent on overseas production of tires. Nevertheless, the United States came within an eyelash of losing its last remaining tire company without blinking; so enamored were its leaders of a vision of globalism that they were gulled into a false sense of security. After all, the French, the Italians, the Germans, and the Japanese were all our allies; nothing to worry about there.

For that matter, why worry about international competition from Japan and the European Community? After the Goldsmith deluge, Goodyear, long dominant as the world's leading tire producer, now vies with Bridgestone for second place; both companies have been bested by Michelin, the world's largest tire maker thanks to its U.S. acquisition. What a contrast to the start of the 1980s, when half of the world's dozen leading tire producers were American.[12]

The Goodyear saga highlights the two faces of national security. The most obvious is the defense role. As the owner of an aerospace company, Goodyear was involved in top-secret government contracts. That very aerospace company was sold twice in the four years after Goldsmith's raid to investors in France and Japan successively— two countries that have targeted the aerospace industry for special attention.

Goodyear's core business, tires, also boasted a critical linkage to the national defense: providing mobility for the armed forces with the production of radiators, tires, and fan belts for tanks, trucks, cars, and other vehicles. In World War II, Goodyear developed synthetic rubber, protecting the country from the risk of depending on countries unable to produce or deliver the natural product. Natural rubber is grown within ten degrees of the equator, where obvious transportation difficulties—not to mention unstable and unreliable governments—could cripple production and delivery in wartime.

But U.S. government officials were unimpressed. "I heard Mac Baldrige [then secretary of commerce] say, 'We looked at Goodyear for national-security reasons and felt it was of no consequence,'" recalled Mercer.

Baldrige reflected the view of the Reagan and Bush administrations that for the most part ownership didn't matter, as long as goods were readily available at reasonable cost. Mercer argued in vain that, if all the tire producers were foreign-owned, even if they left their productive capability in the U.S., chances are that they would leave most of their research and development overseas. "If things got tight for the foreign investor," he conjectured, "they would neglect their operation here, and the U.S. would be sitting ducks." The public, the commerce secretary, and the government had become complacent, he explained; as long as everything is working now, we don't have to worry about the future. "Washington won't listen," Mercer said. "As they get in their car, the fan belt is working, the radiator belt is working, the motor-vibration mounts are working, and the tires are working. They don't think they need rubber. There is no substitute for rubber."

That leads to the second category of national security: economic security. Is the United States so rich and powerful that it can afford to lose an $11-billion corporation?

"Up to the LBO [leveraged buyout] we had increased market share and were the leader in R and D," said Mercer. "In contrast, Michelin had lost $1 billion in three years, and got bailed out by the

French government. At the same time, Bridgestone spent $2.6 billion—the very same amount it cost Goodyear to buy out Goldsmith—and acquired Firestone.

"One senator told me, 'You should have bought Firestone.' I answered, 'Senator, do you believe our Justice Department would allow me to buy a competitor?' Yet any foreign competitor can buy a company and I can't."

ANY FOREIGN COMPETITOR:
HOSTILE FOREIGN RAIDERS

"Any foreign competitor," however, like the tourist abroad, acts quite differently in a foreign country than he does at home. Japan's response to the American raiding party of T. Boone Pickens revealed how a nation can support "free trade" abroad while it sternly manages its economy at home. The Japanese responded not by opening up their system but by considering changes in their securities laws to protect themselves from "sneak attacks" by corporate raiders. The new rules, said a spokesman from the Finance Ministry, would make stock transactions more visible and prevent hostile corporate raiders from acquiring shares secretly.[13] Any claims that the rules would open the system up for foreign investors remains to be seen, since only three such bids in nineteen years have been advanced.

The United States provides a remarkable contrast as the only country with virtually no policy toward hostile raiders, foreign or domestic. In 1988, the GAO reported that foreign investors had become more aggressive, spending a record $15.5 billion in hostile takeovers of American companies in the first six months of that year, which represented 75 percent of all foreign acquisitions.[14] Foreign companies spent an additional $4.7 billion on friendly takeovers, and some $68.7 billion was spent by American companies purchasing American companies during the same period.

There is no question that the total number of foreign hostile takeovers and takeover attempts was increasing dramatically, perhaps encouraged by Goldsmith's profitable move on Goodyear. The largest hostile foreign takeover during this period was launched by a Canadian company, the Campeau Corporation, which spent $6.6 billion to acquire Federated Department Stores. Campeau's empire collapsed several years later, and with it a large part of the U.S. retailing industry.

FREEDOM FOR WHOM? THE FREE MARKET
AND HOSTILE TAKEOVERS

The same year as the Goodyear struggle, Japan's Dainippon Ink and Chemicals Inc. spent $540 million to buy Reichhold Chemicals, and Switzerland's Ciba-Geigy Ltd. spent $227 million to acquire Spectra-Physics, Inc., a laser manufacturer. Concern grew over the rapid acquisition of defense-related companies, as did the figures: in the first six months of 1988, thirty-seven military-related industries were objects of foreign takeovers—friendly and hostile. Did such takeovers and the shrinking number of American-owned military suppliers endanger national security?[15]

Goodyear's experience provided the impetus for congressional interest; in fact, the loss of jobs at Goodyear's plant in Lincoln, Nebraska, spurred the interest of that state's Senator James Exon, who cosponsored the Exon-Florio amendment to the 1988 Omnibus Trade and Competitiveness Act authorizing the president to block any acquisition perceived to jeopardize national security. Unfortunately, the bill depends on presidential interest, and, as has been shown, President Bush has demonstrated little inclination to follow through on the bill's legislative intent.

Goodyear suffered through difficult times as a result of the Goldsmith onslaught. During this period, to be sure, the entire industry was suffering setbacks as a result of the recession and the decline in the U.S. auto and rubber industries. But in the first quarter of 1991, Goodyear posted the largest losses in its ninety-three-year history.[16] Not until early 1992 did the company finally begin to show signs of recovery.

In the last analysis, overseas investors were clearly winners, and American citizens, losers. The Goodyear experience showed how foreign and domestic financiers controlled purchases that affected national security, and how unprepared America's leaders were to avert the consequences.

CHAPTER III

Exon-Florio

THE UNUSED WEAPON

The question that we always get is how we define national
security.
> —Stephen J. Canner, director of the
> Treasury Department's Office of Investment,
> chairman of CFIUS

The people who sit on CFIUS have blinders on.
> —A former government official who served on CFIUS

Congress's effort to enable the government to block foreign acquisitions that imperil national security underscores an old lesson: that it is futile to give the president more power than he intends to use. Since enactment of the Exon-Florio amendment, which gave the president this power, it has been invoked only once, to block the acquisition of an aircraft-metal-parts manufacturer by a company owned by the People's Republic of China. Even though the president eventually vetoed this sale, the government took four months to evict the Chinese from the premises.

Other countries in the industrialized world have no need for an Exon-Florio amendment. Critical technologies are nurtured and protected as a matter of national policy. This is a major economic objective of leaders of government and business, who resist the sale of a cutting-edge technology with all possible vigor.

Exon-Florio was one of two bills involving foreign investment to reach the floor of the House and the Senate in the fall of 1988. Both were strongly opposed by the Reagan administration and foreign investors, who sent hundreds of lobbyists to Capitol Hill. Their major target was a proposal by Representative John Bryant, a Texas Democrat, that would require major foreign investors to disclose their financial interests in their American acquisitions, some of which were multi-layered to conceal their real owners. Representative Bryant argued that it was impossible to discuss foreign investment in the United States without knowing the extent of that investment and the identity of the real owners, noting that virtually every other industrialized nation required far better information on foreign investments. But foreign investors saw the Bryant amendment as the first step toward restrictions on their American acquisitions, and their lobbyists, led by Elliot Richardson, denounced the proposal as xenophobic and protectionist, arguing that it would send the wrong signal to foreign investors and discourage the flow of foreign money, on which the United States had become dependent. The measure twice passed the House of Representatives, but was blocked in the Senate. Perhaps because the Bryant amendment drew their major fire, the administration and the foreign investors reluctantly accepted the Exon-Florio amendment to an omnibus trade bill, which gave the president the authority to block any foreign acquisitions that could imperil national security, without declaring a national emergency under the International Economic Emergency Powers Act. Foreign acquisitions could also be blocked by regulators if they violated antitrust, environmental, or securities laws.

FOREIGN INVESTMENT: A TROJAN HORSE?

When former CIA Director William Casey publicly expressed his fears about foreign investment as a "Trojan horse"—friendly on the outside but fraught with potential danger within—his warnings were widely ignored, except perhaps by the intelligence community. His fears, which presaged Exon-Florio, were based primarily on the rising incidences of technology transfer that he was gleaning from intelligence reports not available to the general public. Several years after Casey's death, mounting evidence led many members of Congress to realize that his words were not so farfetched after all.

The Exon-Florio amendment was a reaction to growing congressional fears that foreign acquisitions were sometimes motivated by a desire to obtain technology, and sometimes resulted in the takeover of technologies considered critical to national security. Joseph L. Parkinson, chairman and CEO of Micron Technology Inc., a manufacturer of semiconductors, told Congress that foreign acquisitions were sometimes search-and-destroy missions that enabled foreign competitors to dominate an industry. "When they go about attacking an industry, from our perspective, they use every means available," Parkinson said of his Japanese competitors. "This would include dumping. In my mind, now that they have so many U.S. dollars and we are running such massive trade deficits vis-à-vis Japan, the other easy way to attack an industry is to simply buy it."

Parkinson noted that by 1988 the Japanese had sharply reduced the semiconductor business of such major American manufacturers as Texas Instruments, which moved its production to Japan; Motorola, which got out of D-RAMs totally; and Intel, National Semiconductor, and Mostek, the last being the leading producer of the previous decade. These leaders had been replaced by Nippon Electronic Corporation, Hitachi, Toshiba, and Mitsubishi. "Technology is a fast-moving train," said Parkinson, "and you have to be going full speed just to stay on it. It is very easy to destroy the American D-RAM or any other industrial capability. It is very hard to revive it."[1]

"There is little doubt," added a Congressional Research Service report three years later, "that foreign investment is an important vehicle for the transfer of technology abroad." But, reflecting the conventional wisdom, the report acknowledged that "Most economists believe, however, that the United States can do more to improve its national welfare and its international competitive position by working with other countries to gain an international agreement on foreign investment standards and practices than it can by intervening in the foreign investment process."[2]

Even before Exon-Florio, the government had persuaded some foreign investors to abandon or change the conditions of their proposed acquisitions of American companies to satisfy national security interests. Early in the 1980s, the government became concerned with the proposed $110-million sale of New Hampshire Ball Bearings to its chief Japanese competitor, Minebea.[3] Ball bearings were long regarded as critical to the national defense, especially in conventional warfare. The issue went straight to CFIUS, the Committee on Foreign Investment in the United States, the Treasury-led interagency group created in 1975 in response to concerns that Arab investors were buying up too many American companies. At the time of the Minebea proposal, CFIUS had no authority to block foreign acquisitions of American companies, and could only review cases brought before it. The committee approved the sale; however, the Pentagon's concerns led to a stipulation that production of defense-related products would remain in the United States.

Fujitsu's intended purchase of an 80-percent stake in Fairchild Semiconductor Corporation in the spring of 1987 aroused similar concerns and the first major controversy over a foreign investment. The impending purchase marked one of the most important foreign investments involving the potential transfer of cutting-edge American technology, research, and expertise to Japan in decades. Opponents of the sale contended that the investment would make Fujitsu the leading semiconductor firm in the world, while Fairchild's defense-electronics subsidiary provided more than $100 million of high-speed circuitry annually to the defense community. Ironically, Fairchild was owned by a French company, so one foreign investor would merely have replaced another. Though it was virtually certain that CFIUS would approve the sale, Fujitsu eventually withdrew its offer, unwilling to continue negotiating in the glare of negative publicity generated by Commerce Secretary Baldrige.[4] Also, Japan was understandably upset that no one had objected to foreign ownership when the owner was French, but it suddenly became a national-security issue when the Japanese entered the picture.

Next came the Toshiba incident: four members of Congress smashed a Toshiba product on the Capitol steps to protest that company's sale of submarine technology to the Soviet Union. Footage of the event ran repeatedly on Japanese television; it remains a sore spot in U.S.-Japan relations to this day.

The Exon-Florio amendment was introduced in 1987. Originally, it gave the president the authority to block a foreign acquisition that would imperil "national security, essential commerce, and economic welfare." Supporters of the bill pointed out that nearly every other nation routinely reviewed proposed foreign acquisitions with regard to both national and economic security. This measure was strongly opposed by the administration as an affront to free trade, and by foreign investors who hinted that if the measure passed they might well take their money elsewhere. Indeed, the opponents fastened on a key phrase, asserting that the amendment would have a "chilling effect" on urgently needed foreign investment. They saw the measure as a strategy that could be unfairly used by U.S. companies to delay or even prevent hostile takeovers by foreign investors. In any event, such legislation was unnecessary, critics said, because the government had adequate tools to protect itself.

Their position was voiced by Commerce Secretary Baldrige, who told the Senate Commerce Committee that "In today's global economy, the various economies around the world are interdependent. That becomes more true every day. The second truth, I believe, is that today in this interdependent world economy investment is trade, and trade is investment. . . . We as an administration—and I will say, this was my personal opinion before the administration took a position, Mr. Chairman—we are opposed to the Exon proposal because we think it will mean a diversion away from the principles that we have been trying to espouse around the world and the other nations, which is national treatment for investment, open investment policy, and everything that goes with it."[5]

Senator Exon was dumbfounded. "Do you understand that the Exon amendment says and says only that nothing must happen, that this is only a tool to place in your hands, and if you agree with the President of the United States, to do something in case a national security matter would present itself?"

Secretary Baldrige disagreed, calling the proposal "an example of vast overkill" and citing its "chilling effect on trade."

Besides, Baldrige added, "national security" was invoked by every industry seeking government protection. "Everybody in the USA is in a national security business," he scoffed. "Making buttons, you need them on soldiers' uniforms. Making shoes, soldiers have got to walk. You would have the line stretched all the way from here down to my office."

Maybe so, but other countries protect their security interests anyway, even if that means refusing to extend reciprocity to the United States. "There is a lot more than a chill out there in the real world," Senator John B. Breaux, Democrat of Louisiana, told Secretary Baldrige. "There is an ice storm out there. I mean, our own U.S. Trade Representative has a 100 page listing here of countries from A to Z, from Argentina to Zimbabwe, and everything in-between. And every one of them that is on this list from our own Trade Representative has some kind of requirement that when a foreign country invests in Argentina to Zimbabwe to France to Canada to Australia to the OPEC nations, that there be somebody in their government to take a look at it from a national security standpoint, or from a cultural standpoint, or from an economic standpoint."[6]

Senator Pete Wilson, California Republican and later governor, agreed. "I would say that I think the point is well taken that foreign practices have been infinitely more restrictive than anything that is being proposed here, and it has not chilled enormously even our investment in those countries. And we are taking a hell of a lot greater risk."

RENT-A-TANK: A NEW MILITARY STRATEGY

A heartfelt appeal for Exon-Florio was made by Goodyear CEO Mercer. He warned that, without Exon-Florio, "We might wind up having to go to rent-a-plane or rent-a-tank services if we do not have the ability of an industrial base in this country to do the kind of job that is needed in the event of an emergency."[7]

The investment banking community strongly disagreed with Mercer. Several argued privately that white elephants like Goodyear were vulnerable to takeover attempts for good reason. The prevailing theory at that time, shared by the hard-line free-traders dominating the White House, was that, if Goodyear had left itself open to outside attack, then it deserved the "discipline of the marketplace" imposed by the raiders, whether foreign or domestic. Representing their views to Congress was Richard Darman, former deputy Treasury secretary, then an investment banker with Shearson-Lehman Brothers, and soon to become OMB director in the Bush administration. Darman told the committee that the Exon amendment was, "at least potentially, a radical reversal of U.S. policy favoring increasingly open investment regimes. . . . It is going to have an adverse effect on U.S. interest rates and growth, to the extent that it discourages that investment."[8]

Strongly influenced by the views of the investment-banking community and by international investors, the Reagan administration induced its most influential appointees and allies to oppose the bill. This opposition was best expressed by Treasury Secretary Baker, in a letter to Senator John Danforth, a member of the Commerce Committee, urging him to take the high road. "I share wholeheartedly your concern that the Exon Amendment would, if enacted, have a chilling effect on foreign investment in the United States," Baker wrote. "It would put the United States in the company of those countries whose investment climates we are trying to improve. With respect to Congressional concerns over national security, the United States already has sufficient legislation to protect our national security interests."

Paul Volcker, chairman of the Federal Reserve System, then weighed in with a warning that, "Given the enormous size of our budget and current account deficits, and the prospect that they will not soon be eliminated, any measure that discourages new foreign investments in the United States or causes the liquidation of existing investments is likely to exacerbate downward pressure on the foreign exchange value of the dollar and to put upward pressure on U.S. interest rates with negative effects on the overall rate of productive investment in our economy."[9]

Clayton Yeutter, the U.S. trade representative, also cautioned that "the notion that governmental review may be necessary to determine the economic effects of foreign direct investment in the United States runs directly contrary to our belief that investment flows which respond to market forces provide the best and most efficient mechanism to promote economic growth here and abroad."[10]

Perhaps because the administration and the lobbyists for foreign investors were preoccupied with quashing the Bryant amendment, and perhaps because national security was harder to resist politically, the Exon-Florio amendment to the Omnibus Trade and Competitiveness Act of 1988 won approval in a compromise that was ultimately accepted by the administration. The compromise deleted the words "essential commerce" from the grounds on which the president could block the foreign acquisition of an American company. Instead, the House-Senate conference report stated that "national security is intended to be interpreted broadly without limitation to particular industries." Thus, foreign acquisitions that could affect national security must be reported to the government; if not, they could be divested at any future time. If an acquisition was reported, the statute provided ninety days for the review and investigation, then a presidential decision.

Responding to newly emerging concerns over the erosion of the defense industrial base, the legislation also gave the president latitude to consider domestic production needed for projected national-defense requirements. Specifically, Exon-Florio allows for the assessment of the capability and capacity of domestic industries to meet national-defense requirements, including the availability of human resources, products, technology, materials, and other supplies and services; and assessment of the control of domestic industries and commercial activity by foreign citizens as it affects the capability of the United States to meet the requirements of national security. The statute also requires that information be treated confidentially and be protected against public disclosure under the Freedom of Information Act.

But merely giving a president the authority to block foreign investments on national-security grounds is no guarantee that the power will be exercised. Not surprisingly, President Bush has ignored Exon-Florio: Out of the many cases heard by CFIUS, only one acquisition has been formally blocked by the White House in the three years since the law took effect. Several more were shelved as a result of "jawboning," persuading the parties that the sales would ultimately be blocked, according to economist Stephen J. Canner, director of the Office of Investment at the Treasury Department, and chairman of CFIUS.

No wonder Exon-Florio was dubbed the "Lawyers' Full Employment Act," after the act's major beneficiaries, the lawyers and lobbyists specializing in international practice. For a while, alleged several members of CFIUS, even swimming-pool companies were registering, but eventually foreign investors wised up and the number of filings diminished.

FREE TRADE VS. NATIONAL SECURITY

For President Reagan, the measure presented something of a challenge, underscoring a potential conflict between the two guiding principles of his administration: free trade and national security. Nevertheless, the Reagan administration delegated enforcement of Exon-Florio to CFIUS, not hitherto known for its vigor in challenging foreign acquisitions. "Prior to Exon-Florio, we were a coordinating agency," said Canner. "Now we're a mechanism."[11] The group had been set up by President Ford in 1975 to review foreign investments that might have major implications for the United States national interest, and to coordinate the implementation of U.S. policy on international investment. Its members included representatives from the Departments of Treasury, State, Commerce, Defense and Justice; the Office of the United States Trade Representative; the Office of Management and Budget; and the Council of Economic Advisers.

Despite the dramatic surge of foreign investment in the thirteen years prior to Exon-Florio, CFIUS had seen fit to review only thirty cases. For that reason, critics dubbed the interagency group a "paper tiger." It was argued that the old CFIUS was too inactive to meet the new challenge of foreign investment. By comparison, the new CFIUS reviewed over 650 cases between enactment of Exon-Florio, in October 1988, and March 1992. Of these, twelve were subjected to detailed investigations, two proposed acquisitions were withdrawn, and one was blocked by the president, on the recommendation of CFIUS. Nevertheless, the ambiguity of the statute made enforcement tenuous. "The question that we always get is how we define national security," Canner said. "The answer is: case by case, from the various perspectives of the interests of the agencies, and within the context of Exon-Florio, which says that we should define it broadly."

But a former government official who served on CFIUS felt that the agency, in keeping with its administration mandate, was not sufficiently broad in its interpretation of the law. "They are narrowly focused," the official said. "The people who sit on CFIUS have blinders on."

Bernard Ascher, who represented the USTR on CFIUS, said: "CFIUS is doing its job within the limits of Exon-Florio. We're not going to satisfy every critic. The definition of national security is a big problem. It could fit into all situations. Any definition would be unnecessarily restrictive, and hurt the economy. On products, national security is looked at in terms of the scenario of the next war. For example, do you need warm clothing, or pots and pans? This has never adequately been dealt with."

The following acquisitions went to the final stages of CFIUS review:

(1) The Last Silicon Wafer: Monsanto-Huels

The first CFIUS investigation under the Exon-Florio amendment occurred in December 1988, barely two months after the measure was passed, and involved the proposed sale of the last American-owned manufacturer of silicon wafers for the commercial semiconductor market, and the only American commercial producer of eight-inch wafers. The case was important because it meant keeping an American component alive and well in this particular critical industry.

The Monsanto Company, an American manufacturer, proposed to sell its Monsanto Electronic Materials Co. to Huels AG, a subsidiary of West Germany's VEBA AG. The investigation was initially requested by the Department of Defense, and seconded by the Department of Commerce. The Defense Department sought to assure that SEMATECH, the U.S. semiconductor research-and-development consortium, would be guaranteed access to Monsanto's silicon wafers; that Monsanto's technology would not be transferred abroad; that the Monsanto subsidiary could remain an active member of SEMATECH; and that the administration would be informed of any change in Huels' ownership. Representative Florio called the wafers "building blocks for all the sophisticated equipment required for national defense."

The investigation touched off a furor with the disclosure by the Bureau of National Affairs' "Daily Report for Executives" that some Treasury officials said their agency planned to "undercut" the Exon-Florio amendment. This disclosure prompted letters by Treasury Secretary Nicholas Brady to both Senator Exon and Representative Florio assuring them that such was not the case.[12] "I was surprised to see these allegations," Brady wrote, because they "flatly contradict the Department's policy and actions. The strong support of the Treasury Department and the Administration for an open investment policy is well known. That policy is based on the pragmatic belief that foreign direct investment is good for the United States. But we have made clear that national security concerns may necessitate an exception to this openness." Brady assured the lawmakers that, "In my view, Treasury and the entire Administration have been scrupulous in executing both the letter and spirit of Exon-Florio."

CFIUS eventually persuaded Huels officials to provide written assurances to Secretary Brady that they would maintain production in the U.S. for five years, conduct research and development in the United States and not transfer the technology for five years, and make silicon wafers available to the U.S. semiconductor industry.[13] As a result, CFIUS unanimously recommended that the president not block the proposed transaction, and on February 3, 1989, President Bush concurred with that decision. The president based his decision of "nonintervention" on the thorough investigation by CFIUS, which addressed all the national-security concerns, "including reliability of supply, technology transfer, and the relationship of the transaction to the semiconductor industry research consortium, SEMATECH."

The sponsors of Exon-Florio were not pleased. Representative Florio warned that, because a large block of the stock of VEBA AG was held in bearer certificates, no one could determine who the ultimate owners of Huels were, so that it was impossible to make a finding on national-security grounds. The congressman also was disturbed that a VEBA subsidiary, VEBA Oel Libya, held oil interests in Libya. Backing Florio, twenty-nine congressmen signed a letter to President Bush expressing their "deep concern" and urging him to block the proposed transaction on the grounds that it "poses a serious threat to both our economic competitiveness and our national security." Moreover, CFIUS had no authority to enforce or monitor the written assurances provided by Huels, which were "only as good as the bond paper [they were] printed on," in the words of a Commerce Department official.

(2) The Nuclear Trigger: General Ceramics-Tokuyama Soda

The second investigation, initiated in March 1989, illuminated the mechanics of jawboning. Requested by the Departments of Commerce, Defense, Energy, and Treasury, it involved the proposed $59.4 million acquisition of General Ceramics Inc. by Tokuyama Soda Co. Ltd., a Japanese chemical manufacturer. General Ceramics manufactured, among other products, ceramic beryllium components used in making the triggering devices for nuclear weapons. The New Jersey–based manufacturer held a contract with the Department of Energy at the Oak Ridge Y-12 Weapons Plant, a defense-related facility where plutonium and uranimum are refined for use in nuclear warheads. CFIUS unofficially informed Tokuyama Soda and General Ceramics on April 14 that it planned to recommend that President Bush block the sale unless the classified Oak Ridge contract was removed, and Tokuyama temporarily withdrew its offer. "The company is now trying to deal with the matters that were raised," said Harry S. Axt, General Ceramics' secretary and treasurer.[14]

Under pressure from the government, the contract was renegotiated, and on May 23 General Ceramics announced that it had agreed to assign its classified contract, together with related assets, to a U.S.-owned company acceptable to the Energy Department. "It was clear that MITI [Japan's Ministry of International Trade and Industry] was heavily involved," said a Senate aide who is an expert on CFIUS. "MITI advised Tokuyama Soda to spin off the nuclear-weapons-component division. Tokuyama Soda didn't even know it was getting such sensitive weapons technology." Tokuyama Soda refiled, and CFIUS cleared the sale two weeks later.

(3) High Voltage: Westinghouse-ABB

The third Exon-Florio investigation, also initiated in March 1989, involved a joint venture between Westinghouse Electric Corp. and ASEA Brown Boveri Ltd., a company created by the merger of the ASEA Co. of Sweden with Brown Boveri of Switzerland, to manufacture, distribute, sell, and service high-voltage electrical-transmission-and-distribution equipment in the United States. The investigation was requested by the Departments of Commerce and Defense, after consultation with the Department of Energy. They were concerned that the proposed joint venture, called Westinghouse ABB Power T&D Co., would have the power to limit the availability of high-power electrical-transmission equipment. At the outset, many commentators expressed the view that joint ventures were outside the scope of Exon-Florio, but CFIUS felt otherwise and conducted the investigation. They ended up recommending that the president approve the joint venture, and President Bush did so on May 17, when the White House issued a statement that "ABB reconfirmed its intention to continue the manufacture, servicing, repair, research and design in the United States of these high voltage transformers."[15] As with the Huels-Monsanto case, these guarantees cannot be enforced or monitored by CFIUS.

(4) Scared Away: Tachonics-Lalbhai

The fourth Exon-Florio investigation, begun in July 1989, involved the proposed acquisition by India's Lalbhai Group of Tachonics Corp., a subsidiary of Grumman Corporation, which manufactures gallium arsenide, used to manufacture semiconductor chips. For reasons neither explained nor understood, the Indian company withdrew its offer shortly after the investigation began. "CFIUS scared off the Lalbhai Group," said a government official who works closely with CFIUS.

(5) Space Shot: Fairchild-Matra

The fifth investigation, also begun in July 1989, involved the proposed acquisition by France's Matra SA of three divisions of Fairchild Industries, which had just been purchased by the Austrian-controlled Banner Industries. The Fairchild divisions, Fairchild Communications & Electronics Co., Fairchild Control Systems Co., and Fairchild Space Co., produced hardware and software for aerospace systems and spacecraft. Some of the government contracts held by the three divisions were classified. Initially, the Commerce Department requested the investigation, with support from Defense. After a thorough investigation, CFIUS unanimously approved the transaction. President Bush concurred with CFIUS's recommendation, and decided on August 18 not to block the transaction. "In consultation with the Department of Commerce, Matra developed a comprehensive export control management system that was deemed satisfactory," a White House statement said, and noted that the president had decided there were adequate safeguards to protect sensitive technologies from unauthorized transfer outside the United States.[16] The Department of Defense, through the Defense Investigative Service, established a proxy board to identify the classified technologies and withhold them from the French owners.

(6) What Warrants Presidential Intervention: MAMCO-CATIC

The sixth investigation, the only one that led to a presidential veto of a proposed foreign acquisition, involved the acquisition by China National Aerotechnology Import and Export Corporation (CATIC) of MAMCO Manufacturing Inc. of Seattle. On November 6, 1989, CATIC, which is owned by the Chinese government, notified CFIUS of its intention to acquire MAMCO for approximately $20 million. MAMCO machines and fabricates metal parts for use in commercial aircraft, including tail and wing assemblies and various small parts, such as fittings. The Boeing Co. is MAMCO's largest customer, accounting for 85 to 90 percent of its business. MAMCO had no contracts involving classified information, but some of its machinery is subject to U.S. export controls. On November 30, prior to CFIUS's decision, CATIC completed the acquisition by acquiring all of MAMCO's outstanding shares. Exon-Florio does not prohibit the parties to a transaction under review from completing an acquisition before receiving government approval, "although prudence would argue against closing a transaction before receipt of the clearance letter."

Just four days after completion of the sale, CFIUS informed CATIC that it would in fact investigate the transaction.[17]

To everyone's surprise, given the low level of technology involved, on January 19, 1990, CFIUS unanimously recommended to the president that he seek the extraordinary measure of divestment. On February 1, Kenneth A. Keller, MAMCO's president, said: "I would be amazed if there were a recommendation against allowing the transaction to stand. I was not aware of anything that we do here that would have any possible impact on national security." Some senior government officials were arguing against nullifying the MAMCO sale, partly to avoid angering China.[18] However, there were indications that CATIC had been used by the Chinese government for some of its intelligence operations inside the United States. On February 2, the president ordered CATIC to divest itself of its interest in MAMCO. In announcing this decision, President Bush said that there was "credible evidence" that CATIC's acquisition of MAMCO might impair national security. Several areas of concern were raised, the most credible of which was a concern that CATIC would use MAMCO as a base for intelligence activities in the U.S.

One congressional staff member suggested, "There was concern that the new owners could have gotten onto the floor of a Boeing plant." The administration was alarmed by an alleged violation of U.S. export-control laws in 1984, when CATIC purchased two CFM-56 General Electric aircraft engines. An administration official said that, "Because China had violated an agreement with the British not to take apart another engine in an effort to learn its manufacturing secrets, the United States imposed stringent controls on the 1984 sale." Nevertheless, the Chinese had reportedly disassembled the engines to learn their technological secrets.

Vic Cohen, special assistant to the assistant secretary of the Navy and a CFIUS representative, called the president's action "phony," because "CATIC already owns five to ten other companies in the United States. CFIUS should have turned down all the other acquisitions."

(7) Breaking the Code: UniSoft-CMC

The seventh Exon-Florio investigation involved the attempted acquisition by CMC Ltd., an Indian-government-owned computer-maintenance-and-support company, of London-based UniSoft Group PLC. This transaction was subject to Exon-Florio because of UniSoft's U.S. subsidiary, UniSoft Corp., which designs custom applications for a sophisticated software package used by both the military and commercial customers. The technology includes a digital encryption standard, used to encode data transmission, which is subject to U.S. munitions controls. UniSoft had no classified contracts with the U.S. government, but was a subcontractor to firms that used its services in the manufacture of military products under classified contracts. The investigation, initiated at the request of Defense and Commerce, was intended to determine whether UniSoft had sufficient controls in place to ensure that the restricted technology would not be exported. Another concern was that, during UniSoft's customizing of Unix for U.S. defense contractors, it might have gained access to classified information that could then be transferred to its new owners. CFIUS ultimately found no problems in the transaction, and President Bush approved the sale on May 2, 1990.[19]

(8) How an American Company Used Exon-Florio to Get a Better Deal: Norton-BTR

The eighth Exon-Florio investigation was requested by 119 members of Congress. In a letter to President Bush on April 19, 1990, they expressed their concern over Great Britain's BTR (British Tire and Rubber) PLC's $1.64-billion, $75-a-share hostile bid for the Norton Company of Worcester, Massachusetts. This firm, which employs sixteen thousand people at 113 plants worldwide, is a leading manufacturer of abrasives, advanced ceramics, performance plastics, and chemical-process products. The congressional letter urged that Exon-Florio be used to investigate the takeover because it involved "critical national security" and U. S. "international conpetitiveness."

"Frankly," continued the letter, "we do not believe that any takeover of Norton would be in our economic security or national security interest. It is absolutely essential, however, that no action of any kind be taken without assuring that there are very carefully developed plans to protect the capability that Norton has pioneered through years of investment." Senator John Kerry, Massachusetts Democrat, in a letter to President Bush on April 2, 1990, urged that the transaction be blocked because Norton was "one of the pillars of the Massachusetts economy" and "is central to the advances in materials sciences in the 1990s that are critical in our country's key industries, especially communications, transportation and aeronautics. Norton's unique expertise regarding diamond film, an important emerging strategic material, has great potential for military and other classified applications. Norton has been an active development contractor with the Department of Defense, the Department of Energy, the Defense Advanced

Research Projects Agency, the U.S. Air Force, the Navy and others in the defense/aerospace field."

Senator Kerry urged the president "to take a somewhat broader view of what constitutes national security," and noted that "our nation is only secure militarily if it is strong economically, industrially, technologically. Al Joseph, a physicist and former executive with Rockwell who was one of the developers of gallium arsenide, explained that Norton was the leading U.S. manufacturer of the ceramic balls that went into bearings, and that the company's ceramic bearings were the main ones used in the space shuttle, and helped determine the lifetime of the shuttle in space.

Not trusting the federal government to act in its interests, the Commonwealth of Massachusetts quickly enacted a law on April 9, 1990, intended to protect Norton from the hostile takeover, by requiring that the board of directors be staggered over a three-year period to assure continuity. Thus ended the BTR PLC's bid, but Norton later arranged a friendly takeover by France's Compagnie de Saint-Gobain, which offered $90 a share, gave Norton assurances that the company's headquarters would remain in Worcester, and promised to retain the current management. That no one protested the French takeover prompted questions from many quarters about the misuse of Exon-Florio—namely, waving the banner of national security as a cover for extracting a better deal.[20]

(9) A Technology Cop-out:
Semi-Gas Systems–Nippon Sanso KK

The ninth Exon-Florio investigation, and one of the most controversial, involved Japan's Nippon Sanso's proposed $23-million acquisition of Semi-Gas Systems Inc. of San Jose, California. Semi-Gas was a subsidiary of Hercules Inc., a Wilmington, Delaware, company primarily involved in aerospace and chemical research.

Semi-Gas is the world's leading producer of "gas cabinets," which purify and distribute gases needed for the production of semiconductors; these are crucial to the manufacture of basic-memory semiconductor chips. A cabinet system is a complex group of technologies that includes not only a large enclosure—or cabinet—but also valves, pipes, purifiers, regulators, manifolds, monitors, and additional technology. Semi-Gas had one-third to one-half of the U.S. market for gas cabinets, and its customers included SEMATECH. Semi-Gas was also beginning to break into the Japanese market.

Officials from SEMATECH strongly opposed the sale on the grounds that it would provide the Japanese with access to enhanced technology, which SEMATECH and Semi-Gas had developed jointly. A high official at SEMATECH's headquarters, pointing to a chart of the consortium's enterprises, explained that "Semi-Gas has intimate access and intimate knowledge of all our equipment. In terms of intelligence, they know what fuels run each piece of equipment, and the gas supply required. Semi-Gas impacts the time lines. We can't work with a company that's foreign-owned unless there is no alternative. Semi-Gas will give broad based intelligence to its new owners. It will cause a loss in our timing and create tremendous difficulty for us in recreating technical expertise."

It was early 1990 when Hercules made public its intent to auction off Semi-Gas, and to leave the semiconductor-equipment field. In April 1990, Nippon Sanso made its offer to buy Semi-Gas. Hercules received at least two other offers for Semi-Gas as well, and the management of Semi-Gas made a proposal to purchase its own company. SEMA-TECH, considering Semi-Gas as an important technological link in a wide range of production capabilities, saw the relationship between themselves and Semi-Gas as part of a wider distribution network that had technological and economic ramifications not only for the consortium but for the entire U.S. information-technology industry. SEMA-TECH opposed the sale and lobbied hard against it, not only because their scientists believed that the technology developed through Semi-Gas was unique, but also because they knew replacing Semi-Gas as a supplier would be costly. "It will take [other companies] six months to get up to speed," the SEMATECH official cautioned. "Foreign owners will be six months ahead of us. Six months means we will be running $100 million behind. Semi-Gas is that central to SEMA-TECH."

Others disagreed. Terry Swanson, president of American Specialty Gas Technologies, a U.S. firm recently acquired by a French company, said that such an estimate was "ludicrous, frankly. It's not as if it's the end of the earth and you can't make integrated circuits anymore if they [Semi-Gas Systems] didn't exist."[21] On October 10, 1990, the Subcommittee on Science, Technology and Space of the Senate Committee on Commerce, Science and Transportation held hearings on the sale, and government and industry officials gave assurances that important technology would not be directly given to Nippon Sanso. Addressing both the sale and the safeguard issue, Senator Albert Gore, Democrat of Tennessee and chairman of the subcommittee, charged that "The acquisition of Semi-Gas will cause real damage to SEMATECH, which has provided the company with both contracts and major technical assistance."

"The sale of Semi-Gas Systems to Nippon Sanso," concluded the

Congressional Research Service (CRS), "may restrict or curtail the supply of cabinets and processing equipment for the SEMATECH consortium. While there are U.S. companies which may provide replacement technologies within the U.S. semiconductor industry, there is a lack of consensus regarding the quality, timeliness and cost of the replacement technology." In addition, "It is clear that the cabinet distribution system developed by Semi-Gas was in part assisted and underwritten through the SEMATECH connection, and that these advances proved attractive to Nippon Sanso."[22]

CFIUS ultimately decided that Semi-Gas neither produced a technology that had a direct military application nor was the sole source of the technology it manufactured. CFIUS also concluded that the acquisition would not prohibit or restrict important technologies from reaching SEMATECH, and felt that there were adequate safeguards to prevent any potentially proprietary breakthroughs from being used by Nippon Sanso against American companies. In July 1990, CFIUS advised President Bush that the sale of Semi-Gas to Nippon Sanso should not be blocked.

CFIUS's decision touched off a dispute among policymakers and information-technology industry leaders, a great many of whom disagreed with the CFIUS recommendation. The decision was viewed as the latest example of CFIUS's failing its congressional mandate by rubber-stamping foreign acquisitions of critical technologies. Michael Smith, former (acting) USTR, said: "The CFIUS process was prostituted in a major way by the Semi-Gas decision. The company is going for a song. Nippon Sanso is getting $100 million worth of U.S. technology. CFIUS discounted the SEMATECH testimony, while the Nippon Sanso testimony was taken seriously."

CRS noted that this decision raised two general issues.

The first was whether CFIUS had used a "moving" definition of national security when considering whether to review individual cases. "That is, it did not use a benchmark definition consistently from case to case, but instead considered specific national security considerations unique to each case. There may be merit in applying such a methodology for reviewing cases. It provides flexibility for policymakers reviewing sales of companies ranging from tool and die manufacturers to semiconductor equipment suppliers. But this same degree of flexibility has frustrated others in industry who do not know exactly what criteria are being used to judge which sales may violate 'national security.'"

The second issue was one of transparency. Because CFIUS deals with sales of companies, which are proprietary in nature and may involve national-security considerations, its meetings are closed and its proceedings not made public. "Again, these policies and actions have merit, and CFIUS is mandated by law to make its recommendations to the President," the CRS noted. "But one of the repercussions of these closed meetings is that other interested and affected parties—such as SEMATECH and members of Congress—are informed of decisions after they are made. This has caused friction between legislative and executive branch policymakers and government and industry leaders."[23]

After CFIUS made its recommendation to the president in July 1990, the Justice Department's Antitrust Division also reviewed the case and on January 3, 1991, filed a civil action to block the sale on the grounds that it would give Nippon Sanso an unfair market advantage under U.S. antitrust laws. The complaint alleged that the transaction would give Nippon Sanso a 49-percent market share in the United States, and that "actual and potential competition" in the "market and manufacture and sale of gas cabinets in the United States will be eliminated." The Justice Department lost in the United States District Court for Eastern Pennsylvania, and decided not to appeal.

The Semi-Gas acquisition also raised the question of the expenditure of U.S. tax dollars for the benefit of foreign corporations. Companies like Semi-Gas developed their technologies with federal money. SEMATECH, which worked with Semi-Gas, enjoys federal support through DARPA, which provides half of its $200-million annual budget. The sale of Semi-Gas means, in essence, that federal money will have supported the development of technological breakthroughs for a company now being bought by a foreign competitor. But critics of this point of view argued that there was no evidence Nippon Sanso would use the sale to underwrite large-scale technology transfer, and also that it was misleading to say that federal funds had directly provided a vital technology to a foreign competitor.

Another issue involved the concern that the sale of Semi-Gas fell into a larger pattern of technology acquisition by foreign companies eager to obtain the best and latest technological innovations; in this case, many felt the sale represented part of a broader plan by Japanese electronic and semiconductor companies to target important technologies for acquisition and ultimately to drive out U.S. competitors. Nippon Sanso has purchased other companies in the semiconductor-equipment field, and is in a strong position in the U.S. and international markets. Yet, apart from the issue of market share and antitrust, widespread disagreement prevailed in government and industry over whether this was part of a larger "conspiracy."[24]

Unfortunately, Semi-Gas was not an isolated case. CFIUS's failure to address the sale of more than seven hundred additional firms clearly showed that the government lacked both direction and a strategy to block takeover maneuvers by foreign firms, particularly where critical technologies were concerned.

(10) The Better Deal: Norton–Saint-Gobain

The tenth CFIUS investigation in April 1990, was initiated solely because CFIUS had investigated the Norton-BTR transaction. After fending off a hostile takeover by Great Britain's BTR PLC, which offered $75 a share, Norton found its white knight in France's Compagnie de Saint-Gobain, which manufactures plate glass, windshields, and low-tech ceramics. Saint-Gobain offered $90 a share, along with assurances that it would retain the current management, keep the company's headquarters in Worcester, Massachusetts, and maintain the company's philanthropic program.

(11) Enforcement Delay: MAMCO-CATIC

The eleventh investigation, in July 1990, was a reprise of the sixth, and confirmed the earlier result: CATIC's divestiture of MAMCO. The divestiture was completed on July 26, 1991.

(12) Nuclear Machine Tools: Moore-Fanuc

The twelfth CFIUS investigation, in October 1990, involved Fanuc, a Japanese-owned company, which sought to acquire Moore Special Tools, Inc., a Bridgeport, Connecticut, firm that held classified contracts with the government. Moore was also near bankruptcy and in desperate need of outside capital. The policy issue involved a decision on whether the public interest would best be served by allowing a U.S.-based company with technology vital to the national security to come under foreign influence or control, or by allowing the company to fall into bankruptcy, and possibly losing access to the technology in question altogether. Moore manufactures precise machine tools, two of which are sold annually, on average, to the Energy Department for use in its nuclear-weapons program. Those machine tools are used to manufacture parts that affect the explosive force of nuclear weapons and control the risk of accidental detonation.

There was general agreement that this transaction involved "national security" within the meaning of Exon-Florio. But CFIUS was still reportedly divided on whether or not to block the transaction, and the issue was ultimately referred to the heads of the eight agencies that make up CFIUS, plus the Department of Energy. These Cabinet officers recommended that the president not block the transaction, which was instead modified. Fanuc agreed to acquire 40 percent (less than half) of the outstanding shares of Moore, and to appoint only two of Moore's five board directors. However, the proposal provided that Fanuc could appoint a third director, and thereby control the board of directors, if the company failed to become profitable after two years. The decision not to block the sale appeared to be prompted by Moore's impending bankruptcy, with no American buyer to be found. Nevertheless, the proposed sale created a storm on Capitol Hill, and Fanuc withdrew its bid. Its Washington attorneys said that the withdrawal was due at least in part to congressional concerns.[25]

CFIUS's decision not to block the sale "calls into question the effectiveness of the CFIUS process," in the view of Kevin Kearns, now a Fellow at the Economic Strategy Institute in Washington. "CFIUS is not working as Congress intended," said Kearns, noting that, although Fanuc originally sought a minority stake in Moore, this did not mean Fanuc would not have access to Moore's expertise and technology: "Often, minority stakes as low as five percent will give a foreign investor access to technology." He reminded members of Congress that, since the agreement allowed Fanuc to become the major shareholder under certain circumstances, it was possible Fanuc could take over the company within two years. If Fanuc did so, it would run into difficulties complying with the Atomic Energy Act, which prohibits the U.S. government from contracting with foreign nationals. What would happen then if Moore, regarded as the world's best maker of ultraprecise machine tools, came under the control of a foreign national and could no longer deal with the U.S. government? "We would have to settle for second best for our nuclear weapons program, or pay inordinate costs to reestablish Moore's capabilities inside the Department of Energy," Kearns concluded.[26]

Subsequently, three other controversial transactions took place which CFIUS declined even to investigate. On March 19, 1990, CFIUS approved the proposed acquisition of up to a 25-percent interest in Titanium Metals Corp. of America (TIMET) by Toho Titanium Co. of Japan and its principal shareholders, Nippon Mining Co. and Mitsui and Co. TIMET provided about 50 percent of the titanium purchased by the Department of Defense, and was considered vital to the aerospace industry. CFIUS's decision, the focus of considerable criticism, was reportedly based on a compromise by which the Japanese companies and TIMET gave assurances that they would not transfer advanced technology to Japan. Congressional critics of the sale included Senator Bingaman, House Majority Leader Richard Gephardt, and Representative Helen Bentley, Maryland Republican.

Members of Congress were also critical of CFIUS's decision not to investigate the proposed sale of Union Carbide Chemicals & Plastics to Japan's Komatsu Electronic Metals Co. Ltd. The American company manufactured polysilicon, a material used in the manufacture of silicon wafers. A leading critic of the deal was former Defense official Frank Gaffney, who argued that Union Carbide was the only U.S. producer that met Defense Department requirements for ultrahigh-purity polysilicon, needed in key defense applications. Union Carbide maintained that there was at least one other U.S. manufacturer, and that the company had no contracts to supply the U.S. government with the product. Former Representative Doug Walgren, a Pennsylvania Democrat who was then chairman of the technology subcommittee of the House Energy and Commerce Committee, asked the GAO to investigate why CFIUS had failed to investigate the transaction. A leading advocate for foreign investors, Bradley Larschan, observed in testimony before Congress that "The GAO report was instructive as to the dilemma CFIUS frequently faces: whether to allow an acquisition or to risk the closure of a company."

A Defense Department official involved in CFIUS told the GAO that "the case presented a choice between two alternatives—Union Carbide's closing down its operation in high purity polysilicon production or Union Carbide's acquisition by Komatsu. He stated that acquisition of UCC&P by Komatsu would be preferable. . . ." He noted that it was unlikely Komatsu would close the facility, and that, if the facility *were* closed, the 1983 Mutual Defense Assistance Agreement between the United States and Japan would allow the U.S. government to enlist the aid of the Japanese government to compel Komatsu to supply U.S. military needs.

The third controversy involved the proposed sale of Perkin-Elmer Corp. to Japan's Nikon Corporation. Perkin-Elmer was the last major American manufacturer of machines for etching silicon chips, and its biggest customer was IBM. After a year-long controversy, Nikon suspended its acquisition discussions, citing congressional reaction, and Perkin-Elmer was purchased by a U.S. buyer.

EXON-FLORIO: EXIT AND REPRISE

Because of a legislative glitch, the Exon-Florio amendment expired in the fall of 1990, but both CFIUS and the Association for International

Investment (AII), which represents a group of foreign investors in the United States, urged foreign investors to regard the glitch as temporary, which it was, and to conduct their business as if the law were still in place. The legislative glitch—Congress's failure to renew the Defense Production Act, to which Exon-Florio had been added—provided an opportunity for an assessment of the legislation and its implementation. This process uncovered the difficulty of applying the Exon-Florio criteria, which required: (1) a link to national security; (2) a finding that credible evidence indicated that the foreign interest might take action that threatened to impair U.S. security; and (3) a finding that provisions of law, other than the International Emergency Economic Powers Act, failed to provide adequate authority to protect the national security.

Although the Exon-Florio amendment did not define "national security" (nor did the proposed implementing regulations, issued in July 1989), the accompanying conference report noted that the phrase was to be interpreted broadly, and without limitation to particular industries. The regulations touched off a debate between those who supported a narrow definition, which would include firms that did a majority of their business with the Department of Defense, and those who favored a broader definition, which would include industries and firms whose business was driven by the civilian commercial sector but, because of their leading-edge technologies, were important to overall defense-technology leadership. A GAO report to Congress on February 26, 1991, said, "We did not find evidence that the absence of a specific definition of national security affected CFIUS' ability to investigate investments."

As for the second element of a CFIUS decision, the question of whether there was credible evidence that a foreign interest might take action that threatened to impair national security, the GAO noted that, although the intelligence agencies and the Departments of Commerce, Defense, and State searched their records for evidence of unauthorized technology transfers, "the past CFIUS cases indicate that it is inherently more difficult for a CFIUS agency to argue that foreign firms from allied countries may threaten national security." As the report indicated, the one case the president had blocked involved an investment from the People's Republic of China. The GAO also stated that it was unclear whether anticompetitive behavior on the part of a foreign firm would constitute the type of threat to national security envisioned under the credible-evidence provision. "Examples of such types of anti-competitive behavior might be withholding from U.S. competitor firms supplies of the most technologically advanced components or engaging in cartel-like practices to damage U.S. competitors."

Regarding the third key element, which required a finding that other U.S. laws were inadequate to protect the national security, the GAO report noted that "none of these laws can protect against a foreign-owned firm's decision to close down a U.S. factory or to change the firm's product line or research direction."[27]

Most important, the GAO concluded that CFIUS did not examine larger questions in the public debate over foreign investment in the U.S., including how much of the defense industrial base had been acquired by foreign-owned firms; which industry sectors, technologies, or types of firms, if any, should be preserved for U.S. ownership; why some U.S. companies had found it desirable to discontinue operations in certain high-technology sectors; or how to assess the direction and effects of technology transfers accompanying foreign acquisitions. "These questions need to be addressed at a higher policy-making level and in a broader context than the case-by-case approach presently afforded by CFIUS," the report advised.[28]

The foreign investors, who had fought Exon-Florio, also raised questions about its implementation. Their objections focused on the attempt to link "economic security" with "national security"; the potential for abuse of Exon-Florio in hostile takeovers; and the politicization of the process. The AII acknowledged that the decision in certain instances was clear-cut, such as the General Ceramics–Tokuyama Soda transaction, in which the Department of Energy contracts relating to nuclear-weapons production were seen as squarely within Exon-Florio's scope.

The strongest objection from the foreign investors was leveled at the broader interpretations of the legislation that linked "national security" to "economic security," which had also prompted considerable disagreement within CFIUS. In Nippon Sanso KK's attempted acquisition of Semi-Gas Systems, a key issue was whether "national security" covered semiconductor research, and whether it also extended to at least some of the noncritical suppliers of this research. "CFIUS would appear to have engaged in a debate having more to do with U.S. international competitiveness than traditional conceptions of national security," AII asserted. The foreign-investor group contended that "national security" should be defined in terms consistent with U.S. commitments under its international-treaty obligations, including its numerous bilateral treaties of friendship, commerce, and navigation. "We believe that, on balance, CFIUS has struck a reasoned and principled approach to ascertaining the national security," AII said.[29]

Lobbyists for foreign investors also feared that the use of Exon-Florio as a device to fight off hostile takeovers would be "substantial," since unwilling target companies could exaggerate their importance to the national security. In BTR's attempted takeover of Norton, AII said, the American company stressed its importance to the national security. However, when France's Compagnie de Saint-Gobain, the white knight, came along, the American company played down Norton's importance to national security.

Finally, the foreign investors objected to the "politicization" of the Exon-Florio process, regarding the political intervention by Congress as one of the more troublesome aspects. AII noted that CFIUS had initiated its investigation of BTR's proposed takeover of Norton at the behest of 119 congressmen who wrote to the president. "We are troubled by the exertion of large-scale pressure on CFIUS," said AII, whose clientele is made up primarily of European investors, with only one Japanese company, Hitachi. The group's chairman, Elliot Richardson, stated that "Such political pressure on government regulators is both undeserved and counterproductive. It casts doubt on the integrity of the process and erodes the confidence of international investment policy."

Overall, however, AII concluded that "Exon-Florio has worked well, not only in terms of the review and investigation process, but also because Exon-Florio has involved an interagency mechanism for the scrutiny of and compliance with other laws that did not previously exist."[30]

Others were not so sanguine, believing that CFIUS remains a paper tiger that responds to the administration's commitment to free trade at the cost of national security. They pointed out that only one foreign acquisition was blocked during more than three years of Exon-Florio, and only twelve formal investigations were initiated. Representative Gephardt noted that CFIUS had ignored congressional pressure, though such pressure had led some foreign investors to withdraw their proposed acquisitions. "However, we cannot continue to rely on case-by-case Congressional pressure to make up for the failure of the Administration to view the issue of foreign investment in something other than an ideologue's vacuum. . . . We have to ask whether CFIUS is doing its job" when it approves all but one acquisition, Gephardt said.[31]

Kevin Kearns urged that government play an active rather than a reactive role in monitoring foreign investment in critical industries, and that CFIUS should gather as much information as possible on foreign investment and closely follow trends so that it was prepared to pre-empt any foreign takeovers that were potentially threatening to national interests. Kearns urged that CFIUS's evidentiary standard be changed from an emphasis on the "character" of the foreign firm to the effect of an acquisition on the nation's technological base. He also urged that CFIUS identify those industries that were most critical to our nation's defense and economic health and competitiveness, and that all foreign investors investing in critical industries report their intentions to CFIUS before approaching a targeted firm. The chairmanship of CFIUS, he suggested, should be changed from a Treasury official, "too often too solicitous of foreign interests because of the need to finance the budget deficit with foreign investment," to someone from Commerce or Defense.[32]

"Foreign takeovers of U.S. companies have become a cause of concern among Americans," Kearns said. "The feeling is growing that the United States is losing control of its economic sovereignty, and with it, the ability to act independently in both national and international political matters. A revised CFIUS process is one important way to address these concerns and to ensure that the national technological security of the United States is adequately protected."

The real problems with Exon-Florio surfaced repeatedly during its first three years, the most important of which was White House hostility, since the president and his top advisers were driven by the need to attract foreign capital from abroad to finance the deficit. Exon-Florio was a creature of Capitol Hill; it was wholly sustained by congressional interest, and represented a clear expression of congressional desire to protect the nation's defense industrial base from further erosion through foreign acquisitions. The bill's legislative history indicates clearly that economic and national security were meant to be considered; if the concept of separation of powers were working according to the textbooks, many more acquisitions would have been stopped. But things don't work that way. If the president isn't interested, the congressional intent doesn't much matter, especially on a trade issue that still seems relatively remote to the general public. Even the most dramatic acquisitions, such as those involving nuclear power, attracted scant public attention.

When the president finally stopped an acquisition, his act was meaningless except in a symbolic sense, since it took place after the fact: the MAMCO purchase by the Chinese had gone through well before the CFIUS process kicked in, and it took four months to remove the buyers from the plant. MAMCO represented a fairly low-tech company being purchased by a country whose brutality against pro-democracy demonstrators had angered the American public; imagine an undesirable acquisition of a technology that really mattered! Also, MAMCO was not a critical industry. Stopping the purchase was as phony in its own way as the Norton–St.-Gobain fiasco. Under pressure for going easy on the Chinese after Tiananmen Square, President Bush saw MAMCO-CATIC as a way of showing some backbone. Indeed, if CATIC was a vehicle for espionage, why did the White House allow the Chinese to purchase at least five other companies in the U.S., including a steel company (Phoenix Steel Corp., outside Wilmington, Delaware)?

Exon-Florio also failed to address the agonizing problem faced by many companies under scrutiny: what to do when they faced a real financial crisis. What were companies like Perkin-Elmer or Moore supposed to do when the only capital available to save the company from extinction was offered from abroad? Where was the government's help in raising capital, finding domestic buyers, and remaining viable? Would companies be discouraged from security-related work if they knew it would limit their future financial freedom?

Most important of all was the question of whether Exon-Florio, if implemented according to congressional intent, would compel companies to fold rather than be acquired by foreign investors, thereby losing the technology for the U.S. as well as everyone else involved. And, in the last analysis, what truly constituted a financial threat? Were some of these companies really in trouble, or were they merely tempted by the profits to be gleaned from selling out at inflated prices?

Because Exon-Florio failed to come to grips with the basic questions raised by companies at risk, its effectiveness was greatly diminished and it became almost insignificant. Americans would rather compete with foreign investors than restrict them, and they would rather see U.S. funds in more plentiful supply for critical industries. Exon-Florio should be taken seriously as congressional recognition of a very real problem. But without White House support the law remains unenforced, in silent testimony to Congress's general impotence in matters of trade and security.

CHAPTER IV

The Eyes of the Dragonfly

THE FSX—TECHNOLOGICAL GIVEAWAY OR MODEL FOR THE FUTURE?

To buy an F-16 off the shelf would be like marrying a middle-aged lady when you are young.
> —Toshinori Shigeie, director,
> National Security Affairs Division,
> North American Affairs Bureau,
> Ministry of Foreign Affairs, Japan

It will cost the Japanese two to three times as much per plane to coproduce the FSX as it would to buy the F-16. . . . Clearly, they want that technology so that they can build not just the FSX but an aircraft industry.
> —Senator Lloyd Bentsen,
> chairman of the Finance Committee

THE TOKYO PERSPECTIVE

The man to see in Japan about the FSX is Seiki Nishihiro. A tall man with iron-gray hair, he presides as vice-minister over the Japan Defense Agency in a dignified, stern manner. His Tokyo office is decorated in beige tones, and features a massive conference table surrounded by elegant brocade-covered chairs. A bonsai tree rests on the windowsill, while in a prominent place next to Nishihiro's desk stands a large paper-shredder.

For the better part of the 1980s, Nishihiro served as the lead negotiator on the FSX, a new, advanced fighter plane to be developed and produced jointly by the United States and Japan. The FSX, which stands for Fighter Support Experimental, would be the successor to the F-1, Japan's indigenous support fighter, and the F-16, America's highly acclaimed aircraft. It would be manufactured by Mitsubishi Heavy Industries, Ltd., and the General Dynamics Corporation for the purpose of Japan's national defense in the 1990s.

The FSX soon became mired in an international dispute that raised questions about military dependence and interdependence, the sanctity of agreements, and the relationship between national and economic security. It became a rallying point for a variety of groups that perceived the issue as the latest in a series of Japanese trade victories, threatening the aerospace industry with the fate of VCRs and semiconductors. Critics accused the Japanese of ripping off American avionics in an effort to establish their own industry; the Japanese, it was alleged, were investing capital and a much smaller share of technology. Critics noted that, unlike America's automobile producers, who had been justly criticized for poor quality and failure to respond to the needs of consumers, the nation's aircraft industry was hailed as a world leader. The performance of U.S. aircraft in the Gulf War more than vindicated this view.

For their part, the Japanese argued that they were contributing important technology in their own right, and deserved to be full-fledged partners in this enterprise. Tokyo sought to refute the accusation that the Japanese were just copycats who improved on American products, and claimed that the Europeans were anxious to become their partner in avionics, if America was not. Besides, if Tokyo wanted to develop an avionics technology, who was America to stop them? Moreover, the Japanese thought they had a deal, involving the honor of those who had made it.

The dispute represented a series of firsts: the first time national security and economic security met over a trade issue, the first time an American president was forced by Congress and by his own bureaucracy to expand his definition of national security to include trade and economic objectives along with military and strategic concerns, and the first time Congress had imposed its will on an issue of this kind. It was also the first time the free-traders in the Reagan and Bush administrations were forced to confront a public airing of Japan's challenge. Thanks to the FSX, a public debate was finally launched about developing a U.S. strategic-technology policy without its being immediately shot down as industrial policy.

Recalling his numerous frustrations as lead negotiator didn't lighten Nishihiro's mood. His tone, typical of Japanese officials involved with the FSX, conveyed deep disappointment in his American allies, who, in his view, had reneged on their agreement to codevelop and coproduce an advanced fighter aircraft. He understood that the Americans were responding to intense political pressure at home, but couldn't figure out why his counterparts could not deflect—or at least stonewall—the critics. After all, a deal is a deal. Japanese officials expressed a sense of betrayal, all the sharper since no signs of trouble had emerged during the first three years of negotiation. In Japan, gentlemen are bound to uphold agreements no matter what happens; when they cannot uphold their commitments, they suffer a loss of face, much more devastating in their culture than in ours. Nishihiro lost face with his own colleagues over the FSX negotiation, and he spoke at length about his experience. For more than an hour, the bitter words still tumbled out as he reflected on his years with the FSX. "The FSX did not come to a successful conclusion," he began. "When the U.S. and Japan decided on the FSX, to coproduce the FSX, there were two reasons: one, to promote mutual dependence; and two, to let Americans save R and D money."

There was a time when things really were that simple, and few cared how these agreements emerged from the conference table. Military men on both sides made commitments based on narrowly defined interests. In this case, the Americans were trying to save defense money and in fact were under orders from Congress—namely, the Nunn-Quayle amendment to the Defense Production Act—to do just that.[1]

The era of FSX negotiations also coincided with the "Ron-Yasu" years, when President Reagan and Prime Minister Yasuhiro Nakasone shared a close, informal relationship—too close, some said—based on personal rapport and mutual trust. It was easy to see how agreements could be drawn up without close attention to detail.

Beneath the surface, however, the United States had a more compelling reason for undertaking the agreement: a desire to prevent the Japanese from producing their own fighter. According to U.S. defense officials, negotiators were given explicit instructions from the Reagan White House at the earliest stages of negotiation, in 1985–86, to try to get the Japanese to coproduce F-16s—they had already coproduced F-15s—and forestall any independent effort on their part. The easygoing, relaxed environment of the Reagan years quickly shifted when George Bush entered office and found himself unable to deliver on his predecessor's commitments.

The FSX was a sleeper issue for the newly inaugurated president. Public fears of a technological giveaway fueled a major dispute that forced Bush to send negotiators back to the bargaining table in February 1989, scarcely a month after he took office. In the end, the U.S.

came away with a better deal but Japanese resentment intensified, rupturing the U.S.-Japan relationship and marring the long-term development of the aircraft.

For the first time, U.S. leaders were forced to face what has since become a familiar issue: what do you do when a valued ally is also your most formidable economic competitor? (Especially when the most compelling reason for that alliance, the Soviet threat, had receded in importance).

By the time Bush entered office, the political climate had changed for both the Japanese and the Americans. A growing sense of national pride in their technological achievements impelled Japanese leaders to demonstrate their new prowess; at the same time, they were tired of the cliché that Americans created and invented new technologies while Japanese drones translated the blueprints into products. For the Japanese, the FSX was different.

"Codevelopment is an exchange of technologies between our two countries," Nishihiro said. "There are not so many new technologies to be exchanged. The U.S. can learn from us if they want to. For example, in Japan we save money by keeping prototypes [building an entire plane] to a minimum by using simulation. The U.S. can learn from that.

"There are some opponents in Japan who feel we were giving away the technology without receiving anything in return," continued Nishihiro, who shared many of his colleagues' claims—heatedly disputed by U.S. opponents—of Japanese superiority in such technologies as phased-array radar, gallium arsenide, and advanced composite materials, which produce lighter, stronger, and larger aircraft wings that can carry more missiles. Active phased-array radar can "see" in any direction; this is why its advocates in Japan often compare it so poetically to the "eyes of the dragonfly," for it can spin around the radius of the aircraft instead of facing in only one direction.

The Japanese particularly emphasized that the U.S. could learn from Japan's advanced manufacturing methods and more cost-effective ways of developing weapons systems. "The American way is not cost-effective," said Mr. Nishihiro. "The FSX is a good example of how we—the Japanese government, that is—differ on R and D. We do not have to develop new technologies; we gather new technologies and tailor them to our own modifications.

"You should let your private sector do the basic research, then wait before your government launches new technologies," continued Nishihiro. "The Japanese private manufacturing sector puts large funds into R and D. . . . We are always watching what they do in order to utilize what they are doing for our own military R and D. That is why we can do R and D less expensively than the U.S. where the process is reversed. For example, the Air Force, in developing its next-generation fighter, concentrates all of its efforts in R and D to have weapons system. The U.S. government pays 100 percent. You should prioritize more."

Was the FSX a one-way street, with Japan pouring technology into a U.S. product? What were the Japanese getting in return? None of the Japanese officials mentioned engine technology, or computer software, which later turned out to be the crux of the FSX debate, but they did admit to wanting U.S. expertise in "systems integration and know-how," the complex process of combining technologies to manufacture military aircraft.

Nishihiro stressed that his views stemmed "purely from national-security concerns," not technological ones. Indeed, his experience with the FSX so scarred his view of the U.S.-Japan relationship that he began to question Japan's military dependence on the United States, although Nishihiro was typical of many Japanese defense officials in his strong anti-Soviet views.

"Japan is a country whose dependence on American external deterrence is the highest among allies," continued Nishihiro. "You will note that there are now grave doubts in Europe about America's abilities in external deterrence. We can't link Japan's defense and security any more with the American nuclear force. Japan is more concerned about this than Europe. We face Soviet forces in the Far East and we do not have enough military capability to have parity with the Soviets in the Far East. We need more."

All of the Japanese involved with the FSX were quick to try to allay U.S. fears that the agreement was just another example of Japan's predatory trade behavior, with the FSX a vehicle for entering the lucrative global avionics and military-exports industries. Nishihiro pointed out that the Japanese had a "firmly established policy against military exports." Other Japanese trade and defense officials supported this view, although the boundary line between military and civilian uses is so fuzzy that it is difficult to assess the realities of this policy.

Hiroshi Morikawa, secretary general of the Defense Production Committee of the Keidanren—Japan's major business trading group, with close ties to the government—argued that the government "never even thought in terms of exporting the FSX. The export of arms to us is a serious political issue. This is not something the business community should lightly talk about, if ever."

Morikawa argued that Japan would never be an arms exporter in view of the insurmountable political difficulties involved, noting that the public accepted as national policy the prohibition against it—

no matter that certain groups in the business community, as some suspected, wanted to move in that direction. Morikawa added that even if this policy were changed, Japanese weapons were extremely expensive and not competitive in the international marketplace, because of the low volume.

Sitting back in his chair and gazing out the window of his office high above downtown Tokyo, Morikawa then pointedly asked his U.S. visitor about American misconceptions concerning Japan: "I don't know why Americans don't think Japan extends reciprocal treatment toward U.S. products. You see the foreign cars all over the streets . . . Saabs, BMWs, Mercedes. We don't buy *your* cars because they're junk. That doesn't mean we don't buy foreign cars."

"I'll grant you cars," replied his visitor, who drives a Toyota. "But Americans manufacture many other high-quality products that Japan could use, but are not in evidence anywhere in Tokyo. Take appliances. My washer and dryer haven't been repaired in ten years. They're top-notch products. Yet the most elegant high-rise condos here display laundry hanging from the terraces. Even middle-class citizens in Japan don't seem to have dryers or dishwashers, appliances that would be basic for U.S. families."

"You don't understand our culture," responded Morikawa, himself a wealthy industrialist. "We like our laundry to dry in the sun," implying almost a religious significance to this act, "and my wife would be insulted if she couldn't hand-wash the dishes every night."

The translator, herself a hardworking mother of two, lifted her eyes to the ceiling in disbelief at Morikawa's avowal of his wife's passion for doing the dishes.

The "no, not ever" public stance of Japan's leaders toward the international arms market doesn't mean they haven't thought about the issue; in fact, Japanese leaders often portray themselves as moderates, staving off the hawks from resurrecting the old World War II military machine. But many Japanese still see military exports as a possibility, or a lost opportunity. In any event, it is clear that Japanese leaders are engaged in a private conflict over this issue, with some bureaucrats in the defense and trade bureaucracies supporting increased military production, and others, in the Foreign Ministry, budget office, and Ministry of International Trade and Industry (MITI)— along with pacifist political forces—in vigorous opposition. Michael Green, a scholar and journalist who has spent many years in Japan, has written about this fierce, internal debate over "*kokusanka*," or "developing the capability for autonomous production of weapons."[2]

Well aware of Japan's ability to "spin on and spin off" between consumer and military technologies, Americans feared that Japan would somehow use the technology it acquired from the FSX to compete with the U.S. in the field of commercial aircraft. This is not an unfounded fear, given Japan's ability to move so easily between the two worlds. One good example is the adaptation of carbon tungsten, first used for tennis racquets, fishing rods, and golf clubs, now used in the production of jet wings for the FSX, according to Japanese officials.

Motoo Shiina, a former member of the Diet and one of Japan's most respected defense experts—in fact, he's often referred to as the "Sam Nunn of Japan"—attempted to dispel America's fear of commercialization: "The FSX is not a commercial airplane. Commercialization is remote, because the way fighters fly and the way commercial aircraft fly is so different." Shiina's views were later supported by U.S. defense officials.

Shiina argued that security conditions, *not* commercial ambition, drove Japan's desire to build the new aircraft on its own soil. "Senator Bingaman asked me why we can't buy aircraft engines off the shelf," said Shiina, asked why Japan would spend two and a half times the cost of each aircraft for the experience of building it in Japan. "With commercial aircraft we can buy engines off the shelf and send them home to repair. In a contingency situation, such as a battle, we couldn't send the engines home for repair and then wait for them to come back. Without coproduction we wouldn't get repair technology."

Still, coproduction was far from Japan's initial interest in producing its own fighters *and* its own engines. Shiina recognized this, and described the political problems within the government that led to the agreement to codevelop the aircraft. "We have had a hard time suppressing the crowd who wanted indigenous development," he said, "the Air Force and the indigenous companies. For *economic* reasons it might have been plausible to buy FSX planes off the shelf; it isn't plausible here *politically*." In other words, in Japan, nationalism and corporate interests prevailed over economics.

In fact, Shiina, along with many others—including the Reagan administration—regarded coproduction and development as a coup for the United States, in view of the strong pressures inside the Japanese government for manufacturing independence. "Indigenous development would mean that Americans would have no control over the product, the process, the new technology, and development," he added. "If we get really hostile, we could buy the engines from Europe. The president of Rolls-Royce told me, 'If the Americans are foolish, you are always our customer.'" But Shiina believed that intransigence toward the U.S. would be a mistake. "The U.S.-Japan alliance is very important to us. There is no alternative for Japan. Our Asian neighbors regard us as a threat. They remember the last war."

Tokyo was profoundly disappointed over the failure of the Pentagon to deliver. The Japan Defense Agency (JDA) drew much of its political strength from its long-standing relationship with the Pentagon, and its top officials couldn't comprehend why the Pentagon had failed to protect them against what they viewed as America's emerging trade hawks. More to the point: Americans didn't fully understand the internal political struggles in Japan that resulted in the decision to coproduce the FSX. Buying aircraft "off the shelf" directly from the United States was never an option, according to Japanese public officials.

Evidence suggests that in the early 1980s the Japanese military establishment had just about decided to build its own plane as a matter of national pride as well as national security. A previous effort at indigenous production had resulted in the manufacture of the notorious F-1 aircraft, which was known for its poor performance and spurned by Japanese pilots. But Japanese leaders regarded this failure as a challenge, not a deterrent, and looked forward to trying again. Finding the atmosphere receptive, another powerful political force weighed in: Mitsubishi Heavy Industries began an intensive lobbying effort to persuade the government to produce aircraft at its facility in Nagoya as a last-ditch attempt to save the plant and its five thousand jobs. In fact, Mitsubishi was outspoken in its desire to produce the aircraft by itself; it most decidedly did not want coproduction.

Many later viewed Washington as having been too sympathetic to Japanese interests—a criticism Ronald Reagan did nothing to dispel when, in the fall of 1989, he visited Japan as a private citizen to make two speeches for the unseemly speaking fee of $2.5 million. By the time negotiations began in earnest, "off-the-shelf" purchases were rare even for developing countries; industrialized countries almost always demanded a share of the production or, at the very least, an "offset"— an agreement by the seller to purchase an often unrelated product. The F-16, for example, was coproduced by no fewer than nine countries (excluding Japan), all of whom then purchased the aircraft.

The struggle over the FSX within the Japanese government began in the early 1980s. Nakasone, the prime minister at the time, was a strong advocate of an autonomous defense capability for Japan. Reagan encouraged the development of the aircraft, citing the Soviet threat and echoing his budgeteers' view that the U.S. could no longer afford the expense of defending Japan. Reagan's message quickly took root in a country eager to expand its successful economy. By 1980, Japanese leaders were well along in the development of semiconductors and other defense-related products. Nakasone's allies included business leaders and defense officials; his opponents, the fiscal conservatives in the Ministry of Finance, believed that moving into the defense business was an unnecessary luxury if the nation did not also move into exporting defense products.

Whereas Japanese leaders monitor U.S. politics closely, most American leaders haven't a clue about what propels domestic politics in Japan. This was especially true of the internal struggles over the FSX, which revealed something even more significant: the sense that the U.S.-Japan bilateral alliance was much more important to Japan than it was to the United States. What Americans saw as an isolated trade dispute had a more profound effect on the Japanese and left scars that have yet to heal. "When the U.S. sneezes, Japan catches cold," said Shinichiro Ohta, director of the Aircraft and Ordnance Division of MITI. "The Japan-U.S. relationship is the most important relationship to us in dealing with world economic problems. There is a consistent government policy to maintain bilateral Japan-U.S. relationships. That is the axis on which we build relationships."

(Pinned on the anteroom wall outside Ohta's office was a large English-language cartoon with characters labeled "Tech busters" wearing masks and big hats, and carrying missiles and charts. The top caption reads "E = MC squared"; the bottom, "We ain't afraid of no spies.")

The internal politics of the Japanese government involved a heated interagency debate, in which the budget, trade, and foreign-affairs agencies in government fought the defense agency. In Japan, defense agencies are not as prestigious as they are in the United States, and civilian agencies generally have greater influence; moreover, defense agencies share national-security power with the Foreign Ministry, where a special office for national-security policy is located. The best and the brightest of Japanese youth slated for public service go to MITI, the Ministry of Finance, and the Ministry of Foreign Affairs, and not to the JDA. All the more reason why the FSX was so important to the JDA: it represented the agency's first real victory, which is why losing made them even more bitter at the American defection.

Another striking contrast with the United States is that the major trade agency in Japan, MITI, participates in national-security decisions, whereas the U.S. Department of Commerce and Office of the U.S. Trade Representative typically do not. MITI participated from the beginning in the FSX negotiations, while Commerce and the USTR fought hard for a voice, and only entered the deliberations late in the game. At the time of the FSX dispute, the head of the Defense Agency procurement office at JDA came from MITI on loan, and it was assumed that he retained his loyalty to the trade agency. (Although there is some mobility among agencies in Japan, officials have their "home address," remaining loyal to the agency that originally hired them.)

Japanese officials were also distressed by what they considered America's reneging on an agreement contained in an MOU (memorandum of understanding). After all, America was a trusted ally, not given to breaking its promises. In addition, there was a strong undercurrent running through the Japanese ministries at the time, of sensitivity to what was perceived as American racism toward the Japanese. "If the FSX was on a NATO issue," said Tomoyoshi Uranishi, the chief economic planner for the Ministry of Finance, responsible for the defense budget, "we wouldn't have had the same problem, because the U.S. has closer links with Europe. They regard Europe as their homeland."

As a result of the FSX, some Japanese now view the United States as an unreliable ally. From Reagan they heard they must share the weapons burden and build their own defense weapons; from Congress and their U.S. critics, they were encouraged to continue to buy U.S. defense technologies off the shelf to reduce the U.S.-Japan trade deficit. The result was a buffeting from all sides, and an inclination to avoid joint agreements in the future.

The FSX disappointment provided justification for Japan's trade hawks, who have advocated more defense independence for years. "This stimulated the wrong kind of nationalism," said Kiyofuku Chuma, an editorial writer with the *Asahi Shimbun*. "Until the FSX, the Japanese were content to let the United States assume the global role, and protect them from the Soviet threat, and Japan could remain more local. Up until now, this thinking has been appropriate. From now on, this role is not suitable because of Japan's changing relationship with the United States."

By "the wrong kind of nationalism" Chuma was hinting at a revival of the militarism that had led to Pearl Harbor and World War II. "There is a strong movement to change the executive order in Japan which bans exporting military equipment except to the United States. As a result of the exception for the United States, weapons could be sent to the United States, then sold to other countries. This doesn't seem to make sense any more to Japanese, who feel, 'Why not export directly to NATO or ASEAN?' As a result of this thinking and because of the joint agreement with the United States, people in industry are thinking about ways to get around the executive order."

For this reason, Chuma remains one of the few Japanese who question Japan's position on the FSX: "The real question with the FSX is the economy of scale. There is a plan at the present to build 100–150 FSX planes. That is all that would be needed by Japan for its own defense. I am worried that down the road they're going to say that we have to make 300 planes to be cost-effective. My opinion is that Japan should import these planes instead of coproducing them. If you can't export them—that is, if the executive order is not changed—they will be too expensive to produce here. If there is pressure for exporting these planes there will be even greater tension in the U.S.-Japan relationship, because then Japan really will be competing with the U.S. military-aircraft industry.

"And finally," said Chuma, "it is not really necessary for Japan to be number one in everything, especially when it has become number one in semiconductors and such a lot of other industries. Does Japan really need these [FSX] technologies? There is very little discussion here about this."

In contrast, the question of why Japan needed FSX technologies was central to the debate in the United States—something Japanese leaders failed to see. The FSX issue only heightened the growing suspicion of Japan as an economic juggernaut bent on an inexorable path toward worldwide economic domination. What other reason, asked some FSX opponents, could the Japanese have for focusing on military avionics?

In Japan, the focus was on military independence in an era of global demilitarization. For geographic reasons, Japanese military leaders still regarded the Soviet Union as an immediate security threat, and these Cold War–hardened leaders were made even more anxious by what they saw as American naïveté in being taken in by Gorbachev's rhetoric. The increase in Japan's defense budget was one clear indicator of the military's success, but it also reflected Washington's pressure on Japan to assume a larger share of the military burden. By executive order the Japanese defense budget had been capped at 1 percent of the total budget. This ceiling was instituted by the Cabinet in 1976 and adhered to until 1987. By 1990, Japan had exceeded this cap to rank third in the world, behind the United States and the Soviet Union, in military expenditures.

Another theme that emerged with disturbing frequency among the Japanese was a palpable contempt for U.S. technology. "If you can't make decent cars, how can we trust your avionics?" ran this argument. "There is less confidence now in U.S. technology; there is a feeling among the Japanese that the U.S. could not make the next generation of jets," said Chuma. "Where the U.S. cannot fulfill its role, the Japanese Defense Agency will increase its role. This trend will continue as we enter the 1990s."

Japan believed the United States was forcing it to accept outmoded military aircraft, an accusation that later turned out to be inaccurate. "To buy an F-16 off-the-shelf would be like marrying a middle-aged lady when you are young," argued Toshinori Shigeie, director of the National Security Affairs Division, North American Affairs Bureau, Ministry of Foreign Affairs, using an analogy that has been quoted widely by Japanese negotiators. "The F-16s are not appropriate. The F-16 is a good lightweight fighter but it was developed in the mid-1970s. The F-16s are too old for the 1990s. Their takeoff, their short turnaround, is not adequate."

In response, U.S. negotiators asked, "Why should you climb Mt. Fuji alone when you could start with a partner halfway up?" One of the many misunderstandings that plagued the FSX, the idea of purchasing F-16s off the shelf, was never really an option for the U.S. either; instead, critics offered the option of the F-18, a newer version of the F-16, or the even newer ATF, an advanced tactical fighter being developed in the United States for use in the 1990s.

The major misunderstanding between the two countries involved differing attitudes toward national and economic security. To the Japanese, economic stability went hand in hand with national security; you couldn't have one without the other. In contrast, the American vision of national security since World War II was limited to military technology and geopolitical strategies. Americans rarely connect the loss of commercial technologies with the loss of military technology until it is too late. Yet studies from the Defense Science Board, a prestigious group of scientists and corporate leaders advising the secretary of defense, have made this a major issue in a series of reports throughout the 1980s on defense technology and industrial cooperation.

The issue boiled down to interdependence versus dependence, terms that held different meanings in the U.S. and Japan. Over the years, the U.S. gradually abdicated many of its national-security technologies, such as the manufacture of semiconductors and components, to Japan; 80 percent of all semiconductors used in the United States, for example, are made offshore, mostly in Japan or in Japanese plants in other parts of the world. As long as America felt rich and powerful and relations with Japan remained strong, the United States didn't feel heavily dependent; after all, it didn't matter if we depended on Japan for semiconductors if Japan depended on us for its military security. Also, Japanese leaders have deliberately directed their efforts toward technological independence, while their U.S. counterparts tended to rationalize their growing dependence into a romanticized notion of interdependence.

Suddenly the comfort level changed: American debts mounted and trade deficits with Japan climbed. Japan's economy soared, but the Japanese still felt economically insecure, even poor, in relation to the United States. These conflicting attitudes exploded over the FSX: the United States failed to understand why the Japanese wanted to add avionics to their trade juggernaut, and the Japanese were shocked at U.S. resistance to rising interdependence. New trade frictions with Japan only exacerbated the misunderstanding.

"Americans should be more confident," said Dr. Seizaburo Sato, professor of political science at the University of Tokyo, one of Japan's most accomplished national-security experts and a longtime government adviser. "They have more leverage. They have a huge market without which other countries could not survive. They are huge and powerful and gifted and full of natural resources.

"Japan can produce better-quality components than the U.S. can," he continued. "The U.S. has to depend on supplies from Japan. They don't like it. That's the price of interdependence. That means better and more efficient allocation of resources. It means you are more vulnerable. The U.S. is used to fighting enemies; you are not accustomed to dealing with others on whom you are dependent. It is a source of psychological trouble for the United States. Japan is used to depending on the good will of others.

"Japan is desperately dependent on the United States for food. The United States can depend on the loyalty of Japan. For the United States this new dependency is a good thing. Ownership doesn't matter in a growing age of interdependence." In actuality, after President Nixon imposed an embargo on the export of soybeans to Japan, Japanese leaders embarked on a program to diversify their sources of food and raw materials to avoid the inevitable control that comes from dependence.

THE VIEW FROM WASHINGTON

Ownership did matter to critics in the United States, who were angered by the FSX deal. Quiescent during the Ron-Yasu years, criticism erupted as the MOU became public; the FSX soon became a rallying point for a variety of groups that perceived the issue as the latest in a series of Japanese trade victories.

"What we're seeing," said Representative Les Aspin, Democrat of Wisconsin and chairman of the House Armed Services Committee, "is the emergence of an entirely new concept of national security. It embraces economics and competitive commercial relations."[3]

What's more, many Americans—including captains of industry—now expected their government to guarantee that connection. "The MOU gave avionics to Japan," charged Bernard Schwartz, CEO of the Loral Corporation. "This was a surprise to the electronics industry. If American electronics are so good, why should they be negotiated away? The FSX ran counter to U.S. interests. There will be a cumulative negative impact of this deal and it sends a negative signal to the defense community." Not to mention the aerospace industry, continued Schwartz, who pointed out that aerospace and commercial aviation remained one of the few American industries boasting a trade surplus—$19 billion, to be exact, resulting from the export of $33 billion worth of goods.

"Last month I learned that the Japanese were making commercial fuselages from military plans. If they do in aerospace what they did in electronics, we're in big trouble," said Schwartz. He belongs to a group of industrialists called DPACT, Defense Political Advisory Committee on Trade, who called on Secretary of Defense Richard Cheney in a futile attempt to change his mind on the FSX deal. DPACT complained to Cheney that the FSX was not a good deal, and objected that their industry was not consulted on the MOU. Visibly upset, according to Schwartz, Cheney responded that this was the best deal they could have gotten, but agreed that from then on, the Defense Department would take the views of major subcontractors into consideration.

Opponents of the FSX deal were galvanized by an influential article in late January 1989 in the "Outlook" section of the Washington *Post* by Clyde Prestowitz, a former Japan expert and adviser to the secretary of commerce in the Reagan administration. The article ran less than a month after the FSX announcement. Japan would gain $7 billion worth of U.S. technology, argued Prestowitz, with the U.S. getting very little in return. "Under the agreement . . . the General Dynamics–built F-16, currently one of the Air Force's hottest fighters, will be stripped and virtually redesigned into a new fighter for deployment by Japan's Defense Agency. . . . General Dynamics will provide all the technology—developed at an estimated cost of $7 billion." What General Dynamics would get in return was a scant "$440 million in subcontracting work from Mitsubishi on four development prototypes, possibly a share of component manufacture . . . of 130 planes, a possible transfer of allegedly advanced Japanese radar and composite-wing technology and possible royalties on future production of $75–150 million."[4]

The fight against the FSX was launched by a small group that revolved around Prestowitz. Increasingly frustrated with U.S. impotence in ongoing trade negotiations with Japan on items ranging from semiconductors to rice, Prestowitz resigned from Commerce and published an account of his experiences in *Trading Places*, a book that became an influential work on the unbalanced U.S.-Japan relationship.[5] The FSX deal was also opposed by some key operatives on the Hill, including: Kevin Kearns, a young State Department officer previously stationed in Japan, on leave to the Senate Foreign Relations Committee; Charles Smith, an aide to Senator Alan Dixon, Democrat of Illinois; and Ed McGaffigan, who worked as a key legislative aide on science and technology issues for Senator Bingaman. Also working behind the scenes to influence the administration were Tom Murrin, at Commerce; Deborah Wince-Smith and William Graham, from the White House Science Office; Michael Smith, at the USTR; Dr. Pat Choate, a vice-president at TRW Inc. working through the Defense Manufacturing Board, an advisory group at the Pentagon; and Malcolm Currie, head of Hughes Aircraft and chairman of the Defense Science Board at DoD.

Much to everyone's surprise, this rearguard action of unlikely allies stopped the government and forced the FSX issue into the open. Pro-FSX forces were represented by former Secretary of Defense Frank Carlucci, an investment banker. Supported by the State and Defense Departments, Carlucci argued that by working together, "the U.S. government and industry will have ready access to Japanese technology that would otherwise be unavailable; that the F-16 has already been co-produced to varying extents in eight other countries since 1979, and in its present form does not represent leading edge technology"; and that export controls were sufficient to prevent other technologies from being transferred. At a congressional hearing, Carlucci objected most vociferously to "trade policy driving defense."[6]

Caught off guard, President Bush stalled the FSX agreement and put the MOU off for a month. This gave forces within his administration time to mobilize against the agreement, and also allowed congressional opponents to gain momentum on Capitol Hill. Within the administration only the Pentagon and the State Department urged quick approval; as usual, the State Department was fearful of harming U.S.-Japan relations, while the Pentagon was anxious to meet its prior commitments to Japan and avoid what it regarded as the worst option, indigenous development. Lobbying Bush against the agreement were officials from an impressive array of agencies: the Commerce Department, the White House Office of Science and Technology, USTR, the Treasury Department, Energy, and the Central Intelligence Agency. The CIA's technical staff warned the president that the deal represented a significant transfer of technology to Japan. On Capitol Hill, thirty-five senators issued a statement indicating their unhappiness with the agreement, portending trouble. The GAO produced a devastating report supporting congressional concern about a technological giveaway.[7]

Under pressure from Japan to make a decision by March 31, the end of its fiscal year, Bush met with the National Security Council on March 15 to discuss the issue. Three distinct positions emerged from the NSC meeting. White House Chief of Staff John Sununu, a former professor of engineering, and USTR Carla Hills urged that the deal be scrapped and Japan urged to buy F-16s off the shelf. DoD representative William H. Taft IV, deputy secretary of defense, Secretary of State James Baker, and National Security Adviser Brent Scowcroft argued that the original agreement be left intact, while Secretary of Commerce Mosbacher ended up somewhere in the middle, proposing that the deal should proceed with safeguards. The Japanese also weighed in with the added claim that the U.S. was invoking national-security arguments to gain economic advantage.

To his credit, and to the astonishment of those who regarded the administration as soft on trade issues, President Bush sifted through the conflicting advice and political pressures and decided to force Japan to revise the FSX deal. The issue boiled down to production versus development: how much of each, and where. The original agreement reached in November 1988 guaranteed U.S. contractors 40 percent of the *development* budget, plus access to the secrets of advanced Japanese radar gear and composite materials. This sounded good until closer scrutiny revealed the catch: the U.S. companies were restricted to *development*, not *production*, where the real money is made. The Bush administration demanded that the United States get 40 percent of the *production*, with full assurances that American firms receive 40 percent of the $5–10 billion in production contracts for at least 170 fighters to be deployed in the late 1990s. This would force Japan to buy U.S. aircraft engines and keep critical engine technology in the United States.

Engine technology now emerged as one of the most critical issues of technology transfer involved in the FSX. The U.S. still held the lead in the international marketplace, and American companies zealously guarded the technological secrets that enabled them to retain that lead. Expressing their grave concern, some U.S. companies, including such industry leaders as Pratt & Whitney, privately warned that the FSX would turn out to be the vehicle through which valuable engine technology would be quietly shifted to predatory Japanese companies.

Their concerns proved warranted. In danger of losing the FSX, the Japanese government finally agreed on April 11 to modify the FSX agreement to ensure that 40 percent of the FSX work—development *and* production—be performed in the United States. Ten days later, however, Japan quietly put strings on their 40-percent concession that revealed their major interest in U.S. engine technology. At a secret meeting with State Department officials, Japanese Ambassador Nobuo Matsunaga insisted that, in return for the 40-percent concession, Japan be guaranteed half of the work on the aircraft's engines. This meant *sharing* advanced U.S. engine technology with Japan, when the point of the concession was to allow the U.S. to *sell* engines to Japan.

Two weeks later, on April 27, President Bush announced a new agreement, which made everybody unhappy. Japan's leaders claimed they were forced to make all of the concessions in negotiating the deal to appease Congress. Critics in the U.S., especially those in Congress, vowed to scotch the agreement by May 31, their deadline for accepting or rejecting it.

Editorial opinion was mixed on the FSX issue. *Business Week*'s editorial board headlined the FSX as a "Deal We Should Knock Out of the Sky," the "kind of shortsightedness that let the U.S. give Japan the technology for everything from VCRs to semiconductors," and an "agreement [that] will finally give Japan the basis it needs to start a full-fledged aircraft industry by the mid-1990s." Similarly, a *New York Times* editorial called the agreement "The Pentagon's Handout to Japan," asking "why does Japan insist on a deal that apparently makes no military or commercial sense for either partner?" On the other side, the Washington *Post* applauded the agreement on the grounds that, "if the United States now tried to back out of its fighter aircraft deal with Japan, it would do severe damage to both the Japanese government and itself." Nor, the *Post* added, "should the Commerce Department be allowed to disrupt a reasonable foreign policy to which a country is already committed."[8]

President Bush unveiled the new agreement with the promise that it would protect U.S. jobs and technology. This time the joint design *and* production of the new-generation fighter plane would be shared by the United States and Japan, with the U.S. getting about 40 percent of the production as well as the development. New clarifications included restrictions on U.S. companies' turning over to Japan software source codes, which are the basis of programs that enable pilots to control aircraft and weaponry electronically. Two groups of codes include: (1) those used in flight computers, which translate the pilot's commands into actual instructions to parts of the plane; and (2) those used in the mission computer, which control the weapons, navigation system, radar, and electronic counter-measures. Originally, the Japanese had wanted access to both codes, but U.S. negotiators argued they had never agreed to provide those for the flight computer. The Japanese did not make a public issue of it, knowing these would be relatively easy to get once joint production began. Computer experts privately admit that codes are very hard to control and that when engineers work together it is difficult to protect them.

"Let me tell you a hidden crisis in Silicon Valley that's not discussed," said a high-ranking executive with a computer company. "When you make a chip, the most important part of the process that is your intellectual property is the mask that gets layered on the silicon; that's what makes it a chip, with all the electronic circuits. Well, you have to realize that there are a lot of young engineers in Silicon Valley firms who do the design of chips, but almost all of the FABs [the factories that manufacture chips] are Japanese. So usually what you do is you hand over a tape, and the tape basically tells the manufacturer, who might be Fujitsu, or Hitachi, or NEC, or Toshiba, how to manufacture the chip, but it doesn't tell you the design rules. It doesn't give you the intellectual property.

"Well, it turns out—and this has come out in Silicon Valley as kind of a scandal—that when you work in a partnership with a vendor he can take advantage of you. You get palsy-walsy. It's a young Japanese engineer. He speaks English well; he has a family like you. And he says, 'Come on. Just give me your schematics, and instead of waiting for your tape I'll go back and get this done in two weeks instead of three.' So you hand him the source code, which is your intellectual property. And you please your boss by getting something done in two weeks instead of three. And this is a big problem. It happens all the time, and no company out there will admit it."

THE CONGRESSIONAL FIGHT

In Congress, signs of trouble emerged well before the FSX went public. The issue quickly became a vehicle for Congress to air its collective dissatisfaction with White House trade policy dating back to the Reagan years, and with Japanese trade practices dating back indefinitely. One year before the MOU appeared, key congressional aides and their bosses were building a case for congressional involvement. Some represented their constituents' interests; others spoke for a national interest. Republican Senator John Danforth, Capitol Hill's leading trade expert, spoke for both. Why wasn't the FSX being produced in the United States, he asked, considering the rising U.S.-Japan trade deficit, the national-security considerations, and the strong comparative advantage held by the U.S. in aircraft manufacture? McDonnell Douglas and General Dynamics—the two major prime contractors competing for the job—were located in St. Louis, Missouri, which Danforth had represented since 1976.

One of the leading science-policy experts on the Senate staff, Ed McGaffigan, was instrumental in forging congressional opposition to the FSX. His skepticism was based on Japan's motives in entering this joint venture in light of America's comparative edge. "Japan will spend $8 billion to produce 130 aircraft," he reflected. "That means $60 million an aircraft, while we can produce them for $25 million apiece. The Japanese are denying us our comparative advantage because they want to get involved in knowledge-intensive industries like aerospace."

The question is why? McGaffigan argued that Japan wanted to build a fighter and skewed the competition so that it would be built in Japan. "They played games," he said. "They developed a requirements document, called a paper plane, with unrealistic requirements that no one could meet. One idiotic requirement was that the plane take off in 110-degree heat. It has only hit 110 degrees once in the last century in Japan." Perhaps the Japanese were prescient about building aircraft for operations like Desert Shield, but that would mean exporting the aircraft for military actions, not using them solely for the defense of Japan.

McGaffigan's arguments were later buttressed by evidence, including reports issued by MITI, indicating Japan's intention to move into the aerospace industry throughout the last decade. The latest assessment, from the consulting firm of Booz Allen & Hamilton, projected a sales increase in Japanese aerospace equipment from $7 billion in 1988 to $29 billion by the year 2000.[9]

Other strategies included playing competitors off against one another—namely, McDonnell Douglas against General Dynamics. According to McGaffigan, these prime contractors were asked to compete by handing over their data. At no point were the subcontractors, who do a large part of the work—and who stood to lose a large part of the work—involved in the decision.

As subcontractors complained privately to their congressional representatives and the issue heated up, Congress pressed the president for a better deal and for more congressional involvement in the final agreement. On May 11, 1989, after the Senate Foreign Relations Committee narrowly approved the FSX agreement, Senator Robert C. Byrd, Democrat of West Virginia, introduced an initiative to give Congress a more active role in monitoring the project. The Byrd amendment, which was passed overwhelmingly by a vote of 72–27, reflected the widespread mistrust prevalent in Congress toward the White House's ability to protect U.S. technology from a series of one-way trips to

Japan. It also reflected Congress's growing frustration with Japan, fanned by the Toshiba incident and by the belief of many of its members that Japan's trade practices were at least partly to blame for America's steadily declining world competitiveness. The resolution imposed stringent conditions for monitoring the agreement right through its development and production phases, specifically forbidding the transfer of certain jet-engine technology to Japan or—recalling Toshiba—through Japan to third parties.[10]

At the same time that the Senate overwhelmingly approved the Byrd amendment, it narrowly defeated another amendment (52–47), offered by Senator Alan Dixon, to kill outright U.S. participation in the FSX project. The debate evoked the full range of congressional hostility to the FSX—to Japanese practices, and to the full range of what many considered the laissez-faire, "don't worry, be happy" trade policies characteristic of the Reagan years. With Reagan out of office and hopes high for Bush, Congress let off steam, and then voted with the president against the amendment.

"Do you have any illusions about the Japanese wanting to dominate that [aerospace] market?" Senator Lloyd Bentsen, chairman of the influential Senate Finance Committee, asked his colleagues. "To be premier in that market? To develop that kind of competitive force in that product? . . . Look at the numbers. It will cost the Japanese two to three times as much per plane to coproduce the FSX as it would to buy the F-16. . . . Clearly, they want that technology so that they can build not just the FSX but an aircraft industry.

"Japan means to dominate any sector of the economy that is at the high end, calling for top research, top salaries and long-term top profits . . . ," charged Bentsen. "In contrast to our attitude after World War II, Japan seems bent on subordinating everything to running $50 to $60 billion a year trade surpluses, even to the point of excluding superior imports and endangering the national security of the United States."

Reflecting the widespread feeling among many senators that the FSX represented an opportunity for Japan to redress the trade deficit and reciprocate U.S. defense expenditures in Japan, Bentsen added: "Right now it costs us $5 to $7 billion a year for the United States to maintain its forward presence in Japan. Our purpose is to defend the democracies of Asia. Japan pays less than half of that." The view predominated in the House debate as well, with the FSX providing a fresh opportunity to question U.S. commitments in Japan.

In Bentsen's view, the U.S. budget deficit would be considerably reduced were it not for the nation's commitments to Japan. "You spend 1 percent [of your budget]; we spend 5 percent," he told a group of Japanese businessmen who were criticizing the U.S. budget deficit. "We keep 55,000 American troops in Japan. It costs us a substantial amount of money. You are the No. 2 economic power in the world; yet, we pay about $1,000 per person per year for defense while our Japanese counterparts pay about $163. . . . If we spent the 1 percent you spend instead of the 5 that we spend we would have a substantial budget surplus. If we spent 1 percent you would have chaos in Japan because 53% of your income comes from the Persian Gulf and you would not have the American Navy down there to keep those sea-lanes open."[11]

The opposition was bipartisan, as many Republicans joined Democrats Bentsen, Dixon, and others who feared what the FSX technology transfer and the policies that allowed it would mean for their country. Senator Alfonse D'Amato, Republican of New York, raised the issue of selling off the nation's vital assets. "Talk about the economic colonization of America," said D'Amato. ". . . we are not talking about the purchase of sushi and Sonys, and Toyotas. We are talking about the sale of our industrial base. . . . Are we going to continue to sell and give away the technological achievements that in so many cases we, the United States, have discovered and have literally frittered away. . . . My dad is a veteran of World War II. . . . He said to me, 'Son, it sounds to me like this is Pearl Harbor without bombs.' "

D'Amato reserved most of his fury for the executive branch—his own party—and admitted the deepening dependence of the nation on Japan, which inhibited all areas of bilateral policymaking. "Every area of the executive has sold out," he charged. "The Defense Department should hang their heads in shame. What nonsense to talk about technological flowback. . . . We are superior in all these areas, and yet we have make-believe comity. Is it because we are afraid that we may be held hostage as a result of the great economic clout that Japan has? If we continue to conduct ourselves in this manner and give away our industrial base and technological achievements, what will the future hold?"[12]

One of D'Amato's fellow Republicans, Senator John Chafee of Rhode Island, a former secretary of the Navy and a leader of the internationalist wing of the Republican party, took issue with the full-blown rhetoric sweeping the Senate. In his view, the opposition to the FSX was unrealistic in view of the Japanese refusal even to consider buying U.S. aircraft off the shelf. How do you force someone to buy something he has no intention of buying in the first place? "I have a house to sell," said Chafee, offering his colleagues a down-to-earth analogy. "People are not buying it. What is the matter with them? They are not paying the price I am asking. Something is wrong and I

think I have a right to sue them." Others responded that this was not
a consumer issue; that the decision not to buy U.S.-produced aircraft
was orchestrated by the Japanese government, not by Japanese taxpayers or consumers, whose views on the issue might differ when confronted with the price tag.

Chafee argued forcefully for accepting the FSX deal and rejecting
the Dixon amendment, marshaling the facts that finally prevailed in
the Senate:

• The Japanese had the money and patience to develop their own
aircraft, just as the British and French had done; they wanted to
develop their own aircraft; and, accordingly, U.S. rejection of the FSX
would be regarded as a gigantic favor to groups in Japan lobbying for
indigenous development. All things considered, Japan's decision to
coproduce the FSX represented a concession to the U.S. for which
Americans should be grateful.

• The U.S. work share under the new agreement represented $2
billion, or twenty-two thousand man-years of employment in the U.S.

• Codevelopment would erase 5 percent of the trade deficit with
Japan.

• Japan was assuming a greater share of the defense burden by
contributing $6.2 billion to this program.

• The F-16 technology to be transferred under the FSX agreement
did not represent the leading edge of U.S. fighter-aircraft technology.

• The transfer of technology has precedent in the transfer of F-
16 technology to Belgium, Denmark, the Netherlands, Norway, Israel,
and Turkey, all of whom have coproduced parts of the F-16.

In both the House and the Senate debates, none of the defenders
of the FSX deal echoed the Japanese argument that the U.S. would
benefit from Japanese technology. Instead, their arguments ran along
traditional foreign-policy and national-security lines, generally following the State Department reasoning: that Japan was a valued ally; that
we made the commitment to defend Japan as a bulwark against the
Soviet Union; and that we stood by that commitment to prevent the
rise of militarism that cost so many American lives in World War II.

Senator Bill Bradley, Democrat of New Jersey, a fiscal expert who
was regarded at that time as a potential candidate for president or
vice-president, strongly opposed the Dixon amendment on the basis
of hard-nosed realities. Convinced that the Japanese were hell-bent on
developing their own aircraft industry, Bradley argued that the U.S.
was lucky to get a codevelopment deal and should welcome the opportunities it offered. Even if the Japanese ran down a neighborhood of

blind alleys and made years of mistakes, he figured, "10 years from now the Japanese aerospace industry would be further ahead than if we co-develop with them." Looking forward, Bradley added that the way to address our trade problems with Japan was through expanding exports, and not by reneging on an agreement that "was signed in 1987, delivered in 1988 by one President, reviewed and renegotiated by another President," and "signed on the line" by the Departments of Defense, Commerce, and State.[13]

In the end, the Dixon amendment split the Senate virtually in half, between those who agreed with Senators Bradley and Richard Lugar, Republican of Indiana, who supported the agreement, and those in the Dixon camp, who urged a showdown with Japan. Lugar told his colleagues that this was not the time to "reorder the entire relationship with Japan . . . but to stay with Japan and the $2.5 billion of business and the jobs" that came with the FSX.

Dixon disagreed. "This deal was a secret deal negotiated mostly in the dark," he said. ". . . it is a bad deal for America. Last year, we had a $54 billion trade deficit with the Japanese . . . but we have . . . a $19 billion surplus in commercial aviation and aerospace.

"The 'S' in FSX stands for 'sucker,' " said Dixon, who wondered why America never used her greatest negotiating tool of all—her rich markets—to greater avail in forging trade deals with her competitors: "I say, 'buy the F-16' and for those who come here and say that the horse is out of the barn, for those who come here who say the deal is done, I say if they will not buy the F-16s, we will not buy their cars, their cameras, their color TV's and their telephones."[14]

The Dixon amendment to reject the FSX agreement was defeated. Most curious among the votes were the yeas of Bingaman, one of the leaders of the anti-FSX group in the Senate, and Bentsen, who passionately opposed the FSX in speeches on the Senate floor. Both senators said they were satisfied with White House assurances that the technology would be protected, and that Americans would receive a larger share of the work.

To Senator Joseph Biden, Democrat of Delaware, the FSX deal revealed two strong "signals" from Japan to the United States: "Our market is not open to your finest products," and Japan is "not interested in helping to bring down the United States trade deficit."

Representing the administration's point of view, Republican Minority Leader Robert Dole of Kansas—ironically, a state that depends on aircraft production—argued forcefully against the Byrd amendment on the grounds that it violated the separation of powers. Giving Congress the power to negotiate technology transfer is just another way to kill the FSX, Dole said. Congress had already been consulted by the Reagan and Bush administrations; to give Congress more power would be tantamount to allowing them to negotiate, further "chipping away at Presidential powers . . . in foreign policy areas, and now in trade areas."

The strongest opposition to this view came from another Republican, Representative Marge Roukema of New Jersey. "The Congress is an equal partner in matters pertaining to foreign, defense and trade issues," she contended. Congressional action "does not denigrate the role of the executive branch. . . . If it is bad policy the Congress must act."[15]

The House debate followed similar lines, with Representative Stephen Solarz, Democrat of New York, leading the fight to support the White House FSX position, against a liberal California Democrat, Representative Mel Levine, leading the opposition.

The House debate reflected grass-roots concerns. Representative Dan Glickman, Democrat of Kansas, represents the city of Wichita, home to a flourishing aircraft industry. That industry, said Glickman, directly employs forty thousand people, who, along with the tens of thousands of others who work for supporting businesses, have "strong reason to be concerned about the fire sale of American aviation to the Japanese."

Congress was not alone in fearing that the FSX agreement would help Japan develop its own aircraft industry. A report by the United States National Academy of Engineering, for example, concluded that, "through 1995–2000, the main competition from the Japanese aviation industry will be in aircraft parts and components."[16] Additional evidence was offered by the GAO and the Congressional Research Service, indicating that "the avionics, flight control, and radar subsystems of the FSX have potential for 'wide commercial application' as components of future commercial aircraft."

Very few rose in the House to defend the FSX deal, but there must have been a great deal of hidden support, because, when the debate ended and the votes were taken, the agreement went through. Although Congress had fought for and won a role for itself in trade and competitiveness issues, in the last analysis members remained well aware of political realities in seeking to avoid a direct confrontation with the president—especially when they didn't have the votes. In effect, they had it both ways: they were able to go along with the president, but also to vent their anger and send a strong message to the White House. An amendment to the House bill, the Bruce amendment, required the GAO to monitor in detail the execution of the agreement. On July 31, 1989, President Bush vetoed the amendment as he'd vetoed the Byrd amendment; injecting the GAO into the agreement, he said, trespassed on his constitutional powers as president. In mid-September, the Senate failed by one vote (66–34) to override the president's veto on restrictions, and the deal went through. General Dynamics and Mitsubishi finally crawled through the rubble to sign their own agreement on February 21, 1990.[17]

INTERAGENCY BATTLES

Congressional pressures had forced Bush to renegotiate the deal, however, proving that the Japanese were prepared to make greater concessions than originally thought. In the Defense Authorization Bill of 1988, for example, Congress had previously tried to force the issue by inserting an amendment specifying that the Commerce Department be consulted on all national-security-related negotiations encompassing trade. The language was tailor-made for the FSX, but widely varying interpretations of what constituted "consultation" positioned the Commerce and Defense Departments for heavy combat. As Senator Danforth pointed out, "The basic problem with the FSX from the beginning was that this was something that was brought about by the Department of Defense, with zero input from the Commerce Department and zero input from the U.S. Trade Representative."[18]

Mixed signals from the executive branch on the FSX were confusing to everyone involved, and left the impression both here and abroad that the U.S. government's machinery for dealing with coproduction was inadequate. This was a major finding in a Defense Science Board report, submitted to the Secretary of Defense in 1990, but subsequently sequestered by him on the grounds that it was not for public consumption.

In day-to-day negotiations with a foreign power, a nation is best served by a government that speaks with one voice, is prepared to follow through on its agreements, and is backed by some degree of consensus from its citizens. The FSX showed how counterproductive it was to have several agencies in the same government engaged in open conflict.

For their part, defense officials claimed they had never received any directions from their superiors to change their approach to conducting international business by including the trade agencies or their congressional overseers. All of a sudden, they found themselves negotiating a complex agreement in the midst of a volatile political environment, buffeted on one side by advocates of preserving the industrial base, on the other by defenders of the status quo in U.S.-Japan relations. Their vulnerability during this period was increased because they were negotiating a highly controversial international agreement without a leader—the hearings over John Tower's nomination as secretary of defense were ongoing for much of this period.

DoD spent three years negotiating the FSX deal with the Japanese, and when the political climate changed they found it hard to accommodate to those changes. "We negotiated the FSX for thirty-six months," recalled Richard Donnelly, assistant deputy undersecretary of defense and head of the Defense Department's industrial-base program, "For thirty-five of those thirty-six months, no one asked, 'What will this do to our industrial base?' There is too much of a stovepipe structure in DoD. There is just tokenism on the industrial-base issue. I came in to do damage control. We need to do international agreements with the Commerce Department."

Unlike Japan, where the agencies speak with one voice despite fierce internal conflicts, American officials reflected myriad opinions and wide range of individual entrepreneurial activity. Defense officials were far more comfortable with their Japanese military counterparts, with whom they had regularly negotiated for many years, than with their colleagues on the trade side of the U.S. government, whom they had never met. From the very beginning of the FSX negotiations, Japanese trade officials from MITI sat alongside Japanese defense officials at the table, while on the U.S. side only defense officials took part.

The Defense effort was led by the DSAA, the Defense Security Assistance Agency, the agency primarily responsible for negotiating international agreements at the Pentagon. DoD was originally approached by the Japanese in what some officials in hindsight contend was not a quest for a coproduction agreement at all, but "licensed development." Real codevelopment is different, according to one of the leading negotiators from DSAA, Glenn Rudd: "Most codevelopment is done with the Europeans, and that's on the basis that we both have a need, we both agree to put in a certain amount of money, and we both agree to use the end product. We [the United States] never intended to use the FSX."

DSAA's efforts were supported by the State Department and its representatives based at the U.S. embassy in Tokyo. Rust Deming, a political counselor at the embassy, was heavily involved in the three-year negotiation, and shared his views at an interview in his light, airy office overlooking downtown Tokyo. "People on the Defense side were not used to trade rhetoric," he said. "They began to wonder about the stability of the U.S.-Japan alliance. Congress uses inflammatory language. It gives ammunition to those in Japan who want to see Japan play a more independent role, to do more indigenous development. We were lucky to be able to put it together. It was a gratuitous controversy."

Operating under orders from the White House, DSAA negotiators were taken aback by the intense criticism over their handling of the FSX. In their view, they got the best deal possible given the very tough set of circumstances that began with Japan's unrealistic demands and requirements. In addition to requiring that planes fly in 110-degree heat, said John Tyler, one of the chief DSAA negotiators, there were "peculiar mission requirements," such as fast takeoff, range, and a host of other prerequisites which eliminated any remaining hopes for off-the-shelf sales of existing U.S. aircraft. American negotiators spent a fair amount of time talking the Japanese out of some of those requirements.

"One involved the thickness of the glass in the cockpit," recalled Tyler. "They wanted to be able to take a bird strike—a big bird—at high speed, so that the cockpit would not shatter. Of course, no one had ever experienced this before. They hadn't done their research on bird size and frequencies, and they certainly hadn't done the proper research on what happens when you build the glass that thick—you get distortions.

"We took a team over and demonstrated all this, showing why it was such a bad idea. They considered that extremely threatening, the fact that we were chipping away at the credibility of their own experts; they didn't like that, the fact that we were focusing on real knowledge and real expertise."

Finally, in frustration, the Japanese negotiators told the Americans to forget it: the " 'only thing we need to buy from you is part of the engine and the ejection seat. Everything else we can do ourselves.' I'll never forget his wave of the hand," said Tyler.

No one ever knew the extent to which these requirements were phony, politically motivated by bureaucrats who were pushing indigenous development. In support of that view, we know that, at least in the early stages, these negotiations did not seem to be conducted in the typical Japanese manner, a pattern that usually includes a high degree of consensus arrived at by casting a wide net among as many participants as possible. In contrast, these FSX requirements seemed to be developed solely by engineers, with no input from air-force experts or bureaucrats from the operations or planning sides of the government. Even more telling was the fact that the Japanese, who typically research issues to death, came unprepared to defend their operational requirements—like birds crashing into cockpits—with their usual mountain of data. If any final proof were needed, the dismissiveness with which Japanese negotiators were prepared to abandon the codevelopment scheme bears further consideration.

Some critics suggest that this indicates the Japanese were never seriously concerned about operational matters, but viewed the FSX as just a training ground for R & D, and for acquiring aircraft-design technologies in which they were deficient. The key objective all along, say these critics, was to develop capacity for their own fighter aircraft. Unlike the United States, the Japanese feared dependency, and they clearly didn't want to have to rely on the U.S. for a key technology vital to their national security. One knowledgeable avionics-technology expert involved with the FSX argued that the Japanese never intended to produce the FSX in any substantial quantity, but instead would eventually produce a very different aircraft for which there would be no U.S. production participation.

"You have to understand that Japan has not bought an airplane from anybody since World War II," remarked Captain Andy Button, USN, a quiet-spoken former flier who headed up the FSX team in Japan. Button later wrote a superb paper based on his three years of negotiating the FSX, recounting the step-by-step scenario of the negotiations. He concluded it was clear that the Japanese were starting from a very rigid perspective on the FSX that required their total domination of the project. Explaining how their views stemmed from their negotiating style, Button admitted that "from the outset of discussions . . . the Japanese made it quite clear that they must retain leadership and control of the program."[19]

The negotiations might very well have broken off at the early stages of negotiations in 1987, were it not for high-level political involvement. Secretary of Defense Caspar Weinberger entered the fray and talks resumed, but even so, negotiating a joint-development agreement with a group of Japanese who considered themselves force-fed was far from idyllic. When the U.S. team at last came close to a final agreement in October 1987, Japanese negotiators tried another end run, with a proposal to establish a set of new preconditions for the MOUs. The U.S. team's instructions did not take into account the new set of conditions, and their leaders cabled home frantically, asking for guidance and new instructions.

The supporting team back home, headed by Tyler, came to the rescue. "It was one of those funny times," said Tyler, "when there were a lot of people absent in the building. If there's anything that I feel proud about with the FSX, it was that I took the message and I drafted a reply and I got it out of the building in twenty-four hours, in one workday. And it was in that message that we tabled the idea of

The Eyes of the Dragonfly   99

saying, 'Okay, fine, we want 40 to 60 percent of the production work done in the United States.' And that's how all that business got started. We made a counteroffer and started the bargaining process. That's where development, production, and work shares first came into the picture. If the Japanese hadn't come in with this set of preconditions, then Commerce and Congress would never have entered the picture." This all took place in the midst of negotiations over the Strategic Defense Initiative, SDI. "We had just concluded a very brutal and nasty negotiation of an MOU having to do with SDI," Tyler added. "Frank Gaffney had crammed some things down Japanese throats which were extremely unpalatable, and they were very upset. It stiffened the Japanese hide on the FSX in terms of: 'We're paying for this R and D and therefore it belongs to us.' " (Gaffney, then deputy assistant secretary of defense for international security policy, is now director of the Center for Security Policy.)

Nothing occurs in in a vacuum. Besides Star Wars, the negotiation for the sale of AWACS (Airborne Warning and Control System) to the Japanese was also ongoing. DoD staffers feared that Japan would renege on AWACS agreements with the U.S.; a great deal of money was involved, as well as the fear that the Japanese would start building their own AWACS.

By June 1988, U.S. negotiators had concluded and initialed (but not signed) the FSX MOU and delivered it to their Japanese counterparts for approval. Enter the Commerce Department. "We were stupefied," recalled Joan McEntee, one of the three key Commerce officials responsible for negotiating the FSX. "We asked, 'What about the trade implications of the FSX agreement? How hard did you push?' They answered, 'Our job was to make the agreement and preserve the U.S.-Japan relationship.' Their concerns were military and strategic. We brought the other piece of the puzzle. From the beginning the Department of Defense had great animosity toward the trade issue. We were coming in at a late date and upsetting their agreement. It took them a long time to accept that we had a seat at the table, that we had something to contribute."

The indignation of Commerce officials like McEntee was puzzling, for this was the first time Commerce had been involved in a defense agreement. Their concern was encouraging, however. Commerce officials were now driven by a new interest in competitiveness, and by budding opposition to the agreement on Capitol Hill, specifically from a group of Senate staffers. Their initiation to the FSX began at a defense briefing in December 1987. "Glenn Rudd and the chief negotiator for General Dynamics said, 'This is the best deal we've ever cut with the Japanese,' " reported Charles Smith, legislative aide to

Senator Dixon. "Kearns, McGaffigan, [Senator John] Heinz's guy, and I started asking questions, and the more answers we got, the less happy we were."

What upset the Hill staffers was the Defense Department's interpretation of "consultation." "It teed us off," Smith continued. "[They] said that Commerce could look at the deal and ratify it. They could look at it, but DoD would not give the agreement to Commerce. They knew Commerce would disapprove of the deal from the trade and technology-giveaway standpoint."

DoD officials acknowledged that they were stonewalling Commerce and the Hill, explaining that they were under strict orders from lawyers in their own department, who were also engaged in a turf battle: the acquisition lawyers against the international-program lawyers. John Tyler emphasized that "We got firm guidance from our lawyers: 'Do not show Commerce a copy of the MOU. You can brief them, but do not give them a copy.' We gave them the same briefing we'd used with industry." Tyler added that the briefing should have been adequate for Commerce; that their late entry into the FSX amounted to nothing more than "pole vaulting over mouse droppings."

Suspicion grew steadily among the Capitol Hill–Commerce Department allies, fueled by DoD's refusal to show the FSX document to representatives of their own government. The others felt that the Defense Department must be covering something up, including the Japanese motives. "DoD knew the FSX wasn't the plane they needed to defend themselves," said Smith. "The problem the Japanese had was that in order to have an aircraft industry they needed systems-integration technology. The FSX deal gives them that. They can take all the black boxes now and launch an industry. The F-18 is a better plane. It has two engines. The F-16 has only one engine. The Japanese knew they could work a better deal with General Dynamics [than with McDonnell Douglas, which makes the F-18]."

"Bullshit," responded Tyler, when asked about this viewpoint. "That's one of the great red herrings. Fighters use a rigid-airplane technology, whereas the commercial airliner is extremely flexible. Everyone has seen the pictures of the wings flapping on the 747. The whole approach to design and to systems integration is different. It's not directly transferable. You can make the argument that building airplanes is building airplanes. But the basis for a commercial aerospace industry? Bullshit."

Commerce officials added another item to the debate over Japanese entry into the aerospace industry: adequate reimbursement. "I don't think that we're afraid that Japan will develop an aerospace industry that will be competitive, because the competition could benefit us all," noted John Richards, a twenty-five-year veteran of the Commerce Department and key member of the FSX team. "We are concerned that they develop an industry that is purely based on U.S. technology that's been transferred without receipt or benefit of that transfer of technology. That means either significant reimbursement for it, or an opportunity to share in any technology improvements that are provided in Japan."

Richards pointed out another subtlety that escaped many observers close to the FSX: the difference between guarantees and assurances. Assurances rely on trust; guarantees imply close scrutiny and enforcement procedures. U.S. negotiators knew that there would be specific aspects of the aircraft that would be developed during the production of the FSX, and that the U.S. should have access to that technology, especially if it was based on technology developed in the United States. "Assurances," analyzed Richards, "are not quite the protection that a guarantee would provide. It would have been better to have guarantees. However, you can't have a guarantee on the flow of technology without identifying the specific technology, and the procedures and costs associated with bringing it back to the U.S." Richards was hopeful that the assurances were clear enough and the good will between the two countries was sufficient to provide a mechanism for the flow of technology on a timely basis back to the United States.

Assurances or guarantees make no difference to defense officials, who argue that pinning down precisely 40 percent of the development work share is impossible, regardless of the terminology in the agreement. "I defy any U.S. official or member of Congress or senator to state precisely what any U.S. Air Force or U.S. Navy or U.S. Army development program is going to be precisely within a percentage point," said one official. "This is why we operated within a range: General Dynamics and McDonnell Douglas would have settled for around 30 to 35 percent, and upped the range to 35 to 45 percent. Yet we were trying to pin this down, and it's a phony damn number. Anyone who does this kind of work, building airplanes, knows that."

Information and misinformation about the FSX began to appear at a slow and steady pace. As word on the flaws of the deal emerged, DoD seemed to retreat from its original position, and finally insisted that the FSX represented a security agreement alone, which meant that trade considerations were peripheral. Senator Dixon then began a national campaign pointing out inadequacies of the FSX deal; Senator Bingaman traveled to Japan to present his questions on engine technology to the Japanese; and Senator Bentsen added his support to the inquiry.

DoD underestimated the Congress, as well as the Commerce Department. The results of the GAO report, which concluded that the FSX was a bad deal, riveted the Congress with its findings that the U.S. was ahead in most of the technologies the Japanese claimed as their own contributions to the development of the FSX; and that DSAA's history of protecting the outflow of U.S. technology to foreign countries had long proved the agency to be an inadequate defender. An earlier GAO report, in 1982, criticizing DoD's negotiation of the sale of F-15s to Japan, concluded that, when subjected to the pattern of Japanese persistence in negotiation, DSAA would back off and give up U.S. technology. DSAA's defenders argued that this was consistent with the agency's traditional role, dating back to the 1950s, of encouraging our allies to help us reduce our defense burden by manufacturing their own weapons systems. Military sales, licensing, and coproduction were all regarded as acceptable ways of reaching that goal.

DoD argued that congressional signals were conflicting. On the one hand, Congress berated the Pentagon for the FSX technology giveaway; yet, legislation such as the Gramm-Rudman-Hollings amendment and the Nunn-Quayle amendment expressly encouraged thrift through the codevelopment of weapons systems. The Nunn-Quayle amendment, which favored sharing the cost of development with our NATO allies, was later expanded to include Israel, Egypt, Japan, South Korea, and Australia.

The group most surprised by Bush's reversal on the FSX and his support of the Commerce position was the Japanese themselves. "What are you doing here?" one Japanese negotiator asked a Commerce Department official who had recently entered the FSX talks. "The same thing MITI is doing for you," answered the official. For once, the Japanese were caught off guard by the political changes in the administration. They neglected, in the words of one Commerce official, "to activate their Chrysanthemum Club," a reference to the coterie of academics, lobbyists, and government officials that consistently advance Japan's interests in America. They also failed to realize how close Commerce Secretary Mosbacher was to President Bush, and how the Tower hearings left DoD with virtually no access to the White House, so that Mosbacher's access to the President on this issue went virtually unchallenged. While the Tower hearings were in progress, Mosbacher sat down with John Sununu and the President and told them they were going to have a problem with Congress.

In spite of the President's personal relationship with Mosbacher, and in marked contrast to the situation in Japan, Commerce remains a second-tier agency, far below the Defense and State Departments in status and power. This helps explain the continuing second-class status of trade policy, which the Office of the United States Trade Representative was created to address. Commerce would most likely have remained in the shadows on the FSX issue but for a coalition of agencies that fought to link trade and national security. One of the coalition's leaders was Dr. William Graham, science adviser to President Reagan. In June 1988, Graham drafted a Science and Technology Agreement designed precisely to prevent the kind of technology transfer represented by the FSX. The Science and Technology Agreement provided a policy framework that talked about an equitable, two-way flow of knowledge and technology in which each party to an agreement contributes technologies commensurate with its capabilities and strengths. Reciprocity and "balanced relationships" are the principles behind this agreement, which provided Graham with the legal basis for his opposition to the FSX.

Graham questioned Japanese claims relating to their technological contributions: "Phased-array has been in use for a long time. Many military systems use them. Pave Paws, a big coastal warning radar system, is a phased-array system used to safeguard ABM systems. We're developing new phased-array radars that are well in advance of what the Japanese are working on.

"We're also being naïve on composite-wing technology. It is not clear if it is feasible or efficient. The only legitimate claim on the FSX from the Japanese is their manufacturing system. It's the culture. In our society, engineering is in the universities. Our students' role models are professors, exotic researchers. Factory-floor product engineers are the lowest grade in our system. In Japan, engineers want to be on the factory floor."

Armed with these arguments, Dr. Graham tried to enlist the help of Colin Powell, the President's national security adviser. To Powell, it was a question of turf, and he was reluctant to challenge the secretaries of state and defense on this issue. Graham also expressed his concern about Japan's unreliability in adhering to agreements, based on his long experience with patents. "The U.S.-Japan agreements are asymmetric," he explained. "In patents, secrecy is critical because of defense. Japan agreed. The Patent Treaty passed through the Diet, and then Japan refused to implement the treaty for thirty years. This compromised U.S. security. After thirty-two years of nonimplementation, it was the U.S.'s fault that patent secrecy was not implemented. We finally reached an agreement on April 8, 1988.

"To the Japanese," continued Graham, "cooperation is another form of competition. It always ends up as one-way technology transfer, product improvement, and increased competition. It's a winning strategy. They chose General Dynamics because they already had an agreement with McDonnell Douglas on the F-15. MITI was already sucking the brains out of McDonnell Douglas. *Why are U.S. companies allowing this?*"

Graham's views were buttressed by an avionics expert at DARPA (Defense Advanced Research Projects Agency), who bitterly criticized the sale, off the record, in terms of its national-security as well as its competitiveness problems: "Aircraft know-how is highly classified. We're not going to give them the software for electronic warfare, because it makes the difference in winning a war. The Israelis won the Six-Day War because they were able to jam signals of enemy aircraft . . . because of their expertise in electronic systems."

This scientist was certain that there were definite commercial applications involved with this supposedly exclusively "military" technology: "The FSX has commercial applications. It is the military-aircraft companies that became dominant in commercial technologies. We have the best engine technology—GE and Pratt & Whitney—going into the FSX. The engine companies are really worried."

A battle ensued between the two groups: the State and Defense Departments on the one side, and representatives from the White House Science Office, the Commerce Department, the Treasury Department, the Departments of Energy and Labor, and the USTR's office on the other. Though not everyone in DoD agreed with the department's FSX position, the department muzzled the opposition and presented a united front. The opponents hammered away at the technology-giveaway issue.

Even giving away old technologies can hurt America's competitiveness and national security, argued Deborah Wince-Smith, now an assistant secretary at the Commerce Department. "We don't give the Soviets technology that's two or three generations old, because it still gives them capability."

Strengthened by their allies on Capitol Hill, the coalition in the executive branch succeeded in dividing the administration and opening the issue to a public airing. The net result was that, for the first time in its history, the Commerce Department established the right to be involved in military-coproduction agreements. Legitimizing Commerce's role also linked national security and trade on an operational as well as a rhetorical level. Agreements following the FSX, such as one on the coproduction of a Korean fighter jet, involved former adversaries from both departments who swallowed their grievances, at least in public, and forced themselves to work together.

Privately, however, the FSX issue still rankles, with DoD officials arguing breach of trust. "When you go home and catch your husband in bed with another woman you may keep him, but will you ever really trust him?" asked John Tyler, still bitter about Commerce's invasion of his department's turf, and what he regarded as serious breaches in security. "The civilian agencies outvoted us," he charged. "Many of them were vituperative on the FSX. . . . They issued an interdict against talking to the press and everyone agreed that no one would talk to the press. Instead there were tremendous leaks to the trade press. It was obviously the Commerce Department that leaked copies of the MOU, which was secret and classified, to the press. It's a felony to leak documents.

"In the post-FSX era we are still not whole," Tyler added. "Now we have to negotiate with Commerce on implementing the FSX and a variety of other agreements. The U.S. is no longer regarded as a reliable ally by Japan."[20]

DoD's reaction to the FSX paralleled the reaction in Japan: both felt blindsided by "trade hawks" in the U.S., newly liberated by the exit of President Reagan, whose inattention to competitiveness issues was widely criticized. In one of the most interesting sidelights on the issue, it appeared that DoD's longtime relationships with the Japan Defense Agency were much stronger than any of its linkages with other U.S. government agencies. Indeed, one defense official blamed the problems with the FSX on the fact that Commerce had never developed linkages with MITI to parallel theirs with the Japanese military.

All this, however, is sheer conjecture, and fails to take into account the lopsided disparity between Commerce and MITI—Commerce remains an agency with little power which has never been encouraged or allowed to play a role anywhere near that of the all-encompassing MITI. Correspondingly, defense in Japan is decidedly subordinate in status and power to the trade and budget agencies. Any parallels between Commerce and MITI are therefore unrealistic.

DoD finally began winning the battles—after all, the FSX agreement did go through—after Richard Cheney was confirmed as secretary of defense, and administration pressure to consummate the deal intensified. Cheney immediately supported the pact, impressed the FSX team at DoD with his quick grasp of the issues, and went to work on the Hill to bring the matter to closure. The final resolution owed much to his close attention and to his ability to wield clout so quickly after assuming office. It also showed the relative power of Defense vis-à-vis the Commerce Department: when Defense was leaderless, Commerce could exert its influence; when secretaries are pitted against one another, the power of Defense far outweighs the agency representing the business community. This issue sent a clear message to advocates of industrial strategy: for the near future, they would be wise to put their eggs in the Defense basket.

THE FSX AND THE PERCEPTION GAP

"There was a big perception gap with regard to the FSX that reminded me of an anthill," recalled Rust Deming, the political counselor in the U.S. embassy in Japan. This perception gap exacerbated the conflict and led the players to work at cross-purposes; their confusion was especially striking when contrasted to the Japanese.

One school of thought held that FSX was an old technology; nothing was being given away that the Japanese did not already have or could not develop on their own. The other school said, "Old technology yes," but developed at taxpayer expense; moreover, our aerospace industry was still a world leader, and should we be handing over our competitive edge to a competitor?

It was obviously not possible to determine technological answers in a political vacuum, but the FSX controversy represented a real contribution in that it aired the questions that should have been asked routinely in all cases affecting the nation's industrial base:

- To what extent was the FSX a technological giveaway?
- Did the final decision further erode the defense industrial base?

The Japanese ask these questions *before* they begin negotiating; to them, the economy and its technological base were the basis for entering into negotiations. In the United States, it took a full-blown crisis to elevate such questions to public discussion.

One of the real difficulties facing the FSX was the information gap. DoD and its allies argued that their critics were wrong: the FSX was not a giveaway, but a net benefit to the country. The president and chief operating officer of General Dynamics, Herbert F. Rogers, echoed these views, adding that his company was "an instrument of U.S. government policies, not a creator of them." He also feared that, if the agreement collapsed, his company would lose the business, there being "little doubt that Japan will go it alone and/or use European technical assistance."[21]

The information that galvanized Congress came from the GAO, the agency that serves as the lawmakers' major research-and-auditing arm, which gave Pentagon negotiators deserved low marks for acting solo and neglecting to consult other agencies in the F-15 agreement. The GAO recommended that, since DoD had exhibited no concern in this case over the impact of technology transfer on U.S. manufacturing and trade, in future negotiations the views of departments other than Defense should be solicited "before transferring advanced U.S. technology with wide commercial application."[22]

Asked to examine the FSX seven years later, the GAO found little improvement in the negotiating posture, concluding that, "in negotiating the FSX program, DoD and State did not coordinate with or solicit the views of the Commerce Department or other economic policy-making agencies. In response to the law, DoD provided a cursory briefing to Commerce . . . near the conclusion of the bilateral negotiations" . . . telling the GAO investigators that it was "inappropriate to bring Commerce into full consultation and coordination at that time because the MOU negotiations were virtually complete." The GAO drew the same conclusion as it had in the 1982 coproduction agreements on the F-15: "that the Departments of Defense and State had too narrow a perspective to adequately address the economic, industrial, trade and labor interests of this country."[23]

The GAO research effort also emerged with the volatile conclusions that: (1) the technology that the U.S. expected to get from Japan was already in use in the United States, was well known to the aerospace industry, and in some cases was ten to twenty years old; and (2) not only wasn't the U.S. getting much from Japan, but we risked giving away "valuable systems integration skills," an area in which the Japanese were notably deficient. Specific technological conclusions focused on composite-wing technology and phased-array radar.

In the area of composite-wing technology—making the entire wing of an aircraft out of composite materials (carbon fibers and resins baked together) for greater strength, lighter weight, and durability—the GAO found Japanese claims unsubstantiated and the agreement "high risk": "DOD and industry officials do not have solid information as to whether or not Japan can really produce the wing as planned." In addition, the study found, "The U.S. industry's basic knowledge of advanced composites is superior to Japan's" in terms of "demonstrated and proven capability in composition production and application to military aircraft."[24] Interestingly, the GAO found that the "consensus among industry experts was that General Dynamics—the prime U.S contractor for the FSX—is *behind* some other U.S. aircraft manufacturers in composites technology because the F-16 aircraft has few composite components."

Aware of its technological weakness, General Dynamics astutely insisted on joint production of co-cured wings with the Japanese. In effect, they insisted on working side by side with Japanese technicians, because they knew they would have to learn everything from start to finish if they were going to get the true transfer value of the process. "If you're going to engage in technology transfer with Japan, you've got to be working with an astute American company," remarked one Pentagon official involved with the FSX, "and I wouldn't want to be pressed to name too many of them."

The "eyes of the dragonfly," or phased-array radar technology, also failed the test of GAO scrutiny. A phased-array radar system uses computers to track several different targets simultaneously. In this case, the GAO found Japanese data inadequate; DoD attempts "to obtain information . . . have been largely unsuccessful because Japanese officials have refused to release detailed test and evaluation data." Claims without data are difficult to evaluate, but the lack of data certainly raises red flags. The GAO noted, however, that this, too, was a technology well known to U.S. companies, including Hughes Aircraft and Texas Instruments, and that "U.S. industry was not standing still and is making considerable strides to reduce module costs."[25] Several years later, phased-array radar emerged as the heart of the Patriot antimissile operation during the Gulf War, enabling the Patriot to destroy incoming Scud missiles with its superior, computer-driven accuracy.[26]

The question of whether Japan was ahead of the U.S. was answered by conflicting information. Air-force avionics engineers claimed that the Japanese had less overall radar experience, while citing the statement of the deputy director of the Air Force's Wright Research and Development Center warning that "it would be wrong to assume that the U.S. is significantly ahead of Japan" given Japan's "proven capability in electronics."[27] In any case, the government-to-government agreement doesn't entitle the U.S. to the radar technology but merely enables the U.S. to purchase it after it is developed by Japan. Further, should we decide to purchase it, we will have no idea of the cost of the technology, since this is not addressed by the agreement.

The real advantage to Japan of the FSX agreement lies in the acquisition of systems-integration technology, called by experts the "epitome" of technology in this area, the system that pulls together the complexities of integrating all the software and making it connect to the hardware. Not many countries have experience in integrating avionics; the U.S. has developed this advantage, because as a nation it has invested more heavily in military systems. The FSX, like the F-16, depends more on systems integration, because it is, in the words of

Erland Heginbotham, of the Institute for Defense Analyses, a "fly-by-wire aircraft, aerodynamically unstable and therefore dependent on computers to stay in the air." For this reason, the FSX would not be viable as a commercial aircraft.

What experts did agree on with respect to Japanese contributions to the FSX were: their manufacturing skills, which allowed them to do things more cheaply and more efficiently than the U.S.; their ability to miniaturize; and their head start in a technology known as CFD, computational fluid dynamics, computer simulations of airflows over surfaces and their effects on aerodynamics, turbulence, and other related issues.

FINALE AND NEW BEGINNINGS

As any good mystery buff knows, to solve a murder you need to look for both motive and opportunity. The mystery driving the FSX debate revolved around why the Japanese, known for their business acumen, would want to spend two and a half times more for a fighter plane than it would cost them to buy it "ready-made." Their motives occupied a good chunk of the debate: Did Japan want to launch a world-class aircraft industry? Do the Japanese want to drive the U.S. out of the aircraft business? Do they eventually want to produce and export military aircraft in violation of their constitution? And—the ever-present subliminal question—does Japan want to revive its prewar military machine?

The motives are all there, but the answer lies in the opportunity to keep jobs and protect the industrial base. Governments create their own comparative advantage in market share, jobs, and technology, and no better example of that can be found than in Japan. Japan promoted the FSX and insisted on production in Japan primarily to save the five thousand jobs at Mitsubishi's Nagoya plant, and to enhance their expanding industrial base. All other motives may play a role to some extent, but Japan has always been very clear about its goals: jobs and the industrial base take top priority, and government intervention to protect them takes precedence over trade relations, international good will, and just about everything else. Japanese leaders are not constrained by fears of criticism for practicing industrial policy; on the contrary, their predominant ideology accepts government as a legitimate tool for protecting the industrial base, and they don't have to waste time defending such action. Most important, economic stability and national security go hand in hand in Japan; that linkage is axiomatic.

What we can learn from the FSX experience is particularly relevant in the following areas:

(1) Link Economic and National Security

After the blood-letting, the FSX negotiations brought a new order to the U.S. It was the first time economic security and national security were linked so publicly in the councils of government, and that a chief executive was forced to expand his definition of national security to include trade and economic objectives.

In highlighting the nation's inadequacies, the FSX brought many of our leaders into a mode of thinking more in keeping with that of the Japanese. "We should not be shy about economic and competitive relationships; the Japanese are not shy about them," advised Representative Mel Levine. "Until 1989, the only parts of the administration dealing with the FSX were the Pentagon and State, not Commerce or the USTR. It is significant through which lens the policymaker looks at Japan."

Others echoed his view. In fact, the linkage between economic stability and national security seems so obvious that many wondered why it had never occurred to anyone before. "While it is appropriate for Japan and other countries to consider their economic interests when addressing defense issues, it is just as appropriate for the United States to do the same," wrote Frank Conahan, representing the GAO's position—really wishful thinking—on the FSX.[28]

(2) Negotiate in the National Interest

The smart money says that coproduction and joint investment are the wave of the future in an increasingly globalizing economy. At its best, coproduction represents the Elysian fields of international relations: it ensures that by sharing technologies countries enhance progress for all, acquire new technologies, and improve their own technologies in the process. In the best of worlds, an added benefit includes the fostering of international understanding as workers from both countries labor side by side toward a shared goal. Theoretically, the synergy of partnership creates benefits for both parties; it is the most efficient way to expand each nation's resource base.

At its worst, joint production can lead to a nightmarish scenario very much like the FSX situation, which was marred throughout by just about everything that could go wrong, including lack of trust, mixed signals, broken promises, cross-cultural problems, shaky ground rules, and inadequate information.

The FSX showed that at the very least, joint-production agreements *must* be grounded in an atmosphere of trust. The Japanese had good cause to feel betrayed, especially considering their traditional ways of doing business. They conclude deals on the basis of a hand-shake, easier to manage in a culture grounded in homogeneity, mutual trust, dynastic relationships bonded by family ties, and interlocking networks within industries, within government, and between business and government. Losing face in such a tightly ordered society is a thousand times worse than it is in our more fluid and anonymous culture. Yet the Japanese negotiate with one another very differently from the way they negotiate with *gaijin*, or foreigners, who are never allowed into the inner circles of those relationships of trust or their more formal industrial frameworks, the *keiretsu*. Americans often exhibit naïveté about this closed world, and then overreact when confronted with the consequences.[29]

The Japanese were also caught off guard by the intensity of the reaction to the FSX caused by changing U.S. attitudes toward Japan. Breach of trust would never have been a problem if trust between the two countries had not been steadily eroding throughout the 1980s. Accustomed to American acquiescence on trade issues, the Japanese were suddenly confronted by serious political resistance, triggered by the FSX. Public opposition accelerated as the FSX became a symbol of unfair Japanese trade practices on a range of issues, from rice to semiconductors to beef. The issue would have been more easily resolved if the Japanese had been more accustomed to tougher trade practices on our part—as they were with the Europeans—and if they hadn't been so successful in convincing America's leaders that the $40–50-billion trade deficit was truly "intractable." Most Americans have never really believed these numbers were set in stone; in fact, the FSX raised the question: How much would the trade deficit be reduced if the Japanese conceded aerospace to the U.S., and concluded the FSX agreement with that in mind?

That would never have happened, because by this time Japanese views toward America had also changed, as had their negotiating position. Expectations that the Japanese would suddenly become altruistic about the trade deficit bore no relation to current reality or past behavior; it was certainly not the pattern of Japanese trade practices, and not the way nations do business in general.

Besides fostering mutual trust, joint-production agreements stand a greater chance of success if they are conducted within an atmosphere where adequate information is available. Improved information enhances trust and puts negotiations on a more professional basis. Either way, Americans felt cheated once they looked at the data gap. Sufficient evidence already existed that the Japanese fully intended to enter the aerospace business, and anyone familiar with industrial history could bet the family fortune on their success.

What technologies did the Japanese really have? What were they really offering? What technologies did we have to give away, license, or sell to participate in this deal? No answers to these questions were clear to anyone, especially the public, and this led to the biggest question of all: On what basis were DoD officials operating, given data gaps as wide as the Grand Canyon? After all, the GAO's information spelling out the U.S. advantage in FSX-specific technologies came from defense officials and contractors. If the GAO could collect this information in three months, where had everyone else been during the three-year formal negotiation period? On the basis of his experience opposing the FSX agreement on Capitol Hill, Kevin Kearns concluded that the President would be better served in all of his negotiations with Japan if he designated a competing team of negotiators, to ensure that he would receive alternative views.[30]

(3) Safeguard the Industrial Base

Congress recognized the importance of the industrial base to the country's national security and tried, in the Defense Production Act, to force the administration to safeguard technologies vital to its survival. In a highly explicit directive attached to the National Defense Authorization Act for Fiscal Year 1989, Congress ordered the secretary of defense to "consider the effect on the defense industrial base of the United States, and regularly solicit and consider . . . recommendations of the Secretary of Commerce in this regard" before negotiating MOUs.[31]

One of the act's sponsors, Representative Mary Rose Oakar, Democrat of Ohio, and chairman of the Economic Stabilization Subcommittee, which has jurisdiction over the Defense Production Act, rose up during the FSX debate to protest what she considered the administration's flagrant disregard of that directive. "Established procedures for protecting the U.S. defense industrial base were not followed in arriving at this FSX agreement," she charged. Accordingly, "the defense industrial base will suffer as a result . . . of giving $8½ billion worth of technology wholesale to Japan, which has a trade surplus. We have an enormous deficit and our national security is going to be jeopardized to boot."[32]

One of the problems in trying to preserve the industrial base is a lack of consensus on just what constitutes the industrial base, and why it is so important to the nation. What is certain, however, is that our

major competitors—namely, the European Community and Japan—
protect their industrial bases and their critical technologies as insurance policies for the future.

(4) Make Government Competitive

At the core of the ongoing and unresolved debate over U.S. competitiveness is the role of government, which turns out to be the most
striking lesson of the FSX. The differences between Japan and the
United States in terms of their negotiating capabilities produced some
stark and chilling contrasts: The Japanese set their goals clearly; broad-
ened participation by including representatives from trade, budget,
and defense agencies; and, despite their internal struggles, came to the
bargaining table if not with total consensus at least with a united front.
The U.S. lacked all of those attributes, and suffered as a result.

The Japanese are better able to defend their industries because
their government has the capacity to follow through. Also, in their
value system economic growth and stability takes top priority. In
contrast, the U.S. system of rugged individualism and separation of
powers works in exactly the opposite direction, pitting agency against
agency, with little direction from the White House. Defense and State
faced off against Commerce and a host of other agencies, airing their
differences and struggling for turf. Defense Department officials had
never even met their counterparts in the trade sectors. Through no
fault of their own, U.S. defense officials were out of touch with trade
issues, whereas in Europe and Japan these issues are an integral part
of defense officials' mandate. No wonder the nation's industrial base
eroded so badly during this period.

There is also no doubt that the U.S. was also hurt by the inadequacy of its technology assessment capability. For years, Senator Bingaman has been trying to establish a DARPA office in Tokyo for the
purpose of averting "technology surprises," as well as to improve the
sharing of information between U.S. industry and government. The
funds are there, but the office is not.

In the end, defense officials sadly concluded that relations with
Japan would never be the same. Trust had been breached, and bad
feelings abounded on both sides. They also feared that Japanese purchases of military equipment would decrease in retaliation for their
treatment over the FSX issue. These fears proved prophetic. A year
after the agreement was signed, the FSX was bogged down in delays,
huge cost overruns, and technical problems that threatened to weaken
the project. Each side blamed the other for the difficulties, in almost
an instant replay of their previous conflicts.[33]

When Congress entered the struggle, it only added to the public impression of disarray. Ultimately, Congress was unable to override the president's veto and the FSX went through, but the damage both to the national image and to the U.S.-Japan relationship could have been avoided if the administration had acted more responsively to congressional intent, and if the bureaucracy had functioned more smoothly and communicated more consistently. Bureaucratic inadequacies can be corrected, but the nation will have to learn to reorient its thinking to accept government's role in protecting technology and the industrial base before these problems can be effectively addressed.

CHAPTER V

Computer Chips or Potato Chips

PERKIN-ELMER AND THE CRITICAL-INDUSTRIES DEBATE

We found ourselves in the position of having a technology
for an industry that had moved to Japan.
                    —Horace G. McDonell,
                            chairman and CEO of Perkin-Elmer

I don't think technology policy is on anyone's agenda.
                    —Andrew Grove, president of Intel

THE RESCUE MISSION

As the world prepared for war in the late 1930s, the United States abruptly found itself cut off from its major source of precision optics, manufactured only in Germany, by corporations including Zeiss and Bausch & Lomb. The optics were needed for bombsights, periscopes, and other military hardware vital to the national defense. To fill this manufacturing void, the government encouraged the creation of the Perkin-Elmer Corp., which soon became one of this country's leading manufacturers of precision optics.

The Connecticut-based manufacturer again made headlines fifty years later as both the manufacturer of a key element of the Hubble space telescope, and one of two U.S. producers of state-of-the-art photolithography equipment used in the manufacture of semiconductor chips. The equipment is manufactured in Perkin-Elmer's Norwalk plant, in a facility that looks like a cross between a spaceship and a pottery barn: huge, silent, football-field-sized rooms bathed in an eerie yellow light. Men and women in sterile white laboratory coats, masks, caps, and foot coverings bend over large, shiny machines. While they work, an assortment of machines slowly polish concave pieces of glass and claylike substances. To keep these "clean rooms" sterile enough for the sensitive and sophisticated machinery they house, the air is filtered constantly, the floors are swept four times a day, and all workers and visitors must suit up like surgeons.

The photolithography process at Perkin-Elmer combines the "stepping and scanning" of silicon wafers into a fast and effective system called Micrascan. Micrascan represents an attempt to leapfrog technology. Perkin-Elmer long dominated the "scanning" lithography process, until the "step-and-repeat" photolithography camera—invented by GCA, a U.S. company—replaced the scanning technology, over which it was a vast improvement. Perkin-Elmer failed to respond to this challenge, however, and continued to produce and sell scanners, even though they were being phased out; this put the company at the lower end of the semiconductor-equipment business. After trying unsuccessfully to develop its own step-and-repeat process, Perkin-Elmer instead moved ahead with Micrascan. IBM, the company's major customer for this process and the sole supporter of the technology's development, enjoyed a long-term relationship with Perkin-Elmer—until 1989, that is, when Perkin-Elmer decided that, despite IBM's support, its photolithography division was a money loser and should be sold. The division had been losing money for years.

Perkin-Elmer's problems stemmed from the company's difficulties in bringing its new technology to market fast enough to keep pace with their Japanese competitors, and from a certain complacency in its own corporate culture that had resulted in a slowdown in research during a critical period. By the time Perkin-Elmer decided to sell, two Japanese companies already dominated the "stepper" (step-and-repeat) market: Nikon with 70 percent, and Canon with 20 percent (GCA held the remaining 10 percent). Nikon, a highly successful Japanese multinational, had essentially taken over the business, and scared off potential investors, who rightly feared competing against the Japanese. This became a serious problem for both Perkin-Elmer and other companies who were trying to capitalize their next-generation technologies.

To the consternation of IBM, which feared the consequences of relying on a Japanese competitor to supply a major component of its product, the company's extensive search turned up no American buyers.

"We scoured the U.S. looking for a potential buyer," said Horace

G. McDonell, Perkin-Elmer's chairman and CEO, in a luncheon meeting in his private dining room overlooking the wooded landscape of the Norwalk plant. "We spent nine months looking, and found none. One company said they'd take us for a dollar. Only when we'd exhausted every U.S. alternative did we contact Nikon." McDonell attributed the division's financial difficulties to the capriciousness of the semiconductor market. "It is such a volatile industry. The semiconductor market doesn't go fast and slow, it goes forward and reverse."

According to a knowledgeable industry analyst, no one wanted the company because it was a "sick puppy—with an old product line, and a high-risk new product in an equipment industry in which the Japanese had become dominant. Why would anyone want it? The real question is, why did Nikon want it?" Answering his own question, the analyst continued, "Nikon was willing to pay for the latest IBM technology, which it knew it would be getting with the purchase of Perkin-Elmer."

When negotiations began in earnest and Nikon emerged as the only serious buyer, the pending sale hit the headlines and became a *cause célèbre*. After all, Nikon was also Perkin-Elmer's major competitor. The controversy reflected the nation's growing anxiety about the flood of foreign acquisitions of American assets—particularly its critical technologies—and what this meant for the nation's future. IBM considered Perkin-Elmer's technology critical to the manufacture of components needed for its computers, and feared the loss of the technology to foreigners, especially the Japanese, whom they considered the firm's major competitors. They were especially concerned about Nikon's close ties through its *keiretsu* relationships to other companies and competitors in Japan. In the final analysis, IBM executives refused to allow Nikon to purchase a technology in which IBM had invested so heavily, because they knew, on the basis of experience, that they would lose not only the technology but access to that technology as well.

This year-long struggle was the second major public debate over the long-term consequences of the sale of a critical technology to overseas investors. (The first was the aborted sale of Fairchild Semiconductor to Fujitsu.) Questions raised over Perkin-Elmer continue to confound American leaders in Congress and the executive branch.

One group of questions targeted the private sector: Should government come to the aid of a company whose management some experts considered inept? How deeply committed were the semiconductor and computer industries to the principle of protecting their domestic suppliers? How effective were the corporate executives who managed the company? Unofficially, the Bush administration took the view that, if the technology was truly crucial to IBM, that company should bear the cost of keeping the technology in American hands. Ultimately, IBM—with considerable behind-the-scenes help from DoD—put together a consortium that did just that.

Meanwhile, McDonell found himself in the middle of a firestorm, his company a victim of the nation's inability to invest in itself even for long-term national-security interests. Most Americans had never heard of semiconductors, much less photolithography; what right did they have to protest his responsibility to buy and sell in the best interests of his stockholders?

"We found ourselves in the position of having a technology for an industry that had moved to Japan," McDonell explained. Reflecting the view of many corporate executives in the semiconductor industry, McDonell felt that the government had failed to appreciate the Japanese challenge or the importance of the semiconductor industry when action was still possible. "The semiconductor market is wrapped in mortal combat between the U.S. and Japan. We are in a war with Japan. We keep looking for theories, when we should be swinging."

McDonell found himself abandoned by his industry as well as his government. When the situation looked bleakest, and it appeared as if the technology would finally be sold to Nikon, McDonell's fellow CEOs offered nothing but empty rhetoric. "The industry screams bloody murder, but they all buy Japanese tools," he said. "The semiconductor industry wants protection, but they refuse to protect their suppliers. They want cheap machines, and a laying off of the risks."

Nor were the media helpful. Perkin-Elmer was depicted as selling out, handing over to overseas competitors a technology that was critical to national security. "We were crucified in the press," McDonell recalled. But some experts contended that Perkin-Elmer had created its own crisis. "The management is incompetent," Robert Noyce remarked in an interview in Washington, D.C.'s Occidental restaurant shortly before his untimely death. "They had the lion's share of the market. They knew nothing about the industry and became dependent on government." Another expert from the semiconductor industry, who asked not to be identified, likened the plight of Perkin-Elmer to "a story of neglect. There was no spending on development. They depended on the Defense Department, and developed a 'handout' mentality. There was a time when Perkin-Elmer was the best. Horace lost his edge. He let the wonderful new Micrascan technology languish."

There was no getting around the fact that the Japanese were offering superior products at lower prices, with better service—or that those products were being subsidized and protected in their own markets. It was the story of the auto industry all over again.

SEMATECH drew up a joint development program to make Micrascan more competitive, but insisted that the ownership remain in American hands. It was only when Goldman, Sachs & Co., the company's investment adviser, had failed to find a serious American buyer that it began looking overseas.

Nikon expressed an interest, but feared an American backlash. Nikon is part of the Mitsubishi Group, which had recently bought control of Rockefeller Center, and found itself enmeshed in widespread criticism for purchasing this American landmark. "Generally speaking, under the present political situation it will be very difficult for any company outside the United States to acquire Perkin-Elmer," said Nobuo Itoi, head of Nikon's semiconductor-equipment division. "Even if we obtained the government's permission, there is the issue of public sentiment."[1]

Even though McDonell acknowledged that "political limitations" might make the sale impossible, Perkin-Elmer and Nikon executives met in the Netherlands on November 7, 1989, at the Amsterdam Hilton, to discuss a joint venture. McDonell and his colleagues insisted that the U.S. be given access to Japanese technology in exchange for Perkin-Elmer's sale of the U.S. technology, assuming government approval of the transaction was forthcoming.

"After the meeting in Holland and the public enragement, Nikon waved off," McDonell recalled. "MITI directed them to wave off." Perkin-Elmer's seemingly last, best chance was lost. The company was desperate. The corporate executives sought the aid of Bush-administration officials, including Commerce Secretary Robert Mosbacher and Deputy Secretary Tom Murrin. Mosbacher also sought to involve USTR Carla Hills. Others who helped were Allan Bromley, the President's science-and-technology adviser; J. Michael Farren, undersecretary of commerce for international trade; and Craig Fields, head of DARPA. Bush-administration officials blamed the semiconductor industry for not investing in itself; if Perkin-Elmer were worth saving, they argued, the private sector would move in. Government had no business intervening in the marketplace. "Nothing attracts capital better than the promise of success," Bromley told a Senate subcommittee hearing.[2]

Meanwhile, at a secret, off-the-record meeting in Washington between McDonell and officials from DoD and IBM, the vise tightened on Perkin-Elmer. McDonell was told that DoD would no longer send *any* business to Perkin-Elmer if he sold off the photolithography division, because the "company would not be regarded as a reliable company to trust for advanced work related either to IBM or to DoD."

Despite these warnings, the Perkin-Elmer board decided at a meeting in early December to close down the photolithography unit if no purchaser could be found by the end of the year. "We had to stop the bleeding," McDonell said. "That brought IBM to realize that this could go under. We came within an eyelash of closing the whole thing down."

When it looked as if Perkin-Elmer was serious about closing down or trying to find another Japanese investor, IBM redoubled its efforts to find an American buyer. In a global economy, why should a huge multinational corporation like IBM care about the loss of a small supplier like Perkin-Elmer? As long as they could buy the technology, what difference did it make? Plenty, to IBM's leaders, who were watching the trend lines and had themselves taken leading roles in government and industry efforts—such as SEMATECH, the Defense Science Board, and the Semiconductor Industry Association—to meet these new challenges. They could see the rate of foreign acquisitions in their field accelerating rapidly, and could project the potential effects of such sales on the well-being of their company. Examples abound of benign acquisitions that eventually resulted in lost technology, lost technological leads, and declining market share for U.S. firms. Some of these foreign firms won through sheer competitive superiority, others through shrewd licensing arrangements and acquisitions; but many gained their edge by manipulating international trading rules with behind-the-scenes help and support from their governments.

IBM could also look across the seas to learn the lessons of dependency. Hard on the heels of the Perkin-Elmer crisis came the impending sale of ICL, P.L.C., Britain's only manufacturer of mainframe computers, to Fujitsu. The sale chilled U.S. computer makers, who feared the same fate as ICL, a company that followed the classic pattern of dependency. Over time, ICL found it was much cheaper to buy foreign components and contract out research and development than it was to manufacture or finance R & D at home. They turned to Fujitsu, then a leading competitor, for their chips, circuit boards, and complex cooling systems. Eventually, ICL found its designs of hardware were driven not by the requirements of the marketplace or the need to outperform its competitors, but by the needs of Fujitsu. Meanwhile, executives at Fujitsu determined the rate of ICL's development by managing the flow of parts to ICL—how many, and when they could be bought. Pretty soon, ICL was buying, not leading-edge, but last year's technology from Fujitsu.[3]

ICL confused dependency with interdependency, and allowed

itself to become swallowed up in the process—all in the interests of short-term gain. The pattern—and the location—recalled the British film *The Servant*, with ICL the master and Fujitsu the servant. In the film, the master becomes overly dependent on his servant, who becomes increasingly demanding until, ultimately, the two exchange roles. ICL became the servant officially in July 1990, when Fujitsu agreed to purchase 80 percent of the company for $1.29 billion.

To avoid falling into this pattern, IBM was able to arrange a consortium of American buyers that kept Perkin-Elmer's lithography division in U.S. hands. Enter Papken S. Der Torossian, an Armenian emigrant from Syria who was the head of the Silicon Valley Group, a low-tech company that specialized in making machines to clean silicon wafers and coat them with chemicals. Torossian was interested in purchasing Micrascan. "IBM said, What can we do to help?" McDonell recalled. IBM orchestrated a consortium that included Perkin-Elmer, IBM, and the Silicon Valley Group, which would have a controlling equity position in the new company, called SVG Lithography Systems, Inc. The Silicon Valley Group paid $20 million for about two-thirds of the division. But Perkin-Elmer kept approximately a 20-percent share, and IBM agreed to make an equity investment of less than 20 percent to assist in meeting the fund requirements needed to develop the sophisticated machines. IBM also agreed to purchase more than $10 million worth of equipment, and make available to the new company's customers an advanced material known as an optical resist, which is needed for the step-and-scan machines. Some industry analysts wondered aloud where, in this era of scarce "patient capital," a small company like SVG could obtain $20 million—or, who was really underwriting this acquisition?

"There is no one in the world today that has an equivalent technology to the Perkin-Elmer system," Der Torossian said. He added that the machine would easily produce chips that stored as much as sixteen million bits of information, and would ultimately be capable of producing chips able to store as much as 256 million bits.[4] IBM agreed to provide the new company with substantial equipment purchases in future years, and financial support of SVG's research-and-development programs. "We continue to do what we can to strengthen the infrastructure on which we and others depend," said IBM President Jack D. Kuehler. "Perkin-Elmer has been supplying leading-edge tools, and we want to see that continue."

SEMATECH agreed to spend $5 million over several years to improve the technology, with Noyce voicing his support: "We must direct our national vision, our national will, and our national resources toward creating an environment that allows the American free-

enterprise system to flourish." Buoyed by IBM, SEMATECH, and
Perkin-Elmer involvement, Torossian expressed his confidence that
"this venture will have the support required to become a global leader
in lithography-exposure equipment." Time will tell.

<h2>CRITICAL TECHNOLOGIES AND
THE DEFENSE INDUSTRIAL BASE</h2>

Thanks to widespread publicity, the Perkin-Elmer story drew to a close
with a happy ending, at least in the short term. But what about the
next Perkin-Elmer? Who will write the happy ending for the next
threatened technology? How many high-tech companies in trouble can
attract a year of media coverage before anyone pays attention? Is that
what they want? Horace McDonell loathed the negative publicity he
had weathered over the Perkin-Elmer sale: most CEOs prefer the freedom to buy and sell without being second-guessed by the public.
Custom and law dictate their role: to protect the firm—not the government, not society, not the industry at large, and certainly not national
security, as vague and ill-defined as that concept is in relation to U.S.
commercial activities.

If the public is inattentive, who is going to protect America's
security interests next time? Before and after Perkin-Elmer, most of
the high-tech fire sales have taken place well out of public view, often
concealed by the sellers and the buyers, ignored by the government,
and rationalized by the prevailing ideology of the time: that neither
government nor industry should protect assets in a global economy,
where ownership no longer matters. Ironically, it was America's most
globalized multinational, IBM, that rescued Perkin-Elmer. If a shared
consensus really existed about the decreasing importance of ownership
in the world marketplace, why was IBM so concerned about the sale
of a relatively small supplier to a highly reputable Japanese company?

Finally, what is a critical technology? Did Perkin-Elmer's Micrascan process fall into this category, worthy of public attention, government protection, or private rescue, and who should decide? Or are
semiconductors and semiconductor technologies so "low-tech" by
now that they fall into the category of "commodity," where there are
so many producers competing for business that no one has to worry
about availability?

Witness the sharp contrast between the Japanese attitude toward
technology, and the U.S. response to Perkin-Elmer. While McDonell
was searching for a U.S. buyer and the public debate swirled around
whether or not the technology was worth saving, the Japanese already

had their answer: a buyer, ready, able, and anxious to buy the company. The difference: the Japanese were buying the *technology*, not the *company*; the long-term dividends, they knew, would soon eclipse the red ink, and even if they didn't, the risks were well worth the investment. The question of who decides what is critical didn't even arise: technology and security are so ingrained and intertwined in Japanese political culture that the nuances are irrelevant.

"The U.S. never connected the loss of commercial technologies with the loss of military technology," said David Sanger of the Tokyo bureau of *The New York Times*, who covered Perkin-Elmer and other such sales. "With regard to Japanese national security, history is proving them right. Economic stability comes first, then security, then national security. The choices are all made in the budget. The U.S. chose Star Wars, not semiconductors."

The same pattern emerged in the FSX agreement. The Japanese didn't need the FSX to protect Japan; F-16s or their successors would have more than adequately met their security needs. But they wanted the technology for a future in aerospace manufacturing, and in that context the extra costs didn't matter. In the United States, the reverse is true. Politically, the case can be made for long-term investment only for strictly military technology; supporters of technologies less directly related to military hardware find it harder to argue successfully that they are related to the national security.

Several government agencies have grappled with this issue, and expended considerable resources defining critical industries and technologies. The energy is soon dissipated, however, in the inevitable controversy over exactly what to do about preserving those technologies. The debate disintegrates over the issue of protectionism, and all action is quickly abandoned. U.S. politics is so open, especially in contrast to politics in Japan or even Western Europe, that anything smacking of protectionism seems much worse here, because it is brought to the surface so quickly—primarily by U.S. lobbyists for foreign multinationals, or U.S. multinationals dependent on cheap foreign components. When it comes to strategic industries, admitted Lee Iacocca, the outspoken chairman of Chrysler, "I am a protectionist. . . . A patsy is somebody who won't protect himself."[5]

Even the great free trader Adam Smith was a protectionist, argued the scholar Peter Schweizer, when it came to critical industries eighteenth-century-style, like "sailcloth and gunpowder." Two hundred years ago, Smith warned of the "corrosive effects" of excessive dependence on foreign goods. Smith advocated the support of certain domestic producers for the "national good," and believed free trade should serve the state, not vice versa.[6]

Amid the national debate over protecting critical industries, several influential reports have managed to surface in spite of the White House's best efforts to minimize the issue. Some identify critical industries, while others link the twin issues of the eroding industrial base and U.S. competitiveness. The first warning shot came from the Defense Department in 1988, when, in a rare move, the department actually went on the offensive and in two consecutive reports warned of the nation's increased dependency on foreign suppliers and the dangers of losing technological capability through unrestricted foreign investment.[7]

"Security concerns are not resolved by domestic manufacturing facilities that are dependent on technologies controlled by other nations," concluded the highly controversial Pentagon report known as the "Costello Report." In this view, loss of control is inherent in foreign ownership, because offshore owners tended to take control of critical manufacturing technologies. Several of the "endangered species" named in the report included machine tools, semiconductors, and electronics-manufacturing equipment.[8] Deeply out of sync with the Reagan administration, this report marked the first and last time the Pentagon officially linked national defense to economic stability; thereafter, the agency was careful to stick to military hardware.

The fact that the Costello Report ever surfaced owes a great deal to the shrewdness of its timing: its publication date of July 1988 suggests it was planned for the waning days of Reagan's lame-duck presidency. The salvo also owes a great deal to the leadership of Costello himself. It was he who advocated the notion—highly unpopular at the White House—that national defense was strongly linked to the preservation of the industrial base. In fact, the term "industrial base" is often used interchangeably with "defense" to emphasize the importance to national security of a solid manufacturing base. Costello knew from his days at General Motors how badly technology needed a manufacturing base, and tried in vain to convince his political and military colleagues: "The key is how to maintain your industrial lead if you don't have the base to support you. I liken this to a 120-story building. You need the hundred stories to support the top twenty floors."

Where U.S. industrial strategy went wrong, added Costello in an interview shortly after he left office, was in not looking at markets—not linking the power of military procurement to future commercial gain. "We have one commodity that no other nation has," he said, "a market. We don't look at it as an asset. It is not to be used for the benefit of foreigners."

Drawing an inverted pyramid on a sheet of paper with markets at the top and manufacturing base at the bottom, Costello described the process: "We spend a hell of a lot of money on semiconductors through SEMATECH. We never look at the market. HDTV [high-definition television] is a segment of the market. You can't have a product without a market. The Department of Defense has that market. DoD is the only one with that market. If we had mandated superconductivity for ship-propulsion systems, it would have put the U.S. in a leading role."

Instead, Costello argued, the nation ignored its manufacturing base, and lost high-value technologies as a result. "We gave up optics years ago. Now there's a process that eliminates grinding. You can't have technology without a manufacturing base. You can't fight a war with pizza parlors. Industrial ceramics is used in semiconductors. Kyocera now controls 70 to 80 percent of hermetically sealed packages for semiconductors." Though he described himself as a middle-of-the-roader walking the line between the "free-traders and Fortress America," Costello recalled former CIA Director Bobby Inman introducing him as "Mr. MITI." His answer to the free-traders, he recalled, was this:

"Fortress America is an impossibility. But industry must play a role in protecting the manufacturing base. In the past, we protected components. We paid a premium, but we knew that. Industry must open its eyes. We need a strong infrastructure. We have resources Japan doesn't have: cheaper energy, now cheaper labor, and natural resources.

"I'm told, 'Buy all your memory from Japan.' That leaves me little flexibility with the product. Unless I'm making the product, I can't put logic on the chip. That's a piece of real estate on the chip. Some level of vertical integration is needed to maintain our technological lead."

The Costello Report was followed several months later by that of the Defense Science Board (DSB), linking technological loss to blunting the national strategy of deterrence. The DSB criticized the uncoordinated nature of defense acquisition policy and national economic policy, and called for the creation of an industrial-policy council to assure a more formalized linkage between national economic policy and military strategy. Most important, the DSB warned of the dangers of the nation's deepening dependence on "foreign resources for critical components of our weapons systems" and the need to formulate a policy to assure the availability of industrial and technological resources on which military operations rely.[9]

Although a number of studies supported the Pentagon's conclusions, none was more influential and alarming than *Deterrence in*

Decay, a study issued in May 1989 by the Center for Strategic and International Studies (CSIS), a conservative think tank closely linked to the intelligence and defense communities. Expressing many of the DSB's points and recommendations, the CSIS's report charged that at least eighty thousand firms had stopped doing business with the Pentagon since 1982: some went out of business, including twenty thousand small firms, while others turned from military to commercial pursuits, thanks to import penetration and disastrous DoD acquisition policies. (The total number of defense-related firms is estimated at 250,000.) The irony is that this occurred while the defense procurement budget—which should have some influence over the retention of the defense industrial base—rose from $54.9 billion to $89 billion in FY 1989, "a record defense build-up that in other markets would have attracted a legion of entrepreneurial and growth-hungry commercial enterprises."[10]

The defense community's concern originated with a study on precision-guided munitions, according to James Blackwell of CSIS, who wrote the deterrence report, which found twenty to thirty weapons systems dependent on foreign suppliers. This "plumbed the depths of dependency," said Blackwell, and started some serious thinking about its implications: "Precision optics traced the dependency chain of any system that depends on optics—the M-1 tank, the Bradley infantry-fighting vehicle, any small tank—and we asked, 'Where are the suppliers?' When we looked, we found that at the fifth or sixth level we were down to only two companies making lenses." The same is occurring in the ammunitions industry.

Bernard Schwartz, CEO of Loral, went public on the issue in support of the CSIS findings. Schwartz used the eighty-thousand figure as a launching pad for a serious lobbying effort to get the government to look more closely at the loss of subcontractors, and especially the acquisition of those companies and technologies by foreign investors. "The original license for the semiconductor was sold to Japan for $10,000," he alleged. "We need a change in attitude from protecting the consumer to protecting our industrial strength.

"If we allow Perkin-Elmer technology to leave the country for the exclusive proprietary playground of the Japanese or the Germans, something is terribly wrong. 'Why shouldn't IBM buy Perkin-Elmer?' is the wrong question. The real question should be 'Why shouldn't Perkin-Elmer mean something to the United States?' Why should IBM carry the burden of the United States? Why shouldn't pension funds, labor unions, and other investment funds do this? I would like to buy Perkin-Elmer. If it means Loral has to invest to maintain U.S. strength, the stockholders wouldn't like it. We are asked to be disproportionately responsive. Why shouldn't the government be responsive as well?" Schwartz also raised the question of reciprocity, emphasizing that other nations besides Japan kept tight hold of their critical technologies: "In 1989, I could not buy a division of Schlumberger. It was a French computer company, and I couldn't buy it."

Why keep critical industries? The CSIS attacks the conventional response, which recalls the industrial miracle of World War II, when the "arsenal of democracy" was able to "mobilize" its industrial base rapidly for wartime production—namely, 296,000 aircraft, 1,201 naval vessels, 64,546 landing craft, 86,333 tanks, and 42,585 billion rounds of small-arms ammunition. But economic realities and the development of nuclear weapons have rendered mobilization a lesser goal, "a short-range problem motivated by large-scale combat"; indeed, in both Vietnam and Korea no such mobilization build-up occurred, primarily because the nation could still rely on defense production facilities used for World War II. Mobilization has been replaced by deterrence, the postwar foundation of U.S. national-security strategy.[11] Defense analysts evaluate their readiness for war from a variety of perspectives, including: surge production in emergencies, industrial preparedness, and emergency production. All points of view focus on the industrial base, critical industries and technologies, and their relationship to defense production.

What does the loss of subcontractors mean, especially when no one knows when and to whom they are being sold? Unless the media pick up the story, the public will never be informed; in some cases, the media remain the only warning system for DoD officials as well. This was the case with the impending sale of Avtex, a small company near Front Royal, Virginia, which bore the distinction of being the nation's only producer of rayon of sufficiently high quality to be used in aerospace equipment. Avtex threatened to close, because it found it could not meet water-pollution regulations and still stay in business. Alarm bells rang in the Pentagon, according to one official involved in preventing the closure. "What came to our attention was that Avtex was a sixth-tier supplier to the Defense Department," he recalled. "They are the only producers of aerospace-grade rayon that goes in the nozzles of every strategic missile we own or produce, most of the tactical missiles, and the shuttle as well. So this plant, which showed the vulnerability of the defense industrial base, would have shut down all our missile production and shuttle production for over two years.

"We didn't even have any idea that that kind of vulnerability existed," he added. "We don't have a data base that lets us understand that this is a sole-source producer at a sixth-tier level." The prime contractors have some notion of what is going on, but they generally cannot gather information beyond the second or third tier. Prime contractors, for example, may subcontract out engines, avionics, landing gear, and parts for wings, but these subcontractors would be considered second-tier companies—more important than rayon for nozzles, but without that rayon the primes as well as the subs risked delays in meeting their production schedules.

"DoD owns sixty ammunition plants, doing business with twenty thousand prime contractors," explained DoD official Richard Donnelly. "Most of our problems are at the supplier level. If we could behave as a commercial customer, we'd be able to say, 'Here is what we need.' We're trying to behave more like commercial customers, getting out of the specifications-and-standards business." But the Pentagon is limited in its ability to do so, leaving itself in a vulnerable position. "A lot of us thought that, during the Reagan arms build-up, when we bought more weapons and equipment, there would be more technological development. Instead, there is manufacturing uncertainty of one to two years, and problems with the availability and stability of capital, and as a result we are producing tomorrow's weapons on yesterday's technology.

"We try to discriminate between foreign sourcing and foreign dependency, and also foreign components," added Donnelly. "The terms are thrown around too loosely. What if we're cut off from these resources? What if we have a war? More serious is technological dependency. Semiconductors you can dump in a suitcase. The real dependency is the infrastructure issue. We're now second best. Japan over the last ten years has left behind copying and begun innovating. Will our foreign suppliers ultimately share back with us their latest developments? And what is it that stays here?"

Under the influence of leaders like Costello and Donnelly, DoD undertook a study using the production of one tank to focus on the Pentagon's ability to get a handle on the depth of the problem of industrial preparedness. "We were looking for bottlenecks in production," said an official who worked on the study. "What you find is that the prime contractor's ability to produce a hundred [tanks] is constrained by his inability to get components. And that's what industrial-preparedness planning tries to do. But it is very labor-intensive and quite costly to maintain a detailed understanding of the production capability of a complex weapons system. When you get down to the sixth tier, you don't have the manpower, or the time, really, to have a comprehensive set of data to understand the deficiencies we've got. And that's why we really don't understand what the vulnerabilities in the industrial base are to national security."

This means that the nation's military security rests on an almost nonexistent early-warning system for bottlenecks in military production. In the case of Avtex, the Pentagon and NASA rushed in and instantly came up with the money to keep the plant alive. Instead of planning, this was reactive, seat-of-the-pants decisionmaking in which a government subsidy saved a plant that was essentially noncompetitive because NASA was not about to shut down its shuttle production and DoD could not afford to live without missiles.

THE ROLE OF DETERRENCE

The real problem with the body of thinking on critical industries is that everything was viewed in the context of the Soviet Union as the enemy, a concept no longer as relevant today. In that world view, "deterrence" meant the ability to maintain "a large, ready strategic nuclear force to strike at the Soviet Union."[12] It meant matching the Soviets, not soldier for soldier, or gun for gun, but technology for technology; or, better yet, matching U.S. technologies against our enemies' soldiers and guns.

Thus the defense industrial base was judged not so much on its ability to mobilize as on its capacity to provide "material" for the common defense of the United States—through its readiness in manufacturing, production, technology, research, development, and availability of resources. To deter the enemy, the industrial base must also have "crisis flexibility, peacetime efficiency and technological competitiveness."[13] But the Soviet Union is no longer the enemy; "they are no longer the evil empire, they are on 'Night Line' all the time," remarked an assistant secretary of defense. Without an identifiable enemy, how can combat readiness through an industrial base be sold as a viable issue?

The answer is that readiness means being prepared for conflicts or skirmishes that cannot be predicted, such as Iraq's invasion of Kuwait and its threatened attack on Saudi Arabia. Crisis flexibility means the ability of defense industries to convert quickly from peacetime production to wartime, not an easy task but one tested all too frequently in low-level conflicts. As CSIS points out, the 1973 Arab-Israeli War showed what happens when this "surge" capability is missing: "U.S. war reserve stocks in tanks and antitank guided missiles . . . in a very short time were so severely depleted that weapons in the hands of U.S. active forces were taken and given to the Israelis to prevent the utter defeat of a valued U.S. ally."[14]

The Gulf War appeared to demonstrate great crisis flexibility, but no one knows how depleted U.S. stores will be at the next conflict's end. Aircraft, materiel, and weapons systems used in the Gulf were all products of the 1980s defense build-up, and as defense budgets decline, how will the nation provide for future security needs? Also, the Gulf War produced a new enemy and some very different scenarios from those on which current security policy is based.

One thing remains constant, however: the attrition of critical industries through indiscriminate sales, overseas competition, and lack of government interest. A clear mission of DoD is to preserve the defense technology base so that the nation can gear up in times of crisis.[15]

"Even if it never builds anything with it," said Martin Libicki, a defense analyst with the the Industrial College of the Armed Forces, "in some future time, if the skies get dark or if [a Russian leader] gets overthrown, or whatever, we have the basis from which to rebuild a defense structure." If we don't have that capability, deterrence becomes a less potent force, but without the Soviet Union looming as a major threat, there no longer seems to be a compelling reason to stay with that view. The question of what will take its place has not been answered, and the absence of a replacement keeps defense officials nervous. "I was talking with an ex-boss of mine," recalled Libicki, "and we were discussing back and forth the notion of coproduction in Europe. I said, 'In a perfect world,' and I was about to say, 'we wouldn't care where defense products were made'; but then I thought, In a perfect world we wouldn't be making defense weapons, would we?"

MAKING LISTS: GOVERNMENT'S ROLE IN PROTECTING CRITICAL TECHNOLOGIES

The impetus for forcing government to take a more active role in protecting critical technologies came from Capitol Hill, led by Senator Bingaman. Reflecting congressional impatience with the White House's repeated rebuffs and failure to establish priorities, Bingaman took the view that, if the executive branch wouldn't deal with the question of critical technologies, then Congress would legislate those priorities. He had the authority to initiate legislative efforts through his position as chairman of the Subcommittee on Defense Industry and Technology of the Armed Services Committee.

Bingaman began by asking which industries and which technologies were important for national security, which were being targeted by Japan, and which were either lost or in danger of being lost. Frustration with DoD's lack of planning and national perspective fueled his efforts to get an answer, which in turn led to his request for a list of critical technologies and a plan to go with that list. Bingaman's chief aide in what turned into an ongoing effort was his science adviser, Ed McGaffigan, who was also instrumental in the organizing the congressional opposition to the FSX agreement. On the Hill, a growing technology-policy caucus includes Representative George Brown, Jr., Democrat of California, in the House, and Senators Gore and Nunn.

Aided by Pentagon officials like Costello and his allies, Congress finally addressed the issue of critical technologies directly in the Defense Authorization Act of the Defense Production Act of FY 1989. Among other provisions dealing with the industrial base, Congress called on the secretary of defense to review acquisition policies, keeping in mind their impact on the defense industrial base; established a Defense Industrial Base Office in DoD; and, most important of all, required the secretaries of defense and energy to identify twenty critical technologies that demanded a concentrated effort to maintain the lead.

The legislation required that the departments set goals for developing the chosen technologies, compare the positions of the United States and the Soviet Union in developing the technologies, and cite the potential contributions that U.S. allies could make to the technologies.[16] The law did not establish new barriers to foreign access to American technology, nor did it provide new safeguards against foreign competition for American companies—other federal laws gave the president authority to block foreign takeovers when the transaction was considered a threat to national security, and required the Pentagon and the Commerce Department to approve certain sales and transfers of technology that might be a threat to national security.

The list finally emerged the following March (1989) with twenty-two technologies designated as critical to national security and "the long-term qualitative superiority of U.S. weapons systems." These technologies were selected on the basis of four criteria: an ability to enhance the performance of proven types of weapons systems significantly; a potential for creating new capabilities or systems; a potential for improving the reliability, availability, and "maintainability" of weapons systems; and "affordability."

But lofty and ambitious goals cost lots of money if they're to be taken seriously. Identifying critical technologies was only the first step; Congress also "tasked" the Defense and Energy Departments to plan efforts to finance research-and-development strategies to promote those technologies. Not surprisingly, the report did not include an estimate of the cost of such efforts, but the sum was likely to run in the billions of dollars. Directly, or indirectly, that money would have to be allocated by Congress.

The list was subject to change depending on events—"a Sputnik-like surprise, or an unexpected surge in terrorist activity could affect the technologies selected." Or politics. Some defense officials privately expressed their surprise that the list did not put more emphasis on space technology or high-definition television. Senator Bingaman said he was "hopeful that the plan would not only force us, as a nation, to think strategically about how we spend billions of research dollars every year, but will also strengthen coordination among agencies toward achieving that goal."

The following year's critical-industries plan, hailed by Senator Bingaman as a "significant improvement" over the 1989 plan, again found Japan ahead in several of the critical technologies: semiconductor materials and microelectronic circuits, machine intelligence and robotics, superconductivity, and biotechnology materials and processes.[17] The section on semiconductor materials found Japan was "significantly ahead" of the United States in four key areas of chip making, and "capable of making major contributions" in a fourth area, protecting chips against the damaging effects of radiation.[18]

Bingaman expressed disappointment in the lack of meaningful follow-up: DoD did not designate a lead agency for each of the technologies as called for in the FY 1990 Defense Authorization Bill. This meant the report was still a report, and not a plan of action with "specific time frames with specific resources," such as funding commitments for DARPA, the Strategic Defense Initiative, Energy, NASA, and the National Science Foundation to each of the technologies. Aggregate funding was identified as slightly over $3 billion for nineteen of the twenty critical technologies, a significant increase over the $2-billion figure the year before.

Without meaningful action, the lists became ends in themselves, issued to mollify congressional criticism of government's failure to halt the slow attrition of the nation's technological leadership. Unless accompanied by concrete action, they would soon look like wards of the state abandoned at the orphanage of neglected issues. That view was disputed by Charles Herzfeld, an engineer and entrepreneur who had just been appointed director of defense research and engineering several months after the Critical Technologies Plan was issued. Noting the lack of substance displayed by his office's prior statements to Congress, he indicated that he had already begun to lead an effort at DoD to develop a defense technology strategy and "action plan."[19] Exactly what that action plan would entail was not clarified, but as the Pentagon's new research czar he knew he would have to come up with something. In an interview in his office shortly after he was confirmed, Herzfeld shared his ambivalence about what to do:

"Both extremes are wrong," he posited, "those who are alarmists and those who are not paying attention to the issue. In the world economy you can buy almost anything. There are lots of alternative sources. You have to make sure those sources are reliable . . . and that there is no excessive dependence. If the damage is nominal—if there is a 5-percent increase (or 5-percent loss to foreign competitors)—then there is nothing to worry about. My concern with foreign investment is that most of the design work stays at home."

When Costello served at DoD, he made sure the design work "stayed at home" by using the Pentagon's purchasing clout as leverage. When Michelin bought Uniroyal Goodrich, he recalled, "I told them that they had to manufacture and design the tires here, as well as bring the basic technology here," if they wanted to keep DoD's business. "That way," he said, "we used our leverage to control the market, drive a harder bargain, and keep the value-added here."

Herzfeld viewed such strong-arm government intervention with some discomfort. "I share a suspicion of government," he said—"that government would be good at that. Yet government has been good at favoring investments. Ever since the Whitney rifle, 'lay' technologies have been funded by the government. Gunpowder started Dupont. Government does invest. It invests $50 to $70 billion, or the GNP of a small country." But other countries do better, he added. "The French government gave every household a free terminal. That's how they pushed HDTV [high-definition television]. Our government can help in setting standards. There are no FCC standards for HDTV. That's the reason HDTV is not successful in the United States." Unfortunately, Herzfeld was unable either to put together a meaningful plan for critical technologies, or to negotiate the increasingly Byzantine bureaucracy of DoD's "improved" acquisition bureaucracy.

Indeed, why was HDTV left off the critical-industries list? Many defense officials argued for its inclusion, recognizing its importance in security-related weapons systems, medical technology, and many other related products. The answer reveals the one criterion for inclusion on the list that is never stated publicly: political acceptability. When the debate over critical industries was raging in Congress and the Pentagon, editorial writers and cartoonists across the country loved lampooning the issue, virtually united in their opposition to what they viewed as a frivolous and wasteful effort to send taxpayer dollars into a technology that was mistakenly viewed as merely an improved television screen—one that would render the blades of grass at a football game clearer to the viewer. Typical of the genre was a cartoon by Henry Payne, of the Scripps Howard Newspapers, showing the marriage of an obese groom to an equally corpulent bride. The groom sported the label "big business"; the bride, "big government." A preacher named "Congress" recites the vows, while clutching a kicking and screaming taxpayer, over the caption: "Anyone knowing why the groom (who hasn't made a television in years) and the bride (who hasn't balanced a checkbook in memory) should not be joined in the production of high-definition TV, speak now or . . ."

With that kind of editorial opposition, neither Congress nor the Pentagon wanted to risk supporting HDTV; it was difficult enough to convince the public and the White House that identifying critical technologies did not constitute "industrial policy." But, at the same time that the U.S. was engaged in the debate over what was critical and what was not, the Japanese government was organizing industrial expenditures for HDTV that soared well above the $900-million mark; nothing frivolous about HDTV to Japanese industrial leaders, who predicted big dividends in the twenty-first century.

The computer-chip advocates in the White House finally scored a minor victory when Congress adopted a provision of the Defense Authorization Act that required the White House to issue its own critical-technologies report. On April 25, 1991, departing from a long-standing policy, the White House issued its own critical industries list, consisting of twenty-two areas of technological development deemed "critical to the national prosperity and to national security."[20]

The report was applauded on the hill by Senator Bingaman, who pointed out that this represented the first time that the "White House has identified priorities in technology." Unfortunately, there was "still a raging dispute between those who put out this report and others in the White House over the government's role in meeting this challenge." Under pressure from conservative Republicans, the White House ultimately disavowed the report, which was written by its own technology experts. Another dispute involved the Critical Technologies Institute, mandated by Congress and funded for $5 million for FY 1990. The White House delayed setting up the institute for nearly a year; today, it is widely regarded as ineffective.

Significantly, the critical-industries lists from the Pentagon also included two technologies that figured prominently in the FSX sale: gallium arsenide and phased-array radar (the latter appeared on the 1989, but not the 1990, list). The FSX sale went forward without any discussion of what those technologies—or any technologies—meant to the defense industrial base. Richard Donnelly, who recalled his frustrations at DoD with the absence of industrial-base considerations in the FSX negotiations, supported the identification of critical technologies as a productive step, but argued that the industrial base was the real issue behind the critical-technologies lists: "The Senate was telling us to have a plan . . . get us thinking more in terms of manufacturing technologies. We started talking about the infrastructure's ability to produce technologies. You start with the technology, then branch out to manufacturing. You can't duplicate SEMATECH all over the place. Just because something is critical doesn't mean that federal dollars are necessary." In other words, the country's leaders must be more selective; it is not a question of the numbers of companies failing, but what sectors of the economy they represent and how those sectors are doing.

Saving critical industries, said Donnelly, is like the old military metaphor of wing-walking: "If you're wing-walking, and if you're about to let go, make sure you're holding on to something."

"Holding on to something" pinpoints the major problem with the critical-industries lists. Once you've identified critical technologies, what then? What policies should be followed to halt further slippage? What agencies will oversee those efforts? What kinds of incentives will best promote corporate efforts to sustain and nurture the technologies? And how does trade policy figure into the equation: what trade policies should support the overall policy to retain critical technologies? In other words, even the most sophisticated lists, by themselves, are doomed to be ineffective unless they impel such actions as establishing barriers to foreign access when that poses a security threat, or providing safeguards against unfair foreign competition. A similar analogy applies to improving data bases: although a critical need exists for better and more timely information, data collection alone can be an expensive and time-consuming academic exercise; to be meaningful, it must be accompanied by plans, programs, and policies.

Judging from Perkin-Elmer and many similar, less publicized sales of critical technologies, the last of the above questions has largely been ignored, despite increasing agreement among defense officials that trade policy and security policy need greater linkage. Government sat by and virtually ignored the loss of U.S. companies engaged in the very technologies they had labeled as critical to the national defense. Perkin-Elmer's photolithography process clearly came within the purview of critical technology, yet the company and its technology could easily have been sold to Nikon.

Perkin-Elmer revealed the nation's schizophrenia over two basic themes: the benefits of economic interdependence through globalization, versus the country's growing dependence on economic competitors for its national defense. With the relaxation of East-West tensions and the triumph of democratic capitalism, worldwide gains for freedom sparked a new euphoria in the United States. The spirit was infectious. To some it seemed that in this era of glasnost international economic competition had gone the way of Bolshevism, and that a new global economy had emerged in which market forces and international cooperation were replacing national interests, and lines of ownership and control were becoming increasingly blurred.

Yet, while this is doubtless a worthy goal that may someday come to pass, it is in fact still a long way from reality. America's leading trading partners may support the ideal of global cooperation in principle, but in practice they often act quite differently; otherwise, America would not be the only industrialized country in the world with virtually no policy toward foreign acquisition of its assets or high-level attention to the issue of what constitutes a critical technology and how to save it. "Are other nations acting first in their own economic self-interests?" asked Tom Murrin when he was deputy secretary of commerce. "The major problem with the past decade's growing internationalization of technology is that we are not seeing many other nations adopting the role of global citizens when it comes to economic competition."

Perkin-Elmer symbolized the current debate over what constitutes national security, and the argument for linking national defense to trade and investment policies. The case capped a decade of trade policies that saw hundreds of companies vital to the nation's industrial base acquired by foreign interests who appreciated their value and leapt at the new opportunities. And who saved Perkin-Elmer? A private U.S. multinational, IBM, a company that is widely regarded as the most global of U.S. companies. Global, but scared nonetheless of relying on a Japanese company for a crucial component of manufacture.

Many companies that manufacture critical technologies have been sold, or had their technologies licensed, without the scrutiny they deserve. Biotechnology ranked high, for example, on the 1989 and 1990 critical lists, yet in 1990 Genentech, the nation's leading biotech company, was sold to the Swiss multinational Hoffman-LaRoche. The few who raised questions about this deal were criticized as alarmist; after all, the Swiss are our allies, and Genentech will benefit from the infusion of capital. Alarmist? The Swiss won't allow foreign nationals to buy property in their country, much less companies involved in leading-edge technology.

Nor will the would-be purchasers of Perkin-Elmer, the Japanese, allow foreign nationals to buy technologies they have determined are critical to their national welfare, and myriad other, low-tech industries, such as leather, fisheries, energy, agriculture, and natural resources; anyone lucky enough to jump the hurdles and buy a Japanese company might find himself with a Japanese partner owning the majority share of the firm.

Robert Perkins, a Chrysler vice-president who sought to negotiate a leasing arrangement for Gulfstream, a corporate jet manufactured by the company, negotiated with MITI. At the third meeting, he recalled, MITI officials told him that he needed a Japanese partner. At the fourth meeting, they informed him that the Japanese partner would own 51 percent of the leasing company, and at the fifth meeting, they told him who Chrysler's partner would be. Chrysler finally said "no thanks," and abandoned its plan.

Asked about the Chrysler case, Japanese officials acknowledged the restrictions on Chrysler's activity in their country: "We had to stop them; we knew they would fail." Don't capitalists have the freedom to fail? Not in a managed economy like Japan's, where reciprocity between trading partners takes a back seat to national objectives. American business leaders find this practice galling, especially in view of U.S. policy, which allows Japan—and everyone else—to invest freely without government screening.[21]

The major criticism of the lists is that they overemphasize military production, although the White House list emphasized economic security as well. Even many military experts agree that "The strength of national defense depends on the underlying strength of the industrial base, now eroding in sector after sector," in the words of a Pentagon report suppressed ostensibly because of the Gulf War. "The same events that have so altered the international political terrain make it clear that the military and economic dimensions of national security are inseparable. It would be a historical irony of major proportions if the U.S., having secured the first through its steadfast defense of freedom, were to lose the second through its failure to integrate the two."[22]

CHAPTER VI

Realeconomik

THE CONVERGENCE OF NATIONAL SECURITY AND ECONOMIC INTERDEPENDENCE

> We have no eternal allies and we have no perpetual enemies.
> Our interests are eternal and perpetual, and these interests
> it is our duty to perform.
> —Viscount Palmerston, foreign secretary
> of England, in 1848

> We'll always have dependencies. We've got to change this to
> interdependency. It's okay if I buy D-RAMs from someone,
> as long as that person needs me for microprocessors.
> —Mike Kelly, director of manufacturing, DARPA

THE NEW GLOBALISM

A diagram of the General Dynamics F-16 fighter aircraft looks like a miniature United Nations, with several dozen components from all over the globe. Fuel pylons come from Denmark, Indonesia, Israel, and the U.S.; wing panels from the Netherlands and the U.S.; flaperon seats from Belgium and the U.S.; aft fuselages from Greece, Turkey, Belgium, and the U.S.; jet engines from the U.S., Turkey, and Belgium; and ventrals from South Korea, Israel, and the U.S.[1]

One of the genuine heroes of the Gulf War, the F-16 is a truly international product and an international effort. It is also an archetype of many similar global-defense products, showing how U.S. policy has intentionally, by design and congressional mandate, internationalized its defense industrial base. High-minded goals included the desire to arm our allies, strengthen them against their enemies, share our own technology, and learn new technologies and manufacturing methods.

Initially, the U.S. armed its allies with its own products, but gradually other nations wanted to arm themselves and reap the profits offered by a healthy defense industry. When the U.S. wanted to continue to sell its own products, the price often included coproduction.

Budget constraints have forced the U.S. to consider cost above other factors driving procurement: if you can buy it cheaper, go ahead, even if it means sacrificing "Made in America" companies and products. Lower-cost labor, targeted trade and investment practices, and higher productivity have led to the purchasing of foreign components that are all too often cheaper and better than U.S. products, particularly those from companies that have become increasingly inefficient thanks to steady, noncompetitive business from the Defense Department.

During the 1980s, DoD came under heavy criticism for sloppy and corrupt purchasing practices. Indeed, the term "defense mentality" has become synonymous with laziness, cost overruns, and a general lack of competitiveness—and sometimes downright fraud—referring to suppliers who have long since ceased to worry about the discipline of the marketplace or about especially vigorous oversight. The $600 toilet seat became a symbol for defense procurement, making it far more difficult for the Pentagon to win support for legitimate expenditures.

To a lesser extent, the U.S. has been forced to internationalize by countries whose trade positions strengthen their negotiating hand. These countries often insist that the U.S. company or government "offset" its profits with purchases from the same countries. At times, offsets can exceed profits—especially if the purchaser has no use for the products in question—but companies argue that in the long run winning market share will offset these losses, which they say can also be reduced by creative accounting practices and tax policies.

The mélange of policies that led to increased internationalization is widely regarded as a positive development, in which the rest of the world could profit from freer trade by putting into practice the theory of comparative advantage. If Japan made better, cheaper semiconductors, aircraft-wing composites, and visual displays, all the better. Each country would develop its own market niche, and in the long run everyone would benefit, because market forces make more efficient manufacturing decisions than government bureaucrats, industry leaders, or politicians. The new world order also encompassed foreign policy: the more interdependent nations became, the less likelihood there would be of war; trading relationships would cement security relationships.

During this period of globalization, another development occurred that went virtually unnoticed: the wall collapsed between the defense industrial base and the industrial base. "There are few industries that are exclusively defense industries" any more, said Donald Atwood, deputy secretary of defense, observing a trend that has been largely ignored by his fellow policymakers. "DoD has a legitimate interest in the defense industrial base, but at the same time globalization has made us irretrievably dependent on foreign sourcing."

The ultimate irony was that the U.S. became "irretrievably dependent" during a period that represented the greatest military budget increase in history of a nation in peacetime—a wartime build-up without a war. U.S. defense procurement rose by 100 percent, to a level as high as it was during the Vietnam War. But without a critical-industries policy to influence decisionmakers, cost factors invariably predominated in many procurement decisions, thus accelerating the move toward internationalization and its byproduct, increased foreign dependence.

The response to foreign dependence served up a bland stew in which the flavors canceled themselves out; policies that were intended to *promote* U.S. industry led instead to further internationalization—and foreign dependence. For example: Congress passed a number of "Buy America" laws, along with a provision in the Defense Production Act directing the president to limit the production of weapons systems to domestic manufacturers, within five years. The same Congress then turned around to give the secretary of defense the authority to waive many "Buy America" restrictions, and funded dozens of programs to stimulate R & D and codevelopment of new weapons with NATO allies.

Such inconsistencies inevitably led to problems in U.S.-Japan relations. The Japanese were understandably upset by the controversy provoked by the FSX agreement: why did the United States, they asked, accept with equanimity coproduction with its Western European allies, and then challenge a similar agreement with the Japanese? (Actually, the FSX went further than NATO agreements, in that the Japanese were asking the U.S. to codevelop a plane that the U.S. had no interest in acquiring for itself.)

National emergencies also breed inconsistency, when winning takes precedence over reducing foreign dependence. During the Gulf War, for example, the Defense Department debated waiving prohibitions against purchasing non-U.S. antifriction bearings for fear that U.S. manufacturers could not produce sufficient quantities for the ground war. U.S. manufacturers had already lodged complaints against the Navy for buying Swedish bearings and not abiding by those prohibitions, originally granted as a response to the U.S. bearing industry's arguments of unfair foreign competition.[2] The bearing industry had already taken a beating in 1983, when Treasury officials allowed the sale of New Hampshire Ball Bearing to the Japanese-owned Minebea Co., on the grounds that the sale would not compromise national security. The bearings industry can take cold comfort from the fact that they are not alone; the U.S. government has never stopped a sale to foreign investors on the grounds that losing a technology would constitute a threat to national security.

Globalization has also revealed inadequacies in U.S. technological development, especially in comparison with our major trading parters. It is painfully clear, for example, that Japan and the European Community have proved much more skilled at commercializing and producing technologies with civilian as well as military applications than the U.S. In other countries, particularly Japan, without public debates on whether government intervention is necessary or "industrial policy" is desirable, encouraging strategic technologies is a way of life. In World War II, for example, Yamaha, a manufacturer of musical instruments, shifted from producing pianos to aircraft parts, then went back to pianos after the surrender.

It is not a way of life for the United States, which remains content to keep civilian and military technologies separate despite all evidence linking them. Of the twenty "critical technologies" identified by the Department of Defense in 1990, fifteen are dual-use, including micro-electronic circuits, software, robotics, photonics, superconductivity, and biotechnology. Japan not only leads in many of these technologies, but exports them to the United States for both civilian and military uses.[3]

U.S. policy fosters dual-use technology for military-security reasons, such as microelectronics and computers. But only in rare exceptions has the government provided public money to foster the development of commercial technologies or their applications. This is the key difference between the U.S. and Japan. In computers, for example, DoD funded university research in parallel processing through DARPA, even paying for the early products of start-up companies seeking to commercialize these new innovations. But for strictly commercial (as opposed to military-specific) computers, such companies were then on their own in the marketplace. In Japan, the process *begins* with the global commercial market as the prime objective.

Devastated by war, Japan and many of our NATO allies lacked the wherewithal to assume the role of either defending the world or funneling a lion's share of their resources into solely defense-related products; indeed, the Germans and Japanese were barred by law from developing a strong military capability. But they could rest secure in the knowledge that the United States would shoulder most of the responsibility for defending them against their common enemy, the Soviet Union, in exchange for keeping their own military presence to a minimum. The U.S. promoted and accepted this arrangement, since it suited the nation's postwar and Cold War foreign policy needs; no one wanted to see a re-emergence of the German or Japanese military traditions, even if it meant continued heavy expenditures on our part. At the same time, the long-term economic consequences of this world view tended to focus U.S. attentions and the nation's massive procurement budget on a somewhat narrower military view of defense, ignoring the defense industrial base and the issue of technologies related to—but not exclusive of—weapons or related products.

From the postwar years up to the 1990s, the emphasis was on superior military products, distinct from commercial products, leaving other nations free to focus on the marketplace. U.S. leaders focused on the very real threat of the Cold War and burgeoning Soviet military power, but were not responding at the same time to another vital national-security threat: the decreasing competitiveness of U.S. industries, particularly those involved in critical technologies. The United States' attitudes and policies in this area reflected great optimism on the part of its leaders and a feeling of economic superiority to the rest of the world—superiority unwarranted by the nation's rising budget deficits and foreign debt. In essence, while the world's economic express sped in one direction, the U.S. traveled the opposite way, often dissipating its vast economic and political resources. Thus, in the 1980s, while the U.S. negotiated the FSX agreement, the European Community supported the development and production of its own product, the Airbus, developed by an EC consortium, Airbus Industrie. Though it was widely criticized at the time by free-traders—mostly Americans—as a twenty-year financial drain, the Europeans are now enjoying the fruits of its commercial success—a quarter of the world's market for commercial jets—while the U.S. and Japan are stalled in an unproductive and conflict-ridden venture with virtually no commercial or military spin-off for the U.S. Similarly, MITI supported Nikon's efforts to build semiconductor optical steppers in spite of many generations of failure, while the U.S. government watched Perkin-Elmer flounder.

Many observers argued that the U.S. had lost its self-sufficiency in weapons production even before the Vietnam War, as corporations closely identified with the defense industrial base expanded into the international arena. Today, the contours of the defense industrial base are driven more often by the needs and policies of large multinational corporations, whose decisions often supersede those of nation-states—even countries as large and powerful as the United States.

The contours of the defense industrial base are also influenced by political conflicts within the defense industry, where a form of "class warfare" rages between U.S. prime contractors and the tens of thousands of smaller subcontractors that depend on the primes for their health and welfare. Large electronics and aerospace companies, for example, look for global partners as well as overseas subcontractors. This strategy opens foreign markets for their products, allows them to buy cheaper components, and helps them hold down prices and avoid fighting with DoD and Congress over cost overruns. Smaller companies argue that awarding defense business to foreign firms threatens their own existence. They warn that Asian and European firms seldom share their business, and that if they go out of business the defense mobilization base will further erode.[4] Excessive reliance on foreign subcontractors is a short-term strategy, they maintain, since foreign subcontractors raise their prices as soon as they corner the market. The conundrum continues: the primes then complain, as they have recently, that thousands of their U.S. suppliers have gone out of business, forcing them to depend on foreign suppliers.

Globalization is a fact of life, destined to continue and grow. This is reinforced by a new theory rationalizing the relationship between ownership and internationalization that has taken hold in the wake of an influential article in the *Harvard Business Review* by Robert Reich, a Harvard professor known in the past for his strong advocacy of industrial policy and government intervention in the marketplace. Departing from his former views, Reich now argues that ownership no longer matters in the global economy; what is important is how a corporation's behavior matches U.S. national needs: where its workers are hired and employed, and where its research, development, and engineering are located. U.S. corporations that export jobs and technology are far less valuable to the nation than foreign firms that bring jobs and technology to our shores. "Fifty-five percent of IBM's world employees are now foreign," argued Reich, "and the percentage is growing. . . . All told, more than 20 percent of the output of U.S. firms is now produced by foreign workers on foreign soil." At the same time that American firms increasingly locate their R & D and their engineering and complex fabrication facilities abroad, foreign firms have stepped up their investments here, hiring tens of thousands of American workers and locating labs and factories in the U.S. According to recent figures, foreign firms have invested the same amount of money in R & D in the United States as have U.S. firms. Many of these firms—particularly the Europeans—prefer to locate R & D close to the markets; moreover, they are eager to hire Americans and bring technology to the United States to prove they are good corporate citizens. Reich admits that Japanese firms are less likely than Europeans to hire Americans for high-ranking jobs, and are more likely to keep high-value components and R & D at home, but some, like Sony, are becoming more global in their approach.[5]

In this new world order, American interests no longer seem definable in narrow national terms. Reich argues that "the profitability of 'U.S.' corporations is beside the point" in an era of cross-border investing; and the "standard of living of Americans . . . depends far more on what it is that they *do* than it does on the assets they own." That American citizens control a corporation is no guarantee that the corporation will provide U.S. citizens with high-value jobs, or otherwise act in U.S. interests. Nor should it. Not even the most patriotic executives, says Reich, are "authorized by shareholders to forgo profitable opportunities abroad for the sake of improving the skills and competitiveness of the American workforce."[6]

Part of the problem in analyzing whether ownership matters is defining what constitutes a U.S. corporation. Decisions turning on corporate nationality have become increasingly important in direct proportion to the surge in foreign investment. In some cases, nationality seems confusing, as with the Ohio-based Honda Accord, which represented the leading auto import in Japan in 1988. How should government deal with Yamazaki Mazak, a Japanese machine-tool company with a $110-million screwdriver operation in Florence, Kentucky, when the company asked the Commerce Department to tighten up on Japanese machine-tool imports?[7] Sony, Thomson, Phillips, and other foreign multinationals are busily engaged in trying to get U.S.-government funding on the grounds that at least their affiliates are U.S. companies, creating jobs in the U.S.

In these cases, definition is everything, including criteria based on "incorporation papers, ownership shares, location of facilities and employment, citizenship of management and employees, reinvestment or repatriation of profits."[8] Others consider tax revenues the determining factor. The distinction can translate into millions of dollars, involving the potential denial of "national treatment" to a foreign corporation. A company that is clearly a "foreign company," for example, in certain cases can be denied government grants, access to technology, and tariff relief. Within the current confusing state of affairs, each case demands a unique response, depending on the criteria relevant to that situation. Buy America provisions in government procurement, for example, are based not on foreign ownership, but on content:

products must have at least 50 percent U.S. content. The Defense Department's Foreign Owned, Controlled or Influenced (FOCI) criteria seek to ensure that a corporation's productive capability will be at the government's disposal during national emergencies, and that no unauthorized transfers of technology that could impede national security will occur. Domestic U.S. airlines must abide by a regulation—weakened by the Bush administration—that air carriers be at least 75-percent owned and controlled by U.S. citizens, who must also make up two-thirds of their board of directors and management.

Internationally accepted exemptions to broad definitions of corporate nationality include "national security and economic benefits." These, too, are somewhat murky concepts that can be channeled to anyone's advantage, depending on the skills and clout of a company's advocate. A leading advocate of a relaxed interpretation of Exon-Florio is Elliot Richardson, who heads the Association of International Investors in America. Mindful, perhaps, of all those companies incorporated in the Netherlands Antilles and other tax havens, Richardson argues that "one is operating under the wrong premise even to use the term 'foreign corporation,' because that assumes that the foreign corporation belongs to a country where it is incorporated, whereas it really belongs to the country where most of the shareholders are located. Some multinationals are integrated so well the host country doesn't think of them as 'foreign'; and, indeed, the multinational often doesn't respond to its host country." A more sophisticated approach, advises Richardson, would view multinationals as "centers around which decisions are made, where no country can claim first loyalty from the company, and where a company's first loyalty is to the shareholder. Northern Telecom—a Canadian multinational—resents being called a foreign corporation. The majority of its employees are here. The point is that the entity is accountable, country by country, to its subsidiary in that country."[9]

From the public's point of view, the confusion over definitions renders public policy inert. This means that, even though there are national security and economic benefits issues, they raise more questions than U.S. leaders are willing to answer.[10] United States leaders are also unwilling to tackle the task of what constitutes a U.S. corporation from a political point of view; for example, should U.S. subsidiaries of foreign corporations be considered U.S. corporations and be allowed to intervene in the political process even if they are clearly controlled by foreign parents?[11]

"The legal definition of a company is not the real definition," argued an official from DARPA, "because it does not tell you where the real decisions are made." "The real question is, 'Who is the banker?' "

added Judy Larsen, a computer expert with Dataquest. "The real issue," says Ken Blalick of the Carnegie Corporation, "is one of corporate governance. Who are the shareholders? The institutional investors, the pension funds? We need a definition of the broader stakeholders—such as labor, local government—and until the major trading partners agree on a common definition, discussion is irrelevant."

From a corporate point of view, the new internationalism helps develop markets, adds flexibility to the manufacturing process, and lowers costs. Otis Elevator Co., for example, a division of United Technologies, was able to "save $10 million in design costs" and "cut its development cycle from four years to two" through "global deployment." Its newest, state-of-the-art elevator, the Elevonic 411, was developed by six research centers in five countries. Systems integration was done at the company's home base in Farmington, Connecticut; the motor drives that make the elevators ride smoothly were designed in Japan; the door systems in France; the electronics in Germany; the small-geared components in Spain.[12]

Ideally, the new globalism should protect national security if it works as it's supposed to, rendering ownership irrelevant and discounting public policies aimed at protecting security-related technologies. A foreign-owned firm, for example, that trains Americans and does its weapons manufacturing in the United States does more for U.S. security than an American-owned firm producing weapons and risking nationalization in another nation. For that matter, many argue that there are plenty of laws to take care of emergencies: the U.S. can always nationalize a foreign firm or—as it did with Iraqi firms—confiscate its assets when it presents a security threat.

CAVEAT GLOBALIST: INTERDEPENDENCE
AND NATIONAL SOVEREIGNTY

The new globalism presents a picture of peace and prosperity, where nations take one another's interests to heart and competition takes a back seat to cooperation. Globalism presumes a world in which there is universal acceptance of these values, where nationalism has broken down and given way to a new world order—in short, a world that does not yet exist. The remarkable international coalition forged by President Bush in the Gulf War represented a triumph for globalism in international relations, but sparse evidence exists to show that national interests have become extinct in commercial relationships. Nationalism has in some cases been superseded by regionalism, but the emerging regional coalitions are often, if anything, even more powerful protectionists than their nationalistic predecessors. Watch the rising protectionism in the European Community, or in the less formalized alliances between Japan and the nations of Southeast Asia—or even between Japan and the EC—to see the effects of regional strength on trade and investment issues.

In much the same way that Europe figured out that nation-states would be stronger than the 300-odd duchies of the Holy Roman Empire, regional entities today present a more formidable challenge than do nations. In 1990–91, for example, the GATT almost collapsed over the EC's protection of its farmers—Belgian farmers allied with French farmers proved far more potent than Belgian farmers alone—while the U.S. struggled without much success to introduce investment issues onto the agenda. Though certainly an improvement over prewar trade chaos, the GATT round of trade talks hardly represents the comprehensive world order its founders and supporters intended it to be: today, almost half a century after its inception, the GATT finds itself confronting similar problems in managing the world trading system to those the United Nations treats in global government: it is better than nothing, an excellent framework of goals and objectives, occasionally surprising, and constantly improving, but not nearly enough on which to base the erasure of national borders from the trading map.

Political nationalism also seems alive and well, despite rumors of its early demise. Indeed, some of the most exciting—as well as chilling—developments appear to be occurring around the globe in the name of nationalism. Countries in Eastern Europe long subjugated by the Soviet Union have broken away to return to nation-statehood. Within the Soviet Union, the Baltics and other regions declared their national independence within days of the aborted coup in August 1991, with the Ukraine and other republics following suit before the end of the year. Some of the recent European nationalisms look as frightening as they did in their prewar configurations—Serbs versus Croats, the ugly anti-Semitism that has recurred along with the revival of Eastern European statehood, and the antiforeign violence plaguing a reunited Germany.

There are few signs that citizens are willing to subject their newly acquired national independence to the demands of an idealized global economy. Indeed, the very concept of a global economy is "hidden behind a set of euphemisms . . . 'coordination,' 'harmonization,' or 'negotiation,'" according to economist John M. Culbertson. "But the bottom line is . . . that the nation is not able to apply its own, independent policies in pursuit of its own ideas of what will work, and its own goals and values. Given the enormous range of ideologies and customs among today's nations . . . it seems that actually to bring the homogenization of mankind implied by the 'global economy' would require a miracle."[13]

If we accept the Panglossian premise that joining the global economy means increased reliance on the commercial and political good will of our allies, then Americans should also be aware of some troubling problems that intrude themselves on this scenario, including:

(1) The Reliability of Allies

The new globalism posits that it doesn't matter who owns our assets, because our allies will supply us with products, components, or whatever we need in peace and war; in other words, if we can buy it, we don't have to make it.

Or do we? Our history is replete with the risks of dependence on overseas suppliers, even when they are our most "reliable" allies and trading partners. Two Japanese suppliers, reflecting their nation's concerns with U.S. involvement in the Vietnam War, refused to supply parts for the war effort. Nor has the United States always proved such a reliable ally even to its best friends. Witness a recent case in which the U.S. refused to allow the sale of a Cray supercomputer to an Israeli university, despite a longtime relationship with Israel, the nation's only democratic ally in the Middle East. No reason was given, even though Cray supercomputers are sold worldwide and are commonly used in European and American universities. Brian Silver, the professor from the Technion Institute in Haifa who tried vainly to purchase the computer for his university, visited Washington and walked the corridors of the Pentagon as well as the State and Commerce Departments in a Kafkaesque effort to find out why his request was denied. No one gave him a straight answer, but the "subliminal message" he received was that the Pentagon feared the Israelis would tap into this technology to create more accurate missiles or, worse, a doomsday weapon. Silver's answer to them: How much more accurate would those missiles be than the ones "we used ten years ago to destroy an Iraqi nuclear reactor?" Besides, he added, Technion intended to use the Cray for "unclassified academic research."[14]

The most famous case concerning the "reliability" of allies involved the U.S. refusal to release computer technology to French President Charles de Gaulle in order to prevent him from testing atomic weapons. Rejection of a request from a proud and powerful leader like de Gaulle showed the true meaning of his dependence on the U.S.

Identifying "reliable allies" is highly problematic. Specifically, how do we define our "allies," and how do we know if they will remain U.S. allies two or four or ten years from now? Also, even if our allies are reliable in terms of safeguarding our technologies, what about the companies based within their borders? Toshiba? Imhausen? Kongsberg?

There are also different categories of allies, chosen according to the nation's geopolitical needs at given moments in time. Few wish to be reminded today of how hard the U.S. cultivated Iraq as an ally in the 1980s, when Iraq fought Iran, and Iran was considered the nation's archenemy. During that period, U.S. policymakers turned a blind eye to some particularly heinous Iraqi violations of human rights, despite the best efforts of William Safire, the prescient *New York Times* columnist, who pounded away at Saddam Hussein's genocide against the Kurds, as he did against the German government's laissez-faire attitude toward companies that built chemical plants—"Auschwitz in the sand"—for Libyan dictator Muammar Qaddafi and the Iraqis.

No doubt the German government, in allowing these sales, also considered Iraq an ally. According to information uncovered in February 1991 by Congress, German companies were heavily involved in supplying Saddam with a host of products for his arsenal: over ninety German companies engaged in high-tech sales to Iraq, Libya, Syria, and Iran, with Iraq the biggest winner.[15]

American executives were not exactly choirboys during this period either, nor could federal oversight be characterized as vigorous. In the five years before the Gulf War, the U.S. approved sales of $1.5 billion in advanced technology and products to Iraq, including a sale of $695,000 in advanced data-transmission devices just one day before Iraq invaded Kuwait.[16]

U.S. support of Saddam involved more than the standard diplomatic back-patting: we armed, traded with, and transferred technology to him without looking too closely at his qualities as a long-term ally; Iraq's war with Iran was enough. "When the war's over," warned Senate Majority Leader George Mitchell, Democrat of Maine, "there is one lesson we must never forget: the dictator we help today may turn his weapons on us tomorrow. For ten years, U.S. policy favored Iraq. We can't repeat that kind of mistake."[17]

U.S. policy, driven by the "ownership doesn't matter" theory, also allowed Saddam Hussein to invest in U.S. high-technology assets. Iraq's assets are "believed to be worth about $1 billion," charged Representative Cardiss Collins, Illinois Democrat, chairman of the subcommittee that conducted the investigation. "Blocking Iraq's assets and its acquisition of U.S. technology and equipment must be the highest priority of our domestic enforcement agencies." A worthy goal, but one that came too late to make a difference. Iraq had long since joined the investment party of the 1980s, discovering along with many other governments and companies, that investment was the best of all possible ways to transfer technology: You don't need an export license; protective tariffs and other barriers melt gracefully away; if you're lucky, states will pay you to come; and companies rest easy knowing they have all the rights and privileges of American firms.

Until world conditions change, that is. One of the Iraqi acquisitions, an Ohio machine-tool company with the unlikely name of Matrix Churchill, Inc., was seized one month after Iraq's invasion of Kuwait, when it was revealed to be an Iraqi company whose president, Safa Habobi, was Saddam Hussein's brother-in-law. Carefully concealed behind the façade of a parent company in London, the real owners would never have been identified—thanks to lax U.S. policies regarding disclosure and the absence of a serious screening process for national security risks—were it not for the gimlet eye of the Customs Service. Customs officials identified the company as a security risk and seized its assets, charging that it had been bought by Iraqi leaders to acquire sensitive high-tech equipment in the U.S. For example, Matrix Churchill—with the approval of the Commerce Department—sent equipment ostensibly to be used for building a fiberglass factory for the Iraqi oil industry, but with dual-use capability for missile casings. Evidently, Matrix Churchill represented the latest in a series of Iraqi efforts to acquire military technology and weapons in the U.S. through the vehicle of investment.[18]

Seizing the company after the fact was necessary but came too late. First of all, the technology had most likely long since been transferred to Iraq, perhaps to be used against U.S. troops and their allies. And second, in another twist to defense dependence, U.S. defense contractors who had developed relationships with Iraqi firms found their production cycle disrupted at a critical time by the severing of those relationships. Stanley Aviation, a defense contractor from Aurora, Colorado, found itself in such a quandary. The company had bought a machine tool from Matrix Churchill that malfunctioned in October 1990, well after the Ohio subsidiary had been closed down by the U.S. Treasury Department. This meant that no one was around to repair the machine, nor could Stanley get parts, since the Treasury also blocked the importation of spare parts from the parent company in England. The situation became even more convoluted when it was found that Stanley was making F-14 parts for Grumman, in addition to doing other vital defense work.[19]

There are degrees of "allies," and, of course, at no time did U.S. leaders consider Iraq in the same category as Japan, the NATO countries, or even the nations of Latin America. Yet some troubling issues arise when allies we regard as genuinely "reliable" turn out to be fierce economic competitors. Even if we are chastened by our experience with Iraq and become more discriminating in the future about choosing our trading partners, we know that even the best of friendships with bona-fide allies can turn sour with a sudden shift in world conditions. In this scenario, our continued reliance on the "kindness of strangers" proves most naïve.

Trade tensions between the U.S. and Japan in the late 1980s produced a bitter reaction from the Japanese, many of whom were frustrated by what they considered U.S. domination of their affairs. Underestimating the lingering psychological effects of the Japanese defeat in World War II, U.S. diplomats were late in realizing some of the inherent problems in the U.S.-Japan alliance and found themselves unprepared for some of its ruder manifestations.

One such jolt came with the appearance in Japan, in 1989, of *The Japan That Can Say No,* a book co-authored by two icons of the Japanese establishment, Shintaro Ishihara, a best-selling novelist and member of the Diet, and Akio Morita, the articulate chairman of Sony and the most famous Japanese executive in America. Before Ishihara's part of the book was published two years later in a considerably watered-down American edition—Morita was too embarrassed by the bad publicity to allow his section to appear in English—an unauthorized photocopied translation of the entire original whipped through Washington, D.C. It riveted the attention of everyone lucky enough to get a copy, mostly members of Congress, academics, journalists, and key members of the executive branch. The CIA, DARPA, and electronics industry lobbyists are variously credited for translating and distributing the bootlegged version. What gripped readers was the book's unvarnished view of what Japan could do to the United States through its rapidly growing commercial leverage. Japan could "bring the United States to its knees within six months," wrote Ishihara, simply by withholding semiconductors. Even the sanitized version published in 1991 by Simon & Schuster spent many weeks on *The New York Times'* best-seller list, fascinating American readers with its new and more realistic portrayal of Japan as first and foremost a mercantile state, and its argument that Japan should toughen its trade stance on the grounds that the entire U.S. nuclear arsenal depended on Japanese chips.[20] Although many pointed out that Ishihara represented a right-wing fringe element in Japanese politics, his views still scared Americans, particularly since his following seemed to be growing in size and influence, notably among the young. Unwittingly, Ishihara provided Americans with a healthy dose of skepticism, leading many to question the long-term reliability of an ally that harbored such deep-seated hostility.

Japan's behavior as a member of the Desert Storm coalition reinforced these concerns. Despite the efforts of Prime Minister Kaifu, Japan, which is highly dependent on Middle Eastern oil, only reluctantly supported the war, and only after considerable public debate, then refused to send even hospital ships into the war zone; a call for medical volunteers produced virtually no results. Fear of the resurgence of militarism in Japan offset that nation's desire to play a more substantial role in the community of nations; the result was a public posture of ambivalence. These cross-currents in Japan's internal politics played out against that nation's deeper and more long-standing mercantilism: the view that there was no need to go to war over oil, since it can always be bought on the open market. Most controversial was the effort it took to get Japan to fork over even a small part of its financial commitment to the effort. To put this in context, the initial Japanese commitment—not the actual check—of $4 billion was considerably less than the $6.6 billion Matsushita paid to acquire United Artists. Confronted with rising U.S. resentment over the issue, extensive arm-twisting on the part of the White House, and, finally, the desire to join the victory celebrations, Japan finally paid its full $13-billion share of the cost of the war.[21]

Mutual misunderstanding abounded throughout: Japan, with some justification, never quite understood why Americans were so anxious to risk reviving the militarism that led to World War II, especially since they were required, under the constitution produced during the MacArthur occupation, to remain demilitarized. Americans, for their part, were growing restive with their postwar bargain, in which they retained primary responsibility for protecting Japan's national-security interests, leaving the Japanese free to concentrate on economic issues. Opinion polls after the war reflected the depth of public sentiment. A *Business Week*/Harris Poll conducted one month after the war, for example, revealed that 73 percent of the American public believed that Japan had got away without contributing its fair share to the coalition effort in the Gulf, and 31 percent now regarded Japan as "not very reliable" as an ally.[22]

The following year, the fissures worsened, exacerbated by a trip to Tokyo by President Bush, who was accompanied by a group of American businessmen attempting to persuade Japan to open its markets. In the wake of this trip, America was assailed by leading Japanese politicians, including Yoshio Sakurauchi, Speaker of the lower house of the Diet, who said in January 1992 that Americans were being relegated to the role of "Japan's subcontractors," because they were "lazy," and a third of them couldn't read. Prime Minister Kiichi Miyazawa criticized Americans for losing their work ethic. He chastised

U.S. college graduates for going to Wall Street rather than into manufacturing.

The reliable-ally theory also raises the question: why are our allies trying to reduce their dependence on us at the same time that our dependence on them is rapidly increasing? "Japan's dependence on American defense technology is higher than Europe's dependence," stated a recent Defense Science Board study. "Yet as its no—foreign parts H-2 rocket and earlier go-it-alone FSX designs show, Japan is taking steps to reduce its dependence on American systems and subsystems."[23] The same trend appears to be growing in the European Community. For decades the Europeans "depended on U.S. defense technology in a way that is unacceptable and unthinkable to most Americans," concluded an OTA study. ". . . military dependence enhanced European security . . . and became a means of acquiring technology that could be used to rebuild their industrial bases. . . . Using U.S. technology as a base, they learned to build systems at home, systems that usually cost more and were somewhat less capable than systems available through U.S. foreign military sales programs." In the last analysis, the Europeans accepted a high degree of dependence to become more independent, for, "over time, the Europeans have been able to decrease their dependence on the United States substantially."[24]

"The good guys and the bad guys change over time," concluded the astute Tom Murrin, former deputy secretary of commerce in the Bush administration. "The worst-case scenario concerns military matters. We become dependent for sources of critically needed equipment on foreign sources. It may be in the self-interest of those foreign sources not to be dependable. Alexander Hamilton warned us about that two hundred years ago."

(2) Military Preparedness

Interdependence benefits the national defense in a variety of ways. It can bring down costs and allow DoD to keep an eye on technological developments from abroad. A problem arises, however, when the U.S. can only buy a product overseas: the risk grows greater as the choice of suppliers narrows. One major risk involves military preparedness in emergencies. DoD has to be able to respond quickly to threats to the national security: wars, skirmishes, and information revealing rapid technological advances in the hands of our enemies. Faced with the sale by Toshiba and its Norwegian partners of milling machines to the Soviet Union, DoD was suddenly confronted with the problem of how to deal with suddenly quieter Soviet submarines: how to detect them, and what to do about matching this new threat with appropriate technology of our own. "Techno-military competition is an interactive process of measure and countermeasure," concluded a high-level Pentagon task force. "DoD has to . . . be able to pulse its supplier base and get responses quickly. This base must be tightly linked, and completely accessible. . . . Its action-reaction loop must be tight."[25]

Foreign dependence puts the system at risk by loosening the links between producers and users, and assigning less importance to military needs. This relates to the reliable-ally theory: "Foreign firms are less sensitive to military needs, less responsive to any defense emergencies we may face, and harder to monitor in general." Defense officials also claim that foreign firms can be slow to respond to their timetables, such as "on-time" deliveries that may be critical in wartime. Since these firms often function beyond the reach of U.S. laws, DoD may find it cannot, for example, use the Defense Production Act to get deliveries on time from foreign companies, regardless of pressing needs. Desert Storm turned this fear into reality when DoD officials found themselves forced to rely on the intervention of cooperative foreign embassies who, in turn, were able to "influence" occasionally recalcitrant suppliers in their countries to give the war top priority.

Relying on foreign firms for chips occasionally puts DoD in another security bind: foreign suppliers cannot work on these products without access to sensitive information, which, according to Pentagon officials, is more likely to leak from foreign producers than from domestic companies. One more problem of great concern, the subject of private discussions among U.S. intelligence officials, is the possibility of the insertion of a "mole" (or electronic saboteur) on a chip; this might not be discovered for years, but could do great damage depending on where the chip was located—in a jet engine, a smart missile, or merely information storage. Communications and control systems are also highly dependent on semiconductor technology. In cryptography, for example, collecting intelligence as well as protecting existing communications depends on the availability of the most advanced generation of supercomputers and semiconductor devices. For these among other reasons, the National Security Agency decided to build its own semiconductor plant near its site at Fort Meade, Maryland. Building a semiconductor FAB from scratch today costs more than $500 million, about sixteen times the cost of a decade ago.

Once a foreign producer corners the market, it is normal for him to exercise all the available options the market allows to retain his competitive edge. One of his strategies may involve delaying the delivery of his technology, or not producing it in a timely fashion. The problem of time lags has surfaced in commercial as well as military acquisitions, and is closely linked to the problem of on-time deliveries:

purchasers often can't tell whether they are being denied state-of-the-art products through suppliers' conspiracy or ineptitude, or through the vicissitudes of the market. The result is the same in any case: an interruption in production, or the production of less competitive products. Unfortunately for those "upstream and downstream" in the production process who are dependent on the product, it is often too late to buy back the technology.

A study from the National Defense University by Martin Libicki provided fresh evidence that a major risk of dependence was the threat of reduced access to leading-edge technology. "A Cray computer executive estimated that there was a six month lag in getting chips into American supercomputers; others put it at a year or two. . . . An AMD [Advanced Micro Devices, Inc.] official observed that they were going to get the leading-edge semiconductor manufacturing equipment later than comparable Japanese customers did, and some types they would not get at all. . . . Domestic firms were receiving their DRAM allocations only in dual-inline packages; Japanese customers had greater access to the more advanced surface-mounted versions." The report also raised the question of additional barriers to offshore products: "language and cultural barriers . . . different orientations . . . more benign environments . . . more interested in commercial applications," and less inclination than U.S. firms to "look for military applications of their technology."[26]

Increased awareness of this problem has not solved it; on the contrary, the gap appears to be widening in defense as well as civilian-related technologies. Automakers report one-to-two-year delays in getting state-of-the-art machine tools from Germany. Producers of sophisticated computers and phone equipment have experienced late deliveries of high-speed chips from semiconductor divisions of their Japanese competitors. The gap is widening between the home and foreign introduction of Japanese chips and packaging technologies; chip manufacturers report delays in getting steppers and other related equipment.[27] Japanese companies at home reportedly show preference for Japanese affiliates in the United States; U.S. companies cite NEC's ability to obtain the latest Japanese-made equipment from Nikon Precision, Inc., for its plant in Rosedale, California, while they have been unable to obtain such equipment.

Even if the United States does not officially care where plants are located, other countries recognize the importance of keeping critical technologies within their borders. Xerox, for example, had to locate a factory in Japan in order to get etching equipment for print leads, according to officials at the Defense Department. DoD officials also complained that, when Nikon and Canon sold steppers to American companies, the ones they sold within the United States didn't have the same tables or level of accuracy as the ones they kept in Japan. Without the right tools, companies find it hard to go up the learning curve: one of several reasons the U.S. has remained ahead in software, according to some experts, is that U.S. companies managed to keep their tools at home.

The GAO has found that Japanese companies were withholding critical parts from U.S. manufacturers to give themselves an advantage over their American competitors. These charges have been heatedly denied by the Japanese, but the GAO collected dozens of examples, among them complaints from U.S. makers of flat-panel displays, critical to lap-top computers, and from manufacturers of medical devices and some military equipment, who charged that they couldn't get the latest Japanese parts for advanced versions of their products.[28] Japanese suppliers tell these manufacturers that the parts "are in short supply," according to James Hurd, CEO of Planar Systems Inc. of Portland, Oregon.[29] In the fast-moving world of computer technology, even a delay of a few months can be decisive in the race to be competitive, while declining competitiveness affects military preparedness.

(3) Holding On to Our Technological Edge

Michael Maibach, the government affairs manager for Intel, is one of the most eloquent spokesmen for high tech in the nation's capital. In 1992, he entered the Republican primary to run for the Silicon Valley seat of Representative Tom Campbell, who was campaigning for the Senate. Maibach quickly won the support of a large group of electronics-industry leaders, many of whom shared his views on U.S. competitiveness issues. The year before, holding in his hands a five-and-a-half-pound lap-top computer, he discussed the reasons for recent U.S. technology losses:

"This Compaq computer is the fastest-selling lap-top PC in the country. It uses an Intel 286 chip and a sixteen-bit microprocessor. Everything else is made in Japan. The overall box is made by Citizen Watch. Compaq didn't have the technologies, because they are not in the consumer-electronics business. They don't make ten million watches a year, like Citizen Watch. By making watches, Citizen Watch knows about miniaturization, flat-panel displays, and power management in a small area. The bottom line is: as consumer electronics and computer electronics merge, the U.S. is at a distinct disadvantage, because it no longer has a consumer-electronics business."

Maibach linked the loss of the television industry in the United States to the loss of the lap-top computer. "When you lose the television industry," he explained, "as we did as a result of dumping (from twenty-eight U.S. companies in 1967 to five in 1977 to one, Zenith, in 1987), you lose computers because you lose the technology for making screens."

It's the old story: U.S. companies pioneered the lap-top computer, and Japan perfected and commercialized it. American companies fell asleep for nearly a decade, from 1982, when the first ten-pound lap-top was introduced, to 1991, when they found Toshiba in control of half the world market for lap-tops. Meanwhile, Japanese electronics companies dominated the technologies critical to the manufacture of lap-tops: liquid-crystal-display screens, floppy-disk drives, and memory chips. The reason? The Japanese concentrated on such consumer-electronics products as calculators, camcorders, and watches, enabling them to perfect the miniaturization techniques necessary for producing notebook-sized computers. By 1991, U.S. companies were scrambling to enter joint ventures with Japanese companies. Whatever comes of these ventures, the Japanese now "control the key lap technologies . . . and seem destined to dominate in the laptop era"—all because they understood technology linkage.[30]

The missing links in the technology chain evoke a familiar epigram from *Poor Richard's Almanack*, published in 1785: "For Want of a Nail, the Shoe was lost; for want of a Shoe, the Horse was lost; for want of a Horse, the Rider was lost; being overtaken by the enemy all for want of Care about a Horse, a Shoe, a Nail." As we approach the twenty-first century, the lines become more blurred between fighting wars and trade wars, between economic and military strength, and between commercial and military products.

Today, Poor Richard travels by air in skies that look more threatening each day. Aviation remains one of the few U.S. industries with a trade surplus. "It could be a $400-billion industry in the 1990s," said Mike Kelly, then director of the defense manufacturing office at DARPA and the chief overseer of SEMATECH and HDTV. "But in ten years, if you're going to stay ahead, you are going to need engines, advanced composite materials, and electronics. Japan is ahead in advanced composite materials and electronics. The U.S. is ahead in engines, but worried." Even where the U.S. is clearly ahead, as in supercomputers, the picture can be deceptive: Cray, the leading producer of supercomputers, is totally dependent on imported chips from Japan.

Norman Augustine, the CEO of Martin Marietta, argues that certain technologies require priority for this very reason. "Japan is already at a higher level than we are with sixty-four-megabit chips," he said. "Japan was out building sixty-four-megabit chips while we were doing financial engineering."[31] Martin Marietta is one of the nation's leading defense firms, and one of the most important players in the Gulf War, supplying parts for the Patriot missile and night-vision systems. "There is a lot of foreign content in military systems," he added, "such as missile-guidance systems. All chips are made in Pacific Rim countries; optical components are made in Scotland. There are examples all through electronics. I would worry about that. Nobody does much. DoD has its hands full supplying itself. Government almost always awards to the lowest bidder."

Giving up even one step along the technology chain can lead to permanent losses. "If we decide we're not in the sixteen megabits business," added Mike Kelly, "then it means we're not in on the follow-on, the sixty-four megabits. . . . In HDTV the displays are the critical factor. If we lose that, we'll lose the hardware and the software. You can't focus on islands but on interconnections."

One of Kelly's colleagues at DARPA agreed, adding forcefully that, if U.S. manufacturers of high technology abdicated to overseas producers, they risked their own future: "You lose labs for the next generation; you lose trained workers; and the host country sucks out the knowledge base."

"Intel laid off five hundred people," recalled Maibach, referring to his company's experience with Japanese dumping of D-RAMs. "We lost human capital. They knew the technology. They went off to other jobs. We can't get back into this business, because we lost the people. We could design new chips but not manufacture them, because we don't have the trained work force. We don't want to put new capital into D-RAMs, because we don't know if they'll start dumping again."

For all their public promises about technology accompanying investments abroad, foreign firms often keep their leading-edge technologies at home until they have solidified their competitive edge. Hitachi, Ltd., for example, makes four-megabit computer memories in its Japanese factories, according to Paul Blustein, of the Tokyo bureau of the Washington *Post*, but will not start manufacturing those chips overseas in its U.S. and German plants until it is well along in its sixteen-megabit series.[32] From Hitachi's perspective, there is nothing inherently wrong with this strategy; it is simply good business practice.

The United States has seen its advantage eroded in a number of key areas, often the victim of foreign acquisitions, coordinated strategies by its economic competitors, and current difficulties in raising the capital to commercialize its inventions. U.S. technological slippage was epitomized by the case of Kubota, Japan's largest manufacturer of agricultural machinery. Kubota, which had never produced anything more complicated than a tractor, surprised the U.S. electronics industry when it announced its first advanced minicomputer was ready for export. How did Kubota move up the technological ladder so swiftly from tractors to supercomputers? By investing in several computer companies in Silicon Valley and later in Massachusetts, and then moving the blueprints to Japan. Some of those companies, like MIPS Computer Systems—where Kubota had initiated its high-tech U.S. investment with a 20-percent stake in MIPS' innovative semiconductor technology known as reduced-instruction set computing (or RISC)— had enjoyed support from DARPA. This led inevitably to questions from critics about whether this was an efficient use of taxpayer dollars. Kubota's strategy, perfectly legal, traces the path of technology transfer through investment: the design, chips, and software were all American; the product, and later the profits, Japanese.[33] Just what this exported technology contributed to the further blunting of America's competitive edge is anyone's guess. Many U.S. companies found themselves forced to follow the same path: unable to find home-grown investors with a longer view than the quarterly payoff, they looked to the deep pockets and clearer vision of their offshore competitors.

Why does it matter, as long as we can buy technologies cheaper from abroad? The most troubling consequence of this argument, common among budget-minded policymakers, is that it lulls the nation into a false sense of national security, and takes away the urgency to invest in new technologies. "There's a big difference between being dependent on a foreign company for a component and dependent on a foreign company for an industry—particularly an industry strategically important for our future economic and military security," warned Dr. Richard Van Atta, of the Institute for Defense Analyses.

(4) Connecting Technology and Manufacturing

Part of the problem lies in the dichotomy between manufacturing and innovation in the U.S. You can't have one without the other. Talk of a "defense industrial base" conjures up visions of smokestacks belching pollutants into the air, grimy steel mills, and federal money being poured down a rathole. No one associates the futuristic landscape of a semiconductor FAB or a Los Alamos superconductivity lab with the tedium of an assembly line, a marketing plan, or the nitty-gritty of making products. In the case of semiconductors, for example, much of the critical technology resides in the manufacturing process; then, like the shoe and the horse and the nail, a synergy soon follows: manufacturing technology provides the "underpinning of the ability

of the semiconductor industry to compete in the world market . . .
[then] provides the revenues for firms to support research and
development."[34]

In other words, technology develops best with a profitable commercial base: the higher the profits, the more money can be spent on
R & D, which in turn can lead to even more lucrative products.
Conversely, without a commercial base, technologies risk low productivity, low demand, and loss of world market share and eventually
domestic market share. Scholars John Zysman and Stephen S. Cohen
argued and documented this point eloquently in *Manufacturing Matters*; so did another influential work, *Made in America*, by a team of
scholars from M.I.T.[35] Although many in the U.S. recognized this
connection years ago, the Japanese acted on it, expending a growing
percentage of their semiconductor profits on research and development
at the same time they made sure that sales would increase to support
that research. The results for the U.S. are now history: the U.S. semiconductor industry steadily lost market share, military dependence
increased, and commercial dependencies increased as well.

For anyone who missed the lesson of technology and manufacturing, the point was driven home in December 1991, with the announcement that U.S. firms had leapfrogged their Japanese competitors in
HDTV by showing that digital television was feasible, as against ana-
log waves. Once again, Americans were on the cutting edge, but would
not be there to reap the profits since the nation had lost its television
industry over a decade before. Without a manufacturing base to support innovation, the best the inventors could hope for was royalty and
license payments from those companies that still produced television
sets.

(5) Retaining Engineering Know-how

The Kubota case debunked the view of those who scoff at the foreign
challenge, arguing that in wartime the U.S. can always nationalize its
foreign assets.

"If the Iraqis want to build a tank plant, it would be okay because
we can always nationalize it; that's the argument," said Norman Augustine. "My caveat is that whatever is foreign-owned ought to have
a self-sustaining capacity. If the manufacturing is here and the engineering in Japan, every two and a half years—the life cycle of semiconductors—you fall a generation behind. We need to have a plan. It
could be denying or preventing foreign ownership. Or it could mean
back-up plans for military hardware. This means accessing domestic

sources and the capability for manufacturing military hardware. Foreign ownership is okay for trucks and tanks. Where technology is changing fast, you need something different."

Many security specialists agree that the power to nationalize provides little protection if the engineering know-how remains abroad. Chuck Kimzey, director of the now-defunct Defense Manufacturing Board, raised the example of the Italian-owned Baretta plant:

"Baretta, which manufactures nine-millimeter handguns, was required to build the plant here [in La Plata, Maryland]. The general intuitive feel is that, if you've got the production capability here, then we can appropriate. The question is, even if we appropriated the physical plant, where would we get the know-how to run it? It is the engineering know-how that is the real issue. Where does the engineering expertise reside? How do you make changes—to double or triple or quadruple production, to integrate American or other machine tools into a manufacturing system that we didn't design? The issue is not simply where the production facility is; it's where the engineering is."

(6) The Importance of an American Component:
Dependence vs. Interdependence

A nation does not have to make 100 percent of a product; it can make as little as 10 percent of a product, as long as it retains the technology and the capacity to make that product in times of crisis. Sometimes these products are not profitable but are critical to the existence of other industries. Producers claim, for example, that there is no money in D-RAMs, but defense experts argue that the nation's economic and military security depend on them. To be truly interdependent, the nation must invest in whatever technologies it needs to keep its competitive edge.

But working out the details of interdependence stumps the experts. How much market share does an industry need to remain in business? What kinds of volume, market share, and profit margins are necessary for an industry to keep its technological lead and at the same time attract capital?

"We'll always have dependencies," said Mike Kelly. "We've got to change this to interdependency." To accomplish that, the U.S. must make sure it retains the leverage to assure the flow of needed military equipment and supplies. This means the nation should attempt to diversify its dependencies so that others are as dependent on the U.S. for components as the U.S. is becoming on its trading partners. "If workstations are the industry of the future," Kelly continued, "then we need D-RAMs. It's okay if I buy D-RAMs from someone, as long as that person needs me for microprocessors."

That kind of interdependence hasn't occurred; in fact, quite the reverse. Once the world's leader in high technology, the U.S. today imports 97 percent of the silicon wafers needed for microelectronic circuits, used in advanced military hardware. Also imported: 97 percent of ceramic substrates, 95 percent of bonding wire, 80 percent of scanning electronic microscopes. One company, Kyocera, dominates the manufacture of ceramic substrates, which are used for certain defense and space applications, and that company is based in Japan.

In the case of D-RAMs, the U.S. has deepened its dependence on Japanese producers without any effort to offset that dependence with other products. Once dominated by U.S. producers, by 1986 the leading Japanese electronics manufacturers controlled 80 percent of the world D-RAM market and had surpassed all U.S. producers except IBM in technology. Many scholars and journalists have analyzed the reasons for this loss—predatory and aggressive pricing on the part of the Japanese manufacturers, U.S. slippage, inconsistent government policies, the financial and distributory advantages of Japanese cartelization and vertical integration[36]—but the most salient point is that it happened, and without any effective action on the part of the U.S. There were plenty of negotiations and policies, but, lacking as they were in both timeliness and consistency, they were doomed to cancel one another out.

Without comprehensive policies and effective government leadership, industry fell back on its own resources and decided to take matters into its own hands. Under the leadership of Sanford Kane of IBM, seven semiconductor producers organized a consortium, U.S. Memories, which sought to offset the industry's growing dependence by encouraging long-term investment by U.S. computer companies in U.S. D-RAM manufacturers. Immediately following the organization of U.S. Memories, D-RAM prices suddenly dropped—coincidentally?—and a D-RAM glut appeared on the world market; the flooded market produced a sharp drop in the enthusiasm of cost-conscious but shortsighted U.S. companies for investing in their future independence. Computer makers in the consortium, like Hewlett-Packard and Apple, found cheap D-RAMs from the Far East too hard to resist, and U.S. Memories too hard to support; also, it was alleged that representatives from Japanese companies were privately hinting to their U.S. customers that chips would become harder to get if competition from U.S. Memories became a reality. Not surprisingly, U.S. Memories folded in early 1990. The obituary notices were followed within days by an announcement from Japan's six largest D-RAM producers (who are also Japan's largest computer-makers) that they were cutting production and raising prices. Another coincidence? At the postmortem of the seven original companies, only IBM and DEC (Digital Equipment Corp.) were willing to lend their support and invest in U.S. Memories to preserve an American presence in a vital industry even if it meant paying more in the short run to help build up U.S. capability.

"It's true that there's no money in D-RAMs, but you're stuck," remarked Mike Kelly, for the U.S. must retain an independent capability in that vital technology if it wishes to remain a successful player in the twenty-first century. "The loss of superconductivity [by itself] is not bad," added Kelly; "it's the loss of the technology that gets you to superconductivity. You have to strike a balance."

Not in the eyes of the government, however. Serious discussion about rising dependence takes place all the time within agencies like Defense and Commerce, but the follow-up is nil. At the White House in the 1980s there was virtually no sense of which sectors of the U.S. economy were critical to national security—such as energy resources, banking assets, and land—for fear that national security would be used as an excuse for protectionism—a not totally unfounded concern.

What about U.S. dependence on foreign banks? Lost in the wake of the S-&-L crisis and the general malaise that accompanied it is the question of increasing foreign ownership of banking assets and what that means to the national security. Should there be a U.S. component in banking? Not according to U.S. policy, where the banking industry has suffered from the same philosophical myopia about foreign acquisitions that fed the deregulation that brought it to its present ruinous state.

Does this matter? Will U.S. citizens and U.S. companies get the same treatment from the Bank of Tokyo or Deutsche Bank when it comes to business loans or home mortgages that they do from Citicorp or the bank down the street? Perhaps better, judging from the rise in lending that accompanied these purchases, but a trend line as steep as this one raises some vital questions. First of all, will the banks follow the U.S. Memories pattern? When foreign banks monopolize the market, will interest rates shoot up, loans go down, and service decline? Perhaps even more important is the relationship between banking and economic success, a lesson learned from observing the rise of the Japanese banks as the centerpiece of the *keiretsu*. How can the U.S. continue to compete effectively with these fast-paced changes in the global banking environment? The failure to recognize the necessity for an American dimension in banking can only accelerate the dependency that has become characteristic of this era of neglect.

"THEY ARE NOT US": ANOTHER LOOK AT COMPARATIVE ADVANTAGE

The surge of foreign investment in the U.S. has occurred in some measure because of the nation's recent inability to invest in itself. This represents a marked departure from past practice, which abounds with success stories of government investment in new and critical technologies. In the 1930s, airmail put the airline business aloft; in the 1950s, 75 percent of all computers were purchased by the government; in the 1960s, 70 percent of all chips went into military equipment. Industry after industry can point to initial boosts from government that put them on the map. And, conversely, took them off the map—the case with the airlines, the computer, and the chip industries. Because it is the nation's largest purchaser, government's investment policies can put an industry in orbit or destroy it through inattention, lax trade policies, and noncompetitive buying practices. Misdirected or not, government power is considerable when it comes to industrial health.

The 1980s era of laissez-faire ignored past successes and viewed government in a new light, heavily influenced by the doctrine of "comparative advantage." Simply put, this theory spoke to visions of an international economy, in which nations did what they did best, according to their natural advantages. If the Middle East was rich in oil reserves and Japan was not, Saudi Arabia could focus on producing oil while Japan made VCRs and other products more in keeping with its own advantages—a hardworking, productive, and well-educated labor force.

Influenced by this perspective, U.S. policymakers were content to abdicate a certain degree of self-sufficiency in order to promote the new world order, a vision they had promoted from the heady days of the postwar period to the present. If other countries were beating us in auto production, steel, computer chips, and machine tools, so be it; this just meant that we would have to search harder for products more suited to our own natural advantages. A dose of self-flagellation accompanied this view, much of it deserved. "Corpocracy" became the watchword of the late 1980s: U.S. corporations were caricatures of bloated bureaucracies, overpaid and shortsighted executives, and fickle stockholders who deserted companies in a flash at the slightest hint that dividends might be cut for R & D. Surely, these firms neither needed nor merited government help in the form of handouts or protection against foreign competition.

The doctrine of comparative advantage worked well in simpler times, when countries with forests cornered the lumber industry; those with oceans, fishing; and so on. Holding to this view obscures how this theory works today, as other governments adopt the former U.S. model and determine their own comparative advantages. Japan is a prime example: this nation—with almost no natural resources, vulnerable geographically to a host of predators, and highly dependent on other countries for energy—has, through a mix of public and private strategies, established itself as the premier manufacturer of automobiles as well as many other high-value technologies. Similarly, the Europeans concentrated on machine tools, commercial aircraft, and other technologies that had little to do with either their natural or comparative advantages, but a lot to do with their future industrial strength.

In other words, governments, not the invisible hand, made the difference in the fast-paced international marketplace in the capitalist world; nations that ignored that global fact of life did so at their own peril. Ahead of their time in recognizing that development in the early 1980s, Laura Tyson and John Zysman argued that "comparative advantage is not static but dynamic, and government policies that influence the comparative advantage of particular firms in particular sectors can alter the pattern [of] advantage over time." In the case of the U.S., the reverse occurs: "policies work to reduce our economic well-being over time," thanks to "market distortions induced by the policies of a foreign government" and ignored by our own. Using the semiconductor and automobile industries, the authors traced Japan's winning strategy in gaining a "long-term competitive advantage" over U.S. and European competitors long before it ever became a political issue. In fact, by the time it became a political issue, it was too late to reverse the trend. "In the presence of such distortions . . . [which] may impose unacceptable adjustment costs on the U.S. economy . . . the presumption that markets automatically work well is called into question. . . ."[37]

Tyson argued several years later for a U.S. strategic investment policy on the grounds that "They [foreign corporations] are not us." Particularly when it comes to legitimate national-security concerns, government should resort to more stringent remedies to block takeovers and prevent the concentration of suppliers. In a critique aimed at debunking Robert Reich's "Who Is Us?" thesis, Tyson argues that ownership of U.S. assets *should* matter, on the grounds that "We are us"—that, despite "decades of substantial foreign direct investment by

U.S. multinationals, the competitiveness of the U.S. economy remains tightly linked to the competitiveness of U.S. companies." U.S. companies still locate most of their operations within the United States; U.S. parents account for "78 percent of total assets, 70 percent of total sales, and 74 percent of the total employment of U.S. multinationals."

In other words, despite the tales of U.S. *maquiladoras* shipping jobs across the Mexican border, hemorrhaging globalism, and the "Company A and Company B" thesis, the data show something quite different when they track real companies, not hypothetical examples. In fact, like foreign multinationals, U.S. firms locate their higher-paying, higher-end jobs at home, as well as the bulk of their R-&-D budgets. "The average share of R & D activity undertaken by global companies outside their home countries is quite small. For Japanese companies it is negligible. . . . The leadership of American companies remains overwhelmingly American." Despite globalization, then, a "disproportionate share of U.S. multinationals, especially their high-wage, high-productivity, research-intensive activity, remains in the United States."[38]

When foreign firms have behaved "most like us," or acted in U.S. interests by substituting the more traditional "screwdriver" operations for plants that bring jobs and technology, Tyson argues, this has occurred only because U.S. policy has "encouraged them to do so," often through methods too subtle to document. Trade frictions, for example, brought many firms to the U.S.—firms that otherwise would have preferred to stay home and export their products—to ensure their future access to the nation's rich markets. The Europeans have always been more strategic on this issue. When Nissan located in France, for example, the host country demanded and got 80 percent local content. Even the British, the most laissez-faire-minded of the Europeans, "encourage" a variety of locational, content, and technology factors when foreign investors locate in their country. Recently, the Europeans have become more specific in their demands, deciding to forgo ownership in exchange for technology in the production of integrated circuits: They will "define origin . . . by the country where the 'process of diffusion' takes place." This new policy "encouraged" Japanese and American producers to establish semiconductor-fabrication plants in Europe.[39]

WHO IS IN CHARGE?

The criteria for the new globalism that regard companies in terms of the jobs, technology, and engineering they bring to the U.S., rather than nationality, make sense up to a point. That point fades, however, with the realization that no one is there to monitor whether foreign companies are living up to those expectations (or U.S. companies either, for that matter).

"Who is us?" is irrelevant without knowing "Who is in charge?" In the U.S., that question often remains unanswered, given the nation's fragmented, often *ad hoc*, approach to managing trade and investment problems. With the rapid turnover of trade officials, whose tenure in office averages less than two years, there is virtually no one with a sufficient grasp of history to preserve past gains or to prevent future losses. No wonder the U.S., unprotected by consistent leadership, so often finds itself ignored with impunity in the world trading system.

If government were powerful enough to intervene on questions as detailed as whether jobs, technology, or know-how were sited domestically, then perhaps ownership would not be important enough to make a difference, and more global criteria could be applied. At this point, at least in the United States, government agencies do not gather sufficient information to make policy on this issue, nor do they have the political will to ask questions or require answers. Moreover, the public sector all too often finds itself no match for the giant multinational corporations, whose budgets and power exceed those of most nations. The result, then, is that, with no one in charge, the nation has abdicated its industrial and technological future to the forces of the marketplace—a marketplace where other industrialized nations, well schooled in the lessons of comparative advantage, are very much in charge of their own destinies.

The U.S. must update its view of globalism to include the concept of a greater degree of independence within an interdependent world. The nation needs a new theory that progresses from *comparative* to *competitive* advantage, and that theory must cover "not only trade, but foreign investment," wrote Michael Porter, one of the country's leading thinkers in this field. "What a new theory must explain is why a nation provides a favorable *home base* for companies that compete internationally. The home base is the nation in which the essential competitive advantages of the enterprise are created and sustained. It is where a company's strategy is set, where the core product and process technology is created and maintained, and where the most productive jobs and most advanced skills are located. The presence of the home base in a nation has the greatest positive influence on other linked domestic industries and leads to other benefits in the nation's economy." What is clear is that other nations provide a "home base" more conducive to competitiveness than the U.S.[40]

From their home base, nations compete furiously for competitive advantage in high-profit, strategic technologies. The clashes that result from "technoglobalism" are worse than trade friction, because they involve rivalries among multinationals as well as rivalries among nations and regions whose market systems greatly influence their ability to compete. Japan, for example, does not want to give up the set of domestic laws, policies, and regulations that led to its worldwide successes in lap-top computers, D-RAMs, and HDTV. The EC and the U.S. chafe at their inability to penetrate that system or compete with different sets of rules. Even though Canada and the U.S. have joined together in a free-trade zone, the disequilibrium between their differing health-insurance systems and agricultural subsidies still gives them problems.[41]

TRUST BUT SOLIDIFY: FACING GLOBAL REALITIES

"We have no eternal allies and we have no perpetual enemies. Our interests are eternal and perpetual, and these interests it is our duty to perform," advised Henry John Temple, Viscount Palmerston, foreign secretary of England, in 1848. Paraphrased repeatedly over the years as "Nations have no friends, only interests," and attributed to a number of world leaders, most prominently Charles de Gaulle, Palmerston's advice has held up over the years as a rationale for coldhearted realpolitik.[42]

The U.S. needs a new vision, a "realeconomik" that addresses its need to regain economic ground; otherwise, its role as a world leader will surely diminish over time. Until Iraq, most Americans were unaware that for the last decade their leaders had sacrificed energy self-sufficiency in order to purchase cheaper foreign oil. Talk of energy exploration and conservation soon followed the realization that interdependence didn't necessarily work in the mercurial environment of the Middle East.

It is true, of course, that no nation is an island, entirely self-sufficient and able to determine its own national strategies without regard to its neighbors, its allies, and the community of nations. However, some nations are less dependent and more secure than others, the degree largely determined by the health of their industrial base and technological advancement. It is the nature of interdependence that makes the difference, particularly when one side is more dependent on the other. The United States and Latin America, for example, are highly interdependent, yet the United States has far more power within that relationship. When Latin America wants to exert its influence, it often does so through negative means—angry demonstrations, defaulting on debts—often the only recourse of the powerless. Similarly, the colonies and Great Britain were highly interdependent; yet, as soon as they could, the colonies broke away from the shackles of the mother country. The moral is that in an interdependent world, there are better and worse sides on which to place the destiny of a nation.

CHAPTER VII

Gulf Lessons

FROM SMART BOMBS TO SMART POLICIES

If we can make the best smart bomb, can't we make the best VCR?
> —Senate Majority Leader George Mitchell

Because of the war there is much more of an appreciation of defense dependence.
> —Senator Jeff Bingaman

ARMS AND VCRS

The nation had the right idea in the eighteenth century and for almost two hundred years afterward: to build up the nation's military and economic independence and to link the two. Alexander Hamilton understood firsthand the danger of excessive reliance on foreign suppliers.[1] Hamilton's philosophy prevailed throughout the nineteenth and most of the twentieth century until the mid-1960s, when the government abandoned past policies in favor of a more global, less sovereign approach. As a result, "U.S. high-technology industrial leadership has diminished greatly, and . . . reliance on foreign sources for defense-related materials, components, subsystems, and production technologies is increasing," concluded defense analyst Jacques Gansler, in a high-level report prepared for DARPA.[2]

A number of policies and constraints in the U.S. and abroad combined to produce this new dependence: cost factors, increased zeal on the part of U.S. leaders for "free trade or arms cooperation with Allies [that] has led to trade policies, offset arrangements, transfers of U.S. technology and other actions that ultimately harm U.S. industry and increase foreign penetration of U.S. markets."[3]

The issue of America's growing dependence on foreign technology emerged during the Gulf War, despite a swift, relatively bloodless (for the United States) victory and the dazzling performance of the U.S. military (against a third-rate power). Why worry? many asked. The Sidewinders worked fine, most of the Iraqi Scuds were intercepted, and there was no evident interruption of supply lines to impair operational readiness either on the ground or in the air. Besides, things have changed since the War of Independence; military self-sufficiency is no longer as necessary as it was when the government put Eli Whitney in business. In other words, why quibble with success?

But the Gulf War underscored America's growing technological dependence on overseas sources. "Because of the war," noted Senator Bingaman, "there is much more of an appreciation of defense dependence." The technological virtuosity that vanquished Iraq and impressed the world owed much of its success to the products of foreign companies: almost all the optical glass used in reconnaissance satellites came from Germany, gallium-arsenide chips used in radar and satellite receivers from Japan, and five parts of the Abrams tank, including the optics in the gunner's sight and an ingredient in the seal, were made by foreign companies.[4] Many other critical weapons systems also owed their production to components from abroad or from foreign companies located in the United States, including the F-16, the F/A-18, sonobuoys, and Sidewinder missiles.[5]

At the request of Senator Bingaman, the GAO analyzed two weapons systems used in the Gulf War and assessed their foreign dependencies. In the report, issued one month before the war ended, the GAO found that both systems had been studied five years before by the Joint Logistics Command (JLC) at the Pentagon and were found *at that time* to have significant foreign dependencies. It was no surprise to the GAO to find that nothing had been done in the interim, and that the same dependencies existed today, despite the JLC's conclusion that dependency was a function of production capacity—factors that could be overcome with "time and money"—not lack of technological capability. Components in a weapons system were found to be "foreign-dependent" if the loss of some or all foreign sources would most likely result in domestic demand exceeding domestic production capacity.[6]

As the discussions of foreign dependence unfolded, so did more examples. Allied officers had to send to Paris and Tokyo to get special battery packs to "power their command and control computers"; Teledyne executives enlisted the cooperation of French diplomats to fill a rush order for "one of the most critical items of Desert Storm," a transponder that beamed electronic signals necessary for differentiating between enemies and allies; and U.S. government officials sought help from the Japanese embassy to fill shortages for critical parts for display terminals used to analyze intelligence data. In addition, tactical cockpit displays came from the United Kingdom, and video panels as well as vital components for search-and-rescue radios and navigation systems came from Japan, according to a private briefing report from the Commerce Department in April 1991.[7]

Although many of the weapons were made in the U.S., an increasing number of parts were manufactured abroad, such as semiconductors and computer equipment from Japan, Southeast Asia, and France, and avionics from Great Britain. Budget pressures discouraged the Pentagon from maintaining the kind of stockpiles necessary in wartime, and for the first time in its history the U.S. found its military readiness compromised by serious shortages. "We were sweating bullets," a Bush-administration official told Stuart Auerbach of the Washington *Post*, "and the military was sweating bullets, too." Defense procurement officials also admitted they often had no idea where parts for U.S. weapons came from, since there were no data bases tracking either the sale of subcontractors or the origin of critical components. Auerbach also wrote of a luncheon interview with Taizo Watanabe, a spokesman for the Japanese Foreign Ministry, who admitted that the cooperation his country provided ran contrary to the "strong strain of pacificism in Japanese society," but "verified that we are a very reliable source" for the U.S. defense industry.[8]

The Gulf War vindicated the Defense Science Board, the GAO, the Congress's Office of Technology Assessment, the Pentagon, the Commerce Department, and several congressional committees that had warned that the military faced increasing technological vulnerability. This time, the U.S. was fortunate that its allies shared its security concerns; other scenarios might not produce the same results.

Among the perplexing questions that emerged from the Gulf War was why American industry could succeed so well with Patriot missiles and fail so dismally in the manufacture of VCRs, ovens, and commercial products. "The Raytheon Corporation . . . which built the Patriot anti-missile system that destroyed the Iraqi Scuds, has had a tough time in the consumer marketplace with its Caloric stoves and Speed Queen washing machines," wrote Andrew Pollack in *The New York Times*. "If we can make the best smart bomb, can't we make the best VCR?" asked Senate Majority Leader Mitchell in his response to the president's State of the Union message in January 1991.[9]

The public airing of the connection between VCRs and missiles indicated a growing public awareness of the importance of commercialization to national security. For years, U.S. policy intentionally held to a narrow definition of national security, and the mandate was perfectly clear: to support the development of military products. All talk of commercial spin-offs, spin-ons (when commercial technologies benefit the military), dual-use technologies, and the health of consumer electronics was ignored in light of the urgency to develop the military; commercialization was a luxury, not a goal, and certainly not a goal of the Defense Department. So, while Japan and the European Community were developing VCRs, wide-bodied aircraft, and other products that flourish in peace and war, the U.S. concentrated only on military technology, funneling an increasing percentage of its research-and-development funds through DoD into military production. These policies further blunted U.S. competitiveness in two ways: they drew valuable capital and scientists away from consumer electronics and other commercial technologies, and they produced a decade of deficits to pay for the military build-up that ultimately won the Gulf War.

After the war, industry leaders indicated their growing awareness that America was being outclassed by Japanese and European competitors in key technologies—robotics, silicon manufacture, liquid-crystal displays, structural ceramics, and memory chips. One problem was misdirected research funds: the U.S. spent two-thirds of its research money on defense, but only .2 percent on high technology with commercial applications. Japan, on the other hand, spent 5 percent of government research funds on nonmilitary products, and Germany spends as much as 15 percent.[10]

Military spending and patterns of procurement and acquisition often inhibited the progress of U.S. industry, and led to another form of dependence: businesses that are so encumbered by DoD restrictions that they cannot branch out into more commercially viable areas. Manufacturers complained, for example, that Pentagon restrictions on composite materials prevented them from developing materials as advanced as those now found in golf clubs and tennis racquets. Many of the specifications were developed a decade before those products came on line, in contrast to other countries that tend to standardize their products faster. In short, military specifications—called MIL-SPECS—often strangled companies that might otherwise have expanded into commercial markets.

The most ironic outcome of the Gulf War was the realization that the prowess of the Patriot and Tomahawk missiles was based on technology that was in some cases more than a decade old, and less advanced than the oldest home computers. The computer chips in the Tomahawk and Patriot missile systems, as well as those in sensors on helicopters, were manufactured by Intel, which stopped making chips for the Patriot in 1985. Without discrediting the U.S. role in the Gulf victory, many experts commented privately that Iraq's equipment was

even more outmoded than our own, despite all the arms sales from
Germany, the U.S., France, and the Soviet Union. The United States
was fortunate in its choice of an enemy. Had Iraq been a worthier
opponent from a technological point of view, the war might have
proved far more difficult to win.

As impressive as it looked, the obsolescence of U.S. weaponry
was apparent to the experts, who spoke of "museum pieces" and
"1970s technology" as they identified new opportunities for increased
defense spending. What looked dazzling on television clips, they
pointed out, was full of glaring shortcomings: the failure to track all
of the Scud missiles, laser bombs that were "useless on cloudy days,"
and the failure at times to distinguish friendly from unfriendly fire.[11]
The war was a useful trial run for the nation's arsenal, leading defense
officials to advocate increased funding for even more advanced weapons—weapons that would save lives as well as money by relying more
heavily on the technologies of automation and robotics.

Unfortunately, the other lesson of Desert Storm—the need to
close the gap between military and consumer products—went largely
unheeded, for political reasons. Even though the Pentagon's increased
dependence on the commercial marketplace for advanced technologies
proved that VCRs and Patriot missiles had a lot in common, and even
though there were plenty of outside experts willing to go on record
to drive that point home, the political obstacles proved almost as
formidable as the Scuds. Talk of "industrial strategies" and "technology strategy" was heard in the inner circles of government but rarely
brought out in the open, for fear that the talkers would be tarnished
by the notorious I-phrase "industrial policy." In public, defense analysts stuck to strategies that were narrowly defined in terms of weapons
systems, while those in the defense establishment who supported dual-
use technologies like flat-panel displays and semiconductors usually
kept their views to themselves.

Continued adherence to separating military and commercial technologies perpetuates the Pentagon's investment in weapons systems at
the expense of commercial products. Some critics argue that this policy
doesn't even meet military needs, since it leads the Pentagon to favor
proven technologies over newer, more experimental ones that might
be more powerful on the battlefield as well as in the marketplace.
Weapons take years to develop, by which time the technologies on
which they were based may be obsolete. This means that companies
in the weapons business are tied to the Pentagon and stuck with technologies that have long been obsolete in the nonmilitary marketplace.
These businesses—especially electronics manufacturers—must then
watch their overseas competitors forge ahead of them in design, market

share, and profits. Imagine their frustration when they see the Pentagon first seeking out their foreign competitors to buy their most advanced chips, then forced into the position of negotiating with foreign embassies to meet battlefield needs.

"DoD's challenge is to break the association between defense contracting and the inability to compete in commercial markets," wrote defense scholar Martin Libicki. "The Japanese are more successful in the long run because they gear their products to commercial applications. Consider shape-memory metals. An American corporation, Raychem, leads in the technology selling about $30 million worth of couplings and fittings to military users. Japan's leader, Furukawa Electric, is looking for applications in louvers, rice steamers, fishing-lines and dentistry. Their market may be smaller now, but whose path offers the most certain route to long-run technological superiority?"[12]

Linked to this challenge is the debate over spending priorities: how to match military spending with social spending, national security with economic security. "A secure nation must have a well-housed, well-fed, well-educated people, and it must have a productive economy and a strong infrastructure," said Senator Mark Hatfield, Republican of Oregon. "America today is truly vulnerable on many of those fronts, because we have diverted our resources over the years to create this major outstanding military organization."[13]

The Gulf War also forced Americans to take a good hard look at how the linkage between VCRs and Patriot missiles weakened their global competitiveness. The two most important powers besides the United States, Germany and Japan, tried hard to maintain their role as trading states, with Japan trying especially hard to distance itself from Desert Storm. These nations would continue to develop their prospering civilian industries, while the U.S. assumed leadership for producing the weapons, most of the soldiers, and a large chunk of the funds that went toward safeguarding a world in which oil supplies flowed freely and commercial development could flourish. Following the war, an increasing number of Americans expressed their uneasiness with this new configuration of political and economic power, which revealed a future of awesome responsibilities, deepening dependencies, and continuing economic losses in the world market.

The aftermath of Desert Storm saw serious trade disputes arise between the U.S. and Japan, unparalleled in the post–World War II period. These were exacerbated by Japan's ambivalence toward helping to pay for the war, and also by an unfortunate incident in Tokyo in which Japanese officials threatened to arrest U.S.-government employees at a trade fair if they persisted in their refusal to remove six bags of rice from the display table (placed there to symbolize Japan's refusal to import our rice). It was Japan doing business as usual, but this time the television cameras were running, and the ensuing worldwide publicity cost them dearly. The following month, MITI officials instructed the private and public sectors to nurture the fraying U.S.-Japan relationship.

As unprecedented as the public incident was a long-overdue wake-up call from U.S. business. The conservative, traditionally free-trade National Association of Manufacturers called on the president to conduct a comprehensive re-examination of the nation's relationship with Japan. The NAM had finally acknowledged that the trade deficit wasn't so "intractable" (Japan's word) after all, and, though it was not the group's intention to blame Japan for U.S. economic problems, there was substantial agreement that the "fundamental policy assumptions seem shaky and may be wrong and certainly need to be re-examined."[14] Hard on the heels of the NAM came Lee Iacocca's call for more government restrictions on Japanese autos; Japanese officials quickly responded by pointing out how dependent Chrysler had become on imported parts from Japan.

On the plus side, the crisis in the Persian Gulf created a fresh awareness of America's strong value system and its unique leadership role in the world community. To continue in that role, the U.S. must also be able to act decisively, as President Bush did in mobilizing world opinion and resources against Saddam Hussein's invasion of Kuwait. U.S. troops counted themselves fortunate to be backed by a technological infrastructure—"museum pieces" and all—that supported the nation's military strength; this infrastructure, in turn, owed its existence to the military build-up of the 1980s, and in some cases to technology that was more than a decade old. Will the nation retain its leadership position if it neglects to nurture its technological lead in the world economy?

SMART POLICIES

Why has America allowed other nations to blunt its competitive edge? Perhaps it is because America has never lost its sovereignty in the twentieth century, unlike its more protectionist major trading partners—the French, the Japanese, and the Germans. Coincidentally, the British, who managed never to lose their sovereignty during the two world wars, also preceded the United States in their policies of laissez-faire capitalism and government complacency toward critical industries. The results of their experience should give U.S. leaders pause: the familiar pattern of lost technological strength—the British invented penicillin and radar, but the Americans commercialized them—an eroded manufacturing base, the loss of empire, and a reduced standard of living.

In other words, if we have smart bombs, we can have smart policies. And just as those bombs found their way with precision to such finite targets as elevator shafts, policies can direct their energies from the trivial to the critical. The key is to continue to think globally, but to act realistically. This means reviving a notion of the national interest that incorporates both global concerns and the preservation of U.S. sovereignty. Smart policies of the future would be sure to:

(1) Differentiate Between Dependence and Vulnerability

Growing interdependence among nations represents a positive development, making the world a better place than it was in the 1930s. The hope is that resources will be spread around with more equity, poor nations can lift their standard of living, and world trade will expand, to the benefit of all. A degree of dependence is acceptable, and even desirable; after all, families can work well in a framework of mutual emotional and economic dependence, and even nations can accept a certain amount of dependence on one another. At a certain point, however, dependence can become a matter of deep public concern when one of the parties is rendered *vulnerable*; in the case of nations, that means vulnerable to military attack, economic hardship, or political and social instability.

Vulnerability also can involve sacrificing sovereignty for the sake of interest rates, product development, and standard of living; the loss of control in these areas, though less drastic than wars and social instability, can still be discomfiting. If ignored, it can lead to more serious stages of dependency, especially when increasing interdependence has not evolved to right the balance. If the U.S., for example, gave up all self-sufficiency in supercomputers, and if that loss were not offset by a matching technological dependency on the part of Japan, the equation would become unbalanced, to the detriment of the U.S.

Judging from the standard indicators, the United States appears to be falling into a state of deepening vulnerability—losing by degrees a measure of control over interest rates, its standard of living, and product development. Our increasing dependence on foreign suppliers and foreign investors makes us look more and more like the classic model of a developing nation as defined in the body of scholarship on dependency. "Most would agree," wrote Vincent A. Mahler, "that an LDC [less developed country] would be considered externally dependent to the extent that some or all of the following are true":

- "... *devote[s] considerable resources to the servicing of foreign debts.*" External or foreign debt has always been a leading indicator of dependency status, and the U.S. has joined the company of LDCs in this category. The world's leading creditor nation as recently as 1982, the U.S. now lives with a foreign debt of close to $1 trillion, more than the external debt of Brazil, Argentina, and Mexico combined; the U.S. is now the world's leading debtor nation, the only industrialized nation in the world with a foreign debt, and the only industrialized nation in history to achieve debtor status in peacetime. As this figure climbs geometrically at the rate of about $100 billion a year, the United States spends precious resources servicing the debt, money that could otherwise be spent more productively. Unlike the nineteenth century, when three-quarters of inward foreign investment went toward building the canals, the mines, and the infrastructure that contributed toward the nation's miracle of industrialization, today the figures are reversed. Today's money goes toward interest payments, not infrastructure; foreign investors own 30 percent of the nation's debt, a figure that is still climbing, with no end in sight. Increasing foreign investment in Treasury notes, and the policies that encourage such investment to defray the budget deficit, only serve to deepen the nation's debt and dependence.

- "*[play] host to a relatively large stock of private foreign investment from corporations based in developed countries, and this investment is highly concentrated by source.*" Over the course of its history the U.S. has long been host to direct foreign investment, and by and large this has been beneficial, because it has been diversified; industries have developed with a mix of investors and nationalities, without threatening to reduce the U.S. component in those industries. This is no longer true; it is becoming clearer that foreign investment is in many cases part of national or corporate strategies aimed at targeting specific assets or industries. The U.S. movie industry, semiconductor industry, tire industry, and many others have all experienced such targeted investment policies from abroad.

- *develop an "internationalized bourgeoisie" or "comprador elite" which "constitute the means of transmission of external influences into domestic politics.*" The term "comprador," which comes from the early Portuguese trade with China, originally referred to native employees of foreign trading companies. This measure of dependency, "the emergence of a co-opted elite," is "perhaps the most frequently cited consequence of a high level of external dependence." This elite "uses its leverage achieved from its internationally reinforced position ... [and] ... can be expected to emphasize the production or import of 'luxury' consumption goods at the expense of more substan-

tive development.''[15] Today's "internationalized elite" exerts its influence on U.S. domestic politics. The more than one hundred PACs
representing U.S. subsidiaries of foreign multinationals that have now
registered with the Federal Election Commission exist in direct contra-
vention of U.S. laws barring the participation of foreign nationals in
U.S. elections. Using records from the Department of Justice's Foreign
Agents Registration Act, economist Pat Choate identified expenditures
of $400 million per year—$100 million in Washington, D.C., alone—
spent on lobbying efforts by American representatives of the Japanese
multinationals and government agencies. Choate also identified dozens
of top trade officials from the Carter, Reagan, and Bush administrations who constitute the U.S. internationalized elite, serving as agents
for foreign governments and corporations. No "comprador" elite of
anything like this magnitude—in terms of foreign personnel and expenditures—exists in either the European Community or Japan.[16]

Of course there are vast differences between the United States
and the LDCs in terms of GNP, national wealth, and other factors.
But the indicators of dependency represent a trend line that should be
reversed before it becomes irreversible. The U.S. recognized the high
price of debtor status in the late nineteenth century and took steps
to reduce its dependency on Europe. Those steps, and their success,
coincided with America's transition to a great industrial power.

Late-twentieth-century signs of increasing dependencies and a
concurrent loss of power occur with enough regularity to remind us
of the increased vulnerability that accompanies the subservience of
sovereignty to global markets. On March 12, 1990, for example, the
lead article in *The Wall Street Journal* announced that the Federal
Reserve Board had lost much of its control over U.S. interest rates,
largely because "events in Japan and Germany increasingly tie[d] its
hands." Blamed for rising interest rates for the last seventy-five years,
the Fed has seen its power gradually "slipping away to markets in
Tokyo and Frankfurt." As the Fed loses this power, "the U.S. is losing
some of its control over its economic destiny."

It's globalization all right, but with other countries calling the
shots. U.S. firms "barely think about anything but Japanese firms"
before Treasury offerings. By 1991, U.S. citizens owed Germany and
Japan over $350 billion in Treasury debt—not a good idea by anyone's
standard—and all signs pointed to a growing unwillingness on the
part of those countries to continue financing U.S. budgetary excesses.
Treasury officials worry before bond offerings that foreign investors
won't invest, or that they will stall and force interest rates to rise;
afterward, they worry that foreign investors will sell their bonds. Their

concerns reach the White House and executive agencies like Commerce, Defense, and the USTR, and influence all trade policies, including those that have nothing to do with T-bills. Treasury and White House officials extend themselves to avoid offending foreign investors, for fear of retaliation. How did we get into this unseemly state of affairs? The "budget deficit and low savings rate have addicted the U.S. to foreign capital, so foreign investors increasingly dictate the terms."[17]

As America sank itself into this new condition of financial dependency, so can it find its way out—by encouraging savings, reducing deficits, and concentrating on how to channel investment capital into semiconductors instead of junk bonds and Trump Towers. But first Americans and their leaders must abandon the view that this dependency is merely a natural outgrowth of the global economy, and instead recognize that reacting to Bonn and Tokyo does not represent genuine interdependence by anyone's standards. "World power and influence have historically accrued to creditor countries," argued Benjamin Friedman in *Day of Reckoning*. America's slump into debtor status "cannot help but alter America's international role."[18]

(2) Recognize When and Where Ownership Matters

Those who cannot appreciate the impact of key technologies on the nation's economy and national security are living in a dream world. America's aerospace industry, for example, may rise or fall on its access to leading-edge semiconductor chips and supercomputers. Similarly, America's defense may succeed or founder, depending on its ability to produce these technologies in the event of a sudden reduction or absence of reliable suppliers. With fourteen hundred semiconductors in a B-1 bomber, does the nation really want to rely totally on Japan— or any other single nation—for its chips? Is it really in the nation's interest to go out of the semiconductor business? The National Security Agency (NSA) understood the dangers of vulnerability when it built its own semiconductor FAB. NSA's willingness to pay more than $350 million for a semiconductor plant indicates, if nothing else, that leaders of the intelligence community understand when and where ownership matters; they understand that in the last analysis ownership, above all other factors, determines where management, R & D, and jobs are located.

Unfortunately, the U.S. follows a totally nonselective approach in its policy toward foreign ownership, and remains the only industrialized nation in the world to adhere to this policy. The result is a steep trend showing the U.S. selling its assets faster than it is selling its goods; in fact, the surge of foreign investment owes much of its life force to the nation's need to pay for imported goods by selling off its permanent assets. Conventional wisdom posits that selling off nonliquid assets doesn't matter in the global economy—and in fact is highly desirable—if the new owners use those assets productively; on the other hand, paying off ballooning interest payments from steadily accumulating foreign debts is not productive either, and is in fact downright harmful to the nation.

In separating the two forms of investment, conventional wisdom—and U.S. policymakers—fail to discriminate between healthy, direct foreign investment and foreign investment that has exacerbated the nation's foreign-dependency problem and harmed its long-term security interests. In an influential article in *Foreign Affairs*, the investment banker Felix G. Rohatyn, senior partner of Lazard Freres & Company (the firm that represented MCA in the sale to Matsushita), tackled the issue of "America's Economic Dependence" and argued the reverse: Selling off valuable, permanent assets will prove more costly and damaging in the long run than burgeoning interest payments.

". . . if the United States sells $1 billion in 10-year U.S. bonds to pay for $1 billion of imports, we can ultimately repay the bonds for $1 billion plus interest; on the other hand, if a U.S. company is bought by foreign interests to pay for the same $1 billion of imports, the result is very different. That same company, 10 years from now, may be worth $5 billion or $10 billion; it is creating permanent and growing remittances of profits, dividends and technology abroad. The cost in terms of national wealth is ultimately much greater."

Rohatyn's theory of increasing economic dependence is closer to the Japanese and European way of thinking. He can't understand, for example, why no effort has been made to "redefine . . . categories of investment for the current era," such as investments in media, banks, and sensitive defense industries. An adequate defense industry, he says, "does not consist solely of the capacity to manufacture weapons; it includes the production of all kinds of sophisticated electronics, communications, special materials and many other types of high technology. . . . Foreign . . . control of financial institutions involves our international posture. Control of the media [practically all book publishing is now foreign-owned] can affect public opinion and our political system. Control of manufacturing will affect the know-how and technology around which much of future growth will be created."[19]

Along with Rohatyn, an increasing number of Americans question why the United States remains the only industrialized nation that continues to allow unlimited foreign control and ownership of its domestic business. Foreign investment has traditionally been welcomed as good for the U.S. economy, but the benefits have carried too high a price, forcing American leaders to base their decisions on fear— that foreign investors will pull their investments—rather than on the strength and freedom of movement that have been America's trademark.

(3) Establish Criteria for Defense Vulnerability

Hamlet's options seem simple by comparison: to protect or not to protect; to intervene or not to intervene; to support industries or not to support them. Almost everyone agrees on the basic premise: that America is becoming dependent on foreign investors and foreign suppliers to a degree that may harm its long-term security interests. Disagreement arises as soon as the discussion turns to developing a set of criteria for assessing dependency. This is perfectly natural, because criteria imply action, and action means preferential treatment for certain industries at the expense of others.

In the defense area, criteria are an especially touchy issue, since the ever-present concern for "national security" encourages many industries to claim the defense mantle. Predictably, the refrain of the "naked soldier" warbles on in full voice: the textile industry argues for protection on the grounds that soldiers need uniforms; the footwear industry, shoes; the food industry, meals; construction, housing; etc. Debunking the "naked soldier" argument is easy, but it can also discourage serious attempts to address the issue. It has led to a barrage of criticism of protecting technologies that our competitors have long safeguarded, on the grounds that some of these technologies—semiconductors, for example—are now so common that they should be considered commodities. Since they can be bought on the open market and are in plentiful supply throughout the world, the argument goes, they are not worthy of government investment or protection.

Despite the formidable political risks, some efforts to define criteria have emerged that are worth considering. The shrewd Norman Augustine, CEO of Martin Marietta, has advanced the idea that defense warrants a national industrial strategy. "Certain technologies should have priority," he said. "We launch commercial payloads into space. We're competing against the Chinese. They have support from their government. *They're not more efficient*—it's four times more expensive for us to produce. I asked them [the Chinese]: 'Do you have third-party liability? Medical care for employees?' " Other experts note, along similar lines, that the side that wins a war is the side with the last antenna standing, and that in this regard leaders need constantly to watch out for such technologies as semiconductors, optical systems, exotic power supplies, sensors, specialized materials, and cross-section composites, among others.

Defense vulnerability relates to the changing nature of war, which since the Iron Age has become increasingly related to technology. The new code phrase among defense officials is "technology surprise": technology that has developed *sub rosa* in a way that affects the balance of power. Up until very recently, for example, the greatest fear of imbalance focused on the U.S.-Soviet relationship; knowing that the Soviet Union could not be matched in either troop strength or quantity of hardware, U.S. security policy rested on technological superiority and a qualitative edge. The Toshiba incident in 1987 threw that assumption into sharp relief, and with it the conundrum of globalizing technologies. Toshiba bore the brunt of the controversy, even though a Norwegian company was also involved: together, the Toshiba Machine Co. and the Kongsberg Vaapenfabrikk Trading Co., a Norwegian state-owned firm, sold submarine-milling machines to the Soviet Union that enabled it to build quieter submarines and diminish the U.S. technological lead. Before the sale, U.S. defense leaders were never worried about the fact that the Soviets had several times as many submarines as the U.S.; American subs had quieter propellers, because they were built with superior machine tools and manufactured according to superior systems integration. With one simple illegal export, Toshiba and Kongsberg cost the U.S. millions of dollars in technology loss, as well as untold security losses; it was just a case of two countries narrowing the qualitative edge between two other countries and irretrievably tipping the balance of power. Having learned from this, defense officials are now troubled about "technological surprises" from supercomputers—machines that produce billions of calculations that may mean the difference between a Stealth fighter's finding its way to a target faster than an enemy craft and making sure nothing comes back.

The conundrum? Today, U.S. defense equipment cannot be produced without foreign machine tools. DoD cannot backtrack and purchase only U.S. machine tools, especially if their acquisitions experts testify that doing so would mean shooting themselves in the foot, choosing a second-rate American product over a first-rate Japanese product. Therefore, we must devise a new strategy to address the very different nature of security needs. The first step is not to deny the nation the best available technology but, rather, to begin developing criteria for maintaining a certain degree of U.S. capability in critical industries. A modest set of criteria could include:

• *The rate at which state-of-the-art technology changes.* The basic design of shoes has not changed in the last two hundred years, but semiconductors change on the average of every two and a half years. Therefore, an independent capability in semiconductors is a critical need.

• *The time frame for mobilizing an independent manufacturing capability.* For example, tank engines don't take long to tool and build, but helicopters do. In light of this criterion, it would not be advisable to lose the U.S. capability to manufacture helicopters.

• *Market share.* This is one of the factors in assessing the nature and necessity of government involvement. One of the most widely discussed and creative attempts in this genre is the 4/50 rule, the brainchild of Theodore Moran of Georgetown University, who has written widely on defense dependence. Moran warns of the consequences of U.S. dependence: delay, denial, gouging, and manipulation. His theory, which can be applied to foreign acquisitions, focuses on market concentration and suggests that, if an industry is sufficiently dispersed, no one country or company could manipulate U.S. access to defense-related products. Using a standard antitrust measure for determining the strength of any monopoly or oligopoly, Moran settled on the following threshold: four companies, four countries, and 50 percent of the market. In other words, if four companies or four governments control less than 50 percent of a market, they would be unable to collude with one another to manipulate and control the market. In the case of foreign investment, Moran argues that this criterion should be applied by the Treasury Department's screening committee, CFIUS, as a realistic test for foreign acquisitions that threaten national security, though the test need not be rigidly applied.[20]

These criteria look too much like protectionism for classical economists, even those who accept national security and defense as a "public good," worthy of government attention. The instrument is not sufficiently precise, argued Robert Z. Lawrence, an economist specializing in trade at the Brookings Institution. "Leave defense industrial policy up to defense planners; give them the money, and do not use trade protectionism as an excuse."

Economic criteria alone do not protect technology, since the focus on market concentration doesn't take other factors (like technology transfer) into account. But such economic criteria do represent a start, even if they only raise the issue to a higher level on the national agenda. Additional criteria could then be added: military, technological, and financial.

These additional criteria could take the following forms:

• *The need for a national component.* Using the critical-industries list, determine that a certain percentage (10 to 30 percent, for example) must remain under U.S. ownership for national-security reasons. This means that, once that threshold has been reached, companies cannot be acquired by international investors, nor can their production, research, or development be sited offshore or contracted out to foreign corporations.

• *Differentiate among technologies and develop support for them:* critical technologies, lead-time technologies, and building-block technologies (such as machine tools).

• *Identify spin-on and spin-off technologies.* Combine military and civilian objectives. Develop joint ventures between defense and civilian agencies to determine which technologies will bring long-term civilian as well as military benefits. Support industries with a view toward commercializing defense wherever possible; make products less exotic, more marketable, and more cost-efficient. These criteria would reward defense contractors for simplifying designs, diversifying products, reducing costs, and producing products that either "spin on" or "spin off" the commercial industrial base.

• *Establish a vulnerability index.* Using Viscount Palmerston's rule of valuing the national interest over friendship, assume no nation can be trusted eternally to provide all the nation's needs in certain industries. Differentiate between interdependence and vulnerability in technologies, and bring back a national component in those technologies.

• *Establish a country/company test.* When investors or suppliers come from U.S. allies, no one investigates them too closely, even if they are owned by foreign governments. Over one-fifth of all foreign investment in the United States, for example, represents government-owned enterprises, and central banks—primarily in Germany and Japan—have surpassed private lenders as the major purchasers of U.S. Treasury notes. Since these governments have agendas that are often very different from those of private investors, the U.S. government should begin to take a closer look at where such differences might prove critical.

(4) Collect Information: A Prelude to Policy

Even if everyone agreed on the perfect set of criteria, these would be unlikely to have much effect, for two reasons: the inadequacy of data, and the widespread ambivalence about the ability of government to apply the criteria effectively or evenhandedly. Every report that emerges concludes shamefacedly that no one has a clue as to the extent of foreign dependencies, only that they exist. "Washington can now barely monitor international trade and investment activities of U.S. businesses, and Washington is nearly blind when it comes to determining what foreign corporations are doing in the United States," concluded a cover story in *Business Week* on "The Stateless Corporation."[21]

High-level defense officials admit to the lack of systematic information, as well as the tendency to ignore information that has already been collected at considerable taxpayer expense. Nearly everyone agrees that there is a crisis in the making, even as dust gathers on the reports that make this point. The Joint Logistics Command's (JLC) study on foreign dependencies was gathered in 1986 and ignored until the GAO revisited the issue in 1991. No doubt the GAO report will suffer a similar fate, joining the legions of industrial-base studies of the past decade and their recent critical-industries companions.

DoD collects virtually no systematic data on defense dependencies, on sales of subcontractors to overseas buyers, or on foreign sourcing or foreign items used in weapons systems. The only sources of information are the prime contractors themselves, whose information is often as spotty as the Pentagon's. One commonly heard rationalization for not collecting information is the protection of proprietary data. In its 1991 study, the GAO found what it called a "stovepipe effect" in DoD, which the agency defined as a lack of interaction between defense officials involved in industrial preparedness and those assigned to acquisition. The GAO found itself relying for information on officials attached to specific weapons systems. Here, too, the information gap was profound. Even the officials dealing every day with the Abrams tank and the Hornet aircraft were blissfully unaware of the previous JLC study!

Without systematic information gathering, government cannot make sensible policy on defense dependency, nor can it assess how and where to help industries on which the nation's national security and economic stability depend. Information is sorely needed on the next generation of technology: Where is it occurring? Are transplants—U.S. subsidiaries of foreign corporations—conducting research? What kind of research? Critics allege that there is virtually no research in transplants on next-generation technology. Without comprehensive data, there is no way of knowing.[22]

(5) Intervention Without Protectionism: Passive Globalism

At issue is the extent to which government should intervene in the marketplace to assure that a necessary component of key industries and technologies remain in American hands. Critics argue that government intervention is doomed to failure, because the government, unable to balance its checkbook, can hardly be expected to take effective action to guarantee the nation's industrial strength. They maintain that government intervention would be based on political considerations rather than economic imperatives. Besides, they say, a nation as rich in natural resources and human capital as the U.S. does not have to rely on government intervention to win in the marketplace.

The bad rap accorded government intervention often turns out to be well deserved. Recent attempts to protect U.S. industry have by all accounts failed to meet their goals, and in some cases have harmed the very industries they were designed to save. Not that protectionism alone is the problem—although the word is guaranteed to produce universal negative reactions—but, rather, the half-baked, fragmented, ill-conceived, and untimely policies that pass for government intervention. One form of protectionism deemed politically acceptable was the VRAs (Voluntary Restraint Agreements) given to the machine-tool and automobile industries, by which foreign companies accepted voluntary limits on their exports. VRAs helped those industries in the short term, but did little to strengthen them in the international marketplace. General Motors, for example, used the profits from the VRAs in the early 1980s to diversify, investing in an aircraft and a data-processing company.

Other countries quickly figured out which industries were most likely to muster the political clout necessary to achieve policies like VRAs, and responded by investing heavily in those industries. Honda, Nissan, and Toyota moved quickly to locate plants in the United States, bringing hundreds of auto-supply companies with them. Supported by their own country, showered with hundreds of millions of dollars in incentives by the states, and in possession of a superior product, the Japanese auto firms soon surpassed U.S. companies on their own turf. U.S. firms were forced to engage in joint ventures, with the Japanese companies keeping much of the value-added components. Similarly, machine-tool investments followed the Houdaille petition to the International Trade Commission; television companies flocked here after protectionist signs appeared in the late 1970s; and today, extensive investments in semiconductors are made simultaneously with rancorous U.S.-Japan semiconductor negotiations.

Additional high-tech investments occur with increasing rapidity, no doubt well ahead of any action on defense-dependency recommendations. Foreign investors know they have a five-to-ten-year window of opportunity to establish themselves before anyone figures out their strategy. Some of them recognize that they now have to invest to compete in U.S. markets, and strongly believe they are making a contribution to U.S. technology. "We are not here to eat your lunch," said the Washington, D.C., vice-president of Plessy, a British-based multinational, at a conference on Capitol Hill in the summer of 1989. "We just spent $650 million in foreign investments to be able to sell in your markets. We want to help you and collaborate and get you into world markets." Others argue that foreign investors who can surmount all the barriers of locating abroad to invest in the United States—and still beat Americans on their own turf—have proved many times over that they are much more competitive than the U.S. industries they have targeted.

Foreign investors also benefit from the fact that Americans have not quite caught on to some of the hidden motives of foreign investment, especially when that investment is timed to defuse trade frictions and pre-empt congressional action. One week after the Commerce Department accused Japanese manufacturers of dumping flat-panel display screens, for example, the Sharp Corporation of Japan announced on February 21, 1991, that it would begin producing some of the screens in the United States; by 1993, the company planned to manufacture a half-million screens, or one-third of the U.S. market, in the U.S. A year before, a Sharp official was quoted as saying his company would move production to the U.S. only "when it becomes a necessity politically."[23] Following the pattern of many foreign investments, Sharp planned only a "screwdriver" operation, a plant that would perform final-assembly operations of its simplest screens. The most sophisticated and difficult technologies for producing the flawless ten-inch computer screens from silicon and for color displays would remain in Japan. The most recent of the technology losses to Japan, flat-panel displays follow all the familiar patterns of U.S.-inspired passive globalism:

- Invented in the United States, the technology promises to be a multibillion-dollar industry of the future, with demand sharply rising all over the world.
- The Japanese quickly grasp the potential of this industry and proceed to commercialize it at a much more rapid rate than their U.S. competitors.
- At the first sign of protectionism, Japanese companies invest in assembly plants in the U.S.
- Once this has happened, local politicians become protectors, to preserve jobs and forestall congressional action. U.S. companies then find themselves at odds, effectively canceling one another out in the political and economic arenas. Computer companies like IBM and Apple clearly did not want to pay more than they were spending on

the new, thin screens from Japan to support what they regarded as a second-rate industry in the U.S.

• The 10 percent solution. Following the Exon-Florio amendment requiring Treasury review of security-related foreign investments, some foreign investors now rely on an entirely new strategy to avoid U.S.-government scrutiny: holding their investments under 10 percent. In this way, they are able to acquire technology, play a role in management, and still establish a beachhead in the U.S. market. These strategies work very well, since the U.S. remains the only industrialized country that still separates trade and investment policies. Thus, foreign investment is never scrutinized for its negative effects in the same way that trade is examined, leaving investment relegated to a fairly low level of policymakers. No wonder most leaders remain oblivious to their competitors' trade-related investment strategies.

Countries also seem to benefit from other forms of U.S. protectionism: import restrictions and tariffs. Both are widely regarded as ineffective, because they make industries less competitive by keeping them on the dole and discouraging them from becoming internationally competitive; in fact, U.S. firms may continue to make shoddy products if their markets are guaranteed and their competitors are kept at bay.

Japan's protectionism involves a much shrewder strategy, geared to making its industries internationally competitive. The Japanese restrict both investment and imports, and are highly focused on industries they regard as critical. They waste little time deciding which industries are critical and which are not; like the Supreme Court's pornography test, they "know it when they see it." And their protectionism looks tough-minded: they impose quid pro quos in the form of improved products in return for government largesse; one would never catch MITI doling out VRAs for free only to emerge with declining market share.

The kind of half-baked protectionism practiced by the United States is more likely to strengthen foreign competitors or provoke retaliation than help a specific U.S. industry. But protectionism of any kind is not the answer by itself. U.S. policy needs to be more comprehensive in scope, more targeted toward segments of industries, and more long-term in its thinking. It also needs to be focused on the vital questions of criticalness and vulnerability. "I want government to protect my technology," said Bernard Schwartz, CEO of Loral. "I'm restricted in terms of what I can do as a businessman. I do not understand why government can't also tell me what is bad with regard to national security." A congressional study in late 1991 did recommend some form of protectionism—for infant industries, to enable them to prosper before being exposed to foreign competitors.[24]

Intervention must also follow a long-term strategy, so that industries can plan without fearing changes that will disrupt their production cycle. Corporate planners need to know that trade laws will be enforced with consistency and targeted industries supported without annual wrangles over their criticalness. Many would also welcome strong commitments from the highest levels of government, including and especially the White House.

TOWARD A VIABLE U.S. TECHNOLOGY POLICY:
DARPA AND SEMATECH

DARPA, the government agency that plays such an important role in the success of technology development through research support and promotion, comes closer than any other U.S. agency to the activities of MITI, the ubiquitous Japanese trade agency that seems to work such magic for that nation's industrial development. Little-known outside the defense community, DARPA's accomplishments in promoting defense-related technologies form an impressive list, including: artificial intelligence, semiconductors, computer workstations, and interactive computing. Among the specific military accomplishments are the research that led to the Stealth aircraft's ability to shield planes from radar detection, sensors used for submarine tracking, and artificial gills that extract oxygen from the ocean for use in submarines.

DARPA quietly resolved the debate on dual-use technologies by simply supporting them. Some specific programs with industrial applications, in addition to SEMATECH, are: high-definition television, budgeted at $30 million over a two-year period; superconductivity—materials that lose their resistance to electricity at high temperatures and are used in high-speed computers as well as military sensors—$25 million; neural networks—computers modeled after the brain—$33 million; and MIMIC—microwave and millimeterwave monolithic integrated circuits for communications systems, involving the development of advanced chips using gallium arsenide—$67 million.[25]

DARPA was the first government agency to appreciate the importance of computers, viewing them not merely as calculating machines but as advanced systems that would form the basis for environments of the future. Computer makers like DEC owe their existence to DARPA's early support, as do almost all of the major university-based computer-science departments. In fact, DARPA created the modern computing field, justifying its subsidies to improve the supplier base with the rationale that the agency represented the largest consumer in the world, the Pentagon, for which it was merely acting as agent. "We operate the same way any large customer does," said a DARPA official, speaking on condition of anonymity. "We need a strong supplier base. The major computer-science departments were created by DARPA investments. We orchestrated the interface among them. DARPA was the major user and major source of innovation. We crossed the boundaries of bureaucracy."

Subsidizing technologies of the future doesn't mean throwing money away indiscriminately. DARPA's budget—$1.2 billion a year, or 3 percent of the Pentagon's R & D budget, and 1 percent of total federal R & D funding—forces it toward a policy of selectivity, which means orchestrating, consensus building, networking among scientists, and a host of other strategies that accompany funding. Actually, DARPA's investment in the computer industry amounts to a very small fraction of the $300-billion U.S. computer industry, but the agency's impact on computers and supercomputers has been substantial, particularly in computer graphics, networking, personal computing, and parallel computing.[26]

Seed money from DARPA also led to commercial successes by helping companies leverage their government-funded innovations into private venture capital. DARPA funded projects from Berkeley and Stanford, for example, that were so successful they later became three of the nation's most profitable computer companies: Sun Microsystems, MIPS Computer Systems, and Silicon Graphics Computer Systems. "We help identify projects, then get the community together," said another DARPA official. "The trick is not subsidizing, but consensus-building."

DARPA also plays Dutch uncle in its attempt to keep defense suppliers viable. Mike Kelly, the agency's director of manufacturing and the man who oversees SEMATECH, described his dealings with a group of electronics companies: "There were ten companies supplying DoD for radiation-hardened electronics. I brought them in here, saw them for five minutes, then left. Before I left, I said, 'In two hours, I want you to tell me which three of you want to stay in business.'" To those who find this approach draconian, Kelly answers: "Small companies have to compete in a global marketplace. If you lose, you lose your industrial base. What does that do to your life-style and your service industries?" In other words, there isn't enough business for ten companies, but three companies could compete successfully in the new global environment. Is it better for DoD to force the number down, or watch all ten fold in the face of foreign competition? Kelly believes the same pattern is true for semiconductors, with companies competing at horizontal levels while Japan is organized vertically. "Of the twelve to fifteen thousand companies supplying the semiconductor industry, very few make money. One-half of them should go out of business."

Kelly, who spent ten years in academe and fifteen years in industry before coming to DARPA, also runs roughshod on companies he considers too lazy to innovate. This time it was the aeronautics industry that came in and said, "We need help." "I asked if they represented the industry," recalled Kelly. "They said 'yes.' I said, 'When was the last time you made a commitment to design a machine?' I said, 'I [will] invest when you tell me what commitment you're making to your suppliers in terms of orders so that those companies can make a commitment to R and D. They have to be part of a family.' "

DARPA, like SEMATECH, began subsidizing with an eye toward product development and markets—early proof of Japanese influence on U.S. policy. Kelly estimated that the U.S. spent 50 to 60 percent of its R & D subsidies on pure research, unrelated to products, while Japan spent 80 percent of its R & D money on product-related research. Many of the DARPA scientists favored their agency's new direction, and advocated expanding its functions to capitalize on prior achievements.

DARPA's subtle shift toward dual-use technologies brought many detractors, throwing the hitherto obscure agency headlong into controversy. As attractive as this policy proved to many on Capitol Hill and in the defense technology community, its new visibility drew the unwelcome attention of the White House, which definitely did not want another MITI, or any agency that even dreamed of "industrial policy." The ax fell in 1990, when Dr. Craig I. Fields, a brilliant young scientist and fifteen-year veteran of DARPA, was fired from the directorship of the agency. Fields had offended the formidable White House free-trade troika—Chief Economic Adviser Michael J. Boskin, Chief of Staff John Sununu, and Budget Director Richard G. Darman—with his open advocacy of public support for HDTV and other technologies not solely defense-related.

Fields' job had been saved earlier that year by a coalition of sympathetic government officials, including Tom Murrin at Commerce, along with several of the nation's leading scientists who rallied to his defense. All the nation's Nobel Prize winners combined, however, couldn't protect Fields from White House wrath after his decision to invest in Gazelle Microcircuits, a small firm producing chips manufactured from gallium arsenide. DARPA invested $4 million in the Santa Clara company in exchange for future profits and royalties from products developed with these funds. In addition to these benefits, DARPA insisted on a degree of control over the company: namely, a nonvoting seat on the board of directors, and a say in preventing future purchases of the company or its technology to a foreign company. Should a foreign company try to purchase Gazelle, DARPA could arrange for a domestic company to buy the company or buy back its own investment.

Foreign investment in high technology was the driving force behind DARPA's controversial move. The agency was deeply concerned about recent Japanese purchases of thirty of the 151 high-tech firms producing semiconductor equipment, and sought to prevent yet another such acquisition of technology developed in the U.S. with U.S. funding. Having already supported research in gallium arsenide, DARPA saw no sense in losing that technology to Japan for want of venture capital. After all, would the Japanese subsidize a technology only to allow an overseas investor to snap it up and bring it to market? DARPA leaders also wanted to avoid the classic mistake of the VRAs: government largesse without a quid pro quo linked to industrial competitiveness.

Gazelle followed the classic pattern of a small firm that tried to expand, couldn't find venture capital in the U.S., and was forced to turn to Japan. The company wanted to expand its production beyond military uses and mass-produce its chips for workstations, personal computers, and communications systems. The president of Gazelle said Japanese investors had already been in touch with him when a representative from DARPA, a scientific officer named Arati Prabhakar, visited the firm and asked if they would like to be a guinea pig for a new experiment: government as venture capitalist.

The experiment went straight from guinea pig to sacrificial lamb. The White House regarded such direct government investment in a private corporation as nothing short of state-supported socialism and reacted accordingly. The irony was that although many thought the fight represented a dispute between Fields and the White House, Fields was not acting alone but in concert with Congress. Congress had specifically authorized DARPA to invest $25 million over a two-year period in a new plan, called "flexible agreements," through which DARPA could act like a venture-capital firm helping to support winning technologies, enabling the agency to cut the red tape that would otherwise tie it up under the old rules. In other words, DARPA's powers were expanded by Congress to engage in private-entrepreneurial activities, but when it actually happened the White House went into shock. "Nobody has gained but our military enemies and our economic competitors," remarked Senator Gore, recapping the incident at a Senate Armed Services subcommittee hearing.

Fields' firing highlighted the national schizophrenia about subsidizing high technology in the interests of national security, along with the increasing confusion over the blurred lines between military and commercial technologies. Was DARPA funding for computer technology all for naught if the computer technology ended up more in workstations than in guided missiles? What if the nay-sayers had ruled the day when DARPA funded projects that led to bank cash machines, computer graphics, or parallel-processing technologies?

Fields' successor, Victor Reis, learned from Gazelle, and in his testimony before Congress in 1991 was careful to stick to DARPA's military mandate; his testimony contained many examples of how DARPA research benefited the Desert Storm effort.[27] The irony of Fields' firing was that by the late 1980s, the Pentagon was already spending hundreds of millions of dollars on generic manufacturing technologies with potential civilian as well as military applications. SEMATECH stood as the outstanding example; another Pentagon program, ManTech (for Manufacturing Technology), provides funds for technologies from machine tools to automatic machinery for making military uniforms, $130–200 million per year from 1980 to 1990.

The White House was not happy about the agency's direction, however. Fearful that ManTech had deteriorated into a source of pork-barrel largesse for Congress, the White House in 1991 decided to attempt to cut ManTech's budget by two-thirds, stripping away initiatives in photolithography, machine tools, and other high-tech fields.[28] But, despite its problems, DARPA seemed to survive the budget ax, probably because of its long-term legitimacy in the field of military objectives, which enabled the agency to maintain government support for its activities in "precompetitive" (before products are ready for the market place) generic research on dual-use technologies. Congress provided $50 million for this research in the FY 1991 Defense Authorization and Appropriation Acts, in an amendment sponsored by Senator Bingaman. Following DoD's 1991 critical-technologies report, DARPA allocated this funding to six consortia, including two of the key areas in which the U.S. was lagging behind Japan, optoelectronics and SRAM technology.[29]

Without White House support, congressional initiatives in high-tech funding specifically geared to civilian research have added direction to the issue, but not enough money to make a real difference. One such effort was an attempt to introduce a civilian DARPA: a short-lived proposal for an agency to be named CARPA (for Civilian Advanced Research Projects Agency) was seriously discussed and later abandoned on Capitol Hill. Instead, a more cautious approach involved renaming the old Bureau of Standards—called the National Institute of Standards and Technology (NIST) as of 1988—and giving the new agency the mission of coordinating policy on industrial technology and stimulating innovation in the private sector. NIST, which is part of the Commerce Department, funds projects through a new program known as Advanced Technology Program, or ATP, which was initially budgeted at $10 million a year. Compared to DARPA's $1.2 billion, and considering the nation's urgent needs, this figure seems paltry. Still, it represents a new beginning: at least the White House has accepted the concept of funding high-technology projects that are specifically civilian-oriented.[30]

What if DARPA "sticks to its knitting"—a common phrase among DARPA critics—never veering from narrowly focused military research? Critics of this strategy argue that placing too much stress on military over commercial research was exactly what hurt the nation's industrial competitiveness in the first place: military requirements tend to make products too expensive to be transferred to civilian technologies, and military priorities have already siphoned off too many scientists, engineers, and government funds into weapons production instead of VCRs and fax machines.

The separation between military and civilian becomes especially blurry when the Pentagon finds itself forced to rely on components from abroad after they lose their own critical technologies through neglect—the very condition of technological dependence Fields was trying to avoid with the investment in Gazelle. "You can't have a material industrial base producing goods that are only used for the military," said Robert C. McCormack, deputy undersecretary of defense for industrial and international programs. "We make our own chips, and they are the most expensive in the world."

DARPA's wings were clipped temporarily, but the debate is ongoing. The agency's success in what *Science* magazine calls "beating swords into . . . chips" will probably continue, given the commitment of the agency's scientists, whose longevity in government service means their views have a fighting chance to prevail over time. Their vision is echoed at government labs across the nation by scientists who express frustration at putting so much effort into innovation only to watch overseas competitors move in at key stages and commercialize those innovations. They want to help industry commercialize; industry is reaching out to the labs; but the issue is still too controversial to erupt into the open, especially after what happened at DARPA.

One of DARPA's great successes is SEMATECH, by far the most interesting and successful of the current crop of consortia, whose model of government-industry cooperation holds considerable promise for the future. A five-year, $2-billion project, SEMATECH was founded in 1987 at the behest of defense officials, semiconductor suppliers, and chip makers. The investment was substantial, but at least the risk was shared—$100 million a year from the semiconductor companies and $100 million from government. SEMATECH represented an exciting development for the U.S. in that it focused primarily on research related to the manufacturing process. Its purpose, to help semiconductor-equipment manufacturers compete more effectively in global markets, was carried out through the expedient of helping U.S. producers solve technical problems that they could not solve on an individual basis. In a capital-intensive industry, SEMATECH provided funds for capital-starved companies and lowered the risk of individual failures.

A sense of excitement pervades the SEMATECH FAB in Austin. The labs are humming, white-coated men and women in small groups bend over machines of enormous complexity, bright graphics decorate the walls, and a feeling of urgency reminiscent of the early days of NASA is palpable. SEMATECH regards itself as competitive without being protectionist; its scientists are hard-eyed realists about what can and cannot be achieved. But the old excitement over what Americans can do when they put their minds to it is infectious, and it is tempting to dream about the potential for applying the SEMATECH formula to dozens of other critical technologies.

"SEMATECH attacks the problem of manufacturing," explained Turner Hasty, chief operating officer. "Nuts-and-bolts technology is the problem of manufacturing. Our basic mistake is that we tend to isolate product development and research from the factory. When we organized, we had a wall between manufacturing and research. We've since taken the wall down."

The purpose of this ambitious enterprise was daunting: to get suppliers and manufacturers to work together to increase the supplier base and reduce the industry's dependence on foreign manufacturers.

Up until then, computer makers and semiconductor suppliers had been locked in combat over foreign dependencies; computer makers preferred to buy cheaper components from abroad, while semiconductor manufacturers struggled to convince them to take a longer view and spend more to ensure a greater degree of self-sufficiency at home.

Another sticking point involved the reluctance of individual companies within the same industry to work together if it meant revealing company secrets. Convinced finally by Japan's D-RAM dumping campaign of the early 1980s, the fourteen U.S. electronics firms that formed SEMATECH decided they had to work together or they would fail separately. "Our emphasis was on the supplier network," said Hasty. "We watched this happen to consumer electronics. You can't resuscitate consumer electronics, because we've lost the infrastructure. We were seeing this happen to semiconductors."

The founders of SEMATECH wisely decided to learn from the Japanese. The key was "precompetitive organization." "We've reached the stage where we can have consortia in the precompetitive stage," reported Charles Herzfeld, director of the Office of Research and Engineering at DoD. "The weakness is that, unless our large companies develop a taste for long-term investing, these efforts will not pay out." Government support of precompetitive technologies also circumvents the old industrial-policy debate about putting government in the role of picking winners and losers. "If we pick generic, precompetitive technologies, like high-performance computing," explained Burgess Laird, a scientist at Los Alamos, "we're not picking winners or losers. If the private sector puts up the money, the industry picks the winners. High-performance computing has many industrial uses. It's the only thing on which we can get Gore and Sununu to agree."

Conversely, if we lose high-performance computing, we risk losing additional critical industries. "Advanced computers are the heart of American technology," said James O'Connell of Control Data, a leading U.S. computer company. "You lose that and you've lost everything. Supercomputing and semiconductors are two sides of the spectrum: semiconductors are the seed corn of electronics; super-computers are the ultimate expression of the American computer industry."

SEMATECH was fortunate in the choice of its first leader, Robert Noyce, one of the nation's most prestigious scientist-entrepreneurs. Noyce revolutionized American electronics with his invention of the integrated circuit, or semiconductor chip, which made it possible to store volumes of data on a chip smaller than a fingernail. The "chip" propelled the computer age forward by downsizing computers from city-block-sized facilities to "lap-tops" today, and made possible such information-age products as microwave ovens, pocket calculators, exercise machines, Nintendo games, computerized flight plans, and thousands of products for military and commercial use. Noyce also cofounded Intel, today the nation's third-largest manufacturer of chips. It galled Noyce to think about the loss of his invention to overseas competitors through what he viewed as a combination of lax government policies and a disorganized private sector.

Noyce quickly recognized two problems which informed his passion for SEMATECH. The first problem focused on the inability of U.S. companies to move from the lab to the marketplace; the second was the Japanese challenge. "Our mission is moving research into the manufacturing process," he said of SEMATECH. "Government is great at doing one-of-a-kind research that you can't produce. The Japanese perfected manufacturing. We want to keep suppliers alive.

That means getting suppliers and customers to work in their common interest. It means working on the use of computers to control manufacturing processes.

"The U.S. does well in design-intensive tasks," he continued. "In that sense, we have an advantage over the Japanese. Where we lose is in the commodity product. With D-RAMs, we lost our commodity product through dumping. Japan lost $4 billion; we lost $2 billion. Americans couldn't tolerate the loss and quit. They went back to designing E-PROMs [erasable-program read-only memory], which the Japanese started dumping one year later." By then, the U.S. had smartened up: "It was easier to file the second dumping suit than the first."

Noyce also viewed SEMATECH as a bulwark against unfair Japanese trade practices, and under his leadership the consortium led lobbying efforts to toughen government's role in protecting his industry. "The Japanese have defeated many industries," said Noyce, "but they weren't getting anywhere until government got into the act. Their businesses were not able to compete with American business." After Noyce's death in 1990 (W. J. Spencer became the new CEO), SEMATECH representatives fought unsuccessfully to combat the purchase of Semi-Gas by a Japanese company on the premise that its sale would give their Japanese competitors access to the blueprints of every single project at SEMATECH.

The semiconductor industry decided that one of the best ways to compete with Japan was to emulate them in two areas: 1) introducing U.S. producers to the concept of "precompetitive competition," providing U.S. manufacturers with a technological edge so that they could compete better in the marketplace; and 2) strengthening their supplier base and developing long-term relationships between producers and suppliers. At their $250-million Austin-based FAB, a SEMATECH official described how "precompetitive competition" worked in practice:

"We looked at what the Japanese were doing better, and SEMATECH copied from Japan," explained Joe Stroop, SEMATECH's senior communications manager. "NEC and Hitachi engage in ferocious competition, but they recognize the value of pooled research. It is better for SEMATECH to fail once than for fourteen companies to fail fourteen times."

The two concepts are connected. Japanese manufacturers engage in precompetitive bidding, a stage during which producers could still criticize their suppliers, who thus benefited from timely and honest feedback. U.S. producers, on the other hand, tend to keep their suppliers at arm's length, with very little feedback; instead, they concentrate on their customers. The faulty U.S. system invariably leads to weaker products, because the supplier doesn't know what's wrong with his product until he loses the business to overseas competitors and it is too late to recover. Fact-finding can give a manufacturer a competitive edge, perhaps a six-month head start that can make the difference in a company's survival in the marketplace.

SEMATECH tried to reverse the routine pattern of secrecy, stiff competition, and lack of cooperation among manufacturers by bringing suppliers together and attempting to iron out the technical problems that were driving them out of the global marketplace. Member companies rotate their top scientists and engineers into the Austin plant, where they work with fellow member companies as well as the permanent SEMATECH staff. "We've demonstrated that we can sit together with thirty to forty experts from industry and come up with a consensus," explained Avtar Oberai, head of SEMATECH's Competitiveness Division. "SEMATECH takes one nugget and invests a member company's money for one idea. For example, eight years ago, the U.S. had over 70 percent of the market for lithography. Ten years ago, it was 100 percent. Now we have 20 percent of the market, and only two companies are left: GCA and Perkin-Elmer. GCA went bankrupt two and a half years ago, and they're back in business now. We've made tremendous progress with GCA. All fourteen member companies focused on making world-class equipment. We're not out of the woods yet, but two years ago it was Nikon all the way; nobody would have touched GCA equipment two years ago. Today, because of SEMATECH, GCA is viable."

How was this done? "We improved their technology," explained Oberai. "We took their machine out on the floor and told them how to improve. We did marathon runs on the machine." In a "marathon run," technicians take an existing problem "tool," put it in a "clean room," and run it till it works.

The hardest job for SEMATECH involves working on the attitudes of member companies, some of whom have yet to be convinced that they must share their technology if they want to solve their problems. When GCA submitted to SEMATECH's joint development program, its machines were performing at 50 percent of the level of the Nikon product. Within two years they were up to 80 percent, and still climbing. "We convinced GCA it was in its own interests to improve," continued Oberai. "Japan will buy inferior equipment and help companies compete on the world market. We try to make U.S. chip buyers buy less than the best and then improve it."

In the summer of 1990, SEMATECH's efforts in GCA's behalf bore fruit with the introduction, a year ahead of schedule, of a new piece of equipment, a state-of-the-art stepper.[31] Additional successes keep emerging to support SEMATECH's mission and the taxpayer's investment. But there are also disappointments. "The world's silicon capability, now split between Europe and Japan, is our biggest disappointment," admitted Hasty. SEMATECH failed to convince the government to stop the sale of Monsanto's silicon-wafer division to the German company Huels, thus losing the U.S.'s last domestic supplier. "Now it's a Mexican stand-off. Monsanto is still in St. Louis, but American industry has no control. There is no reason why Huels can't shut down their Monsanto division. Now Japan is double-dumping, selling silicon wafers at 20 percent under what they were selling for in Japan."

"I went to CFIUS," recalled Tom Seidel, director of SEMA-TECH's manufacturing methods division. "The Monsanto people said silicon was a commodity. I said, 'I tell you it is not a commodity.' The guys who said it was a commodity won. Does it matter if it is located here? Qaddafi found out with those chemical plants that location didn't matter if you didn't have the technicians."

Long experience with Japanese competitors has convinced SEM-ATECH scientists like Seidel that a degree of U.S. ownership matters in their industry. What will happen if we lose semiconductors? "The Japanese will get the manufacturing and they will design the specs and the chips," says Hasty. "The ability to generate wealth is still in manufacturing and the selling of goods. The fallacy of the theory of 'You can always buy these things' is, 'Where do you get the money?' Especially if the only way to generate wealth is buying and selling products. Today, we're buying products and selling assets."

A NEW WATCHWORD: INTERDEPENDENCE

A new theory would focus on three factors: criticalness, accountability, and vulnerability. The nation's future economic and national security depends on its ability to identify these three factors and follow them through with meaningful policies in the areas of trade, defense acquisition and procurement, and the large umbrella covering economic competitiveness. These policies could begin with:

• A serious effort at exploration, definition, and consensus building to identify critical industries and the technologies upon which these industries depend. In the spring of 1990, the Department of Commerce identified twelve emerging technologies, noting that, in comparison with Japan, the U.S. was *losing badly* in advanced materials, biotechnology, digital-imaging technology, and supercomputers; and *losing* in advanced semiconductor devices, high-density data storage, high-performance computing, medical devices and diagnostics, optoelectronics, and sensor technology. The nation was holding firm in artificial intelligence, sensor technology, and flexible computer-integrated manufacturing, but not gaining in those fields.[32]

• Once they are identified, a recognition that ownership of critical industries does matter, and that America needs to own enough of those industries to produce what it needs if supplies were cut off. This means combat readiness as well as "lifelines"—how those industries and technologies relate to other industries and to the defense industrial base.

• A recognition that jobs alone do not make a nation strong; that ownership matters in the areas of engineering and product design, systems integration, know-how, intellectual property, stock ownership, and the location of corporation leaders and the board of directors. The question of who is the equity owner should be paramount, given that the equity owner determines how resources are allocated, how research-and-development money is spent, and where the company will go.

• A "trust-but-verify" policy for sharing technology. Recognizing that if joint ventures are the wave of the future, the U.S. must get its fair share in those ventures. Technology diffusion benefits everyone, and borders should ideally be meaningless in the worldwide exchange of ideas. But is our nation getting access to its partners' technologies at the same time that it is licensing away its own? Reciprocity is only beginning to achieve legitimacy in the trade lexicon; it needs to become more of a reality in negotiating coproduction agreements.

• A "trust-but-share" technology policy. Too often the U.S. finds itself at a marked strategic disadvantage simply because its leaders fail to insist on a fair deal. In the FSX deal, American leaders insisted on mutual sharing of technologies only after Congress, the Commerce Department, and a number of other agencies forced the issue onto the national agenda. The idea of "two-way technology transfers" is one way to ensure strategic as well as economic balance, but such a policy requires tough-minded trade negotiators who are given the mandate to follow through on technology agreements as closely as their colleagues in arms control.

• A multilateral reconciliation of investment policies that recognizes existing asymmetries of access, antitrust, and financing practices. If this is not possible in a timely manner, then U.S. policy must adjust unilaterally to its competitors' aggressive trade-and-investment practices. America must meet these new challenges with greater speed and flexibility, and in a manner congruent with its own unique value system. This means figuring out a way to invest in itself, finance its critical industries, reverse its deepening dependence, and learn how to commercialize its own inventions.

• Most important of all, a recognition that a stronger federal-government presence is needed as gatekeeper, arbiter, integrator, and protector for critical industries. Other countries rely more heavily on their governments for these roles, to their pronounced economic advantage. All too often, the U.S. has lost industries because its own corporations have canceled one another out in the political arena: computer companies need cheap, imported semiconductors; a constellation of companies depended on components produced by Toshiba; high-tech companies sell, license, or trade off their high-value-added technologies so that they can expand and grow with foreign capital. Add to that the wars among the states to lure industries with tax incentives and other blandishments and you have pluralism run rampant—draining dollars and resources in unnecessary intranational competitions virtually unknown in the European Community or in Japan.

National sovereignty, even among the most powerful nation-states, is a new ball game; multinationals find they can shape policies more effectively than ever before. "There has been a reversal of roles between government and the corporation. Governments act as if they are fully sovereign within their own borders . . . but stateless corporations have increasingly learned to shape national climates by offering technology, jobs and capital. . . . Governments and nations that fail to create the right climate will find their living standards and well-being short-changed."[33] Dealing with that fact of life represents one of the biggest challenges of our times. To turn it to our advantage requires the highest level of strategic thinking available on the national level. The individualistic, state-centered, *ad hoc* policymaking that might have worked in the past is clearly inadequate today.

CHAPTER VIII

A Matter of Degree

WHY HER MAJESTY'S GOVERNMENT
REDUCED THE KUWAITI INVESTMENT
IN BRITISH PETROLEUM

In the conflict of British Petroleum and the government of
Kuwait, we balanced the interests of BP and Her Majesty's
government. The chances of conflict would be small, but the
effects are large. The fact that there were foreigners in the
company had no effect except insofar as it is *against the
national interest.*
> —Stephen Burbridge, secretary to the
> Monopolies and Mergers Commission, U.K.

As a member of OPEC, Kuwait would be likely, as it has
been in the past, to support OPEC's objectives. . . . In these
circumstances . . . we believe Kuwait would seek to influence
BP's policies in its own interest . . . [and] against the public
interest.
> —Monopolies and Mergers Commission[1]

NATIONAL SECURITY AND LAISSEZ-FAIRE

While the United States debated the pros and cons of how and when
to take action against foreign cartels, the British acted speedily against
a foreign investor whose actions they considered a threat to their
national interest. The case involved the oil and energy reserves of the
government-owned British Petroleum (BP) company, Britain's largest
company and the third-largest oil company in the world; the investor,
the government of Kuwait; and the "matter of public interest . . . the

ability to operate independently and free from external government influence."[2]

To keep BP firmly under British control, the British government reduced Kuwait's interest in the company from 22.5 percent to 9.9 percent. In contrast to the more laissez-faire U.S. policy toward foreign investment in strategic industries, the British seized the issue, elevated it to national importance, and acted aggressively and in a timely manner to protect its national interests. Energy was a critical industry, they determined, and British access was threatened by the rising level of foreign investment, especially since the investor was a foreign government, not a private investor. Differentiating between foreign governments and individuals would be considered heretical by U.S. leaders. Also out of bounds for U.S. policymakers but confronted directly by the British was the issue of scale: the point at which a foreign investment becomes undesirable—namely, when it threatens an industry's independence and global competitiveness. The U.S. still has no such criterion for foreign investors, and would rather see an industry—however important—lost to foreign competitors than saved through any strategy that smacks of "industrial policy."

The British became passionate when faced with the risk of losing control of BP. Losing control meant the risk of losing jobs, technology, and profits. With operations in seventy countries, BP employs 126,000 people, 28,100 in the United Kingdom. Founded as the Anglo-Persian Oil Company in 1909, the company slowly expanded over the years in much the same way the Kuwaiti oil business was expanding: from upstream oil operations (exploration and production) to downstream activities (marketing and distribution) and increased diversification into related products, such as petrochemicals.

BP's long and unhappy experience with the Middle East added to its suspicion of Kuwait. In 1951, the government of Iran nationalized the company's interests there, forcing BP to rely more heavily on other Middle Eastern countries; Libya and Kuwait soon followed the Iranian example in throwing off colonial ownership and exploitation, nationalizing BP's assets there as well. Their reverses in the Middle East were offset, however, by their discovery of gas and oil fields in the North Sea and in Alaska, leading to the acquisition of Standard Oil of Ohio—an acquisition unopposed by the U.S.

With BP's expansion into the North American market and Kuwait expanding its downstream operations, they went from a manager-employee relationship to one of direct competition. As a founding member of OPEC, Kuwait was indeed a formidable competitor: OPEC countries at that time accounted for one-third of the world's proven reserves of crude oil, and the Arab countries accounted for the bulk of production within OPEC. Specifically, Kuwait held 10 percent of the world's existing oil reserves and 2 percent of total world production; Kuwaitis also were secure in the knowledge that these reserves would last 200 years.

The British move to reduce Kuwaiti involvement was based mostly on hypothetical considerations, and revealed the British government as eager to protect a critical industry from harm or extinction. It also showed that a nation can strategize in its own interests and still remain committed to a policy of free trade and investment. Although even the most ardent opponents of government intervention in the United States support antitrust enforcement, the issue would have followed a very different path here: the Kuwaiti government would have bought into a critical industry with very few roadblocks; CFIUS would have cleared the purchase, saying it presented no threat to national security (probably because the Kuwaitis were our allies); and public opposition would be nonexistent, since the public would not know of the sale until it was a *fait accompli*. Indeed, the Kuwaitis have invested extensively in the United States, including the energy business.[3]

The British recognized the critical nature of British Petroleum to the nation's economic and security interests. Deeply involved in oil extraction, refining, marketing, and trading, BP is the largest producer of oil and holder of oil reserves in the United States as well as the United Kingdom.[4]

What triggered the alarm bells in Whitehall was the sudden and speedy acquisition of BP stock by the Kuwait Investment Organization (KIO), the investment arm of the Kuwaiti government in London, during the autumn and winter months of 1987–88. Similar to the surge of foreign investment in the United States, the Kuwaitis' move was in response to "Black Monday," when the stock market crashed and many assets, including BP, seemed a bargain to countries with strong currencies, deep pockets, and long-term investment horizons. Kuwait knew a bargain and seized the opportunity, expanding its holdings within four short months from under 10 percent of the company to 22.5 percent. These purchases made Kuwait the largest individual beneficial shareholder in BP by far, dwarfing the next two largest shareholders: the Prudential Corporation, which held 1.8 percent, and Her Majesty's government, which held 1.7 percent.

What galvanized British leaders into action? After all, what is wrong with Kuwaiti investment in an international energy company? The Kuwaitis, along with the Saudis and other OPEC investors, know the oil business; they have a long and relatively trouble-free tradition of investing in Great Britain; and the British have traditionally welcomed foreign investment, including investments from the Arab world.

With their preference for liquidity—for portfolio investments rather than direct investments—Arab investors present less of a threat to the host country than investors seeking to sink deep roots into the society.

As it turned out, the British were prescient. The Gulf War rendered Kuwait a tragic battleground, a victim of Iraqi aggression and no longer master of its own fate. What if the Kuwaitis had used their investment in BP to win a negotiated settlement from Saddam Hussein? What if the secrecy surrounding Kuwaiti investments affected the location of the shares and they ended up in Saddam Hussein's unfriendly hands? What if Hussein then used those assets to purchase even more deadly weapons to be used against the British, the Americans, Saudi Arabia, and all the nations fighting against him? With Kuwait's leadership dispersed, who would represent their interests? And would this representation be legitimate and in the best interests of the company, not to mention Great Britain's national interest?

The Gulf War vindicated the British concern, which in 1988 centered on the opportunities for influence that accompany the rights of ownership. At British Petroleum, ownership rights are not a matter of speculation; they are spelled out specifically in company rules ensuring that investors holding substantial amounts of stock can exercise a controlling interest in the company. "The Kuwaitis' interests in Britain were reduced to 9.9 percent on the grounds that, with 10 percent of the company, an investor could convene a corporate meeting and have a material influence on the actions of the company," recalled Stephen R. Burbridge, secretary to the Monopolies and Mergers Commission, in an interview in his New Court office in London. The commission, which advises the secretary of state for trade and industry, is a purely advisory, independent, investigative body, financed by the government but not part of it.

"The concept of material influence is written into the act [governing antitrust], and we are always engaged in discussing what constitutes material influence," continued Burbridge. "Material influence is used to prevent the exploitation of a monopoly position. There's a difference between complete control and partial control. The commission is normally concerned with full takeovers. The Kuwaiti Petroleum Company interest rose swiftly on purchases of daily business, and occurred over a four-month period." Indeed, it rose so swiftly that the possibility of a full takeover became imminent, causing the British leaders to think more seriously about the question of degree, or whether there should be a limit on foreign investment in the energy industry.

What spurred Parliament and the government's initial request for a commission investigation was the speed with which the Kuwaitis raced to acquire BP stock, along with the British realization that this was a race with no finish line in sight—no ceiling or percentage limitation on the escalating Kuwaiti buys. As the 20-percent range hove into sight, opportunities for Kuwaiti influence expanded. ". . . if you own 25 percent, you can block an emergency meeting of the company," explained Burbridge. "If you have 16.7 percent of the company, you have the right to two members on the board of directors."

At this point, the problem of potential "material influence" emerges, continued Burbridge: ". . . we recognize that sometimes you can achieve control over a company with a minority interest. The rule of thumb about the quality of a merger is when a combined company would have more than 25 percent of the market, or £30 million."

THE BUY-OUT: DIPLOMATS AND TRADERS

The investigation would never have proceeded if the Kuwaitis had responded to signals by British-government officials warning them off the BP investment. Indeed, why should the Kuwaitis respond? Shares of BP were being offered to the general public as part of a company policy to divest some of its holdings amid widespread investor interest from North America, Japan, and Europe. "Black Monday," on October 17, 1987, suddenly intruded, leading to a drastic markdown of all shares, including BP. As a result, investor interest evaporated—except in Kuwait, which, taking the long view, "indicated to the market that it was a buyer for as many shares as it could obtain at the then favourable price."[5]

Through the KIO, the Kuwaiti government saw its share in BP rise swiftly, with purchases on a daily basis. From October 30 to November 23, the KIO increased its shareholding role to over 10 percent of BP's equity; by December 30, it was 19 percent; by March 11, it was 22.5 percent.

A serious difference of opinion marked BP's and Kuwait's recollections of the period. BP alleged that at the time of the stock offer its "objective was to distribute the shares widely, with no single holding in excess of 1 percent." In fact, BP indicated that it had "always considered that a 5 percent shareholding by any one shareholder was undesirable and that a Kuwaiti shareholding of 10 percent or more gave rise to considerable concern about the continued independent role of the company." Kuwait challenged that view, saying that BP's objective that "no single shareholding should exceed 5 percent" was never conveyed to them.[6]

Since Kuwait seemed to have misunderstood the signals, British officials made diplomatic contact with that country on November 23 to be apprised of the Kuwaiti government's short- and long-term intentions. At a number of meetings, ministers expressed their "concern at the continuing purchases of shares while stressing that it was the *extent* of the holding, and not its fact, that posed problems."

At these meetings, Kuwait assured BP and government representatives that, since KIO had no intention of interfering in the management of BP or of seeking representation on its board of directors, there was no need to give KIO the "demeaning" instructions to limit its purchases. British government officials responded by telling both the commission and Kuwait that assurances were not sufficient to assuage their concerns about the expanding size of the Kuwaiti investment.

WHY KUWAIT?

The Kuwaitis raised the issue of why they in particular were being targeted. What warranted their exclusion from an increased investment in British Petroleum? Was this just another form of British racism? The old colonial prejudices once again? Resentment at escalating Kuwaiti wealth and British decline? What proof did the British have to justify their lack of trust in Kuwait's assurances that this investment was passive, that they had no intention of using ownership to control the company? And if there was a ceiling on the scale of investment, why hadn't this been clarified in the initial offering?

Of greatest concern to the British was the reality that there was no such thing as a private Kuwaiti investor. The government of Kuwait controls, owns, and manages all investments and investment organizations. The BP buyer, the KIO, is a subsidiary of the KIA, the Kuwait Investment Authority, a Kuwait-based public corporation wholly owned by the state of Kuwait. All investments at home and abroad are the property of the state of Kuwait, and all profits from those investments flow back to the state, supposedly for the benefit of its citizens, who are concerned about the financial security of future generations once their oil runs out.

The economy of Kuwait proved another source of concern to the British. Despite its rich oil reserves, Kuwait had consciously shifted away from its dependence on oil revenue to more reliance on income from overseas investments. This meant that Kuwait would continue its current policy of aggressive expansion of outward investment, focusing on the refining, chemicals, and downstream oil operations that would enhance its oil business at home. In fact, Kuwait was looking more and more like the colonial power Britain used to be, living off its investments and the labor of others. Kuwait was now a mixed, industrialized economy, turning its rich natural resources to work for its own interests, rather than steadily dissipating them for the good of a mother country.

As a former colony, Kuwait had learned its lessons well, and had no trouble dispensing with some of the free-trade tenets—such as "reciprocity"—that did not work in its part of the world. Although Kuwaitis invest freely all over the world, they do not permit foreign investment in their own critical industries (especially energy) or in noncritical industries unless a Kuwaiti national is the majority owner. In the United States, for example, the Kuwaiti government drills for oil on federal land thanks to its ownership of Santa Fe International, an engineering and architectural firm.[7] Lack of reciprocity in investment has become standard practice all over the Arab world, but emerged as a subissue in the BP acquisition, with British officials complaining that, "although there appeared to be no barrier in Kuwaiti law, there were considerable practical obstacles to the involvement of foreign companies in the development of Kuwaiti oil reserves and no effective way for a foreign company to buy shares in KPC [Kuwait Petroleum Company] or its subsidiaries."[8]

The secrecy surrounding Kuwaiti investments also brought some grief to commission investigators, who tried to make sense of the investment picture. "In order to put the investment in BP in perspective we asked Kuwait for certain information on the approximate value of KIA's ten largest quoted investments and for details of KIO's top 15 investments in the United Kingdom other than BP," they said. Hardly proprietary information, but the Kuwaitis stonewalled: "The Government of Kuwait declined . . . but told us that the BP holding . . . would exceed . . . any other individual holding . . . in [the] United Kingdom."[9] Estimates of Kuwait's assets in Asia and the West following the Iraqi invasion reached the $100-billion mark; the fear of a mass liquidation of those assets to finance the Gulf War sent shudders throughout world money markets.[10]

At that point, the British needn't have worried about Kuwait's solvency, assured as they were by the state's representatives that the KIO paid cash, had no liabilities, could rely on the state to pay all expenses, and could afford to take a much longer view of the market than most other investors. They could also look at Kuwait's impressive investment history to see how BP would benefit from their deep pockets: their holding in Daimler-Benz, valued at $1 billion in 1987, had doubled in only one year. Similar assurances demonstrated their total lack of interest in control: KIA held an interest of 14.9 percent in the

Royal Bank of Scotland, but did not sit on its board or take any part in its management.

THE GOVERNMENT VIEW

Her Majesty's government weighed in through its Department of Energy with strong views opposing the Kuwaiti investment. One of the primary objections concerned OPEC's extensive and well-documented record of interfering with the forces of the market in restraint of free trade. "In the early 1970s, Kuwait was one of the first [OPEC nations] to cut back oil production and push up prices," testified the department. "In recent years, it has continued to hold output significantly below capacity in support of prices," which ran counter to the British position that "questions of production and pricing should be left to the market."[11]

Kuwait's promises of nonintervention in BP's management activities were also dismissed by energy officials, who pointed to Kuwait's heavy-handed involvement in its investments in Spain. There was nothing "passive" about Kuwait's role in these enterprises: "The investment activity in Spain . . . afforded examples of the way in which KIO had sought to influence the policy of companies in which it has a shareholding." These included encouraging the sale or merger of corporate assets against the will of existing company management (Union Explosivos Rio Tinto); using a significant shareholding as a lever to obtain board representation (Union Explosivos Rio Tinto, Banco Central); calling an Extraordinary General Meeting in order to overturn existing management policy (Banco Central); the rapid sale of shareholding despite a declared policy of long-term investment (Banco do Vizcaya); and a hostile takeover bid (Ebro).[12]

Energy officials feared Kuwait's equity ownership would follow the Spanish pattern; indeed, there was no reason to think otherwise. In their view, this could lead to undue influence over BP policy through "blocking resolutions at shareholders' meetings or by convening such meetings and then carrying motions unwelcome to the BP board," and to the replacement of directors.[13]

OWNERSHIP AND INFLUENCE: THE RELATIONSHIP

The British raised many noteworthy public-interest issues related to ownership and sovereignty through their Kuwaiti experience. These included:

(1) Strategic Significance

BP's involvement in petroleum extraction and trading was "of strategic significance in both economic [world oil market] and political senses," said British officials in defending their opposition to Kuwait's acquisition. This included BP's "continued ability to operate successfully in a commercial manner unconstrained by governmental interference."[14]

(2) Influence of Foreign Cartels on BP's Production and Development

OPEC's influence on world oil markets prompted at least a glance at the lessons of history. OPEC's past and present behavior gave new meaning to the word "cartel." Its global reach affected the world economy in ways no other monopoly had ever dreamed of. Nothing in OPEC's past suggested that in the interest of BP's corporate health it would refrain from its traditional practices of price-fixing, market manipulation, and production agreements. Nor would it refrain from exercising its influence through one of its founders and charter members, the emirate of Kuwait. "Given OPEC's efforts to persuade other producing countries to support, via production controls, world oil prices favourable to OPEC members . . . conditions might arise in which Kuwait would attempt . . . under pressure from fellow OPEC members, to constrain BP's oil production and development activities in the North Sea . . . or by delaying new developments."[15]

More specifically, although Kuwait was not always in sync with OPEC's policies, its role as a ringleader in OPEC gave the British pause: Kuwait led the drive for nationalization of foreign oil assets, joined with other Arab oil producers in the 1973 oil embargo against the United States and the Netherlands, and cut back its production during the 1979–80 Iranian revolution to take advantage of the loss of Iranian oil.

(3) Dependence

Should OPEC or Kuwait succeed in damaging BP's North Sea business, Britain would be forced "once more to become dependent on the Middle East for oil, as it was in the 1970s."[16]

(4) Competition

Kuwait's new role as a direct competitor of BP raised a specter of a different sort. Normally, competition in global markets brings benefits to all parties: companies become more efficient, consumers benefit from lower prices, and governments can relax in the knowledge that multiple sources, not monopolies, provide for critical industries and products. In this case, however, the opposite scenario threatened, since the competitors were to be housed under the same roof. Kuwait, a producer state, traditionally allied itself with high-reserve countries, encouraging a long-term demand for OPEC oil and discouraging the development of high-cost, non-OPEC reserves, such as those in the North Sea and in Prudhoe Bay, Alaska. From Kuwait and OPEC's point of view, BP also presented a threat to their competitive position: OPEC and Kuwait enjoy low-cost, highly regulated production, whereas Great Britain relies on high-cost, unregulated production.

Clearly, Kuwait and OPEC's interests collided with BP in a number of areas, spelling future disaster for BP. BP regarded Kuwait as a serious competitor in three major trading areas: "exploration for oil, gas and new energy sources, trading in oil, and investment in downstream activities." Buttressed by official government policy, BP's future strategies to develop and exploit North Sea oil to the maximum extent possible were "expected to be in conflict with those of . . . Kuwait . . . a principal supporter of OPEC and a commercial trader in the same product markets."[17]

BP also expected Kuwait to reverse BP's purchasing policy that discriminated against Kuwaiti crude since its high sulphur content raised the cost of production at the refining stage. On the basis of Kuwait's aggressive entry into the penetration of downstream markets in Europe and elsewhere in order to guarantee outlets for its crude, BP argued that Kuwait would not waste much time before exerting its influence over BP's purchasing policies. The ability to "operate in an independent and flexible manner in relation to the purchase of crude was essential to its commercial success," said the company. "The risk that that freedom might be materially constrained was . . . regarded by BP as a matter of serious public interest concern."[18]

Moreover, BP worried that Kuwait, through its rights as a major investor, could constrain the company's ability to raise capital and to make corporate acquisitions that might conflict with Kuwait's corporate or national interests.

And what about the dilemma of giving a direct competitor access to company technology? Similar competitive collisions presented themselves here as well: Unlike Kuwait, Britain was not awash in oil, and, to reduce its costs in production and refining, had developed new technologies to retrieve that oil. Kuwait's oil business, on the other hand, relied on extensive conventional techniques. How would this play in the corporation's future? Would Kuwait try to curtail BP's expenditures on research and development to bring costs down and enhance its competitive position? Or would Kuwait adopt those technologies in its own business, further reducing its own costs and cutting into BP's global competitiveness?

(5) International Reputation

Even if Kuwait did nothing, BP claimed it would be hurt by its alliance with the country, since the perception by other companies and governments throughout the world would change and affect its ability to engage in high-risk investments and purchases in non-OPEC areas. Its reputation hinged on the perception by the rest of the world that BP was an "independent company and not aligned with a major OPEC power." This extended to all of BP's activities, but especially in the United States, where the Kuwaiti connection was "a particularly important point," and where "BP was the largest producer of indigenous crude oil and holder of the largest reserves."[19]

The linkage of BP and Kuwait had already proved troublesome to the company because of "political factors"; BP documented complaints from government agencies and companies in Iran, Abu Dhabi, Venezuela, and Japan as well as the United States, who now regarded BP as a less attractive joint-venture partner, trading partner, and investor.[20]

NATIONAL SECURITY: THE DIFFERENCE BETWEEN
FOREIGN GOVERNMENTS AND PRIVATE INVESTORS

In one of the best statements to date on the difference between individual foreign investors and foreign governments who are also investors, the British called into question the practice of placing national assets in the hands of another sovereign state, in this case "a sovereign state which was itself involved in the politics of the oil market and the politics of the Middle East." Prophetically in light of the Gulf War, British corporate and government leaders also took into account the time frame of the investment, which they assumed, quite reasonably, would extend into the future. From that perspective and with the wisdom of hindsight, Kuwait's "investment was very different from that of an ordinary investor," and even though it would be difficult to predict how that nation would further its commercial goals, it was a virtual certainty that in any Middle Eastern power conflict, Kuwait's investment in BP would be "subordinated to its wider interests" as a sovereign state.

The Gulf War also vindicated British concerns about the security of the energy supply, a concern that was regarded by many at the time as unduly alarmist. Although government officials worried primarily about what Kuwait's mercantilist policies would inflict on BP, no one predicted that Kuwait itself would become the victim of a vicious and brutal political siege, losing control, at least for a short period, of its territory and its oil assets.

Troubles in the Gulf also spoke to the earlier criticisms of giving the Kuwaitis access to sensitive information. Members of the board of directors of BP enjoy access, as a matter of course, to politically and commercially sensitive information involving the company's world-wide strategies. Although the British were primarily concerned at that time with economic conflicts of interest, they mentioned the inherent temptation for Kuwait to share such information with fellow members of the OPEC cartel. What if those data had fallen into the hands of the Iraqis during their occupation of Kuwait?

A nation's security rests on its ability to harness the private sector to work for its interests in a crisis. What happens if a foreign government owns a vital component of the private sector and that nation's interests conflict with those of the host country? BP predicted that its crisis management would be severely impeded by the Kuwaiti investment: "In the event of a crisis of the kind experienced in 1973 and 1979 the interests of the United Kingdom and BP on the one hand, and Kuwait and other OPEC states on the other hand, would conflict. . . . There could be little doubt that the Government of Kuwait would use its holding in BP to further its own immediate interests and not those of either BP or the United Kingdom . . . in order to enhance OPEC's manipulation of the world market."[21]

NATIONAL ASSETS AND NATIONAL SECURITY

BP, the British government, the labor unions, and other oil and chemical companies all offered their views, which were generally supportive of the move to exclude Kuwait from a dominant role in BP. Kuwait fought bitterly to retain all of its holdings. Kuwaiti officials assured the British that they had no other motive than making money, and would refrain from exerting any influence over BP; in fact, state policy was "not to interfere with the management of companies" in which they held a portfolio interest.

The Kuwaitis also accused the British of double-dealing: expressing gratitude, on the one hand, to the KIO for putting a floor on BP's falling stock price, then objecting to the dimension of their purchase.[22]

Look at their record, Kuwaiti officials said, to judge whether they stood by their word: On no occasion had their government or investment agents declared themselves passive portfolio investors—as they did with BP—and then changed their minds to become direct investors. In Spain, where they took direct control, Kuwait's intentions were spelled out up front, and were welcomed by the Spanish authorities. In fact, if they went back on their word, it would destroy their own international reputation and restrict their ability to invest freely.

The Kuwaitis also addressed BP's concerns about damage to the company's reputation as an independent oil producer and trader. Again, they said, look at their record: holdings in Santa Fe and Hoechst, a German company in which they held a 20-percent interest, did not appear to have appreciably sullied the international reputations of those companies; in fact, both had benefited from their Kuwaiti association.

Promises were not enough, however, concluded the royal commission, which agreed with most of the government's premises about the Kuwaiti purchase. Kuwait's assurances, though honorable in their intent, had "no legal effect" on the decision to declare that a "merger situation" existed and could be blocked by law.[23] The British government quickly accepted the commission's findings and forced the Kuwaitis to reduce their investment from 22.5 percent to 9.9 percent—thereby reducing their opportunity to influence the company.

Significantly, the *potential* for influence was sufficient to justify reducing the Kuwaiti investment; it was not necessary to show an actual act of bad faith, or a record of influence. Merely the "ability to control or materially influence the policy of BP" justified the decision, even in the absence of a legal definition of what constituted "material influence," which was left to be judged on a case-by-case basis.

The issue of foreign shareholders—not even foreign governments—also influenced the commission, which concluded that "foreign shareholders [were] less likely to attach importance to matters which may affect United Kingdom interests."[24] What disturbed the commission was the secrecy behind so many foreign investments—the lack of data about the actual owners, the size of their holdings, and their nationalities—although this doesn't seem to bother British trade officials, particularly when the investors are regarded as allies of the U.K. "We are so open we don't know how many U.S. companies are here," said J. C. S. Christen, director of the Invest in Britain Bureau of the Department of Trade and Industries. "We think there are between two and three thousand U.S. companies. That is our estimate."

Even if the Kuwaitis did not exert direct influence over BP, the commission feared the subtle influences of stockholders with large equity interests. The commission also didn't believe Kuwait's allegations of double-dealing, concluding that ". . . the Government of Kuwait could have been in no doubt that the increasing size of its holding was unwelcome to the United Kingdom Government."[25] Even BP was actively divesting its own shares, for reasons very similar to its objections to Kuwait's investment: to release the company from the perception of being under government influence and not free to act in its best commercial interests.

In strong terms, the report sustained the view that Kuwait's interests as a member of OPEC collided with British interests in strategic as well as economic terms for most of the oft-stated reasons. Seeing only a few short years into the future, the British conjured up this possibility:

"Kuwait may come under pressure from its larger neighbours to join them in a more aggressive approach to the oil market. Moreover a future Government of Kuwait may be less well disposed towards the United Kingdom or the West . . . [and] feel under no obligation to abide by the statements of intent which have been made in respect of the shareholding in BP. It could even feel compelled to abandon them in the overriding interests of its own country . . . and at a time of a major crisis in oil supply or for powerful political reasons, we believe the Government of Kuwait would feel obliged to put tangible benefits to its oil and political interests before a potential risk to its investments."[26]

In August 1990, Saddam Hussein invaded Kuwait with an eye toward its rich oil reserves, its access to the sea, and its overseas wealth, in the mistaken belief that the West would not intervene. British concerns were fully justified, even as it fought alongside other Western countries to defend Kuwait's sovereignty, in pointing out that governments were not the same as private investors. In that light, the decision to reduce Kuwait's share in BP turned out to be right for the interests of Britain and its allies; it was as much a decision to preserve Britain's rising energy independence as to promote her economic security against the threat of unfair, cartelized international competition.

CHAPTER IX

Selling Our Science

FOREIGN CORPORATIONS AND
THE UNIVERSITIES

It's important for universities to be open.
> —Dr. Paul Gray, former president,
> Massachusetts Institute of Technology

There's one area in which we have a trade surplus—
exporting America's ideas and brains.
> —Bernard Schwartz,
> chairman, Loral Corporation

America's great research universities are reservoirs of intellectual capital, fueling technological innovations the world over. Although most of this research is federally funded, American companies, driven by a desire for quick profits and a reluctance to make long-term investments, have often been slower than their foreign counterparts to avail themselves of this great natural resource by commercializing the discoveries. Ironically, taxpayer-supported research at American universities has sometimes enabled foreign competitors to outperform American companies.

The relationship between American universities and foreign corporations presents a dilemma. Those who support sharing federally funded research with foreign companies point to the globalization of research. They claim that it is impossible to restrict the flow of scholarship, and would be counterproductive to try. They note that the community of scholars is worldwide, and that research in remote academic outposts has often aided scholars in the world's great research centers. International conferences and the constant flow of ideas across international borders attest to the fact that no nation has a monopoly on ideas, research, or scholarship. University officials say that involving academicians in the commercialization of their research helps bring the academy into the real world, in a process that also generates needed income for academic institutions and underwrites additional research.

Critics, however, say that the issue is neither research nor scholarship, but commercialization. The flow of research toward commercial ends is usually not free, but paid for by grants, contracts, or membership in a university's industrial liaison program (ILP), which allows a company to acquire the fruits of a university's research. In addition, the universities, which hold the patents on government-funded research, often license foreign as well as American companies to manufacture products based upon their research, thereby further restricting U.S. access to commercialization and whatever research fruits derive from this process.

Some critics even contend that this marriage of industry and the academy has skewed academic research by introducing the ethics of the marketplace where it plainly doesn't belong. This has led scholars to be reluctant to share their data, and prompted new conflicts of interest among academicians who have a financial as well as professional interest in the outcome of their scholarship. Such a marriage also has the trappings of anticompetitiveness, in that it mostly benefits large, rich multinational corporations, financially able to join these programs, at the expense of smaller domestic companies that lack the funds necessary to participate.

Of all foreign entities, Japanese interests have forged the closest ties to American universities, leading some to praise their generosity and others to criticize their opportunism. In the last decade, Japanese multinationals have poured more than $4.5 billion into U.S. scientific, educational, and economic policy endeavors. By comparison, total U.S. corporate financial support for American education in the same period came to $5.9 billion. In a study commissioned by the Center for Public Integrity, economic analyst Stephanie Epstein estimated that Japanese companies had spent four times more than their nearest rival, the Germans, who were followed by the Saudis, the Swiss, the Canadians, and the British. Her research indicated that the money was largely intended to fund American university research on advanced technologies, to hire away leading American scientists, to sway American opinion, and to finance think tanks whose policy studies were generally sympathetic to Japanese interests.[1]

But others dispute such charges, arguing that the impact of these contributions is minimal. Daniel Steiner, vice-president and general counsel of Harvard University, which received $93 million from Japanese sources between 1986 and 1991, described how the university protects itself: "For all outside support we insist upon conditions that maintain our independence. Professorships that are endowed or donated are only in fields in which we are interested. The donor has no say on who gets the appointment. Sponsored research grants are accepted when a scientist here is interested in working in the field, and, as in all of our research agreements, the scientist is free to publish all research results and make them available to everybody."

Despite such assurances, however, government officials, who have traditionally viewed foreign access to American research with equanimity, expressed their concerns in May 1991, when they protested a Japanese-government effort to enlist leading American scientists in a project aimed at achieving breakthroughs in computer design. Japanese officials made overtures to scientists at several universities as well as at Bell Laboratories. The ten-year project, informally called the Sixth Generation Computer Project, seeks to develop innovations such as using light instead of electrons to perform high-speed computer calculations, modeling computers after the human brain, and linking together thousands of smaller computers to form a parallel-processing system.

Eugene Wong, associate director of the White House Science Office, stated publicly that the Japanese project seemed to "pose a serious competitive threat" to the United States. He warned that American universities, generally considered to be world leaders in computer-science research, should be concerned about the consequences of accepting foreign support for their research, and that many American professors were "uncomfortable" about accepting foreign funding but still "rationalized" it in order to keep the funds flowing. The White House science adviser, Allan Bromley, meanwhile informed Japanese officials that a 1988 U.S.-Japan science agreement required that such large-scale international research projects be coordinated through official channels and that direct contacts with American laboratories were inappropriate. And Deborah Wince-Smith, assistant secretary of commerce for technology policy, said flatly, "We've asked MITI not to do it anymore." MITI had in fact unsuccessfully sought White House permission the previous year.[2]

The conflict over foreign money echoed ongoing arguments over the extent to which business interests in general should influence university research. Shouldn't scholars be left alone to do their research, untainted by pressures to bring a product to market? Ideally, the academic culture supports a value system that rejects commercial influences, preferring an environment that supports freedom of inquiry. But, in reality, the ivory-tower concept of a university, removed from

materialistic and other pragmatic concerns, was never altogether accurate. Universities have always relied on the sponsorship of commerce
and industry and often tailored their work to the needs of the marketplace, just as Michelangelo relied on the Medici, and Mozart on the
patronage of kings. In recent years, however, such activities have become more common—and some say intrusive—and are increasingly
encouraged by universities, as a means of compensating for a decline
in private philanthropy and a growing uncertainty about government
aid in the face of growing budget deficits. And if much of that money
comes from overseas, well, that's where the money is. Daryl E. Chubin,
a senior analyst with the Office of Technology Assessment, a government agency that advises Congress on science and technology issues,
quipped that "publish or perish" was being replaced with "profit or
perish."[3]

Through the years, the wedding of industry and academe has
paid off handsomely for foreign corporations. Thanks largely to their
access to American-university research, Toshiba Inc. developed a new
technology for recording images on disks, the Toyota Motor Company
devised new engineering-stress sensors, and the Asahi Chemical Company computerized its manufacturing processes.[4]

The United States government underwrites the lion's share of the
nation's research, including more than 80 percent of all academic
research. In 1991, the government's total research budget was $66.4
billion. Of this amount, $11.6 billion went for basic research, $51.8
billion for applied research and development, and $3 billion for re-
search-and-development facilities. Of the basic research, $10.6 billion
went to civilian projects. On the other hand, most of the applied
research and development, $37.8 billion, went for defense-related proj-
ects.[5]

In Japan, by comparison, most scientific and technological research is conducted by private corporations rather than academic institutions, and the international community of scholars does not enjoy
the same access to the research that is afforded by American academic
institutions. Kojio Kobayashi, former chairman of the Nippon Electronic Corporation, "credits access to MIT research for much of NEC's
success in computers."[6] NEC is one of more than a hundred Japanese
companies that paid up to $100,000 a year in 1990 for annual mem-
bership in ILPs that provided members with prepublished papers,
ready access to university laboratories, a chance to acquire exclusive
rights to patents held by the university, and help in overcoming technological problems in developing their products. NEC has also endowed
two chairs at M.I.T., one of the sixteen chairs endowed by Japanese
corporations at roughly $1.5 million each.[7]

"Some Japanese support for research is predatory," said Chalmers Johnson, professor of international relations at the University of California at San Diego. "It is to buy research they can't get otherwise."[8] In December 1990, for example, it was revealed that M.I.T. had signed a $10-million contract to teach Japanese scientists how to replicate a laboratory where futuristic media products were being developed. The objective was to duplicate the creative atmosphere at M.I.T.'s Media Laboratory, where young scientists pursued creative ideas merging computers, television, and films.[9] Researchers at the media lab have also found ways to send movies over telephone lines, so that, instead of going to video rental stores, people will be able to call a number and have movies transmitted to their television sets. They have developed a technique they call interactive television, which allows viewers to use a computer to tailor television shows to their liking, focusing on one item in a news show or selecting a camera angle for a sports event.

Critics viewed this deal, between M.I.T. and both Nihon University and the Japanese industrialist Chiyoji Misawa, as the sale of expertise in one of the few areas of computer science in which the Japanese were lacking: the ability to build a creative environment to generate new ideas. They noted that the agreement did not even require the Japanese to publish all the results of their research, as M.I.T. does. But others defended the agreement; they said it was preposterous even to think of taking a "protectionist attitude" toward science, and viewed the university, and the world, as benefiting from having a Japanese counterpart to the M.I.T. Media Laboratory. How else, they asked, could the U.S., with its shortage of funds, hope to compete with the Japanese in the development and marketing of high-definition television, except in a partnership arrangement?

The M.I.T. Media Laboratory costs $10 million a year to operate, of which $3 million comes from federal funds. Dr. Amar Bose, who teaches electrical engineering at Harvard and is also founder and director of the Bose Corporation of Framingham, Massachusetts, said, "If you ask whether this is going to diminish ultimately the U.S. competitive position, the answer is 'yes.' "[10]

There has been an explosion of foreign-held patents based on research developed by American institutions. In 1987, 46.6 percent of U.S. patents were issued to foreign companies, with nearly one-fifth going to the Japanese firms Canon and Hitachi.[11] Both companies are members of M.I.T.'s ILP, similar to programs at Stanford, the University of California at Berkeley, Texas A & M, and even smaller schools such as Ohio University at Athens and the University of Florida at Gainesville. Participant companies have access to new research as much as a year or more before it is made public. Most controversial, perhaps, the corporate members come to the academic institutions to help solve technological problems and develop commercial products.

Since taxpayers support most scientific research at academic institutions, some in Congress and in the university community have questioned whether the taxpayers should pay for research that is tailored to the needs of foreign corporations—especially if those foreign corporations gain access to the research before their U.S. counterparts. Representative Ted Weiss, a liberal Democrat from the West Side of Manhattan and one of the major congressional critics of ILPs, spoke out on this issue. "Our major concern," he said, "is that these liaison programs provide privileged access to federally funded research . . . sometimes even before the research is completed. They're selling off federally funded research, before it's even completed, to the Japanese, German, and other foreign companies, and that's just wrong. The question is whether U.S. taxpayers want our limited federal dollars to be used on research that will make foreign companies more competitive against American companies."

His concern was echoed by Bernard Schwartz, chairman of Loral. "There's one area in which we have a trade surplus—exporting America's ideas and brains," Schwartz said. "It's extraordinary that we're allowing this to happen. We're dealing with a protagonist [Japan] that views trade competition as trade war. They're predators." Schwartz did not distinguish between government-funded and privately funded research. "Even if it was not federally funded, we should not sell our research. We need a general recognition in the United States that we are in a war, and we need to develop strategies that give us an advantage. Why should we help Japan develop its industry, and become our competitor?"

Dr. David Noble, professor of history at Drexel University and a leading academic critic of the programs, considers them a mercantile scam bordering on the unpatriotic. "The universities are currently selling publicly funded research, generated and paid for by American taxpayers on the explicit assurance to Congress that such research would be of direct benefit to the American economy," Dr. Noble charged. "By doing so, M.I.T. and the other universities who have indeed accepted M.I.T.'s industrial liaison program as their model, are betraying the public trust. . . . Instead of retaining control of inventions crucial to the health of the American economy, they are contributing directly to the alienation of increasing numbers of patents held by foreign corporations who are members of the ILP and similar programs." In 1991, Dr. Noble settled a long and bitter lawsuit against

M.I.T., which he charged with denying him tenure because of his criticism of ILPs. M.I.T. denied the charge.[12]

Responding to such criticism, the university published a report in May 1991 warning against the dangers to both the university and the nation of a shift toward "intellectual protectionism." This report suggested at the same time that M.I.T. faculty members give American companies first crack at the results of their research.[13] But some academic leaders have expressed their discomfort with the accelerating closeness between their world and the world of commerce. The clarity improves with experience: witness the prohibition against publishing on the Japanese side of the Pacific at the NEC-M.I.T. media lab. "I have often heard it said within the scientific community that everyone gains from this marriage of academic and commerce," reflected Sheldon Krimsky, associate professor in the Department of Urban and Environmental Policy at Tufts University and chairman of the Committee on Scientific Freedom and Responsibility of the American Association for the Advancement of Science. "Nothing can be further from the truth. I do not dispute the claim that there are some gains, but there are some losses. Some of these losses involve values and practices that are essential to the integrity of our scientific institutions and to the public confidence in science."[14]

Dr. Krimsky challenged the conventional wisdom that open borders and the free flow of research enhanced scientific inquiry; on the contrary, he said, industry's needs often held up scientific advances. "Trade secrets," he asserted, "and the refusal to share data and biological reagents in a timely fashion have increased." He warned that the use of public funds to support proprietary knowledge could delay important discoveries about new treatments, or delay the publication of data that questioned certain accepted treatments. In addition, the commercialization of biomedical science has spawned new kinds of financial entities between universities, their faculty, and private companies, producing blatant conflicts of interest. "Faculty members engage in research on the efficacy of drugs or therapeutic procedures while they hold substantial equity or are the principals of firms seeking to market these products," said Dr. Krimsky. In some cases, he noted, universities were also partners in the enterprises. "This three-part relationship between scientist, university and firm, in which each is financially linked to the other, is a recipe for conflicts of interest." Dr. Krimsky also cited corporate funding of academic science for skewing research toward short-term product applications, and away from basic science.[15]

Dr. Erich Bloch, former director of the National Science Foundation, challenged that view on the grounds that the advantages of an industry-university research partnership far outweighed the disadvantages. "For many years the National Science Foundation has actively promoted industry-university research cooperation and has encouraged other forms of 'public-private partnerships' in science," Dr. Bloch said. Such partnerships unite researchers on the frontiers of science with those on the frontiers of industrial applications, to their mutual benefit. "But there are disadvantages and potential problems. No doubt about it," he added. "University-industry relationships could result in withholding of information which inhibits the openness of communication. Industry-university relationships could result in a biased interpretation of results. The lure of commercial success or scientific recognition could result in fraud, misconduct and the exaggeration of research results, independent of the industry-university relationship."[16]

Many academic leaders contend that these programs are part of the open flow of ideas and cross-fertilization among scholars that are essential to academic research. Such programs bring scholars into the real world of commerce, and also generate income. Unfortunately, the decline in private philanthropy has led them to seek corporate funds— for a price. "We look to corporations for substantial financial support," said Dr. Paul Gray, former president of M.I.T., "and our industrial liaison program is a way of lubricating that process. Research depends on openness, and restraints could kill the goose that lays the golden egg." Dr. Gray said that ILPs "facilitate" a company's acquisition of research, but do not offer the research on a private or exclusive basis, because nonmembers are welcome to the research— after it has been published.

The M.I.T. ILP is the prototype. It was created in 1948 as part of a broad effort to spur the postwar economy. However, 70 percent of the 281 existing ILPs at forty-one academic institutions were created after 1980.[17] That was the year Congress enacted the University and Small Business Patent Procedures Act, a Carter-administration initiative that gave universities proprietary rights to patents developed with federally financed research—whereupon the universities licensed companies to develop products based upon the patents. It seems paradoxical to some that, although the universities defend industrial liaison programs on the grounds that they encourage openness and a free exchange of ideas, they give member companies patent licenses that prevent other companies from developing those technologies, thereby restricting the free exchange of scientific and technological research. By comparison, the Japanese government retains ownership of all ideas emerging from work it sponsors, and it has licensed that technology chiefly to its own industries.[18]

Universities market these programs with the lure of giving corporate members a technological edge. The M.I.T. program's brochure advertises that since its founding:

The M.I.T. Industrial Liaison Program has helped its members stay at the leading edge of advances in science, engineering, and management, allowing them to assess the potential of emerging technologies for the marketplace. In the rapidly changing world of business, the Program can be a particularly valuable resource to tap in making crucial business and technical decisions.

The Industrial Liaison Program places at the disposal of industry the expertise and resources of all the schools, departments, centers and laboratories of M.I.T. It can assist its member organizations in making strategic business and technical decisions and help them identify business opportunities by:

- Augmenting industrial research and technical efforts with information, perspective and background;
- Facilitating access to the expertise of M.I.T.'s faculty and research staff;
- Providing information on the latest developments in almost any area of science, engineering and management;
- Establishing links to M.I.T. resources, including libraries, laboratories, and the M.I.T. Press;
- Informing members of the latest patent licensing opportunities at M.I.T.;
- Notifying clients of special lectures, events and educational opportunities at M.I.T. relevant to the business community;
- Introducing member organizations to the Institute's pool of talented undergraduate and graduate students.[19]

The brochure advises:

Upon joining the M.I.T. Industrial Liaison Program, each member company is assigned an individual Liaison Officer as its principal on-campus contact. The Officer is readily available to management and members of the research staff who seek to use the expertise of M.I.T. faculty to explore leading-edge technologies or to discuss specific technical problems.

The Liaison Program is a pro-active service designed to help member companies take advantage of the rich resources of the

Institute. The Liaison Officer visits the member organization regularly, initiating contacts, following the organization's activities closely, and looking for opportunities to offer M.I.T.'s consultation. He or she becomes acquainted with the organization's business, technology, market and structure. It is the Officer's goal to reveal M.I.T. as an accessible and responsive resource, with a thoughtful and informed faculty who are interested in the concerns and activities of member organizations.

In addition to such outreach, the program also encourages a company's "in-reach," through a "working contact." "A designated working contact within a member company is critical to the organization's successful use of the I.L.P. This person's role is to visit M.I.T., to keep informed about the program, and to help company management and research staff make use of it. The Liaison Officer communicates regularly with the working contact to keep abreast of company activities."

The program strives for a harmony of research and its application. "Liaison Officers can arrange for representatives from member companies to meet with individuals on M.I.T.'s faculty and staff. Through these meetings, members can confer with the Institute's experts on campus about current research on anything from international finance to computer architecture. Officers can also arrange for faculty, who frequently travel to many parts of the world, to visit member companies."

In return for their participation, M.I.T. awards points to each faculty member: one point for each unpublished article that is made available to the member companies, two points for a phone conversation or a brief on-campus visit, and at least twelve points for a visit to the company. Each point is worth $35. The money is used not for personal expenses but, rather, for professional purposes, such as travel to professional conferences, and supplies and equipment.

M.I.T. itself has expressed concerns about U.S. competitiveness. "Increasingly, Americans are concerned about the competitiveness of U.S.-based industries," Dr. Gray wrote in 1989. "We at M.I.T. share this concern. In 1986, we appointed a commission of sixteen members of our faculty to examine the productivity of eight industrial sectors in the U.S., Japan, and Europe. 'Made in America,' a book presenting the results of this study, was published in May by the M.I.T. Press. Not only does it identify several weaknesses common to these sectors in the U.S., it suggests imperatives which could improve our productivity and international competitiveness."[20]

But does M.I.T.'s program, along with similar programs at the

40 other universities, undermine that very competitiveness? In 1989, the M.I.T. program had 291 member companies, of whom 161 were American and 130 foreign. The foreign members included 56 Japanese corporations, 13 French, 13 Italian, 6 Canadian, 5 each from Finland, Germany, Sweden, and Switzerland; 4 each from the Netherlands and the United Kingdom; 3 each from Brazil, Norway, and Venezuela; and 1 each from Austria, Belgium, Colombia, Denmark, and Korea. The program produced gross revenues of $8–9 million, against expenses of $4–5 million.

"Revenue is not the only value," Dr. Gray responded. "It's an opportunity for the faculty to understand the nature of the interests of industry, a window into the industrial world, the world we're preparing students for."

M.I.T. receives $640 million a year from the federal government for research. The institution's Lincoln Laboratory, which explores military applications of electronics, is fully funded by the federal government with $400 million, and only a small fraction of its work is listed in the ILP directory. The federal government also finances $240 million in on-campus research, which is unclassified and available to corporate members. An additional $15 million comes from state and local governments, and $45 million from private industry.

M.I.T. takes the position that, if American companies fail to use the resources of the institution, and if foreign companies thereby gain an advantage, the Americans have only themselves to blame. Dr. Gray noted that "Foreign companies are bigger users than American companies, some of which are not assiduous in following research developments." However, this is not entirely by chance. M.I.T. has an ILP office in Tokyo, the program's only foreign office, which solicits Japanese corporate members. Dr. Gray noted that Japanese universities have no such outflow of research, even to their own companies. "It is startling to me that the Japanese universities have had no consequential relationships with corporations, foreign or domestic," Dr. Gray said. "So you have this curious situation in which a host of Japanese companies have closer relationships with American universities than with their own universities."

Was there a problem of technology transfer? "Sure, no question about it," Dr. Gray said. "Integrated circuits were invented here; the Japanese built on those inventions." But, like other officials at universities with ILPs, Dr. Gray believes that such transfers are an integral part of research. "I don't think that any society can keep bottled up for very long secrets on technology that it wants to apply."

Of 107 universities reporting foreign funding, 41 identified 281 different liaison programs, according to the General Accounting Office. The universities reported that these major programs had 2,848 U.S. member companies (85 percent) and 496 foreign member companies (15 percent). Three universities accounted for 379, or 76 percent, of the foreign companies: M.I.T., the University of California at Berkeley, and Texas A & M.[21]

Carnegie Mellon University, which did not begin its industrial liaison program until 1989, distinguished between research that was funded by the government and research that was privately financed. Dr. Richard Cyert, the university president, said: "We have had a lot of foreign firms interested in participating in some programs not paid for with public funds, and are now opening them up. We tried to keep this solely for domestic firms, but haven't been able to raise the money we need. We think that the results of our federally funded research should go into the public domain."

Frank J. Giunta—director of industrial liaison programs at the University of California at Berkeley, which has 350 corporate members, of which 15 percent are foreign—said, "Some companies are very intimately involved in the research they support." Corporate contributions range from $5,000 to millions of dollars, Giunta said: "It's a matter of the support that the company chooses to give to the university." Did Berkeley's programs undermine U.S. competitiveness? "That's a very interesting question," Giunta said. "Since all our research is published in the open literature, we believe that these programs are neutral in technology slippage." Berkeley's programs were limited to the engineering departments, whereas M.I.T.'s applied across the board.

Nancy Hay, Stanford University's assistant director for foundation and corporate relations, said, "Our 'affiliates programs' are entirely different from M.I.T.'s." There were fifty-two foreign companies out of a total of about 325, and about half of the foreign companies were Japanese. The companies pay up to $50,000 for membership. Foreign companies were excluded, however, from the university's Center for Integrated Systems, each of whose twenty-five members pays $120,000 to join and $750,000 over a three-year period. "We decided not to encourage Japanese companies to join, because of the technology problem," Hay said. "But they can join our affiliates programs."[22]

Congressman Weiss, who is chairman of the Human Resources Subcommittee of the House Government Operations Committee, which held hearings on the issue, jousted with Dr. Gray about whether these programs undermined American competitiveness. He reminded the educator that in 1985, when Gray sought increased federal funding, he had told the House Science and Technology Committee that such funding would enhance America's competitive role. Weiss recalled that Gray had told Congress: "In recent years the Japanese have not often seized from us positions of scientific leadership, but they have often succeeded in superior implementation. Thus, stronger relationships that bridge between U.S. industry and basic research can be seen as matters of national interest to be encouraged and fostered by Congress."[23]

Weiss asked Gray to reconcile that statement with the fact that foreign corporations made up 45 percent of M.I.T.'s ILP. Gray responded that most of the effort that goes into bringing a scientific idea to the marketplace in the form of a commercial product "occurs not in the university setting and is not aided in detail a great deal by the basic research that has occurred in the university, but it depends on what happens in the corporation. If the Japanese are indeed eating our lunch, as some have suggested, it occurs not because they have a superior scientific research program, and I suggest it occurs not because they have access to the superior program of scientific research that exists in this country, but because they have been much more assiduous and much more effective at implementation, at the process which takes an idea and translates it into something which affects the market." Gray noted, for example, that the VCR was developed by the Ampex Corporation, an American company, which wrongly concluded that it could not be developed as a consumer product. "The Japanese picked up on that idea and by being prepared to invest in that process over a period of many years, a kind of time horizon that most U.S. corporations have found unacceptable, developed the VCR at a price level which makes it possible for most families to buy." He added that the Japanese now owned 80 percent of the VCR market, as opposed to no VCR production in the U.S.[24]

Congressman Weiss, noting that 86 percent of M.I.T.'s research funds came from the federal government, asked, "Are you at all concerned that American taxpayers are paying for research whose results are being sold to private industries that will not necessarily benefit the American public?" Gray replied that "all the results of the research sponsored by the Federal Government or by private industry are in the public domain. The Industrial Liaison Program does not provide exclusive access to those results. It does provide facilitated access."

At the very least, it would seem, American companies should enjoy the same access to federally funded research as foreign firms, and be exempted from the special fees for membership in industrial liaison programs. Similarly, any federally funded research tailored to help a foreign company should also be tailored to help its American competitor. American companies and American taxpayers have already paid their dues, in providing the federal funds that underwrite the research. Moreover, Americans have made both the financial and intellectual investments that created America's great academic institutions. By increasing the cost of this research to foreign companies, the academic institutions could offset the money they would lose from American companies.

Dr. Frank Press, president of the National Academy of Sciences, and Dr. Bloch contend that foreign beneficiaries should pay more to support American research; they see "cream skimming."[25] William Norris, founder and former chairman of Control Data Corporation, focused on the Japanese, who, he said, were reaping the rewards of America's investment of billions of dollars to develop the nation's academic institutions, and academic atmosphere. In that light, Norris said, Japanese membership in industrial liaison programs "is not a fair deal. It took us a hundred years to build those universities. If the government continues to let universities work with Japan, let the Japanese fund 25 percent of the National Science Foundation budget. Let's charge them. They're getting a free ride."

The relationship between foreign corporations and American universities raises more questions than it answers. Still, the globalization of research should not be used to justify the sale of taxpayer-funded research to overseas competitors. If it is indeed impossible to restrict the flow of scholarship, let that scholarship flow freely, without cost, to American and foreign users alike. American companies should not be disadvantaged. Research financed by American taxpayers should be in the public domain.

CHAPTER X

The Casino Economy

WHY AMERICA ISN'T INVESTING IN ITS CRITICAL TECHNOLOGIES, AND OTHER ANOMALIES OF GLOBALISM

We've got a casino economy. There are big stakes, and we just throw the dice on the table.

—Kenneth Courtis, senior economist, Deutsche Bank (Asia)

Look at the Japanese. They're willing to take out hundred-year mortgages. They are perfectly willing to commit their grandchildren. . . . In Japan, money is cheap, but technology is forever.

—Carl Ledbetter, president of ETA

VISIONARIES AND WALL STREET

"Six years ago, we decided to take a look at the future," recalled Martin Marietta's CEO, Norman Augustine. "We knew we needed advanced technology to win new business, and we had exciting ideas for research. We were so enthusiastic, our president went up to New York and met with a group of [investment] analysts." The message to Wall Street was that management had decided to invest heavily in research and development to realize the company's full technological potential.

Instead of joining in the excitement, Wall Street recoiled in horror. "The analysts literally ran out of the room and pulled their stock," Augustine continued. "We went down eleven and a half points in five days. The decline continued for two years. They didn't want us to spend on R and D. The analysts and stockholders hoped we would be broken up and sold to the Japanese."

The executives from Martin Marietta were equally shocked. "Why do they act that way?" asked Augustine. "The average share turns over every eighteen months. If it takes five years to pay off R and D, and owners will only own you for eighteen months, why should they care?"

In light of this experience, why didn't Martin Marietta fold, break up, or succumb to a takeover instead of surviving to share the glory for the performance of the Patriot missile during the Gulf War? Careful to explain that he wasn't with the company at that time, Augustine credits management with standing up to Wall Street and sticking to its decision to invest in research. Ignoring the investors, "the management of the company had the courage to spend over $1 billion over five years, and everybody applauded it, including [eventually] the analysts."

Even the numbers turned out right: "Today, our backlog in orders is $12 billion. Everyone says we're brilliant, even the analysts who ran out of the room."

Augustine promotes "patient management" to compensate for the absence of "patient capital"—long-term investment capital not subject to the demands of the quarterly report. Its scarcity is a common complaint of the high-tech community. Martin Marietta was unusually fortunate to have a team of managers who withstood the pressures from their investment bankers. "Patient management wants to do what's right for the long term," he explained.

Not every company is so lucky. Only a company like Martin Marietta, with an arsenal of defense contracts, deep pockets, and tough-minded executives can survive such an onslaught. More typical was the experience of ETA, a producer of supercomputers spawned by Control Data. When ETA folded, Cray of Chippewa Falls, Minnesota, became the last surviving supercomputer company in the United States. The questions raised by the demise of ETA highlighted the critical-industries issue: how could the nation allow a company producing a technology of the future to expire without fighting for it?

The answer lies in Wall Street, and the haphazard financial system to which the nation entrusts its critical industries. The ETA experience showed the vulnerability of high-tech companies, which may need more nurturing than the current U.S. financial environment can provide. Control Data was founded by William Norris, a Navy cryptographer who had helped break the German code for submarine warfare. At its creation, the model he created seemed ideal for both ETA and Control Data: a step toward vertical integration, in which companies finance related technologies, the very model that had propelled the dramatic postwar economic success of Germany and Japan.

Unfortunately, in this case, the transplant worked like palm trees in Alaska. As successful as it was, Control Data wasn't Mitsubishi, with a bank and hundreds of other interlocking companies to provide a wellspring of funds. ETA was totally dependent on the financial fortunes of its parent, for better or worse: when Control Data was cash-rich, ETA flourished, but when Control Data ran into trouble, ETA was closed down as the company's biggest cash drain.

"As a cash transaction, I can't criticize them," recalled Carl Ledbetter, former president of ETA. "As a technological transaction, it was fatal." ETA had already spent $490 million developing a supercomputer without a government contract, but needed $800 million more to stay in business. "We were beating Fujitsu, NEC, and Hitachi in the same period of time. In the first year of shipments, we sold $110 million worth of products: thirty-four machines. ETA had 800 to 850 employees, costing $100 million a year. All three Japanese companies combined shipped less than thirty-four machines, even though all three companies individually had more employees. That meant that, whatever financial pressures were on ETA, Japan had three times as much; they were three times worse off than ETA. Yet Japan never would have considered shutting down those companies."

Ledbetter also claimed that ETA's technology was "superior to what everyone in the world was doing. In an industry in which Japan has an eighteen-month lead in semiconductor and printed-circuit-board technology, ETA had a lead of three years to everything Japan was doing." Ledbetter's assessment of his company's achievements was corroborated by one of the nation's leading supercomputer scientists, who also blamed Ledbetter (off the record) for not responding to the market:

"ETA developed the best technology and the best manufacturing process anywhere in the world," he said. "They were doing board-routing automatically while Cray was using housewives in Chippewa Falls to do it manually. I told them [ETA], 'You can't stamp out supercomputers like cookie cutters if nobody wants to buy them.' Ledbetter got mad at me. He wasn't listening to his customers. His computer caused the user to go to a lot of trouble that was not warranted. There were other alternatives. . . . The product was not applicable. It did not respond to the market. To fix it would have been easy. They could have put Cray out of business."

According to Ledbetter, the federal government agreed that his product was superior but did little to help the company, either by purchasing their product or by pushing them to develop a more competitive product. "The federal-government officials who considered buying the ETA product told us we were competitive, our technology was good, and that they needed the leverage [of another supercomputer company] against Japan and the other vendors," recalled Ledbetter. But talk is cheap; the government still didn't buy their product.

Ledbetter said that the business-and-government environment in Japan fosters leading-edge technologies and focuses on the long term. "We have a fatal fascination for quarterly reports," he said. "Look at the Japanese. They're willing to take out hundred-year mortgages. They are perfectly willing to commit their grandchildren. That's a view we don't have. Our financial decisions were forced by Control Data's financial crisis. In Japan, there would have been another choice: . . . MITI would have forced purchases. That is so antithetical to our free-enterprise market . . . although we do it with great frequency—as with NASA—if the projects are big enough. In Japan, money is cheap, but technology is forever."[1]

The U.S. government not only did little to save ETA, but inadvertently worked against the company's survival. ETA was both too big and too small for its own good. It wasn't a big enough science project to sustain the kind of large-scale public support enjoyed by NASA, Star Wars, or the human-genome enterprise. But it was too small to generate the kind of funds that it needed to become profitable within the limited time frame required by Wall Street and its corporate parent.

Wherever ETA turned, it faced U.S. policies inimical to its survival. Most important, government proved unwilling to follow its time-honored practice of supporting several vendors of the same product, which typically assured that competition would keep prices down and quality up. In view of what Ledbetter described as disenchantment among government officials with Cray's high prices and monopolistic behavior, why wasn't there more of an effort to nurture competition in the supercomputer industry? "There is a quota system for vendors," explained Ledbetter, "deliberately created competition for torpedo manufacturers, but there is no such thing with the computer industry."

Ledbetter, a well-heeled mathematician turned entrepreneur, also blamed risk-averse government officials for failing to stick their necks out: "The problem is civil bureaucrats. They are not terribly well paid; they only get $89,000 to run a federal agency. Why should they take a risk? With a Cray, they're safe. There is a saying in the computer business that no one ever got fired for buying an IBM. The same is true of Cray. Cray has 80 percent of the world market, excluding Japan. Few were willing to put the risk into the work ETA needed."

Another U.S. policy prevented ETA's expansion into world markets, this one under the rubric of national security: export controls.

Fearful that unfriendly foreign nations might tap into American-controlled weapons research, the government prevented ETA from getting an export license to ship supercomputers abroad. The company fought the decision by guaranteeing to the government that its own employees would set the machinery up and keep an American supervisor on the site at all times. "If we don't physically put our hands on it, it will stop running irreparably," promised Ledbetter, but to no avail. "The Department of Commerce, NASA, and Defense were not qualified enough to understand that we could do that." Had they understood, "there would have been money available to ETA in the sale of just a few machines. In Japan, export licenses are much easier to get. The Bush administration wants a free market but cuts off one part of the market that would be useful, that would make resources available to us." Those in Defense and Commerce who supported strong export controls argued that companies like ETA expected them to take a great deal on faith: how could they evaluate the trustworthiness of ETA's on-site personnel?[2]

What kinds of losses emerged from ETA's untimely end?

First the technological loss: Supercomputers are used throughout a variety of product lines, from weapons systems to toasters. Even the most ardent free-trader would agree that having only one company, Cray, is not the most desirable situation, either for Cray or for the country (especially since the Cray supercomputer is filled with chips from Japan).

Then there was the loss of expertise, one of the ripple effects of technological loss. "We dispersed the human capital immediately," said Ledbetter. "Some went to NEC, others to Fujitsu. One key person went to Cray. I sent him to Rollwagen [John A. Rollwagen, of Cray Research], and said, 'Keep the guy for America,' even though we were still competitors."

After personnel came the product chain. ETA insisted on using semiconductors manufactured in the U.S. by a Honeywell plant in Colorado Springs; the loss of ETA meant lost business for Honeywell. Finally, there was the loss from spent resources: Control Data's $490-million investment, plus the incalculable resources expended in training and educating personnel for high-tech production. "Our way is to fire eight hundred people and hope they stay in U.S. companies," said Ledbetter. "That's inefficient. It's like plowing a cornfield under, three days before harvest time. It is an expensive way to fertilize."

The ETA saga reveals how easy it is to lose critical technologies in an environment that fails to appreciate their importance. Key technologies might survive in the U.S. if other industrialized nations allowed the marketplace to determine their technology priorities. But they don't. While U.S. policymakers ponder, industry after industry, technology after technology, depart for nations that understand the importance of investing in themselves, and providing a business environment conducive to financing technologies of the future.

Stark contrasts between the U.S. on one side, and Japan and the European Community on the other, reveal a pattern of financial anomalies that consistently work against our nation's interests. These anomalies include different banking and antitrust laws, costs of capital, and tax inequities that amount to whopping advantages for foreign corporations—also referred to as "imbalances" and "asymmetries." Add to this the leveraged buy-out party of the 1980s, the quarterly returns demanded by Wall Street, the idiosyncratic U.S. corporate culture which plays into the Wall Street syndrome, and the relatively high cost of capital in the U.S.—at least until 1991. Finally, there is the government, contributing a mélange of policies and attitudes that confuse investors and fail to address the new global realities. The results speak for themselves: the U.S. is falling behind other nations in its capacity to invest in critical industries, preserve its standard of living, retain its technological edge, and guarantee economic stability and national security.

Although most Americans regard Japan as their major competitor, the Europeans bear watching as well, for they have caught on to the Japanese model. Europeans can now laugh at the misbegotten predictions that their Airbus would never fly. U.S. trade negotiators have shifted from ridiculing the Airbus to criticizing it as a case of unfair subsidization.[3]

The superior attitude of Americans toward the Airbus dominated the thinking of the postwar period right up to the 1990s, and continues despite all evidence to the contrary: it says that government intervention doesn't work and government investment is even worse. The evidence? Look at the breeder reactor, synfuels, and other examples of trendy, politically inspired government investments in boondoggles that never amounted to anything.

U.S. official attitudes toward Japanese industrial policy displayed even more naïveté, if that was possible, and ultimately proved more harmful to U.S. interests. The Japanese were far more strategic than the Europeans, especially vis-à-vis U.S. industries. Americans, flushed with their own postwar success and a sense of their own hegemony, rationalized that the system that had yielded the Japanese economic miracle could never work in the U.S.: Americans were unaccustomed to the level of material sacrifice accepted by the Japanese people, who saved a high percentage of their earnings to provide cheap capital for industry and accepted a lower standard of living in consequence. They rarely complained publicly about their tiny apartments, their lack of home appliances and other amenities common in American households, or about having to pay much more for Japanese-produced VCRs and other consumer-electronic gadgets than Americans had to pay. It is ironic to see Japanese tourists in New York City flooding the consumer-electronics stores and purchasing Japanese-made cameras, VCRs, and other products at far lower prices than they would have to pay back in Tokyo. Few Japanese officials complained when MITI forced them to buy Japanese computers that were clearly inferior to those made by IBM and other U.S. producers. MITI knew they had to practice protectionism until their own computer industry was up to speed.[4]

U.S. computer executives who understood what was happening fought these practices bitterly, but to no avail: the Japanese steadfastly refused to enter the free market until they determined they were good and ready. Even those who engaged in joint ventures were often held at bay. "We had a joint venture with C. Itoh," recalled William Norris. "They put a 15-percent import duty on us. You can't compete with a 15-percent import duty. Our business was data services. We couldn't get into their markets. We set up a data center. We couldn't take the service out of Tokyo for six years. By the time they let us in, it was too late; they had already developed their data services. It was a $100-million investment we had to forgo. The only person in government who recognized the problem was Prestowitz [Clyde Prestowitz, an adviser to former Secretary of Commerce Malcolm Baldrige]. We had no U.S.-government support."

In other words, it took the Japanese eight years to develop their own data-services industry, but they persevered until it was competitive. The Europeans are following suit. In the spring of 1991, for example, EC officials admitted publicly what had clearly been their practice: to protect their auto industry from the Japanese until 1999, when they predicted their own automobile producers would be able to compete. They were "learning," EC officials said, "from the mistakes of the Americans." Spending a month in northern Italy confirmed that they meant what they said: not a single Japanese car was spotted around the hill towns of the lake country during that period, although Japanese dealerships in the area were open for business.

The results again proved how shortsighted and misguided were U.S. attitudes. The Japanese economy is half the size of that of the U.S., yet exceeds ours in capital investment, both public and private. In 1989, the Japanese spent $549 billion on capital investment, as opposed to $513 billion in the U.S. "Toshiba invested 10 percent of its profits in R and D," explained Kenneth Courtis, senior economist for Deutsche Bank Capital Markets (Asia). "That's $250 million, or equal to Harvard University's entire research budget." Based in Japan, Courtis is one of the world's shrewdest analysts of Japanese technology-and-investment strategy. "We've got a casino economy," he cautioned. "There are big stakes, and we just throw the dice on the table." Courtis continued: "The U.S. economy is in a Ricardoian era [after the nineteenth-century icon of free-market economists, David Ricardo], closer to a market economy," continued Courtis. "Japan is structured, with a clear understanding of the national interest. They have a clear understanding that Japan has to go up the technological ladder; it is the new product lab of the world. That is a strategic necessity. Their sequence goes in three steps: first the new product lab; then the internationalization of the life cycle of the product; then the distribution of the product in sequence around the world."

The most pernicious problem in the U.S. is the attitude that says this doesn't matter. The 1980s saw a peculiar confluence of attitudes that accepted the "capital-poor" condition of U.S. technologies, yet at the same time revered entrepreneurs Donald Trump and Henry Kravis for raising untold amounts of capital for casinos, hotels, and leveraged buy-outs of biscuit companies.

What is most surprising is that Americans, who invented competition among products, can't yet conceive of competition among nations to preserve those products. "You can't leave anything to chance," cautioned Courtis. "In the abstract, it doesn't matter who owns what. But, in reality, ownership is very important. In Japan, the brains of the companies are in Japan and that's where they're staying. It is imperative to break out in key technologies. Technological decisions are made at the home base. Controllership of key technologies is vital; *you can't leave things to chance*. It does matter. Japan won't let foreign investors buy their key technologies. You don't buy because you're a Boy Scout. The Japanese buy as part of an overall strategic plan of where they're going."[5]

PATIENT CAPITAL, RISK CAPITAL, AND VENTURE CAPITAL

Virtual agreement exists among U.S. executives about the shortage of capital, particularly long-term capital. They quickly part company, however, when it comes to the reasons for this dearth, the kind of capital they need, where to get capital, and the level of government intervention required to solve their problems. The divisions among them explain why so little has been done about the problem.

The figures support the individual experiences of CEOs like Augustine and Ledbetter. Venture capital, for example, has declined by 28 percent since 1986, making the venture-capital industry today almost totally dependent on institutional sources such as pension funds. In 1983, institutional funds provided 79 percent of venture funds; in 1988 this rose to 92 percent. Managers of pension funds tend to be cautious about investing in innovation and unproven technologies— a reaction to poor decisions made in the 1980s.

Some say there was too much capital throughout the 1970s and early 1980s, and "too many inexperienced people chased wrongheaded risks in biotechnology and gallium arsenide—wrongheaded because the real time to market and the capital dollars required proved beyond the means for venture funds," wrote George Jenkins, a venture-fund manager. Across the board, there is a tendency toward reducing risk and encouraging greater portfolio maturity among fund managers, who would rather "leverage already established companies than finance nascent ones. We want to repot seedlings rather than plant seeds."[6]

Many point to the tax system as the major culprit. Though the tax-reform legislation of 1988 streamlined the confusing and inequitable U.S. tax system, it also spelled trouble for critical technologies. The elimination of the capital-gains incentive removed the motivation for individual investments, "and seriously eroded the availability of early stage, high-risk capital from wealthy individuals, traditionally a most important source of seed money."[7]

"We need patient capital," said J. Richard Iverson, president of the American Electronics Association, who sees this problem as central to the survival of the electronics industry in America. "Every study says the real problem is the cost of capital. Now the issue is patient capital. The pension funds have no loyalty. One takeover announcement, and pension funds drop. The banks are even worse. Pension funds want a return next year. No one wants to make investments that pay off in ten years."

"The lack of capital," warns Iverson, "means companies are underinvesting in productivity improvement. With the added dimension of reduced defense budgets, there ain't no business. In 1989, Japan outinvested us by $49 billion in plant and equipment. In 1988, 109 firms considered industrial-base firms, one-half of them electronics firms, were acquired by foreign investors."

The answers point to a revision of the capital-gains tax, in the view of Juan Benitez, former acting deputy undersecretary for technology at Commerce, and onetime owner of a high-tech company in Texas. "A few years ago, the capital-gains tax on a long-term investment was 15 percent. Today, it's equivalent to ordinary income, or 30 percent. That's a twofold increase on our taxation rate of capital gains. Also: the risk-reward ratio has substantially decreased. A few years ago, you could write off losses; now the relief is limited. That means that not only do you have to pay a higher tax for your capital gains, but at the same time you can suffer more of a loss if you're out there making investments of a somewhat risky nature. We have no risk-tolerant capital whatsoever."

Turning to Asia is the first response of capital-starved high-tech firms, who want to grow but can't find American investors willing to stake them. Apple cofounder Stephen Jobs, who founded a computer company called NeXT, Inc., accepted $100 million from Canon in exchange for a 16.7 percent equity stake. Investors from Europe, Taiwan, and Japan scour the United States for the high-technology companies that spawn innovations for which Americans are famous; there is no dearth of foreign investors willing to risk capital for inventions that may pay off many times over in future profits. Future-minded foreign investors buy technology, not the company.

American entrepreneurs feel they have no choice but to look to Asia, recalling Willy Sutton, who said he robbed banks because "that's where the money is." Their job is to make a profit, not public policy. "If somebody feels it is un-American to sell technology to Japan, then all they have to do is give us the money," said Larry Boucher, president of Auspex Systems. Boucher, who produces equipment that helps users get information on a computer network, traded some of his company's technology and equity for $12 million from two Japanese firms. "It will be of no value to me to have the technology if I can't get it to market," he concluded. Auspex also raised an additional $14 million from U.S. investors.[8]

OFF BALANCE: HOW ASYMMETRIES WORK
AGAINST U.S. INTERESTS

The devaluation of the dollar and high capital-gains tax that followed led to the inexpensive sale of U.S. assets. The Japanese benefited most from the free fall of the dollar, a drop of at least 50 percent against the yen over the period 1985–1990. This sudden financial gain worked to the advantage of Japanese investors, who aimed their sights at golf courses, real-estate trophies like Rockefeller Center, cattle ranches, and a range of technologies.[9] "Putting the cheap-dollar policy and the high capital gains tax policy together—a 50% drop in the currency and a 50% drop in the P/ES [price-earnings ratio]—has cut the price of

American innovations by around 75% to Japanese and some European buyers," wrote George Gilder. "The result is a deadly undervaluation of critical U.S. assets that is moving the foundation technologies of the information age step-by-step to Japan."[10]

Like tax policy, the lowering of the dollar didn't occur accidentally: it was the result of a conscious policy on the part of the U.S. Federal Reserve Board, the Treasury, and the Congress to help American exporters. Exporters with clout, that is: the government was responding to producers of textiles, paper, steel, and other commodities at the expense of high-technology industries. High-tech producers lost market share and equity value during this period, while their counterparts in Japan were gaining. In Japan, Nippon Steel cut steel output and moved into semiconductors and computers; the shipbuilder NKK started producing D-RAMs; Kawasaki Steel produced advanced semiconductors; and the tractor manufacturer Kubota produced advanced minicomputers.[11]

Politically it made sense. High-technology industries were concentrated in Silicon Valley, around Boston, and in isolated spots around the rest of the country. High tech was no match for the heavily populated industrial states, the politically powerful South, and the combined power of the Pacific Northwest lumber interests. Lobbyists for high tech were also relatively new to the political arena; nor were their bosses as aware of the potential effects of fiscal, monetary, and trade policy on their well-being.

Even companies that tried to stave off foreign acquirers met with indifference. Materials Research Corporation (MRC), a leading producer of semiconductor equipment, was forced to sell out to Sony in 1988 at a price of $60 million, estimated at 40 percent of the company's annual sales, or about twice what Sony would have paid MRC for new equipment over a two-year period. The president of MRC said that no U.S. buyers were interested, even though he'd spent a considerable amount of time searching for one. Joseph Krenski, the final-assembly manager at MRC, recalled in an interview his company's fruitless efforts to find an American buyer: "We were in the market for years. Sony was the only one that looked at us. We were looking at some future products that we couldn't fund before. We had banks walking around the plant for three years. No one was interested until Sony came around. We tried very hard to find American investors. Sony lets us run the company without interference. Sony did try to put a Japanese flag outside the plant but backed down after resistance from American workers."

The MRC experience echoed that of Perkin-Elmer and many other companies whose stories failed to reach the media. But clearly something was happening to alert the nation that its financial system was clearly off balance if U.S. buyers couldn't be found for technologies that were snapped up in a flash by offshore investors. "When market leaders such as Perkin-Elmer and MRC can't survive under the American brand of capitalism and get shunned by potential U.S. buyers, a major shakeout seems inevitable," editorialized *Business Week*.[12]

Just why is capital more expensive in the United States than in other industrialized countries? How do other industrialized countries produce capital for their new technologies and their industrial bases, while the U.S. comes up short? Why were half the electronics firms in the U.S. defense industrial base purchased by foreign investors in the late 1980s? One answer offered by Richard Iverson is that the "Europeans see electronics as a growing business, while our companies do not."[13]

Bill Emmott, business editor of *The Economist*, contradicts that view, arguing that U.S. business can no longer complain about the cost of capital since by 1991 the cost of borrowing was lower for Americans than it was in Germany: German prime rates rose to 10.5 percent (a result of reunification with East Germany), compared with 8.5 percent in the United States. The Japanese money machine, he emphasizes, was no longer so relevant, given the 40-percent fall in the Tokyo stock market and the scandals affecting several of their major brokerage houses. Dale Jorgensen, an economist at Harvard, agrees, adding that the cost of capital is actually higher in Japan, if the cost of investing—setting up sites, construction costs, labor, land, and equipment—were factored in as well.[14] This fine-tuning of the cost of capital reflects only a recent escalation, however.

The tendency to personalize U.S. problems neglects all the systemic factors that favor fickle, shortsighted, and predatory behavior. Ivan Boesky and Michael Milken didn't represent isolated examples of corruption; they were products of a system that encouraged and supported their behavior—at least for a while—during a period that was critical for U.S. industry. It took fifteen years, for example, for the Japanese to penetrate the U.S. market for automobiles; it might take the same time to create a market for HDTV, but Japanese industry and government will not hesitate to spend whatever time it takes to develop the technology they believe will give their nation an edge in world markets in the twenty-first century. The Japanese can still relax and spend that time to develop products without the pressures that U.S. managers face, primarily because of the availability of capital, and the longer time horizons of their managers and government leaders.[15]

Many critics on both sides of the Pacific focus on interest rates and tax codes, and can't help but berate Americans for not saving more, spending less, and reducing their deficits. Although such criticism is well taken, it neglects the disparities in raising capital that blunt the nation's technological edge and international competitiveness, and put the U.S. increasingly in the company of low-wage countries that produce commodities, raw materials, and low-level services and products.[16]

FOREIGN AID: TAX ADVANTAGES
FOR OVERSEAS INVESTORS

Most Americans are fair-minded; they believe that foreign corporations should not be treated differently from American companies, and that good manners require that foreigners who are our guests be treated as well as our own citizens. Americans have led the world as advocates and practitioners of "national treatment" as a principle of international law, even when this doctrine worked against their interests.

But extending national treatment in a manner that gives foreign corporations a pronounced advantage is another matter entirely—it is the difference between being a good host and allowing the guests to steal the silver. This appears to be the case in the tax treatment of foreign corporations and foreign investors, an issue the Internal Revenue Service began to pursue in the late 1980s. A shrewd foreign investor can use the global economy to considerable advantage, thanks to U.S. laws and uneven enforcement policies. One successful strategy is double-dipping: A foreign corporation buys a company in the U.S. and thereby contrives to assume a substantial debt. The corporation is then in a position to deduct the interest on this debt, in both the U.S. and its home country, by the expedient of creating a third-country "finance subsidiary." All the parent company has to do is make sure the tax treatment in the third country is "favorable"—a relatively easy task, since these third countries are often so delighted to have attracted the subsidiary that taxes are relaxed as part of the "incentive" package.[17]

Foreign multinationals can also avoid sales taxes, through a tax dodge known as "transfer pricing." Coincidentally, this involves the cooperation of other countries as well. Small wonder corporations learned to love the global economy; it not only opens up new markets, but the opportunities for confusing the local tax collector are limitless. A shrewd foreign multinational with conveniently located branches can sell its products through various subsidiaries and not pay a dime's worth of taxes to either its own or the host nations.[18]

Small wonder foreign corporations paid so little taxes even as their assets exploded. Any foreign multinational that found itself paying its fair share of taxes to the U.S. Treasury should probably fire its accountants. The Internal Revenue Service reported that in 1986 foreign multinationals evaded $20 billion in taxes through various ploys, legal and illegal. Foreign corporations reported that they sold $543 billion in goods, but experienced net losses of $1.5 billion on that trade. Even more curious was that, though foreign-owned assets had more than trebled since 1980, and the gross income of foreign multinationals doubled, total tax revenues remained pretty much the same. By 1991, foreign-owned assets in the United States by official estimates exceeded $2.3 trillion; more hard-nosed unofficial estimates put the figure at least 50 percent higher, allowing for still greater under-reporting of foreign assets.[19] Despite the massive acquisitions of the 1980s, "of 36,800 foreign-owned companies filing returns in 1986, more than half reported no taxable income."[20]

Foreign banks were particularly shrewd: In 1986 (the last year for which the IRS had comprehensive data), foreign banks reported $26.3 billion in profits and $25.9 billion in losses. The result: no taxes. How can foreign banks be doing business in the United States for ten years and still not be making money? It's easy to hide profits, if the banks are multinationals with branches all over the world. IRS audits of ten foreign banks in 1989 produced $100 million in added taxes. Conservative estimates of how much the Treasury is losing each year through tax scams by foreign multinationals amounts to about $30 billion.

Of course, foreign multinationals have long avoided taxes by claiming that they only earn their profits in low-tax countries; in other words, their factories in California break even, and their profits are earned in Mozambique. Wherever they're earned, a large share of those profits went to lobbying efforts in state capitals, an investment that paid off many times over in the state-by-state defeat of the unitary tax. States that held out as long as they could against the foreign lobbyists finally succumbed when the pressures became too great: the California legislature, for example, admitted defeat when the combined clout of President Reagan, Prime Minister Margaret Thatcher, and the Sony Corporation, among others, wore it down after a ten-year struggle. Some experts believe that the U.S. federal deficit would be totally eliminated if a federal unitary tax forced foreign corporations to pay their fair share of U.S. taxes.[21]

In response to foreign tax dodges, Congress gave the IRS increased resources and more power to subpoena tax records from foreign parent companies in December 1989; less than a year later, the deficit-reduction bill authorized stiff penalties for foreign companies that understated income on transactions involving their U.S. subsidiaries; and on June 14, 1991, the IRS issued regulations requiring American subsidiaries of foreign multinationals to improve their record-keeping on the prices charged by their foreign parents for goods and services, and to report all transactions with foreign corporations to the IRS. The IRS was also empowered to fine recalcitrant companies $10,000 a month, with no limits on the penalty, and to compel companies to produce their records. Tax agents decided to focus on U.S. subsidiaries of Japanese companies, on the grounds that they appeared to be making more money than they were declaring. Japanese tax experts opposed these efforts, arguing that the IRS had no "concrete guidelines" for determining international transactions; besides, the low rate of return on their investments was genuine, given the tendency of Japanese companies to accept lower rates of profit while they gained a foothold in the U.S. market.[22] Other foreign companies joined with the Japanese in objecting to the new powers of the IRS, on the grounds that they violated bilateral tax treaties.

Armed with new resources, the IRS uncovered more evidence indicating that American subsidiaries of foreign automobile and electronics companies were underpaying federal income tax, and were at least $13 billion in arrears. Representative Richard T. Schulze, Republican of Pennsylvania and the ranking minority member on the Ways and Means Committee's Subcommittee on Oversight, linked foreign tax avoidance and declining U.S. competitiveness, charging "unfair competition" for U.S. businesses. A nine-month investigation by the subcommittee found that of 212 tax returns filed over a ten-year period by American subsidiaries of thirty-six foreign companies, more than half paid "little or no income tax." Another finding revealed that eight foreign-owned electronics companies reported almost $14 billion in gross receipts but paid no federal income taxes. Representative J. J. Pickle, Democrat of Texas, who chairs the subcommittee, railed against the foreign tax dodgers: "Some of the companies . . . have been operating in the U.S. for years and have never sent a check to Uncle Sam for one thin dime in corporate taxes. They have failed to pay taxes despite the fact that they have profited from selling billions of dollars of cars, motorcycles, stereos, televisions, videocassette recorders, microwaves and other products to the American consumer."[23]

Despite these added powers and the expansion of its international staff, the IRS still finds multinational tax dodges difficult to pursue and reports that it is eight years behind in auditing foreign corporations. For example, although transfer pricing is illegal, it is very difficult to prove; and even when proved, it is a monumental pain to fight. Nevertheless, the IRS enjoyed a rare victory over Toyota, which had been overcharging its U.S. subsidiaries on parts, trucks, and cars for years. Toyota paid the IRS $1 billion in settlement fees, although they denied the charges against them.[24]

A curious twist finds U.S. multinational corporations claiming *they* are disadvantaged by improved IRS enforcement against foreign tax dodgers, because the IRS has easier access to their records than to those of their foreign competitors. Foreign languages, the absence of detail required by U.S. law, and the difficulties of tracking the records down in the foreign country all combine to increase the tax agency's difficulties.[25] One can see the unanticipated consequences of this kind of policy: If it is easier to enforce the tax codes against U.S. multinationals than foreign companies, U.S. firms will pay higher taxes than their foreign competitors; this could make them less competitive internationally, and spur them to export more jobs and production abroad.

One of the most important tax advantages for foreign investors, long known to the cognoscenti, is the exemption for withholding tax on portfolio income. Prior to 1984, the U.S. imposed a 30-percent tax, though bilateral treaties reduced the rate for investors in many countries to zero; in 1984, the tax was repealed for all foreign investors. Payments of interest on foreign deposits in U.S. banks were also not subject to the tax. Supporters of repeal argued successfully that the tax was discriminatory in that "large U.S. corporations were able to avoid, primarily through the use of the tax treaty with the Netherlands Antilles, the impact of the withholding tax on their borrowings while the Federal Government and small business could not avoid the effect of the tax."[26]

Opponents countered that exempting interest from taxation would distort investment choices: It risked investors favoring debt over equity and a rise in the cost of capital available in the U.S. The problem has stymied U.S. tax experts, who wish to avoid international tax evasion yet protect the competitiveness of their own banks and companies. Any solution will involve the cooperation of the industrialized nations; in fact, the European Community has already come to the conclusion that an across-the-board withholding tax is the best means of avoiding tax evasion.[27]

Whatever else is shown by the tax inequities, there is no doubt that growing internationalization has created new complexities that the U.S. is just beginning to sort out. Internationalization creates new opportunities for maximizing national advantage, as shown by the inventiveness of foreign corporations in gaining favorable tax treatment by the U.S. government. Some of those tax advantages were inadvertent; some a result of inadequate resources for enforcement of existing codes. To their credit, Congress and the president tightened up on enforcement in the face of mounting evidence of tax dodging.

The goal is to eliminate all tax scams and work toward multilateral cooperation to avoid the flight of scarce capital to the most hospitable nation.

BANKING AND OTHER INEQUITIES

Adam Smith and Karl Marx held one belief in common: the importance of the ownership of the means of production. But what about the institutions that finance the means of production, the banks? Neither Marx nor Smith has been around in the late twentieth century to observe the plight of the U.S. banking industry, beset by a tangled deregulatory environment, then weakened by international competition. Whereas American investors wanted as little as possible to do with their unstable banks, foreign investors recognized the importance of banks to U.S. markets, technology, and production. Aided by the slow U.S. response to the nation's banking crisis, foreign investors took advantage of gaps in the laws to make profits in an uncertain environment.

Exempt from some of the laws and regulations that had harmed U.S. banks and savings-and-loan institutions, overseas investors snapped up a good share of the U.S. banking business. The rapid transfer of the nation's banking assets to overseas investors has emerged as a national-security issue of increasing concern to federal agencies, the Congress, state legislatures, the Federal Reserve Board, and other agencies that regulate banks and S & L's.

The banking industry mirrors the massive influx of foreign investment in the United States. In 1983, two of the three largest banks in the world were U.S.-owned; today all of the top ten banks are Japanese, and only one U.S. bank (Citicorp) remains in the top twenty-five.[28] The Japanese now own 14 percent of U.S. banking assets, a sixfold increase since 1983. The steepest increase in foreign ownership of U.S. bank assets by all countries occurred between 1988 and 1990, from 16 percent to nearly 25 percent, totaling $695 billion. If foreign ownership continues at this rate, nearly 77 percent of the nation's bank assets will be owned by offshore investors by the year 2000—a distinct possibility, since the U.S. remains the only industrialized country with no ceiling on foreign ownership of its banking assets. At this point, foreign bank holdings remain highly concentrated, with the top five foreign banks accounting for over 75 percent of all U.S. banking assets held by overseas investors.[29]

"Economic fundamentals are what really count," warned E. Gerald Corrigan, president of the Federal Reserve Bank of New York, commenting on the economic imbalances confronted by U.S. banks in the international marketplace. In fact, "the only way the rise in net foreign investment in the U.S. can be ameliorated is in a context in which underlying economic imbalances are reduced over time."[30]

The imbalances in banking parallel the globally skewed U.S. financial and trading system in an all-too-familiar pattern of increasing U.S. vulnerability and dependence. With banks, these imbalances can determine survival in both domestic and international environments. It was easier for Japanese banks to expand in the U.S. by acquisition, for example, but virtually impossible for U.S. banks to expand in Japan in the same way. No wonder U.S. banking assets in Japan now total $30 billion in twenty U.S. banks, whereas three dozen Japanese banks hold $370 billion in assets in the United States; in fact, U.S. bank assets in Japan have dropped during the 1980s, the period of Japan's greatest growth in the U.S. bank market.

In the early 1990s, just as Martin Marietta, ETA, and other high-tech companies were having trouble raising capital, U.S. banks sought rescue from abroad. Even Citicorp—the only U.S. bank still in the top thirty of the world's banking institutions—confessed its inability to raise capital by selling a 14-percent equity stake to Prince Al-Waleed Bin Talal, a thirty-five-year-old entrepreneur from Saudi Arabia, for $590 million. Citicorp had been pressured by the Federal Reserve Board to improve its financial position by raising $1–1.5 billion; finding the money wells dry in the U.S., the bank looked abroad. Under heavy criticism, Citicorp proclaimed publicly that the prince had promised he would not try to gain control of the company. The investment made Prince Bin Talal the bank's largest shareholder.

Legal and regulatory inequities added to U.S. banks' competitive disadvantage. For a long time, for example, U.S. laws discriminated against U.S. banks in favor of foreign banks by prohibiting U.S. banks from engaging in interstate banking, whereas foreign banks could operate across state lines. Foreign banks took full advantage of this situation and cornered a large share of the American market for a considerable period of time until the International Banking Act of 1978 eliminated some of the inequities. Even so, many discrepancies remain in force, to the long-term disadvantage of the U.S. banking industry.

A striking case involves the Union Bank of California, the state's fifth-largest bank with assets of $9 billion, which was put on the auction block in 1987. Citicorp's bid to purchase the bank was rejected because of laws prohibiting a New York bank from buying a California bank. Ironically, the laws were enacted to prevent the large banks in

New York and Boston from taking over the country, but they do not prevent foreign banks from acquiring banks throughout the U.S., even though Japanese banks now dwarf their American counterparts. Thus the California subsidiary of the Bank of Tokyo, under no such restrictions, snapped up the Union Bank for $750 million, giving Japanese owners control of four of California's ten largest banks. The Bank of Tokyo is now the largest foreign bank in the United States.

The imbalance was worsened when Citicorp attempted to gain international reciprocity from Japan. While Citicorp was displaced by the Bank of Tokyo, thanks to U.S. laws that welcomed foreign banks and turned their back on domestic companies, the Japanese succeeded for a long time in preventing Citicorp from installing automatic-teller machines at its Tokyo branches. And though the U.S. remains the most open country in the world vis-à-vis international investment, other countries demonstrate far less hospitality toward offshore banks. The reason is that industrialized countries the world over—except for the U.S.—consider banking a critical industry worthy of government attention and protection.

What difference does it make if U.S. bank assets follow the pattern of their fellow critical industries? If they're not competitive, don't they deserve to fail? In a truly global economy, capital would flow freely to and from its best sources, while international regulators ensured equity, national treatment, investor security, and consumer rights. But no such international regulators yet exist, and until such a presence emerges, nation-states would be wise to safeguard a hefty percentage of their banking assets. Otherwise, they risk losing control under a variety of conditions, such as:

• *Tight money.* In times of tight money, foreign banks could give preferential treatment to home-country firms. There is no evidence of this yet, but given the tendency of foreign banks to favor close ties with the subsidiaries of multinationals from their own countries, this is a very real possibility. Foreign banks can be expected to act out of feelings of national loyalty; they could also find themselves pressured by their governments, particularly if they are government-owned.

• *Concentration of assets.* These concerns apply to foreign banks from a single country, where a concentration of assets creates a virtual monopoly. Potential supervisory and regulatory problems could arise from such a situation, particularly if the foreign country finds itself in a liquidity crunch—as happened to some of the oil-rich Arab nations following the Gulf War. When that concentration of assets is controlled from abroad, the nation also loses its cushion in a financial crisis, a lesson the U.S. learned on Black Monday. "More [was] at stake in U.S. banks' slippage than mere national pride," said *The Wall Street Journal*. "In a financial crisis, control of credit often determines the outcome. On October 19, 1987, when the stock market crashed, the Federal Reserve Board of New York leaned on New York banks to meet the cash needs of Wall Street firms. The banks generally responded and a national economic calamity was narrowly averted. But would the banks have acted as quickly if the final decisions had rested in Tokyo or London? It's hard to say."[31]

• *Loss of business for U.S. banks.* Many U.S. businessmen who expected foreign investors to use them in their production efforts were surprised, particularly those who had high hopes for supplying the Japanese auto manufacturers. For the most part, foreign investors have tended to prefer doing business with firms from their own countries, a pattern that also appears to hold true for service industries like banks and insurance companies. The major foreign auto companies— Toyota, Mazda, and Honda—brought hundreds of auto-supply firms with them, along with their own banks. Four Japanese banks, for example, located in Lexington, Kentucky, in order to serve the new Toyota plant and its satellite parts suppliers. Of course, given the uncertain state of U.S. banks and their regulatory problems, one can hardly blame foreign corporations for avoiding them.

• *Predatory practices.* The increase of foreign banks as a critical presence in the United States also enhances their position as potential raiders, both hostile and friendly. "Foreign bankers will act like raiders in selecting which assets of which banks to make a bid," concluded an article in the British magazine *The Banker*. "They will practise tight line-of-business accounting. . . . They will be as divestiture-minded before they make a bid as many UK banks have become afterward."[32]

• *Difficulties in uncovering criminal activities.* Just as IRS officials find it harder to gain access to foreign multinationals evading U.S. taxes than to their domestic counterparts, bank regulators find chasing foreign banks bent on eluding them virtually impossible. The multibillion-dollar scandal involving the Pakistani-based BCCI that unfolded in the summer of 1991 showed just how unequal to the task the regulators were. BCCI gained secret control of several U.S. banks, including First American, the National Bank of Georgia, and the Independent Bank of Encino, California. The bank laundered money from drug smuggling and gun running, among other activities, including funds for the Contras and General Noriega. Senator Kerry raised this issue before the Senate Banking Committee on May 23, 1991, in reference to BCCI:

"... the lack of regulation of foreign banks in the past raises some very serious issues about incursion into the American financial services delivery system of foreign entities about which we know very little, and sources of money about which we know very little. ... This country is coming off a decade of scandal surrounding our financial institutions. ... BCCI ... may represent the biggest financial scandal involving an individual institution ever."

BCCI, widely labeled the "Bank of Crooks and Criminals International," cost depositors and taxpayers up to $5 billion. *New York Times* columnist William Safire blamed "an anesthetized or slow-footed gaggle of lawmen and bank regulators," including international regulators from the "see-no-evil Governments of Luxembourg and the Cayman Islands." BCCI achieved the biggest bank heist in history the usual way: hiring politicians, providing sweetheart deals for them, and involving intelligence agencies for further insulation from government probing. The venerable Clark Clifford, adviser to three presidents, was hired by BCCI to preside over its Washington bank, First American; former President Jimmy Carter received $8.8 million for his foundations; and even former Prime Minister Callaghan of Great Britain turned up on their payroll.[33]

How does the global economy control such chicanery through the international banking system? Or is international banking just a convenient way to circumvent the kind of domestic regulation that would ordinarily identify and prosecute such scams? At a minimum, American banks should have the same opportunity to acquire banks in other regions as do foreign banks, which would require a revision of the banking laws.

Most nations understand the importance of a stable banking system and, except for the United States, the necessity for retaining a degree of national control over that system. In the U.S., concerns are expressed from isolated quarters of the government, rarely in concert, and usually in response to a crisis. One of the most influential government agencies, the GAO, issued a report addressing its concerns about the international dimensions of the U.S. banking industry: "Banking is a sector critical to the functioning of a country's economy. Because of its central role in channeling payment flows to sustain economic growth and transmitting government monetary policy, the banking sector is of special interest to the U.S. government. As foreign entities gain control over an increasing share of U.S. banking assets, concerns have arisen about potential effects on the growth and development of U.S. industry through changes in bank lending practices."[34]

"THE DOG ATE THE EXPERIMENT" AND OTHER
CORPORATE EXCUSES

Many critics argue that the fault lies with corporate attitudes, not with external factors. After all, nothing forced U.S. banks to reduce their operations in Europe in 1990 "despite predictions of an economic boom." U.S. bankers felt they did "not make enough money abroad" to make it worth their while. They blamed the outmoded regulatory system, yet they had succeeded under that very system in the early 1970s, when they expanded their European business just as European, Japanese, East Asian, and other foreign banks are now moving into the U.S.: by meeting local needs and acting aggressively. In the early 1970s, for example, U.S. banks were known for defying local tradition and engaging in the then unusual practice of calling on potential customers.

The number of foreign branches of U.S. banks has dropped, along with their foreign assets; not surprisingly, their credit rating has also fallen. Citicorp, thanks to Prince Al-Waleed Bin Talal, remains the only U.S. bank expanding its operations; all others are reducing their foreign presence. Wells Fargo & Co., the nation's eleventh-largest banking company and one of its most profitable, has eliminated its twenty foreign offices in South America, Asia, and Europe.[35]

Top bank executives responsible for reducing foreign operations regard their decisions as sound: they are acting in the best interests of their stockholders, they say, and according to the best principles of fiduciary responsibility. U.S. bankers complained that they were not making enough money; their view of what constituted adequate profit seemed very much at odds with their foreign competitors'. Foreign banks look toward a more distant horizon, where short-term profits are eclipsed by long-term market share. Far from abandoning the bottom line, foreign banks, like foreign corporations, extend their bottom line beyond three months into the future.

Many analysts look at high-tech investments in the same light, believing that America's failure to invest in itself owes much to corporate indifference and short-term bean-counting. Financial columnist Michael Shrage attacked what he considers the crybaby attitudes of U.S. executives in an article on how " 'The Dog Ate the Experiment' and Other Corporate R & D Excuses." The tendency to blame "forces beyond their control" for their failure to engage in research and development proves more than anything else that "America's top research managers . . . are more interested in passing the buck than making one." Shrage thinks any corporate executive in charge of research and development who can't produce ought to fire himself for incompetence: If he "can't effectively explain, persuade or produce within the general management and external financial constraints, then he should resign." His failure owes more to "squandered resources, mismanaged priorities, and the inability to communicate fluently with either internal or external customers" than to the tougher and more challenging financial environment.[36]

Along the same lines, columnist and TV host Michael Kinsley charges that Japan's equity advantages are a myth, no longer relevant in today's fast-paced international markets. He blames America's poor industrial performance, not Japan's price-earnings advantage: "Investors simply feel that a factory in Osaka is a better bet than one in Chicago, and are willing to pay more for a piece of the action," he writes.[37]

In fact, blaming others for competitiveness problems that begin at home is just one big "excuse industry" with a "defeatist message," added Robert J. Samuelson, one of the nation's most highly respected financial analysts. "The biggest casualty in these crusades is the truth," which Samuelson presents in quite a different light:

• The nation is not capital-short; rather, U.S. managers are short-sighted. Since U.S. companies raise three-quarters of their investment funds from internal sources, they could just as easily decide to invest in R & D as blame Wall Street.

• Government already fosters patient capital; it does not have to do more. "A profitable company that spends $10 on new R & D gets tax breaks worth $5."

• Cost of capital—which Samuelson admits is higher in the U.S. than it is in Germany and Japan—"isn't decisive because too many other things determine whether businesses succeed or fail," such as "less efficient manufacturing."[38]

Many also fear that enhanced public awareness of financial inequities will not lead to correction of those inequities, but to politically easier overreactions. One such overreaction could be tougher trade-and-investment policies; or, in this case, restricting foreign investment. "Limiting a firm's access to foreign capital," cautioned Stephen Canner, executive director of CFIUS, "does not help them with regard to competitiveness."

SELF-RELIANCE—U.S.-STYLE

One executive who did not allow the dog to eat his experiment was John Morley, CEO of Reliance Electric, a U.S. multinational based in

Cleveland with thirteen thousand employees, branches throughout the country, overseas plants in Canada, Mexico, and Brazil, and a joint venture in Japan. Morley prevailed over a corporate parent, over capital shortages, and over a hostile environment to launch a management buy-out that made Reliance a world leader and one of Ohio's must successful companies. One decided advantage was Reliance's status as a closely held private corporation. Another advantage was Morley himself. An astute entrepreneur, Morley not only knew the technology, the markets, and the financial picture, but was sufficiently sensitive to the fluctuating economy of the 1980s to make it work in his own and his company's interests. Above all, his success proved that, with a combination of luck and shrewd timing, it was possible to beat the system.

The tea leaves predicted a very different future for Reliance, which was bought by Exxon in 1979. Morley, an executive with Exxon since 1958, was sent to Cleveland to dismantle Reliance and sell it off; instead, he organized a hundred of the company's managers to buy the company from Exxon. Morley recognized the value of the company and its potential as a viable, money-making international business. "Reliance was never happy to be taken over," recalled Morley in an interview at his Cleveland headquarters. "Exxon paid two times the price of the stock. I was new to the business, the culture, and the company." The ups and downs of the economy worked in Morley's favor. When the economy "took a nose dive and we went through difficult times," it was not propitious for Exxon to move forward with its plans to sell the company. Morley adapted accordingly: "We restructured in the early 1980s, and developed strategies to go forward. By the fall of 1986, Reliance was in good shape, while Exxon meanwhile was going through hard times." At this point, Morley thought it was likely that Exxon would sell the company, and organized management to try to buy it. "I represented management's interest; Exxon got two individual organizations. There were three separate groups [Citicorp, Pru-Bache, and Morley's management group] looking at the acquisition; all of them wanted management's participation. There was an open competition and Exxon made the decision [in Morley's favor] based on price."

Again, the economy and Morley's prescience worked in the company's favor. The company was able to get permanent financing by the end of 1987, and "we were organized for recession. We divested our Toledo scale company to reduce the debt and move into a growth mode. We expanded more aggressively in information technology. We began acting like a global organization. We had success in mainland

China in motors and controls that run motors, power transformers for electrical utilities, and power distributors.

"The LBO [threat] gave us a reason to be focused," Morley continued, "and our strategic evolution focused on markets. We were under pressure to better utilize what we had. We started world-class manufacturing, statistical quality control, just-in-time manufacturing, and total employee involvement in the manufacturing process. Of forty-two plant operations, not one plant is the same as others. We raised production by 50 percent, substantially improved quality, shortened the product cycle time, got as close to the customer as possible, and reduced inventories." Success showed up in the bottom line: "From 1986 to 1989, sales went from $1 billion to $1.4 billion."

Morley belied the patient-capital argument of many of his fellow corporate leaders. None of his innovations required a great deal of capital. "You have to invest in training and do more planning," he reflected; these innovations "were relatively minor compared to yield." If they hadn't planned as carefully and reduced inventories, for example, they "would have needed more capital: we would have needed $200 million more if we were working on inventories of five years ago. We don't make a part until the need is visibly clear. And we don't have to make three batches of a product to know there's a problem.

"The notion is never to let the process stop," he said. "The Japanese have done this for years. The hardest element [in the United States] is cultural change."[39]

Confusion now reigns in the corporate culture with regard to how to cope with anomalies in worldwide financial systems. Corporate executives know something is seriously wrong with their system; whether the fault lies in their stars, in themselves, or in their system is less important than the knowledge of how to survive in the global environment. The problem is how to compete despite a national system that is slightly out of sync with the rest of the industrialized world. And greatly out of sync with Japan.

What U.S. executives can learn from their Japanese counterparts, many argue, is what President Bush referred to in another context as "the vision thing," or how Japanese companies think strategically, as opposed to U.S. companies, which remain glued to their quarterly reports. Kenneth Courtis of Deutsche Bank compared the job experiences of a Japanese woman working first at Salomon Brothers, then at Nomura. "At Salomon," he recounted, "the emphasis was on cash flow. At Nomura, she was constantly screening for corporate Japan. The attitude was that first you find the companies making major strategic moves; then find out what they need strategically; you then satisfy their strategic need; *then you look at the balance sheet.*" Nomura, concluded Courtis, looked at the world from a strategic point of view, not solely a financial one. It was not that Nomura was not profit-oriented; it was just that the company didn't start out from a financial vortex and work its way back, but looked at financial data from a more long-term point of view.

Both Salomon Brothers and Nomura have since gone through hard times, both of them found sadly wanting in the area of corporate ethics. At Salomon, top executives placed illegal bids in auctions for government securities. Nomura was one of seventeen major Japanese brokerage houses that in 1991 admitted compensating favored clients for trading losses in a scandal that shook the Japanese stock market and caused stock prices to plunge.[40]

Many U.S. executives admit they can certainly organize more effectively among themselves, even if they cannot cartelize. At the very least, they can stop inflicting mutual harm. "I sat in a meeting once where we were talking about the concern of Japanese dumping chips in the U.S. and [how] it was wiping out the semiconductor market," recalled Richard Elkus, chairman of Pro-Metrix, a computer company, before the Senate Banking Committee. "In a different room another major industry leader [who was producing the end-use product] was saying, 'if we do something to halt the Japanese inflow of low-cost product, you will make me no longer competitive in my product. . . . I am trying to sell where I need Japanese low-cost semiconductor devices.'"[41]

Though their interests are at loggerheads, corporate leaders in the U.S. must function with their stockholders' best interests in mind; if they don't, they can be prosecuted for neglecting their fiduciary responsibility. They are in business to make profits, not public policy— that's someone else's job. Naturally, in this context, they will try to lobby government to act in their company's interests, even if it means acting against the interests of other U.S. industries.

The net result is a confusion among otherwise patriotic corporate leaders between fiduciary responsibility and the national interest. "If I announced to our shareholders that I am looking even to 1992, I would be out as chairman," complained Bernard Schwartz of Loral in 1990. Commerce official Juan Benitez recalled similar conflicts in his years as a CEO: ". . . what do you do if the guy next door is giving his shareholders a 25-percent return on their money and you're telling them you'll give them 2 percent but in ten years we'll be a great company. How do you deal with that?"

"We need a change of attitude from protecting the consumer to protecting our industrial strength," Schwartz says. "From that will flow a lot of things. I am convinced that our system, our morality, and our attitudes of social justice, of human dignity, will not exist without a strong economy."

Another area of concern among the nation's more enlightened corporate leaders remains the lack of awareness of the interrelationship among technologies. Not surprisingly, the lack of concern translates into an absence of any significant political organization or representation at the highest levels of government. Unlike Japan, no government agency coordinates technologies to ensure economic health and prevent the kind of losses that harm the nation's competitive strength. "The pace at which our industrial base is becoming progressively weaker and weaker is greater than our society realizes," cautioned Donald E. Petersen, former chairman of the Ford Motor Company, "and the link [between industries] that seems so remote to people is so direct." Petersen showed, for instance, how the loss of consumer electronics in the U.S. contributed to the "severe weakening of the auto industry."

"Visualize, if you will," said Petersen, "that in Japan NEC . . . is constantly going to Toyota or Nissan . . . and saying, 'we anticipate that five, six, seven years from now, we're going to be able to do this with compact discs. You might be wanting to plan on it.' There's nobody left in America to come to Ford and say, 'five or six years from now, this technology's going to be commercially feasible . . . and it would certainly play in to the environment of automobiles.' This [lack of] an interrelationship among industries [has a] corrosive effect on our total strength, as we lose first one, then another industry."[42]

Corporate executives express increasing concerns about the loss of related technologies and industries, but do not regard government intervention as the answer. They still see government as the enemy—as tax collector, overregulator, and general nuisance—and philosophically avert any possibility of the public sector in any role other than junior partner. Without a substantial government presence even to coordinate among companies, it should come as no surprise that the U.S. is losing so many firms—many of them, in fact, originally nurtured by government funds. Speaking of how this problem relates to the computer-chip industry, physicist and former Rockwell executive Al Joseph called the system "bad news. Folks who have this technology are scattered. One company has the [circuit] board; another the testing equipment; another the tools. No one is orchestrating the companies and the companies are not talking to each other."

What happens when companies producing critical technologies don't talk to one another? "Japanese companies wait for the U.S. to make mistakes. Then they move in quickly," said a DARPA official, describing the investment his agency made in high-density packaging technology at General Electric, only to watch the company lose interest.

An adviser for Stellar, a small supercomputer company in Massachusetts, recounted the company's desperate struggle to keep afloat in the face of an untenable financial position. "Stellar was caught between a rock and a hard place," he said. "It wasn't big enough to go out and really get capital on the regular market. It was too big for venture-type capital. Stellar was at this peculiar time in an investment life, where it had started off as sort of a little venture-capital company, but had gotten too big for the so-called venture-capital companies. It really needed to go public and become a regular company. There's a vulnerability in the life of a company between a $20-million capitalization and a $100-million capitalization. . . . They couldn't get a $100-million capitalization, but that's what they really needed if they were going to survive."

Meanwhile, the Japanese tractor manufacturer Kubota had begun purchasing similar high-tech companies in Silicon Valley, including a company called Ardent. "So what happened," continued Stellar's adviser, "Ardent came right in and started dumping supercomputer-graphic products in a way that was killing Stellar, but you really couldn't prove injury yet—given the rigorous [legal] test for injury in the U.S. Stellar was being clobbered by the Japanese. Eventually, they threw in the towel and joined up with Ardent. Now the company is called Stardent, and all the technology has gone to Japan." Kubota has become a well-known success story showing how shrewd investments lead to technological prowess. Though it had never manufactured anything more complicated than tractors and other earth-moving equipment, the company is now in the business of producing advanced minicomputers for export.

Small U.S. companies like Stellar find themselves in a bind. To many in government, the pattern is familiar but the solutions are elusive. Start-up firms get in trouble, and Japanese firms come in and buy an equity interest. This interest becomes a legitimate avenue for technological transfer. But small companies have traditionally been an engine of growth in the U.S., particularly in high-tech areas. How will such firms continue to survive, to grow, and to innovate in the current environment?

The issue comes down to the freedom to buy and sell, a foundation of American capitalism and a right no one wants to lose, despite the obvious difficulties. Take the story of John Hall, an eccentric entrepreneur from Silicon Valley who invented a semiconductor technology critical to U.S. military development only to lose it in a tragedy of errors. His story is a precursor of the Stellar pattern. Hall decided in the early 1970s that, in order to profit from his invention and expand his company, Micro Power Systems, he needed more capital; to get it, he sold a large equity interest in his company to Seiko, the Japanese watch-and-computer company. As bright as he was as an inventor, Hall's business acumen left something to be desired. In the early years, Hall was lulled into a false sense of security; his new partners provided him with capital and introduced him to the blandishments of a high-flying life-style in Tokyo that included the companionship of an entertainer whose charms led Hall eventually to divorce his wife. Perhaps recognizing his limitations, perhaps for reasons of its own, Seiko proceeded gradually to take over the company, moving some of the technology to Japan and eventually easing Hall out the door. Years of litigation increased public awareness of Hall's personal and professional plight but did not bring his company or his technology back. Despite his unfortunate experience, Hall was back in Tokyo in July 1989 looking for venture capital for his new company, Linear Integrated Systems, Inc.

The consequences of Hall's adventure amounted to more than just another business deal gone awry. Pentagon-chip experts quoted by *Wall Street Journal* reporter Eduardo LaChica indicated that Hall's inventions had "military significance," and traced "Seiko's upsurge in the powerful computer chips, called complementary metal oxide semiconductors, to his [Hall's] time in Japan in the early 1970s. Before that, they had nothing. But after Hall, they had a lot."[43]

THE BALANCING ACT

Like Hall, U.S. executives and government leaders invariably return to the model of Japan: Japanese management, Japanese corporate financing, and the facilitating role of Japanese government. The more sophisticated now acknowledge the unlikelihood of convincing the Japanese to become "more like us," in the words of author James Fallows,[44] and recognize instead the necessity of coping with a global environment that will not always bend to U.S. preferences. Increased pressure from some sectors of the business community reflects a growing acceptance of government's role in offsetting existing imbalances and leveling the playing field.

"My concern is that if the government of the United States, in particular the President, does not recognize that we are going to have winners and losers . . . if we cannot stop the concept that we have to have losers and therefore winners, we are going to lose everything," cautioned Richard Elkus.[45]

For every chief executive like Elkus, another counters with just as convincing a case against government intervention. Business ambivalence about government often comes from hard experience, just as often from ingrained habit or ideological preference, and sometimes from conflicting needs.

The result is that U.S. industries often cancel one another out politically: computer assemblers against semiconductor producers; auto companies against machine-tool producers. For the last two decades, this has been reinforced by a polarized ideological framework that locks the issue into rather stark and simplistic terms: "industrial policy versus no government intervention."[46] No nuances are allowed, since the merest suggestion of government intervention risked scorn from every point along the liberal-conservative continuum. It took a courageous—or politically suicidal—politician to suggest that government act even minimally during this period. Indeed, it was a tribute to President Reagan's political effectiveness that his promises to "get government off the backs" of the people proved so attractive to such a wide range of constituencies that it took a truly massive effort—such as the campaign launched by Chrysler—to attract government attention; more selective intervention was virtually impossible during this period. Reagan earned his reputation as the "Great Communicator" for convincing Americans that deregulating business, freeing up markets, and reducing taxes would improve their lives.

The effects of this period brought lasting consequences: reduced taxes coupled with increased military expenditures brought deficits and debts that wrenched the nation from the world's leading creditor nation to the world's leading debtor nation; the festival of deregulation, initiated by the Carter administration and implemented by Reagan, severely damaged the banking system, while environmental and workplace hazards grew; and finally, while other countries nurtured their critical industries, the U.S. steadfastly ignored global realities under the rubric of "free trade."

The debate over supporting winners and losers always boiled down to the crudest kinds of choices, and many soon found that the easiest way out was to avoid the issue. That included the issue of national security: namely, how national security was affected by the loss of critical industries. It was easier to avoid the issue in the past, when the military could quietly protect technology in the name of national security. With today's budget constraints and the ever-broadening use of chips, this is no longer possible. "In the mid-1970s 75 percent of the chips went into military systems," said Roger Steciak of Dataquest. "Today, only 11 percent of the chips go into military systems. Besides, today, the technology of the future is in workstations. Military technologies are old technologies which are in jeopardy." Although military agencies are the only government bodies with the legitimacy, the mandate, the commitment, and the budget to support U.S. technology, their best intentions often cancel one another out in the impossible task of keeping expenditures down and technology up.

High-tech companies also suffer politically, especially in comparison with other industries. Geographically, they tend to cluster together, and rarely do they muster the clout achieved by manufacturers whose plants, distributorships, and union locals fan out into multiple congressional districts. The best case for government intervention, the retention of manufacturing jobs, doesn't necessarily apply to semiconductor-equipment manufacturers. "What difference does it make in electronics if there are U.S. manufacturing jobs?" asked Judy Larsen, an executive with Dataquest.[47] "There are no manufacturing jobs in electronics." (Actually, other representatives of the electronics industry claim there are 2.6 million jobs in electronics, including many manufacturing jobs.) Add to that the absence of powerful unions, and once again technology loses out in the competition for government intervention.

In view of the urgency confronting decisionmakers concerned about this issue, a preliminary agenda to preserve America's technology within the current global financial environment could include:

(1) Leadership from the States: Incentives for Directing a Small Fraction of Pension Funds to High-Tech Companies

Some hope of offsetting global financial inequities comes from the state level, especially from states that appreciate the importance of high technology to America's future but see little future in federal help. Christopher Coburn, former science-and-technology adviser to Ohio Governor Richard Celeste, is a leading advocate for using pension funds as "patient capital." He developed a program to divert a small percentage of pension funds into "risk capital" for high-tech ventures. When Coburn began his tenure in 1982, he found the state sadly deficient in helping industries raise money. "We can get money for fast food and real estate," he said, "but not for risk or patient capital." Coburn found that the state was losing companies to other states because of the absence of capital. One company made switching devices for telephones and employed three thousand people; the state lost it to a group of Texas investors who bought it and then moved the plant to their state.

To address this problem, Ohio passed a law in 1983 allowing up to 5 percent of state pension funds to go to venture capital, a figure that now amounts to $2 billion out of the total of $40 billion. Coburn believes that pension funds hold great potential for future development. "How else can companies expand," he asks, "when the cost of capital [was] three to four times higher here than in Japan? In the United States, we have $1 to $2 trillion in pension funds that are relatively unsupervised except by rigid formulas that dictate economic traditionalism." These formulas often allow irresponsible investment in such ventures as LBOs, says Coburn, but when "they are criticized for not providing patient capital, they throw back 'fiduciary responsibility.'"

Coburn concluded that the federal government had a role to play by "tying the states together" and coordinating the investment of even a small percentage of pension funds. "After all, the Europeans have warred against each other and they can do it," he said, referring to the fast-breaking economic successes of the European Community.

The problem with pension funds is that Americans are rightly loath to risk their retirement income on risky ventures—however patriotic or worthy these are, and regardless of the long-term potential of the investment. High tech is still risky, especially in competition with technology in other industrialized countries, where the government's financial backing reduces the risk of investment. Thus, if institutional funds are directed toward critical industries, the federal government will have to offer some degree of insurance against risk. Given the current difficulties of continuing to justify federally insured bank deposits, the backing of critical industries—however worthy—may no longer be politically feasible.

(2) Tax Reform for Technology

Suggested reforms could include a capital-gains tax for investors in high-tech companies; relief from the double taxation of retained earnings and dividends; an equalization of foreign dividend income with U.S. counterparts; and tax advantages for companies that export—to encourage U.S. companies that are too lazy and comfortable in their home markets to globalize. Victor Kiam, the colorful chairman of Remington Products, Inc., who "bought the company because [he] liked the product," suggests that the tax system should "reward long-term investments, not short-term capital gains, by giving tax deductions for capital goods across the board," with the exception of real estate. "These deductions should only be given to bona-fide investments," Kiam emphasized, "with proof of investment in performance, equipment, further development of the product, and plant construction." And, to avoid individual profiteering, "the investment must be in your own business, restricted to corporate entities. That way you avoid situations like General Electric buying up tax credits for other companies."

(3) Restructure Tax Incentives for Critical Technologies

Taxes from overseas operations could be eliminated, suggests Apple Computer Vice-President Debi Coleman, if those profits were "put directly into R and D, property, or plant and equipment" and not for "LBOs or stock repurchases." Otherwise, argues Coleman, there are as of now more incentives for U.S. multinationals to reinvest their overseas profits abroad.

(4) Equalize Accounting Standards

A number of disparities exist in accounting standards, very much as in the cost of capital, which many argue hurt U.S. business. The concept of "good will" (an accounting concept, very nebulous in definition, that factors in a business's "good will" from consumers as a tangible asset for tax and sale purposes) means different things to different nations' accounting systems. "Good-will" standards in Great Britain, for example, are more generous than in the United States; this means that British companies could afford to work on a longer-range basis than U.S. companies, since they could claim more assets than a U.S. company would be allowed to claim.

(5) Direct Government Investment Through Subsidies and Grants

To offset the sale of U.S. industries critical to the nation's future and avoid the departure of companies like ETA, government might consider more direct subsidies to industries in jeopardy. The key would be differentiating among industries that are legitimately connected to the national security and economic future of the nation, and those that are more expendable. Controversial as this would be, U.S. government must face up to the problem and decide which industries it wants to save, which ones the nation can afford to lose, and how much of an

American component must be retained in a critical industry to keep the nation competitive. With many technologies today, the question is no longer one of leveling the playing field, but staying on the playing field.

Among the criteria for selecting industries worthy of government intervention, one idea gaining currency concerns getting the product to the marketplace. "Any idea that does not go to the marketplace should not be supported," emphasized Dr. Al Joseph, the well-known physicist and entrepreneur. "Why would you want to support gallium arsenide without finding out its marketplace? In order for technology to be beneficial, it has to go from research to manufacture to market. High tech is a different community. Japan outspends us on applications. We're still hung up on Nobel Prizes. The infrastructure exists in the United States for research, but the groups are detached from outlets to the marketplace. It is like my avocado tree: the pears drop to the ground, but if the seeds are not planted they will not grow."

(6) Tougher Trade and Tax Policies to Accompany Government Support

If taxpayers are going to invest in critical industries and don't want their money wasted, government will have to bolster its initiatives with additional efforts. That means tougher trade policies enforced *on a timely basis*. Control Data's experience, spending $100 million to break into the Japanese market and being excluded for eight years until the Japanese had developed their own data-services industry, should never occur, especially with a trade partner whose surpluses with the U.S. exceed $40 billion each year.

U.S. budget deficits might also benefit from tougher tax enforcement toward foreign multinationals. The administration and Congress have already moved forward in this area, demonstrating how cost-efficient increased resources for the IRS have proved in recovering tax revenue.

Another innovative suggestion is the idea of a value-added tax on production, to be borne primarily by overseas investors. Known as the BTT, short for "business-transfer tax with payroll-tax offset," this would address the inequities suffered by U.S. producers competing against foreign producers, by imposing a low, value-added tax on production. The BTT would include a companion "border tax" on imported goods and services (U.S. companies pay much higher border taxes in the forty-seven countries that impose them, including all twelve countries in the EC); it would also help U.S. producers by rebating the BTT on exports.[48] Although the BTT might help, it would be very difficult to sell politically, for several reasons: the aversion on the part of Congress and the president to tinker with the tax code after the bruising battles of tax reform; the reluctance of any president to create new taxes; and the growing potency of foreign companies in the U.S. to influence—and in this case kill—legislation affecting them.

(7) A Quasi-Government Agency to Offset the Nation's Capital Deficiencies

Richard Iverson, the electronics executive who makes the strongest case for patient capital, suggests a Ginny Mae–type agency that will provide an infrastructure for the nation's long-term capital needs. Iverson thinks that the imbalances in the cost of capital, plus "free trade, Japanese-style," and the educational system have impeded America's progress. The lack of capital, he explained, means companies are underinvesting in productivity improvement. We never should have lost silicon wafers, gallium arsenide, and copper foil (which is used for every printed circuit board—a reference to the sale of Gould, the producer of 60 percent of the world's copper foil, to Nippon Mining, a Japanese company).

Comsat and the Export-Import Bank have also been suggested as models for a new government agency, whose mandate would address the availability of capital for critical technologies. If the nation accepts the idea of mitigating risk for investment in third-world countries, why not help its own industries?

(8) Deficit Reduction

No grab-bag of solutions would be complete without the oft-cited warning to reduce the federal deficit and increase the nation's savings rates. Though this is very true, it has been repeated so often that the nation has unfortunately become inured to its critical message.

(9) Counterpunch on Patient Capital

It is finally time to stop agonizing about the high cost of capital in the U.S. and begin taking action. To some extent a degree of equilibrium is being restored. Thanks to low inflation, higher productivity gains, and decreasing labor costs, capital appears to be getting cheaper in the United States and more expensive abroad.[49] Whether this trend will continue, encourage more investment in emerging technologies, or offset the competitive disadvantages created by the imbalances of the 1980s, remains an open question.

Americans are still uneasy with the idea of government largess toward industry, even industries critical to the nation's future. Yet, at the same time, neither are they happy with losing the nation's next-to-last supercomputer company, along with other high-value companies being purchased and controlled from abroad.

Naturally, the government cannot save every failing company, but it is time to turn the usual question around: What companies can we afford to lose? How can America invest in itself to secure its future? The only time these questions are elevated to public discussion is when the company involved is so huge, with so many branches across the land, that it becomes a matter of national concern, like Chrysler or Lockheed. Smaller companies, even those with technologies critical to the national defense, might, in rare cases like Perkin-Elmer, attract national attention, but never direct government help.

At the very least, government can play an important role in equalizing the disparities in world finance that have disadvantaged U.S. companies. "80 percent of Japan's capital investment occurring today is targeted to an economy of the future," says Kenneth Courtis, who believes that the "1990s are the make or break decade for America." Where are America's capital investments going? To the future? To the past? No one knows.

The choices are hard—to erase imbalances, to block acquisitions until those differences are removed, or to provide the capital to counter the sale of U.S. technology—but they cannot be evaded indefinitely. If Japan and France could find patient capital to finance their computer industries, why did U.S. leaders accept this period of disparity in the global economy? Surely a nation that invented the computer, the microchip, and a host of other technologies can also figure out how to foster an environment that will enable these technologies to flourish in the future.

Government must be tough enough to avoid the trap of "lemon socialism": supporting "lemon" industries that deserve to fail, while ignoring those with more potential for success. But if government decides to support an ETA, for example, it must demand a *quid pro quo*. This means supporting not only technologies that conform to exotic military specifications, but industries that demonstrate their worth in global markets. This will take leadership, and a changed mind-set about government intervention in the nation's future.

CHAPTER XI

America the Vulnerable

GO-VIDEO AND THE DILEMMA OF
GLOBAL CARTELIZATION

... American companies didn't realize that U.S. antitrust
law gives them the right to sue even for something that
happens in a smoke-filled room in Tokyo.
                              —John Stern, vice-president,
                    American Electronics Association, Tokyo

There is no evidence that trading companies restrict market
access ... for the purpose of protecting *keiretsu* members
from foreign competition.
                    —Masaru Yoshitomi, director-general,
                         Economic Planning Agency, Japan

THE CARTEL IN ARIZONA

In the infectious entrepreneurial spirit of the early 1980s, a young
Scottsdale lawyer and former prosecutor named R. Terren ("Terry")
Dunlap decided to go into business for himself and produce video
programs for corporate meetings and family gatherings. The result
was the founding of Go-Video, the "Go" symbolizing the vans used
in this mobile production company that traveled to professional meetings, weddings, Bar Mitzvahs, reunions, and similar functions that
sought video recordings.

The market was wide open, but the technical difficulties of making cassette copies were soon apparent: wiring machines together was
cumbersome, and the quality of the copies was poor. Dunlap got the
idea to develop a double-deck VCR, an invention that would solve all

his recording problems and preserve the quality of his product. His enthusiasm far outweighed his resources: the company's initial capitalization amounted to $60,000 drawn against personal credit cards. In 1984, after a year of research and development, Dunlap applied for patents in the U.S. and Japan for the dual-deck system—he received U.S. patent protection in 1988—and began to seek a manufacturer for his product.

It sounded easy: a ready market niche, an innovative product, and some start-up capital. But VCRs, as everyone knew, symbolized yet another high-value American product invented here and manufactured abroad. America had already gone out of the VCR business, and coming back was hard to do, as Dunlap was soon to find out. After a seven-year battle against enemies that ranged from Hollywood to Tokyo, Go-Video was finally able to manufacture Dunlap's brainchild, the dual-deck videocassette recorder, or VCR-2. Priced at around $1,000 and chosen by *Popular Science* as one of the best hundred products of 1990, the VCR-2 can play one tape while recording on another, duplicate tapes and retain their high quality, edit from tape to tape, and record two different television programs simultaneously.[1] Dunlap called his product the "first significant American-designed and engineered consumer electronics invention" in fifteen years.[2] There was a catch however: it could only be manufactured abroad; only the "brain" of the VCR-2, a microcontroller on a personal-computer circuit board with seven other semiconductors, is manufactured in the United States (by an Intel plant in Arizona).

Dunlap tried to convince an American company, Zenith, to manufacture the dual-deck VCR in the United States, but was unsuccessful. "I went to Zenith and saw Bruce Huber, the director of sales and management," recalled Dunlap. "I said, 'You've been losing money for years. Take our license and manufacture it and we'll all be heroes. We'll bring back economic competition to the U.S.'

"He said, 'What price competition? We have a great relationship with JVC [a Japanese company]. We buy the product from Japan and sell it in the United States.' He refused to get involved. He was already doing business. U.S. companies are afraid they'll be cut off from their suppliers."

Initially, Dunlap's problems came from American foes, not Japanese. U.S. movie-production companies, cassette manufacturers, and the recording business all feared consumer fraud. Dual-deck recorders, they argued, would make it easy for consumers to duplicate the quality of movies, records, and television shows without having to purchase their products. They had a good point: Dunlap's upstart invention threatened a multibillion-dollar business—the motion-picture industry was said to earn $2.3 billion from videocassette sales in 1986 alone, or 34 percent of its entire domestic revenues. Potential losses riveted the attention and the resources of a formidable roster of Hollywood giants, including MGM UA Communications Group, Twentieth Century–Fox, United Artists, Walt Disney, Paramount Pictures, Orion Pictures, MCA Universal City Studios, Columbia Pictures, and Warner Brothers.

Hollywood was well represented by the articulate and politically savvy Jack Valenti, president of their major lobbying group, the Motion Picture Association of America (MPAA). Valenti argued that "the people who create movies and television programming will not sit idly by" without putting up a fight to prevent the marketing and distribution of the VCR-2 invention, which he termed "another sword thrust right into our belly," and another "piece of evil magic doing the devil's work."[3] Dunlap's response, that consumer fraud was not his responsibility, was legalistic and shortsighted.

Valenti organized not only the U.S. opposition to Go-Video, but the opposition in Japan as well. The plot line, more convoluted than in a Le Carré spy novel, began with Dunlap's fruitless search for a company to produce his product. Finally heeding everyone's advice to "go to the Japanese," Dunlap initiated negotiations with NEC. In January 1985, after the deal was consummated, Dunlap returned to the United States with the understanding that NEC would manufacture the VCR-2. Production schedules had been worked out, champagne bottles uncorked; only the formal details remained.

Suddenly everything seemed to fall apart. NEC executives stopped returning Dunlap's calls. An article appeared in *The Wall Street Journal* announcing a voluntary restraint agreement among members of the Electronics Industry Association of Japan (EIAJ) not to manufacture dual-deck VCRs. Finally, NEC (a member of EIAJ) sent a message to Dunlap that they had decided to bow out of the deal. The EIAJ's decision chilled business on all levels; its rigidly enforced discipline extended to smaller companies outside the cartel, to Korean companies, and to American electronics companies doing business with them.

What Dunlap didn't reckon with was Hollywood's clout in the Far East, and the speed with which the Japanese and Korean companies would respond. In response, Dunlap sued the Hollywood magnates and an array of Japanese and Korean companies, alleging that the motion-picture companies had convinced the Japanese electronics firms to refuse *en masse* to manufacture his product. He contended that this constituted a restraint of trade, and was subject to the Sherman and Clayton Act antitrust laws.[4]

"Immediately after learning of the dual-deck VCR," alleges the 1988 lawsuit, the motion-picture defendants approached the Japanese electronic manufacturers organized through EIAJ, an umbrella group that included all the behemoths of the Japanese electronics industry— Sony, Matsushita, Funai, Toshiba, Sanyo, Hitachi, Mitsubishi, Victor, and Sharp. Soon after, Dunlap's agreement with NEC fell through, followed by a string of unsuccessful attempts to negotiate manufacturing arrangements with Matsushita, Sharp, JVC, and other Japanese and Korean companies. The reason? An agreement that guaranteed that "dual-deck VCRs would not be marketed or manufactured for marketing in the United States" by any of the EIAJ member companies. The Korean companies quickly fell in line, effectively preventing Dunlap from manufacturing the VCR-2 for five years.[5]

The lawsuit alleged "agreement, combination and conspiracy," amounting to potential damages in the millions of dollars. The problem rested with the evidence. Dunlap had ample evidence of an agreement among the Japanese manufacturers: the EIAJ had gone public with its policy, issuing a written directive to member companies ordering them to refuse to deal with Go-Video. Newspaper and trade-publication accounts attributed the unofficial agreement to fears of copyright infringement and the "furor over the ease by which cassettes could be duplicated by consumers from many quarters—producers, software providers, rental outlets."[6]

The motion-picture producers operated openly, and were proud of their victory over Go-Video. Barbara Dixon, a lobbyist for the MPAA, told the Greater Phoenix *Business Journal* that the MPAA had a written trade agreement with the Japanese electronics industry and informal agreements with Korean companies not to manufacture dual-deck VCRs. She was also quoted in *Penny Stock News* stating that the ban extended even to supplying parts for the VCRs, since her group believed that the invention served the sole purpose of illegal tape copying.[7] The MPAA eventually withdrew its formal objection, but did not support Go-Video.

The damages claimed by Go-Video as a result of these agreements included lost revenue and profits from not being able to manufacture, market, or license the rights to their product; legal expenses (at the start of 1991, Dunlap alleged he'd spent $2 million); diminished value of the company; and the inability to raise capital.

Eventually, Dunlap agreed to insert devices in his machines that would prevent cassettes from being copied, a breakthrough that effectively eliminated the American movie industry from his legion of opponents. In 1989, a court ruling rejecting the request of the Japanese companies to dismiss the suit buoyed his cause. He received $2 million in settlement fees from some of the defendant companies, which paid his legal expenses and kept Go-Video in business. Another part of the settlement broke the manufacturing chokehold: Samsung, one of the Korean manufacturers, agreed under pressure to break the boycott and manufacture dual-deck VCRs for Go-Video.

The significance of the court ruling was that it legitimized Dunlap's claim. He was no longer just a lone Don Quixote, tilting at worldwide cartels; he now had the backing of a U.S. Federal Court which, on the defendants' motion to dismiss, found that Dunlap had stated a cause of action (and that his case should not be dismissed before trial) based on an alleged conspiracy mounted by the Japanese electronics industry giants.

Most important, that court meant business. It ordered individual foreign companies to answer conspiracy-in-restraint-of-trade charges in an American court before a federal jury, and prevented the Japanese electronics industry and any other foreign companies from manufacturing dual-deck VCRs on their own while this case was being heard. This ruling prevented the defendants from resorting to the common tactic of protracting the legal struggle indefinitely until the technology was obsolete or the competitor driven out of business.

Until this case, "American companies didn't realize that U.S. antitrust law gives them the right to sue even for something that happens in a smoke-filled room in Tokyo," said John Stern, vice-president of the American Electronics Association and head of its Tokyo branch.[8]

The court also protected Go-Video by assuring them the legal resources to obtain proof and build a case against the Japanese electronics industry—namely, the right to take depositions from Japanese executives. Dunlap's attorney, Joseph Alioto, Jr., went to Japan to take depositions from high-ranking executives of the firms still opposing him, including Akio Morita, chairman of Sony. Of the twenty-six original defendants, all but six had settled with Dunlap.[9]

Dunlap protected himself with massive publicity. He became an expert on Japanese cartels, and spoke out about his experiences. His saga was covered extensively in the print and electronic media—from articles in *Time* and *The New York Times* to appearances on "20/20." But was Go-Video, a company that had sustained net losses of $3.5 million in 1990 and $2.6 million in 1989, any match for the deep-pocketed Japanese electronics firms whose resources could stretch a lawsuit out indefinitely?[10] Unfortunately for Dunlap, Go-Video has lost its most recent challenge, a $750-million suit against the three Japanese electronics firms that had not yet settled—Sony, Matsushita, and JVC—in late June 1991. Dunlap is appealing that decision.

CARTELS AND *KEIRETSU* IN JAPAN: THE AMERICAN
CHALLENGE TO THEIR GLOBAL REACH

Unlike Goodyear, giant Japanese multinationals do not have to worry
about unfriendly takeovers from foreign investors—or domestic investors, for that matter. Most of them belong to *keiretsu*, the coalitions
of member companies that form the backbone of Japan's economic
success. Descendants of the prewar conglomerates that were broken
up during the American occupation, these coalitions bear an eerie
resemblance to their precursors—known as *zaibatsu*—at least in their
economic form. More than half of Japan's hundred largest companies
belong to *keiretsu*, along with nearly all of that nation's choice industries, including banking, insurance, computers, telecommunications,
and semiconductors. About 150 industrial groups that fit the descrip-
tion of *keiretsu* operate in Japan today; they function as corporate
families tightly bound together by custom and tradition, as well as solid
financial ties, such as mutual shareholding and cooperative business
strategies.

As the U.S. takeover expert Boone Pickens discovered, the *keiretsu* protect their companies from unwanted LBOs through a finely
honed system of interlocking directorates and "stable shareholding,"
which means never trading more than 60 to 80 percent of member-
company shares. This cozy arrangement leaves managers relatively
free to conduct their business without fear of raiders, and cushioned
against some of the predatory dangers of the marketplace.

The *keiretsu* claim to offer the best of capitalism and industrial
policy: the discipline of the marketplace remains intact, since the *keiretsu* members compete very fiercely against one another and within
their parent groupings for market share, and there is a government-
backed global safety net for the winners. The contrast between the
Japanese and U.S. systems recalls the parable of the tortoise and the
hare: while Americans hurtled through the 1980s in a frenzy of bound-
less merger and buy-out activity, the Japanese slowly but steadily
continued to build their *keiretsu*-based industries for the future.

The vast majority of *keiretsu* are organized along vertical, not
horizontal lines. An auto manufacturer like Toyota, for example,
would include in its family of companies upstream suppliers (manufacturers of axles, transmissions, and carburetors), as well as downstream
distributors (auto sales outlets and rental outfits). These companies
revolve around a major bank—and often some unrelated businesses—
and are linked by partial stock ownerships rather than outright ownership. Vertically organized industries would not be illegal under U.S.

antitrust law; indeed, in many respects, General Motors and Ford resemble a vertically organized Japanese *keiretsu*, since they own, engage in joint ventures with, and invest in parts suppliers, car rental companies, and dealerships. What are clearly illegal under U.S. antitrust law are horizontally organized *keiretsu*, companies in the same industry—two or more chemical companies, or computer companies—operating in collusion to fix prices and control production. Although horizontally organized *keiretsu* are clearly in the minority in Japan, they are still significant economically.

The major difference between an American conglomerate and a Japanese *keiretsu* is that the latter revolves around a bank, whereas U.S. law prohibits banks from owning industrial assets under the Glass-Steagall Act. This means that the Japanese government, whose central bank backs up the nation's banks, is also indirectly an investor in these industrial conglomerates. Efforts to revise Glass-Steagall, passed during the Depression, have failed for fear of encouraging U.S. companies to organize along such monopolistic lines. The conceptual problems involved in the U.S. relationship to the Japanese conglomerates are hard to unravel. At what point, for example, do *keiretsu* become cartels, collections of companies operating in restraint of trade? (OPEC, a group of government-owned oil companies, is the world's most powerful cartel.) It is clear that the cooperative behavior of firms in a *keiretsu* may violate U.S. antitrust law, although their structure may be perfectly legal. In addition, since there is little enforcement in Japan against either *keiretsu* or cartels—a sore point with U.S. negotiators at the SII (Structural Impediments Initiative) talks—how can such differences be addressed between countries that have become so economically interdependent?

It is easy to be seduced by the idea of the *keiretsu*, even to the point of imagining how to transplant the concept to the United States. How many U.S. industries now struggling to survive would benefit from guaranteed markets, long-term financing, and government backing all at once? Whatever the financial advantages, however, those with long memories recall the pitfalls of monopolies, particularly in terms of individual freedom and democracy. The giant cartels that preceded World War I and World War II in Italy, Germany, and Japan developed freely without the restraining hand of antitrust laws: linking the massive power of government to economic industrial strength, they generated enormous profits, and industries flourished. And the governments that protected them joined the ranks of the most notorious in history.

Keiretsu remain remote to most Americans, who do not yet connect the success of the Japanese system with the decline in U.S. competitiveness. Because the U.S. constitutes the world's largest market, American leaders believe they can still afford to persist in their efforts to convince the rest of the world to bend to their notions of antitrust; the weight of history and the merits of their arguments—that monopolies invariably lead to high prices and poor quality—can't help but prevail in the end. Many antitrust advocates argue convincingly that the U.S. has done better in the international marketplace because of strong antitrust enforcement, which has forced firms to compete vigorously at home and strengthened their ability to compete abroad. Indeed, they blame the lax enforcement of the 1980s for the merger frenzy, excessive corporate debt, and subsequent diminution of investment in corporate R & D and capital improvements.

The historical resistance to cartels grew so powerful in the national psyche that, to guarantee fair competition for future generations, two government agencies were spawned for the purpose of antitrust enforcement—the respective antitrust divisions of the Federal Trade Commission and the Justice Department—just in case one agency fell down on the job. Americans extol to heroic proportions Teddy Roosevelt, the famous "trust-buster" who broke up the monopolies and cartels—not Andrew Carnegie and Jay Gould, who built them.

The surge of foreign investment in the United States convulsed antitrust and banking law when it became evident that foreign nations not only did not share our antipathy to cartels, but viewed them as key to their economic success. Americans could no longer ignore cartels whose operations reached, through rapidly growing investment, into their own economy and political life; and they could no longer afford the luxury of traveling the high road while other nations were moving along a divergent path.

The 1990s heralded a new and disturbing challenge: "change or protect." Americans would either have to move with the times and adjust their antitrust and banking policies, or find a way to protect their assets against further incursions from foreign cartels. The issue of foreign cartelization in America raised three vital questions that defy easy answers:

• How do we reconcile our fierce anticartel traditions with the need to compete in the global economy, where the rising success of cartels throughout the industrialized world is forcing us to question our own business traditions?

• Recognizing our aversion to cartels, how do we treat foreign cartels that operate freely in the United States? How do we know a cartel when we see one, given the secrecy with which some of them operate and the paucity of data on foreign investment? Should foreign cartels be forced to adhere to our laws and traditions?

• Is blaming the foreign cartels another way of avoiding the real reasons for America's competitive decline? Another excuse for protectionist legislation? Another reason for avoiding the tough measures we should be taking on the deficits, on infrastructure, and on education? To what extent is foreign economic success attributable to the superiority of organization within these foreign conglomerates that have unlimited cash for growth; and to what extent is that success due to other factors—higher productivity, and technological and economic superiority?

The purchase of Rockefeller Center by the Mitsubishi Estate Company in the fall of 1989 heralded a new sense of awareness of the global reach of the *keiretsu*. Americans took another look at the low-profile Mitsubishi family of companies and found a highly organized trading empire—"an international dynamo," according to a cover story in *Business Week*, "with hundreds of interdependent companies stretching from Rockefeller Center to Riyadh." The Mitsubishi *keiretsu* included ventures in mining, real estate, chemicals, space satellites, television, consumer electronics, steel, banking, telecommunications, cars and trucks, paper products, and insurance.[11] One year later, another deep-pocketed *keiretsu*, Matsushita, bought another American icon, the movie conglomerate MCA United Artists, for the astronomical sum of $6.6 billion—the largest Japanese purchase ever in the United States.

WOMB TO TOMB IN THE ENTERTAINMENT INDUSTRY: THE MATSUSHITA BUY-OUT OF MCA UNITED ARTISTS

The purchase progressed quietly, behind closed doors, until about a month before the deal was concluded (the purchase was announced by Matsushita in November 1990, and finalized before the New Year). A short time span was critical: it was barely long enough to examine the issues, but left plenty of time to head off political opposition.

Many issues were raised by the purchase, coming so soon after Sony's purchase (the year before) of Columbia Pictures, but the one-two punch of Sony *and* Matsushita buying movie companies crystallized the critical issue they shared in common: antitrust and the power of foreign cartels. Hollywood was strapped for cash, given the increasingly high cost of making movies, and only foreign multinationals possessed the resources to bail out the movie business. Fortunately, they came to the rescue, and by 1990 four out of the seven major American movie studios were foreign-owned. The purchases occurred so quickly that they created a dynamic all their own, sparking a national controversy over ownership of one of the nation's major cultural assets. Many said that, after the Sony purchase, it was only a matter of time before their archrival, Matsushita, bought a movie studio.

What difference did it make? Sony and Matsushita were merely conglomerates buying other conglomerates. The MCA conglomerate included a diverse range of companies connected to the entertainment industry, including the Putnam Berkley Group, a publishing company; Geffen Records; a 49-percent interest in Cineplex Odeon Theaters; Universal Studios in Florida and Hollywood; MCA Television Group; Universal Pictures; Spencer Gifts; WWOR-TV; and a 50-percent interest in the USA Cable Network. Curry Company, which owned the concessions in Yosemite National Park, sparked the only heated political controversy over the sale. Interior Secretary Manuel Lujan, Jr., publicly denounced Matsushita and its U.S. emissaries, Robert Strauss (a former U.S. trade negotiator and well-known Washington lawyer-lobbyist) and former Senator Howard Baker, for not abiding by a prior agreement to convince Matsushita to donate the concession company to the government. Baker and Strauss denied that any such agreement had been reached, and attacked Lujan for Japan-bashing. Lujan, who reflected growing American sentiment against the acquisition, quickly backed down from his original stance under pressure from the White House, which feared antagonizing foreign investors.

The real issue with the Sony and Matsushita purchases involved the degree of control—in both hardware and software—that could now potentially be exercised by two Japanese multinationals over one of America's most internationally competitive industries, entertainment. Both the Sony and Matsushita groups already dominated the hardware industry, the television sets, movie cameras, and all the technological components of the industry: they are both vertically integrated companies geared toward total control of one industry, from factory to consumer. Their purchase of movie studios guaranteed that they would control the software as well—the creative side, the entertainment that had propelled the industry into its flagship position as one of the U.S.'s leading exports.[12]

"They are picking up everything from womb to tomb in the communications field. If you control the production of material, the display of material, and the manufacturing of equipment, you have a significant advantage in the information age," concluded Richard Iverson, who was critical of the purchase. In an era of "high-definition broadcasting," ownership is critical: it means domination of the standards of broadcasting and production. By integrating hardware and software, Sony and Matsushita—fierce competitors themselves—will have a very strong influence on those standards in all future media production and transmission. The standards reach well beyond the entertainment business, into medical imaging, radar, defense electronics, workstations, supercomputers, flat-panel displays for personal computers, and many other industries.

Matsushita occupies a dominant position in the worldwide consumer-electronics hardware market. Its revenues reached nearly $40 billion in 1990, from sales in audio equipment, home appliances, and video equipment, including cameras and recorders. Among its companies are such well-known names as Quasar, Panasonic, Technics, and JVC; its U.S. subsidiary, MECA (Matsushita Electric Company of America), is totally owned by the foreign parent. As of now, the major antitrust issues raised by the Matsushita-MCA purchase remain unresolved:

• *What about the domination of related markets?* Although consumer-electronics and software markets are separate and distinct, they are interdependent. VCRs play movie videos, television sets play programs, and CD players play concerts recorded on CDs. "Hardware needs software," said Akio Morita.[13] Indeed, software comes first: people buy the technology in order to enjoy the software. The victory of the VHS over the Beta format for VCRs proves the competitive advantage enjoyed by the company that dominates the software market. Beta, the superior technology—and one still used by television stations—lost out to the VHS producers largely because of the preponderance of VHS software. Ironically, it was Sony, the producers of Beta, who lost out to its fiercest competitor, Matsushita, because of the latter's superior distribution network.

• *Will Matsushita's acquisition of MCA lessen competition in the hardware markets? Will barriers to entry increase?* These markets have become highly concentrated in the last decade, as well as largely dominated by Japanese and, to a lesser extent, Korean and European companies; the real issue, therefore, is the reduction of competition for international as well as U.S. investors. Matsushita, Sony, and other Japanese manufacturers have already organized into a Japan-EC Round Table, which might further foreclose U.S. options in the consumer-electronics markets.

• *Will Matsushita try to "bundle" hardware and software to-*

gether to create an unfair advantage? Will Matsushita, or Sony, once
they come to dominate the market, sell only some of their products
on condition that we buy other, unwanted products?

• *How will this affect distribution networks?* Another potential
for unfair competition is the possibility of excluding hardware competitors from software outlets. Will first-run movie rentals, for example,
exclude VCRs manufactured by someone other than Matsushita or
Sony?

• *To what extent will Matsushita control new technologies with
dual control over software* and *hardware?* Through MCA, will Matsushita be in a position to configure its software so that it can only
be displayed on hardware developed by Matsushita? Since its purchase
of CBS Records, Sony has directed that CBS Records produce only
software formatted for the DAT format adopted by the cartel, and not
for a competing format offered by Phillips.[14] Other Sony businesses
that could be helped by this hardware-software relationship include
Cable TV, HDTV, and satellite broadcasting. In the case of Cable TV,
Sony could supply as many as thirteen million Japanese households
with programs, cable hardware, and its own channel; the HDTV market could be worth over $40 billion a year by 2010; and satellite
broadcasting could give Sony the opportunity to win equipment and
transmission contracts.

• *To what extent will dual control over both hardware and software reduce competition in software markets?* Will this acquisition
reduce competition in the movie industry or the record business? Will
higher prices in software affect hardware production?

DEEP POCKETS AND THE *KEIRETSU:* COMPETING FOR
THE AMERICA'S CUP IN A ROWBOAT

Go-Video showed how decisions made in the boardrooms of a foreign
cartel could freeze out a U.S. business in the United States. In the
cartel's view, nothing sinister occurred; it was adhering to its own
traditions and code of honor. Other cartels move with equal agility,
striking quickly when opportunities arise. Their "global reach" exceeds all original predictions, and their economic power is only beginning to dawn on political leaders, who have long ignored the
implications of this trend.[15] Japan's largest *keiretsu*, Mitsubishi, represents an industrial conglomerate that has worldwide sales of over $175
billion, with a great deal of cash to invest. Though it drew international
attention with its purchase of 51 percent of Rockefeller Center, the
Mitsubishi *keiretsu*'s network circulates at all critical points in the

economy, from real estate and construction into chemicals, aerospace, cement, cable industries, paper mills, plastics, rayon, glass, cement, and even a brewery.

Mitsubishi's political power has grown in proportion to its economic clout. Witness the power of Mitsubishi Heavy Industries in the fight over the FSX fighter aircraft. Inspired initially to save five thousand jobs at its Nagoya plant, MHI generated sufficient government interest to launch a world-class aerospace industry, and sustained that interest despite the damaging clash with its U.S. ally.

The Mitsubishi cartel sits on a foundation that is the envy of the world. It has everything: money, depth, breadth, and government backing, which means public sector support as well as freedom from antitrust restrictions. "The 28 core members of the Mitsubishi group are bound together by cross-ownership and other financial ties, interlocking directorates, long-term business relationships, and social and historical links," concluded an extensive *Business Week* investigation into the Mitsubishi cartel. "The three flagship members are Mitsubishi Corporation, the trading company; Mitsubishi Bank, the group's banker; and Mitsubishi Heavy Industries, the leading manufacturer. Beyond this core are hundreds of other Mitsubishi-related companies."

Keeping the likes of a Boone Pickens out of this thicket of inbreeding and its governance structure was easy, since the hundreds of companies own shares of one another: 17 percent of the shares of Mitsubishi Electric, for example, are owned by other members of the *keiretsu*, 25 percent of Mitsubishi Estate, 100 percent of Mitsubishi Construction, 37 percent of Mitsubishi Mining & Cement. Pickens attempted to ply his trade as a raider in Japan by investing a 26-percent stake in Koito, an auto lighting-systems company attached through a *keiretsu* to Toyota. "We had no intention of taking over Koito," alleged Pickens, "which is virtually impossible anyway, because between 60 and 65 percent of Koito's stock is locked up by Toyota's *keiretsu*." Koito did not believe Pickens, and refused his request for four seats on their twenty-member board of directors, and for detailed financial records of the company—a right guaranteed by Japanese law to shareholders holding over 10 percent. Koito could always outvote him, but Pickens figured out that the company wouldn't allow him on the board because "they don't want me or any outsider to see the inner workings of the cartel" and its conditions of "indentured servitude," which included, according to Pickens, restrictive business practices and costly perks for top managers.[16]

In American eyes, the real advantage of cartels lies in their access to long-term capital, which empowers companies to draw on resources for long-term growth. No one ever hears Japanese industrialists lamenting the absence of patient capital, the pressure of quarterly reports, or the problems of an eroding supplier base. Deep pockets also give companies a decided advantage in the international marketplace: available capital enables them to purchase new technologies, licenses, patents, and companies in their own country and abroad; a network of captive retail outlets keeps prices high and competition at bay; networks of captive suppliers also keep costs low and reduce uncertainty.

All in all, it's a foolproof recipe for independence of action, reduced competition, and economic success for the home-based companies. And in the case of Japanese investment, cartelization is credited more than any other factor with the *keiretsu*'s success in building up their outward investment portfolio. According to William Holstein, international editor of *Business Week* and one of the leading U.S. experts on the subject, there are four major types of *keiretsu*; all of them are dominated by companies whose names are now familiar to Americans, thanks to their extensive investments in the United States.[17]

The first type of *keiretsu* is represented by the old-school *zaibatsu*, the trading organizations that arose in the 1860s to counter Western colonization and grew to form the backbone of the formidable Japanese military-industrial war machine. Decapitated after World War II by the U.S. occupation, they have re-emerged in economically potent form: Mitsui, Mitsubishi, and Sumitomo are members of this group. Mitsui began doing business in the U.S. during the administration of Ulysses S. Grant.

The other three categories arose after World War II, and also represent attempts to cope with economic renewal following the devastation of war. One postwar group revolves around the banks—Fuji, Daicho-Kango, Sanwa, and Nishi-Iwah—and represents yet another example of an astounding economic success story attributable in part to this type of cooperative organization. The third group consists of "enterprise *keiretsu*," comprising electronics *keiretsu* (such as Matsushita, Sony, and Hitachi) and the auto *keiretsu* (i.e., Toyota). Enterprise *keiretsu* retain their own captive suppliers, like Toyota's Koito.

The fourth group, the "distribution *keiretsu*," may overlap the other groups and include companies from other *keiretsu*, but these are distinguished by being totally dominated by one company. Matsushita, for example, has its own distribution *keiretsu*, with fifteen thousand retail outlets. This ensures that prices will be kept as high as the company wishes, with no discounting; no wonder the Japanese have fought so long and hard to keep American discounters like Toys R Us from opening in Japan. Higher prices allow the company to subsidize overseas investments, or perhaps to keep their own prices abroad below market costs until they can corner market share. This latter practice, called "dumping," is illegal in the United States, but difficult to prove. By the time the government takes the company to court, the targeted company or industry might have long disappeared.

"These groups sometimes compete, but it's more interesting when they cooperate," said Holstein. "In the cartels there are different players from different *keiretsu* at different times. It is a deeply interlocking industrial structure." One of the most important features of that structure is loyalty, companies coming to one another's rescue in hard times—often, in effect, a guarantee against bankruptcy. "When group member Akai Electric Co. ran into financial problems in the early 1980s, it was rescued by Mitsubishi Bank. When Mitsubishi Heavy Industries' shipbuilding business hit rough seas in the mid-1980s, it was able to place unneeded workers with other group companies and raise massive new equity." It is also a perfect formula for warding off unwanted takeovers: when Texaco bought Getty Oil in 1984 and appeared ready to sell Getty's 50-percent share of Mitsubishi Oil to the Kuwait Petroleum Company, several of the Mitsubishi member companies rallied, outbid the Kuwaitis, and kept the company in the family.[18]

The *keiretsu* organization also positions its members in the international investment game. Following the Mitsui and Sumitomo groups—and wary of impending investment restrictions on the EC and U.S. horizons—Mitsubishi executives began to pursue an aggressive investment strategy. After the acquisition of Rockefeller Center, Mitsubishi Corporation, the trading arm of the Mitsubishi *keiretsu*, beat General Electric for control of Aristech Chemical Corp. by paying $877 million. During the same period, other groups of companies from the Mitsubishi family bought Verbatim from Eastman Kodak for $400 million, won a $400-million power-plant contract in Virginia, and financed the $940-million purchase of Pebble Beach, one of the world's most famous golf courses. The Mitsubishi *keiretsu* already owned a substantial number of investments in the U.S., including a television plant, a semiconductor company, an auto-glass plant, and an auto-assembly plant. Outside the United States, Mitsubishi made headlines with an announcement that it was exploring a joint venture with Germany's Daimler-Benz.[19]

One school of thought argues that the *keiretsu* hold far less power to restrict market access than outsiders believe. "If Japanese business practice effectively restricted market access, it would be almost impossible to explain the growing volume of manufactured imports, which jumped by 101 percent in four years from 1985 to 1989," wrote Masaru Yoshitomi, director-general of the Economic Research Institute of Japan's Economic Planning Agency. Yoshitomi also challenges the conspiratorial view of the *keiretsu*'s critics: "There is no evidence that trading companies restrict market access of products produced by foreign companies for the purpose of protecting *keiretsu* members from foreign competition." He argued that the success of the *keiretsu* rested not on monopolistic behavior but on the superiority of their products, consumer and supplier preference for quality and service, similar preferences for long-term relationships between core firms and their suppliers, and business strategies that seek "market-share dominance rather than profit-maximization."[20]

In the American view, traditional monopolies discourage competition, while the *keiretsu* benefit from competition that they generate among themselves. "Core firms continually exercise ratings on suppliers," providing a mechanism by which a "long-term relationship can be compatible with tough competition among suppliers."[21]

Chalmers Johnson, an eminent scholar at the University of California, emphatically disagrees. He sees the *keiretsu* as an instrument of the state geared to the continuous implementation of "Japan's long-standing mercantilist industrial policy." Through "predatory pricing, and rigged distribution and financial systems," the state manipulates its market system "to achieve political goals." The financial *keiretsu*, writes Johnson, serves to segregate the "Japanese financial system into government banks, the postal savings system, local banks . . . and the securities industry," in order to "control domestic interest rates . . . to supply capital to industry at prices well below those available from international capital markets." Distribution *keiretsu*—including some seventy thousand retail stores in the electric-appliances industry alone—"restrict competition and . . . gouge domestic competitors and keep out foreign competitors." Encouraged by the Japanese government, the distribution *keiretsu* include the notoriously inefficient mom-and-pop retailers, a key constituency of the Liberal Democratic Party. Production *keiretsu*, the suppliers and subcontractors of big companies like Toyota and Nissan, are the "shock absorbers of the Japanese business cycle . . . [and] . . . the flip side of Japan's divided and pacified labor movement. . . . Without the subcontractors to squeeze during down swings, big business could not maintain labor peace by giving male heads of households career job security regardless of business conditions."[22]

Despite mounting evidence to the contrary, American leaders cling to the view that the *keiretsu* are traditional monopolies and will soon become obsolete, too inefficient to survive. But the *keiretsu* seem perfectly adapted to their current environment, unlikely to expire in the near future. They are so successful that they are being successfully copied in places like South Korea, where Hyundai, Daewoo, and Samsung groups flourish on the *keiretsu* model; in fact, the Korean *keiretsu* are called *chaebol*, the Korean word for *zaibatsu*.

CRITICAL INDUSTRIES AND *KEIRETSU* READINESS

Unlike the communist systems that collapsed after forty years, the Japanese cartels are based on a pure capitalist model, very different from the West but perhaps better adapted for global competition. In a timely and well-documented article in the *Harvard Business Review*, Charles Ferguson, one of the country's leading computer experts, argues for the same sort of protection for the high-value hardware of his industry, arguing that, "if the U.S. and the European companies continue business as usual, they will either fail outright or become, in effect, local design and marketing subsidiaries of Japanese companies that will dominate a $1 trillion world hardware industry."[23] His endangered list includes such stalwarts as Apple, Compaq, Sun Microsystems, DEC, Xerox, and Hewlett-Packard.

Ferguson's analysis mirrors the case histories of Go-Video and Matsushita, echoing the now-familiar refrain of "invented here, owned and managed abroad." His figures tell the tale of declining market share attributable to the lack of capital: the computer trade balance with Japan slid from a small surplus ten years ago to a $6-billion deficit in 1988 that keeps rising; and the U.S. and European computer manufacturers pay an increasing fraction of their revenues to Japanese components-and-hardware suppliers who come from companies that are also their major future competitors. Within five years, Ferguson predicts, Japanese industry will control 50 percent of the hardware content of worldwide personal-computer systems, following the pattern of semiconductor memories—"a $10 billion market the United States has all but lost."

Today, Ferguson says, the information-systems industry finds itself in the ironic position of being the victim of its own innovative successes, or "technological trajectory." The information industry finds itself moving swiftly into an era of digitalization: cameras, computers, stereos, and photocopiers are all dependent on low-cost standardized technologies assembled from mass-produced components. The victors that will enjoy the spoils of these fast-breaking innovations will be companies that have "access to patient capital, that maintain close links with component and equipment developers, and that can afford huge, continuing expenditures for R & D and capital investment."[24]

Invention is no longer the issue in the 1990s; success comes to companies that can commercialize technologies faster and cheaper. Who can do this better than the *keiretsu*, whose strategic and technical strengths are natural homes for the information industry of the future? Canon, Matsushita, NEC, and Sony are diversified, vertically integrated companies that are also fully absorbed into financial industrial groups. They are perfectly positioned to make "long-term investments in technology and manufacturing, command the supply chain from components and capital equipment to end products, and coordinate their strategic approaches to block foreign competition and penetrate world markets."[25] How can U.S. companies match them in all those critical respects? Particularly the risk factor: investing in high-risk technologies is perfect for large, vertically integrated cartels, whose future would not be threatened by the ups and downs of technological innovation.

Is the cartel arrangement simply a superior form of economic organization, something Americans should emulate if they could change their own culture and society to meet that challenge? Is it a totally legitimate and desirable way of doing business at home and in the world? Not really, argues Ferguson, who adds that, although Japanese companies have demonstrated their excellent engineering and mass-production talents, and have obtained most of their technology through legitimate licensing arrangements, the cartels also have qualities antithetical to American traditions. According to Ferguson, the cartels "collude to force foreign competitors to license critical technologies, to block foreign applications for Japanese patents, and to deny foreign competitors access to technologies and markets over which Japanese industries gain control."[26]

One of the best examples of the *keiretsu* in action occurred in reaction to the failure of U.S. Memories, the consortium of U.S. D-RAM manufacturers that went out of business in early 1990. One week after the announcement, six Japanese D-RAM producers simultaneously announced production cuts and price increases. Their success spoke to the importance of starting early: The closure of the Japanese 16K D-RAM markets to imports and FDI, argued Laura Tyson, "encouraged learning, economies of scale, and investment behavior that were critical to Japan's later success in other semiconductor products."[27] The *keiretsu* worked well for the Japanese D-RAM producers: with government help, it restricted competition, discouraged foreign entry, kept prices high, controlled supply—and built a world-class industry. Next to the global force of the *keiretsu*, U.S. trade negotiators look like they're fighting a pit bull with a fly swatter.

The Ferguson view reflects a growing—and increasingly vocal—

majority in the high-tech community. In opposition sits a smaller but more powerful group who believe that American innovation would be stifled by copying the Japanese cartels. One of the most influential spokesmen for this view is George Gilder, whose book *Microcosm* traces with riveting detail the invention of the microchip and its revolutionary consequences.[28]

Gilder argues that the microchip would never have been invented in a cartel arrangement. The great inventors and entrepreneurs of the integrated circuits—Robert Noyce, Carver Mead, Jack Kilby, and others—did not get their inspiration from ponderous, government-managed programs; their genius was more of an individual enterprise, lightly supported perhaps, but unencumbered by the heavy hand of government regulation and industrial policy. Gilder's research indicates that, "rather than pushing decisions up through the hierarchy, the power of microelectronics pulls them remorselessly down to the individual."[29] In fact, the inventors initially agreed with this philosophy themselves, as evidenced by their early lobbying efforts: In the late 1970s, the leaders of the then embryonic semiconductor industry, led by Noyce, met with officials from the Department of Commerce, specifically to ask for a hands-off policy toward their burgeoning industry. The same group spent a good part of the late 1980s trying to undo this policy, after watching their market share steadily decline in the competitive race against a very different industry-and-government structure. Of the semiconductor-industry leaders, only T. J. Rodgers, CEO of Cypress Semiconductor Corp., agrees with this individualistic approach today. A relentless promoter of this view, Rodgers offers his own small but highly profitable company as proof that the lone ranger formula works—at least for him.

TO CHANGE OR PROTECT:
THE U.S. POLICY CONUNDRUM

While the rest of the world was building up its conglomerates, the U.S. was breaking up its industrial giants. Witness the twelve-year unsuccessful antitrust suit against IBM, the nation's premier computer company, as well as the very similar break-up of AT&T, whose Bell Labs, a victim of the split, led the nation and the world in many areas of advanced research, many with commercial applications. Tom Seidel, now director of SEMATECH's manufacturing-methods division, left Bell Labs after the break-up, along with many of his fellow scientists. "I was ranked the top in my division," he recalled. "Because of the break-up, I got no raise for two years. I had kids in college."[30]

How many *keiretsu* would dissipate their critical resources in this way? Many U.S. businesses complain that the centrifugal direction of U.S. policies repeatedly puts them at a marked disadvantage—at home and abroad—against foreign cartels, while the worldwide influence of those cartels continues to grow unabated. Sony and Matsushita faced no antitrust or any other legal barriers, at home or abroad, in purchasing major movie companies, but the U.S.'s major networks—the only companies with the resources and the interest to compete with the foreign multinationals—were barred from purchasing the companies by FCC regulations prohibiting them from buying television production companies.

Unable to protect its own companies from the inequities wrought by encroaching globalism, the U.S. turns ethnocentric in its attempts to encourage the world to follow its antitrust example. If Japan adopted the U.S. system, so the theory goes, then the *keiretsu* would be dissolved and worldwide competition would become more equitable. Those who adhere to the belief that they can change Japan fail to recognize the global reach of money, power, and corporate culture. Nevertheless, the task of persuading Japan to strengthen its weak antitrust system has occupied U.S. trade negotiators with increasing intensity throughout the 1980s and early 1990s, under the umbrella of "structural impediments to investment." Charles Dallara, assistant secretary of the Treasury, sternly warned his Japanese counterparts in the late spring of 1991 that the U.S. could no longer tolerate the anticompetitive practices of the *keiretsu* system.

Tough talk, but then what? Would the U.S. restrict Japanese investments from *keiretsu* groups? Send all VCRs through Starkville, Mississippi, to be inspected by a single customs official, as the French did in the south of France to protest unfair Japanese trade practices? Eliminate free-trade zones? Cut Kentucky's subsidies to Toyota? By the time U.S. negotiators started playing with a hard ball, they were too out of shape to win the game. The Japanese owned a hefty chunk of the national debt and had virtually overtaken the British as the U.S.'s leading investor; Japan had also become the world's leading capital-surplus nation. From their position of strength, Japanese leaders responded by focusing on America's inability to get its deficits down and its own financial house in order. Government officials were backed by the private sector, with Akio Morita publicly advising them to "say no to the U.S. more often."

Recent events led to a good-news/bad-news conclusion. The good news, that Japan's Fair Trade Commission (FTC) had toughened its stance, was offset by the bad news that, instead of going after their own conglomerates, the commission's first targets were European and

U.S. importers—including Apple Computer Inc., whose thirty-nine offices were raided by FTC agents, and Master Foods K.K., a subsidiary of Mars Inc.—who were allegedly keeping their prices up and forcing Japanese retailers to follow suit.[31]

On paper, Japan's antitrust laws look as tough as U.S. laws; the difference lies in their enforcement. A Justice Department study found that from 1985 to 1988 the U.S. government "found fault with 30% of the cases it investigated, while the Japanese government took action in only 5% of its cases. The average fine in the U.S. was eight times as large as in Japan."[32] Unlike U.S. and European law, the thrust of Japanese antitrust law and policy is geared toward producers as well as consumers, with the scale tipped more often in the direction of the producers. In fact, the position of the Japanese FTC tells the tale: subordinate to MITI, it is more often than not maneuvered into favoring trade over antimonopoly considerations. The agency is also hampered by laws specifically *exempting* cartels from antitrust enforcement.[33]

In the U.S., confusion characterizes the current antitrust atmosphere. This is reflected in the uneven policy responses from the executive branch, Congress, and the courts. The pluralism that has worked so well for America as a political system has not worked as well to strengthen its hand in the current global environment. It has disadvantaged U.S. companies and confused foreign multinationals, who find it difficult to cope with the international irrelevance of our laws and the inconsistency in their application.

To their credit, the White House and the Congress have recognized the problem and begun to address it. As part of his campaign to aid U.S. business, President Reagan relaxed antitrust enforcement to encourage U.S. companies to compete more effectively in the international arena by pooling their resources. Unfortunately, he didn't reckon with the unexpected: the highly individualistic nature of American business, the precipitous drop in the dollar, and the subsequent surge of foreign investment. Though the new policies freed up the entrepreneurial spirit of the business community and enriched those clever enough to take advantage of them, they did little to help U.S. businesses compete against foreign cartels; in fact, they helped the cartels buy U.S. assets! The problem was the nonselective nature of Reagan's business revolution in which some very diverse groups benefited from the relaxation of the antitrust laws, including LBO gamesmen, junk-bond salesmen, and foreign investors with deep pockets and strong currencies.

The move to reduce antitrust enforcement also undercut the free-market advocates, who had long argued that foreign cartels were no threat to Americans since U.S. antitrust laws applied equally to foreign as well as U.S. companies, and if foreign cartels exhibited monopolistic behavior in the U.S. they could be prosecuted. Now U.S. laws had become too malleable, too subject to differential interpretations, and too idiosyncratic in their application. In this more complex environment, litigation ought to be pursued, but only in conjunction with policies that reflect the new facts of life: that the cartels and *keiretsu* are here to stay and will most likely expand, not contract to conform to U.S. views of fair competition.

Another measure from the Reagan administration focused on breaking down antitrust barriers to joint research. Under the provisions of the National Cooperative Research Act of 1984, firms were allowed to cooperate in precompetitive research consortia without risking prosecution. This led to the formation of more than a hundred research consortia, the best-known being the Microelectronics and Computer Technology Corporation (MCC)—a group of twenty companies, now headed by Dr. Craig Fields, the former director of DARPA—and SEMATECH. The idea of research consortia took a long time to come to the United States. Many believe they represent a significant improvement over the rugged-individualist model more characteristic of U.S. corporations, but others fear that companies with highly individualistic traditions will not reveal their choice technologies to their competitors, obviating the purpose of consortia. Worldwide competition may force the issue, one way or the other.

The Bush administration, aware of the nonselective nature of antitrust enforcement, instructed the Justice Department to prevent mergers the agency considered undesirable. By this time, however, the courts were packed with Reagan appointees, many of whom were unsympathetic to antitrust enforcement and highly supportive of the trend toward worldwide cartelization. Still others showed little concern for the problems of foreign investment and U.S. competitiveness, leading to some embarrassing defeats for the Justice Department.[34] Despite its well-publicized failures, the Justice Department still prevails at times without going to court, since companies will either drop their bids or restructure to avoid a government lawsuit.

At long last, the Bush White House tried to ease antitrust restrictions for U.S. joint-production ventures to protect companies against the threat of treble damages in antitrust lawsuits. Unfortunately, the White House found itself so conflicted over the issue that the bill went nowhere, as high-ranking aides fought the old cliché battles over "industrial policy" that had stymied so many of their former trade disputes. The legislation "languished for months on Capitol Hill, in part because the administration had failed to take a clear stand on the matter," wrote Alan Murray and Paul M. Barrett in *The Wall Street Journal*.[35] Commerce Secretary Mosbacher strongly advocated the legislation, in the belief that easing up on antitrust would encourage joint ventures and boost U.S. competitiveness; he was supported by Attorney General Richard Thornburgh. Economic officials in the administration, Budget Director Richard Darman and economic adviser Michael Boskin, opposed the bill on the grounds that it smacked of "industrial policy," which was against administration policy. Darman and Boskin finally agreed to go along with the bill if it was stripped of all measures that could possibly be considered encouraging to joint ventures, or measures that could be construed as financing those ventures.[36]

Noted antitrust expert Professor Robert Pitofsky of Georgetown Law School agrees, in part, with the thesis that the problem cannot be solved by changing the law alone. "The problem is not so much antitrust, but risk-averse lawyers," said Pitofsky. "There are three kinds of industrial organization: mergers, joint ventures, and research consortia. Only one case in the last hundred years was brought against a research consortium, and there never was a single production venture challenged. If United States business stayed away from R and D and production joint ventures, it was not because antitrust blocked the way. [Joint marketing ventures in] sales are a different matter. Those can be noncompetitive.

"The more subtle question relates to our tradition of *not* collaborating," continued Pitofsky. "Why didn't Zenith and all the other companies get together sooner on semiconductors and electronics? Hundreds of companies in the United States—drug companies, engine manufacturers, computer companies—often collaborate on R and D."[37]

In one of their last official acts, the 101st Congress passed the Antitrust Amendments Act of 1990 on October 28, 1990. In its final form, this appeared to tighten antitrust enforcement, not ease it, supporting those who believe that nonaction is better than risking the consequences of being involved with government. The bill continued the trend begun in the days of the Sherman Act: penalties for antitrust violations were increased, while liability standards were tightened. Reflecting inflation, fines rose to $350,000 for individuals and $10 million for corporations (twenty years ago, the maximum fine for an individual was $20,000). The potential term of imprisonment remained unchanged, at three years. With a nod to the foreign cartels, rules on interlocking directorates were somewhat eased. The final act avoided addressing the real problem of U.S. business in its struggle to remain competitive against the foreign cartels, because of politics, with much of the credit going to the accelerated lobbying activity of the foreign investors and their Washington representatives. The original antitrust bill, intended to enhance the competitiveness of U.S. business, provoked such strong opposition among foreign investors that they took the unusual step of asking the Speaker of the House to take the measure off the House calendar.[38]

What galvanized the foreign investors into action was a provision barring eligibility for antitrust protection for joint ventures in which foreign investors held more than 30 percent of any of the companies involved, or for joint ventures located outside the United States or its territories. The reason was the widespread feeling that foreign companies enjoyed an advantage because their governments support rather than penalize joint ventures, and even subsidize ventures that enhance technologies and other products that promise an enhanced share of the global market.

"I see no reason why this bill should unduly favor foreign firms when their host countries keep our businesses out," charged Representative Jack Brooks, Democrat of Texas, chairman of the House Judiciary Committee and sponsor of the bill. "Let's not forget that this type of legislation was initially hailed by American business and the administration under the banner of American competitiveness. I do not want the first word of that nice slogan to somehow be lost or forgotten as the bill moves forward."[39]

Brooks was backed by Democrats as well as Republicans, who hailed the measure as "a large step toward helping U.S. high-tech industries resume their leadership" in world markets—in the words of Representative Norman Y. Mineta, a California Democrat whose district represents many high-tech firms. Representative Carlos J. Moorhead, Republican of California, spoke in favor of the bill as "another logical and important step in the effort to assure that America remains economically strong as we enter the twenty-first century."

Foreign investors did not agree. Their U.S. spokesman, Elliot L. Richardson, said, in a letter asking Speaker of the House Thomas B. Foley, Democrat of Washington, to take the bill off the floor, that he supported the "public policy purposes" of the bill, but that its passage would be counterproductive. The bill "is no doubt motivated by a desire to promote U.S. competitiveness," he wrote, but it would have the opposite effect, "because it would discourage foreign participation in research and development ventures at a time when the U.S. is seeking access to foreign technology."[40]

Prior to the bill's enactment, the Congress heard from many business executives who complained that leading competitors overseas, particularly in Japan, were not subject to antitrust laws as strict as those in the United States, and thus enjoyed advantages in pricing and manufacturing products for the international marketplace. (The White House version of the bill did not exempt companies with foreign investments, seeking to afford foreign companies the same privileges as wholly American companies.) Richardson was joined within the Congress by Representative Bill Frenzel, a Minnesota Republican, who argued that "we are trying to remove investment restrictions around the world" and this bill "discriminates against foreign investment."

"Foreign investors are outrageous in their criticism of this bill," countered Representative Ron Wyden, an Oregon Democrat, who noted that many foreign governments gave their companies far more help than does the United States in the form of subsidies, low-interest loans, and other assistance. Some supporters of the bill added that the act would not bar foreign investors, but merely provide fewer benefits for their ventures.

Despite the efforts of Richardson and the foreign investors, the bill passed the House by voice vote on June 4, 1991. The cartels and the foreign investors prevailed, however, because the act died in the Senate, and no legislation has moved forward since.

Election-year politics in 1992 led the Bush administration to reexamine antitrust policy with regard to the Japanese challenge. In an interview on John McLaughlin's Sunday television show, Attorney General William Barr announced the White House's intention to reformulate antitrust policy to enable the Justice Department to pursue Japanese industrial cartels. The Justice Department at that point was limited by its own guidelines, which restricted enforcement actions to cases in which American consumers were harmed. Barr hoped to expand the policy to include U.S. exporters trying to compete in Japan. Unfortunately, Barr's proposals were short-lived; strong opposition from Vice President Quayle, the State Department, and U.S. Trade Representative Carla Hills proved sufficient to quash the initiative.[41]

The quandary remains. How can the U.S. compete and survive in a global environment saddled with a system that is somewhat out of sync with the industrialized world, and greatly out of sync with our most formidable competitor, Japan? There is no longer any question that the cartel-*keiretsu* system works better in terms of what matters most to corporations of any nationality: producing capital for expansion and increasing worldwide market share. At the same time, U.S. consumers, manufacturers, and prosecutors would never tolerate any form of transplant. Can the U.S. adopt some of the best features of the *keiretsu*, while eliminating its most blatant anticompetitive practices? One view encourages large companies to purchase smaller, related companies, as White House officials wanted IBM to purchase

Perkin-Elmer. This offers the advantage of being legal; it would also offer a greater degree of stability to larger companies, who need more assurance of continuity among their suppliers, while smaller companies could benefit from the financial resources and stability of their larger brethren.

Any attempt to compete even minimally against the *keiretsu* by adopting some of their features seems a long way off politically, considering the inability of Congress and the White House to come to grips with the problem. Without the removal of treble damages from the books—the penalty for companies convicted of antitrust violations—what hope would there be for cooperation in sales or production, even in clear-cut cases in which U.S. market share is seriously threatened? Japanese leaders find America's aversion to more efficient types of industrial organization hard to understand in the face of global realities. "Mike, if you guys think Cray is so important, either you should nationalize it or make it merge with IBM," MITI Vice-Minister for International Affairs Makoto Kuroda told former U.S. trade negotiator Ambassador Michael Smith. "It won't survive otherwise against an NEC, or a Fujitsu, or a Hitachi." Smith agreed, calling the Japanese system a huge "money machine." Money machine or not, Americans still find the cartel-*keiretsu* system too inimical to their own values to adopt, leaving themselves with a dilemma their leaders are only too happy to avoid.

CHAPTER XII

Global Strategies

Economic nationalism started overseas.
 —Robert Noyce,
  co-inventor of the integrated circuit,
  first president of SEMATECH

We can't sell a 486 chip without all kinds of export licenses,
but we can sell all of Intel with no clearance at all.
 —Michael Maibach,
  government-affairs director of Intel

A mythical animal called the "yi" hops around on his single leg. One day, the yi comes face to face with a centipede, and marvels at the insect's hundreds of legs. "Tell me," the yi asks the centipede mischievously, "how do you decide which leg to move first?"

The metaphor evokes the nation's scattershot approach to protecting and promoting its critical technologies. Other industrialized nations resemble the yi: since they are not as well endowed, they are forced to conserve their energies and strategize. They may move slowly, but they move in a single direction.

The idea of "strategic investment"—in which specific technologies are targeted for government assistance—has recently gained currency in the industrialized world. Nations in control of their destiny invest in themselves. They make choices about what will enhance their future, and follow through on those decisions. Conversely, nations that do not invest in themselves find that others soon fill the vacuum.

Japan's MITI has a twenty-year plan for critical technologies and a fifty-year plan for industrial growth. Similarly, the European Community puts enormous resources into high-technology consortia that plan for the future. Only the United States—despite its deepening dependence on other nations—remains unwilling to engage in the long-range planning that will begin to mesh its military and economic interests into a more comprehensive view of national security, more suited to current realities.

The greatest challenge for U.S. leaders is to reconcile the national interest with the global economy—to prepare for a world with blurring borders and rapid change, while still preserving the nation's jobs, technologies, and profits. The key is strategic investment: a nation's commitment to investing in itself first will determine its future ability to invest in other countries, and hence its success in international markets. That means targeting domestic investments, particularly in critical technologies, and following through on those investments with strong support from the public and private sectors. It also means directing resources to that goal, rather than dissipating them in fruitless debate over whether this means choosing winners and losers.

Nations that meet global challenges most successfully meet them from a position of strength. They benefit from an arsenal of strategies that revolve around targeted investments, strategies which include the capacity to regionalize, consortialize, cartelize, strategize, and subsidize. A glance at the new world order reveals how the successful strategies of our major allies and trading partners work in practice.

(1) Regionalize

Despite many struggles and temporary setbacks, most observers agree that multilateralism has triumphed in the industrialized world, at least at the regional level. The Europeans have buried years of internecine warfare to create an economic union that is a model of regional cohesion, bringing extraordinary benefits to participating nations, large and small. Their achievements in raising the standard of living, most dramatically in the poorer countries like Italy and Spain, bode well for the European Community's future success and growth. The EC has succeeded remarkably well in winning respect on many trade issues as the legitimate representative of member nations. In trade battles over television programming, for example, U.S. negotiators no longer challenge France or Germany as they have in the past, but deal with the totality of the European Community.

The miracle of the EC is its philosophy of inclusion and expansion. Its goal to add another dozen nations to the twelve core members will most likely be realized within the next decade. Today, the reality of a united Europe, with its enormous economies of scale, its elimination of trade and investment barriers, its efficient markets and increased global demand for its goods and services, moves ahead as a formidable political and economic alliance. If the EC fulfills most of

its original 285 directives—by 1991, it had achieved more than half—
it will be the largest unified market in the world. In fact, the EC
reached agreement at its meeting in Maastricht in December 1991 on a
common currency and regional central bank by 1999.[1]

The long-term effects of the EC have yet to be analyzed, but
preliminary observations indicate that, despite internal difficulties, the
Europeans have gone further toward realizing Jean Monnet's dream
of a united Europe than anyone could have predicted. After all, the
EC arose from the ashes of World War II, the Cold War, and hundreds
of years of religious and social strife. Europe's triumphs in economic
cooperation deserve much of the credit for encouraging, by example,
the revolutions in Eastern Europe; those nations, having cast off com-
munism, now struggle with forms of capitalism modeled after Europe
and the United States. Although Europe's successes at this point are
mostly economic, many predict that the EC's preliminary triumphs in
reducing trade barriers and encouraging technological cooperation
will eventually lead to a greater measure of political unity, and perhaps
a more lasting peace.

Similarly, in the Far East, the Japanese have moved toward closer
ties with the NICs (Newly Industrializing Countries), particularly in
Southeast Asia, through expanded trade and investment. Japan has
invested billions of dollars in auto factories and electronics plants in
Malaysia alone, for example, gradually displacing the U.S. as the major
power in the region. Japanese leaders believe that regional economic
development promises to reduce their dependence on U.S. markets—
a new objective emerging from their worsening trade relations with
the U.S. Japan and the NICs, like the Europeans, must struggle to
overcome centuries of ill will. Recalling their histories of Japanese
occupation, the Koreans, Chinese, and Taiwanese are especially resis-
tant to a more formal regional entity, which they fear would be dominated by Japan. Japan's strategy of investing heavily in those countries
may prove the best route toward a different form of regionalism.

The success of regionalization has enhanced the economic clout
of the Europeans and the nations of East Asia, but what about their
trading partners and political allies? Does their good will spill over?
Yes and no. Politically, the benefits are evident. A united Europe at
peace represents a great advantage to the United States, still haunted
by memories of two European wars and still paying for troops to keep
the peace. Trade wars are far better than shooting wars, although
trade wars, especially if they involve scarce resources, can turn very
quickly to bloodshed. Economically, no one knows for sure, but talk
about "Fortress Europe" frequently reflects fears that the European

Community will abandon the principles of free trade and multilateralism that have forged the relationship between the U.S. and Europe since World War II.

In the final analysis, regionalization also means that the United States will have less influence, as these regions become less dependent on American aid and trade. The U.S. response, to move toward more regional arrangements in its own hemisphere, most notably with Canada and Mexico, reflects the nation's awareness of these global trends.

(2) Consortialize

Japan and the European Community have long put into practice the concept that "technology is destiny." They also saw the United States win World War II, achieve the highest standard of living in the world, and become the leader of the free world, all through technological preeminence grounded in a solid industrial base.

America's working definition of national security has always encompassed enconomic growth. But recently this has been forgotten, as many technologies invented in the United States, from computer chips to VCRs, were commercialized abroad thanks to new forms of foreign industrial organization and the unwillingness of U.S. leaders to recognize them, adopt them, or adapt to them. Our trading partners have discovered, for example, that one of the most successful methods of commercializing new technologies is through consortia: organizations of companies engaged in joint research, development, and manufacturing, most of the time with government help. Consortia take different forms, depending on the country and the companies involved. A few have, indeed, failed to achieve immediate success, but, despite those short-term failures, America's major trading partners appear to be increasing their support of consortia as a strategy for channeling investment into product development.

Japan, for example, has established more than seventy-five research consortia throughout the country, all committed to making improvements in the wide range of technologies Japan has identified as critical to its industrial future. With Japanese consortia, which go back to the 1920s and 1930s and operate at the prefecture level, the emphasis is on the application of technology, not on research for its own sake. They are linked not to universities but to corporations that will benefit from the innovations they generate. As with all forms of business-government activity in Japan, no one knows the exact extent of government involvement, or even the level of government or business subsidies.

The Europeans have followed the Japanese model and established consortia to help leading industries match their international competitors. Industries targeted for special attention in Europe include semiconductors, computers, biotechnology, energy, and aircraft. EUREKA, JESSI, ESPRIT, Airbus Industrie, and the many others are all precursors of organizational arrangements that will be commonplace in the twenty-first century. Despite their different structures and uneven track records, the Europeans have given no sign that they will abandon their consortia; instead, they will search out ways to increase and improve upon them, as well as protect them from outside competition: when Fujitsu bought the British computer firm ICL, the company was unceremoniously bounced from JESSI.[2]

One of the most successful of the European consortia, Airbus Industrie, includes aerospace companies from Britain, France, Germany, and Spain. Despite U.S. trade experts' conventional wisdom that it would never work, the joint venture surpassed McDonnell Douglas for second place in world markets in 1991, and appeared to have positioned itself as a serious challenger to Boeing, the U.S. company occupying first place. Braced with success from its effort in commercial aircraft, the EC will soon embark on developing its own hypersonic aerospace plane, representing another serious challenge to a field in which the U.S. has long held the technological lead.

The Airbus also owes its success to the dowry that comes with marrying into a consortium. "Airbus . . . has become a competitor, growing enormously in the last decade, as a result of what we estimate to be . . . about $25 billion in subsidies," reported Under Secretary of Commerce J. Michael Farren, at a hearing before the Joint Economic Committee Subcommittee on Technology and National Security in February 1992. Farren attributed the pending McDonnell Douglas sale of a 40 percent equity stake to a government-backed firm in Taiwan as a "symptom of what arises from these enormous government subsidies," and described the Airbus consortium as a "foreign competitor that has the deep pockets of four government treasuries available to it which . . . [are] willing to, if necessary, give aircraft away in order to keep production on line."

Consortia represent the best projection of a nation or region's commitment to invest in itself. While U.S. leaders debated the pros and cons of SEMATECH, of DARPA's involvement in SEMATECH, and of government investment in high-definition television, the Japanese and the Europeans established dozens of organizations to advance technology. In November 1991, the Japanese announced the opening of the first high-definition television station.

Consortia in Japan and, to a lesser extent, in Europe also benefit from looser enforcement of antitrust laws. They can conduct joint research, development, and even manufacturing activities without worrying about the treble damages U.S. firms face when they enter into such arrangements. When SEMATECH, U.S. Memories, MCC, and the relatively few consortia that operate in the United States were created, their founders were forced to spend a considerable amount of time clearing up antitrust questions, whereas their counterparts abroad could concentrate on the main tasks of research and development.

(3) Cartelize

Cartels are anathema to Americans, and for good reason. A cartel's concentration of economic power is a threat to consumers and free markets, and sometimes even to democratic governments. But Americans must recognize the development of cartel-like structures overseas, assess their impact on American competitiveness, and create a strategy to counter and compete with them. In Japan, the *keiretsu* and the cartels are related to the consortia, and derived from long traditions of cooperative business arrangements. Whatever the variations in form and function, the results are the same: powerful combinations of corporate networks, with sizable financial resources and airtight distribution systems. Japan's largest *keiretsu*, Mitsubishi, operates a conglomerate of hundreds of companies linked by financial ties, interlocking boards of directors, and cross-ownership of stock to ward off takeovers. Mitsubishi's annual sales of $175 billion produce cash for its affiliates, which embrace many industries. Most important, like other *keiretsu*, Mitsubishi revolves around its own bank, the Mitsubishi Bank.

Other nations cope with *keiretsu* by screening foreign investment through "antitrust reviews." These reviews are never called "screening," which might leave them open to criticism as unfair trade practices. Indeed, even many free-trade advocates in the United States now argue for "antitrust reviews," as the only legitimate way to counter Japanese competition.

American antitrust traditions grew from the belief that monopolies destroyed competition. This was partially the case in Japan, where competition proved strong in domestic markets and—as intended—weak in the global marketplace. Depending on the industry, six or more *keiretsu* compete fiercely against one another for market share in Japan; in addition, companies within the *keiretsu* are often encouraged to compete among themselves. But the winners face the world with a united front and a supply of capital patient enough to wait for the second coming.

(4) Subsidize

Do they or don't they? No one ever knows for sure, but the varieties of industrial and government organization practiced by our trading partners function perfectly for "targeted-investment" strategies. Airbus Industrie was subsidized. MITI probably subsidized its leading-edge technologies. Subsidies may be outright gifts of cash; they may not even be visible to the naked eye. Often, they amount to little more than quiet persuasion, as when government agencies "convince" the private sector to invest in critical industries. MITI, for example, "persuaded" Japanese companies to invest $900 million in HDTV; any U.S. trade agency that attempted to "persuade" domestic companies to pour $900 million into HDTV research would have been laughed at. Indeed, U.S. advocates of HDTV *were* laughed at, and one Defense Department official, Craig Fields, was fired for publicly promoting the idea.

Nations subsidize when they want to take advantage of an emerging technology. One example being watched closely is superconductivity, which holds the promise of dramatically reducing the amount of heat required to power any product that uses electricity. The applications of this technology encompass civilian as well as military needs, and the potential appears limitless: scientists envision very small components supplying the power for supercomputers as well as trains, nuclear reactors, and aircraft carriers. The energy and cost savings would be enormous if this new technology, which many believe is similar in potential to the invention of the semiconductor, is successful.

In the superconductivity laboratory at Los Alamos, scientists admire the Japanese approach and credit it with overtaking U.S. efforts. "While others sit back, the Japanese government is proactive," said Larry Blair, a scientist at the lab. "For a while, we had a lead over the Japanese. We had a huge meeting with Reagan. He said, 'This is a test; can we compete?' The discovery was made in 1986 by IBM in a Swiss lab. By June 1990, the Japanese were ahead. At the beginning, everyone had an equal shot. The Japanese community is sensitive to the claim that they are the replicators and we are the innovators. They are using superconductivity to prove they can innovate, that they are good researchers, too."

The nuts and bolts of close government-business collaboration

were key, continued Blair, although the exact amount of the Japanese
subsidy was unknown. "The Japanese government formed an international center for superconductivity. Major industries were told they
had to be members. The entry fee was $800,000. The dues were $1
million a year. They converted a power plant on the docks for a
research lab. It was put up very fast . . . in eighteen months. I asked,
'What was the rent?' No one knew. They said they'd work out the
details later."

Whatever the method, a clear pattern of government subsidies
for critical industries is evident throughout the industrialized world—
including, to some extent, the U.S., though subsidies here are more
furtive or linked directly to the military. Today, when U.S. trade
negotiators become aware of foreign subsidies whose success puts
our industries at a pronounced disadvantage, they typically respond
by complaining after the fact through the GATT or other multilateral
organizations. Their responses fall short of meeting the nation's current needs. Timing is everything: by the time U.S. trade representatives initiated a serious challenge at the GATT meeting in 1991 against
subsidies to Airbus, the consortium had leapt to the top of the
charts.

(5) Strategize

Like the Christmas carol about the partridge in the pear tree, other
nations' strategies add up to a rich holiday gift package: the consortia,
regional entities, and cartels, individually and together, help nations
choose what they want to be and what they want to manufacture in
the twenty-first century.

All those factors came into play in Japan's strategic decision to
promote a domestic computer industry and compete against the U.S.
giant IBM. "Japan had about as much of a comparative advantage in
supplying computers as she had in selling oil," wrote computer expert
Marie Anchordoguy. Driven by the fear of dependence on foreign
computer makers, Japan decided to designate computers as a "strategic
industry"; this brought the attention of government to bear on domestic producers until they became technologically competitive. The Japanese idea of strategizing ran the gamut: "Government protection of
the domestic computer market, strengthened by the behavior of firms
in Japan's keiretsu, helped shift demand to domestic machines [still
inferior to IBM's] and thereby handed domestic makers market share
that, in a free market, would have been IBM's."[3]

Japan has also shown remarkable flexibility when it comes to
swimming with the currents of global change. After investing almost

$600 billion abroad in the second half of the 1980s—much of it in the U.S.—Japan suddenly found itself confronted with a declining stock market and an economic slump in its home market. Instead of following the U.S.'s "not to worry and relax with globalism" approach, Japan quickly shifted its strategy in late March 1992 to bring its money back home. In lockstep, Japanese banks announced they would lend less to foreigners, corporations indicated they planned to build fewer plants abroad as well as cut back on their foreign acquisitions, and Japanese investors began to sell off their American securities. What was most impressive about this shift was Japan's dexterity in dealing with a national crisis, which by American standards was minuscule: Japan still remained the world's largest creditor nation, with a $103 billion trade surplus, 40 percent of it with the United States. At the same time, many were chilled by the realization that Japan's new policies left the U.S. in an increasingly exposed position, owing to its accelerated dependence on Japanese investment and Japanese capital to finance its deficits, satisfy its greed, and provide "patient capital." No one could even guess at the long-term impact of the new policies on U.S. interest rates or the U.S. economy, but there was widespread agreement that some impact was inevitable—that the U.S., having sacrificed a measure of its economic sovereignty on the altar of internationalism, was now chronically vulnerable to the effects of such decisions made beyond its shores.

GLOBAL THREATS AND THE U.S. RESPONSE: MORE HARMONIZING, LESS PROSELYTIZING

Meeting the global challenge means facing up to current realities by developing our own set of strategies. Some may lead the nation toward matching the European and Japanese methods; others may point to more direct confrontation; in still other cases, the U.S. may want a response tailored to its needs and culture. Whatever happens, the new world order calls for a very different policy response from U.S. leaders: more harmonizing with the rest of the world and less proselytizing.

The U.S. is not accustomed to being a follower. But our allies and trading partners have repeatedly indicated that they plan to continue on the course that has brought them success, and if that doesn't jibe with U.S. views, more's the pity. Clearly, our allies will not accept the degree of domination that the U.S. has enjoyed since World War II; other nations may follow our military and political lead, but not our economic lead. Why should they? American budget, trade, and current-account deficits are hardly a model for the rest of the world; nor is the nation's eroding industrial base, or its cavalier treatment of critical industries.

To think globally and at the same time act in the national interest, Americans and their leaders must undergo an attitudinal shift. To begin with, the concepts of a national economic strategy and internationalism are not incompatible. "Economic nationalism started overseas," remarked Robert Noyce. The Japanese, for example, have proved themselves masters in the art of national economic strategy, but in some respects they are more highly internationalized than the U.S. Japanese companies have moved more aggressively to expand world markets, they certainly have an international investment strategy, and their technology strategy is more international in scope. Internationalism in the United States has recently assumed a more reactive stance: verbal support for the GATT and other multilateral organizations; a naïve assumption that the invisible hand of the international marketplace will make better decisions than the heavy hand of government; and a misbegotten policy that runs on the theory that foreign ownership of vital assets doesn't matter.

Strategizing is a sophisticated form of "industrial policy," which means many things to many people. Opposition to "industrial policy" has distorted the issues and sapped the nation's ability to preserve and protect its critical industries. Today, the question is not *whether* to support critical industries, but *how* to support them. Even the Japanese would like to see the United States adopt a consistent industrial strategy, if only to stem the ongoing criticism of Japan. "I think the U.S. needs some sort of industrial policy," said Makoto Kuroda in 1989.[4] "In fact, the U.S. already has an industrial policy," wrote Bruce Scott, in the *Harvard Business Review*. "It's just hidden, inconsistent, and self-destructive. What it needs is a policy that says . . . it is more important to succeed in electronics than in citrus, tobacco or beef."[5]

In the process of trying to succeed in global markets in electronics, or even in beef and citrus, some of the nation's most precious values clash with the new world order. Property rights, for example: the right to buy and sell without government intervention. Of course, impediments to sales have always existed—laws that bar insider trading, export controls, "trading-with-the-enemy" laws, securities regulations, and antitrust requirements. But the trend is toward liberalization: very few laws restrict overseas investment in the United States, and export controls have been liberalized considerably as the Soviet threat has receded.

A realistic agenda for the U.S. that harmonizes with the rest of the world, yet still conforms to our unique value system, culture, and politics, would include efforts in these areas:

REGIONALIZE: ENHANCE STRENGTH THROUGH
REGIONAL COOPERATION

One of the first efforts in this direction, the U.S.-Canada Free Trade
Agreement, eliminated many barriers to trade and investment, and
represents an important step toward the creation of a North American
economic union. The U.S. fought hard for this regional pact. Despite
initial and continued resistance from the Canadians, who feel they are
being shortchanged, this regional alliance will probably continue to
serve the interests of both nations. Efforts toward the same kind of
arrangement with Mexico met with stiffer resistance from groups in
the United States, especially labor unions, fearing a loss of jobs to
Mexico, and environmentalists, who worried about the weakening of
pollution controls. The White House persisted, however, and beat
back congressional opposition, and is now negotiating a North American Free Trade Agreement that would include Mexico. Some analysts
predict similar efforts at economic unity with Latin America, but,
judging from the Mexican experience, it will be difficult to convince
Americans of the economic benefits of such a venture. Still others seek
an economic union with Japan, based not on regional but on economic
interests.

In spite of its efforts to regionalize as well as to promote multilateralism through the GATT, the United States has moved in the opposite
direction within its own borders. Instead of maintaining a strong posture as a nation-state, the U.S. has retreated to a form of governance
reminiscent of the earliest days of the Republic, when the Articles of
Confederation allowed the states to pre-empt the federal government
on many vital issues of international trade policy. Today, the states,
desperate to attract new jobs and capital, vigorously compete against
one another for foreign investment, with little thought of whether
those investments are beneficial for the country as a whole, or for the
domestic industries they threaten to displace. The states compete by
offering incentives to investors that total hundreds of millions of taxpayer dollars: Kentucky beat its competitors and won a Toyota plant,
for example, after offering that company $325 million worth of low-
cost bonds, new roads, job-training programs, and other blandishments. Foreign governments and foreign multinationals enjoy the benefits of disarray among the states.[6]

The states' taking the lead in international investment and trade
policy poorly equips the U.S. for the challenges of the twenty-first
century, because the federal government is demoted to a secondary
role in reality as well as in the eyes of our trading partners and allies.

"I don't care what your Congress does on the foreign-investment issue," said a leader of the Keidanren in the summer of 1989, referring to pending legislation in the trade bill that required improved data collection on foreign investment. After all, he noted, "I have forty-two state offices in Tokyo."

Each state competes for investment, never questioning whether its hefty incentive packages—$93 million from Pennsylvania for Volkswagen, which eventually left—serve the best interests of the taxpayers, or how companies in other states might be affected by such subsidized competition. How did Tennessee's recruitment of Komatsu, for example, affect John Deere and Caterpillar, the other major earth-moving manufacturers in the United States?

Any state, individual, or locality can sell just about anything (except a nuclear-power plant and certain other restricted defense-related industries) without interference from the federal government. "We can't sell a 486 chip without all kinds of export licenses," said Intel government-affairs director Michael Maibach, "but we can sell all of Intel with no clearance at all."

In this fragmented environment, hardly anyone is left to guard the nation's critical technologies and defense industrial base, which explains why so many high-technology and defense-related companies have been bought and sold on international markets with no one in Washington even counting how many companies have been sold, or to whom. The states have been joined by investment bankers and other entrepreneurs, who regularly travel abroad to recruit investors for land, hotels, and all manner of companies, high- and low-tech. In the U.S., the depreciation of the dollar and the shortage of capital help these agents broker their deals; no one is there to register a protest when national needs conflict with such sales.

The shortcomings of the Articles of Confederation eventually led to its replacement by the Constitution, which strengthened the most important functions of the federal government: commerce and the national defense. In fact, the commerce clause of the Constitution was designed to prevent states from dealing on their own with foreign governments, and from imposing obstacles to the free flow of goods within the United States. Today, our major allies and trading partners have not only strengthened their national governments but also created regional entities that present formidable competition to our own negotiators. In the new global environment, how will Montana fare in negotiations with Mitsubishi, the EC, or even a multinational like Thomson, owned by the French government and backed by the clout of the EC?

Montana should not be negotiating directly with Mitsubishi, the

EC, or Thomson. Nor should any state. If this is such a desirable practice, why don't we see officials from French provinces, German *Länder*, or Japanese prefectures combing the United States looking for American investors for their critical industries? Why aren't they offering hundreds of millions of dollars to lure U.S. investors to purchase companies within their borders?

To enter into a regional union, a country must first act as a strong nation-state. Strong nation-states do not permit individual units within their jurisdiction to engage in activities that risk harm to the national interest. Europe succeeded in uniting only after its nation-states became strong economic leaders in their own right; not until then were they able to relinquish some national power in the interests of the region. For the U.S. to succeed in the long run with its plans to regionalize, it must first streamline its functions as a national government.

A good start would include these initiatives:

• *A federal ceiling on state giveaways to foreign corporations.* Toyota, backed by its rich *keiretsu*, didn't need $325 million as much as Kentucky needed those funds for its own citizens. Foreign multinationals intending to locate in the U.S. make their decisions primarily to corner the U.S. market and avoid tariffs. Since they have every intention of locating with or without incentives, why dissipate U.S. resources in this way? In 1988, a number of state governors, including Henry Bellmon of Oklahoma, tried to persuade their colleagues to place a ceiling on the incentives offered to foreign investors, but to no avail.

• *Timely information collection about what is bought and sold.* Japan restricts foreign investment in its high-technology industries, and even in low-technology industries deemed critical to the nation's future—mining, natural resources, energy, fishing, leather, and certain foods, such as rice. No doubt these restrictive practices have hurt Japanese consumers and caused massive international criticism. But at the same time, the Japanese made singular progress in acquiring and developing technologies of the future. Although much of their success stems from their domestic investment policies, they are also careful about which investments leave their own country. The first step is knowing what they have and what they don't. "We have our own Bryant amendment," admit Japanese officials privately, referring to the unsuccessful U.S. bill to improve information on foreign investment.

In contrast, the U.S. government has extremely limited knowledge about the extent of foreign investment, or the reasons for heavy losses in certain key industries. Are these losses attributable to the recession, to declining defense budgets, or to careful targeting on the part of foreign governments? Reports from the Departments of Commerce and Defense offer different figures, with widely varying criteria concerning the kinds of companies that are tallied. The Defense Department hasn't a clue as to how many defense subcontractors below the second-tier level have been sold, or to whom. The intelligence agencies have attempted to play a role in keeping track of what is bought, sold, or lost, but this has proved controversial; there is still not sufficient political or public support to carry forward a new mandate for economic competitiveness and national security.[7] In any event, it is a matter of national importance that the government gather this information in a timely and public manner, and disseminate it to policymakers so they may decide what to do about the loss of defense-related firms.

Information gathering is no longer sufficient to meet the security needs of the nation. The question is what to do about it. How is U.S. business brought into the decision process? How are business needs coordinated with those of the federal government? Of the individual states? Who determines whether this is a really good deal, or whether U.S. technology is being sold, or given away at bargain basement prices? And who differentiates between companies owned by private investors and those owned by foreign governments, whose agendas might conflict with our own national needs?

CONSORTIALIZE: THE AMERICAN ANSWER TO CARTELS

The rising Japanese challenge has shaken the U.S. antitrust system to the roots of its trust-busting tradition. Clearly, the new world order better suits the *keiretsu*. Even if American corporate leaders could overcome the quarterly-report mentality, the threat of treble damages still hangs over them if they organize among themselves to match the *keiretsu*'s global reach.

Many U.S. officials take a somewhat judgmental approach to the *keiretsu*, in the belief that they are nothing less than monopolies in restraint of trade; that they are wrong, unfair in their practices, highly restrictive to outsiders, monopolistic in the worst sense of the word, and a bane to the Japanese consumer. Though all those criticisms have merit, they are also highly insular and ethnocentric. After all, the Japanese do not share the American experience: they have not lived for the last one hundred years with American antitrust traditions; and they see nothing wrong in organizing for profit and for global market share. If that means that their consumers will have to continue to sacrifice for the long haul, that's their choice. Indeed, there is practically nothing in recent Japanese political life to indicate that the voters are apt to rebel to obtain cheaper VCRs—or to secure U.S. approval. Quite the reverse: despite their status as the world's largest creditor nation, the Japanese still feel the need to continue sacrificing.

If Americans consider *keiretsu* competition morally "wrong," that means they feel they have the right to try to force change. Yet, in the spring of 1991, when U.S. negotiators attacked the restrictive practices of the *keiretsu* during trade talks with Japan, the Japanese responded along the lines of "If it ain't broke, why fix it?"

The *keiretsu* will not change fast enough to make a difference to U.S. national interests. They may revise their practices slightly, but no number of FTC investigations, court cases, or antitrust actions from the Justice Department will force wholesale change—however valuable such actions are in alerting the public to the impact of the *keiretsu* in the U.S.

But even if the *keiretsu* will not change, U.S. industries should certainly not begin to organize along the lines of Hitachi, Mitsubishi, or Fujitsu. That kind of organization goes against the history, traditions, and politics of the American people. IBM is the only U.S. multinational that even begins to approach the size of a Japanese conglomerate. But U.S. companies with the ambition and resources to become another IBM would think twice about expanding to that size, recalling the recent twelve-year-long antitrust action weathered by IBM that ended in 1982—during which time the company's Japanese competitors flourished unimpeded by their government.

So, in view of these constraints, what *can* the nation do to compete with the cartels in the international marketplace, and to prevent them from acquiring critical U.S. industries and technologies? The best approach is always the positive one: to adopt the best features of the *keiretsu* and reject the negative ones. A few examples:

• *Ready cash.* U.S. policymakers should focus on the capital supply for critical technologies, and enact changes in the tax code to create incentives to direct money toward investment in those vital industries. Policymakers should also recognize and address imbalances in the world financial system and try to level the playing field for U.S. companies. These problems must be addressed, and soon, to halt the outflow of technologies and companies.

• *Superior organization.* Antitrust laws should be overhauled with global competitors in mind. The National Cooperative Research Act of 1984, which eliminated antitrust damages for joint research, spawned at least three hundred consortia. Joint research-and-development activities should continue to be encouraged, not discouraged by outdated laws that do not meet current needs. Treble damages should be eliminated as a penalty for coordinated R & D; in view of world realities, the issue of joint production and sales under certain circumstances might also be revisited.

• *Global reach.* When foreign cartels begin to extend their influence into the U.S., as Go-Video demonstrated in court, U.S. officials should take swift action to blunt their impact. The FTC investigation into the impact of the *keiretsu* in the U.S. might be worth its cost to the taxpayers if it dragged the government into this issue, and forced some concrete response to cases like Go-Video, which otherwise take years to resolve. Tougher U.S. trade positions would help; they would certainly solve the mystery of why we don't use our power over market access to greater advantage. So would limited restrictions on sales to foreign investors of U.S. companies that are vital to national security. When a company is the last remaining producer of a vital technology, someone in the U.S. government should be alert to the consequences of its loss and prevent its exit. The legislation is there, in Exon-Florio, but, alas, the national will is not.

None of these suggestions should stop the U.S. from continuing to press for multilateral solutions to antitrust problems; that would be the optimal way to reconcile antitrust practices and provide a forum to resolve disputes. Unfortunately, such an international forum is a long way off.

The best response to the growth in world cartelization, and one that is in keeping with American values, is the encouragement and development of consortia—organizations that can match many of the benefits of the cartels without adopting their obvious faults. "The real threat is not that Japan, Germany, and Asia have better manufacturing, but that they have the infrastructure in place," said Robert Costello. "Government, academia, and business are working together. Consortia are one of the answers. We must pool our resources to counter our competitors. We can always become the most advanced third-world country in the world. The choice is ours. . . . If you're not the lead dog, the scenery never changes."

Pooled resources have always been part of the American tradition. In farming communities, for example, a few days after a young couple married, the whole town would turn out for a barn-raising. More recently, and on a different scale, efforts like the Manhattan Project or the man-on-the-moon space venture represented a form of cooperation that looked very much like today's industrial consortia.

Pressed mostly by industry and by pockets of sympathetic government officials, the U.S. is slowly catching on to the idea of accelerating consortial arrangements. And, similar to the atomic threat that led to the Manhattan Project—or the Sputnik scare that galvanized the space program and led to the creation of DARPA—SEMATECH and other technology-based consortia are running scared from their dramatic loss of technology and global market share. "We used to be 60 percent of world market share; today, we're only 35 percent," said Tom Seidel, director of manufacturing methods at SEMATECH. "Erosion was the reason SEMATECH was formed. It's one thing to make chips, and quite another to find markets for them."

Consortia can take many forms. They can restrict their operations to private companies, like U.S. Memories; business and government can go into partnership together, the SEMATECH model; or, as in the case of the production of the F-16 fighter plane, government can orchestrate the private sector, serving as both impresario and conductor.

The U.S. government has always nurtured various forms of consortia, but without the fanfare or formality of the European model. Antitrust constraints, belief in free trade, competitive fears among U.S. industries, and many other factors conspired to restrain the growth and development of consortia, at least in comparison with those in the European Community and Japan.

Since the U.S. is so new to the business of consortia, success still depends on such minimal requirements as the ability to stay in business. SEMATECH has managed to survive, despite considerable opposition, while U.S. Memories folded. All of the recent consortia—SEMATECH, MCC—were created primarily in response to the Japanese challenge in advanced electronics.[8]

"Consortia need three things to succeed," said SEMATECH's founder, Robert Noyce: "Industry supplying the people and the technology; government deciding the appropriate level of investment; and, to maintain the public's commitment, the decision to support consortia only in areas of national importance. History shows that industry and government can work together. Look at agriculture and space. But first we must develop the need and the national will."

Today, consortia need an especially high level of public and political support. Thanks to the indefatigable efforts of Noyce, public support for SEMATECH grew exponentially in the first years of its existence, despite regular complaints from critics that it was not worth $100 million a year in taxpayer support, and despite difficulties in communicating its highly technical achievements to the general public. Consortia are still too new to the American experience for any final determinations about their long-term impact, but the survival and successes of SEMATECH foretold a healthy future for consortia in that mold.

SUBSIDIZE: INVEST IN TECHNOLOGY

The old cliché about success having many parents while failure is an orphan applies to the demise of U.S. Memories, a consortium of private companies formed to combat Japanese domination of D-RAMs. There was no shortage of theories explaining why the orphaned U.S. Memories failed: the prices were too high, the products inferior; the leadership was inadequate; member companies were disloyal; member companies refused to send their best scientists to the consortium; and, most importantly, the companies were too greedy and shortsighted, preferring dependence on foreign components to taking a chance on the future. But there was one major omission at the postmortem: the absence of government. Unlike SEMATECH, U.S. Memories did not have the benefit of government's presence to introduce the presence of national interest into the project, to mediate the conflicts that were sure to impinge on the group's initial enthusiasm, and to provide the deep pockets necessary to sustain such capital-intensive industries.

Deep pockets means subsidies, a word that sends chills down the spines of political leaders trying to balance budgets in tough economic times. It conjures up visions of socialism and a planned economy. Critics fear, with considerable justification, that subsidies would be given to the technologies with the most political clout, rather than those that are most crucial to the nation's economic success. Critics also question whether government bureaucrats would be adept at choosing between "winners" and "losers."

The U.S. government nevertheless does provide subsidies, for a variety of reasons—moral, economic, political, and security. The government finances measles shots for poor children to prevent epidemics. It supports commercial aerospace for security reasons, and for the profits that industry will generate for companies who will then pay higher taxes, provide jobs, and offset the trade deficit. Some industries locate in a certain state or congressional district just because they believe that the clout of its senators and representatives will keep the money flowing. And government has paid billions of dollars for exotic weaponry in the name of national security.

The U.S. government boasts a long tradition of investing in industries with a strong relationship to military security, beginning with its financing of Eli Whitney. Since World War II, the defense budget has provided financing for technological innovation, reaping benefits not just for the United States but for the world. In the Reagan years, the defense build-up increased the budget for military R & D—from $15 billion to $40 billion—but the broader technological benefits were lost in the focus on high-tech weapons. Critics repeatedly made this point, though to no avail. Kosta Tsipis, of M.I.T., pointed out: "I don't build a house so I can develop the faucet. While the radar and aircraft jet engine was something that you could . . . transplant from the military to the civilian, when you start going into ballistic missiles and Stealth aircraft and things like that . . . there's very little that spins off military R & D into the civilian sector."[9]

Subsidies give government the power to choose among competing interests, and to influence otherwise private commercial dealings among companies that would prefer to conduct business without much involvement from the public sector. At Los Alamos, New Mexico, this issue is underscored by the experience of supercomputers. The powerful Cray supercomputers are not large, but stand isolated in a football-field-sized room; another, equally large room underneath is filled with generators supplying the electricity for the Crays. How will the U.S. support these technologies of the future? Will the cooperative research-and-development efforts among Department of Energy labs and U.S. companies supported by the 1989 Technology Transfer Act match the Japanese efforts to invest in technology?

How does the U.S. attract the interest of private investors in technologies that will not pay off for ten years? Pilot programs on superconductivity focus on individual companies, but how long can those companies continue investing in a technology without re-sponding to their stockholders? Or the marketplace? And what happens if the U.S. government or private investors do not invest in technology either in its precompetitive phases or later, on its way to market? "The problem is not what happens to individual companies; they're not as important as whole industries," explained Larry Blair of Los Alamos. "We found this out with Canon and Nikon in the camera business. When you lose market segments, you lose the industry. The greatest uncertainty is, what industries can we lose if we lose superconductivity? One industry we risk is electric motors. At some point, there should be a limit to our complacency."

Some experts feel the U.S. has already lost the superconductivity competition because of the loss of one of the basic building-block industries necessary to the development of that technology: large electric motors. "The discussion is irrelevant," concluded Alf Andreassen, vice-president for information systems at AT&T. "Because of the threat of antitrust action, large power plants had disappeared. After that, the market went away. Then there were no engineering students; they left the field. Now we are missing the engineering students that speak this language. Business enterprise is synergistic with a lot of things. Advanced work is cut off. They thought we could always buy it from the Austrians. Government didn't even know it had lost the market. The shadow was cast that long. It seemed as if we had it, then it was gone. What's left is only at an M.I.T. lab. Fifteen years ago, this was a thriving commercial enterprise."

STRATEGIZE: INVEST IN LEADERSHIP

Subsidies do not mean everything, although some technologies without a direct relationship to security have received government sustenance in the name of national defense, such as highways and education. In general, subsidies mean selecting which industries are critical to the nation's future, then deciding how to organize government and the private sector's resources most efficiently to help them compete in global markets; otherwise, experience has shown repeatedly that such industries won't survive.

The U.S. seems to have no trouble investing in what is known as "big science," ambitious projects viewed as critical to the advancement of knowledge, the expansion of the frontiers of science, and winning Nobel Prizes. The cost of the space station, the superconducting super-collider, the human genome, and the relativistic heavy-ion collider—four of the nation's most important "big-science" projects—totals $50 billion. Yet smaller research projects, with perhaps equally important challenges for the nation's future, often go begging, or go offshore, for want of capital. How can the U.S. president extol the manned landing on Mars promised by the $30-billion investment in a space station, but view even fractional commitments to advanced robotics, gallium arsenide, or any of the other critical technologies as "industrial policy"? It is time that national values shifted slightly, not to halt "big science" but, rather, to focus on additional frontiers of science—such as computer science and artificial intelligence—that contribute to the nation's industrial future.

Corporations must also assume greater responsibility for maintaining their investments in R & D, even in the face of recessions and declining defense budgets, and especially since their trading partners have maintained a higher level of R & D in real terms despite similar setbacks. U.S. firms would be wise to organize more effectively to press government to shift some of its resources from military to civilian technologies, and to sustain a permanent tax credit for R & D.[10]

Timing is a critical factor; the nation cannot wake up in the year 2000 and retrace all the steps that go into developing advanced technologies. How will the loss of HDTV or superconductivity affect other industries? The nation should debate these issues and break the stalemate of current policy. Targeting investments will bring long-term economic benefits that form the basis for national security. Some concrete suggestions for realizing these goals include:

■ An Export-Import Bank for Technology That Is Related to National Security

An Ex-Im–type bank for technology would reduce the risk for capital-intensive industries that need patient capital, in much the same way U.S. companies are insured against risk when they invest in unstable parts of the world. The government would limit the risks taken by investors by becoming an insurer against catastrophic losses.

■ A National Security Production Board for Coordinating Government Aid to Critical Industries

Such a board, modeled after its World War II predecessor on defense production, would expand current notions of defense to include the defense industrial base.

■ An Expansion of International Divisions in Domestic Agencies

If they already exist, international bureaus in existing agencies should be expanded; if they do not exist, they should be created for all agencies dealing with foreign direct investment or trade-related issues. These divisions should be included in all MOUs (memoranda of understanding), bilateral treaties, joint ventures, and other dealings previously left to one agency.

■ An Endangered Technologies and Industries Act

Just as Congress and the President have seen fit to protect the spotted owl, the snail darter, the condor, and the bald eagle, perhaps it is time to offer similar protection to preserve the backbone of the nation's economic future—in other words, an endangered-species act for critical technologies and industries. The legislation could start by taking DoD's annual critical-industries lists off their dusty shelves, and mandate strategies to keep them alive and well. That could mean subsidies, tougher trade policies, and perhaps even prohibitions against foreign purchases or offshore siting. As with any compromise, no one will be perfectly happy, but at least the issue will climb to a higher rung on the national agenda, and the process of preserving these technologies will begin in earnest.

■ Explore an American Version of MITI

A Japanese trade official who addressed a group of Washington-based trade experts was asked if the United States should pay Japan the ultimate compliment and adopt some of Tokyo's trade policies. "Not at all," he said adamantly. "What works for us will not work for you."

Perhaps not, but Washington still has much to learn from Tokyo. One possible innovation is a Cabinet-level agency that would formulate and implement policies related to trade, investment, and technology. This could replace the Tower of Babel of agencies that now share fragmented responsibilities in these areas. Such agencies, often at cross-purposes, sow confusion through mixed signals that confound both American entrepreneurs and our trading partners.

They could be replaced by a single executive-branch agency that would set long-term goals and either incorporate or direct many of the trade, investment, and technology functions now filled by the Treasury Department, the Commerce Department, the USTR, CFIUS, the Export-Import Bank, the Defense Science Board, DARPA, the National Institute of Standards and Technology, and other agencies. Indeed, the Office of the United States Trade Representative was itself created— under President John F. Kennedy, in 1962—in recognition that America's trade interests were not adequately represented by existing agencies. They still are not.

An American-style MITI would have to rest on a national-security rationale to win political acceptability: an agency with the goal of promoting and preserving a strong defense industrial base. There is indeed a growing recognition that economic and military security are intertwined. A danger is that such an agency could become too powerful, and create a system that would not be responsive to the many political cross-currents that are the hallmark of our democracy. Although our present system may be too responsive to campaign contributors and influential lobbyists, it is also more open to political and social movements like women's rights and environmentalism, for example, to which the Japanese government is virtually impervious.

Another option would concentrate trade and investment goals within the Defense Department. MITI, in fact, grew out of the former

Japanese Munitions Ministry. Commerce may have the mandate, but Defense is the only agency with adequate resources, since national security remains the only concept with the legitimacy to justify government involvement. Defense analyst Jacques Gansler advocates using "defense as a demonstration case for future industrial strategy policy development . . . in order to allow the nation to regain its full competitive advantage." Defense already has the structure and is accustomed to implementing industrial strategy, and its "influence permeates the U.S. economy."[11] Defense also is responsible for one out of every four manufacturing jobs and jobs in research and development. It has created, or played a major role in the development of, such industries as jet aircraft, computers, communications satellites, numerically controlled machine tools, and computer-controlled production.

The problem is how to control the Pentagon to make sure it does not become a sinkhole for government funds. Defense is endlessly criticized for failing to wean industries from the public trough, and for keeping them captive and noncompetitive. In fact, the Office of Technology Assessment blamed the military build-up during the Reagan era for driving the nation into a condition of international indebtedness, military overcapacity, and increasing U.S. dependence. With the exception of the Costello Report and the work of the Defense Science Board and DARPA, Defense has tended to restrict its vision of national security to weapons systems.[12]

An American version of MITI could restructure defense procurement to remove the barriers between military and commercial technologies. This would better reflect current global realities and help shore up the defense industrial base. Indeed, restructuring defense procurement should be done very carefully, to avoid some of the mistakes of the past, such as luring companies into a condition of defense dependency in which they produce high-cost, low-volume products solely for the Pentagon. It was ironic that U.S. companies lost out in the field of consumer electronics during the 1980s, when the Pentagon spent $40 billion on consumer-electronics equipment; during this same period, European and Japanese companies poured billions into revamping their companies to produce advanced products that included commercial markets.

Whenever possible, the massive purchasing power of government should be directed toward building up U.S. industry and revitalizing the industrial base. Such a policy would amount to nothing but rhetoric unless all major procurement decisions were influenced by industrial-base considerations. A few examples of past and future decisions: How did the Navy's decision to buy liquid-crystal displays for the war rooms of submarines from Japan rather than from U.S. companies affect that industry? Wouldn't it have been better to bolster American companies, instead of resorting to trade complaints after it was too late to save the industry? Looking to the future, how can the military's $1.5-billion annual budget for semiconductors—likely to expand despite the drop in the defense budget—be used to help the U.S. semiconductor industry?

Of course, any solution that dares to suggest an enhanced government role is destined to run up against a barrage of criticism, much of it legitimate. From the private sector, the typical response runs: "How can you trust such important decisions to government bureaucrats, many of whom are either fools, overzealous, or corrupt?" Would those decisions be made for political rather than economic reasons? Less legitimate comments take the form of: if they were smart, they'd be working for us and making more money. Or, how can we trust members of Congress, who bounce checks, run deficits, and respond all too quickly to their PAC masters?

Despite such criticism, government remains the only vehicle capable of addressing such problems. Every major industrialized nation uses its government to achieve these ends, and the United States must become competitive in its governance if it is to become competitive in its products.

■ Presidential Leadership

What's wrong with this picture? The U.S. semiconductor industry, battered by foreign—primarily Japanese—competition and rapidly losing market share, finally gets the attention of the government. To help the industry, U.S. taxpayers fund SEMATECH with $100 million a year over a five-year period. SEMATECH takes its responsibility seriously, organizes the industry, and launches a massive effort to recoup its losses by perfecting its technology. Labs at SEMATECH work around the clock to help member companies become competitive, and security at SEMATECH is so tight that when the Nikon repairman comes to repair one of their machines, he is blindfolded and led by the hand until he reaches the exact site of the machine he is scheduled to fix.

But the U.S. government in effect removed the blindfold when it allowed the sale of Semi-Gas Systems to Nippon Sanso. Semi-Gas produces equipment for gases used in the production of chips and supplies all the labs at SEMATECH. As a result, a Japanese company now holds the blueprints for all the SEMATECH labs, making it privy to the proprietary secrets of member companies. In effect, the sale of Semi-Gas virtually gave Japanese competitors certain technologies that

American taxpayers funded for the very purpose of competing with the Japanese.

How did this happen? Instructed by the White House that the sale did not violate national security, the Treasury Department directed CFIUS to allow Nippon Sanso to purchase Semi-Gas. After the CFIUS decision, the Justice Department lodged an antitrust challenge to try to stop the sale on the ground that it would put too much power in the hands of a single supplier.[13] Are the Treasury and Justice Departments working for the same government? Is this the U.S. version of a good-cop/bad-cop routine? Or is U.S. policy just totally confused and unco-ordinated?

A number of similar decisions demonstrate the conflicts as decisions to buy and sell U.S. companies vital to the national security in effect cancel out other government decisions to bolster U.S. competitiveness. A change in the definition of national security to include economic competitiveness might prevent such sales by strengthening the Exon-Florio amendment, but without White House support the strongest language in the dictionary wouldn't prevent the lax implementation of this law.

The Semi-Gas sale and the FSX fiasco both underscore the need for presidential leadership, as well as a Cabinet-level agency to coordinate trade and competitiveness policies. Funding DARPA activities with billions of dollars over the years, then preventing that agency from saving the very technologies it had funded, seems the height of foolishness.

The real problem is that the agencies have a conflict of goals that leads to a conflict of interests. The Treasury Department, which is the lead agency in carrying out the Exon-Florio amendment, is also responsible for the federal debt and deficit and other fiscal woes. This clash of interests leads to a foregone conclusion. Treasury officials' top priority is to finance the budget deficit by enticing foreign investors to purchase Treasury securities. At the same time, they bear responsibility for evaluating foreign investments for national-security purposes. Fearful of offending foreign investors and scaring off their T-bill purchases, Treasury officials turn a blind eye toward foreign investment and allow virtually all sales to go through.

The U.S. government needs to rejuvenate its capacity for dealing with critical technologies. Some new beginnings could include:

• Lead from the top. Only the White House can sort out the confusion among the agencies, elevate trade to a higher status, and end the incessant turf battles.

• Appoint a national-security adviser who is not solely political or military, but could bridge the gap and encompass trade issues. Similarly, the National Security Council, no longer preoccupied with the Soviet threat, could direct more of its considerable talents toward retaining critical industries, defining what is critical, and devising a strategy for targeting investments.

• Replace CFIUS with a *Commission* on Foreign Investment in the United States. CFIUS, unfortunately, has retained the "paper tiger" image affixed to it before Exon-Florio strengthened its mandate. And for good reason: The committee is a joke; it does not protect the nation's critical industries, nor does the secretive way it conducts business allow for public debate and scrutiny. It's time to face the fact that CFIUS wastes the taxpayers' money at the same time its existence holds out the false hope that the nation's interests are protected from predators.

CFIUS should be abolished, and its funds channeled to create a bipartisan, five-person, independent regulatory commission, appointed by the President and Congress. An analytical staff would research the issues and fill the yawning data gap on foreign investment and critical industries. Its decisions would be binding, not advisory like those of the International Trade Commission. Even in an antiregulatory environment, such an agency would raise the level of oversight of the nation's industrial health, and would make it harder for the White House to ignore the rush of foreign purchases that threaten the national security.

Acting as a buffer, such a commission would actually help the President withstand the cross-pressures within his administration, and as well from foreign finance ministers threatening to hold back their purchases of Treasury bills. In fact, this is what the nation really needs to deal with the indifference and intimidation that have been characteristic of the CFIUS process.

• Augment the government apparatus for shaping U.S.-Japan policy. Inspired by the FSX fiasco, Robert Pear of *The New York Times* found that decisions about Japan were "often made by one or two agencies acting alone, without fully considering the views of other agencies which belatedly register their objections . . . [and that] United States policy toward Japan is so confused and uncoordinated that many American officials say they cannot figure out how it is made or why economic concerns are regularly subordinated to military and political objectives. Relatively few people in the United States Government focus on Japan, and even fewer can read Japanese. They are invariably outnumbered by their counterparts in the Japanese government, which has a large cadre of experts on the United States."[14] Not to mention an army of lobbyists, who spend more than $400 million a year to influence U.S. politics, and take full advantage of the U.S. government's inadequacies on trade and investment issues. The imbalance of resources between the two countries would not be so serious were it not for the high stakes involved: Japan is now the world's largest creditor nation, with a currency that has more than doubled in value since 1985, and a trade surplus with the U.S. ($43.4 billion in 1991) that accounts for a rising share of the United States' worldwide trade deficit.

■ Know Thy Neighbors (and Trading Partners)

If the U.S. decides to adopt a more strategic view toward its own industries, it has to become realistic about its trading partners. America, for example, remains the only nation that separates trade and investment policies; accordingly, it acts as if everyone else in the world followed that shortsighted view, despite massive evidence to the contrary. The location of Toyota, Nissan, and Honda plants across the U.S. originated in a Japanese investment strategy that was an element of that nation's trade policy. An even clearer example of the linkage between trade and investment policies emerged when U.S. negotiators finally forced the Japanese to reduce their trade barriers against beef and citrus products. In response, Japanese investors rushed to buy U.S. cattle ranches, beef-processing plants, and citrus groves; this meant that the Japanese would be exporting to themselves, making their previous concessions symbolic at best.

The sale of cattle ranches represented a private transaction, but the result was another in a long string of examples of U.S. policies canceling themselves out. The logical conclusion is not necessarily to stop other nations from such strategic decisionmaking, but to formulate a national investment strategy of our own. That means not only targeting U.S. industries identified as critical to the nation's future, but also adopting tougher trade policies that *include* foreign investment and preserve critical technologies. Current U.S. policy remains foolish and wasteful. Why subsidize avionics through the defense budget for decades, only to watch the FSX deal risk the loss of a technology that represents one of the nation's last industries with a trade surplus?

Knowing one's neighbors also means knowing their rhetoric. While the U.S. was trading off the FSX technology, Japanese trade negotiators continued to call their $43-billion trade surplus with the U.S. "intractable." Why intractable? By how many billions of dollars would a better deal have reduced that "intractable" trade deficit? U.S.

military aircraft are still the best in the world, as evidenced by their performance in the Gulf War; the F-16, which Japanese defense officials called a "middle-aged lady," was particularly agile for her age.

■ Know Thyself

Better yet, listen to the experts. A number of reports warning of the erosion of the defense industrial base and the loss of critical industries have emerged from the Pentagon, the Commerce Department, business groups, and Capitol Hill. The problem is that too few have been listening.

One example should suffice. In 1987, the Defense Science Board, a blue-ribbon panel of CEOs, defense experts, and scientists, issued the first of a series of reports, impressive for their substance as well as their vision of the future. This report, reflecting previous warnings from the semiconductor-manufacturing community, outlined what was happening to the industry:

"The principal factor affecting the . . . shift in strength of the U.S. and Japanese semiconductor industries is the fact that the Japanese established a *strategic (long term) goal* and effectively brought together all the *resources* from government, industry and academia, needed to pursue that goal. The U.S., *at its own discretion*, elected not to pursue such an organized focus and structure, and as a result is finding that it is unable to compete in the marketplace as it has been defined by the Japanese. Although this is viewed by some as evidence of impropriety on the part of Japan, it would appear more accurate to describe it in retrospect as a sound business decision and . . . one which could . . . have been available to the United States should we as a nation have chosen to embrace it. The U.S. was . . . once in a position to enforce virtually any semiconductor market strategy it chose, having invented the technology, controlled the leading-edge research, dominated the related education, held the largest world market share, and consumed the majority of the product."[15]

The U.S. remained complacent despite such reports, despite lists of critical industries issued by the Pentagon each year, and despite the continuing loss of such technologies, which made the nation increasingly dependent on its allies and trading partners.

■ Halt the Revolving Door

One of the major reasons that so many policies cancel themselves out is that many former high government officials have become the midwives of the nation's technology losses. Take the example of David

Olive, an economic-and-commercial officer on the Japan desk of the State Department, who left office in 1990, in the middle of sensitive negotiations, to become deputy director of the new Washington office of Fujitsu. Olive, who helped develop the U.S. negotiating strategy on high-tech issues ranging from semiconductors to space stations, took this detailed knowledge to his new job. Meanwhile, U.S. taxpayers had footed the bill for Olive's on-the-job training, foiled again by the country's fuzzy ethics laws and lax enforcement. Lawyers at the Office of Government Ethics said Olive did not appear to have violated the laws, and he was neither prosecuted nor prevented from assuming his new position.[16]

Other officials profited while still in office, including a Commerce Department official who wrote to Honda, Nissan, and other Japanese auto companies proposing to create a trade association to represent their interests after he left office. The official, Robert E. Watkins, had served as the department's deputy assistant secretary for automotive affairs and consumer goods; in his official capacity he had negotiated trade agreements with Japan and other countries.

Americans believe in the principle of corporate proprietary rights. They carefully safeguard secrets through export-license restrictions, and employ a huge patent office to protect innovation. Yet the nation does virtually nothing to close the revolving door in U.S. government that allows trade negotiators with regular access to corporate secrets to move in and out of office and then go to work for foreign governments and foreign corporations. America stands alone among its trading partners in the huge number of political appointees in its federal service: the U.S. has 3,000 political appointees; Great Britain has 150; France, 400; West Germany, 60; and Japan, unknown, but very few. Although our system works to provide more policy flexibility for the president than his counterparts abroad enjoy, in the area of trade policy it helps blunt America's competitive edge. Professional civil servants of long standing and experience serve our major trading partners in trade negotiations, but the U.S. must content itself with trade officials whose average term of service—if they are political appointees—is one and a half years. After their short stint in the government, at least half go to work for overseas firms and governments.[17]

No other industrialized country, either by law or by custom, allows its public officials to share trade secrets with its competitors. This practice raises a number of questions about America's readiness to compete in the increasingly rugged international marketplace. How vigorously will trade officials represent America's interests if, during their short tenure in office, they are looking toward future employment with their present adversaries?

While David Olive and many others left government with knowledge that made them so valuable to Fujitsu and other foreign companies, the White House and lobbyists for foreign investors were fighting
passage of the Bryant amendment to the trade bill. They said they were
safeguarding corporate proprietary rights. The Bryant amendment
didn't force a company to reveal its secret formula for nylon, merely
to supply better information on the country of origin of overseas
investors and the amount of the investment. A watered-down version
of the Bryant amendment, the Exon-Lent bill, finally passed, giving
the GAO and the Census Bureau the power to share in the data
collection on foreign investment. The public was still excluded from
the findings, much to the delight of lobbyists for U.S. subsidiaries of
foreign corporations, who fought for continued secrecy and ignorance.

GLOBALIZE: INVEST IN THE FUTURE

Events have propelled us into a new era in which U.S. interests must
be held paramount. Participation in the global economy shouldn't
mean wholesale capitulation on issues that will determine the nation's
national security and economic health. If a nation can't collect its own
data, protect its national security, and promote its economic interests
without foreign intervention, it begins to look more and more like the
original colonial government its forebears fought so hard to overturn.

Many American leaders mistakenly believe that internationalization is incompatible with an economic strategy based on national
interests. The Japanese have internationalized their world markets and
acquisitions more swiftly than the U.S. during the past decade, yet
Japan branches out from a distinctly national base: Japan is host to
the world's most carefully managed economy in terms of protecting
the national interest, which is openly defined in terms of economic
considerations. In contrast, the U.S. government has taken a more
reactive stance, passively accepting what globalism offers, rather than
moving from a position of strength.

A nation can only globalize after strengthening its economic base
at home. One cannot be an internationalist from nowhere. In the past,
the U.S. has not had to worry about its critical industries, or about the
relationship between economic and military power. The nation enjoyed the highest standard of living in the world; boasted technological
supremacy in supercomputers, software, and other technologies; and
dominated many international organizations. Even when the U.S.
earned the dubious distinction of becoming the world's largest debtor
nation, the country still felt rich and did little to reverse its accumulat-

ing deficits and debts. Indeed, if there was one organizing principle behind U.S. security policy, it was the Soviet threat, and it was in that context that technological competition was first mentioned: when Secretary of Defense Richard Cheney's 1989 report on "Soviet Military Power" admitted that, "although the Soviet Union constitutes the greatest threat to U.S. security, the greatest challenge to the U.S. technology and industrial base will almost certainly come from the United States' own allies." Today, the nation's economic plight and inability to control its budget-and-trade deficits has taken the place of the "Evil Empire" as the greatest threat to the nation's security.

Without a Soviet threat to guide their policy choices, U.S. officials must shift gears: they should accept the new world order, but not allow it to impinge on the nation's own path toward growth and development. America has dominated world events for so long that its leaders may be forgiven the illusion that its pre-eminence will last forever. At the same time, they have neglected economic strength, deluded by the false beliefs that ownership didn't matter, that control of technologies didn't matter, and that market forces would ultimately protect the nation's industrial base.

But America is infinitely adaptable. That has always been the strength of its democratic system. America has benefited from being the most open country in the world, welcoming to its shores entrepreneurs, workers, scientists, and creative artists. America's strength has come from its democratic heritage and its free-enterprise system.

American ideals and values have sometimes blinded us to the trade practices of others, leaving us at a marked disadvantage. After a long period of neglect, America's leaders are beginning to realize that we can no longer ignore global realities if we are to remain competitive in global markets. This means that we must nurture the nation's critical technologies and preserve its industrial base. Both are crucial to military security, and enable the nation to convert quickly, if it must, to its wartime needs.

The challenge is to continue to promote internationalism, but from an American perspective. The goal is to expand America's technological strengths, recognizing the key role that technology has played in the lives and fortunes of nations, with a view toward enhancing America's military security and its economic competitiveness in the twenty-first century.

APPENDIX A*

SUMMARY OF FOREIGN AND U.S. TECHNOLOGICAL CAPABILITIES

Critical Technologies	USSR	NATO Allies	Japan	Others	
1. Semiconductor Materials and Microelectronic Circuits	☒	☐☐	☐☐☐☐	☐☐	Israel
2. Software Productibility	☒	☐☐	☐☐	☐☐	Various Countries
3. Parallel Computer Architectures	☒	☐☐	☐☐	☐☐	Switzerland, Israel, Hungary
4. Machine Intelligence and Robotics	☒	☐☐☐	☐☐☐☐	☐☐	Finland, Israel, Sweden
5. Simulation and Modeling	☒	☐☐☐	☐☐☐		
6. Photonics	☒☒	☐☐	☐☐☐☐	☐	Various Countries
7. Sensitive Radars	☒	☐☐	☐☐	☐☐	Sweden
8. Passive Sensors	☒☒	☐☐	☐☐		
9. Signal Processing	☒☒	☐☐	☐☐	☐☐	Sweden, Israel
10. Signature Control	☒☒	☐☐	☐☐		
11. Weapon System Environment	☒☒☒	☐☐☐	☐☐	☐	Various Countries
12. Data Fusion	☒☒	☐☐	☐☐	☐☐	Israel
13. Computational Fluid Dynamics	☒	☐☐	☐☐	☐☐ / ☐	Sweden, Israel / India, China, Australia
14. Air-Breathing Propulsion	☒☒	☐☐☐	☐☐		
15. Pulsed Power	☒☒☒☒	☐☐	☐☐	☐	Various Countries
16. Hypervelocity Projectiles	☒☒☒	☐☐	☐☐		
17. High Energy Density Materials	☒☒☒	☐☐☐	☐☐☐		
18. Composite Materials	☒☒	☐☐☐	☐☐☐	☐☐☐	Israel
19. Superconductivity	☒☒	☐☐	☐☐☐☐	☐☐☐	Sweden
20. Biotechnology Materials and Processes	☒☒	☐☐☐	☐☐☐☐	☐☐	Various Countries

LEGEND:

Position of USSR relative to the United States

☒☒☒☒ significant leads in some niches of technology
☒☒☒ generally on a par with the United States
☒☒ generally lagging except in some areas
☒ lagging in all important aspects

Capability of others to contribute to the technology

☐☐☐☐ significantly ahead in some niches of technology
☐☐☐ capable of making major contributions
☐☐ capable of making some contributions
☐ unlikely to make any immediate contribution

*From U.S. Department of Defense, *Critical Technologies Plan*, For the Committees on Armed Services, March 15, 1990.

APPENDIX B*

ACQUISITIONS TABLE: CRITICAL TECHNOLOGIES

Company Selling/ Technology Lost	Company Purchasing/ Technology Gained	Item(s) Purchased	$ Amount of Sale/ Investment	Year of Sale
Emerson Radio Corp.	Semi-Tech (Global) Ltd.	electronics	$30 million 20% control	1991
Honeywell Federal Systems	Cie. de Machines Bull	systems integration, computer products, & technical services	$39 million	1991
Institute for Biological R&D, Inc.	Kuraya Pharmaceutical Co., Ltd.	pharmaceuticals	$25 million	1991
King Instrument Company	Otari Electric Co. Ltd.	magnetic tape loader	not disclosed	1991
MCA, Inc.	Matsushita	movies, book publishing etc.	$6.6 billion	1991
National Semiconductor Corp.	Matsushita Electric Industrial Co.	semiconductor	$86 million	1991
Shield Health-Care Centers, Inc.	Kobayashi Pharmaceutical Co., Ltd.	pharmaceuticals	$20 million	1991
Sprague Technologies	Sanken Electric Co.	semiconductor	$58 million	1991
UCAR Carbon Corp.	Mitsubishi Corp.	50% stake— produces carbon & graphite electrodes	$232.5 million	1991
Vertex Semiconductor	Toshiba	advanced integrated-circuit-chip sets for high-performance electronics	$20 million	1991
York Research	Sony Corp.	audio/visual cassette tape	$23 million	1991
Eastman Kodak Co.—Verbatim Co.	Mitsubishi Kasei Corp.	floppy-disk business, digital-cassette-tape business	$200–67 million	1990
Gen-Probe, Inc.	Chugai Pharmaceutical Co.	genetic-probe technology	$110 million	1990

Company Selling/ Technology Lost	Company Purchasing/ Technology Gained	Item(s) Purchased	$ Amount of Sale/ Investment	Year of Sale
Materials Research Corp.	Sony Corp.	semiconductor-coating & etching equipment, high-purity materials & ceramics	$60 million	1990
Rorer Group	Rhône-Poulène SA (France)	pharmaceuticals	$3.2 billion; acquired 68% of firm	1990
Semi-Gas Systems	Nippon Sanso KK	semiconductor-manufacturing equipment	$23 million	1990
Wyse Technology, Inc.	Channel International Corp. (Taiwan)	computer terminals	$267.4 million	1990
Zenith Electronics	Cie. des Machines Bull	computer industry	$635 million	1990
Cincinnati Milacron, Inc.	Osaka Titanium Co.	silicon epitaxial wafers (used in the manufacturing of semiconductor devices)	undisclosed	1989
Cominco Electronic Materials	Johnson Matthey PLC	electronic components, semiconductor materials	$32 million	1989
Electro-Nucleonics, Inc.	Pharmacia AB (Sweden)	pharmaceuticals and biotechnology	$55 million	1989
Encore Computer Corp.	Nippon Mining Co., Ltd.	computer products	31.2% of outstanding common stock	1989
Fairchild Industries	Matra SA (France)	hardware & software for aerospace systems		1989
General Ceramics	Tokuyama Soda Co. Ltd.	ceramic/chemical productions	$59.4 million	1989
Langley Corp.	Fleet Aerospace Corp. (Canada)	aerospace		1989 & 1987
Lyphomed, Inc.	Fujisawa Pharmaceutical Co. Ltd.	pharmaceuticals	$650 million (remaining 70% not already owned)	1989; 1987, 30% was acquired
Monsanto Electronic Materials Co.	Huels AG (W. Germany)	silicon wafers	undisclosed	1989
National Semiconductor Corp.'s National Advanced Systems	Memorex Telex NV	Computer	$250 million 50% interest	1989
Norton Co.	Cie. de Saint-Gobain (France)	ceramics/chemical products	$1.9 billion	1989
Pennwalt Corp.	Société Nationale Elf Aquitaine (France)	diversified manufacturer of chemicals	$1.05 billion	1989

Company Selling/ Technology Lost	Company Purchasing/ Technology Gained	Item(s) Purchased	$ Amount of Sale/ Investment	Year of Sale
Silicon Systems, Inc.	TDK Corp.	integrated circuits	$200 million	1989
Titanium Metals Corporation of America	Toho Titanium Co.	titanium—aerospace	25% interest	1989
Varian Associates	Tosoh Corp.	specialty-metals division	$33 million	1989
Gould Inc.	Nippon Mining Co. Ltd.	computer & electronics	$1.1 billion	1988
Micron Technology	Amstrad PLC (England)	memory chips	$75 million 9.8% of shares	1988
Dana Computer	Kubota Ltd.	compact superconductor	$20 million	1987
Lear Siegler Holding Corp.'s	Smiths Industries PLC	aerospace	$350 million	1987

*Material collected from *Foreign Investment in the U.S.: News and Analysis*, Acquisitions & Mergers sec., BNA International, Inc., Washington, D.C. 1989–1991; the U.S. Department of Commerce, selected reports, 1989–1991; and from data collected for this study by the authors.

APPENDIX C*

ECONOMIC STRATEGY INSTITUTE DATABASE

SELECTED ACQUISITIONS
OF U.S. HIGH TECHNOLOGY COMPANIES
October 1988–October 1991

December 1, 1991

U.S. Company	State	Foreign Acquirer and Country of Acquirer	Keiretsu Affiliation (Japan)	Industry	Product	Date	Mode of Investment	Purchase Price ($m)
1 Moritex	NJ	Ajinomoto Co (Japan)		advanced materials	Fiber optic cable	1989	inv	$0.8
2 Yates Industries/Square D Co		Arbed SA (Luxembourg)		advanced materials	copper foil used in printed circuit boards	1989	div	
3 Facile Technologies, Inc.	NJ	BTR-Nylex Ltd. (Australia)		advanced materials	plastics & rubber manufacturer	1989	acq	$34.0
4 Hyperion Catalysis	MA	C. Itoh Fine Chemical Co., Ltd. (Japan)	DKB	advanced materials	graphite fibril	1991	inv	
5 McDanel Corp	PA	Cookson (UK)		advanced materials	technical ceramics	1989	acq	
6 Products Research & Chemical Corp	CA	Courtaulds PLC (U.K.)		advanced materials	specialty polymers, sealants, adhesives	1989	acq	$281.7
7 NL Spencer Kellogg		Dainippon Ink and Chem (Japan)		advanced materials	resins and primers	1989	div	
8 Sawyer	OH	Fang (Taiwan)		advanced materials	synthetic quartz crystals	1990		$86.0
9 Yates Industries/Square D Co.	NJ	Furukawa Electric Co. (Japan)	DKB	advanced materials	copper foil used in printed circuit boards	1989	div	
10 Micro Mech	MA	Gunze Sangyo Inc. (Japan)	Gunze Ltd.	advanced materials	carbon products and electronics	1991	inv	
11 Reichold Chemicals Inc.	NY	Harima Chemicals Inc. (Japan)	Hasegawa Kosan	advanced materials	resins	1990	acq	
12 Battery Engineering Inc	MA	Hitachi Maxell Inc (Japan)	Hitachi Ltd.	advanced materials	lithium battery cells, serve as back-up power sources	1990	acq	$6.0
13 Micro Mech	MA	Ibiden Co. Ltd. (Japan)	Mitsui	advanced materials	carbon products and electronics	1991	inv	
14 US Chrome	CT	Japan Metals and Chem (Japan)	Nippon Steel	advanced materials	Semiconductor Materials	1990	acq	$32.0
15 Cominco Electronic Materials Inc.	WA	Johnson Matthey PLC (U.K.)		advanced materials	semiconductor materials	1989	acq	$100.0
16 Division of ICI	PA	Kawasaki Steel (Japan)	DKB	advanced materials	high performance plastic	1991	acq	
17 UCC&P	WA	Komatsu Electronic Inc. (Japan)	Komatsu Ltd.	advanced materials	ultra-purity polysilicon	1990	div	
18 AVX Corp.	NY	Kyocera Corp. (Japan)	Sanwa	advanced materials	technical ceramics for semiconductors	1990	acq	$620.0

*Data collected by Linda Spencer, Economic Strategy Institute, December 1991.

	U.S. Company	State	Foreign Acquirer and Country of Acquirer	Keiretsu Affiliation (Japan)	Industry	Product	Date	Mode of Investment	Purchase Price ($m)
19	Southwall Technologies Inc.	CA	Marubeni Corp (Japan)	Fuyo	advanced materials	thin-film coatings	1988	inv	
20	Chemick		Mitsubishi Corp. (Japan)	Mitsubishi	advanced materials	synthetic fibers	1990	acq	
21	Newport Composites Inc.	CA	Mitsubishi Rayon Ltd. (Japan)	Mitsubishi	advanced materials	carbon fibers & resins	1990	acq	$38.0
22	Southwall Technologies Inc.	CA	Mitsubishi Toatsu Chem (Japan)	Mitsubishi	advanced materials	thin-film coatings	1988	inv	
23	Titanium Metals Corp of America	PA	Mitsui & Co. (Japan)	Mitsui	advanced materials	titanium for aerospace industry	1990	inv	$70.0
24	Magnox, Inc	VA	Mitsui Mining & Smelting Co Ltd (Japan)	Mitsui	advanced materials	Magnetic iron oxides	1990	acq	$34.7
25	Alberox	MA	Morgan Crucible (UK)		advanced materials	hermetic barriers	1989	inv	
26	Certech, Inc		Morgan Crucible (UK)		advanced materials	investment castings—molds	1989	inv	
27	Copolymer Rubber & Chemical Corp/Mark IV	LA	NV DSM (Netherlands)		advanced materials	Polymers & synmthetic rubbers	1989	acq	$248.5
28	Division of Titan Corp.		Nippon Iron Powder Ltd. (Japan)	Nippon Mining	advanced materials	ferrite powders	1989	div	
29	Moritex		Nippon Mining Co (Japan)	Nippon Mining	advanced materials	Fiber optic cable	1989	inv	$0.8
30	Titanium Metals Corp of America	PA	Nippon Mining Co Ltd (Japan)	Nippon Mining	advanced materials	Titanium sponges, supplier of aerospace industry	1990	inv	
31	Thermofil Inc.	MI	Nippon Steel Chemical Co. (Japan)	Nippon Steel	advanced materials	Thermoplastics	1988	acq	$25.0
32	Hercules Welding Products	MI	Obara Corp. (Japan)		advanced materials	resistance welding electrodes	1988	acq	
33	Stackpole	MA	Pechiney Corp (France)		advanced materials	electrical discharge graphite	1990		
34	Kleerdex Co.	PA	Sekisui Chem Ltd. (Japan)	Sanwa	advanced materials	polyvinyl chloride sheets	1990	acq	$6.5
35	Wixom Products Inc.	MI	Shinto Industrial Ltd (Japan)		advanced materials	plastic injection molds	1991	acq	$7.3
36	Vulkor Inc.	MA	Showa Elec. Wire and Cable (Japan)	Mitsui	advanced materials	heat-resistant wire	1990	inv	$2.5
37	American Spring Corp.	AZ	Sogo Spring Co. Ltd. (Japan)		advanced materials	precision springs for aerospace	1991	acq	
38	Division of Kuhlman Corp	MI	Solvay & Cie. SA (Belgium)		advanced materials	blow-molded plastics	1990	acq	$45.0
39	High Voltage Engineering	MA/ CA	Sumitomo Electric (Japan)	Sumitomo	advanced materials	fine wire	1988	div	
40	National Magnetics Co.	KY	Sumitomo Special Metals (Japan)	Sumitomo	advanced materials	ferrite magnets for engines	1990	acq	
41	Highland Industries Inc.	SC	Takata Corp. (Japan)	Sumitomo	advanced materials	laminating substrates	1988	acq	
42	Titanium Metals Corp of America	PA	Toho Titanium (Japan)	Nippon Mining	advanced materials	titanium sponges, supplier of aerospace industry	1990	inv	
43	Mini Magnetics	CA	Tokin (Japan)		advanced materials	magnetic materials	1989	inv	$23.0
44	General Ceramics Inc.	NJ/ CA	Tokuyama Soda Co., Ltd (Japan)	Sumitomo	advanced materials	Ceramic and metal packages for ICs	1989	acq	$59.0
45	McCann Plastics Inc	OH	Tonen Chemical Corp. (Japan)	Fuyo	advanced materials	composite resins	1991	inv	$1.5

46	Division of General Atomics	CA	Toshiba (Japan)	advanced materials	Mitsui	Applied Superconetics	1990	acq	$30.0
47	Bodine Aluminum	IL	Toyota Motor (Japan)	advanced materials	Toyota Motor	aluminum castings	1991	acq	$90.0
48	DAP Inc. (USG Corp.)	CA	Wassall PLC (U.K.)	advanced materials		sealant and caulking	1990	acq	
49	Sierracin	CA	Asahi Glass Co. (Japan)	aerospace	Mitsubishi	plastic and composite materials for aerospace	1990	inv	
50	Texstar Inc.	TX	BBA Group (U.K.)	aerospace			1990	inv	
51	Van Dusen Air Inc.	MN	BBA Group (U.K.)	aerospace		aviation parts and supplies	1991	acq	$23.0
52	Learjet Corp.	KS	Bombardier, Inc (Canada)	aerospace		small, medium-sized business jets	1990	acq	$75.0
53	Reflectone, Inc.	FL	British Aerospace PLC (U.K.)	aerospace		flight simulators	1990	acq	$130.0
54	Chase Aircraft Finance	FL	CIT Group Holdings Inc. (Japan)	aerospace	DKB	aircraft leasing	1991	acq	
55	Sierracin Corp	CA	Christoph Tribull (Germany)	aerospace		hi-tech products for aerospace industry	1989	inv	
56	General Plasma Inc (Unit of Alpine Group Inc.)	CT	Derlan Industries Ltd. (Canada)	aerospace		specialty coatings for aircraft engines	1991	acq	$12.0
57	Langley Corp.	CA	Fleet Aerospace (Canada)	aerospace		aerospace and missles	1990	acq	
58	Enstrom Helicopter Corp	MI	International R&D (Japan)	aerospace		helicopters	1991	inv	
59	Crestview Aero Corp/Fairchild	FL	Ishida Group (Japan)	aerospace		aircraft parts	1990	inv	$6.0
60	Swearingen Jaffe	TX	Ishida Group (Japan)	aerospace		aircrafts	1990	inv	$1.5
61	Space Hab	DC	Japan Air Lines Co., Ltd. (Japan)	aerospace	Mitsubishi	space technology	1990	inv	$3.0
62	Fairchild Space Co	MD	Matra SA (France)	aerospace		aerospace hardware, software, and spacecraft	1989	div	
63	Fairchild Communications and Electronics	MD	Matra SA (France)	aerospace		aerospace hardware, software, and spacecraft	1989	div	
64	Fairchild Control Systems Co	CA	Matra SA (France)	aerospace		aerospace hardware, software, and spacecraft	1989	div	
65	Avicom Inc	CA	Matsushita Electric (Japan)	aerospace	Matsushita	audio-visual systems for aircraft	1990	acq	$19.0
66	Power Systems Inc.	CT	Minebea Co. (Japan)	aerospace		aircraft components, electric motors, power supplies	1990	acq	
67	Space Hab	DC	Mitsubishi Corp. (Japan)	aerospace	Mitsubishi	space technology	1990	inv	
68	Space Hab	DC	Mitsubishi Heavy Industries, Ltd. (Japan)	aerospace	Mitsubishi	space technology	1990	inv	
69	Space Hab	DC	Mitsubishi Trust and Banking Corp. (Japan)	aerospace	Mitsubishi	space technology	1990	inv	
70	Trodyne Corp	MA	Morgan Crucible (UK)	aerospace		helicopter rotor blades	1989	inv	
71	Adcole	CA	Nippei Toyama (Japan)	aerospace	Toyobo	space satellites	1991	inv	$4.0
72	Mil-Com Associates, Inc.	CA	Okura & Co. Ltd. (Japan)	aerospace	Fuyo	aircraft	1991	acq	$1.5
73	Metraplex	MD	Racal Electric PLC (UK)	aerospace		instrument-landing devices	1989	inv	
74	Space Hab	DC	Shimizu Corp. (Japan)	aerospace	DKB	space technology	1990	inv	

	U.S. Company	State	Foreign Acquirer and Country of Acquirer	Keiretsu Affiliation (Japan)	Industry	Product	Date	Mode of Investment	Purchase Price ($m)
75	Quincy Technologies Inc.	MA	Teijin Seiki Co. Ltd. (Japan)	Sanwa	aerospace	speed-reduction gears for aerospace	1991	div	$10.0
76	Space Hab	DC	Toyo Engineering Corp. (Japan)	Mitsui	aerospace	space technology	1990	inv	
77	Technical Arts Corp.	WA	Toyo Tire & Rubber Co. (Japan)	Sanwa	aerospace	measuring equipment for aircraft mfg	1990	inv	$2.9
78	Argo-tech	OH	Yamada (Japan)		aerospace	engine fuel pumps	1990	inv	
79	Subsidiary of Whittaker Corp., Bio Whittaker In	CA	Boehringer Ingelheim Inter (Germany)		biotechnology	biotechnology	1991	inv	$23.0
80	Gen-Probe	CA	Chugai Pharmaceutical Co. (Japan)	Sumitomo	biotechnology	disease diagnostic kits	1989	acq	$110.0
81	Lymphomed	IL	Fujisawa Pharmaceutical (Japan)	Sanwa	biotechnology	over-the-counter pharmaceuticals	1989	inv	$30.0
82	Cell Genesys Inc.		JT Immunotech USA (Japan)		biotechnology	monoclonal antibodies	1991	inv	$4.0
83	Cooper LaserSonics	CA	Leonix Corp. (Japan)		biotechnology	surgical and industrial lasers	1988	acq	
84	Dijene Diagnostics Inc.		Mitsubishi Petrochem (Japan)	Mitsubishi	biotechnology	testing devices	1988	inv	
85	Imatron Inc.	CA	Mitsui & Co. (Japan)	Mitsui	biotechnology	medical scanners	1988	inv	$2.0
86	Ketchum & Co., Inc.	CT	Office Commercial Pharmaceutique SA (France)		biotechnology	pharmaceuticals & chemicals	1989	acq	
87	Biomagnetic Technologies Inc.	CA	Sumitomo Metal Industries, Ltd. (Japan)	Sumitomo	biotechnology	magnetic sensitive medical equipment	1990	inv	$9.0
88	IDEC Pharmaceutical Corp.	CA	Zenyaku Kogyo Co. Ltd. (Japan)		biotechnology	anti-idiotype antibodies	1991	inv	$9.5
89	Reliance Universal, Inc.	KY	Akzo NV (Netherlands)		chemicals	industrial coatings	1989	acq	$275.0
90	Polymer International Corp.	FL	Altamira Capital Corp. (Canada)		chemicals	polymers and plastic products	1989	acq	
91	Racon Inc.	WA	Atochem (Groupe Elf Aquitaine (France)		chemicals		1989	acq	
92	Kalama Chemical Inc.	WA	BC Sugar Refinery Ltd. (Canada)		chemicals	fine and specialty chemicals	1990	acq	$46.0
93	Chem-Trend, Inc	MI	Burmah Oil PLC (UK)		chemicals	specialty lubricants	1988	acq	
94	Division of Kearney Industries		Carbone Lorraine (France)		chemicals	graphite based chemicals	1989	acq	
95	Linear Instruments Corp.	NV	Ciba-Geigy Ltd. (Switzerland)		chemicals	ultraviolet detectors for industries	1989	acq	
96	Norton Co	MA	Gie. de Saint-Gobain (France)		chemicals	advanced ceramics, chemical products	1990	acq	$1,900.0
97	Neptco	RI	Cookson Group PLC (U.K.)		chemicals	polymer materials	1988	acq	$40.0
98	Division of DeSoto Inc.	CA	Courtaulds PLC (U.K.)		chemicals	industrial coatings	1990	div	$135.0
99	Dynepco Inc	NJ	Daicel Chem Industries (Japan)	Mitsui	chemicals	ABS resin used in auto, electronic, & electric industry	1988	acq	
100	Division of Koppers Co.	PA	Dainippon Ink and Chem (Japan)		chemicals	polyester resin	1989	div	$78.0
101	United Chemicals, Inc.	VA	Ellis & Everard PLC (UK)		chemicals	chemicals	1989	acq	$58.0

No.	Company	State	Group	Industry	Description	Year	Type	Amount
102	Division of Olin Corp — Fuji Photo Film Co. Ltd. (Japan)	NJ	Mitsui	chemicals	photographic chemicals	1989	div	$480.0
103	Lion Industries Inc. — Harima Chemicals Inc. (Japan)		Hasegawa Kosan	chemicals		1990	inv	
104	Division of Quantum Chem. — Henkel KGaA (Germany)	OH		chemicals	plastics, textiles	1989	div	
105	Division of UCCP — Hoechst AG (Germany)	NJ		chemicals	chemicals and fiber products	1990	acq	
106	Bepex Corp. — Hosokawa Micron Corp. (Japan)	IL		chemicals	chemical processing equipment	1991	acq	$72.9
107	Himont Inc. — Internat. Multi Petrochemical Enterprises (China)	DE		chemicals	polypropylene	1989	inv	
108	Polymer International Corp. — Intertape Systems, Inc. (Canada)	FL		chemicals	polymers & plastic products	1989	acq	
109	Harcros Pigments Inc. — Ishihara Sangyo Kaisha Ltd. (Japan)	IN		chemicals	magnetic iron oxide	1991	div	$15.0
110	Imperial Chemical Industries PLC — Kawasaki Steel Corp. (Japan)	PA	DKB	chemicals	high-performance compounds	1991	acq	$100.0
111	Glastic Co/Nortek Inc. — Kobe Steel, Ltd (Japan)	OH	Sanwa	chemicals	Plastic cores for fiber-optic cables	1988	acq	
112	Division of Domain Technology — Kubota Ltd. (Japan)	CA	Fuyo	chemicals	substrates	1990	div	$10.0
113	Mycogen Corp. — Kubota Ltd. (Japan)	CA	Fuyo	chemicals	pesticides	1989	inv	
114	Hardwiche Chemical Co. — MTM PLC (U.K.)	SC		chemicals	specialty chemicals	1990	acq	$112.0
115	Aristech Chemical Corp. — Mitsubishi Corp. (Japan)	PA	Mitsubishi	chemicals	Chemicals	1990	acq	$877.0
116	Franklin Burlington Plastics Inc. — Mitsubishi Corp. (Japan)		Mitsubishi	chemicals	polyvinyl chloride compounds	1990	div	$10.0
117	Seradyn Inc. — Mitsubishi Kasei Corp. (Japan)	IN	Mitsubishi	chemicals	integrated chemicals	1989		$14.1-21.1
118	Digene Diagnostics — Mitsubishi Petrochem. (Japan)	MD	Mitsubishi	chemicals	diagnostic reagents	1988		
119	Engineers & Contractors Inter. — Mitsui Engineering & Shipbuilding Co. (Japan)	CA	Mitsui	chemicals	petrochemical plant engineering	1991	acq	$3.0
120	Anderson Development Co. — Mitsui Toatsu Chemicals (Japan)	MI	Mitsui	chemicals	specialty chemicals	1988	acq	
121	East Shore Chemical Co. — Mitsui Toatsu Chemicals Inc. (Japan)	MI		chemicals	color formers for heat and pressure sensitive paper	1991	acq	$40.0
122	Himont, Inc. — Montedison SpA (Italy)	DE		chemicals	polypropylene	1989	acq	
123	Powdertech Corp. — Nippon Iron Powder Co. (Japan)	IN		chemicals	ferrite powder	1988	acq	
124	Ketchum & Co., Inc. — Office Commercial Pharmaceutique SA (France)	CT		chemicals	pharmaceuticals, chemicals, and cosmetics	1989	acq	
125	Black & Decker Corp. — Orkem SA (France)	MA		chemicals	chemical adhesives	1990	div	$345.0
126	InFerGene Co. — Perstorp AB (France)	CA		chemicals		1989	acq	
127	Vista Chemical Co. — RWE-DEA AG (German)	TX		chemicals	commodity and specialty chemicals	1991	acq	$1,150.0
128	GAF Corp — Rhone-Poulenc SA (France)			chemicals	surfactant chemicals	1989	acq	$480.0
129	Miranol, subsidiary of Domtar — Rhone-Poulenc SA (France)	NJ	Fuyo	chemicals	surfactant chemicals	1990	acq	
130	Franklin Burlington Plastics Inc. — Riken Vinyl Industries (Japan)			chemicals	polyvinyl chloride compounds	1990	div	$10.0
131	Ford Chemical and Services — Roussel (France)	TX		chemicals	chemicals	1989	acq	
132	Duracell — SAFT (France)	GA		chemicals	lithium batteries	1989	div	
133	Pennwalt Corp. — Societe Nationale Elf Aquitaine (France)	PA		chemicals	industrial, intermediate and specialty chemicals	1989	acq	$1,050.0

U.S. Company	State	Foreign Acquirer and Country of Acquirer	Keiretsu Affiliation (Japan)	Industry	Product	Date	Mode of Investment	Purchase Price ($m)
134 Valent USA (Sumitomo/Chevron)	CA	Sumitomo Chemical (Japan)	Sumitomo	chemicals	agricultural chemical products	1991	jvb	
135 McLaughlin Gormley King Co.	MN	Sumitomo Chemical Co. (Japan)	Sumitomo	chemicals	synthetic pyrethoids	1989	inv	
136 Imre Corp	WA	Takeda Chemical Industries ltd (Japan)	Sumitomo	chemicals	specialty chemicals	1988	inv	
137 George A. Goulston Co., Inc	NC	Takimoto Fat & Oil Co. (Japan)		chemicals	fibre lubricants	1990	acq	$37.0
138 Tennessee Chemical Co.	TN	Trelleborg AB (Sweden)		chemicals	specialty chemicals	1990	acq	
139 East Shore Chemical Co.	MI	Yamamoto Chemicals Inc. (Japan)	Mitsui	chemicals	color formers for heat and pressure sensitive paper	1991	acq	$40.0
140 Exide Corp.	PA	Yuasa Battery Co. Ltd (Japan)	Mitsui	chemicals	Storage batteries	1991	acq	$73.0
141 Esprit Systems, Inc	NY	ADi Corp (Taiwan)		computers	video display terminals and computer systems	1989	acq	
142 General Videotex	MA	ASCII (Japan)		computers	on-line information & database operator	1990	inv	$1.0
143 Hyperdesk	MA	ASCII (Japan)		computers	software-operating system development		inv	
144 Informix, Inc	CA	ASCII (Japan)		computers	informational database software	1990	inv	$6.7
145 Tera Micro Systems, Inc.	CA	ASCII (Japan)		computers	peripheral chips	1990	inv	$2.0
146 Altos Computer Systems	CA	Acer Group (Taiwan)		computers	multi-use computer systems		acq	$94.0
147 Princeton Publishing Labs		Acer Group (Taiwan)		computers	computers	1989	acq	$3.0
148 Denev Robotics Inc.	MI	Amada Metrecs Co., Ltd. (Japan)		computers	three-dimensional graphics simulation software	1991	inv	$3.0
149 Komag Inc	CA	Asahi Glass Co. Ltd (Japan)	Mitsubishi	computers	High-density disk drives	1989	inv	
150 Unisys Corp.'s Timeplex Inc. subsidiary	NJ	Ascom Holding AG (Switzerland)		computers	computer networking	1991	acq	$207.0
151 GS Computer Corp.	CA	British & Commonwealth Holdings PLC (U.K.)		computers	computers	1989	acq	$10.0
152 Xytel Corporation	IL	C. Itoh & Co., Ltd. (Japan)	DKB	computers	computer controlled systems	1991	acq	
153 SRS Network	NY	CGI Informatique (France)		computers	software	1990	acq	$13.0
154 Yourdon	CA	CGI Informatique (France)		computers	software	1990	acq	
155 UniSoft Group PLC		CMC Ltd. (India)		computers	computer maintenance and support	1990	acq	
156 Div. of Control Data Corp.	CT	CSK (Japan)		computers	software		acq	
157 Wavefront	CA	CSK (Japan)		computers	software	1989	acq	
158 Next Inc	CA	Canon Inc (Japan)		computers	software	1990	inv	
159 MetroLight Studios Inc.	CA	Canon Sales Co. (Japan)	Fuyo	computers	computer graphics	1990	inv	$100.0
160 Systemation Inc.	OH	Cap Gemini (France)	Fuyo	computers	computer services	1989	acq	$4.0

#	U.S. Company	State	Foreign Partner	Keiretsu	Industry	Product	Year	Type	Value ($M)
161	Wyse Technology, Inc	CA	Channel International Corp (Taiwan)		computers	computer terminals	1990	acq	$267.4
162	Telemar Resources Information Services		Chikyu Kagaku Sogo Kenkyujo (Japan)		computers	image proc software			
163	Div. of Zenith Electronics Corp	IL	Cie de Machines Bull (France)		computers	computers	1990	div	$635.0
164	Honeywell Federal Systems Inc.	VA	Cie. de Machines Bull (France)		computers	systems inegration and computers	1990	div	$100.0
165	Leading Edge Products, Inc	MA	Daewoo Telecom Co (South Korea)		computers	computers	1989	acq	
166	Island Graphics Corp.	CA	Dainippon Screen Manuf. Co. (Japan)		computers	color graphics	1989	inv	$6.4
167	Digital Dynamics Inc.	CA	Electric Co. Ltd. (Japan)	DKB	computers	audio capability workstations	1991	acq	$3.8
168	Division of Burroughs		Fuji Electric (Japan)	DKB	computers	imaging division			$20.0
169	Kurzweil Applied Intelligence	MA	Fuji-Xerox Co., Ltd. (Japan)	DKB	computers	artificial intelligence	1989	inv	$2.0
170	Auspex Systems	CA	Fuji-Xerox Company (Japan)	DKB	computers	network file servers	1990	inv	
171	Amdahl Corp.	CA	Fujitsu (Japan)	DKB	computers	mainframe computers, computer disk drives		inv	
172	Poqet Computer Co	CA	Fujitsu Ltd. (Japan)	DKB	computers	pocket computers	1989	inv	$40.2
173	Hal Computer System Inc.	CA	Fujitsu Ltd. (Japan)	DKB	computers	computer start-up	1991	inv	
174	Internatonal Components Technology	CA/OR	Furukawa Electric Co. Ltd. (Japan)	DKB	computers	aluminum disk blanks for magnetic disks	1988	acq	
175	IGX Corp.	CA	General Electric Co. PLC (U.K.)		computers	color-separation scanning systems	1988	acq	$150.0
176	Precision Image Corp	CA	Graphtec Corp (Japan)		computers	plotters	1990	acq	
177	Graphics Technology Corp	MA	Gunze (Japan)		computers	computers touch panels	1989	inv	
178	Division of Anacomp Inc.	CA	Hanny Magnetics Ltd. (Hong Kong)		computers	floppy disks	1990	div	
179	Dataproducts Corp.	CA	Hitachi Koki Co (Japan)	Hitachi	computers	computer printers	1990	acq	$160.0
180	National Advanced Systems	CA	Hitachi Ltd/EDs (Japan)	Hitachi	computers	mainframe computers	1989	acq	$398.0
181	HMT Technology Corp	CA	Hitachi Metals Ltd (Japan)	Hitachi	computers	computer products	1989	acq	
182	Info. & Graphics Sys.	CO	Hitachi Software Eng. (Japan)	Hitachi	computers	software	1990	acq	
183	Eaco Computer Inc.	CA	Hong Kong Investor Group (HK)		computers	switch and keyboard products	1991	acq	$0.9
184	General Automation	CA	Integ Micro Product Ltd. (U.K.)		computers	parallel computers	1988		
185	Telenetics, Inc.	CA	Kanematsu-G (Japan)	DKB	computers	peripheral controlers		acq	$3.1
186	Racet Computers Ltd.	CA	Kobe Steel Ltd (Japan)	Sanwa	computers	computers	1989	acq	
187	Cybernet Systems Co.		Kobe Steel Ltd. (Japan)	Sanwa	computers	software	1989	acq	
188	Prairietek Corp	CO	Kobe Steel, Ltd (Japan)	Sanwa	computers	Hard disk drive	1990	inv	$5.0
189	Komag Inc.	CA	Kobe Steel, Ltd (Japan)	Sanwa	computers	Magnetic disk manufacturer	1990	inv	$20.0
190	C-Cube Microsystem		Kubota Co. (Japan)	Fuyo	computers	graphic proc. VLSI		inv	

	U.S. Company	State	Foreign Acquirer and Country of Acquirer	Keiretsu Affiliation (Japan)	Industry	Product	Date	Mode of Investment	Purchase Price ($m)
191	Maxoptix Corp	CA	Kubota Corp. (Japan)	Fuyo	computers	Optical Disk Drive	1991	inv	$3.4
192	Tricord Systems Inc.	MN	Kubota Corp. (Japan)	Fuyo	computers	network servers	1991	inv	$15.5
193	Ardent Computer Corp.	CA	Kubota Ltd. (Japan)	Fuyo	computers	graphics based mini-supercomputers		acq	
194	MIPS Computer Systems Inc.	CA	Kubota Ltd. (Japan)	Fuyo	computers	reduced instruction-set computers	1989	inv	$20.0
195	Maxtor Corp	DE	Kubota Ltd. (Japan)	Fuyo	computers	optical disk drive	1989	acq	$12.0
196	Rasna Corp	CA	Kubota Ltd. (Japan)	Fuyo	computers	CAD software	1989	inv	$9.0
197	Stardent	MA	Kubota Ltd. (Japan)	Fuyo	computers	graphics computers	1991	inv	$60.0
198	Synthesis Software	CA	Kubota Ltd. (Japan)	Fuyo	computers	software for reduced-instruction set machines	1988	inv	$0.8
199	Exabyte Corp.	CO	Kubota Steel (Japan)		computers	8mm tape memory	1991	inv	$6.0
200	Mouse Systems Corp.	CA	Kung Ying Enterprises (Taiwan)		computers	computer-input devices		acq	
201	Counterpoint Computers	CA	Kyocera (Japan)	Sanwa	computers				
202	LaserData Inc.	MA	Kyocera Corp. (Japan)	Sanwa	computers	document image processing	1991	inv	$4.5
203	Cadware Group Ltd.	CT	Kyodo System Development Co. Ltd. (Japan)		computers	software	1990	inv	$1.0
204	Planar Systems	OR	Lohja		computers	EL flat panel displays	1990		
205	Management Technologies Inc	NY	Macquarie Bank Ltd (Australia)		computers	software	1990	acq	
206	Solbourne Computer	CO	Matsushita (Japan)	Matsushita	computers	workstations	1988		$50.0
207	National Advanced Systems	CA	Memorex Telex NV (Netherlands)		computers	computer distribution unit	1989	inv	$250.0
208	Concord Data System Inc.	MA	Memotec Data Inc. (Canada)		computers	modems, network mgmt. system	1989	inv	$21.0
209	ISI Systems	MA	Memotec Data Inc. (Canada)		computers	proprietary applications software systems	1990	acq	$130.0
210	EPE Technologies	CA	Merlin Gerin (France)		computers	power protection	1990	acq	
211	Hutchinson Technology Inc	MN	Minebea Co Ltd (Japan)		computers	computer peripheral components	1989	inv	
212	Inacomp Computer Centers	MI	Mitsubishi Corp. (Japan)	Mitsubishi	computers	personal and small business systems	1991	inv	$2.0
213	Verbatim Co/Eastman Kodak Co.	NC/CA	Mitsubishi Kasei Corp. (Japan)	Mitsubishi	computers	floppy disks	1990	acq	$250.0
214	Kalok Co	CA	Mitsubishi Mining & Cement Co Ltd (Japan)	Mitsubishi	computers	Hard disks	1990	inv	$2.4
215	Sercomp Corp	CA	Mitsubishi Pencil Co (Japan)	Mitsubishi	computers	printer accessories	1990	acq	$11.8
216	Stellar Computer	MA	Mitsui & Co. (Japan)	Mitsui	computers	supercomputers			$1.0
217	Unisys Corp	PA	Mitsui & Co. (Japan)	Mitsui	computers	Electronic computers	1990	inv	$150.0
218	Raster Graphics Inc.	OR	Mitsui Comtek (Japan)	Mitsui	computers	plotters			

No.	Company	State	Acquirer / Investor	Keiretsu	Industry	Description	Year	Type	Value ($M)
219	KCR Technology Inc.	IL	Moore Corp. Ltd. (Canada)		computers	computer peripherals	1989	acq	
220	Computer Graphics		Muto Kogyo (Japan)		computers	digitizers and computer graphic input systems	1990	acq	$13.3
221	Kurta Corp.	AZ	Mutoh Industries Ltd. (Japan)		computers		1990	inv	
222	Honeywell Inc	CA	NEC Corp. (Japan)	Sumitomo	computers	HNSX Supercomputers Inc	1989	acq	
223	Silicon Graphics Inc	CA	NKK Corp (Japan)	Fuyo	computers	Graphics workstations	1990	inv	$35.0
224	Division of Seagate Technology	CA	NMB		computers	composite head recording division	1989	div	$45.0
225	Mountain Computer Inc.	CA	Nakamichi Corp. (Japan)		computers	minicartridge tape drive equipment	1988	acq	
226	Excalibur Technologies	NM	Nikkei Inform. Systems Ltd. (Japan)		computers	software	1989	inv	$0.2
227	Encore Computer Corp.	FL	Nippon Mining Co. Ltd. (Japan)	Nippon Mining	computers	computer products	1989	inv	
228	Areal Technology	AZ	Nippon Sheet Glass (Japan)	Sumitomo	computers	glass disks		inv	
229	GTX	CA	Nippon Steel (Japan)	Nippon Steel	computers	computer equipment	1991	inv	$200.0
230	Oracle Ssstems Corp.	CA	Nippon Steel Co. (Japan)	Nippon Steel	computers	database software	1990	inv	
231	Calcomp Inc.	CA	Nippon Steel Corp (Japan)	Nippon Steel	computers	computer products	1990	inv	$160.0
232	Dataproducts Corp.	CA	Nissei Sangyo Co.	Hitachi	computers	computer printers	1989	inv	
233	Auspex Systems	CA	Nissho Electronics Corp. (Japan)		computers	network file servers	1990	acq	$44.8
234	Graphic Technology Inc	KS	Nitto Denko Corp (Japan)		computers	computerized scanner technology	1989	acq	
235	TEC America Electronics Inc	MA	Oki Electric Industry Co., Ltd (Japan)	Fuyo	computers	computer products	1989	acq	
236	Software Design Tool Division	WA	Oki Electric Industry Co. (Japan)	Fuyo	computers	circuit design software	1991	acq	$174.0
237	Vitelic Corp.	CA	Oki Electric Industry Co. (Japan)	Fuyo	computers	Memory products & Vitelic designs for chips	1989	inv	
238	ISC Systems	WA	Olivetti (Italy)		computers	integrated computer systems	1989	acq	$15.0
239	Delphax Systems	MA	Olympus Optical Co, Ltd (Japan)		computers	high-speed ionographic printers	1990	inv	$46.0
240	Data General	MA	Omron Corp. (Japan)		computers	computers for Japanese market	1991	acq	
241	Corporate Data Sciences Inc.	CA	Polly Peck International PLC (U.K.)		computers	microcomputer peripheral products	1988	inv	
242	Colorocs Corp	GA	Polysar Energy and Chemical Corp (Canada)		computers	Copying machines and printing devices		acq	
243	Mikros Systems Corp	NJ	Renaissance Holdings PLC (U.K.)		computers	Microcomputers for military appl	1989	inv	$90.0
244	Scott Instruments Corp.	TX	Renaissance Holdings PLC (U.K.)		computers	computer peripherals	1989	inv	$207.3
245	Datachecker Sys Inc.	CA	STC PLC (U.K.)		computers	scanners	1988	acq	
246	Computer Consoles Inc.	MA	STC PLC (U.K.)		computers	computer systems	1988	acq	$2.3
247	General Automation, Inc.	CA	Sanderson Electronics PLC (U.K.)		computers	microcomputers	1990	inv	
248	Icon Systems & Software, Inc.		Sanyo Electric (Japan)	Sumitomo	computers	minicomputers		acq	$24.0
249	Iris Graphics Inc	MA	Scitex Corp. Ltd. (Israel)		computers	digital color printers	1990	acq	$1.4
250	Division of Control Data Corp	MN	Shinko Human Create Co Ltd (Japan)		computers	CAD software	1990	inv	

	U.S. Company	State	Foreign Acquirer and Country of Acquirer	Keiretsu Affiliation (Japan)	Industry	Product	Date	Mode of Investment	Purchase Price ($m)
251	Maxi-Switch	AZ	Silitek Corp (Taiwan)		computers	Computer Keyboards	1990	acq	$45.0
252	Ovonic Imaging Systems	MI	Smiths Industries		computers	flat panel displays	1989	inv	
253	Information Presentation Technologies Inc.	CA	Sony Corp. (Japan)	Sony	computers	computer networking products	1990	inv	
254	Edsun Laboratories Inc.	CA	Ssangyong Cement Ltd. (Singapore)		computers	computer graphics	1990	inv	$1.5
255	Calcomp Inc.	CA	Sumitomo Corp (Japan)	Sumitomo	computers	computer products	1990	inv	
256	Integral Peripherals Inc.	CO	Sumitomo Corp (Japan)	Sumitomo	computers	disk drive	1991	inv	
257	Synopsys Inc	CA	Sumitomo Corp (Japan)	Sumitomo	computers	software	1991	inv	$5.0
258	EXSYS, Inc.	NM	Sumitomo Corp. (Japan)	Sumitomo	computers	software engineering tools, AI software	1990	inv	
259	Read-Rite	CA	Sumitomo Metal Industries (Japan)	Sumitomo	computers	thin film magnetic heads	1991	inv	$30.0
260	Level One Communications	CA	TDK (Japan)		computers	local area network chips	1991	inv	$4.4
261	CCT Corp	CA	Tae II Media Corp. (South Korea)		computers	Magnetic disk recording head	1990	acq	$13.3
262	National Micronetics, Inc	NY	Tae II Media Corp. (South Korea)		computers	Computer parts	1990	inv	$4.2
263	Tyan Computer Corp.		Taiwanese investors		computers	electronic workstations		inv	$3.0
264	GraphOn Corp.	CA	Tatung Co. (Taiwan)		computers	computer-window displays		inv	$1.0
265	Kalok Corp.	CA	Techno Venture Co. (Japan)		computers	hard disk drives	1990	inv	$1.0
266	Atherton Technology	CA	Thomson-CSF (France)		computers	computer aided software engineering	1991	inv	
267	FTS Inc.	NY	Thorn EMI PLC (U.K.)		computers	software	1988	acq	
268	Kalok Corp.	CA	Tokyo Venture Capital Co. Ltd. (Japan)		computers	hard disk drives	1990	inv	$0.7
269	University Patents Inc	CT	Vincent Tan (Malaysia)		computers	computers	1989	inv	
270	Computer Associates International, Inc.	NY	Walter H Haefner (Switzerland)		computers	computer software design	1989	inv	$6.5
271	United Tote Inc	CA	Wembly PLC (U.K.)		computers	computer wagering systems	1988	acq	$6.7
272	Integral Systems Inc.	CA	Yamaichi Universal Venture Co Ltd. (Japan)		computers	software	1989	inv	$1.2
273	Supertek Computers, Inc	CA	Yokogawa Electric Corp (Japan)	Fuyo	computers	Minisupercomputers compatibles with Cray computers	1989	acq	$13.5
274	Crosspoint Solutions	CA	ASCII (Japan)		electronics		1990	inv	
275	Integrated Circuit Testing		Advantest (Japan)	DKB	electronics	field programmable gate arrays		inv	

No.	Company	State	Group	Acquirer	Industry	Description	Year	Type	Amount
276	Chyron Corp.	NY		Amper SA (Spain)	electronics	electronic tv production equipment	1991	acq	$10.0
277	Wiltron	CA	Sumitomo	Anritsu (Japan)	electronics	high frequency measuring instruments	1990	acq	$180.0
278	Emerson/ACDC Electronics	CA		BSR International PLC (U.K.)	electronics	modular power switching supplies	1990	div	
279	Emerson/Beckman Elec. Ind. Tech. Div.	CA		BSR International PLC (U.K.)	electronics	passive electronic components and microcircuits	1990	div	
280	Emerson/Doric/Beckman Ind. Products Div.	CA		BSR International PLC (U.K.)	electronics	electronic testing instruments	1990	div	
281	Emerson/Electronic Navigation Ind.	NY		BSR International PLC (U.K.)	electronics	high-power radio equipment	1990	div	
282	Emerson/Powertec/SCI	CA		BSR International PLC (U.K.)	electronics	switching and linear power supplies	1990	div	
283	Thermonics Inc.	NJ		Bowthorpe Holdings PLC (UK)	electronics	temperature sensing devices	1991	acq	$32.0
284	Chancellor Corp	MA		Bruncor, Inc (Canada)	electronics	communications and data processing equipment	1989	acq	
285	Vicon Industries	NY	Nissan Motor	Chugai Boeki Co Ltd (Japan)	electronics	closed circuit TV	1989	inv	$4.0
286	McIntosh Laboratory Inc.	NY		Clarion Co. Ltd. (Japan)	electronics	electronics	1990	acq	$30.0
287	Candela Lasar Corp.	MA		Eddie C.K. Foo (Singapore)	electronics	laser systems	1990	inv	
288	Vantronic Corp	CA		Exicom Ltd (Australia)	electronics	electronic equipment for computer companies	1990	inv	
289	Radionics, Inc	NY		Expanet Int'l PLC (U.K.)	electronics	electronic security systems	1989	acq	$88.0
290	Burndy Corp.	CT		Framatome SA (France)	electronics	electrical and electronic conductors	1989	acq	$325.0
291	Div of Technical Wire Prod.	NJ	DKB	Fuji Kobunshi Kogyo Co. Ltd. (Japan)	electronics	liquid crystal connector div.	1989	div	$5.0
292	Fax division of Burroughs		DKB	Fujitsu (Japan)	electronics		1989	div	
293	Zenith Electronics	IL		Goldstar Co. Ltd. (South Korea)	electronics	television sets (HDTV)	1991	inv	$15.0
294	Dranetz Technologies Inc.	NJ		Hawker Siddeley Group PLC (U.K.)	electronics	electronic testing and measurement instruments	1989	acq	$50.2
295	Continuum Electro-Optics Inc.	CA		Hoya Corp. (Japan)	electronics	pulse solid-state lasers	1991	acq	$20.0
296	Conax Buffalo Corp.	NY		IMI PLC (U.K.)	electronics	electrical products	1989	acq	$33.0
297	Arvin Industries Inc.	IN		Ismanto Wanandi (Indonesia)	electronics	military contractor	1989	inv	$24.0
298	Electronic Metallurgy Co.	PA	Sanwa	Kobe Steel, Ltd. (Japan)	electronics	electric furnace design	1991	acq	
299	Elco Corp of Wickes Co.	CA/PA	Sanwa	Kyocera Corp. (Japan)	electronics	electrical connectors and connections systems	1989	div	$250.0
300	McKenzie Technology	CA	Sanwa	Kyocera Corp (Japan)	electronics	electronic interconnects	1991	acq	$232.5
301	Division of Union Carbide Corp	CA	Mitsubishi	Mitsubishi Corp (Japan)	electronics	carbon, graphite electrodes	1990	acq	
302	Division of Chemtex Inc.	CT	Mitsubishi	Mitsubishi Corp. (Japan)	electronics	manufacture equip. for synthetic fibers	1990	div	$30.0

	U.S. Company	State	Foreign Acquirer and Country of Acquirer	Keiretsu Affiliation (Japan)	Industry	Product	Date	Mode of Investment	Purchase Price ($m)
303	WM Power Prods.	MA	Mitsubishi Electronics (Japan)	Mitsubishi	electronics	circuit breakers	1991	acq	$10.1
304	Power General Corp.		Nippon Densan Corp. (Japan)		electronics	internal switching power supplies	1991	acq	$5.0
305	Exide Electronics Group Inc.	NC	Nippon Electric Industry (Japan)	Sumitomo	electronics	power supply systems	1990	inv	$80.0
306	Arcotronics		Nissei Electric (Japan)		electronics	capacitors	1990	acq	
307	Permacel, Inc.	NJ	Nitto Electric Industrial Co., Ltd.	Sanwa	electronics	pressure-sensitive adhesive tapes for electronics	1989	div	
308	Chemagnetics Inc	CO	Otsuka Pharmaceutical Co, Ltd (Japan)	Otsuka	electronics	Nuclear magnetic resonance equip	1989	acq	$3.5
309	Discovision	CA	Pioneer Electronics (Japan)		electronics	laser disk technology	1989	acq	$200.0
310	Square D Co.	IL	Schneider SA (France)		electronics	circuit breakers/transmitters	1991	acq	
311	Cree Research	NC	Shin-Etsu Handotai (Japan)	Shin-Esu Chem	electronics	blue LEDs for facsimile machines	1990	inv	$2.0
312	ARCO Solar	CA	Siemens AG (Germany)	Shin-Esu Chem	electronics	photovoltaic technology	1989	acq	$40.0
313	Randix Ind.	MA	Starlight International (Hong Kong)		electronics	novelty electronic products	1990	acq	
314	Sheldahl Inc	MN	Sumitomo Bakelite Co, Ltd (Japan)	Sumitomo	electronics	flexible circuits	1990	inv	
315	Cree Research	NC	Sumitomo Corp (Japan)	Sumitomo	electronics	blue LEDs for facsimile machines	1988	acq	
316	Xentek	CA	Taiyo Yuden (Japan)		electronics	power supplies	1991	inv	
317	Emerson Radio Corp.	NJ	Tomei Industrial Ltd. (Hong Kong)		electronics	consumer electronics	1991	inv	$7.5
318	Industrial Circuits, Inc.		Toppan Printing Co., ltd (Japan)	Mitsui	electronics	printed wiring boards	1988	acq	$52.0
319	Electronic Ballast Tech., Inc.		Toshiba Lighting and Tech. (Japan)		electronics		1991	inv	$2.2
320	Veeco Instruments Inc	NY	Unitech PLC (U.K.)		electronics	electric controls	1989	acq	$280.4
321	Interconnection Products Inc.	CA	Wearnes Brothers Ltd. (Singapore)		electronics	solderless terminals and connectors	1990	acq	
322	Industrial Welding Inc.	MI	C. Itoh & Co. (Japan)	DKB	machine tools	industrial welding equipment	1989	acq	
323	Danly Machine		Komatsu Ltd. (Japan)		machine tools	press equipment	1991	inv	
324	National Broach & Machine Co.	MI	Nachi-Fujikoshi Corp. (Japan)	Tokai	machine tools	auto gear	1991	acq	$36.0
325	America's Cutting Tools	WI	Sumitomo Electric Industries (Japan)	Sumitomo	machine tools	carbide tools, reamers and other cutting tools	1991	acq	$1.5
326	Weldon Machine Tool Inc.	PA	Tsugami Corp. (Japan)		machine tools	computer controlled grinders	1991	acq	$1.0
327	Robbins and Craig	CA	Uemura Industries Co., Ltd. (Japan)		machine tools	automated plating and anodizing equipment	1989	acq	$1.4
328	Cincinnati Milacron	SC	Asea Brown Boveri (Switz-Sweden)		robotics	manufacturing robots	1990	acq	

#	U.S. Company	State	Foreign Investor	Keiretsu	Industry	Sector	Description	Year	Type	Value ($M)
329	Precision Instruments Div.	MA	Teijin Seiki Co. (Japan)	Sanwa	robotics	robotics	industrial robot gears	1991	div	$10.0
330	Remote Technology Corp.	TN	Toyo Engineering (Japan)	Mitsui	robotics	robotics	industrial robots	1990	inv	$0.3
331	Transitions Research Corp. (TRC)	CT	Yaskawa Electric Mfg. Co., Ltd. (Japan)	DKB	robotics	robots	robots	1991	inv	
332	Sym-Tek Systems	CA	Advantest (Japan)	DKB	semiconductor equip	semiconductor equip	test equipment	1988	inv	
333	Spectrum CVD	CA	Balzers Ltd.		semiconductor equip	semiconductor equip	front-end equipment	1990	acq	
334	Matrix Videometrix, Inc.	NJ	Bayer AG (Germany)		semiconductor equip	semiconductor equip	materials	1988	acq	
335	EMI, Inc.	CT	Brent Chemicals		semiconductor equip	semiconductor equip	front-end equipment	1988	acq	
336	Olin Hunt	NJ	CIBA-Geigy (Switzerland)		semiconductor equip	semiconductor equip	resistors for semiconductors	1990	acq	
337	AG Associates	CA	Canon (Japan)	Fuyo	semiconductor equip	semiconductor equip	semiconductor production equipment	1990	inv	$3.0
338	Cymer Laser	CA	Canon (Japan)	Fuyo	semiconductor equip	semiconductor equip	excimer lasers, front-end equipment	1990	inv	
339	Lepton		Canon (Japan)	Fuyo	semiconductor equip	semiconductor equip	e-beam, masking for chips	1990	inv	
340	Comp-Aire Systems		Clestra (France)		semiconductor equip	semiconductor equip	clean room technology	1990	inv	
341	MRS	MI	Dainippon Screen (Japan)	DKB	semiconductor equip	semiconductor equip	semiconductor production equipment		inv	
342	PPC Industries		Fuji Electric (Japan)	DKB	semiconductor equip	semiconductor equip	e-beam		inv	
343	Inspex	MA	Hamamatsu (Japan)		semiconductor equip	semiconductor equip		1990	acq	
344	Division of Verteq	CA	Heraeus Amersil, Inc.		semiconductor equip	semiconductor equip	photomasks	1990	div	$25.3
345	Micromask Inc.	CA	Hoya Corp. (Japan)	Sanwa	semiconductor equip	semiconductor equip	photoplates & electronic components—merchant	1989	acq	
346	Division of Monsanto	MO	Huels, AG (Germany)		semiconductor equip	semiconductor equip	8" silicon wafers	1989	div	
347	R & W Ceramics		ICI Australia (Australia)		semiconductor equip	semiconductor equip	semiconductor materials	1990	acq	
348	Siscan Systems	CA	IHI (Japan)	Mitsui	semiconductor equip	semiconductor equip	semiconductor contamination equipment	1990	acq	
349	Division of Combustion Engineering	PA	Imetal (France)		semiconductor equip	semiconductor equip	semiconductor materials	1990	acq	
350	Energy Sciences Inc.	MA	Iwasaki Electric Co. Ltd. (Japan)	DKB	semiconductor equip	semiconductor equip	electron beam equipment	1988	acq	
351	GCA Laser Insp. Equip. Div.	MA	Kobe Steel (Japan)	Sanwa	semiconductor equip	semiconductor equip	laser inspection equipment	1990	acq	
352	AUX Corp.		Kyocera Corp. (Japan)		semiconductor equip	semiconductor equip	ceramic capacitors	1990	inv	
353	Mattson Tech., Inc.	CA	Marubeni Hytech Corp. (Japan)	Fuyo	semiconductor equip	semiconductor equip	wafer fabrication	1991	inv	
354	Ergenics Inc.	NJ	Mitsui & Co., Ltd. (Japan)	Mitsui	semiconductor equip	semiconductor equip	vacuum getters: residual gas removal	1989	inv	
355	Cymer Laser		Nikon (Japan)	Mitsubishi	semiconductor equip	semiconductor equip	excimer lasers, front-end equipment		inv	
356	Perkin Elmer	CT	Nikon Corp. (Japan)	Mitsubishi	semiconductor equip	semiconductor equip			div	
357	Gould	IL	Nippon Mining (Japan)	Nippon Mining	semiconductor equip	semiconductor equip	electrolytic copper foil	1988	acq	$1,100.0
358	Semi-Gas Systems, Inc.	CA	Nippon Sanso (Japan)	Fuyo	semiconductor equip	semiconductor equip	gas purification system	1990	acq	$23.0

#	U.S. Company	State	Foreign Acquirer and Country of Acquirer	Keiretsu Affiliation (Japan)	Industry	Product	Date	Mode of Investment	Purchase Price ($m)
359	Holon		Nippon Steel (Japan)	Nippon Steel	semiconductor equip	semiconductor production equipment			
360	Novellus Systems	CA	Seki and Co. (Japan)		semiconductor equip	front-end equipment, CVD	1988	inv	$1.9
361	Materials Research Corp.	NY	Sony Corp. (Japan)	Sony	semiconductor equip	semiconductor manufacturing equipment	1989	acq	$58.5
362	Advantage Production Technology Inc.	CA	Sumitomo Metal Industries, Ltd.	Sumitomo	semiconductor equip	semiconductor vapor cleaning equipment	1990	inv	$0.5
363	LTX Corp.	MA	Sumitomo Metal Industries, Ltd. (Japan)	Sumitomo	semiconductor equip	integrated circuit chip testing	1990	inv	$24.0
364	Lam Research Group	CA	Sumitomo Metal Industries, Ltd. (Japan)	Sumitomo	semiconductor equip	plasma etching systems—front end equipment	1989	inv	$5.0
365	Therma-Wave Inc. (Japan)	CA	Toray Industries Inc./Shimadzu Corp. (Japan)	Mitsui	semiconductor equip	semiconductor test equipment	1991	acq	$70.0
366	MDA Scientific, Inc.		Zellweger Uster		semiconductor equip	semi-contamination equipment	1988	acq	
367	Midland Bioproducts		Nitto Boseki (Japan)	IBJ	semiconductor equip	semiconductor equipment	1988	acq	
368	Siliconix Incorp.	CA	AEG AG (Germany)		semiconductors	integrated circuits	1988	acq	$10.0
369	Nexgen Microsystems	CA	ASCII (Japan)		semiconductors	microprocessors	1990	inv	$5.0
370	Tera Micro Systems Inc.		ASCII (Japan)		semiconductors	peripheral chips for RISC microprocessors	1990	inv	$2.0
371	Micron Technology Inc.	ID	Amstrad PLC (U.K.)		semiconductors	producers of DRAMs	1988	inv	$75.0
372	Lepton		Canon (Japan)	Fuyo	semiconductors	e-beam, masking for chips	1990		
373	Buss Systems Inc.	CA	Derlan Ind. Ltd. (Canada)		semiconductors	printed circuit boards	1989		$10.0
374	Varian Associates		Ebers Corp. (Japan)		semiconductors		1991	div	$7.5
375	American Specialty Gas Technologies	CA	French Company—name not disclosed		semiconductors	high quality gas for semiconductor products	1990	acq	
376	Carten/Martin	CT	Fujikin (Japan)		semiconductors	valves for processed gas		acq	
377	Via Technologies Inc.		Fujitsu Microelectronics (Japan)	DKB	semiconductors	integrated circuit chips	1989	inv	$10.0
378	Ceraclad		Hitachi (Japan)	Hitachi	semiconductors	ceramic packages	1989	acq	
379	Kollmorgen R&D Ctr		Hitachi Kasei (Japan)	Hitachi	semiconductors	high-density circuit boards		acq	
380	Div of Anacomp Inc	CA	Nikon Metals Ltd. (Japan)	Nikon	semiconductors	thin film disk	1989	div	
381	SEEQ Technology	CA	Huslon Microelectronics Corp. (Taiwan)		semiconductors	semiconductor manufacturing	1990	inv	$52.8
382	Mountain View Research		Ishihara Sangyo Kaisha, Ltd. (Japan)	Mitsubishi	semiconductors	high density circuit boards	1990	acq	$6.9
383	North American Lighting	WV	Koito Mfg. Co. (Japan)	Mitsui	semiconductors	high density circuit boards		acq	$16.5

#	Company	State	Acquirer (Japan)	Parent	Industry	Description	Year	Type	Value
384	Manuf Plant of National Semiconductor Corp	WA	Matsushita Electric Indust. Co (Japan)	Matsushita	semiconductors	semiconductors	1990	div	$86.0
385	Tera Microsystems, Inc.	CA	Mitsubishi Corp. (Japan)	Mitsubishi	semiconductors	chip manufacturing	1991	inv	$0.8
386	Via Technologies	CA	Mitsubishi Corp (Japan)	Mitsubishi	semiconductors	microprocessors	1990	inv	$1.0
387	Powerex	PA	Mitsubishi Electronics (Japan)	Mitsubishi	semiconductors	discrete semiconductors		inv	$4.0
388	Pathtek of Eastman Kodak Co.	NY	Mitsui Petrochemical Industries Ltd. (Japan)	Mitsui	semiconductors	plates injection-molded plastic ICs & 3-d devices	1990	div	
389	Paradigm Technology Inc.	CA	NKK Corp. (Japan)	Fuyo	semiconductors	high speed SRAMs	1991	inv	$5.0
390	DSP Group Inc.	CA	Nikko Capital Co. Ltd. (Japan)		semiconductors	digital signal processing chip sets	1991	acq	$7.0
391	Cabot Beryllium division	PA	Nippon Gaishi (Japan)		semiconductors	semiconductor materials		acq	
392	Division of GE	CO	Nippon Kokan (Japan)	Fuyo	semiconductors	silicon manufacturer		div	$2.0
393	Simtek Inc.	MA	Nippon Steel (Japan)	Nippon Steel	semiconductors	advanced semiconductor products		acq	
394	Aegis, Inc.	CA	Olin Asahi (Japan)		semiconductors	IC packages	1991	acq	$4.3
395	KLASIC PCBAOI product line division of Cincinnati Milacron, Inc	OH	Ono Sokki Co., Ltd. (Japan)		semiconductors	printed circuit boards		div	
396			Osaka Titanium Co (Japan)	Sumitomo	semiconductors	Silicon epitaxial wafers	1989	acq	
397	King Instrument Co	MA	Otari Electric Co, Ltd (Japan)	Sumitomo	semiconductors	Magnetic tape loaders	1990	acq	
398	Planade Energy Systems	CA	Ozaki Electronics (Japan)		semiconductors	high-rise power meters		acq	
399	Panatech Research	TX	Ricoh (Japan)	Tokai	semiconductors	semi. division		acq	$3.2
400	Xetel Corp.	MA	Rohm Co. (Japan)		semiconductors	semiconductor producers	1990	div	$58.0
401	Sprague Technology Inc	CA	Sanken Electric Co Ltd (Japan)	Tokai	semiconductors	Semiconductor	1990	acq	
402	MicroSi		Shin-Etsu Chem. (Japan)	Shin-Etsu Chem	semiconductors	silicon		acq	$2.0
403	Brooktree Corp.	TX	Shin-Etsu Chemical Co. (Japan)	Shin-Etsu Chem	semiconductors	graphic chips	1990	acq	$55.0
404	Advanced Micro Devices, Inc.	CA	Sony (Japan)	Sony	semiconductors	semiconductor	1991	inv	$1.0
405	Prometrix Corp	CA	Sumitomo Corp (Japan)	Sumitomo	semiconductors	Semiconductor measuring equipment		inv	
406	Mosaic Systems Inc	CA	Sumitomo Metal Industries Ltd (Japan)	Sumitomo	semiconductors	Multi-chip modules	1990	inv	$2.5
407	NCHIP	CA	Sumitomo Metal Mining Co. Ltd. (Japan)	Sumitomo	semiconductors	multichip modules	1991	inv	
408	Silicon Systems Inc	CA	TDK Corp (Japan)		semiconductors	Integrated Circuits	1989	acq	$200.0
409	Allegro Microsystems	CA	Tokuyama Soda (Japan)	Sanwa	semiconductors	semiconductors	1990	div	$58.0
410	Signal Processing Technology	CO	Tokyo Inc (Japan)		semiconductors	analog-integrated circuits	1990	div	$6.6
411	Division of Texas Instruments Inc	TX	Toppan Printing Co, Ltd (Japan)		semiconductors	Photomasks	1990	div	$19.0
412	Prostar Inc		Toppan Printing Co, Ltd (Japan)		semiconductors	multi-layered printed circuit boards		acq	
413	Quartz Industrial		Toshiba Ceramic (Japan)	Mitsui	semiconductors	semiconductor materials		acq	

	U.S. Company	State	Foreign Acquirer and Country of Acquirer	Keiretsu Affiliation (Japan)	Industry	Product	Date	Mode of Investment	Purchase Price ($m)
414	Synergy Semiconductor Corp.	CA	Toshiba Corp. (Japan)	Mitsui	semiconductors	high-speed application-specific ICs (ASICs)	1991	inv	
415	Vertex Semiconductor	CA	Toshiba Corp. (Japan)	Mitsui	semiconductors	Semiconductors	1991	acq	$20.0
416	Division of Varian	CA	Tosoh Corp. (Japan)		semiconductors	metals for semiconductors	1989	div	$33.0
417	Weiss Scientific Glass Blowing	OR/CA	Tosoh Corp. (Japan)		semiconductors	glass for IC and semiconductors	1990		
418	BTU-ULVAC, Inc.	CA	ULVAC Japan, Ltd. (Japan)	Matsushita Elec. Industr	semiconductors	wafer processing systems	1991	jvb	
419	Automated Semiconductor Inc.		Uemura Industry Co. Ltd. (Japan)		semiconductors	IC plating	1989		$0.4
420	Sequential Circuits		Yamaha (Japan)		semiconductors	ICs	1989		
421	Armco Steel	OH	Kawasaki Steel (Japan)	DKH	steel	steel processing	1988	acq	$350.0
422	National Steel Corp.	PA	NKK Corp (Japan)	Fuyo	steel	steel manufacturing	1990	inv	$294.0
423	Inland Steel Industries	IL	Nippon Steel Corp. (Japan)	Nippon Steel	steel	Steel	1989	inv	$185.0
424	American Laser Technologies Inc.	OH	Okura and Co. Ltd. (Japan)	Fuyo	steel	laser treated steel sheets	1991	inv	
425	LTV Corporation	TX	Sumitomo Metal Industries Ltd. (Japan)	Sumitomo	steel	steel producer	1991	inv	$200.0
426	Westinghouse	CT	ABB (Sweden-Switzerland)		telecommunications	high-powered electrical transmission equipment	1989	div	$10.0
427	Division of Loral Corp	CA	Aerospatiale (France)		telecommunications	commercial communications and weather satellite	1990	inv	
428	Division of Loral Corp		Alcatel (France)		telecommunications	commercial communications and weather satellite	1990	inv	
429	Division of Rockwell	TX	Alcatel (France)		telecommunications	transmission systems	1991	div	$625.0
430	Wiltron Co	CA	Anritsu Corp (Japan)	Sumitomo	telecommunications	Microwave & telecommunications test equipment	1990	acq	$180.0
431	Phone Mate, Inc	CA	Asahi Corp (Japan)	Sumitomo	telecommunications	telephone answering devices	1988	acq	$8.3
432	ACDC Electronics	OH	BSR International PLC (U.K.)		telecommunications	switching systems	1989	div	
433	Electronic Navigation Industries	NY	BSR International PLC (U.K.)		telecommunications	radio frequency generators	1989	div	
434	Powertec/SCI		BSR International PLC (U.K.)		telecommunications	switching systems	1989	div	
435	Oak Industries, Inc.	CA	Britannia Arrow PLC (U.K.)		telecommunications	electronics and communications	1990	inv	
436	McDonnell Douglas/Tymnet		British Telecom (U.K.)		telecommunications	electronic data communications networks/services	1989	acq	$355.0

No.	Company	State	Foreign partner	Group	Sector	Description	Year	Type	Value
437	McCaw Cellular Communications	WA	British Telecommunications PLC (U.K.)		telecommunications	Telecommunications equipment	1989	inv	$1,370.0
438	TRT/FTC Communications, Inc	DC	Cable & Wireless PLC (UK)		telecommunications	data transmission and telephone concern	1991	acq	$174.0
439	DataAmerica Inc.	VA	Cable and Wireless PLC (UK)		telecommunications	cable and wireless communications	1991	acq	
440	Interactive Media Technologies, Inc.	AZ	Canon States Co. Inc. (Japan)	Fuyo	telecommunications	multimedia integrator	1990	inv	
441	Wakefield Electronics	NY	Diploma PLC (UK)		telecommunications	data communications cables	1990	acq	
442	Resdel Engineering Corp	CA	Doty group PLC (UK)		telecommunications	defense radar systems	1990	acq	
443	Amphenol Corp.	CT	Fujikura Ltd. (Japan)	Mitsui	telecommunications	cable assemblies and connecters		acq	
444	Intelligent Storage		Fujitsu Am. (Japan)	DKB	telecommunications				
445	AT&T-Unix Operations System Group	NJ	Fujitsu, Ltd (Japan)	DKB	telecommunications	Unix system		acq	$15.0
446	Division of Bell Industries		Furukawa Elec. (Japan)	DKB	telecommunications	peripheral and communications equip	1989	inv	
447	Franklin Telecommunications Corp.	CA	Gandalf Technologies Inc. (Canada)		telecommunications	protection and telecommunications	1988	inv	
448	Total Assets Protection Inc.	TX	Girvan Corp. Ltd. (Australia)		telecommunications	communications equip	1989	inv	
449	Kustom Electronics Inc	KS	Glenayre Electronics Ltd (Canada)		telecommunications	telecommunications	1989	acq	$20.0
450	Pactel Company	CA	Great Electronics Corp. (Taiwan)	Mitsubishi	telecommunications	optical communications	1989	inv	$0.8
451	Deltronic Christal Industries Inc.	NJ	Nikon Metals Ltd. (Japan)	Tokai	telecommunications	electric solenoids, relays	1990	acq	$8.0
452	Guardian Electric Manufacturing Co.	IL	Koike Electric Industrial Co. Ltd. (Japan)		telecommunications				
453	Infonet Services Corp.	CA	Kokusai Denshin Denwa Co. Ltd. (Japan)	Mitsubishi	telecommunications	telecommunications services	1990	inv	$3.5
454	Pictel Corp.		Kyocera (Japan)	Sanwa	telecommunications				
455	Zeta Laboratories	CA	Lucas Aerospace (UK)		telecommunications	jamming devices	1989	acq	
456	InteCom Inc.	TX	Matra SA (France)		telecommunications	integrated application solutions/ information switching			
457	Astronet	FL	Mitsubishi (Japan)	Mitsubishi	telecommunications	cellular and telecommunications equip		inv	
458	Amtech Corp.	TX	Mitsubishi Corp. (Japan)	Mitsubishi	telecommunications	recognition systems	1988	inv	$6.0
459	Poly-Optical Prods.	CA	Mitsubishi Rayon (Japan)	Mitsubishi	telecommunications	fiber-optics	1988	inv	
460	Worldcom International Private Lines Services		Motor-Columbus AG (Switzerland)		telecommunications	telecommunications services	1988	acq	$56.0
461	AIM Telephones		NEC (Japan)	Sumitomo	telecommunications				
462	API Telephone Systems		NEC (Japan)	Sumitomo	telecommunications				

	U.S. Company	State	Foreign Acquirer and Country of Acquirer	Keiretsu Affiliation (Japan)	Industry	Product	Date	Mode of Investment	Purchase Price ($m)
463	AT&T-Unix Operations System Group	NJ	NEC Corp. (Japan)	Sumitomo	telecommunications	Unix System	1991	inv	
464	Epitaxx Inc.	NJ	Nippon Sheet Glass Co. (Japan)	Sumitomo	telecommunications	opto-electronic devices and infrared sensors	1990	acq	$6.5
465	Tie-Communications Inc.		Nitsuko Ltd. (Japan)	Sumitomo	telecommunications	telecommunications equipment distribution channels	1991	acq	
466	Mod-Tap System	MA	Oki Electric Cable Co., affiliate of Oki Elec. Ind. Co. (J		telecommunications	communications wiring systems	1991	inv	
467	Com Systems, Inc	CA	Omni Holding AG (Switzerland)		telecommunications	telecommunications	1989	acq	
468	Geophysical Survey Systems, Inc.	NH	Oyo Corp. (Japan)		telecommunications	ground penetrating radar systems	1989	acq	$6.0
469	AT&E Corp.	CA	Seiko Corp. (Japan)		telecommunications	personal paging systems	1991	acq	$20.5
470	Division of Loral Corp		Selenia Spazio SpA (Italy)		telecommunications	commercial communications and weather satellite	1990	inv	
471	Hycom Inc.	CA	Sharp Corporation (Japan)	Sanwa	telecommunications	Telecommunications equipment	1989	acq	
472	Rolm division of IBM	NY	Siemens AG (Germany)		telecommunications	PBX systems	1988		$884.0
473	Executive TeleCard Ltd.	NY	Singapore Telecom (Singapore)		telecommunications	telecommunications	1991	acq	$5.0
474	Times Microwave Systems	CT	Smiths Industries PLC (U.K.)		telecommunications	microwave transmissions for defense	1988		$53.5
475	CXC Corp.	CA	Sony Corp (Japan)	Sony	telecommunications	voice data/interactive communications			
476	Ortel	CA	Sumitomo Cement Co. (Japan)	Sumitomo	telecommunications	fiber-optic lasers	1990	inv	$13.3
477	Kurzweil Applied Intelligence Inc.	MA	Suzuki Musical Instrument (Japan)		telecommunications	automated voice recognition systems	1989	inv	
478	Code-A-Phone Corporation	OR	Technology Applications (Thailand)		telecommunications	telephone answering devices	1990	acq	
479	INFONET	CA	Telecom Australia (Australia)		telecommunications	telecommunications software	1989		
480	AT&T-Unix Operations System Group	NJ	Toshiba Corp (Japan)	Mitsui	telecommunications	Unix systems	1989		
481	Telequest Inc	CA	Undisclosed buyer (Italy)		telecommunications	telephone & telegraph	1988	acq	$0.9
482	Impulse Manufacturing	CA	Uniden (Japan)		telecommunications	radar equipment	1989		$12.0
483	Magellan System Co.	CA	Uniden (Japan)		telecommunications	global positioning receivers	1989	inv	
484	Regency Elec	IN	Uniden (Japan)		telecommunications	radio	1988	acq	$12.0
485	Zonic Corp	OH	A&D Ltd. (Japan)		miscellaneous	signal processors and spectrum analyzers	1988	acq	
486	Bailey Controls	OH	Alenia (Italy)		miscellaneous	amplifiers and controls	1989	acq	

#	U.S. Company	State	Foreign Acquirer	Category	Group	Description	Year	Type	Value ($M)
487	Cypher Data Products	NY	Alps Elec. Co. (Japan)	miscellaneous	Mitsui	electric motors	1989	acq	$5.0
488	REM Technologies Inc.	KS	C. Itoh & Co. (Japan)	miscellaneous	DKB	graphic arts equipment	1988	acq	
489	Opti-Copy Inc.		Dainippon Ink and Chemicals (Japan)	miscellaneous			1990	acq	$131.0
490	Barden Corp	CT	FAG Kugelfischer Georg Schaefer KGaA (Germany)	miscellaneous		Precision ball bearings			$19.0
491	AT&E Corp.		Hattori Seiko (Japan)	miscellaneous	Mitsubishi				
492	Enpak		Japan Storage Battery (Japan)	miscellaneous			1990	inv	$126.0
493	Yamatake-Honeywell		Japanese institutions (Japan)	miscellaneous				inv	$250.0
494	NCNB Corp		Japanese investors (Japan)	miscellaneous		generators			
495	Double Energy Systems	CA	Kamata Corp. (Japan)	miscellaneous		precision die castings	1989	acq	$28.0
496	Diemakers Inc.	MO	Kanematsu Corp. (Japan)	miscellaneous	DKB	scientific instruments and apparatus	1990	acq	
497	Kewaunee Scientific Corp.	VA	Kyoto Electronic Manufacturing Co. (Japan)	miscellaneous		electronic beam processors	1989	div	
498	RPC Industries Inc.	CA	Marubeni (Japan)	miscellaneous	Fuyo				$5.0
499	Robotron		Marubeni (Japan)	miscellaneous	Fuyo	electromechanical components			$4.0
500	Aromat Corp.	NJ	Matsushita (Japan)	miscellaneous	Matsushita	technical services	1991	acq	$16.0
501	American Technical	CA	Meitec Corp. (Japan)	miscellaneous	Mitsubishi		1990	acq	$3.0
502	North American Hitech Group, Inc.	CT	Messerschmitt-Boelkow-Blohm GmbH (Germany)	miscellaneous					
503	Power Systems Inc.	NY	Minebea Co Ltd./IMC Magnetics (Japan)	miscellaneous		power supplies	1990		$13.3
504	Electrosound Group		Mitsubishi Corp. (Japan)	miscellaneous	Mitsubishi	CD's and tape duplicating equipment	1988		$6.0
505	Memory Tech. Inc.		Mitsubishi Corp. (Japan)	miscellaneous	Mitsubishi	printing plate preparation equipment	1988	acq	$5.0
506	Nu-Graphics Equipment	CA	Mitsubishi Kasci Corp. (Japan)	miscellaneous	Mitsubishi				
507	Gain Electronics	NJ	Mitsui & Co. (Japan)	miscellaneous	Mitsui	digital mapping systems	1991	inv	$6.0
508	Navigation Technology Inc.	CA	Nichimen Corp. (Japan)	miscellaneous	Sanwa	measurement instruments	1991	inv	$1.3
509	Adcole Corp.	PA/	Nippei Toyama Corp. (Japan)	miscellaneous	Toyobo Co	components for picture tubes	1988	acq	$4.0
510	OI-NEG TV Products	OH	Nippon Electric Glass (Japan)	miscellaneous	Sumitomo				
511	Motormetic Corp.	NJ	Nippon Seiko (Japan)	miscellaneous	Fuyo	SMT tapes	1991	acq	$3.0
512	Permacel, Inc.		Nitto Electronics (Japan)	miscellaneous	Sanwa	software design tools		div	
513	Div. of Seattle Silicon Corp.		Oki Electric Industry Co., Ltd. (Japan)	miscellaneous	Fuyo				
514	King Instrument Co.	MA	Otari Electric Co. Ltd. (Japan)	miscellaneous		automated magnetic tape loaders	1990	acq	
515	Kinemetrics	CA	Oyo Corp. (Japan)	miscellaneous		vibration instruments	1991	acq	
516	IG Technologies		Pechiney (France)	miscellaneous		industrial magnets	1989	acq	$11.1

	U.S. Company	State	Foreign Acquirer and Country of Acquirer	Keiretsu Affiliation (Japan)	Industry	Product	Date	Mode of Investment	Purchase Price ($m)
517	Telmos		Rohm Co. (Japan)		miscellaneous	anti-friction bearings	1990	acq	$1.5
518	McGill Manufacturing Co.	TN	SKF AB (Sweden)		miscellaneous	spectroscopy	1989	div	$104.0
519	Division of Comstock Group		SPIE-Batignolles (France)		miscellaneous		1988	acq	
520	Acme Printing Ink Co.		Sakata Inx Corp. (Japan)	Sumitomo	miscellaneous	printing ink	1989	acq	
521	Knight Color and Chem. Co.	MN	Sakata Inx Corp. (Japan)	Sumitomo	miscellaneous	printing ink	1989	acq	
522	Midland Color Co.	IL	Sakata Inx Corp. (Japan)	Sumitomo	miscellaneous		1989	acq	
523	Swisstronics, Inc.		Sanko Senzai Kogyo Co. Ltd (Japan)	Kobe Steel	miscellaneous	precision parts		acq	$13.8
524	Icon Systems and Software	CA	Sanyo (Japan)	Tokai	miscellaneous	pressure sensitive tape	1991	acq	
525	TA Industries Inc.		Sekisui Chemical Co., Ltd. (Japan)	Sanwa	miscellaneous		1990	acq	
526	Foxboro Co	MA	Siebe PLC (U.K.)		miscellaneous	process control systems (industrial controls)		acq	$656.4
527	National Machine Systems	CA/	Sony Magnescale (Japan)	Sony	miscellaneous		1988	acq	
528	Judd Wire Inc.	MA	Sumitomo Electric Industries (Japan)	Sumitomo	miscellaneous	irradiated cross-linked wire/cable		acq	$4.0
529	International Pressure Service	OH	Tokyo Tokushu Nekko Co. Ltd. (Japan)		miscellaneous	isostatic presses, thermocouples	1988	acq	
530	Div. of Herco Technology Corp.	TX	Toppan Printing (Japan)	Mitsui	miscellaneous	Industrial Circuits	1988	div	$52.4
531	MRI division of Diasonics	CA	Toshiba (Japan)		miscellaneous	noninvasive MRI diagnostic equipment	1990	div	
532	Toshiba-Westinghouse	NY	Toshiba (Japan)	Mitsui	miscellaneous	television picture tubes	1989	acq	$20-30.0
533	Outlook Technology	CA	Toyo Corp. (Japan)		miscellaneous	logic analyzers	1991	acq	
534	Hoover Group Inc.		Tsubakimoto Precision Products (Japan)	Tsubakimoto	miscellaneous	ball bearings	1990	acq	$64.4
535	Circuit Controller Corp.		Yazaki Corp. (Japan)		miscellaneous	harnesses		acq	$3.8
536	Textube Corp.	SC	Yazaki Industrial Chemical Co. (Japan)		miscellaneous	materials handling systems	1991	acq	$13.0

APPENDIX D

BRIEF CHRONOLOGY OF THE FSX

June 1985–June 1987: High-level discussions between the Department of Defense and the Japanese Defense Agency:

(1) The parties consider the indigenous development of a Japanese fighter aircraft.

(2) Also discussed is the purchase, coproduction, or licensed production of an existing U.S. aircraft.

(3) Japanese officials conclude that no existing U.S. aircraft meets their needs and requirements.

(4) U.S. officials inform Japanese that indigenous development could jeopardize existing bilateral trade-and-defense relationships.

August 1987–May 1988: The secretary of defense and the Japanese defense minister agree that the U.S. and Japan will coproduce a new fighter aircraft and that it will be based on a modified version of General Dynamics' F-16. Discussions begin on a Memorandum of Understanding.

November 1988: Formal MOU on the FSX is signed.

December 1988: Letters are exchanged between DoD and the JDA on development work share and wing manufacturing.

January 1989: Mitsubishi Heavy Industries and General Dynamics sign a License and Technical Assistance Agreement.

February 1989: President Bush puts the FSX decision off for a month, following opposition in Congress, his own administration, and the press.

March 1989 (United States): Senate Armed Services Committee hears testimony. The National Security Council meets. Thirty-five senators voice their objections to the FSX agreement. The secretary of commerce wins a greater role for his department in the FSX agreement, as well as in negotiating future agreements in which allies are given sensitive technology to build weapons. The president insists on changes in the FSX agreement to include more production work for the U.S. before moving forward.

March 1989 (Japan): Japan calls on the U.S. to honor its agreements, charging that the U.S. is invoking national security to gain economic advantage.

In response to Bush's demands, Japanese officials assure the Bush administration that at least 35 percent of the FSX would be produced in the U.S. Seiki Nishihiro, of the JDA, travels to Washington to rescue the FSX.

April 1989: Amid mounting strains between the U.S. and Japan, President Bush announces an agreement to design and build with Japan a new-generation fighter plane for Japan that will protect American jobs and security. The new agreement stipulates: restrictions on the U.S. regarding sensitive software source codes; 40 percent of the development share for the U.S., and "about 40 percent" of the production share. Under pressure from Congress, the White House responds for the first time to calls to expand its definition of national security beyond military and strategic objectives to include trade and economic considerations.

May 1989: Pressure builds in Congress to kill the $7-billion FSX deal, reinforced by an influential report from the General Accounting Office. The report concludes that the agreement was lopsided, since the technology from Japan was already well known to the American aircraft industry. The Senate approves a motion from Senator Robert Byrd giving the Senate a stronger role in monitoring the agreement, and raising the U.S. work share. The Senate defeates a motion from Senator Alan Dixon to kill U.S. participation in the joint venture.

June 1989: The House votes for a resolution sponsored by Representative Terry Bruce conditionally approving U.S. participation in the FSX. Discouraged by the air of mistrust produced by the FSX controversy, military leaders in Japan begin preparing for independent production of advanced weapons.

August 1989: President Bush vetoes legislation imposing conditions on the FSX agreement on the grounds that it violates his constitutional rights and duties. One month later, the Senate fails by one vote to override the president's veto. The FSX agreement is in force.

APPENDIX E*

F-16 COPRODUCTION COMPONENT BREAKDOWN

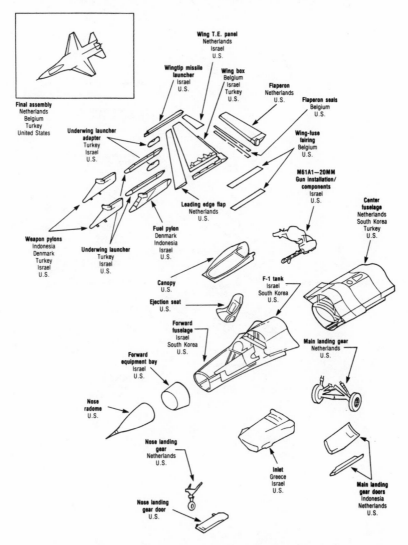

Wing T.E. panel
Netherlands
Israel
U.S.

Wingtip missile launcher
Israel
U.S.

Wing box
Belgium
Israel
Turkey
U.S.

Flaperon
Netherlands
U.S.

Flaperon seals
Belgium
U.S.

Final assembly
Netherlands
Belgium
Turkey
United States

Underwing launcher adapter
Turkey
Israel
U.S.

Wing-fuse fairing
Belgium
U.S.

M61A1—20MM Gun installation/ components
Israel
U.S.

Center fuselage
Netherlands
South Korea
Turkey
U.S.

Weapon pylons
Indonesia
Denmark
Turkey
Israel
U.S.

Underwing launcher
Turkey
Israel
U.S.

Leading edge flap
Netherlands
U.S.

Fuel pylon
Denmark
Indonesia
Israel
U.S.

Canopy
U.S.

Ejection seat
U.S.

F-1 tank
Israel
South Korea
U.S.

Forward fuselage
Israel
South Korea
U.S.

Main landing gear
Netherlands
U.S.

Forward equipment bay
Israel
U.S.

Nose radome
U.S.

Nose landing gear
Netherlands
U.S.

Inlet
Greece
Israel
U.S.

Main landing gear doors
Indonesia
Netherlands
U.S.

Nose landing gear door
U.S.

*From General Dynamics, cited in U.S. Congress, Office of Technology Assessment, *Arming Our Allies: Cooperation and Competition in Defense Technology.* May 1990.

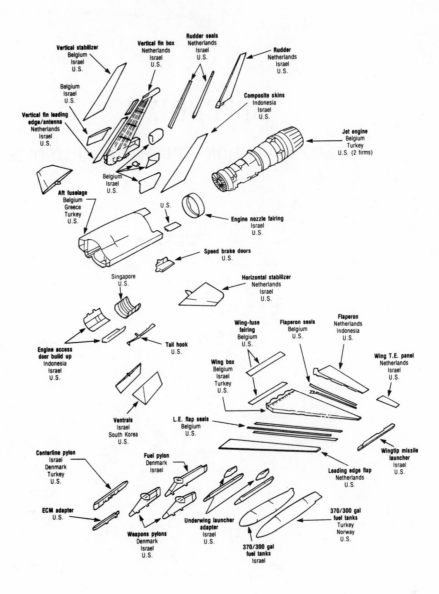

Vertical stabilizer
Belgium
Israel
U.S.

Vertical fin box
Netherlands
Israel
U.S.

Rudder seals
Netherlands
Israel
U.S.

Rudder
Netherlands
Israel
U.S.

Belgium
Israel
U.S.

Composite skins
Indonesia
Israel
U.S.

Vertical fin leading
edge/antenna
Netherlands
Israel
U.S.

Jet engine
Belgium
Turkey
U.S. (2 firms)

Belgium
Israel
U.S.

Aft fuselage
Belgium
Greece
Turkey
U.S.

U.S.

Engine nozzle fairing
Israel
U.S.

Speed brake doors
U.S.

Singapore
U.S.

Horizontal stabilizer
Netherlands
Israel
U.S.

Engine access
door build up
Indonesia
Israel
U.S.

Tail hook
U.S.

Wing-fuse
fairing
Belgium
U.S.

Flaperon seals
Belgium
U.S.

Flaperon
Netherlands
Indonesia
U.S.

Wing box
Belgium
Israel
Turkey
U.S.

Wing T.E. panel
Netherlands
Israel
U.S.

Ventrals
Israel
South Korea
U.S.

L.E. flap seals
Belgium
U.S.

Wingtip missile
launcher
Israel
U.S.

Centerline pylon
Israel
Denmark
Turkey
U.S.

Fuel pylon
Denmark
Israel

Leading edge flap
Netherlands
U.S.

ECM adapter
U.S.

Underwing launcher
adapter
Israel
U.S.

370/300 gal
fuel tanks
Turkey
Norway
U.S.

Weapons pylons
Denmark
Israel
U.S.

370/300 gal
fuel tanks
Israel

APPENDIX F*

THE TOP 25 BANKING COMPANIES IN THE WORLD

1. Dai-Ichi Kangyo Bank Ltd., Tokyo
2. Sumitomo Bank Ltd., Osaka
3. Mitsui Taiyo Kobe Bank Ltd., Tokyo
4. Sanwa Bank Ltd., Osaka
5. Fuji Bank, Ltd., Tokyo
6. Mitsubishi Bank Ltd., Tokyo
7. Crédit Agricole Mutuel, Paris
8. Banque Nationale de Paris
9. Industrial Bank of Japan, Ltd., Tokyo
10. Crédit Lyonnais, Paris
11. Deutsche Bank, Frankfurt
12. Barclays Plc, London
13. Tokai Bank Ltd., Nagoya
14. Norinchukin Bank, Tokyo
15. Mitsubishi Trust & Banking Corp., Tokyo
16. National Westminster Bank Plc, London
17. ABN Amro Holding N.V., Amsterdam, Netherlands
18. Bank of Tokyo, Ltd.
19. Société Générale, Paris
20. Sumitomo Trust & Banking Co., Ltd., Osaka
21. Citicorp, New York
22. Mitsui Trust & Banking Co., Ltd., Tokyo
23. Long-Term Credit Bank of Japan Ltd., Tokyo
24. Dresdner Bank, Frankfurt
25. Compagnie Financière de Paribas, Paris

*From the Treasury Department, citing *American Banker*'s World Bank Survey, 1991, cited in James R. Kraus, "No U.S. Bank Company Among World's Top 20," *American Banker*, July 10, 1991, p. 1.

APPENDIX G

SEVERAL MAJOR EUROPEAN CONSORTIA AND THE TECHNOLOGIES THEY FOSTER

ESPRIT (EUROPEAN STRATEGIC PROGRAMME FOR RESEARCH AND DEVELOPMENT IN INFORMATION TECHNOLOGIES): The emphasis of the ESPRIT program is information technology, with specific projects focusing on microelectronics, information-processing systems, telecommunications, and information technology application technologies. This means software development, computer-assisted manufacturing, robotics, workstations, and a wide variety of computer-connected applications in industry. Taking a page from the Japanese model, ESPRIT also stresses "precompetitive" research, which means connecting what happens in the lab with commercialization, or marketing the products that come from the lab.

RACE (RESEARCH AND DEVELOPMENT IN ADVANCED COMMUNICATIONS TECHNOLOGY FOR EUROPE): Together with ESPRIT, RACE has brought together several hundred companies and university and research institutes in the European Community, linking the work of six to seven thousand research institutes in the EC that work in the area of communications-technology equipment and services. RACE's special mission involves standardizing telecommunications throughout the EC, with worldwide goals in mind: if telecommunications throughout Europe are designed with compatibility in mind, then the internal market will be stronger, and the EC in a better position to conquer a heftier percentage of the world market.

EUREKA (EUROPEAN RESEARCH COORDINATION AGENCY): The mission of EUREKA appears even more broad-based: to bring basic research in science and technology into the marketplace by supporting research *beyond* the precompetitive stage. EUREKA is funded by eighteen countries in Western Europe, including the twelve member states of the EC. To be funded by EUREKA, a project must win the support of at least two countries, and involve collaboration between two or more laboratories. EUREKA's broad mission encompasses many of the technologies the EC has identified with its future, including biotechnology and advanced television.

APPENDIX H*

KEY AGENCIES WITH JURISDICTION OVER INTERNATIONAL TRADE ISSUES

Agency	Function
Office of the United States Trade Representative (USTR) in the Executive Office of the President	Conducts most international negotiations, usually aimed at increasing access to foreign markets. Investigates allegations of unfair foreign trade barriers (sec. 301).
Department of Commerce	Investigates allegations of subsidies and dumping. Conducts export-promotion programs. Lead role in export controls. Conducts studies and advises on competitiveness of individual industries.
U.S. International Trade Commission (ITC)	Determines whether U.S. industries are injured for purposes of determining whether they merit relief from unfair dumping and subsidies (sec. 201). Studies and advises on competitiveness of U.S. industries, including the effect of imports.
Department of Defense	Assists the Department of Commerce in specifying and enforcing export controls. Makes agreements with other nations regarding defense trade.
Department of State	Assists Department of Commerce in export controls; leads international negotiations in export controls.
Department of Energy	Assists Department of Commerce in export controls.
Export-Import Bank of the U.S. (Ex-Im Bank)	Helps firms to obtain financing for exports.

Department of Agriculture   Conducts export-promotion programs.
                                     Leads many international negotiations in
                                     agricultural trade. Collects and
                                     disseminates data. Helps businesses to
                                     obtain financing for agricultural exports.
                                     Administers price-support programs.

*Source: U.S. Congress, Office of Technology Assessment, 1991.

GLOSSARY

Advanced Ceramics—Specialized ceramic materials engineered to withstand high temperatures and other extreme conditions.

Artificial Intelligence (AI)—The use of computer software to make decisions through processes resembling human reasoning.

Avionics—The production of electrical devices for use in aviation, missiles, and astronautics.

Biotechnology—The study of the relationship between humans and machines, especially in terms of physiological, psychological, and technological requirements. As commonly used in industry, the term refers to the production of drugs and other medical products employing living organisms instead of chemical processes. The clearest example is the use of bacteria to produce insulin, or penicillin mold to produce penicillin.

CFIUS (Committee on Foreign Investment in the U.S.)—A U.S.-government multiagency committee, headed by the Treasury Department, that screens foreign acquisitions of American companies. (See Exon-Florio.)

Chip—An integrated circuit device. (See "integrated circuit.")

CoC (Council on Competitiveness)—A group of business and education leaders that conducts research and promotes U.S. competitiveness.

DARPA (Defense Advanced Research Projects Agency)—A Pentagon agency that provides funds for experimental technology projects.

Data Fusion—A process by which machines transform raw data into more usable forms.

Digital Imaging—A process that makes pictures out of dots, as if by a pointillist painter, by recording lightwaves on computer chips.

D-RAM (dynamic random-access memory)—What microchips possess. The ability to store, alter, and retrieve information,

Exon-Florio—An amendment to the 1988 trade bill that authorizes the president to block any foreign acquisition that imperils national security. Invoked only once, in a case involving a company owned by the government of the People's Republic of China.

Fiber Optics—A system that allows the transmission of information in the form of a beam of light through a fine, threadlike piece of transparent fiber.

FSX (Fighter Support Experimental)—An advanced jet fighter plane, based on the F-16, developed by the U.S. and Japan.

Gallium Arsenide—A semiconductor material used instead of silicon.

HDTV (high-definition television)—Offers wider-screen pictures with high resolution that improves their depth, clarity, and detail.

High-Density Storage—Holding a lot of information in a small amount of computer memory.

High-Performance Computing—Performed by fast and powerful computers.

Integrated Circuit—A miniaturized electronic device on which circuit patterns are imposed onto a semiconductor material base. The results are chips, often no larger than a fingernail, capable of containing millions of bits of information or thousands of logical operations.

Integrated Optics—The use of light instead of electricity for circuits and computers.

Keiretsu—A Japanese organization consisting of interlocking ownerships of banks, manufacturers, suppliers, and distributors.

LCD (liquid-crystal display):—A crystal film sealed between two plates of glass, which changes its optical properties when a current is applied. Used most frequently to display readings continuously on digital watches, calculators, and computer screens.

Microchip—An exceptionally small and technologically advanced chip.

MITI (Ministry of International Trade and Industry)—Coordinates Japan's trade policies and manufacturing projects.

Optical Encoding—The use of lightwaves to create codes.

Optoelectronics—Equipment and software used to process information transmitted by light.

Passive Sensor—A device that can detect targets and monitor equipment without emitting a signal.

Phased-Array Radar—A radar technology that allows the pilot to "see" in any direction (360 degrees) through an array of computer chips that allow the device to scan the horizon electronically, instead of the traditional mechanically rotating antennas.

Photolithography—A process used to etch circuits onto chips by using sharply focused waves of light.

Robotics—The technology of using computer-controlled robots to perform industrial tasks, as on assembly lines.

SEMATECH (Semiconductor Manufacturing Technology consortium)—A U.S.-government-and-industry-sponsored research-and-development consortium of manufacturers and suppliers.

Semiconductor—Materials that act as conductors once an applied current exceeds a threshold amount. These materials are formed from elements like silicon, or compounds, such as gallium arsenide, which are used in microelectronic circuitry (i.e., integrated circuits). The properties of these materials can be significantly modified by the addition of small quantities of carefully chosen additives, which then make them useful for integrated circuits.

Signature Control—A method used in creating hard-to-detect weapons. Popularly known as Stealth Technology.

Silicon—A nonmetallic element that is commonly used in the making of computer chips.

Superconductivity—The phenomenon of almost perfect electrical conductivity by certain substances at temperatures approaching absolute zero.

Superconductors—Materials that conduct electricity with almost 100-percent efficiency because they have zero resistance.

NOTES

CHAPTER I
From Slingshots to Computer Chips

1. The report found that the U.S. was holding its own only in the areas of artificial intelligence, flexible computer-integrated manufacturing, and sensor technology; and had fallen behind in the production of advanced materials, advanced semiconductor devices, biotechnology, digital imaging technology, high-density storage, high-performance computing, medical devices and diagnostics, optoelectronics, and superconductors. (U.S. Department of Commerce, *Emerging Technologies: A Survey of Technical and Economic Opportunities*, Spring 1990, p. 13. See also Appendix A.)
2. Stuart Auerbach and Steven Pearlstein, "Aerospace Giant Goes to Taiwan for Edge," Washington *Post*, November 16, 1991, p. C1.
3. Richard W. Stevenson, "Gain for McDonnell Douglas Raises Fears of U.S. Loss," *New York Times*, November 21, 1991, p. D1.
4. Carnegie Commission on Science, Technology, and Government, *Technology and Economic Performance*, Washington, D.C., September 1991, p. 13; U.S. General Accounting Office, International Trade, *U.S. Business Access to Certain Foreign State-of-the-Art Technology*, September 1991, p. 9.
5. U.S. Senate, speech on Senate floor by Senator Ernest F. Hollings, June 4, 1991, Congressional Record, p. S 6967.
6. U.S. House of Representatives, Committee on Energy and Commerce, Subcommittee on Commerce, Consumer Protection and Competitiveness, Representative Richard Gephardt testimony, February 21, 1991.
7. Geoffrey Perret, *A Country Made for War* (New York: Random House, 1989), p. 96, cited in TASC (The Analytic Sciences Corporation), *Foreign Vulnerability of Critical Industries*, report, March 1, 1990.
8. Council on Competitiveness, *Gaining New Ground: Technology Priorities for America's Future*, March 1991, p. 1.
9. U.S. General Accounting Office, *U.S. Business Access*, p. 3.
10. U.S. Senate, Committee on Commerce, Science and Transportation, *Acquisitions by Foreign Companies*, June 10, 1987.
11. Connie Bruck, "Leap of Faith," *New Yorker*, September 9, 1991, p. 71.
12. Steven R. Weisman, "Film Changes After Japanese Buy Studio," *New York Times*,

November 20, 1991, p. 1; Steven R. Weisman, "Hollywood Bows to Sumos and Drops a Film in Japan," *New York Times*, February 5, 1992, pp. C15, 19.

13. See chs. VI and VII for a fuller discussion of the relationship of defense dependence and U.S. allies. See also U.S. Congress, Office of Technology Assessment, *Arming Our Allies: Cooperation and Competition in Defense Technology*, May 1990.

14. Center for Strategic and International Studies, *Deterrence in* Washington, D.C. *Decay: The Future of the U.S. Defense Industrial Base*, May 1989, p. 5.

15. U.S. House of Representatives, Committee on Banking, Finance and Urban Affairs, Subcommittee on Economic Stabilization, *New Industrial Base Initiative*, introductory statement of Subcommittee Chair Mary Rose Oakar (Democrat— Ohio) citing General John A. Wickham, Jr., recently retired army chief of staff, July 8, 1987, p. 2. Earlier, in 1980, the Armed Services Committee of the House of Representatives had warned of the erosion of the defense-industrial base. See U.S. House of Representatives, Defense Industrial Base Panel of the Committee on Armed Services, *The Ailing Industrial Base: Unready for Crisis*, Report, 96th Cong., 2nd sess., December 1980; U.S. House of Representatives, Committee on Armed Services, *Capability of U.S. Defense Industrial Base*, hearings, 96th Cong., 2nd sess., November 1980.

16. Department of Defense, Report to the Secretary of Defense by the Under Secretary of Defense (Acquisition), *Bolstering Defense Industrial Competitiveness*, July 1988.

17. Department of Defense, *Report of the Defense Science Board Study of the Defense Industrial and Technology Base*, October 1988.

18. Although the measure was approved by the House of Representatives in both 1990 and 1991, it failed to reach the floor of the Senate. See Executive Office of the President, *President's Proposed Budget for Fiscal Year 1991*, pt. two, 1990, p. 39. The American Technology Pre-eminence Act of 1991 was passed in the House of Representatives by a vote of 296 to 122, overwhelming enough to override a veto. The administration also strongly objected to a provision authorizing up to $100 million in government loans to help companies commercialize technologies. See Martin Tolchin, "House Plan Fuels Debate on Business," *New York Times*, July 22, 1991, p. D3; U.S. House of Representatives, *American Technology Preeminence Act*, Report 102-134, to accompany H.R. 1989, pp. 20–21.

19. The technologies included computer simulation and imaging, microelectronics and optoelectronics, ceramics, composites, aeronautics, sensors and signal processing, and applied molecular biology. The report also urged that America focus not merely on basic research, but also on the commercialization of that research: "The key to future U.S. competitive success involves a fundamental change in the way U.S. industry competes in the marketplace. U.S. research institutions and businesses must place greater emphasis on deployment of new technologies. Moreover, discovery, development and deployment must be integrated and viewed as concurrent rather than sequential activities. U.S. industry must be infused, from the boardroom to the factory floor, with a relentless desire to constantly improve both product and production methods." (Executive Office of the President, Office of Science and Technology Policy, *Report of the National Critical Technologies Panel*, March 22, 1991.) See ch. V for further discussion of critical technologies.

20. Evelyn Richards and T. R. Reid, "Japanese Overtures to U.S. Scientists," *International Herald Tribune*, May 22, 1991.

21. Department of Defense, *Report of the Defense Science Board*.

22. U.S. Congress, Office of Technology Assessment, *Arming Our Allies*.

23. The Congressional Research Service found that "spot shortages revealed a significant dependency on foreign-made components," and referred to the Defense Science Board report of 1988, which found the U.S. military "dangerously dependent on foreign suppliers." The conclusions of the CRS were reiterated by the OTA and the GAO. See Congressional Research Service, *Persian Gulf War:*

Defense Policy Implications for Congress, by Ronald O'Rourke, May 15, 1991, p. 71.

24. Andrew Pollack, "In U.S. Technology, a Gap Between Arms and VCRs," *New York Times,* March 4, 1991, p. D8.
25. U.S. Department of Commerce, *Implementation of DPA Authorities, Defense Priorities and Allocations Systems,* April 1991.
26. Bernard Baruch, "A Few Kind Words for Uncle Sam," *Collier's,* June 12, 1948, pp. 458–63.
27. Using sources from the U.S. Department of Commerce and *The Wall Street Journal,* the U.S. Council on Competitiveness reported that, "even before the recession, U.S. per capita disposable income, considered one of the best measurements of living standards, had started to decline [measured in terms of the dollar's 1982 buying power]. . . . Other living standard indicators—hourly pay and the net worth of consumers—show similar declines." See U.S. Council on Competitiveness, *Challenges,* July 1991, p. 3. See also Kevin Phillips, *The Politics of Rich and Poor* (New York: Random House, 1990).
28. Martin and Susan Tolchin, *Buying into America: How Foreign Money Is Changing the Face of Our Nation* (New York: Times Books/Random House, 1988).
29. Martin Tolchin, "Union Takes On Chinese-owned Factory," *New York Times,* September 6, 1989, sec. A, p. 14.
30. M. and S. Tolchin, *Buying into America,* p. 1.
31. A group of senators and representatives tried to alert the executive branch to the national-security perils of the Saudi purchase. This "joint venture provides Saudi Arabia with unprecedented influence over U.S. downstream oil operations . . . a guaranteed outlet for Saudi crude . . . at a time when our dependence on foreign oil is growing at an alarming rate," said a letter to Secretary of the Treasury Nicholas Brady from Senators Jeff Bingaman and Howard Metzenbaum, and Representatives John Bryant and Edward Markey. "Should that occur, the harm to the domestic oil production industry could be irreparable . . . [and] could seriously increase U.S. dependence on foreign oil, threaten the viability of the domestic oil industry, and jeopardize the well-being of American consumers." (Letter to Secretary Nicholas Brady, December 9, 1988.) Brady forwarded the letter to CFIUS, which allowed the sale, despite gentle reminders from the legislators that Saudi interests have not always meshed with ours; in fact, they have often collided. Recollections of the Saudi participation in the 1973–74 oil embargo, the artificial oil-shortages of 1978–79, and subsequent price reductions that devastated the domestic oil industry reinforced their point.
32. David Pugliese, "Canada Holds Firm on de Havilland Sale," *Defense News,* July 8, 1991, p. 26.
33. M. and S. Tolchin, *Buying into America,* p. 11.
34. See ch. III for a more comprehensive discussion of the Exon-Florio amendment and the CFIUS process.
35. Linda Spencer, *Foreign Investment in the United States: Unencumbered Access,* Economic Strategy Institute, 1991, p. 1. See also appendices B and C for more detailed lists of sales of companies in the critical-industry category to foreign investors.
36. Martin Tolchin, "Monsanto Unit Sale Faces Inquiry," *New York Times,* December 21, 1988, p. D3.
37. Japanese investors spend $400 million per year in the U.S. See Pat Choate, *Agents of Influence* (New York: Alfred A. Knopf, 1990).
38. At least half of all foreign investment goes unreported, because of failures in the government's system of data collection, which does not consider an investment "foreign," for example, if the money comes from an American bank or some other domestic source.
39. Bingaman amendment to the Defense Production Act of 1987.
40. U.S. Congress, Office of Technology Assessment, *Holding the Edge: Maintaining*

the Defense Technology Base (Washington, D.C.: U.S. Government Printing Office, April 1989), p. V.

41. Ibid.
42. Susan Walsh Sanderson, "The Consumer Electronics Industry and the Future of American Manufacturing," Washington, D.C.: Economic Policy Institute, 1989.

CHAPTER II

Shooting Down the Goodyear Blimp

1. U.S. Senate, Banking, Housing and Urban Affairs Committee, Robert E. Mercer testimony, March 4, 1987.
2. The "partnership loophole" in the Hart-Scott-Rodino Premerger Notification rules enables companies formed as partnerships to avoid filing premerger notices, since partnerships are not considered to have ultimate parent entities.
3. U.S. House of Representatives, Committee on the Judiciary, Subcommittee on Monopolies and Commercial Law, *Mergers and Acquisitions*, hearings, H.R. 35, ser. no. 124, April 3 and 25, 1985, and November 18, 1986.
4. U.S. House of Representatives, Banking, Finance and Urban Affairs Committee, Dennis W. Rich testimony, February 8, 1989, p. 2.
5. U.S. House of Representatives, *Mergers and Acquisitions*, p. 299.
6. Michael Lev, "Goodyear's Pipeline: A White Elephant," *New York Times*, July 8, 1990, p. F4.
7. U.S. House of Representatives, *Mergers and Acquisitions*, p. 308.
8. Ibid., p. 301.
9. Ibid., p. 305.
10. Rich testimony.
11. Company leaders also claimed that these investments paid off: sales grew from $5.8 billion in 1976 to $9.6 billion in 1985; the debt was lowered from 53 percent in 1976 to 28.4 percent in 1985; productivity increased by 30 percent; and the share price of company stock grew at an average compound rate of 14 percent a year. (Mercer testimony, pp. 330–32.)
12. Jonathan P. Hicks, "All About the Tire Industry," *New York Times*, February 11, 1990, p. 8.
13. Mari Yamaguchi, "Japan May Revise Securities Law to Stem Hostile Raiders," Washington *Post*, February 1, 1990.
14. Martin Tolchin, "Hostile Bids by Foreigners on the Rise," *New York Times*, December 27, 1988, p. D1; U.S. General Accounting Office, *Foreign Investment: Foreign Hostile Takeovers of U.S. Firms*, December 1988. Allan I. Mendelowitz, who directed the study, noted that the previous largest hostile takeover was the 1984 acquisition of the Shell Oil Company by the Royal Dutch/Shell Group, a Netherlands company, for $5.7 billion; only five hostile takeover attempts were launched in 1987, four in 1986, three in 1985, and two in 1984. In comparison, there were six major hostile takeovers by foreigners in the first six months of 1988; the two largest were for $6.6 billion and $5.2 billion. These did not include the $5.7-billion acquisition of the Pillsbury Company several months later by Grand Metropolitan P.L.C., a British conglomerate. The Pillsbury board at first resisted Grand Met's hostile bid, but after Grand Met's successful tender offer and a court's declaration that Pillsbury's antitakeover defenses were illegal, the board yielded. Three of the hostile takeovers were by British companies: Batus Industries' $5.2-billion acquisition of Farmer's Group, an insurance company; Beazer P.L.C.'s $1.7-billion acquisition of Koppers Company, a construction-and-chemicals concern, and Tate & Lyle's $1.5-billion acquisition of Staley Continental Inc., a corn-refining and food-services company. Two takeovers were completed by French companies: Hachette S.A.'s $450-million puchase of Grolier,

Inc., a publishing house, and Compagnie de Saint-Gobain's $76-million acquisition of Wolverine Technologies, a vinyl manufacturer.

15. Martin Tolchin, "Tracking a Foreign Presence in U.S. Military Contracting," *New York Times*, January 1, 1989, p. E5.

16. That amounted to an earnings loss of $90.1 million and an operating loss of $30.4 million in the first quarter of 1991; interest payments on its staggering $3.31-billion debt totaled an equally staggering $81.7 million for the first quarter of the year alone. Goodyear blamed its losses on being "weighted down by debt, overcapitalization, and slumping sales," with debt the biggest item. (Dana Milbank, "Goodyear Posts Biggest Loss for Quarter in Firm's History," *Wall Street Journal*, European ed., April 25, 1991, p. 5.)

CHAPTER III
Exon-Florio

1. U.S. Senate, Committee on Commerce, Science and Transportation, *Foreign Acquisitions of Domestic Companies*, hearing, June 10, 1987, p. 28. The Exon-Florio bill originated as an amendment to the Omnibus Trade Act of 1988, where it was specifically designated as an amendment to the Defense Production Act, which is subject to annual renewal.

2. Congressional Research Service, *Foreign Investment: The Exon-Florio National Security Test*, September 26, 1990, p. 1. See also Jose E. Alvarez, "Political Protectionism and United States International Investment Obligations in Conflict: The Hazards of Exon-Florio," *Virginia Journal of International Law*, vol. 30, no. 1 (Fall 1989), pp. 1–187.

3. Martin and Susan Tolchin, *Buying into America: How Foreign Money Is Changing the Face of Our Nation* (New York: Times Books/Random House, 1988), p. 9.

4. Ibid., p. 12.

5. U.S. Senate, *Foreign Acquisitions*, p. 3.

6. Ibid., p. 13.

7. Ibid., p. 27.

8. Ibid., p. 47.

9. Paul Volcker, letter to Senator Ernest F. Hollings, Democrat of South Carolina and chairman of the Senate Banking Committee, entered in the Commerce Committee record, June 9, 1987.

10. Clayton Yeutter, letter to Senator John Danforth, entered in the Commerce Committee record, June 10, 1987.

11. Martin Tolchin, "Agency on Foreign Takeovers Wielding Power," *New York Times*, April 24, 1989, p. D6.

12. Letters dated December 19, 1988.

13. U.S. Congress, House Committee on Energy and Commerce, Bradley Larschan testimony, February 26, 1991, p. 8.

14. Clyde H. Farnsworth, "U.S. Stops Acquisition by Japanese," *New York Times*, April 18, 1989, p. D1.

15. Larschan testimony, p. 10.

16. Ibid., p. 11.

17. Martin Tolchin, "U.S. Will Scrutinize a Chinese Deal," *New York Times*, December 5, 1989, p. D4.

18. Andrew Rosenthal, "Bush Urged to Void Sale of Airplane-Parts Maker to Chinese," *New York Times*, February 2, 1990, p. A9.

19. Larschan testimony, p. 13.

20. Ibid., p. 14.

21. Congressional Research Service, *The Semi-Gas Systems Sale: Technology and National Security Issues*, March 12, 1991, p. 4.

22. Ibid., p. 12.
23. Ibid., p. 8.
24. Ibid., p. 9.
25. Larschan testimony, p. 16.
26. U.S. Congress, House Energy and Commerce Committee, Subcommittee on Commerce, Consumer Protection and Competitiveness, Kevin Kearns testimony, February 26, 1991, p. 2.
27. U.S. General Accounting Office, *National Security Reviews of Foreign Investment*, February 26, 19991, pp. 7–9.
28. Ibid., p. 10.
29. Larschan testimony, p. 20. For a fuller exposition of this viewpoint, see Alvarez, "Political Protectionism."
30. Larschan testimony, pp. 18, 21–22.
31. U.S. House of Representatives, Energy and Commerce Committee, Subcommittee on Commerce, Consumer Protection and Competitiveness, Richard Gephardt testimony, February 21, 1991.
32. Kearns, testimony, pp. 4–6.

CHAPTER IV
The Eyes of the Dragonfly

1. Defense Production Act, 1950, as amended. See Appendix D for a chronology of FSX negotiations. The term "FSX" is spelled either "FS-X," or "FSX." For purposes of simplicity, this chapter uses "FSX," regardless of the style used by individual sources.
2. Michael Green's *Kokusanka: FSX and Japan's Search for Autonomous Defense Production*, Working paper, Cambridge, Mass.: MIT-Japan Program, May 1990, provides an excellent discussion of Japanese internal politics. Green illustrates how fierce were the internal politics over this issue, as well as the winners and losers in the ensuing battles.
3. *Time*, April 24, 1989.
4. Clyde Prestowitz, "Giving Japan a Handout: Why Fork Over $7 Billion in Aircraft Technology?," Washington *Post*, January 29, 1989, pp. D1 and D4.
5. For a fuller discussion of Prestowitz's analysis of the FSX, see the preface to the paperback edition of his book, *Trading Places* (New York: Basic Books, 1989), pp. 5–58.
6. U.S. Senate, Armed Services Committee, Defense and Technology Subcommittee, hearing, March 10, 1989.
7. General Accounting Office, *U.S.-Japan FS-X Program*, May 1989.
8. Editorials include: "The FSX Decision," Washington *Post*, March 17, 1989, p. A18; "The Flaw in the Deal," *New York Times*, May 7, 1989, sec. 3, p. 1; "Why General Dynamics Wants to Fly With Japan," *Business Week*, March 20, 1989, p. 7. Excellent newspaper coverage of the FSX included articles by Clyde H. Farnsworth, David E. Sanger, Thomas H. Hayes, Bernard Weinraub, Steven R. Weisman, and Louis Uchitelle of *The New York Times*; Shigehiko Togo, Fred Hiatt, David Hoffman, Evelyn Richards, Ann Devroy, and Stuart Auerbach of the Washington *Post*; Paul Magnusson, Dave Griffiths, and Neil Gross of *Business Week*; John Greenwald of *Time*; Eduardo LaChica of *The Wall Street Journal*; Daniel Sneider, Michael Green, and David Silverberg of *Defense News*; Pat Towell of *Congressional Quarterly*; and Peter Ennis of *Tokyo Business*.
9. "Japan's Aerospace Industry: Implications for the Global Market," Booz, Allen, 1988.
10. Pat Towell, "U.S.-Japan Fighter Jet Deal Is Cleared for Takeoff," *Congressional Quarterly*, May 20, 1989, pp. 1198–99. An excellent government source on the FSX issue is the Congressional Research Service's *The FSX Technology: Its Rela-*

tive Utility to the United States and Japanese Aerospace Industries, written by John D. Moteff, April 12, 1989. Specifically, the Byrd resolution:

—prohibited any transfer to Japan of certain jet-engine technologies, including computerized fuel controls and the design of the "hot section" of an engine where combustion occurs;

—expressed the sense of the Congress that any agreement covering joint production guarantee U.S. firms at least 40 percent of the value of the production of the planes and spare parts to be used over the life of the FSX fleet; and

—required the secretary of commerce to review the commercial implications of the FSX agreement and required the president to take account of the secretary's views.

11. Congressional Record, 101st Congress, May 16, 1989, vol. 135, no. 62, p. S 5313.
12. Ibid., p. S 5314.
13. Ibid., p. S 5341.
14. Ibid., p. S 5342.
15. Congressional Record, House of Representatives, June 7, 1989, p. H 2391.
16. "The Competitive Status of the U.S. Civil Aviation Manufacturing Industry" (Washington, D.C.: National Academy Press, 1985), cited in ibid., p. H 2369.
17. *Defense News*, February 26, 1990.
18. Congressional Record, Senate, May 16, 1989, p. S 5346.
19. Andrew J. Button, "Cooperation in the Development of the FS-X: An Analysis of the Decision Process," unpublished manuscript, Executive Research Project, Industrial College of the Armed Forces, Fort McNair, D.C., 1989, p. 29. See also Frank S. Turek III, "FSX: An Analysis of the Decision Process Within the Department of Defense," unpublished paper, Department of Public Administration, George Washington University, December 14, 1989.

   For DoD operating instructions for negotiating the FSX, see Department of Defense Directive No. 5530.3, *International Agreements*, June 11, 1987; Title 22, Code of Federal Regulations, pt. 181, #181.1, 22 CFR Ch. 1 (4-1-85 Edition), subchapter S—International Agreements, pp. 448–54; U.S. Congress, Department of Defense Authorization Bill, 1989, Statute #2504, Defense Memoranda of Understanding. This bill orders the secretary of defense to "consider the effect of each memorandum of understanding [with] one or more foreign countries . . . [on] the defense industrial base of the United States."
20. Indeed, Tyler's predictions proved true later on, when Japan indicated its unwillingness to coproduce anything with the U.S. and rebuffed DoD's efforts to create a joint venture. See Michael Green, "DoD Seeks Japanese Cooperation," *Defense News*, July 16, 1990, pp. 7, 12. Perhaps to send a message to the United States, Japan also began seeking greener pastures for joint venturing, such as that between Mitsubishi and the German company Daimler-Benz. For additional articles, see, Bill Powell et al., "Will Aerospace Be Next?," *Newsweek*, March 19, 1990, pp. 36–37; Michael Green and David Silverberg, "Japan Seeks MLRS, Aircraft in Continued Defense Buildup, *Defense News*, May 21, 1990, pp. 1, 8; Richard J. Samuels and Benjamin C. Whipple, "The FSX and Japan's Strategy for Aerospace," *Technology Review*, October 1989, pp. 43–51; and Jeff Shear, "FS-X Fighter Program Hits Turbulence in Cost, Politics," *Insight*, December 17, 1990, pp. 28–29.
21. He also argued that the facts of international economic life dictated "strategic alliances with foreign companies . . . [as a] fundamental part of that strategy" (Herbert F. Rogers, "Why We Backed the FS-X Deal," Washington *Post*, May 3, 1989, p. A27).
22. U.S. General Accounting Office, *U.S. Military Coproduction Programs Assist Japan in Developing Its Civil Aircraft Industry*, March 1982.

23. U.S. General Accounting Office, testimony, *U.S.-Japan FS-X Codevelopment Program*, statement of Frank C. Conahan, May 16, 1989, p. 5.
24. Ibid., pp. 7–9.
25. Frank C. Conahan, letter to Senator Alan Dixon, May 11, 1989.
26. Specifically, the beam of phased-array radar is steered electronically, instead of by a movable dish. Incoming targets are tracked by radar, which also conveys guiding signals to interceptors. An antenna on the interceptor seeks out radar reflections from the target, thus bringing the radar on the ground closer to the action. On-ground computers then send back signals to the Patriot, giving it greater accuracy at its final stages of operation.
27. Conahan testimony, p. 10.
28. Ibid.
29. For excellent discussions of the cross-cultural problems confronting the U.S. and Japan, see Karel Van Wolferen, *The Enigma of Japanese Power* (New York: Alfred A. Knopf, 1989); Richard Halloran, *Japan: Images and Realities* (Rutland, Vt.: Charles E. Tuttle, 1969); and William J. Holstein, *The Japanese Power Game* (New York: Scribner's, 1990).
30. Kearns argues convincingly that the president needs a "Team B," specifically to formulate policies on Japan. See Kevin Kearns, "After FSX: A New Approach to U.S.-Japan Relations," *Foreign Service Journal*, December 1989, pp. 43–48.
31. Congressional Record, House of Representatives, June 7, 1989, p. H 2368.
32. Ibid.
33. David E. Sanger, "New Rift in U.S.-Japan Jet Project," *New York Times*, November 19, 1990, pp. D1 and D18.

CHAPTER V
Computer Chips or Potato Chips

1. David E. Sanger, "Key Technology Might Be Sold to the Japanese," *New York Times*, November 27, 1989, p. 1.
2. *New York Times*, May 28, 1990, p. 20.
3. Steven Prokesch, "Fujitsu to Buy ICL Stake," *New York Times*, July 31, 1990, p. D1.
4. "Perkin Unit to Remain U.S. Owned," *New York Times*, May 16, 1990, p. D15.
5. Lee A. Iacocca, "O.K., O.K., Call Me a Protectionist," *New York Times*, February 10, 1991, sec. 4, p. 17.
6. Peter Schweizer, "On the Other Invisible Hand," *Washington Post*, July 22, 1990, p. C5; Adam Smith, *The Wealth of Nations* (London: Penguin, 1970; first published 1776).
7. The preceding year, the Defense Science Board issued a report on defense semiconductor dependency that presaged the industry's problems as well as the defense concerns. See Department of Defense, Defense Science Board, *Defense Semiconductor Dependency*, February 1987.
8. Department of Defense, Report to the Secretary of Defense by the Under Secretary of Defense (Acquisition), *Bolstering Defense Industrial Competitiveness*, July 1988. The Costello Report was backed up by an impressive literature on the defense industrial base, published throughout the 1980s. Many studies make the point that the U.S. can be dependent on foreign sources without being vulnerable, although there does not appear to be much of an attempt to differentiate between dependency and vulnerability. A foreign-source dependency is generally defined as any militarily useful material that can be purchased outside the U.S. or Canada. One particularly impressive report presaging the findings of the Costello Report was a two-part series issued by the MCDC (Mobilization Concepts Development Center) at the National Defense University, called *Industrial Base US Dependence/Vulnerability*; pt. I, authored by Roderick Vawter, was published in 1986, and

pt. II, released in 1987, was co-authored by Jack Nunn, Martin Libicki, and William Taylor. The significance of these reports is that they relied on data from studies that were conducted in the early to mid-1980s; this means that defense officials knew about defense vulnerabilities and were concerned enough to commission studies addressing these problems. Unfortunately, like many studies, these remained ends in themselves, supporting one of their own conclusions: "Foreign dependencies in weapons systems have not been dealt with in any systematic or effective way by DoD. Little action beyond the studies has been taken to identify the existence of foreign dependencies in specific weapons systems and to pursue effective corrective actions which would result in the creation of alternative domestic sources." (Pt. I, pp. iii and iv.) Pt. I of the report also pointed out that "foreign dependence is a national security issue . . . in terms of our ability to expand production in a national security emergency, either a peacetime surge or a wartime mobilization"; that "no effective organizational responsibility exists within DoD for addressing foreign dependence"; and that DoD could reduce the "impacts of foreign dependency . . . through informed management of system development and procurement" (pp. iv, 12–13). Typical of all studies on this subject, *Industrial Base* criticized the fact that information was "hard to find" and that what was found tended to be "misleading, obscure and hard to assess" (p. v). Although commissioned by DoD, the study laid into the Pentagon as well as the civilian government for confusing and conflicting policies and for not managing this issue more effectively. Both studies give weight to industrial-base considerations and fault DoD and its legislative mandate for not balancing industrial-base considerations with the need to give priority to competition, as ordered by the Competition in Contracting Act.

    The Institute for Defense Analyses also played a major role in the thinking in this area. As early as 1985, Dr. Richard Van Atta wrote a report on defense electronics dependencies, emphasizing that a nation can be dependent on a foreign source without being vulnerable as long as there are sufficient source outlets distributed around the world. However, the report noted that key semiconductor-equipment manufacturers were increasingly concentrated in Japan, and even in single companies in Japan, which truly represents vulnerability. Richard Van Atta, *Technical Assessment of U.S. Electronics Dependency*, Washington, D.C.: Institute for Defense Analyses, November 1985.

9. Department of Defense, Report of the 1988 Defense Science Board Study of the Defense Industrial and Technology Base, October 1988. The DSB highlighted the problems of the eroding defense industrial base and urged the government to "eliminate the apparent loss of leadership in key defense technologies." The report warned that the loss of technological leadership blunted the national strategy of "deterrence . . . [which] relies on convincing a potential aggressor that the U.S. is fully capable of countering any form of aggression."

10. Center for Strategic and International Studies, *Deterrence in Decay: The Future of the U.S. Defense Industrial Base*, May 1989, p. 5. Unfortunately, trying to track the data bases on which the CSIS figures on fifth-and sixth-level subcontractors were based was fruitless, leading to a number of blind alleys at the Pentagon. The material was either classified, suppressed, or destroyed, and had to be taken on faith. One data base, Project Socrates, tried to track these sales, but lost its funding in July 1990. Michael Sekora, the Pentagon official responsible for the list, left the department shortly before his project was deep-sixed. Information collection on the loss of subcontractors appeared as fragmented and inadequate as the collection of foreign-investment data, with officials just as adamant about the necessity for maintaining the status quo. Many defense analysts cannot understand why the Department of Defense does not introduce a reporting requirement so that, at the very least, the agency would have a record of which companies were sold and to whom. No such requirement exists at this time. As a result, DoD officials must rely on the data collected by CFIUS, located in the Treasury

Department. Those data are not available to the public, and are exempt from the Freedom of Information Act.

11. Ibid., pp. 11–12.

12. Specifically, "forward deployed, qualitatively superior conventional forces and theater nuclear forces; a deployable strategic reserve to reinforce U.S. forward commitments and those of U.S. allies; and the ability to preserve the qualitative superiority of U.S. weaponry over the long term" (ibid., p. 10).

13. Ibid., p. 13.

14. Ibid., p. 14.

15. *Deterrence in Decay* also identifies import penetration into critical defense industries as one of the most significant measures of industrial performance and gives the U.S. a low grade in responding to its challenges. Judging from the data, import penetration and foreign acquisitions both seem to create "undesirable foreign dependencies that, during peacetime, could sap the technological competitiveness of U.S. weaponry and that, during wartime, could disrupt the flow of materiel to U.S. or allied forces in combat." Compared with the manufacturing base as a whole in the 1980s, the findings report that fifty-two critical defense sectors experienced significantly more import penetration, particularly in machine tools, industrial machinery, and office machinery. In sum, import penetration grew in 104 of 122 critical defense sectors, while in at least forty-eight of 215 relevant sectors there was "ample reason for concern." What these numbers mean in real terms is that in time of crisis the U.S. might not be able to overcome shortages of critical items, and could not support a war "on the scale of Vietnam without a major mobilization effort to rebuild domestic production." (Ibid., pp. 2, 36.)

16. Martin Tolchin, "Crucial Technologies: 22 Make the U.S. List," *New York Times*, March 17, 1989, p. Dl. The twenty-two critical technologies included microelectronic circuitry; preparation of gallium arsenide and other compound semiconductors; software-design productivity; parallel processing for high-speed computing; robotics; simulation and modeling; integrated optics that use light instead of electicity for circuits and computers; fiber optics, used in telecommunications cables; sensitive radars; passive sensors, to detect targets or monitor equipment without emitting a signal; automatic target recognition; phased arrays, a kind of radar that does not require moving an antenna; data fusion, in which machines process raw data into more usable forms; signature control, which is used in creating hard-to-detect weapons; computational fluid dynamics, in which computers simulate the flow of liquids or gases; air-breathing propulsion, which can improve jet-engine efficiency; high-power microwaves, which can be used as weapons; mobile high-power lasers; kinetic kill energy, a potential use of electromagnetic energy in firing projectiles at high speeds; lightweight composite materials; superconductivity, which can be used to create devices in which electrical resistance is very low; and biotechnology materials and processing.

17. Two new technologies were added, weapon-system environment and high-energy density materials, while others were either combined or—like high-power microwaves and phased-array radar—dropped from the list (George Leopold, "U.S. Faces Tough Competition in Critical Technologies," *Defense News*, July 16, 1990, p. 6). See also Senator Jeff Bingaman, press release, March 15, 1989.

18. While Japan led the U.S. in some key technologies, NATO allies, Israel, Switzerland, and the Soviet Union matched the U.S. in superconductivity, composite materials, biotechnology, machine intelligence and robotics, weapon-system environment, parallel computing, and others. The Soviet Union scored ahead of the U.S. in pulsed power, and matched it in hypervelocity projectiles, weapon-system environment and high-energy density materials. The list, a real apples-and-oranges grab-bag, made little sense from a technological point of view: superconductivity doesn't yet exist; biotechnology is a very broad and applied area of research, whereas hypervelocity is narrow and applied. It is also interesting that,

for purposes of the critical technologies list, even before the passage of the U.S.-Canada Free Trade Pact Canada was not considered "foreign" because of what is known as the "reliability factor." Except for a few highly classified projects, and as far back as the 1940s, Canada has always been considered part of the U.S. defense industrial base, as well as "domestic," from the point of view of Buy America legislation. For a discussion of Buy America legislation on defense, see Department of Defense, A Report to the United States Congress by the Secretary of Defense, *The Impact of Buy American Restrictions Affecting Defense Procurement*, July 1989.

19. Leopold, "U.S. Faces Tough Competition." See also Aerospace Industries Association of America, Inc., *Key Technologies for the 1990s: An Overview*, 1987. The aerospace-industry leaders identify composite materials, very large-scale integration (VLSI), software development, propulsion systems, advanced sensors, optical-information processing, artificial intelligence, and ultrareliable electronic systems.

20. The report cited technologies involving materials and manufacturing, information and communications, biotechnology and life sciences, aeronautics and surface transportation, and energy and the environment. Included in the surface-transportation-technologies section of the report were the development of "intelligent vehicle/highway systems," often referred to as "smart cars" and "smart highways," and electrically powered vehicles, which rely on advances in batteries and fuel cells. The environmental section involved minimizing pollution; recycling; and the treatment, storage, and disposal of pollutants. The report also urged greater commercial use of new technologies, cautioning that "the key to future U.S. competitive success involves a fundamental change in the way U.S. industry competes in the marketplace." (Executive Office of the President, "Critical Technologies,". . . . See also Martin Tolchin, "White House Lists 22 Areas for Nurturing," *New York Times*, April 26, 1991, p. D17.) Additional technologies listed in the report are: materials processing, electronic and photonic materials, ceramics, composites, high-performance metals and alloys, flexible computer-integrated manufacturing, intelligent processing equipment, micro-and nano-fabrication, systems-management technologies, software, microelectronics and optoelectronics, high-performance computing/networking, high-definition imaging and displays, sensors and signal processing, data storage, computer simulation, applied molecular biology, medical technology, aeronautics, and energy technologies.

21. For a fuller discussion of the reciprocity issue, see Martin and Susan Tolchin, *Buying into America: How Foreign Money Is Changing the Face of Our Nation* (New York: Times Books/Random House, 1988), ch. 17, "Coals to Newcastle: Reciprocity in Reverse, or How Kuwait Came to Pump Oil on U.S. Land," pp. 229–38; and ch. 16, pp. 205–28.

22. U.S. Department of Defense, Defense Science Board, *Critical Industries: A New Strategy for the Nation's Defense Industrial Base*, May 1990, p. 15.

CHAPTER VI
Realeconomik

1. See Appendix E. See also U.S. Congress, Office of Technology Assessment, *Arming Our Allies: Cooperation and Competition in Defense Technology*, May 1990, pp. 42–43.
2. David Silverberg, "DoD May Use Foreign Bearings in Event of Desert Shield Conflict," *Defense News*, November 7, 1991, p. 25.
3. See ch. V. See also U.S. Department of Defense, *Critical Technologies Plan*, prepared for the Committees on Armed Services, U.S. Congress, March 15, 1990, p. ES-1.

4. U.S. Congress, Office of Technology Assessment, *Arming Our Allies: Cooperation and Competition in Defense Technology*, May 1990, p. 12.

5. Robert Reich, "Who Is Us?," *Harvard Business Review*, January–February 1990, pp. 53–64; Robert Reich, "Does Corporate Nationality Matter?," *Issues in Science and Technology*, Winter 1990–91, pp. 40–44.

6. Reich, "Corporate Nationality," p. 42.

7. Zachary Schiller and Roger Schreffler, "Look Who's Taking Japan to Task," *Business Week*, June 4, 1990, p. 64.

8. John Kline, "Trade Competitiveness and Corporate Nationality," *Columbia Journal of World Business*, vol. 24, no. 3 (Fall 1989), p. 26.

9. From remarks made at the March 1990 meeting of the United Nations Association, a private group that addresses international issues.

10. It is even less surprising that within this context both national security and economic benefits are often sacrificed to looser interpretations of nationality and political sovereignty. See Kline, "Trade Competitiveness," p. 27.

11. Security-based exemptions rest on the concept of corporate noninterference in the internal affairs of states, which in turn rests on the government's ability to resist outside political influence that might be channeled through a foreign-based corporation. In the United States, foreign political influence has risen dramatically in proportion to the upsurge in foreign investment—so much so that foreign multinationals now control more than a hundred PACs in the U.S. through their U.S. subsidiaries. The justification? That their U.S. subsidiaries should be considered U.S. corporations, even if they are controlled by a foreign parent. See U.S. Senate, Hearing before the Committee on Finance, *Foreign Influence on the U.S. Political Process*, testimony of Susan J. Tolchin, September 19, 1991, p. 52; Martin and Susan Tolchin, *Buying into America: How Foreign Money Is Changing the Face of Our Nation* (New York: Times Books/Random House, 1988), chs. 1, 2, 8, 18.

12. William J. Holstein et al., "The Stateless Corporation," *Business Week*, May 14, 1990, p. 104.

13. John Culbertson, "The New Foreign Ownership in the U.S.: Its Causes and Implications," *Southern Business & Economic Journal*, January 1990, p. 90.

14. Brian Silver, "Computers, and a Sealed Room in Israel," *New York Times*, February 17, 1991, sec. 3, p. 13.

15. Iraq did business with a majority of the companies (Libya came in second), including Imwako GMBH, a company that sold Iraq "magnets for its uranium enrichment plant" and made "technical improvements on SCUD-B missiles." Other sales that warranted congressional attention include: The Messerschmidt-Boelkow-Blohm (MBB) sales list ("fuel air explosive technology, . . . SAAD-16 chemical and missile weapons development plant, combat helicopters, . . . anti-tank rockets, and electronics and testing for Condor 2 missiles"); Pilot Plant's "chemical warfare plant"; Loi Industrial Furnace Facilities' "furnaces for cannon installation"; Walter Thosti Boswai (WTB)'s "Construction of four nerve case plants"; Water Engineering Trading GMBH (WET)'s "Chemical substances for manufacture of nerve gases"; Imhausen-Chemie's "chemical warfare plant"; and Hofberger Bau's "buildings for chemical weapons facilities." See U.S. Congress, Subcommittee on Commerce, Consumer Protection and Competitiveness, Committee on Energy and Commerce, *Iraq's Efforts to Acquire U.S. Technology and the Need for Legislation to Give the President Additional Authority to Seize Iraqi Interests in U.S. Firms*, February 21, 1991.

16. Sales also included: advanced computers, and "graphics terminals that could be used to design rockets and analyze their flights, machine tools, computer mapping systems and imaging devices for reading satellite pictures." A great deal of this technology was later destroyed by allied bombing aimed at Iraq's chemical and nuclear-weapons plants. Commerce Department officials claimed they tried to

tighten their policies after Saddam Hussein "threatened to use poison gas on Israel . . . but were rebuffed in interagency meetings by top officials of the State Department." (Stuart Auerbach, "$1.5 Billion in U.S. Sales to Iraq, Washington *Post*, March 11, 1991, pp. A1, A16.)

17. According to a study published by the Simon Wiesenthal Center in 1991, the White House instructed the Pentagon to yield to the Commerce Department and permit export licenses to Iraq for dual-use technologies that could be employed for war or peace. Citing Commerce documents, the study showed that, between 1986 and 1990, four hundred export licenses for Iraq were approved and only seventy-seven turned down. The approved technologies ranged from computer systems to imaging technology to high-temperature furnaces that could be used in a nuclear program. Stephen Bryen, formerly deputy undersecretary of defense for trade-security policy, confirmed a 1986 National Security Directive that urged the Pentagon to be "more forthcoming on Iraq," listing specific cases where the Pentagon's Defense Technology Security Agency had "obstructed the export of technology to Iraq." Commerce official Dennis Kloske was, in essence, fired several months following the publication of the directive, after testifying before Congress that the White House and the State Department had ignored his warnings to limit American technology to Iraq months before the invasion of Kuwait. The White House denied that Kloske—undersecretary for export administration—was being fired, but Kloske's remarks, distinctly out of character for official Washington, almost invited his dismissal. "I decided to employ the only option available to a bureaucrat," he told Congress. "I tried to tie up all sales in red tape." (Clyde H. Farnsworth, "Official Reported to Face Ouster After His Dissent on Iraq Exports," *New York Times*, January 10, 1991, pp. A1, D2.)

18. Michael Isikoff, "U.S. Seizes Iraqi-owned Tool Company in Ohio," Washington *Post*, September 20, 1990, p. A26; Barnaby J. Feder, "Ohio Company Seized as Iraqi Front," *New York Times*, September 20, 1990, p. D21.

19. U.S. Congress, *Iraq's Efforts*, letter from J. R. McCollough, president and CEO, Stanley Aviation, February 18, 1991.

20. Shintaro Ishihara, *A Japan That Can Say No*, New York: Simon & Schuster, 1991.

21. Paul Blustein, "In Japan, the Politics of Hesitation," Washington *Post*, February 17, 1991, p. C2.

22. A question asking which was the most serious threat to the future of the country— the Soviet military threat or the economic threat from Germany or Japan—drew a 72-percent response on the side of the "economic threat from Japan." The poll also tested public sentiment toward Germany. Even though Germany pledged half as much money as Japan, Japan fared significantly worse: 46 percent of the public said Germany did not contribute its fair share, with about the same percentage favoring stiffer trade practices as a result; 64 percent said that as a result of Japan's behavior they would be less likely to buy Japanese products; and 68 percent felt that the U.S. should take a tougher line on trade with Japan because of the "failure to do more to help the coalition in the gulf." (*Business Week/ Harris Poll*, "Americans Resent Japan's No-Show in the Gulf," *Business Week*, January 1, 1991, p. 28.)

23. U.S. Department of Defense, Defense Science Board, *Critical Industries: A New Strategy for the Nation's Defense Industrial Base*, May 1990, p. 7.

24. U.S. Congress, Office of Technology Assessment, *Arming Our Allies*, p. 36.

25. U.S. Department of Defense, Defense Science Board, *Keeping Access to the Leading Edge: A Consolidated Executive Summary by the Industrial Base Committee to the Defense Science Board*, June 6, 1990, p. 5.

26. Martin Libicki, "What Makes Industries Strategic: A Perspective on Technology, Economic Development, and Defense," National Defense University, April 13, 1989, pp. 13–14.

27. U.S. Department of Defense, Defense Science Board, *Keeping Access*, p. 8.
28. U.S. General Accounting Office, International Trade, *U.S. Business Access to Certain Foreign State-of-the-Art Technology*, September 1991.
29. G. Pascal Zachary, "U.S. Probes Allegations of Withholding of Parts," *Asian Wall Street Journal*, January 21, 1991, p. 1.
30. Deidre A. Depke et al., "Laptops Take Off," *Business Week*, March 18, 1991, pp. 118–24.
31. WMAL-TV, Washington, D.C., February 17, 1991.
32. Paul Blustein, "Japan Inc. Stretches Its Global Foothold," Washington *Post*, March 24, 1991, p. H7.
33. David E. Sanger, "U.S. Parts, Japanese Computer," *New York Times*, September 7, 1988, p. D1.
34. U.S. Department of Defense, Defense Science Board, *Defense Semiconductor Dependency*, February 1987.
35. John Zysman and Stephen S. Cohen, *Manufacturing Matters: The Myth of a Post-Industrial Economy* (New York: Basic Books, 1987); Michael L. Dertouzos et al., *Made in America: Regaining the Productive Edge* (Cambridge, Mass.: M.I.T. Press), 1989.
36. Charles Ferguson, "Computers and the Coming of the U.S. Keiretsu," *Harvard Business Review*, July–August, 1990, p. 66.
37. The formula: insulating their own domestic markets, retaining a secure home base (which leaves plenty of room for mistakes), and pouring lots of resources into research, development, management, and engineering. The Americans did the reverse: instead of reinforcing their strengths and enhancing their ready-made comparative advantages, U.S. companies went for cheap labor, tolerated laissez-faire neglect on the part of their leaders, and ignored modern management techniques that their Japanese competitors adopted with alacrity. (Laura D'Andrea Tyson and John Zysman, *American Industry in International Competition* [Ithaca, N.Y.: Cornell University Press, 1983], p. 34.)
38. Laura D'Andrea Tyson, "They Are Not Us: Why American Ownership Still Matters," *American Prospect*, no. 4 (Winter 1991), pp. 37–48. Tyson uses some data from the work of Raymond Mataloni, Jr., "U.S. Multinational Companies: Operations in 1988," *Survey of Current Business*, 70 (June 1990), pp. 31–44; and John Dunning, "Multinational Enterprises and the Globalization of Innovatory Capacity," paper presented at University of Reading, September 1990.
39. Tyson, "They Are Not Us."
40. Michael E. Porter, "Competitive Advantage," *Harvard Business Review*, March–April 1990, p. 85. See also Michael E. Porter, *The Competitive Advantage of Nations*, (New York: Free Press, 1990).
41. Sylvia Ostrey, a professor at the the University of Toronto and former Canadian trade official, calls this "system friction," or friction among the consumer-oriented, short-term pluralist market economy of the U.S., which favors minimal government involvement; the European social market economy, with its extensive government involvement in business as well as the promotion of social welfare; and the Japanese managerial market economy, unique for its long-term, producer orientation, government involvement in business, and ability to weather external shocks. Recognizing that there can never be any true reconciliation of policies among those systems, she calls for greater multilateral cooperation, especially in the area of investment and technology, where "asymmetry of access to investment and technology"—or absence of reciprocity—is becoming a growing political problem. (Sylvia Ostrey, "Technology and the Global Economy: International Responses," unpublished monograph, International Policy Conference, OECD, Montreal, 1991. See also Sylvia Ostrey:, *Governments and Corporations in a Shrinking World* (New York: Council on Foreign Relations, 1990).
42. Palmerston was advocating British support for the Polish patriots, who were

fighting the partition of their country between Austria and Prussia by the Congress of Vienna. In this case, "England's short-term interests just happened to coincide with their historic values of freedom and independence." (William Safire, "Friends More Than Interests," *New York Times*, February 7, 1991, p. A25.)

CHAPTER VII
Gulf Lessons

1. Geoffrey Perret, *A Country Made for War* (New York: Random House, 1990), p. 96, cited in TASC, "Foreign Vulnerability of Critical Industries," March 1, 1990.
2. TASC, "Foreign Vulnerability," p. 4-2.
3. Ibid., p. 4-3.
4. Andrew Pollack, "In U.S. Technology, a Gap Between Arms and VCRs," *New York Times*, March 4, 1991, p. D8.
5. TASC, "Foreign Vulnerability," p. 4-4.
6. Specifically, the GAO found the following dependencies. In the F/A-18 Hornet fighter, the ejection seat; in the Abrams tank, the optics in the gunner's primary sight; Trimer (an ingredient in the seal connecting the engine and the air-intake system), specialty steel in the doors above the engine, ammunition storage racks; and microcircuits in the ballistic computer. The GAO also found that assembly of the microcircuits for ballistic computers used in the Abrams tank occurred offshore, to lower costs. Extending its inquiry to the production of the four essential parts of the microcircuits—the die or chip, ceramic packaging, lead frames, and bonding wire—the agency found that only the dies were manufactured in domestic facilities by U.S. companies, whose managers warned that U.S. firms were producing less and less of the equipment and materials needed to make the dies. Semiconductor packaging was totally dependent on foreign sourcing for ceramic parts: Japanese firms now control over 90 percent of the U.S. ceramic-packaging market; only one U.S. firm was identified as a potential supplier, Kyocera America, Inc.—a subsidiary of the Japanese parent. Lead frames and bonding wire were also sourced abroad. (U.S. General Accounting Office, National Security and International Affairs Division, *Industrial Base: Significance of DoD's Foreign Dependencies*, January 10, 1991.)
7. U.S. Department of Commerce, *Implementation of DPA Authorities, Defense Priorities and Allocations Systems* (DPAS), April 1991. This system has been in place since 1950, and was intended to expedite production in wartime and bump commercial orders in favor of military ones.
8. Stuart Auerbach, "U.S. Relied on Foreign Made Parts for Weapons," Washington *Post*, March 25, 1991, pp. A1, A17.
9. Pollack, "Arms and VCRs," p. D8.
10. Council on Competitiveness, *Gaining New Ground: Technology Priorities for America's Future*, March 1991.
11. Evelyn Richards, "New Weapons in Works for Future Wars," Washington *Post*, March 3, 1991, p. H1.
12. Martin Libicki, "What Makes Industries Strategic: A Perspective on Technology, Economic Development, and Defense," paper presented at National Defense University, April 13, 1989, p. 52.
13. U.S. Senate, Mark Hatfield testimony, March 19, 1991, Congressional Record, p. S 3480.
14. Clyde H. Farnsworth, "U.S. Is Asked to Review Japan Trade," *New York Times*, March 25, 1991, pp. D1, D2.
15. Vincent A. Mahler, *Dependency Approaches to International Political Economy* (New York: Columbia University Press, 1980), p. 3. Other caveats in Mahler's

typology about large-scale foreign investment in LDCs should prove equally unsettling to Americans who lack the data to examine the extent to which these trends affect them:

(1) "Foreign investment in LDCs, far from serving as a conduit of capital ... actually results in a net drain of capital from host to investor";

(2) "extensive foreign investment means that important sectors of an LDC's economy are subject to the priorities of an outside actor whose interests and objectives may be very different from those of the host country";

(3) "foreign investors play an important and negative role in conditioning internal political structures and policies"; and

(4) "Executive decision making and advanced technology are largely confined to a center based in the industrialized (host) country, with co-opted LDC elites serving as agents of transmission and ... non-elites largely excluded from influence."

16. Pat Choate, *Agents of Influence* (New York: Alfred A. Knopf, 1990).

17. David Wessel and Constance Mitchell, "Fed Has Lost Much of Its Power to Sway U.S. Interest Rates," *Wall Street Journal*, March 12, 1990, p. A1.

18. Benjamin Friedman, *Day of Reckoning* (New York: Random House, 1988).

19. Felix Rohatyn, "America's Economic Dependence," *Foreign Affairs*, vol. 68, special issue (1989), pp. 62–63.

20. "If the company to be acquired did fall within the 4/50 danger zone, and was a non-hostile takeover," wrote Moran, "the U.S. government would impose a requirement that R & D be kept within the United States, with proviso for periodic review." See Theodore Moran, "The Globalization of America's Defense Industries: What Is the Threat? How Can It Be Managed?," paper presented at Georgetown University, October 18, 1989; Theodore H. Moran, "The Globalization of America's Defense Industries: Managing the Threat of Foreign Dependence," *International Security*, vol. 15, no. 1 (Summer 1990), pp. 57–99.

21. William J. Holstein et al., "The Stateless Corporation," *Business Week*, May 14, 1990, p. 105.

22. The Defense Science Board report emphasized that neither DoD nor industry could measure the scope of foreign dependence or identify systems or components that were affected. See U.S. Department of Defense, Defense Science Board, *Critical Industries: A New Strategy for the Nation's Defense Industrial Base*, May 1990.

23. David E. Sanger, "Made in the U.S.A., but by Sharp," *New York Times*, February 22, 1991, pp. D1, D3.

24. U.S. Congress, Office of Technology Assessment, *Competing Economies: America, Europe and the Pacific Rim*, November 1991.

25. Material on DARPA was drawn from interviews and the following sources: "U.S. Technology Strategy Emerges," *Science* (April 5, 1990), p. 20; Joel S. Yudken and Michael Black, "Targeting National Needs," *World Policy*, Spring 1990, pp. 251–88; Robert Kuttner, "Industry Needs a Better Incubator Than the Pentagon," *Business Week*, April 30, 1990, p. 16; Evelyn Richards, "Uncle Sam as Venture Capitalist," *Washington Post*, April 29, 1990, pp. H1, H5; George Leopold and Neil Munro, "Budget Bill Bolsters Tech Base," *Defense News*, November 12, 1990, pp. 3, 53; Andrew Pollack, "America's Answer to Japan's MITI," *New York Times*, March 5, 1990, sec. 3, p. 1; John Markoff, "Pentagon's Technology Chief Out," *New York Times*, April 21, 1990, p. 31; Sandra Sugawara, "Pentagon Agency Invests $4 Million in Chip Firm," *Washington Post*, April 10, 1990, pp. D1, D6; Breck W. Henderson, "DARPA Invests $4 Million as Venture Capital in High-Technology Companies," *Aviation Week & Space Technology*, April 30, 1990, pp. 25–26.

26. "U.S. Technology Strategy Emerges."

27. U.S. House of Representatives, Armed Services Committee, Subcommittee on

Research and Development, statement by Dr. Victor H. Reis, director, Defense Advanced Research Projects Agency, April 23, 1991.

28. "U.S. Technology Strategy Emerges."
29. Other technologies included: ceramic fibers, superconducting electronics, linguistic data processing, and scalable-computer systems. See U.S. Senate, Armed Services Committee, Subcommittee on Defense Industry and Technology, hearing before Senator Jeff Bingaman, chairman, on the Third Annual Critical Technologies Plan, testimony of Dr. Charles Herzfeld, director, Office of Research and Engineering, Department of Defense, and Admiral J. M. Barr, deputy assistant secretary for military applications, Defense Programs, Department of Energy, May 7, 1991.
30. In 1990, ATP awarded grants to eleven out of 250 applicants. These included awards for companies producing goods for computer and communications industries, as well as an $823,000 grant for the Microelectronics and Computer Technology Consortium in Austin, Texas, then headed by Dr. Craig Fields.
31. This prints circuit patterns down to .5 micron. Another company, Genus Inc., also unveiled a machine that "deposits atoms from a gas of vaporized metal to create circuit connections as tiny as 0.4 micron across—far thinner than a human hair." (Otis Port, "Sematech May Give America's Middleweights a Fighting Chance," *Business Week*, December 10, 1990, p. 186.)
32. U.S. Department of Commerce, Office of Technology Administration, *Emerging Technologies: A Survey of Technical and Economic Opportunities*, Spring 1990.
33. Holstein, et al., "Stateless Corporation," p. 105.

CHAPTER VIII
A Matter of Degree

1. Monopolies and Mergers Commission, *The Government of Kuwait and the British Petroleum Company PLC: A Report on the Merger Situation*, presented to Parliament by the Secretary of State for Trade and Industry by Command of Her Majesty, Great Britain, October 1988, p. 65.
2. Ibid., p. 1. See also Monopolies and Mergers Commission, *1989 Review* (London: 1989).
3. See n. 7 below.
4. See British Petroleum, *BP Annual Report and Accounts 1988* (London: Britannica House, 1989).
5. Monopolies and Mergers Commission, *Report*, p. 3.
6. Ibid., pp. 3–4, 45.
7. See "Coals to Newcastle: Reciprocity in Reverse, or How Kuwait Came to Pump Oil on U.S. Land," in Martin and Susan Tolchin, *Buying into America* (New York: Times Books/Random House, 1988), pp. 229–38. In 1982, the U.S. Department of the Interior unsuccessfully challenged the Kuwait Petroleum Company's right to drill on U.S. federal land.
8. Monopolies and Mergers Commission, *Report*, p. 26.
9. Ibid., p. 7.
10. "Trouble Inside Kuwait's Money Machine," *Business Week*, January 21, 1991, p. 44.
11. Monopolies and Mergers Commission, *Report*, p. 27.
12. Ibid.
13. Ibid.
14. Ibid., p. 28.
15. Ibid.
16. Ibid.
17. Ibid., p. 40.
18. Ibid., p. 43.

19. Ibid.
20. Ibid.
21. Ibid., p. 40.
22. Ibid., pp. 46–51.
23. Ibid., p. 55.
24. Ibid., p. 56.
25. Ibid., p. 59.
26. Ibid. pp. 62–63.

CHAPTER IX
Selling Our Science

1. Stephanie Epstein, "Buying the American Mind: Japan's Quest for U.S. Ideas in Science, Economic Policy and the Schools," report prepared for Center for Public Integrity, Washington, D.C., December 1991.
2. The importance of commercialization was emphasized by President Bush, who said in November 1990 that, "If America is to maintain and strengthen our competitive position, we must continue not only to create new technologies, but learn to more effectively translate those technologies into commercial products." That theme was underscored in a White House report the following spring that urged America's academic institutions to help American industry compete globally, and "place a greater emphasis on deployment of new technologies," as well as view "discovery, development and deployment [as] . . . integrated . . . [and] concurrent rather than sequential activities." See Executive Office of the President, Office of Science and Technology Policy, *Report of the National Critical Technologies Panel*, March 22, 1991, p. 4.
3. Calvin Sims, "Business-Campus Ventures Grow," *New York Times*, December 14, 1987, p. D1.
4. Martin Tolchin, "A Debate over Access to American Research," *New York Times*, December 17, 1989, p. E4.
5. The President's Budget for Fiscal Year 1992, pt. two, p. 39.
6. Leslie Helm, "On the Campus: Fat Endowments and Growing Clout," *Business Week*, July 11, 1988, p. 70.
7. Japanese companies that endowed chairs at M.I.T. included Daichi Kangyo Bank (finance), Fujitsu (electrical engineering), Fukutake Publishing (media laboratory), Kokusai Denshin Denwa (media laboratory), Kyocera (materials sciences), Matsushita Bank (finance), Mitsui (international management; contemporary technology), NEC (computers; communications software), Nippon Steel (civil engineering policy), Nomura Securities (finance), TDK (materials), and Toyota (materials). Ibid. See also Pat Choate, *Agents of Influence* [New York: Alfred A. Knopf, 1990], pp. 181–87, for a discussion of Japanese penetration of U.S. educational institutions.)
8. Helm, "On the Campus."
9. Gina Kolata, "M.I.T. Deal with Japan Stirs Fear on Competition," *New York Times*, December 19, 1990, p. 1.
10. Ibid.
11. U.S. House of Representatives, Committee on Government Operations, Subcommittee on Human Resources and Intergovernmental Relations, hearing, *Is Science for Sale? Conflicts of Interest vs. the Public Interest*, June 13, 1989, p. 24.
12. From interview material, but see also David Noble, "The Multinational Multiversity," *Zeta*, April 1989, pp. 17–23.
13. Leonard Silk, "Should Foreigners Share Fruits of U.S. Research?," *International Herald Tribune*, May 25, 1991, p. 9.
14. U.S. House of Representatives, *Is Science for Sale?*, p. 4.
15. Ibid., p. 5.

16. Ibid., p. 174.
17. U.S. General Accounting Office, *Industrial Liaison Programs*, 1988, sec. 3, "Other Characteristics of Foreign Involvement in U.S. Universities."
18. David E. Sanger, "Japan Asks Aid on Next Computers," *New York Times*, March 15, 1991, p. D1.
19. Massachusetts Institute of Technology, *Industrial Liaison Programs*, brochure.
20. Paul E. Gray, "University Research: Who Benefits?," *M.I.T. Report*, July–August 1989, p. 1. For more of his views on the subject, see Paul E. Gray, "Technology Transfer at Issue: The Academic Viewpoint," *IEEE Spectrum*, special report, May 1982, pp. 64–68.
21. U.S. General Accounting Office, *Industrial Liaison Programs*.
22. M. Tolchin, "Debate over Access."
23. U.S. House of Representatives, *Is Science for Sale?*, p. 136.
24. Ibid.
25. Silk, "Should Foreigners Share."

CHAPTER X
The Casino Economy

1. An excellent study of how Japan helped its computer industry grow and thrive in domestic and international markets through selective government intervention is Marie Anchordoguy's *Computers Inc.: Japan's Challenge to IBM* (Cambridge, Mass.: Harvard Council on East Asian Studies, 1989). See also David E. Sanger, "I.B.M. Losing Ground in Japan," *New York Times*, June 3, 1991, pp. D1, D5. Sanger points out that, though IBM had achieved great success in Japan over the years, the company was beginning to suffer declining market share in that nation, in part because of its "decidedly American . . . pedigree," which meant it was "largely frozen out of the public-sector market in Japan—universities, government offices and national laboratories"—leaving the company "little cushion when its commercial business declined."
2. For more on how export controls can hurt U.S. business, see Robert Kuttner, *The End of Laissez-faire* (New York: Alfred A. Knopf, 1991), pp. 197–209.
3. Airbus Industrie is a joint venture of aerospace companies from France, Germany, Britain, and Spain. The large air transports produced by Airbus hold between 150 and 350 seats. See also Congressional Research Service, *The Europe 1992 Plan: Science and Technology Issues*, by Glenn J. McLoughlin, August 23, 1989, pp. CRS 18–20.
4. At the beginning of the 1980s, the U.S. had approximately 85 percent of the computer-systems market, while Japan had less than 5 percent. By 1990, the U.S. share had dropped to 69 percent, while Japan's had risen to over 17 percent. This does not include peripherals (parts and software), in which Japan is gaining even more ground. Nor do these figures include Japan's stake in Siemens or other joint ventures. Most of Japan's growth has come from its own internal computer market, where the U.S. still holds a 40-percent share. (Figures from Tim Miles, senior industrial specialist, Department of Commerce, Office of Computers and Business Equipment.)
5. For additional views on this subject, see Council on Competitiveness, *Japanese Technology Policy: What's the Secret?*, by David W. Cheney, and William W. Grimes, Washington, D.C., February 1991.
6. George Jenkins, "Venture Capital Fund Is Cautious: Who Will Seed Start-ups?," *Harvard Business Review*, November–December 1989, p. 117.
7. Ibid.
8. Evelyn Richards, "In Silicon Valley, a Rebirth of Risk-taking," Washington *Post*, July 29, 1990, pp. H1, and H6.
9. See Martin and Susan Tolchin, *Buying into America: How Foreign Money Is*

Changing the Face of Our Nation (New York: Times Books/Random House, 1988), pp. 1–28.

10. George Gilder, "American Technology at Fire-Sale Prices," *Forbes*, January 22, 1990, pp. 60–64.

11. Ibid.

12. "Bargain Basement Time for U.S. Technology," *Business Week*, January 4, 1989, p. 67.

13. A source of controversy among economists and policymakers continues to be the reason behind the problem of insufficient capital for high-tech investments. One school of thought argues that there are disparities between the U.S. and the rest of the world that work to our nation's disadvantage. One such imbalance involves the price-to-earnings ratio (p/e) in the U.S. versus the p/e ratio in Japan. The average p/e ratio on the New York Stock Exchange in 1989, for example, was 14, while the corresponding figure on the Tokyo Stock Exchange—adjusting for accounting differences—was 40. This means that the average U.S. corporation returned at least $7 on every $100 of equity investment, while a Japanese corporation was only expected to return $2.50. This changed in the early 1990s, with the sharp drop in the Japanese stock market, and a corresponding balance between interest rates in the two countries. However, the disparity that existed during the decade of the 1980s gave Japan a decided edge during a critical period. For an interesting discussion of Japanese stock prices, see Kenneth R. French and James M. Poterba, "Are Japanese Stock Prices Too High?," Working Paper no. 3290, National Bureau of Economic Research, Inc., March 1990. See also Lee Berton, "U.S. Investors Devise Strategies to Value Secretive Japan Firms," *Wall Street Journal*, March 22, 1990, pp. C1, C2. Berton discusses not only the disparities between Japan's inflated p/e ratios—18.3 for Toyota and 30 for Honda, compared with multiples of 8 for General Motors and 6 for Ford—but the secretive reporting practices of Japanese firms. Japanese companies, he writes do not report quarterly results, as they are not required (as U.S. businesses are) to break down their earnings by business segment, and do not feel obliged to inform investors of their hottest profits; in fact, if they make a killing on one product, investors might never hear of it. Money managers sharp enough to figure out the system can make a killing; others can suffer serious losses. As a result of this difference in p/e ratios, "any equity investment that promises to double in value within twelve years would be considered an irresponsible act in the U.S. but worthy of praise in Japan," wrote George N. Hatsopoulos, chairman of the board and president of the Thermo Electron Corporation. Hatsopoulos singles this out as the "overriding factor" responsible for the inability of U.S. industry to incorporate technology into its products; in other words, small wonder that "Japanese managers take a longer view," since the rate of return on equity capital demanded by U.S. stockholders far exceeds the expectations of Japanese stockholders, who are in for the long haul.

    This affects the cost of capital and—more important—the cost of equity. "The cost of capital in general depends on the cost of debt, the cost of equity (which is much higher than the cost of debt) and tax code parameters." See George N. Hatsopoulos, "Technology and the Cost of Equity Capital," paper presented at the National Academy of Engineering Symposium, Washington, D.C., April 5, 1990, pp. 2, 7.

14. Bill Emmott, "The American Money Edge," *Washington Post*, July 7, 1991, pp. B1, B4; Dale W. Jorgenson and Masahiro Kuroda, "Productivity and International Competitiveness in Japan and the United States, 1960–1985," paper delivered at the National Research Council, Committee on Japan, National Academy of Sciences, October 23–24, 1991.

15. See also U.S. Department of Defense, Defense Science Board, *Defense Semiconductor Dependency*, February 1987, pp. 78–79. The DSB makes two critical points about the impossible financial situation of the semiconductor industry in

competing against the more stable, lower-cost capital available to the Japanese manufacturers: (1) "The staying power of the large Japanese industrial entities is suggested by a comparison of the average return on assets of these firms with those of their U.S. counterparts during the era in which Japanese industry was making its major inroads on the world industrial market (the 1970s). It would seem unlikely that any U.S. firm could remain viable for a prolonged period producing a one to three percent return on assets—as has been the case for much of Japanese industry." (2)". . . the average semiconductor manufacturer turns over its entire equivalent ownership (total number of shares divided by annual number of shares exchanged) every six to nine months. A project having a five-year payout is in effect heavily discounted by investors because it will be of direct benefit to owners seven to ten 'generations' in the future. Thus, there is little motivation, in fact little tolerance, for management to seek truly long-term objectives. Rather, management finds itself under continued pressure to produce short-term results. This is in sharp contrast to the basic economic structure of Japanese industry."

16. Some of these critics address disparities in the costs of equity capital, concluding that the cost there, too, has had a considerable impact on long-term U.S. competitiveness. What this means is that the cost of equity in the U.S., the rate at which managers must discount and plan for the future, is not competitive with that in other industrialized nations.

    A cousin of the p/e ratio is the changing debt-equity ratio, which according to some analysts has contributed to the deterioration of the defense industry. The rapid growth of debt in relation to equity in that industry since the early 1980s has resulted from a combination of factors, including: more aggressive bidding by companies, the tightening of the tax code, and tougher procurement policies, which have forced companies to absorb a greater proportion of the cost of weapons development—the last, no doubt, the result of public reaction against lax procurement oversight at DoD which failed to catch the $900 monkey wrenches and $600 toilet seats. In the early 1990s, budget cuts have added to the defense industry's debt problems, a shock after the Reagan defense buildup. (President Bush in his 1992 State of the Union message promised defense cuts that would amount to more than $50 billion by 1997, representing a 30 percent cut since 1988.) In the aerospace industry, all of these conditions led to more than a doubling of debt to shareholders' equity from 1983 to 1990, according to Standard & Poor's aerospace index: from 14 percent to 37 percent. Grumman, for example, climbed from 51 percent to 108 percent of debt to equity. At the same time, the defense industry experienced an increase in institutional investors—pension funds, banks, and investment groups—who brought with them the mixed blessing of new capital on the one hand, and demands for higher short-term returns on their investments on the other. With defense stocks already depressed, pressures to produce higher returns translate into a further limitation on investments in research and development—all part of a long-term trend line in the defense industry. "Since the summer of 1985," testified Joseph Campbell, vice-president of Paine Webber, "defense stocks have underperformed the broader markets by somewhere between 50 and 80 percent. . . . The larger and more sensitive the defense company is . . . dependent on defense company earnings, the more likely the underperformance is to be near 80 percent, the larger conglomerates are closer to 50 percent." See U.S. Senate, Armed Services Committee, Subcommittee on Defense Industry and Technology, Joseph Campbell testimony, September 28, 1989, pp. 77–79. See also Philip Finnegan, "Mounting Debt Threatens Industry," *Defense News*, April 23, 1990, p. 1. On the new trend toward institutional investing in defense stocks, see Philip Finnegan, *Defense News*, June 11, 1990, pp. 1, 28; September 28, 1989, pp. 77–99. See also "The Impact on Defense Industrial Capability of Changes in Procurement and Tax Policy, 1984–1987," *The MAC Group*, February 1989.

17. Raymond S. Haas and John S. Karls, "How Foreign Buyers Can Get Double Tax Deductions," *Mergers and Acquisitions*, July–August 1989, pp. 70–73.
18. Transfer pricing works like this: An item manufactured in Germany at a cost of $80 is sold to an Irish subsidiary for $80. The tax rate in Germany is 48 percent, but because the item was sold to an Irish subsidiary of the same company, no tax is paid. The Irish subsidiary then sells the item at $150 to a U.S. subsidiary, earning a $70 profit. The Irish tax rate is 4 percent; the tax paid, $2.80. The U.S. subsidiary (remember, the parent is still German) sells the item at cost for $150, earning no profit. The Irish subsidiary then lends the money to the U.S. company for future expansion at a tax rate of 34 percent; since the profit was used for expansion, no taxes were paid. (Larry Martz and Rich Thomas, "The Corporate Shell Game," *Newsweek*, April 15, 1990, pp. 48–49.)
19. M. and S. Tolchin, *Buying into America*, pp. 276–77, on gaps in foreign-investment data collection.
20. Robert Pear, "I.R.S. Investigating Foreign Companies over Units in U.S.," *New York Times*, February 18, 1990, pp. 1, 30.
21. M. and S. Tolchin, *Buying into America*, ch. 8, "The 'Juicing' of California: The Influence of Foreign Investors on State Tax Policy," pp. 93–118.
22. Pear, "I.R.S."; Robert Pear, "For the Multinationals a Crackdown on Taxes," *New York Times*, October 30, 1990, p. A23.
23. Robert Pear, "More Tax Avoidance Is Cited," *New York Times*, July 11, 1990, pp. D1, D2.
24. Martz and Thomas, "Corporate Shell Game."
25. Ibid.
26. Advocates also contended that repeal would reduce the level of interest rates for all borrowers offsetting the losses. The tax raised $153 million in 1982, for example. (U.S. Congress, Joint Committee on Taxation, *Background and Issues Relating to the Taxation of Foreign Investment in the United States* [JCS-1-90] January 23, 1990, pp. 75–76.)
27. Ibid.
28. See Appendix F for a list of banks in global competition.
29. Australia, for example, limits foreign ownership to 14 percent of total bank assets. As of 1989, foreign banks held 28.5 percent of the U.S. business-loan market, up from 21.4 percent in 1983. In New York and California, the percentage is much higher; foreign banks in California control 32.4 percent of all business loans. Foreign banks dominate more than 60 percent of the market for "standby letters of credit," used mostly for the extension of trade credits; Japanese-owned banking institutions account for 43.8 percent of this market. Japanese institutions accounted for 53.4 percent of the $40.2-billion increase in U.S. business loans from mid-1987 to mid-1988. (*American Banker*, March 6, 1989, pp. 1, 29. See also M. and S. Tolchin, *Buying into America*, ch. 9, "Foreign Owned U.S. Banks: A Policy Conundrum," pp. 119–30.)
30. E. Gerald Corrigan, "Trends in International Banking in the United States and Japan," *Federal Reserve Board of New York Quarterly Review*, Autumn 1989, p. 1. See also "The Japanese Banks: Emerging into Global Markets," *Salomon Brothers*, September 1989.
31. Robert Guenther and Michael R. Sesit, "U.S. Banks Losing Business to Japanese at Home and Abroad," *Wall Street Journal*, October 12, 1989, p. A12. See also State of Maryland, Senate Committee on Finance, "Foreign Investment in U.S. Banks," Susan J. Tolchin testimony, State of Maryland, Annapolis, Md., July 31, 1990.
32. "Future foreign buyers, like those acquiring industrial concerns, will 'target acquisitions with break-up value in mind,' " added an analyst from Price Waterhouse. See "Enter the US bank raider?," *The Banker*, November 1989, pp. 20–22. *The Banker* also identified fourteen U.S. banks ripe for restructuring and foreign

acquisition, including Chase Manhattan, Manufacturers Hanover Trust, Citibank, Mellon Bank, and Bank of Boston.

33. William Safire, "Breaking the Underworld Bank," *New York Times*, July 11, 1991, p. A21.
34. U.S. General Accounting Office, *Foreign Investment: Concerns in the Banking, Petroleum, Chemicals and Biotechnology Sectors*, May 30, 1990.
35. Michael Quint, "U.S. Banks Cut Global Business As Rivals Grow," *New York Times*, July 5, 1990, pp. A1, D9.
36. Michael Shrage, " 'Uh . . . the Dog Ate the Experiment' and Other Corporate R & D Excuses," Washington *Post*, February 22, 1991, p. C3.
37. Michael Kinsley, "Two American Myths About Japan," Washington *Post*, January 11, 1990.
38. Robert J. Samuelson, "The Excuse Industry," *Newsweek*, December 11, 1989, p. 74.
39. Japanese business and government officials also resist change, particularly when it comes from U.S. trade negotiators. Responding more openly to pressures to reform the antitrust system, one Japanese executive remarked: "You like to say if it isn't broken don't fix it. Well, this isn't broken." See Bill Powell and Rich Thomas, "All in the Family," *Newsweek*, June 3, 1991, p. 36.
40. Associated Press, "Japan Knew of Stock Compensation in 1983," *Investor's Daily*, August 28, 1991, p. 27.
41. U.S. Senate, Committee on Banking, Housing, and Urban Affairs, *Challenges to America's Economic Leadership and How Government and Industry Should Respond*, transcript, September 14, 1990, p. 96.
42. Ibid.
43. Eduardo LaChica, "Chip-making Pioneer in U.S. Found Grief in Seiko Joint Venture," *Wall Street Journal*, May 4, 1990, pp. A1, A5. Sources include an interview with Hall, plus his congressional testimony: before the U.S. Senate, Committee on Commerce, Science and Transportation, *Foreign Direct Investment in the United States*, prepared statement of John H. Hall, March 24, 1988.
44. James Fallows, *More like Us: Making America Great Again* (Boston: Houghton Mifflin, 1989).
45. U.S. Senate, *Challenges*, p. 92.
46. For an interesting discussion of "managed trade" from a global perspective, see David D. Hale, "Global Finance and the Retreat to Managed Trade," *Harvard Business Review*, January–February 1990, pp. 150–62.
47. See also Judy Larsen, "Silicon Valley Fever," *Journal of the American Planning Association*, vol. 53 (Spring 1987), pp. 288–90.
48. Jodie T. Allen, "A New Tax That Even Bush Can Support," Washington *Post*, May 13, 1990, pp. C1, C3.
49. By the first half of 1991, the cost of capital had fallen to 5.9 percent in the U.S., and risen to 6.1 percent in Japan and 4.8 percent in Germany (Christopher Farrell and Ted Holden, "The U.S. Has a New Weapon: Low-Cost Capital," *Business Week*, July 29, 1991, pp. 72–73).

CHAPTER XI
America the Vulnerable

1. Other features of this device include a 155-channel cable-ready tuner, multichannel TV sound, an advanced remote control, and on-screen programming. In their first year of production, ten thousand VCR-2s were delivered in the United States, twenty-five thousand ordered in Europe; VCR-2 was featured on the cover of the catalogue of The Sharper Image, one of the nation's best known consumer-electronics chains.

2. Technology Transfer Task Force, hearing, R. Terren Dunlap testimony, June 7, 1990.

3. *Go-Video, Inc., v. The Motion Picture Association of America, De Laurentiis Entertainment Group, Inc., MGM UA Communications Co., Twentieth Century Fox Film Corp,. . . . Matsushita Electric Industrial Co., Ltd., Samsung Electronics Co., Ltd., et al.,* U.S. District Court of Arizona, CIV-87-0987 PHX RCB, Second Amended Complaint, April 20, 1988, pp. 32–33.

4. Ibid. See also secs. 4 and 16 of the Clayton Antitrust Act (15 U.S.C. # 15, 26), and sec. 1 of the Sherman Antitrust Act (15 U.S.C. # 1).

5. *Go-Video v. Motion Picture Association et al.,*

6. *Audio Video International Magazine,* April 1985.

7. *Go-Video v. Motion Picture Association et al.,* pp. 41–43.

8. Lewis M. Simons, "U.S. Maker of VCR Suing Japanese Firms on Conspiracy Charges," San Jose *Mercury News,* October 23, 1990. Much of the material in this section is based on interviews and court documents, and on excellent articles on the subject, including: Jacob Schlesinger, "At Tokyo Electronics Show, What's New Is Actually Old, or Still in Development," *Wall Street Journal,* October 3, 1990, p. 88; Bill Arnold, "Video Chips to Bridge Image Gap," *EDN,* November 29, 1990, pp. 1, 3; Donna Coco, "The 'Get Up and Go' of Go-Video," *EDN,* November 29, 1990, pp. 1–4; Robert D. Hershey, Jr., "VCR to Beat Was Born (Surprise!) in the U.S.," *New York Times,* July 7, 1990, pp. 1, 19; Stuart M. Dambrot, "High-Tech Toys Are for High-priced Joys," *Japan Times,* October 15, 1990, p. 21; Dennis Wagner, "Go-Video Founder Playing David to Japan's Goliath," Phoenix *Gazette,* July 10, 1990; Larry Armstrong, "This Double-Decker VCR Makes Copying a Snap," *Business Week,* October 8, 1990, p. 156. The 1989 Court decision which found just cause for Dunlap's appeal was *Go-Video Inc. v. Akai Electric Co. Ltd.* 885 Fed 2d 1406. Ninth Circuit, 1989.

9. The six holdouts were the giants of the Japanese electronics industry: Matsushita, Sony, NEC, Sanyo, Sharp, and JVC. In 1990, Go-Video amended its 1988 lawsuit to add patent-infringement charges against these six Japanese companies, alleging that they misused their patents in violation of U.S. antitrust laws to prevent American manufacturers from entering the marketplace. Motions for summary judgment from those companies, arguing that there was not enough evidence to show conspiracy, were subsequently dismissed by the court. The Japanese companies would not negotiate. This meant that the boycott of Go-Video remained in place in Japan, barring potential distributors and suppliers from doing business with the firm. Privately, some Japanese explained that the only reason the EIAJ maintained the boycott was cultural: Unlike the litigious Americans, the Japanese have a strong aversion to lawsuits and are likely to resist ever doing business again with anyone who has sued them. (*Go-Video, Inc., v. Matsushita Electric Industrial Co., Ltd; Panasonic Company, a Division of Matsushita Electric Corporation of America; Victor Company of Japan, Ltd, et al.,* First Amended Complaint, MDL 765-PHX-RCB, CIV 90-0118 PHX RCB, July 20, 1990.) The boycott also raised the potential threat of patent violations and the critical role of timing: with the Japanese patent application still pending, what would prevent Japanese companies from eventually manufacturing dual-deck VCRs on their own in Japan, despite the U.S. court order? This loomed as a very real threat, given the experience of other companies with Japan's reluctant patent system. Texas Instruments, for example, filed a patent application in 1960 in Japan to protect the "integrated circuit"—the basis for the computer chip—co-invented by Jack Kilby, who worked for TI. Japan finally granted the application in 1989; in the interim, TI had had to engage in years of costly litigation against Japanese companies. After winning millions of dollars, TI now faces another legal battle against Fujitsu, which claims that, since the chip it is using bears no resemblance to the original Kilby invention, Fujitsu does not have to continue to pay royalties. The gains the Japanese companies won by enjoying the fruits of Kilby's research

without having to recognize this intellectual property according to fair standards of patent protection are incalculable—certainly hundreds of times greater than the costs of litigation.

10. One U.S. "victor" learned this lesson the hard way. According to an article in *The Wall Street Journal*, an Oregon real-estate developer won a $1.6-million judgment in the U.S. in 1982 against Mansei Kogyo Co., a big cigarette-lighter distributor near Tokyo, and has yet to collect, thanks to the difficulties of enforcement in Japan. In effect, said David Bryant, the developer, "the Japanese people can come over here with all their investments and . . . be immune from our courts." The lawyer for Mansei claimed that the award reflected "punitive damages, a concept not found in Japanese law." See Richard B. Shmitt, "Claimant Against Japanese Learns the Word for Delay," *Wall Street Journal*, December 14, 1990, p. B1.

11. William Holstein et al., "Mighty Mitsubishi Is on the Move," *Business Week*, September 24, 1990, pp. 98–107.

12. As the nation's leading challenger of the *keiretsu*, and as a hardware producer, Dunlap sued to enjoin the Matsushita purchase, but his motion was rejected by the Supreme Court on the eve of the final purchase. Acting for the Court, Justice Antonin Scalia rejected the emergency request without a written opinion. (*Go-Video, Inc.*, v. *Matsushita Electric Industrial Co., Ltd, et al.*, United States District Court, District of Arizona, Complaint, December 6, 1990.)

13. Ibid., p. 17.

14. Ibid., p. 45.

15. See, for example, the classic *Sovereignty at Bay: The Multinational Spread of U.S. Enterprises*, by Raymond Vernon (New York: Basic Books, 1971).

16. Restrictive business practices included the control of profit margins. When Toyota wants to lift its own profit margins, for example, it restricts Koito's. This is how Toyota has built up its admirable cash position, reported at $25 billion in liquid assets—a considerable advantage in global competition. One perk for top managers included a $1-million country-club membership for the president of Koito. Pickens also alleged that Toyota threatened to cut off its purchases if Pickens and his confederates were given a seat on the board, although, if Toyota controlled 60–65 percent of the stock, one wonders why they would need to threaten the company, or why they would want to. (T. Boone Pickens, "Secrets Koito Hoped to Hide by Keeping Me Off Its Board," *Wall Street Journal*, March 28, 1990, p. A19.)

17. William J. Holstein, *The Japanese Power Game* (New York: Scribner's, 1990), pp. 179–81, 199–207.

18. Holstein et al., "Mighty Mitsubishi." Abroad and at home, these families of companies help one another, sometimes running up against local customs and laws. A jury in Oregon's Multnomah County Circuit Court awarded $6.3 million in a wrongful-dismissal suit brought by a former Bank of California official, who charged he was dismissed when he refused to hand over confidential borrower data to the bank's Tokyo parent, Mitsubishi Bank Ltd. Mitsubishi had acquired the Bank of California in 1984. Three years later, Sigitas Banaitis, a manager in the bank's Portland branch, claimed he had resisted attempts by his superiors in Tokyo to obtain financial information about his clients, U.S. grain and scrap-steel shippers, to help sister companies in the *keiretsu* compete against American businesses. The bank, defending itself, charged Banaitis with "poor performance" and denied soliciting confidential customer information from him. Court documents showed that Mitsubishi managed, despite Banaitis' efforts, to get sensitive financial client information faxed to its Tokyo office; it was, therefore, not surprising that the jury found the evidence supporting Mitsubishi's defense "internally contradictory." Unfortunately, this was not an isolated incident: at least six similar claims are now pending against Japanese companies accused of acquiring U.S. companies to gather information and technology that can be used to compete

against other U.S. businesses. See Ralph T. King, Jr., "Ex–Bank Employee Wins $6.3 million in Dismissal Suit," *Wall Street Journal*, March 22, 1991, p. B8.

19. Official figures on Japanese investment belie the extent of that investment, because of the idiosyncratic method of data collection favored by the U.S. government. If foreign investors borrow money in the United States, for example, the investment is not counted in the official tally of foreign investment. Since many recent Japanese purchases are financed in the United States—and this appeared to be the trend in 1989 and 1990—such acquisitions are not counted, thereby undervaluing Japanese investment in the United States.

20. Masaru Yoshitomi, "*Keiretsu*: An Insider's Guide to Japan's Conglomerates," *Economic Insights*, September–October 1990, p. 14.

21. Ibid.

22. Chalmers Johnson, "*Keiretsu*: An Outsider's View," *Economic Insights*, September–October 1990, pp. 16–17. See also Congressional Research Service, *Japan's Industrial Groups: The Keiretsu*, by Dick K. Nanto, November 5, 1990.

23. Charles H. Ferguson, "Computers and the Coming of the U.S. Keiretsu," *Harvard Business Review*, July–August 1990, p. 55.

24. Ibid., p. 56. See also Marie Anchordoguy, "A Brief History of Japan's Keiretsu," and "How Japan Built a Computer Industry," in *Harvard Business Review*, July–August, 1990, pp. 58–59, and p. 65.

25. Ferguson, "Computers."

26. Ibid., p. 64.

27. Laura Tyson, "Managed Trade: Making the Best of the Second Best," unpublished paper presented at Brookings Institution, September 12, 1989.

28. George Gilder, *Microcosm: The Quantum Revolution in Economics and Technology* (New York: Simon & Schuster, 1989).

29. Ibid., pp. 352, 324, 343. Gilder also warns that government organization of technology "poses serious danger to American technological leadership," and blames the "promiscuous culture of Silicon Valley, with workers and engineers constantly moving from one firm to another," for fostering a "wildfire diffusion of technology that compensated for the lack of national coordination." And what about the deep pockets of the *keiretsu*? The patient capital that translates the spark of innovation into commercial success? Gilder's answer is that venture capital is preferable to patient capital, and fits more naturally into American culture. Government became the problem, he says, back in the 1970s, when the "top capital gains rate between 35 and 49 percent, plus state and local levies" led to the extinction of the venture-capital industry.

30. Seidel pointed out an essay he had written on ion implantation in a fourteen-chapter book titled *VLSI Technology*, ed., S. M. Sze (New York: McGraw-Hill, 1985). The other contributors were all AT&T scientists, half of whom had left Bell Labs following the break-up.

31. Jacob M. Schlesinger, "U.S. Call to Open Japan Trade Market May Bring Crackdown on Foreign Firms," *Wall Street Journal*, June 19, 1990, p. A20.

32. Ibid.

33. In 1988, 276 cartels were identified for such protection, including "40 so-called 'sanitary' cartels—involving cinemas, laundries and hairdressers—which were allowed to operate, apparently to ensure that unfettered competition did not threaten public health." The following year, 4,533 cartels were exempted so that they could "pass on the new 3% consumption tax as they saw fit." See Nigel Holloway, "Freeing the Watchdog," *Far Eastern Economic Review*, October 19, 1989, pp. 48–49.

34. In a decision typical of the recent judicial hostility to antitrust enforcement, a federal judge in Los Angeles dismissed a lawsuit initiated by the Justice Department to block a film-industry acquisition by Rank, a British entertainment company. Judge Terry Hatter, a Carter appointee, allowed the $150-million purchase of a film-processing laboratory from News Corporation's Fox Inc. unit. (See *Wall*

Street Journal, December 11, 1990, p. 5.) No doubt Matsushita took heart from this decision before bidding for MCA.

35. The White House also supported a requirement that the courts evaluate the legality of joint ventures with a flexible "rule-of-reason" analysis that, in effect, tended to favor ultimate approval of the ventures. The watered-down legislation disappointed many entrepreneurs, who considered the bill too diluted to offer much protection. The bill still left joint ventures in the risky-business category, because they were not given immunity from antitrust laws, but merely assured that, *if* the company in question filed disclosure notices with the government, and *if* they were found in violation of the laws, they would only have to pay *actual* damages, not triple damages. (Alan Murray and Paul M. Barrett, "Bush Aides Urge Antitrust Restrictions Be Eased for U.S. Firms," *Wall Street Journal*, January 22, 1990, p. A4.)

36. An economic-policy paper prepared for the president's Economic Policy Council argued that the change would nevertheless represent a "strong statement of the administration's support of American efficiency and competitiveness without suggesting a lack of commitment to vigorous antitrust enforcement." In support of its view that radical change was unnecessary, the authors noted an upsurge in joint-production ventures since 1988, including a "venture by Merck & Co and Johnson & Johnson to develop and market new over-the-counter medicines, a venture by Dow Chemical Co. and Eli Lilly & Co. to operate an agricultural chemical concern and a venture by General Electric and Ford Motor Co. to develop a new generation of automobile lighting systems." (Ibid.)

37. For further discussion on this subject, see Robert Pitofsky, "New Definitions of Relevant Market and the Assault on Antitrust," *Columbia Law Review*, vol. 90, no. 7 (December 1990); Harry First, Eleanor M. Fox, and Robert Pitofsky, eds., *Revitalizing Antitrust in Its Second Century* (New York: Quorum Books, 1991).

38. This bill, the National Cooperative Production Amendments of 1990, would have relaxed antitrust laws for joint ventures in manufacturing, and extended a current exemption for joint research and development. The measure, which had bipartisan support, would have extended the National Cooperative Research Act of 1984 (which only covered research-and-development ventures) into manufacturing. It also contained an exemption for Canadian companies in accordance with the Canada–United States free-trade agreement.

39. A similar bill, pending in the Senate and sponsored by Senator Patrick J. Leahy, a Vermont Democrat, and Senator Strom Thurmond, Republican of South Carolina, did not exclude foreign investors from the benefits. See Martin Tolchin, "Foreigners Criticize Venture Bill," *New York Times*, June 6, 1991, pp. D1, D2.

40. Elliot L. Richardson, Letter to the Speaker, June 1, 1990.

41. Stuart Auerbach, "U.S. to Aim Antitrust Laws at Japan," Washington *Post*, February 22, 1992, pp. A1, A14; and Stuart Auerbach and Ann Devroy, "Antitrust Proposal Draws Opposition," Washington *Post*, February 23, 1992, p. A9.

CHAPTER XII
Global Strategies

1. The goal of the European Community in its unification plan—variously called "Europe 1992," "Program 92," the "1992 Initiative," etc.—is "to eliminate or reduce bariers to promote the greater unification and coordination of the political, social, economic and technological policies of twelve western European nations." For a good synopsis of the current literature on EC '92, as well as the plan itself, see Congressional Research Service, *The Europe 1992 Plan: Science and Technology Issues*, by Glenn J. McLoughlin, August 23, 1989.

2. For more specific information on ESPRIT, RACE, and EUREKA, see Appendix G. See also Commission of the European Communities, *Esprit—European Strategic*

Programme for Research and Development in Information Technology—1988 Annual Report (Luxembourg: Office for Official Publications of the European Communities, 1989).

3. Marie Anchordoguy, *Computers Inc.: Japan's Challenge to IBM* (Cambridge, Mass.: Harvard Council on East Asian Studies, 1989), pp. 21, 33.

4. "Five Ways to Fight Back," *Newsweek*, October 9, 1989, p. 72.

5. Bruce Scott, "Competitiveness: Self-Help for a Worsening Problem," *Harvard Business Review*, July–August 1989, p. 119.

6. Martin and Susan Tolchin, *Buying into America: How Foreign Money Is Changing the Face of Our Nation* (New York: Times Books/Random House, 1988), chs. 3, 4.

7. A lively debate over using the intelligence agencies for a more vigorous technology policy occurred in 1990. Defensive about their importance in light of the receding Soviet threat and fearful that their budgets would be cut accordingly, the intelligence agencies were searching for another mission, and this one looked viable; in fact, the NSA and the CIA had already begun to gather "economic intelligence" before Congress initiated the debate on the advantages and disadvantages of such a controversial policy shift. It would work as follows: the NSA would feed the intelligence it received on world trade and financial transactions to the CIA, National Security Council, Treasury and Federal Reserve Board. The advantages of such a scheme are evident. It would address the current data gap and match our foreign competitors, who routinely collect information and distribute it to their national companies, many of whom are government-owned; and it would utilize the NSA's tremendous global-eavesdropping communications network. The NSA has already demonstrated its abilities in cracking codes, identifying terrorists, and tracking the contra-gate money trail. Also, the national-security rationale justifies the collection of economic data for broader security reasons, such as the prevention of the collapse of the banking system or financial markets. The disadvantages are less obvious, and involve ethical, legal, and economic questions. The most troublesome issue involves spying on our allies: even though some of our allies spy on us, Americans embrace a value system that finds such activities distasteful. Another is the question of who gets the information. Should General Motors be the beneficiary of industrial-intelligence gathering? There are also legal barriers in the way of adding functions to the intelligence agencies without changing their charter. The final problem is one of oversight. Who can guarantee that the intelligence agencies, given their uneven record, will not misuse this new power? See Michael Wines, "Security Agency Debates New Role: Economic Spying," *New York Times*, June 16, 1990, pp. A1, A6; Neil Munro, "U.S. Mulls Industrial Spy Role," *Defense News*, May 28, 1990, pp. 1, 35; Robert J. Samuelson, "Spying Won't Boost U.S. Competitiveness," *Washington Post*, January 11, 1990, p. A19; David Warsh, "Using a Spyglass to Keep Track of America's Place in Global Markets," *Washington Post*, June 27, 1990, p. H3.

8. Microelectronics and Computer Technology Corporation (MCC) is a twenty-one-member consortium with a $65-million annual budget whose member companies included General Electric, Digital Equipment, and Motorola. MCC has managed to stay afloat, but has been criticized for "underachievement" vis-à-vis comparable Japanese consortia. See John Carey and Jim Bartimo, "If You Control Computers You Control the World," *Business Week*, July 23, 1990, p. 31.

9. Paul Solman, "Focus: Costs of War," on "MacNeil-Lehrer Newshour," January 31, 1991, New York.

10. While the U.S. is slowing down, private corporations in Canada, Italy, France, and Germany have increased their R & D expenditures from 2.8 percent to 7.5 percent in real terms in 1990, despite slowdowns in their economy. The most sluggish R-&-D expenditures in the U.S. appear to be in the high-risk, cutting-edge technologies that lead to new products. The NSF predicted no real growth

in 1991 for U.S. corporate R & D. ("Business Should Rally Round the Labs," *Business Week*, July 15, 1991, p. 156.)

11. Jacques Gansler, "Needed: A U.S. Defense Industrial Strategy," *International Security*, vol. 12, no. 2 (Fall 1987), p. 48.

12. U.S. Congress, Office of Technology Assessment, *Holding the Edge: Maintaining the Defense Technology Base* (Washington, D.C.: U.S. Government Printing Office, April 1989)—a very impressive report detailing this problem. Another excellent report from OTA supports the view that there is increasing public acceptance of "the idea that troubled American manufacturing industries could use help from their government. A consensus is forming for more focussed government policies to help industry develop and adopt technologies that can boost the competitiveness of U.S. manufacturing." (U.S. Congress, Office of Technology Assessment, *Competing Economies: America, Europe and the Pacific Rim*, November, 1991, p. 11.)

13. Evelyn Richards, "U.S. to Fight High-Tech Firm's Sale," Washington *Post*, December 2, 1990, p. C1.

14. Robert Pear, "Confusion Is Operative Word in U.S. Policy Toward Japan," *New York Times*, March 20, 1989, pp. A1, A8. See Appendix H for a list of key agencies with jurisdiction over international trade issues.

15. U.S. Department of Defense, Defense Science Board, *Defense Semiconductor Dependency*, February 1987.

16. U.S. Senate, Committee on Finance, *Foreign Influence on the U.S. Political Process*, hearing, Susan J. Tolchin testimony, September 19, 1991, p. 52. See also Hilary Stout, "Washington Talk: Capital Ethics," *New York Times*, November 12, 1987, p. B8; M. and S. Tolchin, *Buying into America*, chs. 1, 2, 8, 18; Pat Choate, *Agents of Influence* (New York: Alfred A. Knopf, 1990).

17. Examples of conflicts of interest like the Watkins and Olive cases occur with increasing frequency. Senator Strom Thurmond was so incensed by the resignation of a leading U.S. textile negotiator who went to work for Hong Kong in the middle of negotiations that he sponsored legislation barring government officials from working for foreign governments and foreign companies for one year after they left government service; President Reagan vetoed the bill. See Charles Lewis, *The Office of the United States Trade Representative: America's Frontline Trade Officials* (Washington, D.C.: Center for Public Integrity, 1991). Choate's study, *Agents of Influence*, offers many highly detailed examples of the impact of the revolving door on trade policy.

SELECTED BIBLIOGRAPHY

Books

Abegglen, James C., and George Stalk, Jr. *The Japanese Corporation*. New York: Basic Books, 1985.

Adelman, Kenneth L., and Norman R. Augustine. *The Defense Revolution*. ICS Press, 1990.

Anchordoguy, Marie. *Computers Inc.: Japan's Challenge to IBM*. Cambridge, Mass.: Harvard Council on East Asian Studies, 1989.

Barnet, Richard. *Global Reach*. New York: Simon & Schuster, 1974.

Bhagwati, Jagdish. *Protectionism*. Cambridge, Mass.: MIT Press, 1988.

Blechman, Barry M., and Edward Luttwak. *Global Security: A Review of Strategic and Economic Issues*. Boulder, Colo.: Westview Press, 1987.

Brown, Lester. *World Without Borders*. New York: Random House, 1972.

Buchanan, James M. *Liberty, Market, and State: Political Economy in the 1980s*. New York: New York University Press, 1986.

Burstein, Daniel. *Yen: Japan's New Financial Empire and Its Threat to America*. New York: Fawcett Columbine, 1988.

Buzan, Barry. *An Introduction to Strategic Studies*. New York: St. Martin's Press, 1987.

Calleo, David P. *Beyond American Hegemony*. New York: Basic Books, 1987.

Choate, Pat. *Agents of Influence*. New York: Alfred A. Knopf, 1990.

Conway, Hugh. *Defense Economic Issues*. Washington, D.C.: National Defense University, 1990.

Crowe, Kenneth C. *America for Sale: An Alarming Look at How Foreign Money Is Buying Our Country*. New York: Doubleday & Company, 1978.

Deitchman, Seymour J. *Beyond the Thaw: A New National Strategy*. Boulder, Colo.: Westview Press, 1991.

Derian, Jean-Claude. *America's Struggle for Leadership in Technology*. Cambridge, Mass.: MIT Press, 1990.

Dertouzos, Michael L., et al. *Made in America: Regaining the Productive Edge*. Cambridge, Mass.: MIT Press, 1989.

Destler, I. M. *Making Foreign Economic Policy*. Washington, D.C.: The Brookings Institution, 1980.

Dunning, John H. *International Production and the Multinational Enterprise*. London: George Allen & Unwin Ltd., 1981.

Emmott, Bill. *The Sun Also Sets: The Limits to Japan's Economic Power*. New York: Times Books/Random House, 1989.

Fallows, James. *More like Us: Making America Great Again*. Boston: Houghton Mifflin, 1989.

First, Harry, Eleanor M. Fox, and Robert Pitofsky, eds. *Revitalizing Antitrust in Its Second Century*. New York: Quorum Books, 1991.

Frantz, Douglas, and Catherine Collins. *Selling Out*. Chicago: Contemporary Books, 1989.

Friedman, Benjamin. *Day of Reckoning*. New York: Random House, 1988.

Fucini, Joseph J. and Suzy. *Working for the Japanese: Inside Mazda's American Auto Plant*. New York: Free Press, 1990.

Gamota, George, and Wendy Frieman. *Gaining Ground: Japan's Strides in Science and Technology*. Cambridge, Mass.: Ballinger, 1988.

Gelsanliter, David. *Jump Start: Japan Comes to the Heartland*. New York: Farrar, Straus & Giroux, 1990.

Gilder, George. *Microcosm: The Quantum Revolution in Economics and Technology*. New York: Simon & Schuster, 1989.

Glickman, Norman, and Douglas Woodward. *The New Competitors: How Foreign Investors Are Changing the U.S. Economy*. New York: Basic Books, 1989.

Graham, Edward M., and Paul R. Krugman. *Foreign Direct Investment in the United States*. Washington, D.C.: Institute for International Economics, 1989.

Halberstam, David. *The Next Century*. New York: William Morrow, 1991.

Halloran, Richard. *Japan: Images and Realities*. Rutland, Vt.: Charles E. Tuttle, 1969.

Heilbroner, Robert, and Peter Bernstein. *The Debt and the Deficit*. New York: W. W. Norton, 1989.

Holstein, William J. *The Japanese Power Game*. New York: Scribner's, 1990.

Ishihara, Shintaro. *A Japan That Can Say No*. New York: Simon & Schuster, 1991.

Johnson, Chalmers. *MITI and the Japanese Miracle*. Stanford, Calif.: Stanford University Press, 1982.

Johnson, Chalmers, et al., eds. *Politics and Productivity: How Japan's Development Strategy Works*. Cambridge, Mass.: Ballinger, 1989.

Julius, DeAnne. *Global Companies & Public Policy*. New York: Council on Foreign Relations Press, 1990.

Keohane, Robert O., and Joseph S. Nye. *Power and Interdependence*. 2nd edition. Glenview, Ill.: Scott, Foresman and Company, 1989.

Kester, W. Karl. *Japanese Takeovers: The Global Contest for Corporate Control*. Cambridge, Mass.: Harvard Business School Press, 1991.

Kirk, Elizabeth J., ed. *Technology, Security, and Arms Control for the 1990s*. Washington, D.C.: American Association for the Advancement of Science, 1988.

Kline, John M. *State Government Influence in U.S. International Economic Policy*. Lexington, Mass.: D. C. Heath, 1983.

Kuttner, Robert. *The End of Laissez-faire*. New York: Alfred A. Knopf, 1991.

Libicki, Martin C. *Industrial Strength Defense: A Disquisition on Manufacturing, Surge and War*. Washington, D.C.: National Defense University Press, 1988.

Lincoln, Edward J. *Japan's Unequal Trade*. Washington, D.C.: The Brookings Institution, 1990.

Lodge, George. *Perestroika for America: Restructuring Business-Government Relations for World Competitiveness*. Cambridge, Mass.: Harvard Business School Press, 1990.

Magaziner, Ira, and Mark Patinkin. *The Silent War*. New York: Vintage Books, 1990.

Mahler, Vincent A. *Dependency Approaches to International Political Economy*. New York: Columbia University Press, 1980.

Mattione, Richard P. *OPEC's Investment & the International Financial System*. Washington, D.C.: The Brookings Institution, 1985.

MIT Commission on Industrial Productivity. *The Working Papers of the MIT Commission on Industrial Productivity*. Vols. I, II. Cambridge, Mass.: MIT Press, 1989.

Morris, Charles. *The Coming Global Boom*. New York: Bantam. 1990.

Nau, Henry. *The Myth of America's Decline*. New York: Oxford, 1990.

Nye, Joseph. *Bound to Lead: The Changing Nature of American Power*. New York: Basic Books, 1990.

Ohmae, Kenichi. *The Borderless World*. New York: Harper Business. 1990.

Ostrey, Sylvia. *Governments and Corporations in a Shrinking World*. New York: Council on Foreign Relations. 1990.

Pauly, Louis. *Opening Financial Markets*. Ithaca, N.Y.: Cornell University Press, 1988.

Phillips, Kevin. *The Politics of Rich and Poor*. New York: Random House, 1990.

Perret, Geoffrey. *A Country Made for War*. New York: Random House, 1990.

Poniachek, Harvey A. *Direct Foreign Investment in the United States*. Lexington, Mass.: Lexington Books, 1986.

Porter, Michael E. *The Competitive Advantage of Nations*. New York: Free Press, 1990.

Prestowitz, Clyde. *Trading Places: How We Allowed Japan to Take the Lead*. New York: Basic Books, 1989.

Sampson, Anthony. *The Midas Touch*. New York: E. P. Dutton. 1990.

Servan-Schreiber, J. J. *The American Challenge*. New York: Atheneum, 1969.

Smith, Adam. *The Wealth of Nations*. Bks. I–III. New York: Penguin, 1970. Originally published 1776.

Snow, Donald M. *National Security: Enduring Problems in a Changing Defense Environment*. New York: St. Martin's Press, 1991.

Starr, Martin K., ed. *Global Competitiveness: Getting the U.S. Back on Track*. W. W. Norton, 1988.

Stewart, Michael. *The Age of Interdependence: Economic Policy in an Interdependent World*. Cambridge, Mass.: MIT Press, 1984.

Tolchin, Martin and Susan. *Buying into America: How Foreign Money Is Changing the Face of Our Nation*. New York: Times Books/Random House, 1988.

———. *Dismantling America: The Rush to Deregulate*. Boston: Houghton Mifflin, 1983.

Tyson, Laura D'Andrea, and John Zysman. *American Industry in International Competition*. Ithaca, N.Y.: Cornell University Press, 1983.

Van Wolferen, Karel. *The Enigma of Japanese Power*. New York: Alfred A. Knopf, 1989.

Vawter, Roderick L. *Industrial Mobilization: The Relevant History.* Revised edition. Washington, D.C.: National Defense University Press, 1983.

Vernon, Raymond. *Sovereignty at Bay: The Multinational Spread of U.S. Enterprises.* New York: Basic Books, 1971.

Whitman, Marina. *Reflections of Interdependence.* Pittsburgh: University of Pittsburgh Press, 1979.

Zysman, John, and Stephen S. Cohen. *Manufacturing Matters: The Myth of a Post-Industrial Economy.* New York: Basic Books, 1987.

Newspaper and Periodical Articles, Monographs, Speeches, and Dissertations

Allen, Jodie T. "A New Tax That Even Bush Can Support." Washington *Post*, May 13, 1990, pp. C1, C3.

Alster, Norm. "Sprechen Sie High Tech?" *Forbes*, April 17, 1989, pp. 172–76.

Alvarez, Jose E. "Political Protectionism and United States International Investment Obligations in Conflict: The Hazards of Exon-Florio." *Virginia Journal of International Law*, vol. 30, no. 1 (Fall 1989), pp. 1–187.

Anchordoguy, Marie. "A Brief History of Japan's Keiretsu." *Harvard Business Review*, July–August 1990, pp. 58–59.

———. "How Japan Built a Computer Industry." *Harvard Business Review*, July–August 1990, p. 65.

Associated Press. "Japan Knew of Stock Compensation in 1983." *Investor's Daily*, August 28, 1991, p. 27.

Auerbach, Stuart. "$1.5 Billion in U.S. Sales to Iraq." Washington *Post*, March 11, 1991, pp. A1, A16.

———. "U.S. Relied on Foreign Made Parts for Weapons." Washington *Post*, March 25, 1991, pp. A1, A17.

"Bargain Basement Time for U.S. Technology." *Business Week*, January 4, 1989, p. 67.

Baruch, Bernard. "A Few Kind Words for Uncle Sam," *Collier's*, June 12, 1948, pp. 458–63.

Berton, Lee. "U.S. Investors Devise Strategies to Value Secretive Japan Firms." *Wall Street Journal*, March 22, 1990, pp. C1, C2.

Blechman, Barry M. "Economic Strength and Dependence." in Hugh Conway, ed., *Defense Economic Issues.* Washington, D.C.: National Defense University, 1990.

Blustein, Paul. "In Japan, the Politics of Hesitation." Washington *Post*, February 17, 1991, p. C2.

———. "Japan Inc. Stretches Its Global Foothold." Washington *Post*, March 24, 1991, p. H7.

Brandt, Richard, et al. "The Future of Silicon Valley." *Business Week*, February 5, 1990, pp. 54–60.

Branscombe, Lewis. M. "Toward a U.S. Technology Policy." *Issues in Science and Technology*, Summer 1991, pp. 50–55.

"Business Should Rally Round the Labs." *Business Week*, July 15, 1991, p. 156.

Business Week/Harris Poll. "Americans Resent Japan's No-Show in the Gulf." *Business Week*, January 1, 1991, p. 28.

Calder, Kent. "The Rise of Japan's Military-Industrial Base." *Asia Pacific Community*, November 1982, pp. 26–41.

Carey, John, and Jim Bartimo. "If You Control Computers You Control the World." *Business Week*, July 23, 1990, p. 31.

Clark, Kim B., et al. "When Technology Drives Competition—You Can't Compete on Technology." *Harvard Business Review*, special section, November–December 1989, pp. 94–120.

"The Competitive Status of the U.S. Civil Aviation Manufacturing Industry." Washington, D.C.: National Academy Press, 1985.

Corrigan, E. Gerald. "Trends in International Banking in the United States and Japan." *Federal Reserve Board of New York Quarterly Review*, Autumn 1989.

Culbertson, John M. "The New Foreign Ownership in the United States: Its Causes and Implications." *Southern Business & Economic Journal*, January 1990, pp. 89–98.

Davidow, Joel, and Paul Schott Stevens. "Antitrust Merger Control and National Security Review of Foreign Acquisitions in the United States." *Journal of World Trade*, vol. 24, no. 1 (February 1990), pp. 39–56.

Depke, Deidre A., et al. "Laptops Take Off." *Business Week*, March 18, 1991, pp. 118–24.

Emmott, Bill. "The American Money Edge." *Washington Post*, July 7, 1991, pp. B1, B4.

"Enter the U.S. Bank Raider?" *The Banker*, November 1989, pp. 20–22.

Epstein, Stephanie. "Buying the American Mind: Japan's Quest for U.S. Ideas in Science, Economic Policy and the Schools." report prepared for Center for Public Integrity, Washington, D.C., December 1991.

Farnsworth, Clyde H. "Official Reported to Face Ouster After His Dissent on Iraq Exports." *New York Times*, January 10, 1991, pp. A1, D2.

———. "U.S. Is Asked to Review Japan Trade." *New York Times*, March 25, 1991, pp. D1, D2.

———. "U.S. Stops Acquisition by Japanese." *New York Times*, April 18, 1989, p. D1.

Farrell, Christopher, and Ted Holden. "The U.S. Has a New Weapon: Low-Cost Capital." *Business Week*, July 29, 1991, pp. 72–73.

Feder, Barnaby J. "Ohio Company Seized as Iraqi Front." *New York Times*, September 20, 1990, p. D21.

Ferguson, Charles H. "America's High Tech Decline." *Foreign Policy*, no. 74, Spring 1989, pp. 123–43.

———. "Computers and the Coming of the U.S. Keiretsu." *Harvard Business Review*, July–August, 1990.

———. "Technological Development, Strategic Behavior, and Government Policy in Information Technology Industries." paper prepared for Massachusetts Institute of Technology, 1988.

Finnegan, Philip. "Mounting Debt Threatens Industry." *Defense News*, April 23, 1990, p. 1.

"Five Ways to Fight Back." *Newsweek*, October 9, 1989.

French, Kenneth R., and James M. Poterba. "Are Japanese Stock Prices Too High?" Working Paper no. 3290, National Bureau of Economic Research, Inc., March 1990.

Friedberg, Aaron L. "The Changing Relationship Between Economics and National Security." *Political Science Quarterly*, vol. 106, no. 2 (1991), pp. 265–76.

Gansler, Jacques. "Needed: A U.S. Defense Industrial Strategy." *International Security*, vol. 12, no. 2 (Fall 1987), p. 48.

———. "U.S. Dependence on Foreign Military Parts." *Issues in Science and Technology*, vol. 2, no. 4 (Summer 1986).

Gilder, George. "American Technology at Fire-Sale Prices." *Forbes*, January 22, 1990, pp. 60–64.

Gray, Paul E. "Technology Transfer at Issue: The Academic Viewpoint." *IEEE Spectrum*, special report, May 1982, pp. 64–68.

———. "University Research: Who Benefits?" *M.I.T. Report*, July–August 1989.

Green, Michael. "DoD Seeks Japanese Cooperation." *Defense News*, July 16, 1990, pp. 7, 12.

Green, Michael, and David Silverberg. "Japan Seeks MLRS, Aircraft in Continued Defense Buildup." *Defense News*, May 21, 1990, pp. 1, 8.

Guenther, Robert, and Michael R. Sesit. "U.S. Banks Losing Business to Japanese at Home and Abroad." *Wall Street Journal*, October 12, 1989, p. A12.

Hale, David D. "Global Finance and the Retreat to Managed Trade." *Harvard Business Review*, January–February 1990, pp. 150–62.

Helm, Leslie. "On the Campus: Fat Endowments and Growing Clout." *Business Week*, July 11, 1988, p. 70.

Henderson, Breck W. "DARPA Invests $4 Million as Venture Capital in High-Technology Companies." *Aviation Week & Space Technology*, April 30, 1990, pp. 25–26.

Hicks, Jonathan P. "All About the Tire Industry." *New York Times*, February 11, 1990, p. 8.

Hodges, Michael. "The Japanese Industrial Presence in America: Same Bed, Different Dreams." In Kathleen Newland, ed., *The International Relations of Japan*. London: Macmillan, 1990.

Holloway, Nigel. "Freeing the Watchdog." *Far Eastern Economic Review*, October 19, 1989, pp. 48–49.

Holstein, William J., et al. "The Stateless Corporation." *Business Week*, May 14, 1990, pp. 98–106.

———. "Mighty Mitsubishi Is on the Move." *Business Week*, September 24, 1990, pp. 98–107.

Hufbauer, Gary C., and Kimberley Ann Elliott. "The International Economy with a National Security Perspective." In Barry Blechman and Edward N. Luttwak, eds., *Global Security: A Review of Strategic and Economic Issues*. Boulder, Colo.: Westview Press, 1987.

Iacocca, Lee A. "O.K., O.K., Call Me a Protectionist." *New York Times*, February 10, 1991, sec. 4, p. 17.

"The Impact on Defense Industrial Capability of Changes in Procurement and Tax Policy, 1984–1987." *The MAC Group*, February 1989.

Inman, B. R., and Daniel F. Burton, Jr. "Technology and Competitiveness: The New Policy Frontier." *Foreign Affairs*, Spring 1990, pp. 116–34.

Isikoff, Michael. "U.S. Seizes Iraqi-owned Tool Company in Ohio." *Washington Post*, September 20, 1990, p. A26.

Jenkins, George. "Venture Capital Fund Is Cautious: Who Will Seed Start-ups?" *Harvard Business Review*, November–December 1989, p. 117.

Johnson, Chalmers. "*Keiretsu*: An Outsider's View," *Economic Insights*, September–October 1990, pp. 16–17.

Kearns, Kevin. "After FSX: A New Approach to U.S.-Japan Relations." *Foreign Service Journal*, December 1989.

Kelman, Steven. "The 'Japanization' of America?" *The Public Interest*, no. 98, Winter 1990, pp. 70–83.

Kinsley, Michael. "Two American Myths About Japan." Washington *Post*, January 11, 1990.

Kline, John. "Trade Competitiveness and Corporate Nationality." *Columbia Journal of World Business*, vol. 24, no. 3 (Fall 1989) p. 26.

Kolata, Gina. "M.I.T. Deal with Japan Stirs Fear on Competition." *New York Times*, December 19, 1990, p. 1.

Kuttner, Robert. "The Free Trade Fallacy," *New Republic*, March 28, 1983, pp. 16–22.

———. "Industry Needs a Better Incubator Than the Pentagon." *Business Week*, April 30, 1990, p. 16.

LaChica, Eduardo. "Chip-making Pioneer in U.S. Found Grief in Seiko Joint Venture." *Wall Street Journal*, May 4, 1990, pp. A1, A5.

Larsen, Judy. "Silicon Valley Fever." *Journal of the American Planning Association*, vol. 53 (Spring 1987), pp. 288–90.

Leopold, George. "U.S. Faces Tough Competition in Critical Technologies." *Defense News*, July 16, 1990, p. 6.

Leopold, George, and Neil Munro. "Budget Bill Bolsters Tech Base." *Defense News*, November 12, 1990, pp. 3, 53.

Lev, Michael. "Goodyear's Pipeline: A White Elephant." *New York Times*, July 8, 1990, p. F4.

Levine, Jonathan B., et al. "Is the U.S. Selling Its High Tech Soul to Japan?" *Business Week*, June 26, 1989, pp. 117–18.

Libicki, Martin C. "What Makes Industries Strategic: A Perspective on Technology, Economic Development, and Defense," National Defense University, April 13, 1989.

Markoff, John. "Pentagon's Technology Chief Out." *New York Times*, April 21, 1990, p. 31.

Martz, Larry, and Rich Thomas. "The Corporate Shell Game." *Newsweek*, April 15, 1990, pp. 48–49.

Mayer, Jeffrey L. "Global Interdependence and Domestic Economic Policy." Paper presented to the U.S. undersecretary for economic affairs, Department of Commerce, January 14, 1986.

McLenahen, John S. "The Buying of America," *Industry Week*, June 4, 1990, pp. 61–65.

Milbank, Dana. "Goodyear Posts Biggest Loss for Quarter in Firm's History." *Wall Street Journal*, European edition, April 25, 1991, p. 5.

Moran, Theodore H. "The Globalization of America's Defense Industries: Managing the Threat of Foreign Dependence." *International Security*, vol. 15, no. 1, (Summer 1990), pp. 57–99.

Morrison, David C. "Halting the Erosion." *National Journal*, July 30, 1988, pp. 1968–71.

Munro, Neil. "U.S. Mulls Industrial Spy Role." *Defense News*, May 28, 1990, pp. 1, 35.

Noble, David. "The Multinational Multiversity." *Zeta*, April 1989, pp. 17–23.

Nye, Joseph S. "Independence and Interdependence." *Foreign Policy*, vol. 22 (Spring 1976.

Pear, Robert. "Confusion Is Operative Word in U.S. Policy Toward Japan." *New York Times*, March 20, 1989, pp. A1, A8.

———. "For the Multinationals a Crackdown on Taxes." *New York Times*, October 30, 1990, p. A23.

———. "I.R.S. Investigaitng Foreign Companies over Units in U.S." *New York Times*, February 18, 1990, pp. 1, 30.

———. "More Tax Avoidance Is Cited." *New York Times*, July 11, 1990, pp. D1, D2.

"Perkin Unit to Remain U.S. Owned." *New York Times*, May 16, 1990, p. D1.

Pickens, T. Boone. "Secrets Koito Hoped to Hide by Keeping Me Off Its Board." *Wall Street Journal*, March 28, 1990, p. A19.

Pollack, Andrew. "America's Answer to Japan's MITI." *New York Times*, March 5, 1990, sec. 3, p. 1.

———. "In U.S. Technology, a Gap Between Arms and VCRs." *New York Times*, March 4, 1991, p. D8.

Port, Otis. "Sematech May Give America's Middleweights a Fighting Chance." *Business Week*, December 10, 1990, p. 186.

Porter, Michael E. "Competitive Advantage." *Harvard Business Review*, March–April 1990.

Powell, Bill, and Rich Thomas. "All in the Family." *Newsweek*, June 3, 1991, p. 36.

Powell, Bill, et al. "Will Aerospace Be Next?" *Newsweek*, March 19, 1990, pp. 36–37.

Prestowitz, Clyde. "Giving Japan a Handout: Why Fork Over $7 Billion in Aircraft Technology?" Washington *Post*, January 29, 1989, pp. D1, D4.

Prokesch, Steven. "Fujitsu to Buy ICL Stake." *New York Times*, July 31, 1990, p. D1.

Pugliese, David. "Canada Holds Firm on de Havilland Sale." *Defense News*, July 8, 1991, p. 26.

Quint, Michael. "U.S. Banks Cut Global Business As Rivals Grow." *New York Times*, July 5, 1990, pp. A1, D9.

Reich, Robert. "Does Corporate Nationality Matter?" *Issues in Science and Technology*, Winter 1990–91, pp. 40–44.

———. "The Quiet Path to Technological Preeminence." *Scientific American*, October 1989, pp. 41–47.

———. "Who Is Us?" *Harvard Business Review*, January–February 1990, pp. 53–64.

Richards, Evelyn. "In Silicon Valley, a Rebirth of Risk-taking." Washington *Post*, July 29, 1990, pp. H1, H6.

———. "New Weapons in Works for Future Wars." Washington *Post*, March 3, 1991, p. H1.

———. "Uncle Sam as Venture Capitalist." Washington *Post*, April 29, 1990, pp. H1, H5.

———. "U.S. to Fight High-Tech Firm's Sale." Washington *Post*, December 2, 1990, p. C1.

Richards, Evelyn, and T. R. Reid. "Japanese Overtures to U.S. Scientists." *International Herald Tribune*, May 22, 1991.

Richardson, Elliot L., chairman of the Association for International Investment. Letter to Speaker of the House Thomas B. Foley, June 1, 1990.

Rogers, Herbert F. "Why We Backed the FS-X Deal." Washington *Post*, May 3, 1989, p. A27.

Rohatyn, Felix. "America's Economic Dependence." *Foreign Affairs*, vol. 68 (special issue), 1989.

Rosenthal, Andrew. "Bush Urged to Void Sale of Airplane-Parts Maker to Chinese." *New York Times*, February 2, 1990, p. A9.

Safire, William. "Breaking the Underworld Bank." *New York Times*, July 11, 1991, p. A21.

———. "Friends More Than Interests." *New York Times*, February 7, 1991, p. A25.

Samuelson, Robert J. "The Excuse Industry." *Newsweek*, December 11, 1989.

———. "Spying Won't Boost U.S. Competitiveness." Washington *Post*, January 11, 1990, p. A19.

Sanderson, Susan Walsh. "The Consumer Electronics Industry and the Future of American Manufacturing." Washington, D.C.: Economic Policy Institute, 1989.

Sanger, David. "Japan Asks Aid on Next Computers." *New York Times*, March 15, 1991, p. D1.

———. "Key Technology Might Be Sold to the Japanese." *New York Times*, November 27, 1989, p. 1.

———. "Made in the U.S.A., but by Sharp." *New York Times*, February 22, 1991, pp. D1, D3.

———. "U.S. Parts, Japanese Computer." *New York Times*, September 7, 1988, p. D1.

Schiller, Zachary, and Roger Schreffler. "Look Who's Taking Japan to Task." *Business Week*, June 4, 1990, p. 64.

Schlesinger, Jacob M. "U.S. Call to Open Japan Trade Market May Bring Crackdown on Foreign Firms." *Wall Street Journal*, June 19, 1990, p. A20.

Schmid, Gregory. "Interdependence Has Its Limits." *Foreign Policy*, vol. 21 (Winter 1975–76).

Schmitt, Richard B. "Claimant Against Japanese Learns the Word for Delay." *Wall Street Journal*, December 14, 1990, p. B1.

Schweizer, Peter. "On the Other Invisible Hand." Washington *Post*, July 22, 1990, p. C5.

Scott, Bruce. "Competitiveness: Self-Help for a Worsening Problem." *Harvard Business Review*, July 1989, pp. 115–21.

Shear, Jeff. "FS-X Fighter Program Hits Turbulence in Cost, Politics." *Insight*, December 17, 1990, pp. 28–29.

Shrage, Michael. " 'Uh . . . the Dog Ate the Experiment' and Other Corporate Excuses." Washington *Post*, February 22, 1991, p. C3.

Silk, Leonard. "Should Foreigners Share Fruits of U.S. Research?" *International Herald Tribune*, May 25, 1991, p. 9.

Silver, Brian. "Computers, and a Sealed Room in Israel." *New York Times*, February 17, 1991, sec. 3, p. 13.

Silverberg, David. "DoD May Use Foreign Bearings in Event of Desert Shield Conflict." *Defense News*, November 7, 1991, p. 25.

Sims, Calvin. "Business-Campus Ventures Grow." *New York Times*, December 14, 1987, p. D1.

Solman, Paul. "Focus: Costs of War." On "MacNeil-Lehrer Newshour," January 31, 1991, New York.

Stevenson, Richard W. "Foreign Role Rises in Military Goods." *New York Times*, October 23, 1989, pp. A1, D14.

Sugawara, Sandra. "Pentagon Agency Invests $4 Million in Chip Firm." Washington *Post*, April 10, 1990, pp. D1, D6.

Stout, Hilary. "Washington Talk: Capital Ethics." *New York Times*, November 12, 1987, p. B8.

Sun, Marjorie. "Investors' Yen for U.S. Technology." *Science*, vol. 246, December 8, 1989, pp. 1238–41.

Tolchin, Martin. "Agency on Foreign Takeovers Wielding Power." *New York Times*, April 24, 1989, p. D6.

———. "Crucial Technologies: 22 Make the U.S. List." *New York Times*, March 17, 1989, p. D1.

———. "A Debate over Access to American Research." *New York Times*, December 17, 1989, p. E4.

———. "Foreigners Criticize Venture Bill." *New York Times*, June 6, 1991, pp. D1, D2.

———. "Goals for Military Research Ignite Debate." *New York Times*, September 13, 1991, p. D4.

———. "Hostile Bids by Foreigners on the Rise." *New York Times*, December 27, 1988, p. D1.

———. "House Plan Fuels Debate on Business." *New York Times*, July 22, 1991, p. D3.

———. "Monsanto Unit Sale Faces Inquiry." *New York Times*, December 21, 1988, p. D3.

———. "Tracking a Foreign Presence in U.S. Military Contracting." *New York Times*, January 1, 1989, p. E5.

———. "U.S. Will Scrutinize a Chinese Deal." *New York Times*, December 5, 1989, p. D4.

———. "Union Takes On Chinese-owned Factory," *New York Times*, September 6, 1989, p. A14.

———. "White House Lists 22 Areas for Nurturing." *New York Times*, April 26, 1991, p. D17.

Tolchin, Susan. "Bargain Giant Bought with Cheap Dollars. *Nikkei Business*, May 15, 1988.

———. "Buying into America." In *The Impact of Foreign Investment in the United States*, New York: Touche Ross, a Special Report, 1989.

———. "Cultivating Japan." Washington *Post*, March 6, 1988.

———. "Foreign Investment in the U.S.: A Trojan or Gift Horse? *Japan Times,* May 25, 1988.

———. "Reciprocity, Disclosure, and the U.S. Role in Global Investment." *Mid-Atlantic Journal of Business*, vol. 25, nos. 2 & 3 (January 1989), pp. 79–88.

———. "The United Bazaar of America: Defense Industries for Sale." Washington *Post*, May 31, 1992, p. C4.

Tolchin, Martin and Susan. "Foreign Money, U.S. Fears." *New York Times Magazine*, December 13, 1987.

———. "Hiro-San Goes to Sacramento." *California Business*, March 1988.

———. "The Influence Peddlers." *Japan Newsweek*, January 21, 1988.

———. "States Court Foreign Investors." *Best of Business Quarterly*, vol. 10, no. 1 (Spring 1988), p. 55.

———. "The States' Global Hustlers." *Across the Board*, vol. XXV, no. 4 (April 1988).

———. "U.S. Unions and Foreign Employers: A Clash of Cultures," *Management Review*, March 1988, pp. 47–53.

Towell, Pat. "U.S.-Japan Fighter Jet Deal Is Cleared for Takeoff." *Congressional Quarterly*, May 20, 1989, pp. 1198–99.

"Trouble Inside Kuwait's Money Machine." *Business Week*, January 21, 1991, p. 44.

Tyson, Laura. "Managed Trade: Making the Best of the Second Best." Unpublished paper presented at The Brookings Institution, Washington, D.C., September 12, 1989.

———. "They Are Not Us: Why American Ownership Still Matters." *American Prospect*, no. 4, (Winter 1991), pp. 37–48.

Tyson, Laura, and John Zysman, "American Industry in International Competition." In Laura Tyson and John Zysman, *American Industry in International Competition*. Ithaca, N.Y.: Cornell University Press, 1983.

Ullman, Richard H. "Redefining Security." *International Security*, vol 8, no. 1 (Summer 1983), pp. 129–53.

"U.S. Technology Strategy Emerges." *Science*, vol. 252 (April 5, 1990), p. 20.

Warsh, David. "Using a Spyglass to Keep Track of America's Place in Global Markets." Washington *Post*, June 27, 1990, p. H3.

Wessel, David, and Constance Mitchell. "Fed Has Lost Much of Its Power to Sway U.S. Interest Rates." *Wall Street Journal* March 12, 1990, p. A1.

Wines, Michael. "Security Agency Debates New Role: Economic Spying." *New York Times*, June 16, 1990, pp. A1, A6.

Yamaguchi, Mari. "Japan May Revise Securities Law to Stem Hostile Raiders." Washington *Post*, February 1, 1990.

Yoshitomi, Masaru. "*Keiretsu:* An Insider's Guide to Japan's Conglomerates." *Economic Insights*, September–October 1990.

Yudkin, Joel, and Michael Black. "Targeting National Needs." *World Policy*, Spring 1990, pp. 251–88.

Zachary, G. Pascal. "U.S. Probes Allegations of Withholding of Parts." *Asian Wall Street Journal*, January 21, 1991, p. 1.

Government Documents, Reports, and Congressional Hearings and Testimony

Code of Federal Regulations. Title 22, pt. 181, #181.1, 22 CFR ch. 1 (4-1-85 Edition), Subchapter S—International Agreements.

Commission of the European Communities. *Esprit—European Strategic Programme for Research and Development in Information Technology—1988 Annual Report*. Luxembourg: Office for Official Publications of the European Communities, 1989.

Congressional Research Service. *Commercialization of Technology and Issues in the Competitiveness of Selected U.S. Industries: Semiconductors, Biotechnology, and Superconductors*, by Wendy H. Schacht. June 1988.

———. *Critical Technologies Lists: A Comparison of Published Lists and Legislative Proposals*, by Genevieve J. Knezo. September 17, 1991.

———. *Defense Basic Research Priorities: Funding and Policy Issues*, by Genevieve J. Knezo. October 24, 1990.

———. *The Europe 1992 Plan: Science and Technology Issues*, by Glenn J. McLoughlin. August 23, 1989.

———. *Foreign Direct Investment: Effects on the United States.* 1989.

———. *Foreign Investment: The Exon-Florio National Security Test.* September 26, 1990.

———. *Japanese and U.S. Industrial Associations: Their Role in High-Technology Policymaking.* June 6, 1991.

———. *Japanese Basic Research Policies*, by Genevieve J. Knezo. August 1, 1990.

———. *Japan's Industrial Groups: The Keiretsu*, by Dick K. Nanto. November 5, 1990.

———. *Persian Gulf War: Defense Policy Implications for Congress*, by Ronald O'Rourke. May 15, 1991.

———. *Research and Development Funding FY 1992.* Issue brief. April 22, 1991.

———. *The Semi-Gas Systems Sale: Technology and National Security Issues.* March 12, 1991.

Executive Office of the President. Office of Science and Technology Policy. *Report of the National Critical Technologies Panel.* March 22, 1991.

———. *The Federal High Performance Computing Program.* September 8, 1989.

Executive Office of the President. President's Commission on Industrial Competitiveness. *Global Competition: The New Reality.* Vols. 1, II, 1985.

———. *President's Proposed Budget for Fiscal Year 1991*, pt. two. 1990.

Monopolies and Mergers Commission. *The Government of Kuwait and the British Petroleum Company PLC: A Report on the Merger Situation.* Presented to Parliament by the Secretary of State for Trade and Industry, by Command of Her Majesty, Great Britain, October 1988.

State of Maryland, Senate. Committee on Finance. *Foreign Investment in U.S. Banks*, Susan J. Tolchin, testimony, Annapolis, Md., July 31, 1990.

United Nations Centre on Transnational Corporations. *Transnational Corporations in World Development: Trends and Prospects.* New York-United Nations, 1988.

U.S. Congress. Congressional Budget Office. *Using R & D Consortia for Commercial Innovation: SEMATECH, X-Ray Lithography, and High-Resolution Systems*, by Philip Webre. July 1990.

U.S. Congress. Department of Defense Authorization Bill, 1989, Statute #2504, Defense Memoranda of Understanding. 1989.

———. Public Law #100–456.

U.S. Congress. Joint Committee on Taxation. *Background and Issues Relating to the Taxation of Foreign Investment in the United States* (JCS-1-90). January 23, 1990.

———. Office of Technology Assessment. *Arming Our Allies: Cooperation and Competition in Defense Technology.* May 1990.

———. *The Big Picture: High Resolution System and HDTV.* Draft Report. 1989.

———. *Competing Economies: America, Europe and the Pacific Rim.* November, 1991.

———. *The Defense Technology Base.* March 1988.

———. *Holding the Edge: Maintaining the Defense Technology Base.* Washington, D.C.: U.S. Government Printing Office, April 1989.

———. *Making Things Better: Competing in Manufacturing.* February, 1990.

———. *Redesigning Defense: Planning the Transition to the Future U.S. Defense Industrial Base.* Washington, D.C.: U.S. Government Printing Office, July 1991.

U.S. Department of Commerce. *Implementation of DPA Authorities, Defense Priorities and Allocations Systems.* April 1991.

U.S. Department of Commerce. International Trade Association. *The Competitive Status of the U.S. Electronics Sector from Materials to Systems.* April 1990.

———. *International Direct Investment: Global Trends and the U.S. Role.* Washington, D.C.: U.S. Government Printing Office, 1988.

U.S. Department of Commerce. Office of Economic Research. *Foreign Investment in California.* February, 1990.

U.S. Department of Commerce. Office of Technology Administration. *Emerging Technologies: A Survey of Technical and Economic Opportunities.* Spring 1990.

———. Directive Number 5530.3, *International Agreements.* June 11, 1987.

U.S. Department of Defense. *Critical Technologies Plan.* For the Committees on Armed Services, March 15, 1990.

———. Report to the Secretary of Defense by the Under Secretary of Defense (Acquisition). *Bolstering Defense Industrial Competitiveness.* July 1988.

———. A Report to the United States Congress by the Secretary of Defense. *The Impact of Buy American Restrictions Affecting Defense Procurement.* 1989.

U.S. Department of Defense. Defense Science Board. *Critical Industries: A New Strategy for the Nation's Defense Industrial Base.* May 1990.

———. *Of the Defense Industrial and Technology Base.* October, 1988.

———. *Defense Semiconductor Dependency.* February 1987.

———. *Keeping Access to the Leading Edge: A Consolidated Executive Summary by the Industrial Base Committee to the Defense Science Board.* June 6, 1990.

U.S. Department of Defense. Office of the Under Secretary of Defense for Acquisition. *Defense Industrial Cooperation with Pacific Rim Nations.* 1989.

U.S. Department of the Treasury. *Report to Congress on Foreign Treatment of U.S. Financial Institutions.* National Treatment Study, 1990.

U.S. General Accounting Office. *Challenges to America's Economic Leadership and How Government and Industry Should Respond.* Transcript, September 14, 1990.

———. *Defense Procurement: DOD Purchases of Foreign-Made Machine Tools.* February 1991.

———. *Foreign Investment: Aspects of the US.-Japan Relationship.* July 1990.

———. *Foreign Investment: Concerns in the Banking, Petroleum, Chemicals and Biotechnology Sectors.* May 30, 1990.

———. *Foreign Investment: Foreign Hostile Takeovers of U.S. Firms.* December 1988.

———. *Foreign Technologies: Federal Agencies Efforts to Track Developments.* June 1989.

———. *Industrial Base: Defense-Critical Industries.* August 1988.

———. *Industrial Base: Significance of DoD's Foreign Dependencies.* January 10, 1991.

———. *National Security Reviews of Foreign Investment.* February 26, 1991.

———. *U.S.-Japan FS-X Program,* May 1989.

U.S. General Accounting Office. *U.S.-Japan FS-X Codevelopment Program*. Frank Conahan, testimony, May 16, 1989.

———. *U.S. Military Coproduction Programs Assist Japan in Developing Its Civil Aircraft Industry*. March 1982.

U.S. General Accounting Office. International Trade. *U.S. Business Access to Certain Foreign State-of-the-Art Technology*. September 1991.

U.S. House of Representatives. *American Technology Preeminence Act*. Report 102–134, to accompany H.R. 1989.

U.S. House of Representatives. Statement by Representative Marge Roukema, June 7, 1989. Congressional Record, p. H 2391.

U.S. House of Representatives. *American Technology Preeminence Act*. Report 102–134, to accompany H.R. 1989.

U.S. House of Representatives. Armed Services Committee. Subcommittee on Research and Development. Statement by Dr. Victor H. Reis, director, Defense Advanced Research Projects Agency, April 23, 1991.

U.S. House of Representatives. Committee on Banking, Finance and Urban Affairs. Dennis W. Rich testimony, February 8, 1989.

U.S. House of Representatives. Committee on Banking, Finance and Urban Affairs. Subcommittee on Economic Stabilization. *Defense Department Recommendations to Bolster Defense Industrial Competitiveness*. 100th Cong., 2nd sess. Washington, D.C: U.S. Government Printing Office, 1988.

———. *To Enhance the Competitiveness of American Industry, and for Other Purposes*. 100th Cong. 1st sess. Washington, D.C.: U.S. Government Printing Office, 1987.

———. *Foreign Direct Investment: Effects on the United States*. 100th Cong., 1st sess. Washington, D.C.: U.S. Government Printing Office, 1989.

———. *Foreign Investment in the United States*, Susan J. Tolchin, testimony, November 15, 1989.

———. *Foreign Investment in the United States*. 101st Cong., 1st sess. Washington, D.C: U.S. Government Printing Office, 1989.

———. *Offset Agreements*. 99th Cong., 2nd sess. Washington, D.C.: U.S. Government Printing Office, 1986.

U.S. House of Representatives. Committee on Energy and Commerce. Subcommittee on Commerce, Consumer Protection and Competitiveness. *Iraq's Efforts to Acquire U.S. Technology and the Need for Legislation to Give the President Additional Authority to Seize Iraqi Interests in U.S. Firms*. February 21, 1991.

———. Richard Gephardt testimony. February 21, 1991.

———. Kevin Kearns testimony, February 26, 1991, p. 2.

———. Bradley Larschan testimony, February 26, 1991, p. 8.

———. Subcommittee on Telecommunications, Consumer Protection, and Finance. *Disclosure of Foreign Investment in the United States*. 99th Cong., 2nd sess. Washington, D.C.: U.S. Government Printing Office, 1986.

———. *The Public Policy Implications of Increased Foreign Investment in the United States*, Susan J. Tolchin, testimony, May 8, 1986.

U.S. House of Representatives. Committee on Foreign Affairs, Committee on Ways and Means, Committee on Foreign Relations, Committee on Finance. *Country Reports on Economic Policy and Trade Practices*. Washington, D.C.: U.S. Government Printing Office, 1989.

U.S. House of Representatives Committee on Foreign Affairs. International Economic

Policy Subcommittee. *Foreign Investment in the United States,* Susan J. Tolchin testimony, September 14, 1988.

U.S. House of Representatives. Committee on Government Operations. *The Adequacy of the Federal Response to Foreign Investment in the United States.* Washington, D.C.: U.S. Government Printing Office, 1980.

———. Subcommittee on Human Resources and Intergovernmental Relations. Hearing, *Is Science for Sale? Conflict of Interest vs. the Public Interest.* June 13, 1989.

U.S. House of Representatives. Committee on the Judiciary. Subcommittee on Monopolies and Commercial Law. Hearings, *Mergers and Acquisitions.* 99th Cong., 1st and 2nd sess. Washington, D.C.: U.S. Government Printing Office, 1986.

U.S. Senate. Senator Mark Hatfield, testimony. March 19, 1991. Congressional Record p. S 3480.

U.S. Senate. Senator Ernest F. Hollings, speech. June 4, 1991. Congressional Record p. S 6967.

U.S. Senate. Committee on Armed Services. *Department of Defense Authorization for Appropriations for Fiscal Years 1988 and 1989.* 100th Cong., 1st sess. Washington, D.C.: U.S. Government Printing Office, 1987.

———. *Department of Defense Authorization for Appropriation for Fiscal Year 1989.* Washington, D.C.: U.S. Government Printing Office, 1988.

———. Subcommittee on Defense Industry and Technology. *Manufacturing Capabilities of Key Second-Tier Defense Industries.* 100th Cong., 1st sess. Washington, D.C.: U.S. Government Printing Office, 1987.

———. *National Defense Authorization Act for Fiscal Year 1989.* 100th Cong., 2nd sess. Washington, D.C.: U.S. Government Printing Office, 1988.

U.S. Senate. Committee on Banking, Housing, and Urban Affairs. *Defense Production Act Amendments of 1990.* 101st Cong., 2nd sess. Washington, D.C.: U.S. Government Printing Office, 1990.

———. Robert E. Mercer, testimony, February 8, 1989.

U.S. Senate. Committee on the Budget. *The Bryant Amendment to the 1988 Trade Bill,* Susan J. Tolchin, testimony, March 22, 1988.

———. *Concurrent Resolution on the Budget for Fiscal Year 1989.* 100th Cong., 2nd sess. Washington, D.C.: U.S. Government Printing Office, 1988.

U.S. Senate. Committee on Commerce. *Acquisitions by Foreign Companies,* June 10, 1987.

U.S. Senate. Committee on Finance. *Foreign Influence on the U.S. Political Process,* Susan J. Tolchin, testimony, September 19, 1991.

Reports, Monographs, Court Cases, and Other Sources

Aerospace Education Foundation Study. *America's Next Crisis: The Shortfall in Technical Manpower.* Arlington, Va.: The Aerospace Education Foundation, 1989.

———. *Lifeline Adrift: The Defense Industrial Base in the 1990s.* Arlington, Va., September 1991.

Aerospace Industries Association of America, Inc. *Key Technologies for the 1990s: An Overview.* Arlington, Va., 1987.

Air Force Association, USNI Military Database. *Lifeline in Danger: An Assessment of the United States Defense Industrial Base.* The Aerospace Foundation, 1988.

American Electronics Association. *America's Future at Stake: Winning in the Global Marketplace.*

———. *Development of a U.S.-Based ATV Industry.* Background Information, 1989.

American International Underwriters Insurance. *Japanese Investment in the U.S.: American Responses,* Japan Conference Proceedings, held November 15, 1989.

Americans Talk Security. *A Series of American Voters: Attitudes Concerning National Security Issues.* Vols. 8, 10, 11. Boston: Marttila & Kiley, Inc., 1988.

Booz, Allen & Hamilton, Inc. *Direct Foreign Investment in Japan: The Challenge for Foreign Firms.* New York, 1987.

British Petroleum. *BP Annual Report and Accounts 1988.* London: Britanica House, 1989.

Button, Andrew J. "Cooperation in the Development of the FS-X: An Analysis of the Decision Process." Unpublished paper from the Executive Research Project. Industrial College of the Armed Forces, Fort McNair, D.C., 1989.

Carnegie Commission on Science, Technology, and Government. *Technology and Economic Performance.* Washington, D.C., September 1991.

Center for Strategic and International Studies. *Deterrence in Decay: The Future of the U.S. Defense Industrial Base.* Final report of CSIS Defense Industrial Base Project. Washington, D.C.: Center for Strategic and International Studies, May 1989.

Council on Competitiveness. *Gaining New Ground: Technology Priorities for America's Future.* Washington, D.C., March 1991.

———. *Japanese Technology Policy: What's the Secret?,* by David W. Cheney and William W. Grimes. February 1991.

Council on Competitiveness and the Japan Society. *Technology and Competitiveness: New Frontiers for the United States and Japan.* January 1990.

Ferguson, Charles H. *DRAMs, Component Supplies, and the World Electronics Industry: An International Strategic Analysis.* Cambridge, Mass.: MIT Press, 1989.

Go-Video, Inc. v. Matsushita Electric Industrial Co., Ltd., Panasonic Company, a Division of Matsushita Electric Corporation of America; Victor Company of Japan, Ltd., et al. First Amended Complaint, MDL 765-PHX-RCB, CIV 90-0118 PHX RCB, July 20, 1990.

Go-Video, Inc., v. Matsushita Electric Industrial Co., Ltd., et al. United States District Court, District of Arizona, Complaint, December 6, 1990.

Go-Video, Inc., v. The Motion Picture Association of America, De Laurentiis Entertainment Group, Inc., MGM UA Communications Co., Twentieth-Century Fox Film Corp. . . . Matsushita Electric Industrial Co., Ltd., Samsung Electronic Co., Ltd., et al. U.S. District Court of Arizona, CIV-87-0987 PHX RCB, Second Amended Complaint, April 20, 1988.

Green, Michael. *Kokusanka: FSX and Japan's Search for Autonomous Defense Production.* Working paper. Cambridge, Mass.: MIT-Japan Program, May 1990.

Hatsopoulos, George. "Technology and the Cost of Equity Capital." Presented at the National Academy of Engineering Symposium, Washington, D.C., April 5, 1990.

Institute for Defense Analyses. *DARPA Technical Accomplishments: An Historical Review of Selected DARPA Projects,* by Sidney G. Reed, Richard H. Van Atta, and Seymour J. Deitchman. Vol. I, February 1990; Vol. III, July 1991.

———. *Dependence of U.S. Defense Systems on Foreign Technologies.* December 1990.

———. *Interim Report of the Project on Defense Industrial Cooperation in the Pacific*

Rim. Defense Industrial Capabilities of the Pacific Rim Nations and Means of Cooperation, 1988.

Lewis, Charles. *Office of the U.S. Trade Representative: America's Frontline Trade Officials,* Center for Public Integrity, 1991.

Logistics Management Institute. *Identifying Industrial Base Deficiencies,* 1987.

Mobilization Concepts Development Center. *U.S. Industrial Base Dependence/Vulnerability, Phase II—Analysis.* Martin Libicki, Jack Nunn, William Taylor. Washington, D.C.: National Defense University, 1987.

National Advisory Committee on Semiconductors. *A Strategic Industry at Risk.* November 1989.

Ostrey, Sylvia. "Technology and the Global Economy: International Responses." report, International Policy Conference, OECD, Montreal, 1991.

Salomon Brothers. *The Japanese Banks: Emerging into Global Markets.* September 1989.

Spencer, Linda. *American Assets: An Examination of Foreign Investment in the United States.* Congressional Economic Leadership Institute. 1988.

———. *Foreign Investment in the United States: Unencumbered Access.* Economic Strategy Institute, May 1991.

TASC (The Analytic Sciences Corporation). *Foreign Vulnerability of Critical Industries,* March 1, 1990.

Turek, Frank S. "FSX: An Analysis of the Decision Process Within the Department of Defense." Unpublished paper, Department of Public Administration, George Washington University, December 14, 1989.

INDEX

technology (*cont.*)
    policies on, 200–2, 261–6; White
      House report on, 18, 362
dual-use (civilian and military), 141,
    192–5
"enabling," 12
Export-Import–type bank proposed for,
    313
government support of, 10–12, 164,
    260–1; Bush's opposition, 17; loans
    to companies, 17, 362; proposed
    criteria, 263–4
Gulf War and, 18, 149–50
interrelationship of, 257
lead-time, 185
manufacturing base needed for, 125
manufacturing connected to, 159–60,
    197–8
peaceful uses of, 8
proposed U.S. policy for, 190–202, 261–6
reciprocity in sharing of, 201
spin-on and spin-off, 185
summary of U.S. and foreign capabilities
    in, 325
transfer of: court cases pending, 385–6;
    foreign investment and, 47; by
    foreign purchase of start-up firms,
    258; university ILPs and, 227
U.S. loss of, 4–5, 8–9, 11; table of
    selected acquisitions, 329–48
Technology Forecast Survey (Japan), 18
"technology policy," 16
"technology surprise," 183
Technology Transfer Act of 1989, 311
telecommunications, table of selected
    acquisitions of U.S. firms in, 345–6
Teledyne, Inc., 20, 171
telephone manufacturing industry, decline
    of, 5
television
    high-definition (HDTV), 125, 133–4,
      157, 158, 160, 190, 192, 242, 278,
      297, 299, 359
    interactive, 221
    movies transmitted by home telephone to,
      221
television manufacturing industry, decline
    of, 5, 156–7
television networks, prohibited from buying
    movie companies, 286
Tennessee, 304
Texaco, Inc., 24, 281, 363
Texas A & M University, 221, 228
Texas Instruments Inc., 28, 47, 108
    patent suits in Japan by, 384–5
Thatcher, Margaret, 244
Thermo Electron Corp., 380
think tanks, U.S., Japanese financing of, 218
Thompson, Bruce, 35
Thomson-CSF (French firm), 30
Thornburgh, Richard, 289

Thurmond, Strom, 387, 389
Time magazine, 271
TIMET (Titanium Metals Corp. of
    America), 64
tire and rubber industry, 6
    foreign domination of, 3–4, 41–3
    see also Goodyear Tire & Rubber Co.
Titanium Metals Corp. of America
    (TIMET), 64
Toho Titanium Co., 64
Tokuyama Soda Co. Ltd., 54–5, 67
Tomahawk missiles, 173
Toshiba, 47
    in cartel against dual-deck VCR, 270
    half of lap-top market controlled by, 157
    profits invested in R & D, 237–8
    submarine technology sold to Soviets by,
      48, 90, 153, 183
Toshiba Machine Co., 183
Tower, John, 96, 102
Toyota (Japanese company), 187, 250, 279,
    280, 319, 378, 385
    Kentucky's subsidies to, 286, 303, 305
    transfer pricing by, 245–6
Toys Я Us (company), 280
Trading Places (book), 84
traffic jams, sensors that warn of, 13
transfer pricing, 243, 245–6, 382
transponders, 20, 171
Treasury Department, *see* Department of
    the Treasury, U.S.
Tristar Pictures, 14
Trump, Donald, 238
TRW Inc., 85
Tsipis, Kosta, 311
Tufts University, 223
Turkey, F-16 coproduction by, 138, 351–3
Twentieth Century–Fox (company), 269
Tyler, John, 97, 98–9, 100, 105
Tyson, Laura D'Andrea, 165–6, 284

U.S.-Canada Free Trade Agreement, 303
U.S. Memories (consortium), 162–3, 284,
    298, 310
Ukraine, 147
Union Bank of California, 248–9
Union Carbide Chemicals & Plastics, 65
Union Explosivos Rio Tinto (Spanish
    company), 210
Uniroyal Goodrich (company), 41, 133
UniSoft Corp., 57–8
UniSoft Group PLC, 57–8
United Artists (company), 152, 269
United Kingdom, 27, 166
    antitrust legislation in, 206–7, 215
    decline of, 176–7
    "good will" in, 263
    Gulf War equipment manufactured in,
      20, 158, 172
    Kuwaiti takeover of British Petroleum
      stopped by, 24, 203–16

A NOTE ABOUT THE AUTHORS

Martin Tolchin is a prize-winning correspondent in the Washington bureau of *The New York Times*. Susan J. Tolchin is professor of public administration in the School of Business and Public Management at George Washington University. Together they have written four previous books—*To the Victor: Political Patronage from the Clubhouse to the White House* (1971), *Clout: Womanpower and Politics* (1974), *Dismantling America: The Rush to Deregulate* (1983), and *Buying into America: How Foreign Money Is Changing the Face of Our Nation* (1988).

A NOTE ON THE TYPE

The text of this book was set in Sabon, a typeface designed by Jan Tschichold (1902–1974), the well-known German typographer. Because it was designed in Frankfurt, Sabon was named for the famous Frankfurt typefounder Jacques Sabon, who died in 1580 while manager of the Egenolff foundry.

Based loosely on the original designs of Claude Garamond (c. 1480–1561), Sabon is unique in that it was explicitly designed for hot-metal composition on both the Monotype and Linotype machines as well as for film composition.

Composed by Crane Typesetting Service, Inc.,
West Barnstable, Massachusetts

Printed and bound by The Haddon Craftsmen, Inc.,
Scranton, Pennsylvania

Designed by Cassandra J. Pappas